Chevelon: Pueblo at Blue Running Water

Edited by E. Charles Adams

With Contributions By:

Karen R. Adams
Claire S. Barker
Elisabeth Cutright-Smith
Rachel Diaz de Valdes
R. Emerson Howell
David J. Icove
J.R. Lally
Vincent M. LaMotta
Marycruz Magaña Hernández
Melanie Medeiros
Margaret Shaw
A.J. Vonarx

Arizona State Museum Archaeological Series 211

Arizona State Museum
The University of Arizona
Tucson, Arizona 85721-0026
Copyright © 2016 by the Arizona Board of Regents
All rights reserved.
Printed in the United States of America

ISBN (paper): 978-1-889747-98-9
Library of Congress Control Number: 2016962810

ARIZONA STATE MUSEUM ARCHAEOLOGICAL SERIES

General Editor: Richard C. Lange
Technical Editors: Kelly Alushaj and Alicia M. Vega

The *Archaeological Series* of the Arizona State Museum, The University of Arizona, publishes the results of research in archaeology and related disciplines conducted in the Greater Southwest. Original, monograph-length manuscripts are considered for publication, provided they deal with appropriate subject matter. Information regarding procedures or manuscript submission and review is given under Research Publications on the Arizona State Museum website: *www.statemuseum.arizona.edu/research/pubs*. Information may be also obtained from the General Editor, *Archaeological Series*, Arizona State Museum, P.O. Box 210026, The University of Arizona, Tucson, Arizona, 85721-0026; Email: langer@email.arizona.edu. Electronic publications and previous volumes in the Arizona State Museum Library or available from the University of Arizona Press are listed on the website noted above. Print-on-demand versions of the latest Arizona State Museum Archaeological Series may be obtained from several booksellers on-line.

The Arizona State Museum *Archaeological Series* is grateful to the many donors and supporters who continue to make this publication possible.

FRONT COVER: Upper Left--Figure 10.3 Shell pendants; Upper Right--Figure 6.11a Tonto Polychrome jar; Lower Left--Figure 6.10 Sikyatki Polychrome jar; Lower Right--Figure 8.3 Projectile points; BACK COVER: Figure 1.3 Chevelon Plaza and Roomblock Designations.

Contents

Contents	iii
List of Figures	ix
List of Tables	xii
Appendixes	xiv
Preface *by E. Charles Adams*	xv
Chapter 1: Introduction: General Traits of Chevelon *by E. Charles Adams*	1
Previous Research	2
General Place Description and Relationship to other Homol'ovi Settlement Cluster Sites	4
Nearby Settlements and the Big Picture	7
Hopi Oral Traditions about Chevelon and the Homol'ovi Settlement Cluster	9
Research Interests	10
History	10
Exchange	10
Migration	10
Daily Life	11
Community Organization	11
Social Power	12
Agency and Practice	12
Formation Processes	13
Methodology	13
Excavation Methods	13
Sample Design and Size	14
Chapter 2: Environment *by E. Charles Adams*	19
The Setting	19
Chevelon Creek and the Little Colorado River	20
Plant and Animal Communities	20
Chevelon Canyon	21
Driftwood	21
Paleoenvironment and Paleoclimate	22
Little Colorado River Floodplain	23
Summary	26
Chapter 3: Chronology *by E. Charles Adams*	27
Previous Research	27
Chevelon Chronology	28
Independent Dating	30
Radiocarbon Dating	30
Tree-Ring Dating	30
Ceramics and the Jeddito Yellow Ware Index (%JYW)	30
Superposition and Dating the Room Blocks	31
Stage 1: 1290	31
Stage 2: 1300	31
Stages 3 and 4: 1300-1325	31
Stages 5 and 6: 1350-1375	33
Stage 7: 1325-1390	34
Stage 8: 1375-1390	35
Stage 9: 1390/1400	35

Deposits at Chevelon	36
Kiva Stratigraphy	36
Formation Processes and Human Agency	36
Burning	36
Kiva Deposits and Floor Assembleges	37
Dating Individual Structures	39
Summary	40
Chapter 4: Architecture *by E. Charles Adams*	41
The Basics	41
Building Materials	41
Adobe Bricks	41
Roofing	44
Room Use	45
Storage Rooms	45
Storage Rooms With Bin Features	45
Storage Rooms Without Bin Features	47
Corn Storage Rooms	49
Habitation Rooms	49
Habitation with Ritual Features	50
Structure 124	52
Structure 159	52
Ritual Assemblages within Rooms	54
Piki House	56
Kivas	59
Kiva 248	59
Kiva 279	61
Kiva 252	63
Kiva 901	66
Summary	71
The Household at Chevelon	71
Structures 122-124 and 157-159	72
Domestic Activity	72
Ritual Versus Ritual Closure	74
Structure 509/546 and 510/547	74
Interpretation	75
Structures 268/288/289, 287, 246	75
Interpretation	76
Summary	78
Spinal Room Blocks	78
Plaza Spaces	81
Plaza 200	84
Interpretation	84
Plaza 900 (RB300)	85
Interpretation	85
Plaza 800	86
Interpretation	86
Plaza 000	87
Interpretation	87
Social History of Chevelon	88
Room Block 200	88
Room Block 300	92

Room Block 100	97
Room Block 400-700	102
Summary	102

Chapter 5: Modeling Prehistoric Structural Fires at Chevelon Pueblo *by David J. Icove,*
J.R. Lally, A.J. Vonarx, and E. Charles Adams 105
    Archaeological Study of Ancient Structural Fires 106
        Chevelon Pueblo: A Case Study 107
            Compartment Fires and Southwestern Construction 108
            Hypothesis Development Using Fire Testing 110
            Hypothesis Development Using Computer Fire Models 113
                Scenario 1 113
                Scenario 2 113
                Scenario 3 113
    Conclusions 115

Chapter 6: Pottery *by Elisabeth Cutright-Smith and Claire S. Barker* 117
    Total Ceramic Assemblage 117
        Classification 117
        Chevelon Distributions 118
        Comparisons within the Homol'ovi Settlement Cluster 118
        Interregional Comparisons 124
    Temporal Trends 127
        Building Chronologies: Methodology 127
        Temporal Phase Scheme 127
        Evaluating the Jeddito Yellow Ware Index at Chevelon 128
        Seriation of Excavated Deposits 129
        Temporal Trends in Jeddito Yellow Ware and Winslow Orange Ware Distribution 130
        Temporal Trends in Red Ware Distribution 131
        Temporal Trends in the Distribution of Diagnostic Decorated Types 135
    Spatial Patterns 140
        Spatial Patterns in Ware Distribution among Room Blocks 140
        Spatial Patterns in Jeddito Yellow Ware Distribution 140
        Spatial Patterns in Local Ceramic Distribution 141
        Spatial Patterns in Red Ware Distribution 141
        Conclusions from the Spatial Analysis of Major Ceramic Wares 143
    Patterns Resulting from Room Use 144
        Distribution in Kiva vs. Non-kiva Structures 144
        Material Correlates of Religious Ritual Practice 146
        Ceramic Evidence for Structural Burning Classification 149
        Spatial Trends in Structural Burning 149
        Temporal Trends in Structural Burning 151
        Miscellaneous Ceramic Artifacts 151
    Conclusions 153

Chapter 7: Ground Stone *by Melanie Medeiros and E. Charles Adams* 155
    Methodology 155
    Description of the Chevelon Ground Stone Assemblage 156
        Manos and Metates 160
            Manos 161
            Metates 165
        Piki Stones and Griddle Stones 167

Abraders	169
Polishing Stones	169
Axes	171
Miscellaneous Artifacts	172
Spatial Distribution	175
Temporal Distribution	177
Conclusions	178
Chapter 8: Raw Material Procurement, Technological Organization, and Ritual Use:	
Contextualizing Flaked Stone and Use at Chevelon *by Melanie Medeiros*	181
Terminology	182
Methodology	182
The Assemblage	184
Raw Material	184
Raw Material Utilization	188
Raw Material Procurement	192
Petrified Wood	192
Obsidian	196
Technological Organization	198
Formal versus Informal tools	198
Platform Perparation	200
Biface to Core Ratios	200
Spatial Patterns in the Chevelon Flaked Stone Assemblage	203
Depositional Context	203
Raw Material and Depositional Context	203
Flaked Stone Classes and Depositional Context	204
Variability Across Structures	205
Flaked Stone Classes	205
Projectile Points	211
General Distribution	213
Raw Materials	214
Petrified Wood	214
Obsidian	215
Projectile Point Raw Material	216
Temporal Variation in the Chevelon Flaked Stone Assemblage	218
Temporal Variation in Flaked Stone Classes	218
Temporal Variation in Raw Material Use	220
The Ritual Significance of Flaked Stone in the Chevelon Assemblage:	
Theorizing Social Memory *by Melanie Medeiros and A.J. Vonarx*	221
Enriched Deposits	221
Preceramic Projectile Points and Social Memory	222
Summary and Conclusions	223
Chapter 9: Faunal Remains from Chevelon *by Rachel Diaz de Valdes and E. Charles Adams*	225
Methodology	225
General Faunal Composition	226
Modern Environment	226
The Assemblage	226
Lagomorphs	226
Rodents	232
Carnivores	233
Artiodactyls	234

Aves	236
Amphibians and Reptiles	241
Fish	241
Rare/Unusual Taxa	242
Interpretations	245
Comparisons to other Faunal Assemblages in the Homol'ovi Settlement Cluster	247
Worked Bone	248
Summary	250
Chapter 10: Shell *by Marycruz Magaña Hernández*	251
Methodology of Analysis	251
Genus, Species, and Provenience of the Assemblage	252
The Use of Shell at Chevelon	252
Beads	252
Whole Shell Beads	255
Discoidal Beads	255
Pendants	255
Ring Pendant	256
Bracelets and Armlets	256
Evidence for Manufacturing	257
Artifacts in the Process of Being Manufactured	257
Manufacturing Debris	258
Raw Material	258
Anodonta Manufacture and Use	258
Spatial and Temporal Patterns	259
Comparisons to Assemblages from Other Cluster Sites and Beyond	260
Conclusions	263
Chapter 11: Charred Plant Remains *by Karen R. Adams*	265
Setting the Scene: The Modern Plant Environment	265
Methodology of Analysis	267
Description of the Archaeobotanical Assemblage	271
Domesticated Plants	271
Maize/Corn	271
Type of Maize Grown at Chevelon Pueblo	275
Maize Use Through Time	277
Other Domesticates	278
Wild Plants	279
Subsistence Resources	279
Non-Subsistence Resources	282
Comparison to Other Homol'ovi Settlement Cluster Assemblages	285
Summary and Conclusions	286
Subsistence	286
Non-subsistence	287
Spatial Patterns in the Assemblage	287
Temporal Patterns in the Assemblage	287
Seasonality of Chevelon Pueblo Occupation	287
Chevelon Pueblo and Other Homol'ovi Settlement Cluster Pueblos	288
Changes in Vegetation Between Then and Now	288
Chapter 12: Wood Use Behavior, Resource Procurements, and Construction Technologies at Chevelon *by Margaret Shaw, A.J. Vonarx, R. Emerson Howell*	289

Environmental Context	289
Methodology	289
Species Diversity at Chevelon compared to Modern Driftwood	290
Species Diversity Related to Structure Function and Size	290
Species Diversity Versus Room Use	290
Species Diversity Versus Room Size	291
Species Diversity Related to Structure Roof	291
Species Diversity Related to Time	297
Future/Potential lines of Research	297
Conclusions	299
Chapter 13: What We Have Learned *by E. Charles Adams*	301
Spatial Patterns at Chevelon	301
Temporal Patterns at Chevelon	302
Chevelon Social History	302
Founders	302
First Expansion	303
Second Expansion	305
Migration and Chevelon's Role in the Homol'ovi Settlement Cluster	308
Exploitation of Plant and Animal Resources	310
Wealth, Ritual, Power, and Social Memory	312
Distribution of Rare/Unusual Objects	313
Social Memory	317
Community Ritual and Katsina Religion	318
Ritual Placement	321
Summary – The Meaning of Assemblages of Ritual Objects	322
Chapter 14: Future Directions *by E. Charles Adams*	327
What We Do Not Yet Understand	327
Why They Left	327
Why They Burned Their Structures	329
Jeddito Yellow Ware, Cotton, *Anodonta*, and Turtle Shell	330
Chevelon's Role within the Homol'ovi Settlement Cluster	332
The Homol'ovi Settlement Cluster and the History of the Region	333
Final Thoughts	335
References Cited	337

Figures

1.1.	Plan map of Chevelon showing location of excavated structures	3
1.2.	Topographic map of middle Little Colorado River in vicinity of Chevelon	3
1.3.	Plan of Chevelon showing room block designations	5
1.4.	Location of Homol'ovi Settlement Cluster villages	5
1.5.	Topographic plan of Chevelon	6
2.1.	Topographic map of Chevelon and adjoining areas	24
4.1.	Plan view of storage room with bins (Structure 227)	46
4.2.	Plan view of storage room without bins (Structure 120)	48
4.3.	Plan view of habitation room (Structure 603)	51
4.4.	Plan view of Structure 124, a habitation room with ritual features	53
4.5.	Structure 286 floor assemblage (left). Detailed photo of cottontail rabbits and associated artifacts (right)	55
4.6.	Plan view of Structure 222, piki house	58
4.7.	Photograph of east wall of Kiva 248 showing ventilation tunnel	60
4.8.	Plan view of Kiva 279	62
4.9.	Kiva 279 N1152 profile	64
4.10.	Plan view of Kiva 252	65
4.11.	Profile view of Kiva 901	67
4.12.	Plan view of Kiva 901	68
4.13.	Photograph of trash cone in Kiva 901	69
4.14.	Photograph of oxidized fill with burned roof beams in Kiva 901	70
4.15.	Plan view of room suite 122-124	73
4.16.	Photograph of Structure 157, storage room	74
4.17.	Photograph of Structure 158, burned corn storage room	74
4.18.	Photograph of Structure 159, a habitation room with ritual features	74
4.19.	Plan of suite 268/289/288	77
4.20.	Plan view of Room Block 200 plaza with Kiva 248 and Kiva 279	79
4.21.	Photograph of burned roof to Structure 268, a habitation room	80
4.22.	Plan view of Plaza 900	83
4.23.	Map of Room Block 200 showing initial settlement of Chevelon	90
4.24.	Map of Room Block 200 showing pre-1325 additions	91
4.25.	Map of Room Block 100, 200, & 300 showing growth prior to 1325 C.E.	93
4.26.	Map of Room Block 300 showing layout and Plaza 900	95
4.27.	North (left) and west (right) adobe brick wall of Structure 345	96
4.28.	Map of room block additions around Plaza 000	100
4.29.	Map of Room Block 100 showing added, possibly ritual, structures	101
5.1.	A reconstruction of typical pueblo structure or room in preparation for the 2005 fire tests at Homol'ovi State Park in Arizona. Photograph by D.J. Icove	107
5.2.	A diagram of a typical roof. Drawing by K. Harrison	107
5.3.	Burned corn in Structure 123	109
5.4.	Burned corn in Structure 158	109
5.5.	Typical fire debris found on interior wall in archeological excavations at Mesa Portales (LA145165). Photo by J. E. Lally	110
5.6.	Roof interior of experimental structure showing smoke and fire ignited by torch	111
5.7.	View through doorway of model room engulfed in fire from brush	111
5.8.	Burned roof resulting from room intentionally filled with brush	111
5.9.	Time-temperature plot of heat buildup from brush fire	112
5.10.	Simulation of room fire from hearth with vent open	114
5.11.	Simulation of room fire from hearth with vent closed	114

5.12.	Simulation when hearth ignites material on floor with vent open	114
5.13.	Simulation when hearth ignites material on floor with vent closed	115
5.14.	Simulation with large fuel load, such as brush, with vent open	115
5.15.	Simulation with large fuel load, such as brush, with vent closed	115
5.16.	Heavily oxidized south wall to Structure 123	116
5.17.	Sintered roofing material from Structure 123	116
6.1.	Jeddito Yellow Ware sherds	120
6.2.	Winslow Orange Ware sherds	121
6.3.	White Mountain Red Ware sherds	121
6.4.	Roosevelt Red Ware sherds	122
6.5.	Homol'ovi Utility Ware sherds	122
6.6.	Tusayan Gray Corrugated Jar sherds	122
6.7.	Mogollon Brown Ware sherds	122
6.8.	Puerco Valley Utility Ware sherds	122
6.9.	Location of measurements on Jeddito Yellow Ware bowls to determine banding line width and rim-to-banding line distance	129
6.10.	Whole and reconstructible Jeddito Yellow Ware vessels	138
6.11.	Whole and reconstructible Roosevelt Red Ware vessels	139
6.12.	(a)Homol'ovi Polychrome puki manufactured from a bowl; (b)Red-slipped Jeddito Polychrome bowl; (c)Huckovi Black-on-orange sherd	140
6.13.	(a)Homol'ovi Corrugated jar; (b)Puerco Valley Plain miniature ladle	148
6.14.	Tusayan Corrugated jar	148
6.15.	Puerco Valley Corrugated jar	148
6.16.	Miscellaneous ceramic artifacts	150
7.1.	One- and two-hand manos with multiple use surfaces	167
7.2.	Flat metates	168
7.3.	Piki stones and griddles	168
7.4.	Grooved and flat abraders	171
7.5.	Polishing stones	172
7.6.	Stone axes and maul	173
7.7.	Miscellaneous ground stone artifacts	174
8.1.	Edge-damaged flakes and other expedient flaked tools	186
8.2.	Bifaces and drills	186
8.3.	Pre-pueblo projectile points	186
8.4.	Early Pueblo projectile points	187
8.5.	Late Pueblo arrow points of obsidian	187
8.6.	Hammerstones and pecking stones	187
8.7.	Cores	211
8.8.	Archaic and Basketmaker projectile points and bifaces from Kiva 279	212
8.9.	Obsidian projectile points from Plaza 900/Kiva 901 showing three styles	215
9.1.	Articulated rabbits (cottontail)	231
9.2.	Three articulated cottontails from floor of Structure 286	232
9.3.	Bones of Rodents: Beaver (*Castor canadensis*)	233
9.4.	Bones of carnivores	234
9.5.	Artiodactyla bone	235
9.6.	Bones of ravens and birds of prey	238
9.7.	Articulated raven wing from Kiva 901	239
9.8.	Bones of water birds	240
9.9.	Bones of land birds	240
9.10.	Fish bones	242
9.11.	Animal skulls	245
9.12.	Worked bone	250

10.1.	Whole shell beads of *Olivella dama* and unknown shell	255
10.2.	Shell pendants of *Conus* sp., *Nassarius* sp., *Laevicardium elatum*	256
10.3.	Shell pendants of *Anodonta californiensis*	256
10.4.	*Glycymeris maculata* shell ring and fragment of *Glycymeris gigantus* showing modification	257
10.5.	*Glycymeris* sp. shell bracelets	257
10.6.	Miscellaneous reworked shell	258
10.7.	Manufacturing debris from *Anodonta californiensis* ornament production	258
10.8.	Petrified wood flakes possibly used in the manufacture of freshwater shell artifacts	259
11.1.	Chevelon Creek near Chevelon Pueblo	267
11.2.	The protected "Chevelon Uplands"	269
11.3.	Maize (*Zea mays*) ear that burned in storage Structure 702	275
11.4.	Maize (*Zea mays*) kernels from storage Structure 702	275
12.1.	Wood species diversity at Chevelon: wood use	295
12.2.	Percentage of wood species found in kivas at Chevelon	295
12.3.	Percentage of wood species found in Structure 274 (Kiva 279 fill) at Chevelon	295
12.4.	Species diversity in early and late room blocks	298
12.5.	1899 and 1977 photos of juniper expansion between Acoma and Enchanted Mesa	299
13.1.	Profile of Kiva 279 showing numerous ash dumps	305
13.2.	Structure 286 floor assemblage	324
13.3.	Structure 124 floor assemblage	324
C.1.	Field Sketch of structure and location of human remains	390
C.2.	Skeletal elements represented (shaded)	391

Tables

1.1.	Villages within the Homol'ovi Settlement Cluster	6
1.2.	Number and Types of Rooms Excavated/Tested at Chevelon Pueblo	15
1.3.	Number of Deposits within Room Blocks at Chevelon that can be Assigned a Phase Date Estimated from Analyzed Ceramic Assemblages	16
1.4.	Phase of Construction for Excavated/Tested Structures by Room Block Based on Fill Deposits and Subfloor Deposits	18
3.1.	Phase Sequence for the Homol'ovi Settlement Cluster	28
3.2.	Ceramic Attributes Associated with the Present Chronology for the Homol'ovi SettlementCluster based on LaMotta (2006) and E.C. Adams (2001, 2002)	29
3.3.	Stages of Village Growth at Chevelon and the Archaeological Bases for their Interpretation	32
3.4.	Frequency of Burning in Excavated Villages in the Homol'ovi Settlement Cluster	37
4.1.	Structure Use Types by Location and Prevalent Features	42
4.2.	Selected Artifacts as Part of Floor Assemblages	55
4.3.	Contexts and Types of Axes Recovered from Homol'ovi Settlement Cluster Villages	57
4.4.	Characteristics of Chevelon Kivas	60
4.5.	Room Suites at Chevelon	72
4.6.	Spinal Room Blocks that have been Identified at Chevelon	80
4.7.	Plaza Spaces at Chevelon	82
6.1.	Number, Weight, and Percentage for Each by Ware from Analyzed Ceramics at Chevelon	119
6.2.	Percentage of Wares from Excavated Homol'ovi Settlement Cluster Villages (E.C. Adams 2002: Table 7.1, unpublished tables for H2)	123
6.3.	Number and Percentage of Decorated Wares from Selected Silver Creek and Upper Little Colorado Pueblos	125
6.4.	Ceramic Dates for Deposits at Chevelon Based on Percentage of Jeddito Yellow Ware, Adapted from LaMotta (2006)	129
6.5.	Number of White Mountain Red Ware and Roosevelt Red Ware sherds Within Kiva 274/279 by Stratum	130
6.6.	Number and Percentage of Total Decorated of the Four Most Common Decorated Wares at Chevelon by Ceramic Phase	132
6.7.	Counts and Proportions of Select Temporally-Diagnostic Decorated Ceramic Wares and Types at Homol'ovi I, Organized By Ceramic Phase (LaMotta 2006)	133
6.8.	Number and Frequency of White Mountain Red Ware sherds by Ceramic Phase at Homol'ovi I and Homol'ovi III	133
6.9.	Number and Percentage of Jeddito Yellow Ware sherds by Ceramic Phase	136
6.10.	Number and Percentage of White Mountain Red Ware Types by Ceramic Phase	139
6.11.	Number and Percentage of Selected Wares by Room Block	142
6.12.	Frequency of White Mountain Red Ware sherds by Room Block and Plaza 900	143
6.13.	Percentage of Types for Chevelon Kivas	145
6.14.	Reconstructible Vessels from Chevelon	147
6.15.	Number and Percentage of Burned Jeddito Yellow Ware Sherds by Structure	152
6.16.	Amount and Percentage of Burned Jeddito Yellow Ware Sherds by Phase	152
6.17.	Miscellaneous Ceramic Artifacts from Chevelon	153
7.1.	Ground Stone Assemblage	157
7.2.	Completeness of Ground Stone Artifacts	157
7.3.	Ground Stone Material Type	158
7.4.	Texture of Ground Stone Artifacts	159
7.5.	Burned Ground Stone Artifacts by Type	160

7.6.	Recovery Context for Burned Ground Stone Artifacts	161
7.7.	Burned Ground Stone Artifacts by Structure	162
7.8.	Ground Stone Artifact Reuse	163
7.9.	Recovery Context for Ground Stone	164
7.10.	Mano and Metate Subtypes	165
7.11.	Mano Use Surfaces	166
7.12.	Ground Stone Artifact Type by Structure Use	166
7.13.	Ground Stone by Structure	170
7.14.	Abrader Subtypes	171
7.15.	Polishing Stone Subtypes	173
7.16.	Axe Statistics	173
7.17.	Miscellaneous Ground Stone Subtypes	176
7.18.	Frequency of Ground Stone versus Ceramics by Room Block	177
7.19.	Temporal Distribution of Ground Stone	179
8.1.	Definition of Artifact Types Used for the Chevelon Flaked Stone Analysis	183
8.2.	Summary of Chevelon Flaked Stone Assemblage	185
8.3.	Sources of Obsidian from Homol'ovi and Puerco Valley Villages	189
8.4.	Distribution of Flaked Stone Raw Materials by Structure	194
8.5.	Distribution of Projectile Points by Structure	199
8.6.	Distribution of Platform Type by Flake Category	201
8.7.	Biface to Core Ratios by Raw Material and Temporal Phase at Chevelon, Homol'ovi II, and Homol'ovi III	202
8.8.	Distribution of Flaked Stone Raw Materials by Depositional Context	205
8.9.	Distribution of Flaked Stone Classes by Depositional Context	206
8.10.	Distribution of Flaked Stone by Structure and Depositional Context	207
8.11a.	Distribution of Flake Categories by Structure	208
8.11b.	Distribution of Flaked Stone Tools by Structure	209
8.11c.	Distribution of Cores by Structure	210
8.12.	Distribution of Projectile Points by Raw Material	216
8.13.	Distribution of Projectile Point Raw Materials by Structure	217
8.14.	Chronological Distribution of Structures at Chevelon	218
8.15.	Temporal Distribution of Flaked Stone Classes	219
8.16.	Temporal Distribution of Flaked Stone Class Ratios	219
8.17.	Temporal Distribution of Raw Materials	220
9.1.	General Taxonomic Composition of the Chevelon Pueblo Faunal Dataset	227
9.2.	Use of Excavated Rooms	230
9.3.	General Taxonomic Composition of the Chevelon Pueblo Faunal Dataset	230
9.4.	Lepus/Sylvilagus Ratio and Artiodactyl Index for Homol'ovi II, Homol'ovi III, Homol'ovi IV and Chevelon	231
9.5.	Contextual Data for Turkey and Sandhill Crane Remains from Chevelon	233
9.6.	List of Taxa Defined as Rare/Unusual	237
9.7.	List of Cranial Elements Found at Chevelon	243
9.8.	Articulated Animal Remains Found at Chevelon	244
9.9.	Chi-square Goodness of Fit Test for Ritual vs. Non-ritual Structures	245
9.10.	Chi-square Goodness of Fit Test for Cranial vs. Other Rare Elements	247
9.11.	Bone Tools from Chevelon by Type and Structure Number	249
10.1.	Identification of Gastropods by Family, Genus, and Species	253
10.2.	Identification of Pelecypods by Family, Genus, and Species	253
10.3.	Distribution of Shell Artifacts by Structure	254
10.4.	Shell Distribution by Room Use and Artifact Type	260
10.5.	Distribution of Datable Shell Artifacts by Phase and Structure	261
11.1.	Plants Observed on the Wide Foodplain and in the Drier Upland Area Immediately Surrounding Chevelon Pueblo	266

11.2.	Plants Observed Within and Adjacent to Chevelon Creek in the Vicinity of Chevelon Pueblo, and in the Protected Riparian Location Known As Upper Chevelon Creek, Approximately 5.5 km South of Chevelon Pueblo	268
11.3.	Archaeobotanical Samples Analyzed for this Report, Arranged by Structure	270
11.4.	List of Plant Taxa and Parts Recovered in all Flotation and Macrobotanical Samples Analyzed from Chevelon Pueblo	272
11.5.	Presence of Charred Maize (*Zea mays*) Remains in Flotation Samples from Chevelon Pueblo Structures, Arranged by Time Period	274
11.6.	Maize (*Zea mays*) Kernels and Cob Segments Collected as Macrofossils by Excavators, and Examined by R. Emerson Howell	276
11.7.	Basic Measurements of 182 Charred Maize Kernels Collected as Macrofossils, and Examined by R. Emerson Howell	276
11.8.	Basic Observations and Measurements of 182 Charred Maize Cob Segments Collected as Macrofossils, and Examined by R. Emerson Howell	276
11.9.	Distribution of Evidence of Domesticates in 86 Flotation Samples of Secure Time Period	277
11.10.	Presence of Charred and Uncharred Squash (*Cucurbita*) Seed and Rind Specimens, and Charred Cotton (*Gossypium*) Seeds in Flotation Samples from Chevelon Structures, Arranged by Time Period	279
11.11.	Distribution of Reproductive Parts of Wild Plants in 86 Flotation Samples of Secure Time Period.	280
11.12.	Presence of Taxa with Charred Reproductive Parts (e.g. seeds, fruit) in Undisturbed Floor or Floor Feature Contexts of Different Structure Types and a Plaza Area	281
11.13.	Distribution of Non-Reproductive Parts of Wild Plants in 86 Flotation Samples of Secure Time Period. All Remains were Charred	283
11.14.	Distribution of Taxa with Charred Vegetative Parts (e.g., wood, stems, leaves) in Undisturbed Floor or Floor Feature Contexts of Different Structure Types and a Plaza Area	284
11.15.	Comparative Data on Maize (*Zea mays*) and Cotton (*Gossypium*) Remains from Four Homol'ovi Settlement Cluster Villages Farther Down the Little Colorado River	286
12.1.	Chevelon Species vs. Modern Driftwood	291
12.2.	Wood Species Diversity by Structure	292
12.3.	Wood Species Diversity at Chevelon: Room Size	293
12.4.	Wood Species Diversity at Chevelon: Use	294
12.5.	Roof Samples and Minimum Number of Species	296
12.6.	Primary Beams from Chevelon Structures	297
13.1.	Chevelon Structures with Five or More Unusual/Rare Artifacts Frequently Found in Ritual Structures or Enriched Deposits in Other Homol'ovi Settlement Cluster Villages	304
13.2.	Chevelon Structures with Rare/Unusual Artifacts from Shell, Plant, and Animal Remains	316
13.3.	Chevelon Structures with Floor Assemblages	323
13.4.	Structure Deposits Grouped According to Interpretation of Ritual or Ceremonial Activities	326
C.1.	Inventory of Elements Present	388

Appendix A. Seriation by stratum based on Jeddito Yellow Ware index (%JYW) for all structures excavated in 2003 to 2005 at Chevelon Ruin 363
Appendix B. Distribution of rare/unusual animal taxa at Chevelon by structure 373
Appendix C. Structure 227 skeletal remains by Vincent M. LaMotta 383
Appendix D. Provenience Details for Illustrated Artifacts and Objects 393

Preface

This volume summarizes four seasons of fieldwork at Chevelon by the Arizona State Museum (ASM), University of Arizona, under the direction of E. Charles Adams with capable assistance from associate director, Richard C. Lange. Rich did all of the mapping by total station and created AutoCad maps of the site and individual rooms from these data that are used in this monograph. An exceptional group of graduate student crew chiefs directed excavations for one to four years: Melanie Medeiros, Rachel Diaz de Valdez, Lisa Gavioli Roach, A. J. Vonarx, Chris Roos, Sarah Luchetta, Elisabeth Cutright-Smith, Kacy Hollenbeck, Matt Hill, and Ryan (R. Emerson) Howell. Literally dozens of other undergraduate and graduate students (in particular Marycruz Magaña, Natalia Martinez, Lina Mahmood and Zaid Ibraheem) and volunteers made the fieldwork possible, including in particular Earthwatch volunteers for the 2003 to 2005 field seasons, and high school students who participated in the Student Challenge Award Project (SCAP) during the 2005 to 2006 field seasons. I will mention only a few of the more than 100 individuals who worked at Chevelon. Special thanks to volunteers Cathy Maickel, Roberta Foster, Karen Travers, and Betsy Marshall who contributed not only their time but their exceptionally good humor and tolerance for what were sometimes extreme conditions.

The field lab was extraordinarily managed by Donna Cook with able assistance from Karen Travers and Betsy Marshall. In the end, more than 10,000 bags and 400 boxes of artifacts resulted from the excavation of 39 structures and extramural areas at Chevelon. Although no exact count has been made due to the difficulty of the task, I estimate that nearly 250,000 artifacts were recovered from the 2003 to 2006 field seasons.

The four seasons in the field were complemented by 10 years of lab work with major contributions by Melanie Medeiros, Rachel Diaz de Valdes, Elisabeth Cutright-Smith, Lisa Gavioli Roach, Julia Meyers, and Marycruz Magaña, who used the data for their theses and dissertations. Claire Barker, Samantha Fladd, and Saul Hedquist are presently using Chevelon data in their dissertation research. In addition, several undergraduate students used Chevelon data in their senior theses or independent study projects including Carlita Cotton, Katy Copeland, and Melanie King.

Additional lab work was conducted by Jaye Smith, Riley Duke, Jenny Cano, Elizabeth Carroll, Ed Nassy, Monica Voge, Michele Miekstyn, Alyssa Mazza, Katie MacFarland, and Chelsey Santino. In particular, I want to single out Jay Marshall and Tanya Yang for their extraordinary efforts in organizing and cataloging all of the artifacts excavated by ASM from Chevelon. I also want to thank Rich Lange for his continual efforts to manage all of the databases used for analysis of the artifacts. I am indebted to everyone for their efforts and contributions, as without them this volume would not have been possible.

Samantha Fladd created Figures 4.9 and 4.11. Rich Lange produced the remainder of the line drawings. Jannelle Weakly and the editor photographed all the artifacts except those in Chapter 11. Photographs in Chapter 11 are by Karen Adams. Thank you to Wesley Bernardini, Andrew Duff, and Greg Schachner whose reviews of the manuscript much improved the published version.

Funding of the research at Chevelon came from Earthwatch Institute, Earthwatch's SCAP high school program, ASM, and the National Science Foundation (Grant 0135492). Logistics and general support of the fieldwork were provided by Homolovi State Park, Arizona State Parks, and through manager Karen Berggren and her capable staff. The Park allowed us to store our field equipment and conduct our summer field lab in their maintenance yard. ASM staff also worked with Parks personnel to put on the annual Homolovi State Park open house, which was advertised widely and involved tours of the excavations, exhibition of significant artifacts recovered during the summer in the visitors' center, and tours of other cultural features within the Park on one Saturday in late July each year. We typically averaged more than 200 visitors during open house events.

The project would not have been possible without the ability of the project to stay at the Winslow BIA dormitory each summer from 1986 through 2007. The project wishes to thank the Dorm Board members from the Navajo Nation and dorm principals, Leonard Smith and Helen Higdon, who were gracious hosts and allowed us to make the dorm our home away from home. Finally, I want to thank the Hopi Tribe, the Hopi Cultural Preservation Office (CPO), and all of the members of the Hopi Tribe who visited us during our fieldwork and shared their thoughts and cultural knowledge about their ancestral home. Their involvement deepened our understanding of Chevelon and indeed of the entire region, as a special place that still plays an active role in Hopi spiritual life. In particular, I want to thank Leigh Kuwanwisiwma, Director of Hopi CPO, who supported our work and encouraged visitation by members of his advisory council.

Chapter 1
Introduction: General Traits of Chevelon
E. Charles Adams

Smoke was visible for miles around as the remaining rooms of Sakwavayu smoldered and collapsed. *Sakwavayu* is a Hopi name for both Chevelon and nearby Clear creeks meaning "turquoise or blue river," in reference to their continuous flow of water. Perhaps half of the rooms of the village had thus ended their use by the occupants who had called Sakwavayu their home, but now chose to leave and migrate to large prosperous villages to the north. The people left their homes in Sakwavayu with some sadness but with hope and optimism as they began what they hoped was their final migration to join relatives and friends at Awat'ovi and other nearby villages. It is nearing the end of the fourteenth century and old relationships with villages near and far are changing and the people of Sakwavayu must change as well. They had set their dwellings on fire using whatever was available for fuel, including storerooms full of maize or the long-dried timbers and grass that formed their roofs. Some of the fires raged for hours, creating fiery infernos fueled by maize. Others barely burned before their roofs collapsed from weakened beams brought on by old age or use of cottonwood as principal construction material.

Nearly every exposed beam was torched to close the village, seal the spirits there, and discourage those who might come later from disturbing this place. Nearly every room was closed by its occupants prior to its burning according to family or village custom or practice. All belongings not needed for the ritual, but needed for their next destination and that could be carried were taken by the last occupants. Belongings that could not be taken were left behind, as if placed in storage.

They are honoring a village tradition of burning. Burning is used to remodel rooms by removing old, bug-infested roof members and replacing them with clean, bug-free ones. When their kivas are no longer used, they are often decommissioned by burning and collapsing the roof to the floor to purify the space and prevent others not initiated into the rites performed in the structures from being spiritually harmed by objects and the space. The burning not only purifies it begins to cover and fill the underground structure, a process that may go on for many years as associated sacred objects are alternately discarded and buried in these kiva spaces. This history of the use of fire to close and seal a space was logically used to close and seal the village from those who could disturb it and be harmed by religious and perhaps spiritual energy that remained there.

As the remaining 100 or so occupants set fire to and then left Sakwavayu, these thoughts were undoubtedly on their minds. They may have been surprised at the distance they could still see their village and, even when the fires dimmed, of the smoke that arose from the rooms that were burning. Perhaps the smoke could even be seen from Awat'ovi, 100 km north. It could certainly have been seen from the west at Homol'ovi II (H2) and Homol'ovi I (H1), assuming they were still occupied, at 19 and 16 km respectively.

More than 100 rooms at Chevelon Pueblo, known as Sakwavayu by its Hopi descendents, were burned when its occupants left the village in the late 1300s. The scenario above has been constructed from evidence found by Arizona State Museum (ASM) archaeologists working at Chevelon from 2002 to 2006. Chevelon is a 500-room pueblo community that was occupied from about 1290 C.E. to the 1390s (Figure 1.1). It is situated on a small natural hill ranging from 6 to 8 m high with the permanently flowing, spring-fed Chevelon Creek 100 m east and the floodplain of the Little Colorado River (LCR) less than 50 m north (Figure 1.2). This location protected it from the severe flooding that frequently occurs along the LCR (E.C. Adams and Hedberg 2002), yet afforded it ready access to water and arable land. More detail on the environment will be presented in Chapter 2.

Chevelon Pueblo was not the first occupation of this hill. In his documentation of Chevelon, Andrews (1982) noted pit house depressions just west of the pueblo and associated pottery suggesting an occupation dating to the Basketmaker III (BMIII) period within the Pecos Classification of Pueblo culture in the region. Along the LCR, BMIII dates from about 600 to 825 C.E. (Lange 1998). Other than a bell-shaped pit beneath the 200 room block (RB) that may date to this period, no specific architecture has been located during ASM excavations that can be assigned to previous use of the hill. There is also considerable pottery under RB100 and 200 dating to the Walnut Phase occupation of the area, which dates from 1100 to 1230 C.E. (Lange 1998). Similar situations pertain at H1 and H2. Two burned Walnut Phase pit houses were excavated under the north room block to the central plaza at H2 and ceramics, similar to that found at Chevelon, were also recovered from the surface beneath and mixed in with later fourteenth century deposits at H1. Numerous undocumented Walnut Phase pueblos of five to 25 rooms have been seen by the author within 2 to 3 km of Chevelon, to the east of Chevelon Creek.

Chevelon's 500-room size has been suggested for some time (Andrews 1982), but detailed wall tracing and mapping by the Homol'ovi Research Program (HRP) of the ASM, University of Arizona from 2002 through 2005 confirmed the accuracy of this estimate. ASM was able to document about 375 ground floor rooms and another 125 second-story rooms.

Previous Research

Previous professional research at Chevelon was conducted by Jesse Walter Fewkes in the summer of 1896 when he excavated burials on the north slopes below the pueblo rooms (Fewkes 1898, 1904). Fewkes did not publish a map of the village nor apparently conduct any excavations within its architecture. He did, however, accumulate a sizable collection of artifacts from the burials, including almost 500 whole vessels, which are presently housed at the Smithsonian Institution. Research focusing on the Fewkes vessels has been conducted by Patrick Lyons (2003) and Kelley Hays-Gilpin (Hays-Gilpin et al. 1996).

Northern Arizona University, Flagstaff, did an evaluation of Chevelon including documentation of 465 pot holes, mapping

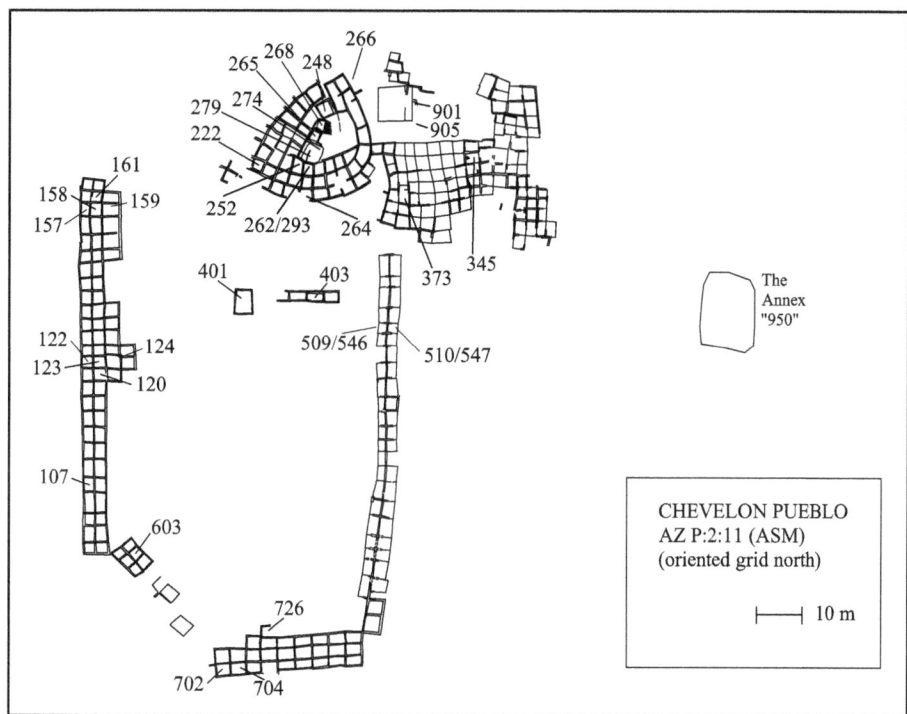

Figure 1.1. Plan map of Chevelon showing location of excavated structures.

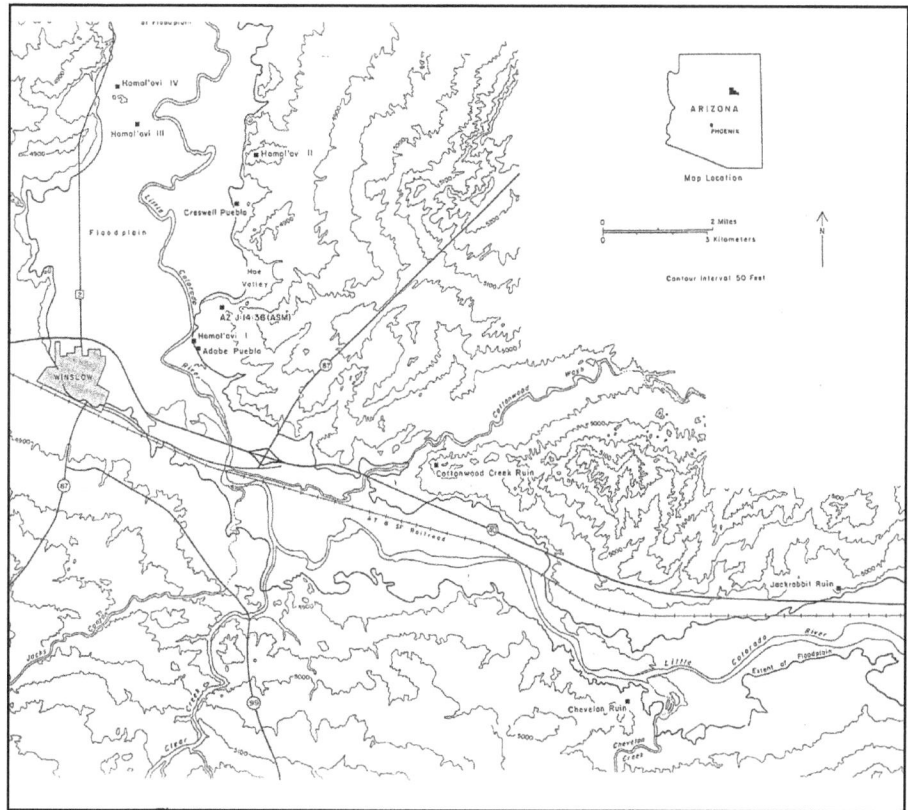

Figure 1.2. Topographic map of middle Little Colorado River in vicinity of Chevelon.

of 234 exposed wall segments, and surface collection of several thousand artifacts including ceramics, flaked stone, ground stone, animal bone, and burned corncobs in 1981 under the direction of Michael J. Andrews (Andrews 1982:69,79). Andrews (1982:Figure 9) divided Chevelon into seven room blocks and three plazas, which he designated 1 through 7 and A to C respectively. He also divided the midden areas in relation to the room blocks for surface collection. ASM has modified these designations by adding two zeros to the room blocks, thus Room Block 2 became RB200, and the plazas were assigned designations 000 for A, 800 for B and 900 for C. Midden areas behind the room blocks received the room block number plus a "99" designation. For example, midden areas adjacent to RB100 are designated as 199 (Figure 1.3).

General Place Description and Relationship to other Homol'ovi Settlement Cluster Sites

The 300 or so occupants of Chevelon were not alone in their occupation along the middle LCR in the 1300s. As I have detailed elsewhere (E.C. Adams 2002), Chevelon is part of a cluster of seven villages situated along a 32 km (20 mile) stretch of the LCR. From west to east, these villages are Homol'ovi IV (H4), Homol'ovi III (H3), H2, H1, Cottonwood Creek Ruin, Chevelon, and Jackrabbit Ruin (Figure 1.4; Table 1.1). I refer to these villages as the Homol'ovi Settlement Cluster (HSC). Chevelon is the third largest village in the cluster, in number of rooms and estimated population, behind H1 and H2 and, at 100 years, one of the two longest lived villages in the cluster, along with H1.

As with H1, the longevity of the occupation of Chevelon caused its role in the HSC to evolve throughout its occupation. More than 20 years of excavations in HSC villages indicates Chevelon was always the second largest village in the community, behind H1, from its founding of about 1290 to about 1365, when H2 was established. As detailed in Chapter 4, Chevelon grew gradually from a founding community of about 50 rooms in 1290 to 100 rooms by the early 1300s to nearly 300 rooms by 1325. Growth seems to have slowed for the next 25 to 35 years before another growth spurt that brought Chevelon to its final 500-room size by around 1375.

Detailed discussion of the place of Chevelon in the HSC has already been presented (E.C. Adams 2002). What will concern us here are the particulars related to Chevelon taken from its perspective. Chevelon's nearest neighbors are Cottonwood Creek and Jackrabbit pueblos, each about a quarter the size of Chevelon. Both were founded about the same time as Chevelon, and along with H1 and H3, formed a string of five pueblos that stretched more than 30 km along the LCR, equally spaced to accommodate local resource needs of the villages (E.C. Adams 2002:7). Chevelon was advantageously situated from the beginning with respect to the other four villages, due to its location at the intersection of Chevelon Creek and the LCR. This provided access to permanent water, a potential to control the direction and flow of this water, access to abundant arable land in the LCR floodplain, and access to riparian resources up Chevelon Creek not present in the LCR floodplain. The availability of a broad hill that protected the Chevelon occupants from the frequent floods in the river was the essential final ingredient

Chapter 1: General Traits of Chevelon 5

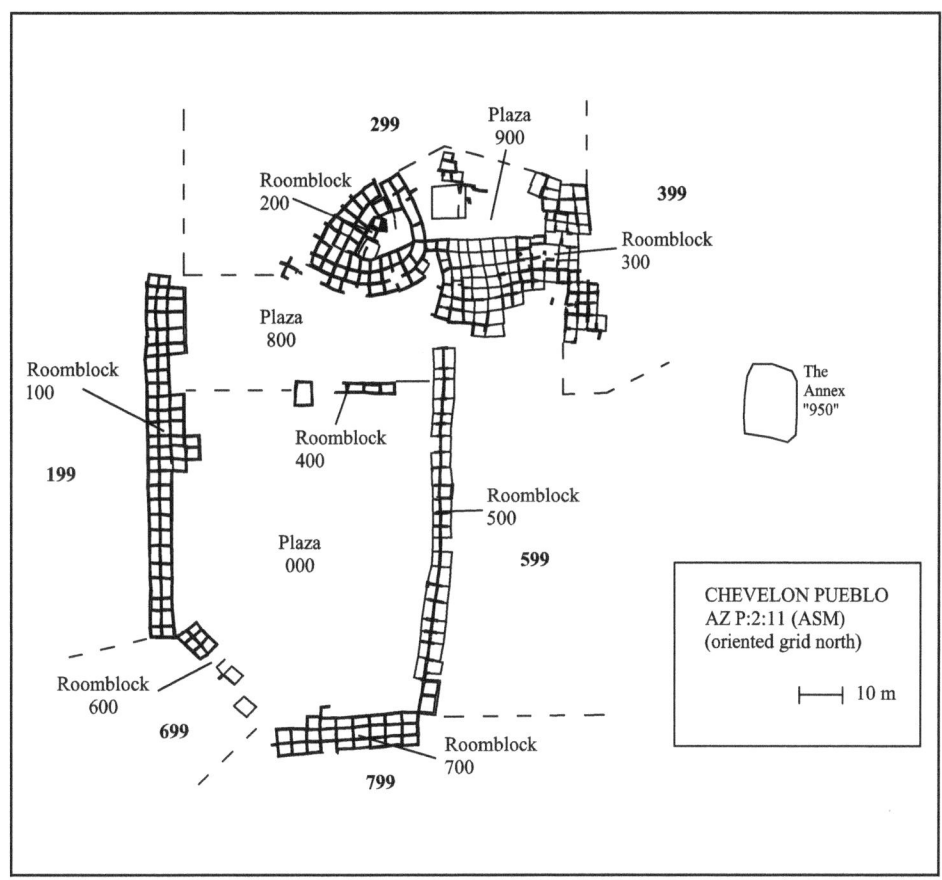

Figure 1.3. Plan of Chevelon showing room block designations.

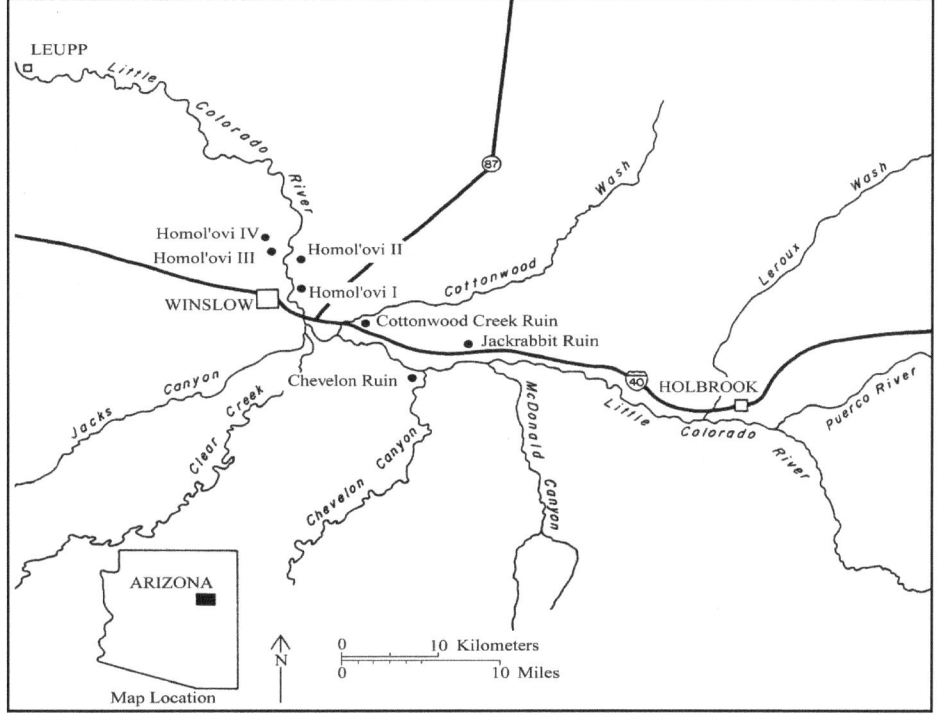

Figure 1.4. Location of Homol'ovi Settlement Cluster villages.

Table 1.1. Villages within the Homol'ovi Settlement Cluster.

Village	No. of Structures	Structures Excavated	Occupation Period
Homol'ovi I	1100	70	1290-1400
Homol'ovi II	1200	34	1365-1400
Homol'ovi III	45	20	1285-1305
			1325-1375
Homol'ovi IV	200	10	1260-1290
Chevelon	500	39	1290-1400
Jackrabbit	120	5	1285-1305
			1350-1375
Cottonwood Creek	120		1285-1360
Total	3285	178	

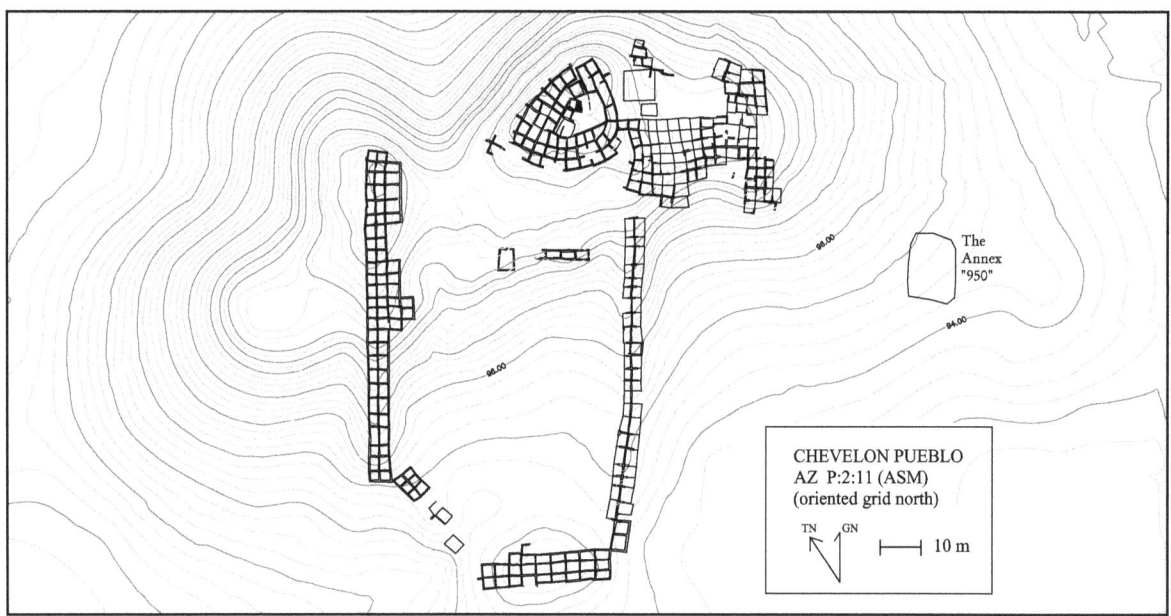

Figure 1.5. Topographic plan of Chevelon.

to its location and subsequent growth (Figure 1.5).

Excavations suggest that by 1325/1330, when Jeddito Yellow Ware (JYW) was introduced to the HSC, Chevelon already had 250 to 300 rooms, second only to H1 in size and much larger than its nearest neighbors (see E.C. Adams 2002:98). Some inhabitants of neighboring Jackrabbit and Cottonwood Creek pueblos, both of which were abandoned between 1350 and 1375, could have added to the increase in population of Chevelon during this period. Evidence accumulated during excavations, however, suggests groups from the southeast, who made Roosevelt Red Ware (RRW), also contributed to village growth after 1365. Evidence for this migration will be taken up in Chapter 4 and Chapter 6.

Prior to the appearance of JYW, Chevelon ceramics were dominated by locally-produced decorated Winslow Orange wares (WOW) and utility wares comprised of Mogollon Brown, Tusayan Gray, Homol'ovi Orange and Gray, and Puerco Valley utility wares (see Chapter 6 for details). I have argued elsewhere that the local production of WOW, as demonstrated by Patrick Lyons (2003), signifies a strong intra-cluster identity and points to the development of a shared tradition and identity distinctive from other clusters, especially the one at Hopi (E.C. Adams 2002). Other indications of strong ties with other members of HSC is the presence at Chevelon of manos and metates from a distinctive stone source near H1 (Fratt and Biancaniello 1993) (see Chapter 7), petrified wood possibly from a source near Jackrabbit Pueblo or as distant as Petrified Forest National Park 55 km east, obsidian from Government Mountain (see Chapter 8), and polychrome pottery from the White Mountain Red Ware and RRW traditions (see Chapter 6), which are far more abundant at Chevelon than at the other HSC communities (E.C. Adams 2002:Table 7.2; Andrews 1982).

Fall-off rates for each of these artifact classes from Chevelon to H1 and H2, suggests intra-cluster trade as the likely mechanism for their distributions. The same can be said for the Shinarump ground stone quarry near H1 and the distribution of artifacts from this source among the HSC villages (see Chapter 7). This exchange, the uniform nature of locally-produced ceramics among the villages, and the mutual dependence on a single water source, water flowing down the LCR from Chevelon and Clear creeks, are argued to make the villages in the HSC mutually dependent (see Chapter 7 in E.C. Adams 2002).

NEARBY SETTLEMENTS AND THE BIG PICTURE

The predominance of JYW, at Chevelon and all other HSC villages occupied after 1325, does not suggest a major change in intra-cluster relationships, but rather a continuation of ties to communities on the Hopi mesas that relate to the origins of most of the cluster inhabitants, including those at Chevelon. As shown by Lyons (2003), these ties are best demonstrated in ceramic design traditions, but also are present in continued trade of white and orange wares made on the Hopi mesas between 1260 and 1325 to HSC villages (E.C. Adams 2002:Table 7.1). As noted above, exchange in a number of non-perishable objects expressed the continuity of ties to one another after production of WOW declined or ceased altogether by 1365.

At Chevelon, as at H1 and H2, JYW came to dominate all ceramic assemblages postdating 1350/1360. I have attributed this substantive increase to the founding of H2 (E.C. Adams 2002). The nearly 90 percent frequency of JYW, among decorated ceramics from H2, point to the origin of its occupants as from Hopi mesa villages. Compositional analysis of JYW ceramics from HSC villages by Bernardini (2005) and Bishop et al. (1988) pinpoint the source of exchange to the Homol'ovi villages as Awat'ovi, Kawayka'a, and other Antelope Mesa villages to the east of modern Hopi communities. According to Bernardini (2005:Table 5.7), 87 percent of H1, 83 percent of H2, 91 percent of Jackrabbit, 100 percent of Cottonwood Creek, and 92 percent of Chevelon JYW ceramics that could be attributed to a Hopi source came from Antelope Mesa villages. The three latest occupied villages, H1, H2, and Chevelon, are also the ones with the highest frequencies of ceramics compositionally produced at the largest Hopi Mesa village, Awat'ovi, with 53 percent, 54 percent, and 41 percent respectively (Bernardini 2005:Table 5.7). Although exchange by individuals within villages with Awat'ovi and other Antelope Mesa villages is likely, down-the-line exchange from H2 to other HSC villages cannot be eliminated as an explanation (E.C. Adams et al. 1993).

Given the above percentages by village of production for JYW, it seems likely that the source of the H2 population was from numerous Antelope Mesa villages, with a substantial number coming from Awat'ovi, although exterior designs, or glyphs, on JYW bowls also implicate Kawayka'a (LeBlanc and Henderson 2009). The presence of extensive exchange of JYW between H1, Chevelon, and other HSC villages, with Hopi Mesa villages predating the founding of H2, suggests that exchange ties between the two areas were more complex. A possible explanation for the pattern unveiled by Bernardini is that H2 occupants initially controlled much of the trade of JYW for cotton, but that later each village established their own exchange ties (E.C. Adams 2002).

The explanation favored here is that exchange relationships between the two areas were predicted on where the populations of specific Homol'ovi villages originated and the continuation of these relationships after JYW began to be produced. Another possibility, proposed by Bernardini (2005), is that the exchange of JYW from different Hopi Mesa villages was a prelude to migration to those villages. This explanation is particularly faulty for H2 given the virtual absence of indigenous ceramics and indications of its introduction of katsina religion to the HSC. The high frequency and strong association of JYW compositional analysis with Antelope Mesa is explained much more parsimoniously as a migration from Hopi to Homol'ovi rather than groups from other regions establishing H2 and then creating strong trade ties with Awat'ovi and Kawayka'a. Bernardini's (2005) other argument, that the diversity of petroglyphs at H2 suggests multiple sources to its population, is also just as easily explained as due to the large and complex group of people who migrated to and settled H2. Hopi villages, today, have extremely complex clan and social groups, and petroglyphs around the villages are equally as complex as any found at H2, also representing the indigenous complexity of the resident villages.

The situation for the other HSC villages is more complicated than for H2, in terms of the sources of their ultimate populations. Numerous lines of evidence, including ceramic composition and decoration, community layout, room architecture, and kiva architecture, have been used to argue that the origins of the founders of all the villages in the HSC came from the Hopi mesas either directly or via secondary migration within the cluster (E.C. Adams 2002; Lyons 2003).

Secondary migration by groups migrating from H3 and H4 is suggested for the founding of H1 (E.C. Adams 2001, 2002, 2004b). The evidence that initial populations from Hopi Mesa villages were supplemented by immigrants with diverse origins comes from trade with neighboring settlement clusters. Ceramics and obsidian, from the Anderson Mesa settlements cluster at H4 and H3, indicate extensive trade and the likelihood that small groups of individuals from Anderson Mesa communities could have joined both villages (E.C. Adams 2001, 2004b).

The diversity of ceramics in foundational and pre-yellow ware deposits at H1 suggests strong relationships with groups north of the Hopi Mesas still making Tsegi Orange wares as well as groups from various ceramic traditions above and along the Mogollon Rim to the south, southwest, and southeast. As with H3 and H4, it appears that these groups were small in size, although perhaps in total, fairly large in number, in that no extensive local production of non-indigenous ceramics occurred in any of these villages. The lack of work at Cottonwood Creek, and minimal work at Jackrabbit, limit the conclusions that can be made about their specific histories. Bernardini's (2005) work on the JYW compositional analysis and rock art from Cottonwood Creek suggest its constituent members were as unique as any in the HSC.

Of all the HSC villages, Chevelon offers the best evidence of continuous contact with settlement clusters outside of Homol'ovi and beyond the Hopi mesas. This evidence will be detailed in the ceramics chapter.

Hopi Oral Traditions about Chevelon and the Homol'ovi Settlement Cluster

Hopi oral accounts of their travels to and through the villages that make up the HSC have been summarized in E.C. Adams (2002), which in itself is a distillation of accounts found in Courlander (1971), Fewkes (1904), and Nequatewa (1936). Although specific clans, such as the Tobacco and Rabbit clans, associate themselves with Chevelon, there is no migration story for Chevelon that is separate from that of the other Homol'ovi villages. Generically, the Homol'ovi area is viewed by the Hopi as a place where many clans gathered as a prelude to their final migration to the various modern Hopi villages (E.C. Adams 2002:6). Hopi oral history refers to Chevelon Pueblo as *Sakwavayu*. According to Fewkes (1904), the area was popular in the late 1800s for collecting turtles and water birds by Hopi for their ceremonies. The many clans living at the Homol'ovi pueblos made their final migration to Hopi villages, occupying the major villages of Orayvi, Songoòpavi, Musangnuvi, Walpi, and Awat'ovi, located at each of the four mesas (Fewkes 1904). According to Hopi oral traditions, groups migrating to the HSC came primarily from the Chavez Pass (Nuvakwewtaqa, or "butte with snow belt") Settlement Cluster, which consisted of three villages, with no more than two occupied at any one time (Bernardini and Brown 2004; Bernardini 2005).

We were visited by numerous individuals, families, and groups from Hopi Mesa villages during excavations at Chevelon. Although interviewed more than a century after Fewkes' work and attribution of clan affiliation, present Hopi are remarkably consistent in their stories of their ancestors who occupied Chevelon. None, however, were aware of the extensive burning of the village nor, evidently, was Fewkes aware of this evidence, as burning is not mentioned in his report (Fewkes 1898, 1904).

Hopi oral history is a misnomer because there is no single Hopi history. Each clan at each village maintains its own tradition of migration. Nevertheless, there is general agreement, among the clan migration traditions from the Homol'ovi area, that migration to Homol'ovi came primarily from the south. Whether from the semi-mythical place called Palatkwapi, or Nuvakwewtaqa, the migrants originated south of the Homol'ovi area. This suggests that groups identified at Chevelon as from the south might be connected to the oral traditions.

Research Interests

Research at Chevelon has focused on several issues of interest to professional archaeologists as well as to the general public. Many of these interests are traditional concerns for archaeology and can be grouped under the categories of history, trade or exchange, migration, and life ways. Other interests are more theoretical in orientation and can be grouped under the categories of community organization, social power, agency and practice, and formation processes.

History

To connect prehispanic archaeology with history can provoke endless debate about what is meant by history. Many would argue that history consists of written records studied and summarized by historians, but every society has a history and it is, in this sense, that I use the word. Hopi oral histories can be considered a type of history (see Lyons 2003). For Chevelon, history will consist of an attempt based on the archaeological record to reconstruct how Chevelon was founded, grew, declined, and eventually was depopulated.

It is impossible to identify individual actors in this history, but it is possible to identify actions of individuals or groups that affected the history of the village. In this sense, the application of concepts based in human agency and practice will help us understand the history of Chevelon. A primary element of reconstructing the history of a place without written documents is to establish a reliable chronology. Traditionally in Southwest archaeology, this has been the purview of ceramics and—to a lesser degree—architecture, ultimately rooted in dendrochronology. Chevelon will be no exception to this case. Chapters 3 and 4 will focus on the chronology and history of Chevelon. Chapter 13 will summarize the results.

Exchange

Relationships between Chevelon and its neighbors are critical to understanding the social context of the village. As noted earlier in this chapter, there is considerable evidence indicating the close relationships among the members of the HSC (E.C. Adams 2002, 2004a). Also touched upon is the exchange between Chevelon and nearby settlement clusters. But there are deeper social meanings to trade that often are ignored in traditional treatments of traded items.

Recently, many have linked exchange as a prelude to migration at various scales (Anthony 1990; Bernardini 2005; Cameron 1995; Duff 1998), highlighting the importance of social relationships prior to migration. Hopi history also points to the importance of social relationships in migrations of the eighteenth and nineteenth century to Zuni (E.C. Adams 1982) during periods of intense social stress brought on by epidemics in the 1770s and drought in the 1860s. For our purposes, exchange of goods will be considered in Chapters 6-10 with discussions of ceramics, ground and flaked stone, fauna, and shell. The nature and timing of this exchange will be discussed in terms of migration and power within the village in each of these chapters and in Chapter 13.

Migration

As discussed in the preceding section, exchange can provide insight into the process of migration in the archaeological record and this seems to be the case at Chevelon. There are, however, many levels to migration, as first noted by Haury (1958) at Point of Pines. Scales of migration affect their visibility in the archaeological record, but perhaps most importantly, migration is a social process that implies a preceding relationship between two areas (sensu Cameron 1995) that as archaeologists, we must explore. Could the presence of extensive migrant groups have prompted conflict with H1 and H2, such as happened with Awat'ovi and the other Hopi villages in 1700 (Brew 1949)? Details of the evidence for migration will be presented in Chapter 6, ceramics, but will also be reviewed in Chapters 3 and 4 as well as summarized in Chapter 13.

Daily Life

Although understanding the daily lives of any prehispanic group is at least a major challenge, this volume will capture an idea of what life was like at Chevelon as its history progressed. What evidence is there for activities that occurred frequently and were essential to the maintenance of life in the village? These practices include processing of food and manufacture of non-food items. Elements to this discussion will be presented in Chapters 6 through 12, which detail the object categories recovered from Chevelon. Chapter 12, on wood exploitation, includes an active sense of human involvement in the decision-making. Similarly, Chapter 5 on burning introduces a better sense of human agency in the affairs of the Chevelon people. In other words, Chevelon people were active participants in forming the archaeological record we recovered from Chevelon and we will attempt to see elements of human agency and social practice in understanding the history of life in the pueblo.

Community Organization

"Community organization" is a broad concept that has become a major focus for archaeologists over the past couple of decades. From the perspective of a traditional culture, community organization is a tangled web of relationships based in religious and social roles that have been earned and ascribed (see Fowles 2013). The Western conceptualization of separating social, economic, and religious roles does not readily pertain to traditional societies. In our attempts to understand community organization at Chevelon, we will try to meld these two practices. Although archaeological evidence containing social information will be described in terms of ritual, economic, or social practices, in Chapter 13, I place these practices into a broader relational structure.

It is important to acknowledge that there are power differentials within every society. Power, in traditional non-western society, is based in religious rites and rituals (or practices) (Bell 1997; Connerton 1989; Rappaport 1979, 1999). Due to their more formal or redundant nature, these practices are often more visible in the archaeological record. It is also within these rituals that social practices and human agency may be more visible. As noted, religion plays a more central role in non-western society and this was certainly the case at historical Hopi and other pueblos encountered by Spaniards in the sixteenth and seventeenth centuries (for Hopi, see Brew 1949) and described by ethnographers in the late nineteenth and first half of the twentieth centuries (e.g., Eggan 1950; Titiev 1944). Therefore, understanding ritual practices at Chevelon will provide insights into more general social practices within the village.

Social Power

As described in the previous section, power is never equally distributed in any society and this certainly was not the practice in traditional Pueblo society (Brandt 1984; Ortiz 1969), specifically Hopi society (Levy 1992; Whiteley 1988), and is not expected to be the case in Chevelon society (E.C. Adams 2002, 2004a; E.C. Adams and LaMotta 2006; E.C. Adams et al. 2004). Development and control of religious ceremonies is a uniform trait for accumulating power in traditional societies (for details see Rappaport 1979, 1999; also cf. Connerton 1989; Mills 2004). As described by Levy (1992), power in Hopi society is based on ownership of religious ceremonies and of the best farmland, in line with such traditions practiced elsewhere (see also Bradfield 1971, 1995). Although access to and control of the best farmland is the practice at Hopi, it does not result in the accumulation of storehouses of food that could be used to distinguish such practices and individuals in the archaeological record (Cameron 1999; Titiev 1944).

The means for detecting religious practices in the archaeological record is quite different (E.C. Adams 1991a, 1994, 2002; E.C. Adams and Duff 2004a; Crown 1994). The history of religious practices at Chevelon can be detailed using the archaeological record and an understanding of formation processes, to be discussed below. Chapter 4 will describe religious structures and Chapter 5 will present evidence for the use of burning as a practice that is often tied to religious power. Chapter 13 will describe several artifact classes that, through their uniqueness, play roles in identifying religious practice in the archaeological record (see Walker 1995, 1996b, 1999; Walker et al. 2000). Chapter 14 will synthesize our understanding of the relationship of religion and ritual practice to social power.

Agency and Practice

Human agency and social practice are popular trends in the present practice of archaeology. Human agency asserts that individuals or small groups have intentional actions that can be detected in the archaeological record through material residues (Hodder and Hutson 2003:101). Here, we shall also consider the possibility that objects can have agency, as discussed by Gosden (2005), Gosden and Marshall (1999), Hodder and Hutson (2003), and Walker (2002). Religious objects are, perhaps, the best examples of objects as agents (Connerton 1989). Objects have personal histories or biographies (Appadurai 1986) that can be reconstructed through various methods first argued by behavioral archaeologists, such as the nature of the context (deposit location, associated objects, etc.) (see Schiffer 1987) Practice theory, also termed social action (Bourdieu 1977; Giddens 1979, 1981), asserts that patterned human behavior, as created through practices within a society, should be readily detectable in the archaeological record and lead us to a better understanding of social, religious, economic, and other practices in human society. An important element of practice is not only its material consequences, but also its identification of space as important in structuring practice.

Connerton (1989) also develops the concept of social memory in similar terms of religious practice and creation of space (see E.C. Adams 2016, for a discussion of social memory within HSC and Chevelon). What is termed "habitus" by Bordieu and "ways of knowing" by Connerton, enables actors or agents to participate, within the milieu of their culture, in ways that cannot be readily described because they are so ingrained within us. Mills (2004), following Weiner (1992), introduces us to the concept of "inalienable possessions." As these are objects belonging to the social group, they are meant to be kept and cannot be exchanged. They confer prestige primarily through the power of associated ritual practices. Religious ritual power, then, can authenticate the authority of corporate groups. These inalienable possessions may be used to authenticate individual, as well as corporate group, identities within societies, such as Chevelon.

Following Bourdieu (1977), Connerton (1989), Hodder and Hutson (2003), Walker (1995) and my own research (E.C. Adams 1991b, 2002), human agency will be viewed through the practice of burning, described in Chapter 5, and practice and agency will be considered through the concepts of social memory, inalienable possessions, and religious rites and practice (Connerton 1989; Mills 2004; Mills and Walker 2008; Rappaport 1979; Van Dyke and Alcock 2003).

Formation Processes

Concern for formation processes, in the archaeological record, has been a practice of research at Homol'ovi from its beginning (E.C. Adams 2002:16-31), with the focus on archaeological deposits rather than larger entities. Schiffer (1987) and others developed the concern for formation processes through the development of behavioral archaeology in the 1970s. For this book, we will focus on the importance of being aware of occupational and post-occupational formation processes. Anything that can happen to an object after it has moved from the systemic to the archaeological record is a formation process. Thus, it could be disturbed or moved by human or natural agency. Object life histories, and other ideas, have been further refined using Homol'ovi data (Walker 1995). The study of object life histories stemming from behavioral archaeology and other disciplines will be helpful in studying agency, memory, formation processes, and other research interests.

METHODOLOGY

E.C. Adams (2002:chapter 3) has already presented a detailed discussion of general HRP methodology. Therefore, the focus here is on sampling design and sample size.

Excavation Methods

Most structures at Chevelon are less than 3 m, in either length or width. In order to have adequate room to work, structures were divided into approximately two equal halves and one was excavated to reveal deposits and stratigraphy, and to produce detailed maps of the structure's profile. If time permitted and the deposits warranted it, the second half of the structure was also excavated with the advantage of knowing the deposits in better detail than in the first excavated half. Frequently, the second half of a structure was not excavated because it had been vandalized and little information could be gained from further excavation.

In the case of larger structures and plaza areas, excavation and sampling proceeded differently. In these cases, 1 m-wide trenches were excavated several meters long to transect either the width or the length of the feature. Because the size of the feature was not known beforehand, the trenches enabled researchers to gauge its size and complexity, leading to a refined sampling design. For kivas, the trench was expanded to include half of the structure in the small kivas and about a quarter of the large kiva, Kiva (K.) 901, in the RB300 plaza. Due to the size and complexity of deposits in (K.) 279 and K. 901, multiple years of excavations were conducted.

Complexity in kiva deposits is nothing new in HSC kivas (Karunaratne 1997; LaMotta 1996; Walker 1995) and their careful excavation was deemed essential for comparison to other HSC kivas and in order to understand the formation processes involved. Plazas were sampled using the same techniques of trenching and in the search for complex surfaces with features that have been found at all other Homol'ovi village plazas. This was less successful at Chevelon, due to a combination of poorer preservation and different use histories for Chevelon plazas (these will be detailed in Chapter 4).

Sample Design and Size

As noted, Chevelon has about 500 total rooms divided into seven room blocks, numbered from 100 to 700, or RB100 to RB700 (Figure 1.3). Additionally, it has four open or plaza spaces, three of which have been numbered RB000, RB800, and RB900. The fourth plaza, which lies within RB200, was not given a separate designation. Details of Chevelon's architecture and settlement growth are presented in Chapter 4. In this section, our concern is how we determined where to excavate and the size of the samples taken (Table 1.2). A total of 39 structures, from all seven room blocks and three plaza areas, were tested and represent about 8 percent of the estimated structures in Chevelon. Table 1.2 lists only 475 structures. It is difficult to estimate the number of second-story rooms and there is no doubt that some were missed in making the room estimates, which were based on wall tracing. Plaza 800 was tested using 108 auger holes, electrical resistivity, and proton magnetometer assessments to identify several features.

Excavations were spread across the pueblo in an attempt to sample spatial variation within Chevelon. Sample size by room block ranged from about 14 percent, in RB100 and 200, to only 3 percent, in RB300, with at least one structure excavated in each of the seven room blocks. Given the large size of the pueblo and the considerable spread of the room blocks that comprise it, the spatial sampling should represent most of the variability in the pueblo, but obviously with only an 8 percent sample, some variability will be missed. There is a recognized sampling bias for RB100 and 200 and against RB300. The low excavation percentage in RB300 is due, in part, to the large estimated number of structures in the room block. Nevertheless, it had the third most structures excavated within it.

Another variable to consider in sampling is perceived room use. Our initial goal was to find and sample three basic structure categories in order to evaluate household and community change: habitation, storage, and kiva/ceremonial. Five structure use types were eventually identified at Chevelon: storage, corn storage, habitation, piki, and kiva. Additional differentiation of structure use will be presented and discussed in Chapter 4. Corn storage is presented as a room use because two of the excavated rooms had more than 60 cm of corn that had been burned and preserved in the many fires at Chevelon. Several other burned corn storage rooms could be identified from surface remains as a result of room vandalism at Chevelon. Other burned storage

Table 1.2. Number and Types of Rooms Excavated/Tested at Chevelon Pueblo.

Room Block	Structures Excavated	Structure Types	Estimated Structures in Room Block	Percent Excavated in Room Block (%)
000	10 sq. m	Plaza	2,000 sq. m	0.5
100	9	4 storage, 2 corn storage, 3 habitation	65	13.8
200[1]	18	7 storage, 1 piki, 5 habitation, 3 kiva, 2 unknown	125	14.4
300[2]	5	2 storage, 1 habitation, 2 kiva	175	2.9
400	1	1 storage	5	20.0
500	3	2 storage, 1 habitation	55	5.5
600	1	1 habitation	20	5.0
700	2	2 storage	30	6.7
800	108 auger holes	Plaza	1,000 sq. m	N/A
900	31 sq. m	Plaza	400 sq. m	7.8
Total	39	18 storage, 2 corn storage, 1 piki, 11 habitation, 5 kiva, 2 unknown	475	8.2

[1]The plaza within RB200 had subsequently been filled with rooms making it impossible to estimate its original size. Thus, no estimates for the RB200 plaza are given.

[2]Structures excavated/tested in RB300 include structures excavated in the plaza, RB900.

rooms did not have corn and this suggests some rooms were specifically set aside for corn storage while others were not. Although in addition to the one at Chevelon, two other piki houses have been excavated in the HSC, one at H3 (E.C. Adams 2001, 2002) and one at H1 (E.C. Adams 2002); their probable rarity would not include them in a sampling strategy. Including corn storage with general storage structures and the piki house with habitation structures results in data recovery from 20 storage structures, 12 habitation structures, five kivas, and two structures of unknown use. Our excavations, in other HSC villages, and data from ethnographic and archaeological research, at Hopi villages, suggests that a ratio of two to three storage structures per habitation structure is typical. Because kiva and habitation rooms typically have more complex histories, the sampling at Chevelon by structure use was biased to increase our knowledge of the village's social history. In addition, sampling in contiguous rooms permitted evaluation of relationships in use of adjacent rooms and the amount of space used by a household.

ASM excavations in the HSC have always focused more on ritual structures than non-ritual structures. For our purposes, ritual structures are places where religious ritual practices took place, which for the most part were in kivas. There are two reasons for this. First, religion and associated religious ritual practices are important elements in understanding pueblo life in the fourteenth century and information from a large sample of religious structures is essential to understanding their variability and the roles they played within the community. In addition, most Homol'ovi kivas were used by corporate groups resulting in artifacts and depositional behaviors that require an adequate sample size to quantify. Of 178 structures excavated in all HSC villages, 26 (14.6 percent) were kivas. Thus, the five kivas represent 12.8 percent of excavated structures at Chevelon, in line with other excavations.

Second, at Chevelon in particular, kivas were the only structures with dense, complex, and deep middens that enabled researchers to evaluate chronological change based on ceramics that could be used to compare deposits from other structures and samples from other villages. It should also be noted that one of the kivas was totally vandalized and contained no intact deposits, while another was only sampled with a shallow 1 m-wide trench and little else is known about it. Thus, only three kivas have been sampled adequately.

Although less is known about RB300 than is ideal, sampling using other criteria is less affected by it. Table 1.3 indicates the estimated age of the deposits, including floor assemblages, within structures based on the percentage of Jeddito Yellow Ware ceramics of total decorated ceramics present (LaMotta 2006). At H1, LaMotta (2006) determined that percentage of JYW predicted the correct order of more than 95 percent of deposits. Its equally successful application at Chevelon is detailed in Chapter 6. Before discussing Table 1.3, it should be stated that 10 of the 32 deposits from RB200 came from K. 274/279 and 11 of the 15 deposits from RB300 came from K. 901. These numbers indicate the size and depth of the deposits in these two structures and their importance, as noted earlier, in helping define the relative chronology of deposits using ceramics at Chevelon. Therefore, 21 of the 53 deposits used in the seriation, or 39.6 percent, came from these two structures and created an inevitable sampling bias.

The other notable trends in the sampling, derived from Table 1.3, are the bias toward RB200, with 22 of the 32 (68.9 percent) non-kiva deposits and the preponderance of Late Homol'ovi Phase (LHP) deposits (31 of 53

Table 1.3. Number of Deposits within Room Blocks at Chevelon that can be Assigned a Phase Date Estimated from Analyzed Ceramic Assemblages.

Phase[1]	RB100	RB200	RB300	RB400	Total
Tuwiuca[2]		1	2		3
Early Homol'ovi	1	9			10
Middle Homol'ovi	1	8			9
Late Homol'ovi	3	14	13	1	31
Total Deposits	5	32	15	1	53

[1]Time periods used to organize Chevelon deposits are derived from detailed seriation of deposits from H1 (LaMotta 2006) and H3 (E.C. Adams 2001) based primarily on percentage of Jeddito Yellow Ware present.

[2]Tuwiuca Phase: 1290-1325/1330; Early Homol'ovi: 1325/1330-1365; Middle Homol'ovi: 1365-1385; Late Homol'ovi: 1385-1400, using criteria and dates from LaMotta (2006).

[58.5 percent]). Excluding the kivas, 19 of 32 [59.4 percent], are from the LHP. Thus, with or without the kiva deposits, the sampling by phase is identical. This is another reason the kivas were used as a dating tool for the rest of the Chevelon deposits. Two Early Homol'ovi Phase (EHP), 7 Middle Homol'ovi Phase (MHP), and 12 LHP deposits come from the kivas. These terms and the Chevelon chronology will be detailed in Chapter 3.

The bias toward RB200, in terms of deposits, is a product of two factors. First, many more structures and deposits were excavated in RB200 than elsewhere in the village because RB200 is the oldest part of Chevelon and therefore has a longer life history than the other room blocks. Not only is the occupation longer, but the number of abandoned and remodeled rooms is also much higher than elsewhere in Chevelon, resulting in a greater number of deposits. A similar situation was encountered in the older parts of H1. Therefore, RB200 offered the best opportunities to recover lengthy chronological information as well as the ability to see change in the organization of the village through time.

The dating bias, toward the LHP at Chevelon, is paralleled at H1 and there was attributed to three factors. First was the inevitable replacement and coverage of earlier deposits by later ones. This could account for only part of the bias, however. The principal bias seems to be caused by the abandonment of many structures during the LHP at H1 and their use as middens. Apparently, earlier occupations did not use structures to such an extent. Finally, the total size of the village population at H1 was apparently much higher and the scope of its use of the pueblo, much broader during LHP. A similar situation seems to have pertained at Chevelon. Prior to the LHP, the village was 250 to 300 rooms. Additionally, use and reuse of all areas, including the oldest parts of the village in RB200 and RB300, removed or destroyed earlier structures and deposits.

Nevertheless, the result of the sampling by phase, illustrated in Table 1.3, is that an adequate cross section of deposits from each phase is present to provide an understanding of village size and growth during its entire occupation with the exception of the Tuwiuca Phase (TP). However, information from architecture can help address this problem because construction dates for many of the rooms are from the TP. Thus, our understanding of village size and layout during the TP will help address some of the shortcomings resulting from a lack of artifacts and deposits.

Table 1.4 lists structures by estimated age of construction to quantify this assertion. In this case, it appears that Chevelon was constructed over a long period of time, but that construction was basically completed by the beginning of the LHP. Earliest construction was in RB200, spreading to RB300 and the northern part of RB100 during the EHP. Major construction occurred around the large southern plaza, RB000, during the MHP. The associated deposits help define the end of use of these rooms and occupation of surrounding spaces, but it is essential to keep in mind that most structures, especially kivas and some habitation structures, had long use lives of perhaps more than 50 years. Issues, such as use-life, will be addressed in Chapters 4, 6, and 13.

Table 1.4. Phase of Construction for Excavated/Tested Structures by Room Block Based on Fill Deposits and Subfloor Deposits.

Phase	RB100	RB200	RB300	RB400	RB500	RB600	RB700	Total
Tuwiuca		17	1					18
Early Homol'ovi	4	1	4					9
Middle Homol'ovi	4			1	3	1	2	11
Late Homol'ovi	1							1
Total Deposits	9	18	5	1	3	1	2	39

Chapter 2
Environment
E. Charles Adams

Tremendous detail about present and past environments in the greater Homol'ovi area has been presented by Lange (1998) and E.C. Adams (2001, 2002) and will not be repeated here except in summary fashion. More detail about the environment, from an archaeological perspective, will be presented in Chapter 8, fauna; Chapter 10, shell; Chapter 11, charred plant remains; and Chapter 12, wood exploitation at Chevelon. Chapter 13 will then summarize, in detail, the picture of the Chevelon area during its occupation.

THE SETTING

The area around Chevelon Canyon and Chevelon Pueblo is located at an elevation of 1490 to 1506 m (about 4900 ft). The founding of Chevelon Pueblo was on top of a 6 to 8 m high hill that has a rather precipitous drop on its north and west sides, but a more gradual slope on its south and east sides, where the pueblo expanded as it grew (see Figure 1.5). Like most hills along the LCR, it is capped with a thick layer, at least 2 m, of gravels held together in loosely compacted caliche. According to Kolbe (1991), these gravels are remnants of the Shinarump Formation, which caps the Moenkopi Formation throughout the study area. The Shinarump is extremely variable in its cementing agents, which range from the hard opaline-silica, used for ground stone, through the soft calcium carbonate (Fratt and Biancaniello 1993). The softer cements are eroded away leaving gravel caps to what are essentially outcrops of Moenkopi Sandstone. Beneath the pueblo, on the top of the hill and along its sides, are gravels ranging from 3 cm to over 15 cm in circumference. This material was used by the Chevelon occupants as raw material for much of their flaked stone processing, with quartzite, used for hammerstones, and chert and petrified wood, used for flaked stone tools (see Chapter 8). This pattern is typical for the entire HSC (E.C. Adams 2001, 2002, 2004b).

The Moenkopi Formation outcrops as layers of laminated sandstone to the west and south of Chevelon and there is evidence of quarrying in these layers for sandstone slabs to construct the pueblo and the mining of clays embedded beneath the harder sandstone for either mortar or pottery. Quarrying for clay is suggested by extensive undercutting of areas where the best clays are located, with less to no undercutting where clays are of poorer quality or do not exist. No raw pottery clay samples were recovered from excavated deposits for comparison, but clays used to construct features or to effect wall repairs derive from clays comparable to those in the nearby Moenkopi Formation outcrops.

CHEVELON CREEK AND THE LITTLE COLORADO RIVER

The Chevelon hill is situated southwest of the intersection of Chevelon Creek with the LCR (Figure 1.2). The springs that feed Chevelon Creek about 10 km upstream from Chevelon Pueblo provide a permanent flow of water that continues for 20 km downstream as the LCR. The permanency of this flow is argued from the abundant fish remains found in the archaeological deposits not only at Chevelon, but also at H1 and H3 (E.C. Adams 2001; McCracken 2003; Strand 1998; see also Chapter 9).

E.C. Adams and Hedberg (2002) have demonstrated the importance and unevenness of streamflow in the LCR drainage, documenting major floods an average of every seven years during the twentieth century. Not only do these floods provide driftwood, so critical for fuel and construction materials, but they also bring sediment that can replenish the floodplain. The downside to the floods is the potential damage they cause to farmland, crops, and human constructs to manage water. No prehispanic water management devices, or systems, have been found during the archaeological research, either through survey, excavations, geophysical work, or aerial photography. They are either buried or removed through erosion and frequent changes in stream channel location. Such rapid changes in location of the actual flow of water in the LCR have been witnessed numerous times since the 1980s, most prominently in 1993, 1995, and 2004. Any movement in location of the flow of water could have a disastrous impact on fields and farmers dependent on the floodplain and water from the river.

The situation for Chevelon Creek is different. Chevelon Creek is located within a canyon cut into the Kaibab and Coconino Formations, which lie below the Moenkopi Formation. Typically, the canyon is less than 100 m across. Extreme flood events have been documented from stream gauges on Chevelon Creek that could have done extensive damage to agricultural systems in the LCR and could have even threatened low-lying areas of the pueblo itself. Fortunately, Chevelon Creek exits its canyon walls about 500 m before the pueblo and the depth of the floodwaters thins considerably. The author has seen the pueblo surrounded with water and, temporarily, an island during floods, but has never seen parts of the pueblo actually inundated. Excavations in the lowest areas of the pueblo did not reveal any flood deposits during or after occupation, suggesting the elevation of the hill was adequate to prevent flooding during the most extreme flood events.

Plant and Animal Communities

Expeditions through this section of the LCR, during the 1850s and 1860s, document the plant and animal communities prior to any Euro-American settlement (Miksicek 1991). Details of plants in the area and in the archaeological record can be found in K. Adams (1992, 1996, 1999, 2001, 2004), K. Adams and LaMotta (2001), Fish (1991, 2001), and Miksicek (1991), and in Chapter 11. Discussions of animals in the region and the archaeological record can be found in Diaz de Valdes (2007), LaMotta (2006), Pierce (2001), Andronescu and Glinsky (2004), McCracken (2003), Strand (1998), Strand and McKim (1996), Szuter (1991), and in Chapters 9 and 10.

In the vicinity of Chevelon, the indigenous plant communities vary from the other villages, due to the presence of Chevelon Canyon. Cottonwoods, willow, and reed are the dominant native plants near Chevelon today, as they were in the 1300s. The nearby upland communities of plants, dependent on less than 200 mm of precipitation annually, were typical of the Great Basin Desert scrub vegetation community, part of the Great Basin Desert Province of the Upper Sonoran Life Zone, which is primarily a treeless grassland dominated by small shrubs, such as shadscale, saltbush, greasewood, sagebrush, and rabbitbrush (Lowe 1964a:37).

Animals best adapted to this environment are rabbits, including cottontail and black-tailed jackrabbit. Faunal assemblages from all the HSC villages, including Chevelon, have 70 to 85 percent rabbits (*Leporidae*), indicating their importance in diet and abundance on the landscape.

Whether along Chevelon Creek or the LCR, unique plants and animals are associated with permanent flows of water. The most important animals are several varieties of fish, turtles, and freshwater mollusks (*Anodonta californiensis*). Fish and especially mollusks are abundant in the Chevelon archaeological record, as discussed in Chapters 9 and 10. Both animals were probably used for food and the mollusk shells were popular for ornaments. An excellent case for multiple uses for *Anodonta* by Chevelon occupants is made by Marycruz Magaña in Chapter 10. Sedges, reeds, and cattails, important plants for rituals and construction at historic Hopi (E.C. Adams 1982), were abundant along the permanent streams and still are today. All are found in the Chevelon archaeological record (see Chapters 9 and 12), with reed occasionally used in roofing, similar to historic roofs at the Hopi pueblo of Walpi (E.C. Adams 1982).

Chevelon Canyon

Chevelon Canyon originates near the crest of the Mogollon Rim, 100 km south of its intersection with the LCR. During its course, it cuts into the Coconino and Kaibab Formations to form sheer rock walls upwards of 100 m deep and sometimes less than 40 m wide. Flow, in its lower reaches, is provided by numerous, large springs that are augmented by seasonal flows from summer monsoonal rains or spring snowmelt (see E.C. Adams 2002; E.C. Adams and Hedberg 2002). Because the Arizona Game and Fish Department constructed a small dam just 100 m east of Chevelon Pueblo, the resultant lake has preserved the indigenous plant community of the canyon less than 5 km from the pueblo. Karen Adams discusses this community in more detail in Chapter 11. Although many species in the floodplain of the LCR are also present in Chevelon Canyon, it has major stands of black walnut and hackberry that are not present in the LCR floodplain. These plants provide additional food sources, building and firewood (see Chapter 12). It is also likely that indigenous fish species, of which five have been documented through the archaeological record (McCracken 2003; Strand 1998), would spawn and maintain viable populations beyond the range of the Chevelon populace. Beaver and muskrat are also known within the canyon. Today, deer and antelope water below the canyon. It is likely, they did so in the past and would have been easily hunted so close to the pueblo.

Driftwood

In Chapter 12, Shaw, Howell, and Vonarx discuss wood exploitation at Chevelon, building on the research into driftwood use at the Homol'ovi villages (E.C. Adams and Hedberg 2002). This topic was also covered extensively in E.C. Adams (2002:46-56). Several major piles of driftwood still remain where Chevelon Creek drains into the LCR channel. At this point, the extreme widening of the stream course encourages the deposition of driftwood carried downstream through Chevelon Canyon from sources within and adjacent to the canyon. One of these piles was sampled in 1996 as part of the research conducted for the E.C. Adams and Hedberg article.

This and other piles are dominated by cottonwood with canyon species of black walnut and hackberry, and higher elevation species found along the edges of the canyon, such as pinyon, juniper, Douglas fir, ponderosa pine, and spruce. Stands of juniper grow within 10 km of the pueblo and could have been harvested, although their presence in driftwood suggests this is the preferred source. Occupants of Chevelon and the other Homol'ovi villages seem to have been opportunists when it came to wood use. The correlation between wood use, documented by Shaw et al., and wood species, documented in driftwood piles at the mouth of Chevelon Canyon, demonstrate that driftwood was the primary source of wood used by inhabitants of Chevelon Pueblo.

Paleoenvironment and Paleoclimate

Detailed discussions of plant and animal exploitation by Chevelon occupants is presented in Chapters 9 through 12 and summarized in Chapter 13. Extensive treatment of this subject can also be found in E.C. Adams (2002:45-58). There is no evidence that the present environment or climate is changed from the fourteenth century, when Chevelon Pueblo was occupied. Certainly, plant and animal communities have been affected by land use and damming of rivers by Euro-Americans since the 1870s. In some cases, such as fish and mollusks, these practices have resulted in their extinction, while beavers, muskrats, and many indigenous riparian plants are now rare. In others, the mix of plants has been drastically altered due to grazing by Old World herbivores.

Nonetheless, the basic ecology of the river versus the uplands, the geology, the soils, and precipitation patterns have not changed. A good sense of the challenges faced by Chevelon occupants can still be obtained from the present environment. Evidence of this continuity is contained in the archaeological record, which for the rest of the HSC is summarized in E.C. Adams (2002). This record indicates a mix of plants used by the occupants that are all still present within 3 km of the village. Cultural choices, made by the occupants of Chevelon, prevent interpreting the exact makeup of the local ecology (e.g., Miljour 2016).

The apparent preservation of plant communities in Chevelon Canyon and of the wetlands around the intersection of Chevelon Creek with the LCR, comparable to their ancestral counterparts, provide insights into the diversity that the environment once provided that is missing from the mainstream of the LCR near the other Homol'ovi villages. Similarly, the paleoclimatic record has been reconstructed for the area based on historic stream flow, the regional tree-ring record, driftwood, and studies of alluvial sequences in the general LCR and, specifically, near H2, H3, and H4 (E.C. Adams and Hedberg 2002; Kolbe 1991; Lange 1998; Van West 1996).

These studies suggest a highly variable climate in terms of annual precipitation and streamflow, but within understood parameters (Van West 1996). In other words, precipitation was always low, but there were years that were even drier and some that were relatively wet. Stream flow was generally low with predictable seasons of increased volume in the spring from snowmelt and during the summer from monsoonal rainstorms. Lange (1998) has detailed this pattern using historic stream gages for nearly the entire twentieth century. However, major floods occurred with regularity either locally or regionally (E.C. Adams and Hedberg 2002). In a sense, all of these patterns combined result in what is normal or average for the area.

The occupants of Chevelon were not the first to live and try to survive along the river (see Lange 1998; Van West 1994, 1996; Young 1996). A 700-year history of farming settlements along the LCR, within the Homol'ovi area, is known and documented from survey and excavations (Lange 1998; Young 1996). The hill on which Chevelon is located was occupied at least twice before. Historic Hopi knowledge and use of the river and Chevelon Creek, in particular, (Fewkes 1904) attest to the continuity and value of this knowledge. I have speculated that detailed knowledge of the Homol'ovi area was essential prior to successfully settling there (E.C. Adams 2002). Thus, Chevelon was settled about 1290 with a complete understanding of the vicissitudes of the river and its tendency to flood. This flooding was always a mixed blessing to groups who lived along, and relied upon the river and its floodplain for existence. Floods might destroy crops or constructions used to manage water, but floods also brought driftwood, alluvium, and organics that improved people's lives. It is even possible that major settlement of the LCR, in the late 1200s, was stimulated by a major flood event that provided much needed wood for construction and fuel (E.C. Adams 2002: 51-56).

Little Colorado River Floodplain

Chevelon occupants, as well as their counterparts in other Homol'ovi villages, relied upon a large floodplain, which in the vicinity of Chevelon Pueblo is nearly 3 km wide, and a permanent flow of water from Chevelon Creek (Figure 2.1). These ingredients provided adequate resources that enabled a viable agricultural strategy that focused on growing maize supplemented with beans, squash, and cotton. Ethnobotanical remains, analyzed from Chevelon (refer to Chapter 11), plus the recovery of several bushels of burned maize, from each of two rooms, underscores the primacy and absolute dependency of Chevelon inhabitants on maize for their subsistence.

In the Chevelon area, unlike the region on the east side of the river between H1 and H2, places other than the floodplain were limited for growing maize (E.C. Adams 2001; Lange 1998). This is caused by the ecology of the region where dominant southwesterly winds remove topsoil from the landscape, to the west and south of the LCR and from the floodplain itself, and deposit it on the north and east sides of the floodplain. The lack of adequate topsoil and low precipitation made the areas more than half a kilometer away from the floodplain, in the vicinity of Chevelon, typically undesirable for any type of permanent settlements reliant on farming.

The longevity of this pattern is underscored by the dearth of archaeological remains of horticulturalists in areas intensively surveyed near Chevelon (Andrews 1982; Lange 1996, 1998), from the introduction of maize over 2500 years ago through the occupation of Chevelon, and even since the beginning of the Euro-American period about 1880. Excavations at the small site of God's Pocket, about 5 km south of Chevelon, recovered maize dating 2500 to 2700 BP, which probably closely approximates the date of local introduction (Huckell 1999).

I have speculated elsewhere (E.C. Adams

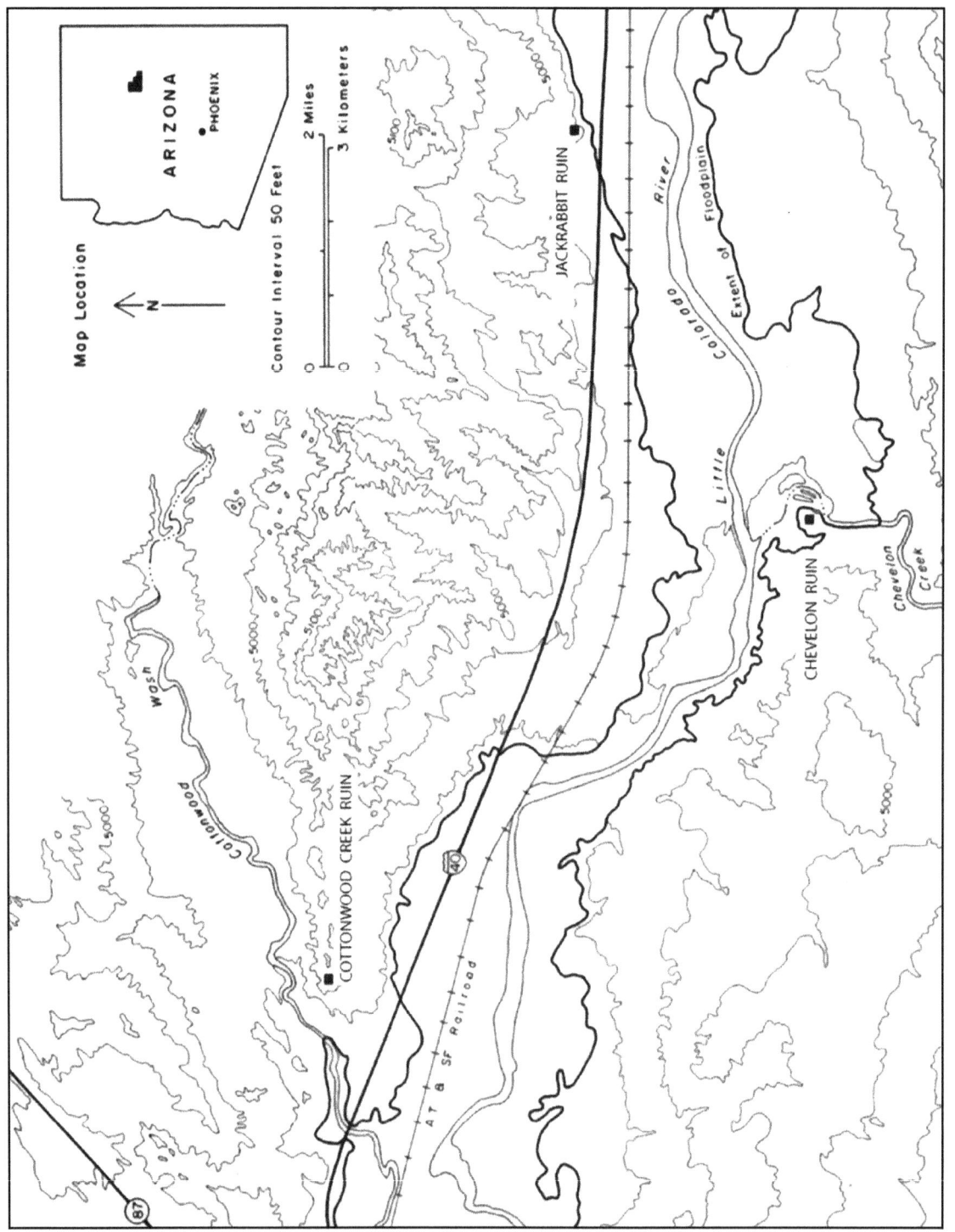

Figure 2.1. Topographic map of Chevelon and adjoining areas.

2002) that farming in the LCR floodplain, in the Homol'ovi area, approximated historic Hopi farming by establishing fields at varying distances from the actual flow of water to minimize risk and maximize yield. By this means, fields could be farmed directly by irrigation, if the level of the water permitted, or by directing or capturing water when flow increased. During instances of higher stream flow, fields adjacent to the stream might be flooded and damaged. In situations where floods were more intense, fields at some distance might survive the flood water while all of those closer to the stream would be damaged or destroyed. Within a floodplain nearly 3 km wide, fields could easily be 1.5 km, and often 2 km or more, from the actual flow of water.

Perhaps the decision on which fields to plant was determined by the extent of seasonal floods in April caused by melting snow in higher elevations. A similar strategy was employed by Hopi farmers into the 1940s, who placed fields in major washes, in akchin situations where runoff from small drainages could enhance precipitation, and in sand dunes dependent only on rainfall. Depending on the precipitation intensity and pattern, almost certainly at least one, and usually two types of fields would be productive using this strategy (Bradfield 1971; Forde 1929; Page 1940). At Hopi, typically 72 percent of their crops were devoted to maize production (E.C. Adams 1982).

As at Hopi, Chevelon occupants had a fourth option: planting near natural seeps or springs (Hack 1942). Every mesa at Hopi relied upon springs and seeps for daily water needs and used them for garden plants (those needing additional water), especially following introduction of Old World plants. A similar situation is present near Chevelon. Numerous springs and seeps are present 1 to 2 km east of the pueblo, on the south side of the floodplain, emanating from outcrops of Moenkopi Sandstone. These were likely present in the 1300s, as several small pueblos dating 1200 to 1250 are located on outcrops overlooking the seeps. This area would have been the source of additional riparian plants, plus an ideal location to plant cotton and other garden crops with salt tolerance.

Although there is always a danger of mapping modern descendents onto ancient groups' behavior, such a model makes sense for the Homol'ovi area. Archaeological survey has found loci of what appear to be areas of intensive farming along the margins of the floodplain and in upland areas between H1 and H2 that date to the HSC occupation (E.C. Adams 2002; Lange 1998). Clearly, the floodplain is being intensively farmed to support the large populations of the fourteenth century. The dynamic flow of the LCR with its constantly moving channel, erosion, and sedimentation, however, has buried or removed most traces of this record.

In a land parched for adequate natural precipitation, where agricultural groups did not permanently settle in the Homol'ovi area until the founding of H4, about 1260, survival is clearly dependent on either harnessing the waters of the LCR or increasing the opportunity for successful production through diversifying farming areas. Given that two Mormon settlements, Sunset and Brigham City, founded in 1876, were both abandoned by 1885, due to their inability to control the LCR; it seems unlikely the people of any of the Homol'ovi cluster settlements with even less technology could do so either (Abruzzi 1981, 1989; E.C. Adams 2002; K. Lightfoot 1984; Walker 1996a). Thus, a modified version of the historic Hopi farming strategy is expected.

SUMMARY

Chevelon Pueblo is located ideally to take advantage of the permanent flow of Chevelon Creek in order to successfully farm the adjacent LCR floodplain. Although natural resources were apparently abundant within Chevelon Canyon, and in much of the floodplain including seeps east of Chevelon Creek, such is not the situation for plant and animal resources in upland areas. A combination of poor topsoil and low precipitation created a more monotonous landscape in terms of subsistence resources. The lack of settlement in this region during any period of time, from the middle archaic to present, underscores the inadequate resources necessary for subsistence to ensure continuous occupation. In terms of inorganic resources, there are adequate building and tool resources, especially in the Moenkopi and Shinarump Formations. This situation pertains to the entire Homol'ovi area.

One question that has not been addressed is whether or not Chevelon occupants sought to or were able to control the flow of water from Chevelon Creek into the LCR. First of all, there is no physical evidence of this and none is expected to survive, given the instability of the river system and the frequent, large flood events that would destroy any evidence. Second, given that the Mormons could not control the waters of the LCR, it is highly doubtful that groups with even less technology could do so. Third, there is no need for the people at Chevelon Pueblo to control or dam water flow. There is no indication that there was ever a lack of water. Gauges suggest that water has always flowed in the lower reaches of Chevelon Creek since 1912, when they were first established. Chevelon Creek is not dammed in the lower reaches until the dam adjacent to Chevelon Pueblo, so flows are unrestricted. Brantley Baird, the owner of the Rock Art Ranch, who has lived on the ranch since 1946 and on whose ranch the springs flow through the lower reaches of the creek, indicates the springs have never dried up, even during the worst drought cycles.

Although an early hypothesis for research at Chevelon speculated that it might be possible that Chevelon inhabitants tried to accumulate social power within the HSC through control of the flow of water to the lower villages; there is no indication they had the technology to do so, even if they wanted to. In fact, to do so might have resulted in conflict with the larger villages downstream, a strong disincentive. Nevertheless, access to unique plants and animals, in Chevelon Creek, could be controlled by Chevelon inhabitants and their interest and ability to do so can be evaluated using the archaeological record. Plants and animals associated with water typically play pivotal roles in Hopi and general Pueblo ceremonies (Parsons 1936), so better access to these objects could enhance prestige and power in the Chevelon community and in the cluster as a whole. Evidence for localized or restricted access to these resources, within Chevelon Pueblo and between Chevelon Pueblo and its HSC neighbors, will be explored in Chapters 9 and 11.

Chapter 3
Chronology
E. Charles Adams

PREVIOUS RESEARCH

Chronology building is foundational to any archaeological enterprise. After all, perhaps the major underpinning to archaeological research is the ability to compare trends over a period of time. The study of continuity and change in objects and settlements enables us to evaluate nearly any research concern. Certainly, the research at Chevelon Pueblo and for the HSC, in general, is based on our creation of chronologies and our interpretation of time. As a result, much research by ASM has focused on developing as accurate a chronological framework as possible (E.C. Adams 2001, 2002; LaMotta 2006; Lange 1998).

Lange (1998) presents the broad chronological scheme for the agriculturally-based groups in the area dating back to 600 C.E. and ending about 1400 C.E. He relies primarily on accepted tree-ring dated ceramics to develop his chronology and then compares the ceramically-derived dates to wet, normal, and dry cycles of precipitation retrodicted from the regional tree-ring record, relying on previous work by Van West (1996). Following Colton (1956), Lange (1998) and E.C. Adams (1991a, 1996) use a broad scheme with two phases, Tuwiuca and Homol'ovi, to define the latest occupation of the prehispanic HSC. Tuwiuca Phase (TP) dates 1260 to 1330 and is named after Colton's Hopi name for H4. Homol'ovi Phase dates 1330 to 1400.

E.C. Adams (2002:59-87) discusses numerous dating techniques that archaeologists use in the American Southwest and those that have worked the best for the HSC. These involve tree-ring based ceramic dating, ceramic seriation within and between Homol'ovi settlements, stratigraphy, and abutment and bonding (E.C. Adams 2002:Table 4.1). This suite of dating techniques will also be used at Chevelon. At H3, I (2001) applied a seriation technique using frequencies of four ceramic wares for all deposits with adequate sample sizes that worked effectively for predicting stratigraphic order for nearly every deposit. Refitting data, percentage of obsidian of all lithics, abutment and bonding patterns within and between rooms, and stratigraphy were used to amplify and refine the ceramic seriation. Ceramic cross-dating and radiocarbon dating were used to assign absolute dates to the deposits.

Although radiocarbon dating is an independent method of dating deposits and sites, E.C. Adams (2001:130-132; 2002:60-63) notes the problems inherent with radiocarbon dating during the fourteenth century. The nature of the radiocarbon calibration curve for the fourteenth century means that for every uncalibrated date there are multiple possible intercepts on the curve. With a moderate to large error range, it is often not possible to distinguish among the dates and, frequently, the date spans the entire fourteenth century.

By increasing the number of targets per sample, LaMotta (2006) has attempted to reduce this error, thus, obtaining two statistically distinct ranges of calibrated dates. Only one of these date ranges includes the true age of the sample and through other means of independent dating, he has often been able to eliminate one of the dates. Using this technique, LaMotta was able to corroborate dates derived from ceramic cross-dated deposits at H1 using 23 radiocarbon samples, 21 of which were processed using multiple targets resulting in high-precision dating.

By combining radiocarbon dating and ceramic cross-dating, E.C. Adams (2001, 2002) and LaMotta (2006) have created a detailed phase sequence for the HSC (Table 3.1) that improves substantially on that proposed by E.C. Adams (1996) and Lange (1998). Table 3.2 describes details of how deposits could be distinguished based on attributes of yellow ware (for the Homol'ovi subphases) and on the basis of tree-ring dated pottery types traded into H1, H2, and H3.

CHEVELON CHRONOLOGY

The detail with which LaMotta (2006) has been able to document yellow ware attributes makes building the chronology at Chevelon that much easier. Because LaMotta (2006) has basically proven that changes in temper, hue, and rim form correlate with time and the percentage of Jeddito Yellow Ware (%JYW) in a deposit, these attributes will not be presented for Chevelon. Instead, %JYW and rim banding data will be used to compare Chevelon ceramics with those analyzed from H1 and H2, which will be detailed in Chapter 6. The task in this chapter is to describe the chronology-building process for Chevelon. Initially, this will take the form of what typical chronology-building tools do not work for Chevelon. Then, I will turn to a discussion of stratigraphic and abutment-bonding data from Chevelon that can be used to paint broad patterns. Finally, tools for chronology-building, specific to Chevelon, will be considered.

Table 3.1. Phase Sequence for the Homol'ovi Settlement Cluster.

Adams 1996; Lange 1998	Adams 2001:134[1]	LaMotta 2006:Table 2.1[2]	Present Chronology
Tuwiuca 1260-1330	Tuwiuca (Founder & Early Phase) 1280-1305	Tuwiuca 1290-1330	Early Tuwiuca Phase 1260-1290
Homol'ovi 1330-1400	Early Homol'ovi (Middle Phase) 1330-1345	Early Homol'ovi 1330-1365	Late Tuwiuca Phase 1290-1325/30
	Middle Homol'ovi (Early Late and Late Phase) 1345-1375	Middle Homol'ovi 1365-1385	Early Homol'ovi Phase 1325/30-1365
		Late Homol'ovi 1385-1400	Middle Homol'ovi Phase 1365-1385
			Late Homol'ovi Phase 1385-1400

[1]This phase sequence is for Homol'ovi III only. The terms in parenthesis pertain only to Homol'ovi III.
[2]This phase sequence is for Homol'ovi I and II only.

Table 3.2. Ceramic Attributes Associated with the Present Chronology for the Homol'ovi Settlement Cluster based on LaMotta (2006) and E.C. Adams (2001, 2002).

Phase	Ceramic Types for Cross-dating	Percent Jeddito Yellow Ware (%)	JYW Attributes[1]	Comments
Early Tuwiuca 1260-1290	Tusayan & Kiet Siel Poly, Kayenta B/w, St. Johns Poly, Jeddito B/o		N/A	Only H4 dates to this Phase.
Late Tuwiuca 1290-1325/30	Pinto, Pinedale & Cedar Creek Polychromes	<1	N/A	Bioturbation will result in some JYW.
Early Homol'ovi 1325/30-1365	Awatovi & Jeddito B/y, Pinnawa G/w, Bidahochi, Fourmile, Tonto & Gila Polychromes	1-39.9	RD: 7.3 mm BW: 11.4 mm Rim Form[2]: 20.1% Paste Color[3]: 64.9% Temper Density[4]: 11.7%	Awatovi B/y has a lower RD and BW, less yellow hue, and a higher temper density.
Middle Homol'ovi 1365-1385	Awatovi & Jeddito B/y, Bidahochi, Paayu, Fourmile, Kechipawan, Gila & Tonto Polychromes	40-71.9	RD: 9.9 mm BW: 12.1 mm Rim Form: 21.7% Paste Color: 82.5% Temper Density: 22.2%	Awatovi & Jeddito B/y appear to be a continuum from analyzed deposits.
Late Homol'ovi 1385-1400	Jeddito Stippled, Engraved & B/y, Paayu, Sikyatki, Tonto, Gila & Kechipawan Polychromes	72-100	RD: 13.7 mm BW: 13.2 mm Rim Form: 32.6% Paste Color: 85.6% Temper Density: 28.9%	This phase is qualitatively different from before & may coincide with H2.

[1] All measurements are from LaMotta (2006) using a sample of 2100 sherds. RD represents rim-to-banding line distance and is measured from the lip of the rim to the top edge of the banding line design that occurs on virtually all %JYW bowls. BW represents the width of this banding line. Numerous studies have shown that through time (later deposits) the banding line grew wider and was placed lower on the vessel wall as the interior design field of bowls changed (E.C. Adams and LaMotta 2002; LaMotta 2002; Levstik 1999; Sigler 2002, Steffian 1995).

[2] This figure represents percent of recurved rims. Recurved or "s-shaped" rims are hallmarks of later yellow wares, thus the frequency of recurved rims increases with time. For example, a study by Levin (1991) of fifteenth century Sikyatki Polychrome bowls revealed that 52.9 percent had recurved rims.

[3] This represents the percentage of %JYW sherds having the Munsell hue of yellow (10YR, 2.5YR, 5Y, 10Y). Smith (1971) among others (Hays 1991) noted the increase in frequency of yellow hues in %JYW and used it as one criterion to distinguish his new type, Awatovi Black-on-yellow.

[4] This represents the percentage of %JYW sherds that are essentially temperless. This trait was noted by Colton and Hargrave (1939) and Colton (1956) in their description of Jeddito Yellow Ware and the later types. Smith (1971) noted numerous sherds from Awatovi with some to considerable temper. He assigned these to his new type, Awatovi B/y.

Independent Dating

As detailed by E.C. Adams (2002), the only independent dating technique to produce reliable results within the Pueblo IV villages is AMS radiocarbon dating.

Radiocarbon Dating

Given LaMotta's (2006) detailed analysis of AMS dated samples to %JYW at H1 and his conclusion that better precision is presently not possible due to issues with the radiocarbon curve for the fourteenth century, no AMS analysis was conducted on samples from Chevelon.

Tree-Ring Dating

As detailed in Chapter 12, 450 specimens of wood have been recovered and identified from Chevelon excavations. Only one of these specimens has produced a tree-ring date— 1244vv—from a primary beam from Structure (S.) 286 (Shaw et al. 2006). This is partly due to many samples not being burned and, thus, poorly preserved for dating. However, over 70 percent of the specimens are cottonwood (see Chapter 12 for details and analysis of species composition). Cottonwood is an indigenous, local species that is seldom datable, due to ring complacency. The remaining samples are mostly of exotic (pines and firs) or poorly dated species (juniper and walnut) that almost certainly are driftwood deposited by flood events (E.C. Adams and Hedberg 2002; Chapter 12). Typically, dates derived from driftwood are unassociated with the construction date of the structure in which they are found and can be more than a century older than the structure (E.C. Adams 2002; E.C. Adams and Hedberg 2002).

The single specimen with a tree-ring date is a Douglas fir used as a primary beam that is missing an unknown quantity of rings. Almost certainly, the specimen is from driftwood transported by a flood, which would account for most of its missing rings (E.C. Adams and Hedberg 2002). Ceramic dating and architectural analysis (discussed in more detail below and in Chapter 6) suggest S. 286, along with the rest of RB200, was constructed during the Late TP, or between 1290 and 1325. The dated specimen certainly does not conflict with this interpretation, but as noted, because it is driftwood, its date has nothing to do with the actual construction of the room or the occupation of Chevelon. Following Adams and Hedberg (2002), the tree-ring date does suggest a flood event after 1244 and prior to 1290 that was of substantial enough volume to deposit driftwood near where Chevelon Pueblo was constructed. The Douglas fir species is not known to grow within 30 km of Chevelon Pueblo suggesting a regional flood event.

Ceramics and the Jeddito Yellow Ware Index (%JYW)

Based on work by E.C. Adams (2001) and LaMotta (2006), the %JYW has been successfully applied to deposits from Chevelon Pueblo (Chapter 6). What this means is that the %JYW of total decorated ceramics is an excellent predictor of the relative age of the deposit that contains it. This has been demonstrated in its ability to accurately replicate the actual order of deposits contained within the same structure at H1, H3, and now, Chevelon, with greater than 95 percent accuracy. It appears that the dating of Chevelon, with respect to %JYW, will be similar to H1 based on the relationship between %JYW and the percentages of tree-ring datable ceramics exchanged to Chevelon. However, due to the higher frequency of White Mountain Red Ware and Roosevelt Red Ware types in the Chevelon assemblage and deep deposits created over many years, some refinement of the actual percentages used in the JYW index for Chevelon is proposed and will be presented in Chapters 4 and 6.

Unlike H1, the excavated deposits and the nature of the settlement of the village allows a more complete understanding of the founding, growth, decline, and depopulation of Chevelon than in other HSC villages. These processes will be detailed in the next chapter on architecture. Dates ascribed to deposits at Chevelon use criteria described in Table 3.2, which are based in the ceramic database derived from previous excavations in the HSC. How this database was constructed will be discussed in the following section.

Superposition and Dating the Room Blocks

Dating the occupation of Chevelon is based on superposition of structures and deposits, abutment and bonding of individual rooms and room blocks, and the type and frequency of various datable ceramics. Unlike H1, Chevelon has relatively little remodeling and superposition of rooms, which allows better understanding of village growth. The growth of Chevelon can be described in various stages, which are summarized in Table 3.3. A brief summary of village growth and the relative dating techniques used to determine it is provided in this chapter. The actual social processes of village growth, structure use, and so forth will be covered in the next chapter along with figures illustrating this growth.

Stage 1: 1290

This stage represents the initial occupation of Chevelon Pueblo. It is manifest as three small spinal room blocks built around and to confine a small internal plaza space in what is termed RB200. Together they create a D-shape because they rest on a small, D-shaped hill covered by a deep gravel layer that is the highest point. Kiva (K.) 248 is associated with this first stage. These room blocks are typically two-rooms wide and five to 10 rooms long. Although some pottery sherds from Basketmaker III (BMIII) and Walnut Phase occupations of the hill are found mixed with later sherds, no intact deposits from these earlier occupations were identified. A bell-shaped pit dug into the gravel bedrock below the pueblo may date to BMIII based on its morphology, but the fill was disturbed by pothunters and contained ceramics from the Chevelon occupation.

Stage 2: 1300

This stage represents the continued development of RB200 by the addition of rooms on the inside of the room block slowly filling in the original plaza space and adding on to the ends of the initial room blocks. Some exterior rooms may have been added at this time. By the end of this stage, the plaza of RB200 was completely enclosed leaving only a small entry on the northeast corner of the room block. All rooms added during this stage have small layers of midden underneath their walls with no JYW. Although, it is possible K. 279 was constructed at this time, it is more likely associated with stage 3.

Stages 3 and 4: 1300 to 1325

To the east of the D-shaped hill, on which

32   E.C. Adams

Table 3.3. Stages of Village Growth at Chevelon and the Archaeological Bases for their Interpretation.

Growth Stage	Room Block	Architectural Details	Archaeological Inference	Estimated Building Date
1	200	3 small room blocks built surrounding a small plaza with at least one kiva	Abutment and bonding	1290
2	200	Infilling of plaza with rooms; possible addition of K. 279	Shallow midden under central rooms. No JYW	1300
3	200, 300	Addition of RB300 on lower terrace surrounding a small plaza (RB900). RB200 continues to infill with probable construction of K. 279	Abutment of RB300 rooms to eastern RB 200 rooms. Western RB300 rooms built over RB200 midden. No JYW	1300-1325
4	100	3 suites of rooms on northern end of RB100 built on small hill west of RB200. Plaza (RB800) created	All excavated rooms have multiple floors. Earliest floors are pre-JYW	1300-1325
5	100, 400, 500N, 700	Major construction of room blocks surrounding south plaza (RB000) constructed to enclose it	RB100 & 700 are built of single spinal room blocks, RB500 of two. %JYW abundant	1360-1375
6	500S, 600	Construction of two spinal room blocks as infilling to complete south plaza enclosure	RB600 and RB500S are spinal room blocks angled to connect preexisting room blocks	1360-1375
7	100, 200, 300	Continued infilling with rooms, additions of 2nd stories, etc. At the same time, some rooms and kivas are no longer being used; some are filled with trash	Abutment of habitation rooms on east of RB100, remodeling in RB200 & 300. %JYW always present; Tonto Polychrome common	1325-1390
8	100	Addition of rooms on the east side of the north half of RB100	Abut to existing spinal room block in stages four and five	1375-1385
9	All	Burning occurs extensively in every room block. No indication of subsequent use suggests it is associated with abandonment of Chevelon	Unburned rooms seem previously abandoned with either middens or no indication of intact roofs. Sikyatki Poly jar on S. 159 floor. Tonto Poly abundant	1390-1400

RB200 is built, is a larger, flat, gravel-covered terrace that is covered by RB300. The dating of RB300 after RB200 is based on two archaeological facts. First, the western rooms to RB300 are abutted to the eastern rooms of RB200, indicating they were built later. Additionally, excavations in S. 373, on the southwest edge of RB300, revealed a deep midden underneath the floor and walls of the room. This midden, which is pre-JYW, came from residents of RB200. The ashy fill of this midden is at least 70 cm deep.

Abutment and bonding of rooms within RB300 suggests spinal room blocks were used to construct the southern and eastern edges to the room block. The northern edge of the room block probably had a single row of rooms. Together, they surrounded a relatively large plaza (RB900) that contained multiple kivas. K. 901 was built during this period. Numerous interior rooms were built using form-molded adobe bricks for all or some of their walls. S. 345/393 and S. 373 are excavated examples. Details on adobe bricks and adobe brick architecture are discussed in the next chapter based on work by Lisa Gavioli and Doug Gann (2006). Thus, two stages of construction are present in RB300, those rooms attached to RB200 and those representing the spinal room blocks on the south and east are stage 3. Rooms added to the interior of the room block, but on the gravel terrace are assigned to stage 4. Limited excavations and reuse of these spaces means only architecture can differentiate between them. The use of adobes in construction is most likely stage 4, which is still pre-yellow ware.

RB200 continued to grow during this period with in-filling of the small plaza and the construction of K. 279. Some rooms may have been added to the outside southern and western edges of RB200 at this time. Little to no midden under their floors suggests this date. Some rooms added second stories. The best evidence for this is an adobe brick structure built as a second story above S. 227, which was probably built at the same time as those in RB300.

RB100 was also begun during this stage. At least two and probably three suites consisting of six to 10 structures were constructed. One interior wall was built using adobe bricks, again, tying their age to this period. Additionally, all excavated habitation structures contained multiple floors with features. The earliest two to three floors in S. 161, for example, were pre-JYW. Numerous sherds from the BMIII occupation, just to the west of RB100, are present in mixed trash deposits in these and other rooms in RB100.

RB800 is the plaza space between RB100 and RB200. Proton magnetometer and electrical resistivity scanning of this open space suggest several large features. Augering of these features and the remainder of this gravel terrace revealed at least one kiva, some potholes, and possible pit house structures from one of the earlier occupations of the hill. There is no indication this plaza was ever bounded on the north or south, except with a few rooms on the southeast that were added in the next stage. Given the presence of occupied structures on each side and the presence of a probable kiva, it is likely RB800 was used as a plaza during this stage.

Stages 5 and 6: 1350 to 1375

This stage represents the creation of the large, south plaza space (RB000) by the construction of RB400, 500, 600, and 700, and a major addition to RB100. All of these additions are characterized by the construction of multiple, lengthy spinal walls in one or two construction episodes. For example, 46 rooms were added to RB100 through a single construction event that added 23 two-room wide structures. Similarly, through two construction events, at least 24 two-room wide structures were built to create RB500. RB600 was built using 10 two-room wide structures built as a single construction event and RB700 was built using 10 three-room wide structures built as a single construction event. RB400 consists only of four rooms, a single room wide, and a kiva, all built as part of a single construction event using the same north wall. Given that some rooms were two stories, 150 to 200 rooms were added to Chevelon to create the south plaza.

The layout of these room blocks permits further relative dating. Close inspection of the southern half of RB500 and RB600 suggests both were added after RB700, RB100 and the northern half of RB 500 were constructed. Both are slightly angled, apparently, to connect existing room blocks. Stage 5 consists of RB100, RB700, and RB500N. Stage 6 consists of the addition of RB600 and RB500S. Only one room involved in stage 6 construction was excavated, S. 603. The difference in age of these two stages is believed to be relatively short, but there is no way to determine what it might be.

All of these additions occurred well after JYW was added to the ceramic assemblage. Tonto Polychrome is the second most common trade ware. A Jeddito B/y jar with an Awat'ovi B/y bowl cover was found buried in the bedrock beneath the floor of S. 120. These were part of the original floor to the room and help date its construction. Finally, the construction of large plaza spaces, as additions to all villages in the HSC occupied after 1350 determined from evidence at H1 (E.C. Adams 2002, 2004a), suggests the dates for the construction of these associated room blocks.

When the south plaza was finally enclosed, the only access to its interior was between RB500 and 300 or through the Plaza 800 area. Although RB700 is built farthest from the top of the hill represented by RB200, it is slightly elevated, resting on a small sand dune. Neither it, nor its junctures to RB600 or 500 appear to have been inundated with floods during or after their occupations. The presence of a second story to S. 509 indicates that at least some of the south plaza room blocks had second stories, although physical evidence is not clear as to how many there are. The most likely areas are RB700 and structures north of S. 509, in RB500.

Only one of the 10 excavated rooms in the latest additions to Chevelon had more than one floor and it had two, providing evidence of a relatively briefer occupation of this area of Chevelon Pueblo than northern RB100, RB200, and RB300. None of the floors cover pre-JYW deposits, although sherds from the BMIII and Pueblo III occupation are present in the RB100 area. The fact that the 10 excavated late structures are all resting directly on the eroded Shinarump gravel deposits indicates these were all new additions.

Stage 7: 1325 to 1390

This stage, which could be inserted at many points in this sequence, represents infilling of rooms in existing room blocks, especially RB300 where structures were added inside spinal room blocks to complete construction in this largest of the room blocks. Second-story rooms were added to many structures in RB200 and 300 during this period as well. Precise dating of these additions is not possible, due to a combination of limited sampling in RB300 and difficulty in dating second-story additions, except when they are adobe, such as the second-story to S. 227.

Stage 8: 1375 to 1390

Evidence for additions to existing room blocks occurs in two excavated rooms, S. 124 and S. 159, that were added to the east side of RB100. S. 124 is one of 13 rooms built east of the original two rooms associated with the spinal room blocks. The fact that they abut to the spinal rooms, suggests all of these rooms were added later.

The RB900 plaza area to RB300 was the site of considerable excavation and revealed details of later construction and remodeling dating to stage 8. K. 901 was built as part of the creation of RB300 when Chevelon expanded in the early 1300s. This is because it was built directly into the deep calichified gravel terrace that characterized the flat topography of the area on which RB300 was built. Use of the kiva stopped well after the introduction of JYW based on midden deposits on its floor, which include Tonto Polychrome. It is estimated that use stopped by 1365 when these deposits were made. The latest midden deposit contained sherds of Sikyatki Polychrome, dating its deposition after 1385. Construction of at least one ephemeral plaza surface with a fire pit and addition of walls to the room block, to the north of K. 901, postdate the latest midden deposits and suggest remodeling to 1390.

While areas of Chevelon Pueblo continued to be used and expanded, other areas were no longer used. This occurred earliest in RB200, where several rooms and two kivas have middens that began during stage 5. Some RB300 rooms have trash associated with stage 6. Even RB600 and RB100 have rooms with midden material, all dating to stage 8.

Thus, it appears during stage 8 that the number of rooms being filled with trash considerably exceeded the number being added at Chevelon.

Stage 9: 1390/1400

Based on the Sikyatki Polychrome jar on the floor of S. 159 and sherds of this type in the upper fill of K. 901, a reasonable guess for the depopulation of Chevelon Pueblo is during the 1390s. This is because recent estimates for the beginning of the manufacture of Sikyatki Polychrome are now about 1385, but possibly later (LaMotta 2006) based on tree-ring dated structures from villages on the Hopi mesas. Certainly, dates ranging from 1385 to 1400 can be argued to contain the actual year when the last occupants at Chevelon finally left. As noted in the previous section, parts of Chevelon had already been depopulated and either begun to be filled with trash from occupants of surrounding rooms, or had floor assemblages associated with room closure together with indications that their roofs had been removed. S. 603 fits this description, for example.

The major and perhaps singular event of Chevelon Pueblo's occupation, however, was the apparent use of fire to burn most, if not all, remaining roofs in the village. Fully 17 of the 39 structures excavated at Chevelon by ASM had roofs that were partly to totally burned as final abandonment acts. There is strong evidence, to be discussed in Chapters 4 and 13, that this burning was a synchronous event, at least as synchronous as archaeologists can determine from the record. Surface indications, mostly due to disturbance from pot hunting, indicate that around 100 structures were burned as part of their closure. Ceramics associated with these terminal structural fires suggest they all occurred near or at the end of the occupation of the pueblo. Whether all were burned at the same time or over a period of time may not be as important as the fact that fire was the choice of most, if not all, of the occupants when they left the village.

As far as can be determined, no other use of any structures burned, at this time, occurred at Chevelon Pueblo. This suggests that this burning was intended to be a terminal act to close individual rooms and the village altogether.

DEPOSITS AT CHEVELON

As alluded to in the preceding section, most structures excavated at Chevelon had little cultural deposition. In all cases, stratigraphy is easy to see and document. The methodology described in Chapter 2 outlines how stratigraphy was recorded. I have previously described (E.C. Adams 2002: Table 4.3) the formation of deposits in the HSC and they are the same for Chevelon.

Kiva Stratigraphy

Deposits in kivas present special cases at Chevelon. Although parts of five kivas were excavated, one was barely tested, one was completely vandalized, and another forms a special case of having been built within a room and had no post-abandonment deposits. K. 279 and K. 901, on the other hand, had deep, complex deposits. Their interpretation will not be treated here, but the nature of the stratigraphy and its relationship to kiva stratigraphy from other HSC villages will be considered. In the HSC, when use of a kiva is discontinued, typically it is formally closed, burned and/or buried (filled with cultural material of a special nature) (E.C. Adams 2016). Formal closure involves placement of objects on the floor or bench(es) of the kiva and often the filling of features with clean sand, sometimes river sand (Karunaratne 1997; LaMotta 1996; Walker 1995; Walker et al. 2000). Kivas are likely to be burned and filled with objects, ash layers, and dense cultural deposits (E.C. Adams and Fladd 2014). The purposes of these deposits will be discussed in Chapters 4 and 12.

Formation Processes and Human Agency

One of the challenges in archaeology is to identify cultural formation processes. Schiffer (1987) refers to this as the systemic part of a behavioral chain interacting with the archaeological record when the culture of interest is still actively forming the archaeological record. At Chevelon, the most clear-cut examples of what today is termed human agency are in burning, kiva deposits, and curated archaeological floor assemblages. Each of these is an example of individuals or groups in the community making decisions that consistently create the archaeological half of the life history equation. Evidence from Chevelon indicates that most such decisions are a result of ritual or religious practices and that these in turn are based on attempts to connect the past with the present, and the present with a perceived future (Connerton 1989; Rappaport 1999). For the time being, the discussion will focus on the nature of these deposits and how they are formed.

Burning

As has already been argued, burning is the most outstanding element of the archaeological record at Chevelon and stands in stark contrast to the other villages in the HSC (Table 3.4). Some of the high frequency of excavated burned structures at Chevelon is attributable to sampling design. For each field season,

Table 3.4. Frequency of Burning in Excavated Villages in the Homol'ovi Settlement Cluster.

Village	Structures Excavated	Structures Burned[1]	Frequency of Burned Structures (%)	Frequency of Burned Non-kiva Structures (%)
Homol'ovi I	70	4	5.7	6.1 (4 of 66)
Homol'ovi II	34	8	23.5	3.7 (1 of 27)
Homol'ovi III	20	4	20.0	13.3 (2 of 15)
Homol'ovi IV	10			0 (0 of 8)
Chevelon	39	19	48.7	45.7 (16 of 35)
Jackrabbit	5			0 (0 of 4)
Total	178	33	18.5	14.8 (23 of 155)

[1]This figure includes kivas: zero at H1; six at H2; two at H3, three at Chevelon.

sampling was structured, in part, by whether or not a structure appeared to be burned from the surface evidence. However, at the same time, an effort was made to excavate unburned structures to present evidence of how their modes of abandonment contrasted with those that were burned. Sampling at the other HSC villages was not governed by any attempts to locate burned structures. However, the pattern of burning kivas at H2 was recognized early in excavations and contributed to the decision to excavate more kivas than a random sample would warrant.

Factoring out kivas creates an even greater contrast between Chevelon and the other HSC villages (Table 3.4). As noted in Chapter 1, it is estimated that about 100 of 500 total structures at Chevelon have been burned. Projecting frequencies for the remaining villages with burned non-kiva structures yields 67 of the 1100 structures at H1, 44 of the 1200 structures at H2, and six of the 45 structures at H3. Regardless of how one measures it, Chevelon stands out among HSC villages in the number of burned structures. The other feature of Chevelon burning that is distinctive is its use as a means of closing a structure and probably of the settlement. Only H2 has a similar pattern; however, burning as a mode of closure is limited to kivas.

Kiva Deposits and Floor Assemblages

Excavation of 21 kivas from other cluster villages identified numerous formal properties or rituals associated with the closure of kivas that are distinctive enough to warrant further discussion to enable comparisons to Chevelon (E.C. Adams 2016; see E.C. Adams 2002 for a detailed discussion of rituals associated with kiva closure). Three kivas at H2 (K. 707, K. 708, and K. 324) can be used to illustrate these patterns. Each of these kivas had numerous objects placed on their floors, almost certainly by individuals who used and "owned" the kiva. In K. 707, a whole corrugated cooking jar was placed over the hearth and supported by two loom blocks (cubical stones used to stabilize looms in kivas still used by Hopi weavers today). In K. 708, a Sikyatki Polychrome bowl with a katsina face, a corrugated jar with a hole carved in its side possibly used to contain snakes, articulated hawk elements, several stone balls, and other objects were placed on the floor or bench (Walker 1995). The roof of each kiva was then burned, collapsing the brush and secondary beam members onto the floor and objects on the floor. In neither case were primary beams found among the burned members and were presumably removed to be recycled into other structures or transported to new kivas on the Hopi mesas as part of memory making (E.C. Adams 2016). K. 708 received a few other objects in its lower fill, mostly other bird elements and stone balls. Thereafter, both kivas filled completely with windblown sand, probably following site abandonment.

K. 324 is similar to the other kivas in having burned roofing material on its floor; however, the kiva was filled with cultural deposits that included numerous rare and exotic artifacts, such as a necklace made from *Nassarius* sp. shell, a species rarely found in the archaeological record of the Southwest (LaMotta 1996), numerous nearly whole pottery vessels, most of the shaped sherds and miniature vessels recovered from H2 excavations, numerous projectile points, crystals, fossils, and various articulated bird elements (Karunaratne 1997; LaMotta 1996). The material placed in the fill of K. 324 was qualitatively and quantitatively different from domestic trash found in structures at H2 or other members of HSC. The deposits in K. 324 alternated between layers rich in ash and layers rich in organic material, mostly too decomposed to identify individual objects other than cobs of maize and worked wood objects (E.C. Adams and Fladd 2014; Karunaratne 1997). The formal nature of these deposits indicates they were purposely structured.

All three H2 kivas have a formality to their closure or decommissioning, including deposits and roof burning, that indicates they were part of a system of behaviors, rites, and ritual practices that were followed in terms of how religious structures managed or owned by social groups within the community were to be processed out of the systemic record and into the history of the village (Connerton 1989).

The situation for kivas at Chevelon can be compared to those at H2. K. 248, K. 279, and K. 901 have similarities to the H2 kivas. Analysis of vandalized deposits from K. 248 and of the structure itself indicates it was similar to K. 324 at H2. Remnant deposits along two walls had alternating levels of ash and organic deposits. Whole and nearly whole artifacts were recovered from fill discarded when the kiva was vandalized, and its roof had been burned with primaries pulled and the remaining roof members on or near the floor of the kiva.

K. 279 is also similar to K. 324 with the exception that its roof was not burned prior to abandonment. This is probably because parts of K. 279 collapsed prematurely, forcing its discontinuation. Perhaps due to the larger size of K. 279, many more individual ash dumps could be distinguished in its fill than in K. 324, which also had been partially vandalized. Whole or parts of articulated animals and rare or unusual objects were common in the fill (Diaz de Valdes 2007; Chapter 9). In general, the deposits in K. 279 do not have quite the formal property of those in K. 324.

The filling of K. 901 is just like the other kivas discussed above, with distinctive ash layers filled with objects contrasted with layers notable for their complete absence of ash and having objects, but of a different nature. Just as with K. 324, the objects recovered from the initial trash cone in K. 901 are qualitatively (such as articulated animal remains, rare taxa, and unusual pottery forms) and quantitatively different from domestic trash found elsewhere in Chevelon, including the two other trash dumps deposited later in K. 901. It also was burned soon after the initial trash cone was completed.

In no cases at Chevelon were objects placed on the floors of kivas as they were in K. 707 and K. 708 at H2. It should be noted that K. 215, K. 558, and K. 901 at H1 had similar formal deposits of ash, whole objects—including animals, and unusual artifacts. As at Chevelon, isolated human remains were typically not involved in kiva abandonment at H1 as they were at H2 (Karunaratne 1997; LaMotta 1996). As at Chevelon, the H1 kivas were not as formally treated, although objects were on the floor of K. 901, and were not burned.

To summarize, kiva deposits at Chevelon have many of the same formal characteristics as their counterparts at H1 and H2. These characteristics are interpreted to be part of cluster-wide practices of how to treat a kiva when it is no longer possible to use it (E.C. Adams 2016; E.C. Adams and Fladd 2014). Analysis of the objects themselves will add more information as to the possible rites involved or their relationship to social power within the various communities.

Dating Individual Structures

Individual structures are dated at Chevelon primarily on the basis of their ceramic assemblages. The use of ceramic seriation to relatively date deposits has been proven to work at H1 and H3 and Chevelon appears to follow the H1 seriation developed by LaMotta (2006), discussed further in Chapter 6. The robustness of the %JYW index has allowed relative and phase dating of each undisturbed excavated structure at Chevelon. In addition, this index allowed narrowing of construction dates for walls built over middens. Details of these dates will be discussed in Chapters 4 and 6.

A major factor in any seriation is sample size. Only deposits having 50 or more decorated sherds were used in the seriation. A secondary biasing effect can be caused by RVs or the presence of reconstructible vessels in a deposit. In some cases, such as S. 120, RVs affected the %JYW index to such a degree that they were removed from the sample so that the %JYW index could be applied. Thus, every deposit was individually evaluated for any sampling biases that might cause it to be misclassified in terms of seriation based only on the criterion of JYW frequency.

Secondary relative dating techniques were abutment and bonding of walls, number of plaster layers, and number of floors. Relative dating of the construction of structures can usually be determined by whether or not they abut or bond to adjoining structures. In the northern three sets of structures in RB100, for example, the rooms are all internally abutted forming a tight group to which the remainder of the room block was later abutted. This interpretation was confirmed by the presence of multiple floor layers and remodeling in S. 159 and S. 161, both habitation structures in the original set of rooms. Additionally, both structures had multiple plaster layers. Depth and number of plaster layers were also used to confirm the lengthy use of S. 252 and S. 262 in RB200. The existence of these structures in RB200 and abutment and bonding had already suggested the structures were probably old, but the plaster data confirmed much greater age for the structures than any other room in the village. There are some caveats in the use of plaster, as it varies by structure use and building material. Interpretation of plaster layers (see Meyers 2007) will be considered in the next chapter on architecture.

Summary

The occupation of Chevelon can be closely determined using tree-ring dated ceramics as occurring from 1290 to the 1390s. It is unlikely these dates are off by more than 10 years in either direction; that is, founding certainly dates between 1280 and 1300 and closure, between 1380 and 1400. The internal chronology of Chevelon, how it grew and declined and, in more detail, when individual structures were built, used, and closed, can be well placed using ceramic seriation. This seriation is based on many years of painstaking analysis (E.C. Adams 2001, 2002, 2004a; LaMotta 2006; Hays 1991; Hays-Gilpin et al. 1996) of more than 100,000 sherds from other HSC villages. Out of considerable additional work, which is summarized by LaMotta (2006), a more precise seriation based on %JYW (yellow-hued variety), has been developed that has been tied into radiocarbon dating and careful examination of the tree-ring dating of key pottery types (Table 3.2). As a result, five phases can now be defined (Tables 3.1 and 3.2) based on seriation of hundreds of deposits using a broad array of ceramic types and wares.

This has resulted in a relatively precise characterization of Chevelon settlement by stage, as detailed above and in Table 3.3. The next goal is to begin looking at individual structures and clusters of structures in order to describe and understand the social processes that affected the archaeological record, as briefly described for kiva deposits in this chapter.

Chapter 4
Architecture
E. Charles Adams

Architecture at Chevelon will be considered in several ways. First, building materials, source areas, structure types, household size, and building strategies will be discussed. These will use various structures excavated at Chevelon to illustrate key points. Second, discussion of room blocks at Chevelon will use excavated structures to buttress arguments about dating, room use, household size, and so forth. Next, kivas and open space (plazas) will be discussed as places for private religious rituals and public performance. Finally, a discussion of the social history of Chevelon will be presented using the previous information. The role of fire in all of these interpretations cannot be ignored, but will receive detailed treatment in the next chapter.

THE BASICS

Building Materials

A typical Chevelon room (excluding kivas) is about 6 to 7 sq. m, in line with average structure size elsewhere in the HSC (E.C. Adams 2001: Table 6.3). Structure size within Chevelon varies some by room block and wall material (Table 4.1). As at H1, structures built of adobe bricks were slightly smaller than their stone masonry counterparts (E.C. Adams 2001: Table 6.3). The prototypical room is built of sandstone masonry quarried from Moenkopi Formation outcrops within 500 m of the village.

The walls are cemented with compositionally heterogeneous adobe made from a mixture of 60 to 70 percent sand, 10 to 20 percent silt, and 10 to 20 percent clay (Gann 1996a; Gavioli and Gann 2006). Little to no organic material was intentionally added to this mix. The source of the adobe is probably the floodplain of the LCR where clay, sand, and silt are regularly deposited and whose composition is variable. Although clays are present in geological formations, they are much more difficult to work and must be ground. The floodplain clays need no such extra step. Lyons (2003) discovered that the most common clay used in ceramics for the local decorated wares was also brought down by the river and deposited in the floodplain.

Adobe Bricks

Adobe bricks, on the other hand, require a slightly different technology using similar materials. Gavioli and Gann (2006) describe and compare the Chevelon bricks to those recovered from H1 and the Adobe Pueblo, a small outlier to H1. Like other villages in the cluster, all Chevelon bricks were made in stone forms. This is determined from surface characteristics and the straightness of the sides and corners of the bricks (see Gann 1996a, 1996b). The same basic recipe of 60 percent sand, 20 percent silt, and 20 percent clay was used in bricks from the three villages. The

Table 4.1. Structure Use Types by Location and Prevalent Features.

Structure Type	Chevelon Structures[1]	Primary Features	Secondary Features	Comments
Storage with Bin Features	227, 286, 269L, 288, 373, 702, 120L	Bin with upright stone slabs	Doorway	S. 702 & 120 bins are much smaller than the others. These structures typically had some artifacts on their floors
Storage with No Bin Features	107, 157, 120E, 122, 161L, 266, 546, 547, 403, 704?	Doorways	Ventilator openings in walls near floor	These structures typically had few artifacts in their fill or floor.
Corn Storage	158, 123	Burned Corn	Doorways	Distribution of burned corn at Chevelon suggests there are many more corn storage rooms
Habitation	222E, 289, 264, 265, 268, 269E, 345, 393, 509, 161E, 293, 603	Hearths	Storage bins	These structures typically had other features and more floor assemblages than storage rooms
Habitation with Ritual Features	159, 124	Hearth	Shrine in 159, bench in 124	These structures are also larger than the average habitation room
Piki House	222L	3-sided hearths		Numerous piki stone fragments in the fill of this structure
Kiva	248, 279, 252, 400, 901, 905	Ventilator system	Hearth	K. 905 was only tested. K. 400 was only outlined by tracing wall surfaces

[1]Some structures were only tested or were upper story structures and could not be assigned to any structure type. Some structures also have multiple floors. For these, L = latest use; E = earlier use.

Chevelon material differed from the other villages in having more variability in color, more gravel in the natural matrix, and by the addition of grass to the brick recipe. While it is believed the gravel may be a natural additive from the soil matrix used, the grass was clearly added as a binder to strengthen the brick (Gavioli and Gann 2006).

Beyond the additives to the bricks themselves, S. 345, the only excavated structure at Chevelon with all adobe brick walls, had vertical stacks of bricks between wooden support posts. Posts are located in the room corners with two additional ones spaced equally along each wall. This architectural feature is unique in the village and HSC. Whether it is a testimony to a lack of faith in the bricks as roof supports, an architectural style imported from another region (such as northern Arizona), or an independent invention at Chevelon is unclear.

S. 345 had a second story, S. 393, but it is unclear from the remaining evidence whether or not the second story room was also constructed this way. An additional unique feature of S. 345 was the diversity of adobe bricks. In addition to three paste recipes resulting in three brick colors, the bricks were sorted by wall (Gavioli and Gann 2006). Abutment and bonding suggests each was constructed independently of the others. S. 393, on the other hand, was constructed of a fourth brick color and recipe, but seemed uniform in the remains of the three recovered wall sections (Gavioli and Gann 2006). Adobe bricks comprised three of the four walls in S. 373, the only other room excavated in RB300. Similar to S. 393, the bricks in these walls used the same paste recipe. Abutment patterns suggest the three adobe brick walls were added to the stone masonry fourth wall.

Surface wall tracing indicates that at least 20 percent of the RB300 rooms were partially, or completely, made of adobe bricks, representing a minimum of 30 rooms. The addition of a few adobe brick second story rooms in RB200 and a single wall in RB100 suggests the total of adobe brick rooms at Chevelon is still below 50, representing fewer than 10 percent of the structures in the village.

The dating of adobe bricks at Chevelon is comparable to H1, with first appearance between 1300 and 1330. In contrast to H1, where adobe bricks were used extensively to expand the village in the late 1300s, adobe bricks at Chevelon seem to have a limited life history with no evidence of new construction using this building technology after 1350 to 1365. For example, none of the 150 or so structures used to build the room blocks creating the large south plaza, after 1365, used adobe bricks.

What then is the meaning of this technology at Chevelon? Gann (1996a, 1996b) traces possible origins of this technology to the upper Little Colorado River (ULCR) area where it is first developed in the 1100s. The relatively widespread appearance of adobe brick manufacture during the 1300s, in places like Awat'ovi and members of the HSC, suggests either the spread of a building technology or the spread of individuals or groups using this technology. The presence of Pinto Polychrome in the early 1300s assemblages at Chevelon is the only other evidence of contact with ULCR groups during this period. The mix of local ceramics does not suggest immigration of groups from the ULCR area, only exchange. The peculiar wall construction, in S. 345, and the variability in adobe brick manufacture suggest the more likely diffusion of this technology, perhaps with direct contact with individuals possessing this knowledge rather than a significant migration of people from the ULCR who practiced this technology. Additionally, the earlier ULCR groups did not use forms to make their bricks, but rather hand-molded their bricks. This also suggests a borrowed technology rather than migration of groups or individuals possessing this knowledge.

Roofing

The roof materials at Chevelon are discussed in more detail in Chapter 12. What will concern us here are the methods of construction and the source of materials. As noted by Shaw, Howell, and Vonarx in Chapter 12, wood was probably acquired locally either through cutting of local species or recovering wood transported through floods. The only possible exception is juniper, which is available in small stands within 5 km and in extensive forests 10 km south of Chevelon. Because juniper also occurs as driftwood, it is not possible to determine the source.

The small size of rooms at Chevelon and throughout the HSC is probably, in part, due to the availability of wood not only for construction, but also for fuel. Cottonwood is the only sizable and locally available species, which means that driftwood provided an important and needed source of useful wood for construction. The limited and unpredictable supply of this wood contributed to a conservative approach to construction. In particular, with the use of spinal room block construction resulting in many rooms being roofed at the same time, the need for uniform roofing material for numerous rooms would likely result in many smaller rooms rather than a few larger rooms. This probably explains the tendency for spinal room block structures to be more uniform than rooms that are added one or a few at a time, which can be bigger. A good example is RB100 where front rooms added later to the room blocks, such as S. 124, are larger than the two rows of earlier rooms built as part of the spinal construction (Figure 1.1).

Room construction typically used only one or two primary beams, which always spanned the narrower of the two room dimensions. At Chevelon, cottonwood was the preferred building material for all roofing elements, accounting for 70 percent of the 450 samples of wood analyzed (Shaw et al. 2006; Chapter 12). Secondary beams were more variable than primaries because the typical piece of driftwood was more suited to use as a secondary than as a primary (Shaw et al. 2006). Depending on size and availability, secondary beams were sometimes topped with wood slabs, usually from cottonwood or ponderosa pine. These slabs are naturally occurring, coming from cleavage planes along tree rings, and were found to be common in driftwood piles. Such construction was preserved in the burned roof of S. 268.

Locally available riparian species of willow and reed (*Phragmites communis*) were typically used as the base elements to closing material, topped by available species of grass or small bushes. Saltbush seems to have been the most popular choice for bushes. A 15-cm, or greater, thickness of earth of similar make-up to wall mortar was then used to cover the organic members of the roof. Total roof thickness, then, was about 30 cm. Roof thickness was comparable, whether a roof was first or second-story, because first-story roofs often had floor features, such as hearths, that required a significant thickness of earth in which to place them. Occasionally, roofing material was slightly carbonized from being in the vicinity of upper floor hearths. Burned primaries were also recycled, such as K. 279. A lengthier treatment of recycling primary beams can be found in E.C. Adams (2016).

Room Use

As discussed in Chapter 1 and in greater length in E.C. Adams (2002), several room uses have been identified in the HSC and at Chevelon. The only addition to structure use at Chevelon is the particular storage structure used to hold corn, possibly other foodstuffs, and plant materials. This category is used at Chevelon due to the discovery of two rooms (S. 123 and 158), used for storage of corn, and the evidence of many more rooms that were visible due to vandalism. In E.C. Adams (2002:127-154), the focus was on the building blocks of HSC society, ranging from domestic and ritual uses of structures to suites of rooms, to multi-family room blocks, to communal spaces and ritual structures. At Chevelon, the approach will be slightly different with similar goals.

Storage Rooms

Storage rooms are typically the typological dumping ground for southwestern archaeologists working in pueblos. This is because these rooms typically have few artifacts and floor, or wall, features to distinguish their use. Thus, by a process of elimination, they fall into this category. They have neither hearths for cooking and heating, nor obvious features associated with religious ritual, such as benches or loom holes. Thus, their use is assumed to be generically storage. Although, this term may be the best catchall for characterizing the use of this space, clearly, more can be said about it and will at Chevelon.

Storage rooms at Chevelon can be divided into three groups based on floor features and material culture. These include rooms with no storage bin features and generally no material culture indicative of use, rooms with storage bin features and frequently having material remains indicative of use, and rooms with burned corn and having no floor features. These three storage room types differ in their location in space and time at Chevelon. Part of these differences could be due to sampling bias and certainly partly due to preservation by burning. Nevertheless, storage structures with bin features appear to be common in the early storage rooms at Chevelon, whereas storage rooms without bins appear to be typical of later storage rooms. Related to this time difference is a spatial difference. Storage rooms with floor features are common in RB200 and 300, occurring in a majority of storage rooms, and are rare in RB100, 400, 500, 600, and 700 (Table 4.1). Given that 11 storage rooms have been excavated in the latter room blocks, the pattern is probably significant.

Storage Rooms With Bin Features

A total of seven structures fall into this category of room (Table 4.1). The two best examples of such rooms are S. 286 and 227 (Figure 4.1). Neither room has a hearth, but both have numerous slab-lined features that seem suited for storage of corn. Similar features were found by E.C. Adams (1982), in his documentation of nineteenth and twentieth century Walpi Pueblo on First Mesa, and are commonly seen in 1900s photographs of Hopi storage rooms, inevitably filled with corn. S. 286 also has two large storage jars on its floor, which could have been used to hold ground corn ready for food preparation. Both structures were abandoned early in Chevelon's occupation, so no corn was recovered in storage. S. 227 ceased use during the Early Homol'ovi Phase (EHP), or before 1365, and S. 286 ceased use during the Middle Homol'ovi Phase (MHP), or before 1385.

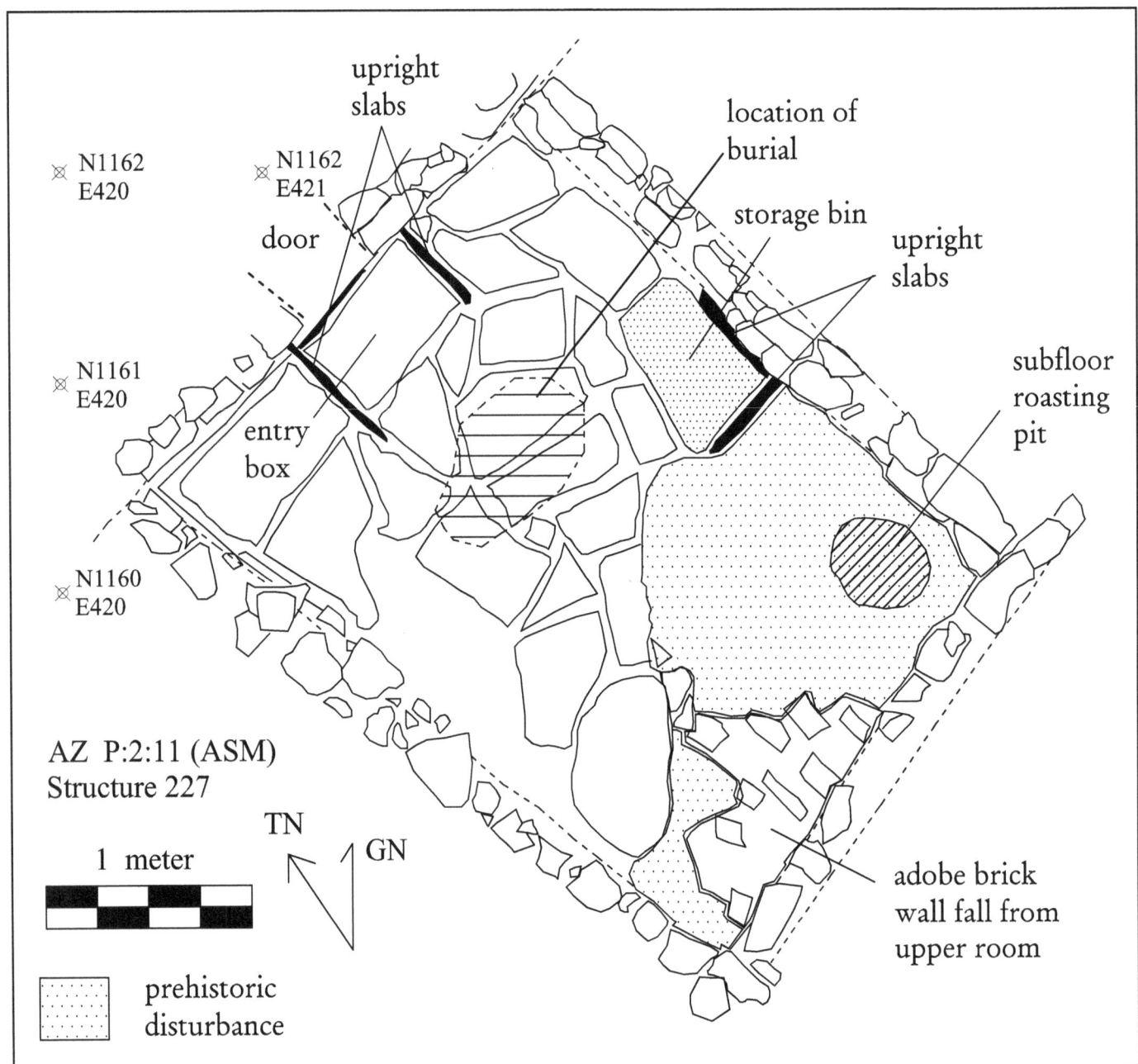

Figure 4.1. Plan view of storage room with bins (Structure 227).

However, their construction certainly dates to before 1330, in both cases, and probably to about 1290 for S. 227, and about 1300 for S. 286.

Both S. 227 and 286 were one to two-story storage units. Both also had distinctive floor assemblages that will be treated later. As with all storage structures, they also had doorways connecting them to adjacent structures; although, in neither case was the use of the adjacent room discovered, due to lack of excavation. Other storage structures having slab-lined bins are S. 702, 120, 373, 269, and 288. The bins in S. 120 and 702 are much smaller than their counterparts in RB200 and 300, and may have had a different use. In fact, the small bins in S. 120 (remodeled use) and 702 resemble small bin features that are common in habitation rooms, which are described below.

Storage Rooms Without Bin Features

The more common storage structure is one without bin features. A total of 11 structures fall into this category (Table 4.1). Storage rooms, such as these, are most common in all Homol'ovi villages and probably represent a generic storage room that can be used for many purposes. It is certainly less specialized than those with bin features. For example, the corn storage structures described below are simply storage rooms without bin features that happened to have corn still in storage when they were burned. At Chevelon, these structures typically have few artifacts, although, S. 120 (original use) is the exception (Figure 4.2). This structure contained two manos and two whole vessels on its earlier floor, including a jar buried in a subfloor feature. Occasionally, bone awls are recovered from the floors of these structures. These are likely tools that have been stored in roofs, as in other Homol'ovi villages (Klandrud 2002), a practice that was also common in historic Walpi (E.C. Adams 1982). General lack of artifacts is probably due either to these rooms being used for storage of food and not implements, or their being cleaned of artifacts prior to Chevelon's depopulation. The manos found in S. 120 are not unique in storage structures at Chevelon, or in habitation structures. They were also found in five other structures in RB100, 600, and 700, two of them storage structures. These manos are generally associated with bin floor features in all structures and appear to be in a storage mode or, perhaps, a structure closure mode. This interpretation will be taken up later.

These storage rooms typically have two types of wall features. Every storage room has at least one doorway and many have more than one. This is true regardless of whether or not the room is a first or second story structure. Storage rooms are usually accessed through a habitation room and, thus, must be connected to it by a door. A second common feature in these storage rooms is what seems to be a ventilator. These features are niche-sized (about 20 cm on a side) and at, or near, the floor. Their use is hypothesized from their location near the floor (where they would not serve effectively to provide light), their small size, and their association with storage rooms. Perhaps they helped dry or ventilate structures filled with stored food. Such ventilation would help dry the corn, reducing the potential for spontaneous combustion or rotting. These features are most common in RB100. They connect S. 157 and 158, 122 and 123, and occur in S. 120. They always occur in the same wall as the doorway, on either side. These vents could easily be blocked, if desired, and the one between S. 157 and 158 had been sealed, while the doorway remained open. Similar features were

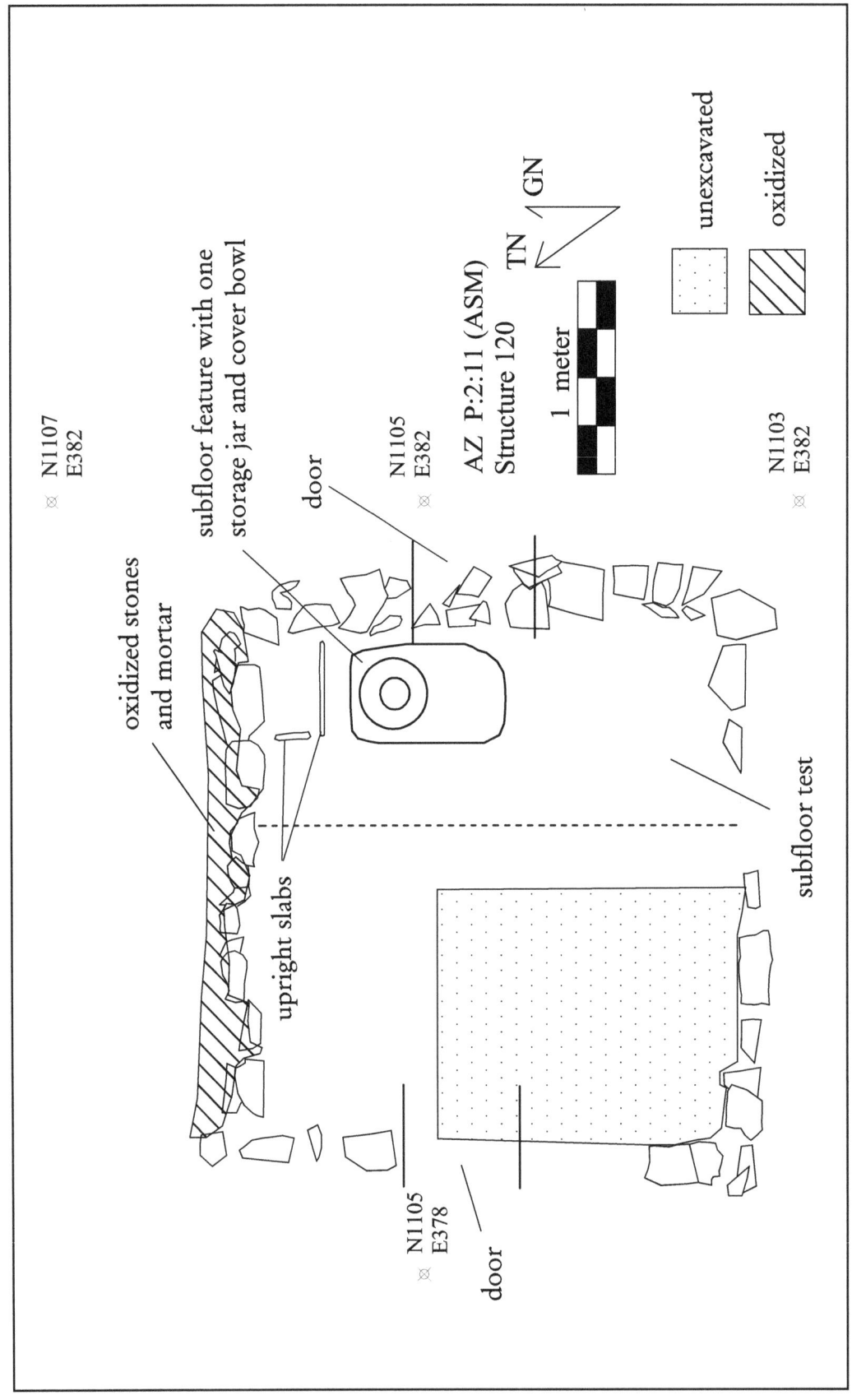

Figure 4.2. Plan view of storage room without bins (Structure 120).

discovered in contiguous rooms in RB100 at H1; however, these were located much higher and while perhaps used for the same purpose as those at Chevelon, could also potentially have introduced light into otherwise dark spaces.

Corn Storage Rooms

Only S. 123 and 158 fall into this specialized category (Table 4.1), although surface evidence at Chevelon points to many more rooms that were burned with corn still in storage. Both of these rooms are in RB100 and lie between a storage room without bins and a habitation structure with features usually found in kivas. Whether or not this is a product of sampling or reflects actual uses of rooms in suites is unknown. In both cases, to get to the back storage room would require walking from the habitation structure through a room filled with corn. It may be that both rooms were typically used to store corn and the back room was simply empty. Pollen samples were taken, but have not yet been analyzed to inform on this question of room use. However, macrobotanical remains from flotation show a clear pattern of use, as detailed in Chapter 11 by Karen Adams. Corn storage rooms seem to have been used only for that purpose, but generic storage rooms, including S. 122 and 157, indicate almost everything else was stored in them.

Both rooms almost certainly were intentionally combusted using the corn. The heat of the fire released enough moisture from the corn to soften the plaster on the walls, leaving impressions of corn cobs (Icove et al. 2008). This fortuitous event allowed determination of the minimum level of corn in the rooms, which was at least 60 cm. Hopi blue corncobs today average 7.4 cm in diameter and 15.2 cm long (D.L. Johnson and Jha 1993: Table 2). Using this size, to get to 60 cm deep requires the corn to be stacked 8 cobs high, 15 cobs long, and 30 cobs wide for a total of 3,600 cobs in a structure, 2.25 m for each dimension. This converts to about 20 bushels of corn on the cob stored in each of these rooms.

Kernels from each cob produce about 59 calories and eaten alone would take about 25 cobs to fulfill a daily need of 1500 calories. For a family of four, this means this store room contained 36 days worth of calories. Of course, the people of Chevelon ate much more than corn, but this provides a means of estimating the level of production and amount of storage that would be required to feed the Chevelon population. Thus, although it appears there was a lot of food in storage at Chevelon, it may not have provided much of a surplus. Additionally, it is not known what time of the year Chevelon was burned, although the high level of moisture released by the fire indicates combustion was relatively soon after harvest. Insects preserved in the burned storerooms could be active year-round and it is not possible to determine whether they were alive or dead when the corn was burned. See Chapter 11 for a more detailed analysis of the maize.

Habitation Rooms

The total of 12 habitation rooms, excavated at Chevelon, provides an excellent source of information about this form of structure. Size was quite variable in the structures. Where excavations permitted a determination, all had at least one doorway and as many as three were found. Room suites will be discussed below. In addition to doorways, by definition, all habitation structures have at least one hearth. Those with multiple hearths all suggest no more than one was in use at a time. This, together with ethnographic evidence, indicates habitation structures were used by single-family units, whatever their size. Habitation structures at Chevelon also typically had at least one slab-lined bin that was set into the floors, but was seldom subfloor. There is no evidence these bins held metates and were in fact dismantled mealing bins. Typically, they are poorly positioned for such use, the stone slabs are too tall, and there is no physical evidence that a metate was ever in place. The presence of bins sets habitation rooms apart from those of other Homol'ovi villages. Of the four habitation structures for which floors were intact (remember, several habitation structures were second story rooms that had collapsed into lower structures, often destroying evidence of floor features) or totally excavated, all had these bins. It is likely these features were used for storage, as typically they were placed either in a corner of the room or adjacent to the hearth. Perhaps those near the hearth stored foods, likely in a ceramic storage vessel ready to be cooked, while those in corners were for longer term or nonfood storage. There is no artifactual evidence to support specific use in any case.

Floor artifacts are relatively common in Chevelon habitation structures, but floor assemblages are still quite sparse. S. 264, 345, 265, 509, and 603 had floor artifacts (Figure 4.3). S. 603 and 345 had manos. S. 345 had half a piki stone. S. 265, 509, and 603 had modest ceramic assemblages of one or two whole, or reconstructible, vessels. As noted in the discussion on storage structures, some of these artifacts appear to be in either storage or structure closure mode. For example, a bowl and jar were found adjacent to the hearth in S. 264. In S. 603, a mano, miniature vessel, and ladle bowl were found in, or adjacent to, the bin. An eagle's foot was found in the bin in S. 345 with the half-piki stone adjacent to the bin. None of these objects appear to be in use mode. This comports with the remaining structures, which have no floor artifacts at all. Only in the three habitation structures, that were later converted to other uses, is there any trash on the floor.

The conclusion from the evidence in the habitation structures, of which only S. 222 (early use), 264, and 265 are burned, is that when a room was no longer to be used, objects were placed in specified positions on the floor. This ritualistic behavior appears to be common across the village. Another lesson from S. 222 is that rooms at Chevelon could have their roofs burned and then be reused. The presence, or absence, of objects left on the floors of structures does not seem to be related to their burning, but rather to a mode of abandonment of the structure. This idea will be returned to in the discussion to follow.

Habitation With Ritual Features

Only S. 159 and 124 fall into this category. In S. 159, this feature is a complex bin in the northeast corner that resembles shrine features described by Hopi (Fewkes 1906) and found elsewhere in the HSC, and on the landscape near H1 and H2 (Lange 1998). In S. 124, this feature is a raised platform or bench along the east wall of the structure. It should be noted at the outset that neither structure was completely excavated. These structures are different from their habitation structure counterparts in several other ways. First, on average they are much larger. Second, they have robust floor assemblages. Third, they are adjacent to burned corn storage rooms. Fourth, they are burned as a result of fires probably set in the corn storage rooms. Finally, they are some of the few structures built into plaza space; in this case, possibly as additions to the east side of RB100. An interpretation of this pattern will be presented later in this chapter. In the

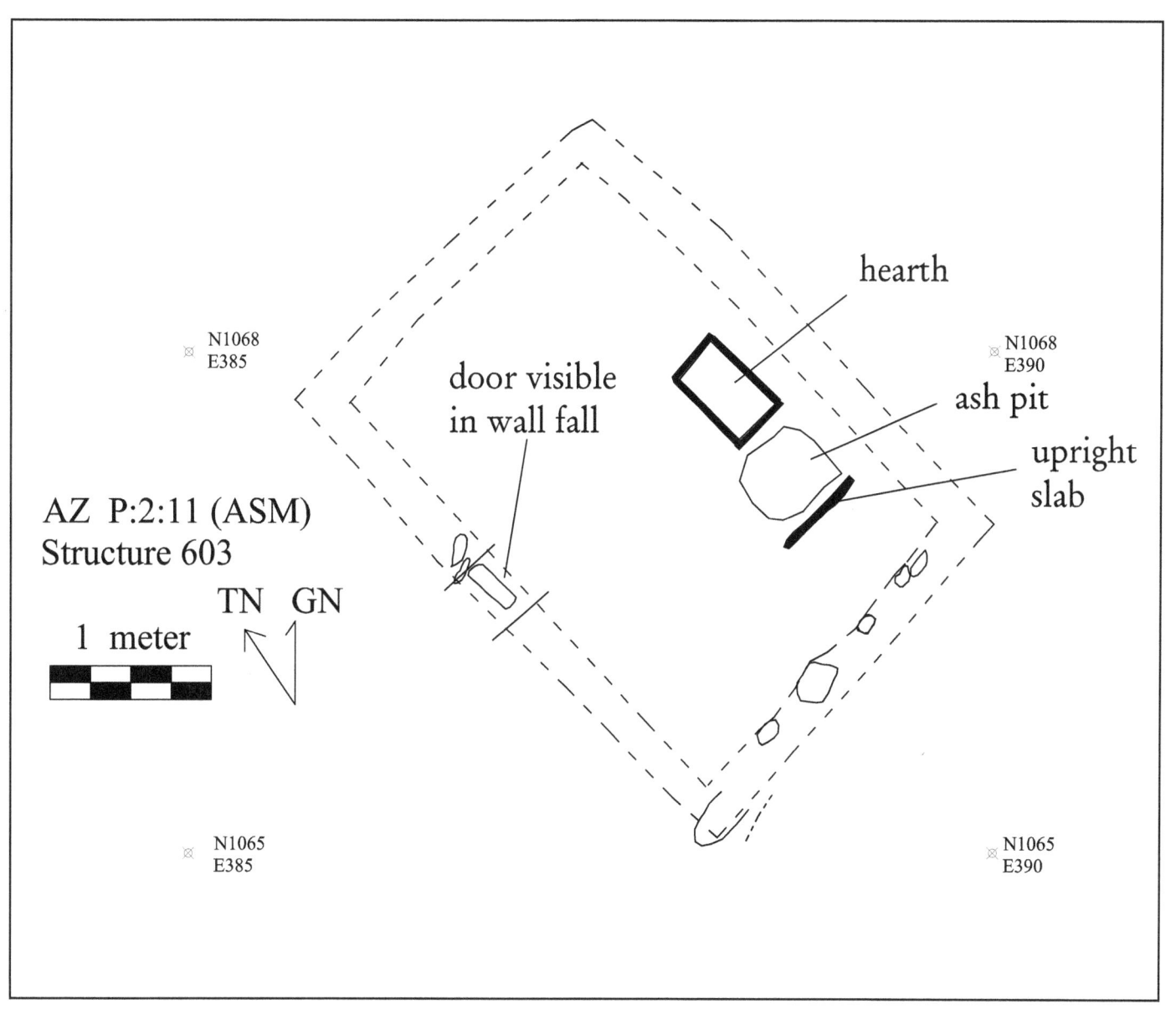

Figure 4.3. Plan view of habitation room (Structure 603).

pages and chapters to follow, these structures are referred to as ritual structures, highlighting the distinctive features that are present. The word *ritual* is used to suggest religious ritual practices likely were staged in these structures either at the household or corporate level. In either case, the rituals were exclusive.

S. 124

S. 124 is to the east of burned corn, S. 123, and connected by a doorway, through which, in all probability, the fire spread from the corn storage room (Figure 4.4). However, the floor of the structure gave no signs of hurried abandonment. Instead, several objects were found in what appears to be storage, much like their counterparts in other habitation and storage rooms. At 9 sq. m, S. 124 is 40 percent larger than the average habitation structure at Chevelon. It was remodeled at least once, when the hearth near the east side of the structure was partly covered with a narrow bench and the active hearth was moved to along the north wall. During its use, prior to and after the remodeling, its north and west walls were plastered white and then yellow. These colors do not carry over to the east wall. At the time of its burning, two manos were left arranged around the hearth and a possible piki stone was placed against the north wall, adjacent to the hearth. A corrugated jar was also recovered from this area, dispersed by the roof collapse. To the west of the hearth and manos was a whole Jeddito Black-on-yellow bowl that had been partly damaged by pothunters, who destroyed the southwest quarter of the structure. The burned roof collapsed onto the structure's floor and included one or two additional manos, which landed near the hearth, suggesting they were arranged near the hatch entry to the structure. An igneous axe, imported from below the Mogollon Rim, was found in the floor fill and was either on the roof when it collapsed or on, or near, the floor. There is no suggestion of use of the structure cavity for any other activity, including as a midden, after the room was burned.

The bench was created by placing several upright slabs end-to-end and filling in behind them. The top of the bench was then plastered. In front of the bench were two features, a hearth and a shallow, circular feature, 10 cm in diameter. The hearth had been partially dismantled and filled with bedrock, seemingly replaced by the larger hearth just west of the doorway in the north wall. The circular feature seems too shallow for a post, so its use remains unknown. The north hearth is large by Chevelon and HSC standards and is similar to ones found in two structures at H1: S. 310 and 504, each having other features and distinctive deposits and floor assemblages that suggest a role in religious ritual. The large hearth size suggests use by a group larger than a typical Chevelon family. The fact that S. 124 had a doorway into the adjacent structure to its north, S. 128, which was probably a habitation structure, could mean the household was large with many members and responsibilities. The large hearth could also mean multiple families used it for preparing large meals needed for feasting. All of this evidence points to S. 124 as being distinctive from other habitation rooms with status gain either through religious ritual, having a large household, its location in plaza space, or some combination.

S. 159

S.159 is in an identical position to that of S. 124. It lies on the east side of RB100 with two storage structures, one with corn, to its west, and another possible structure, to its east. It

Chapter 4: Architecture   53

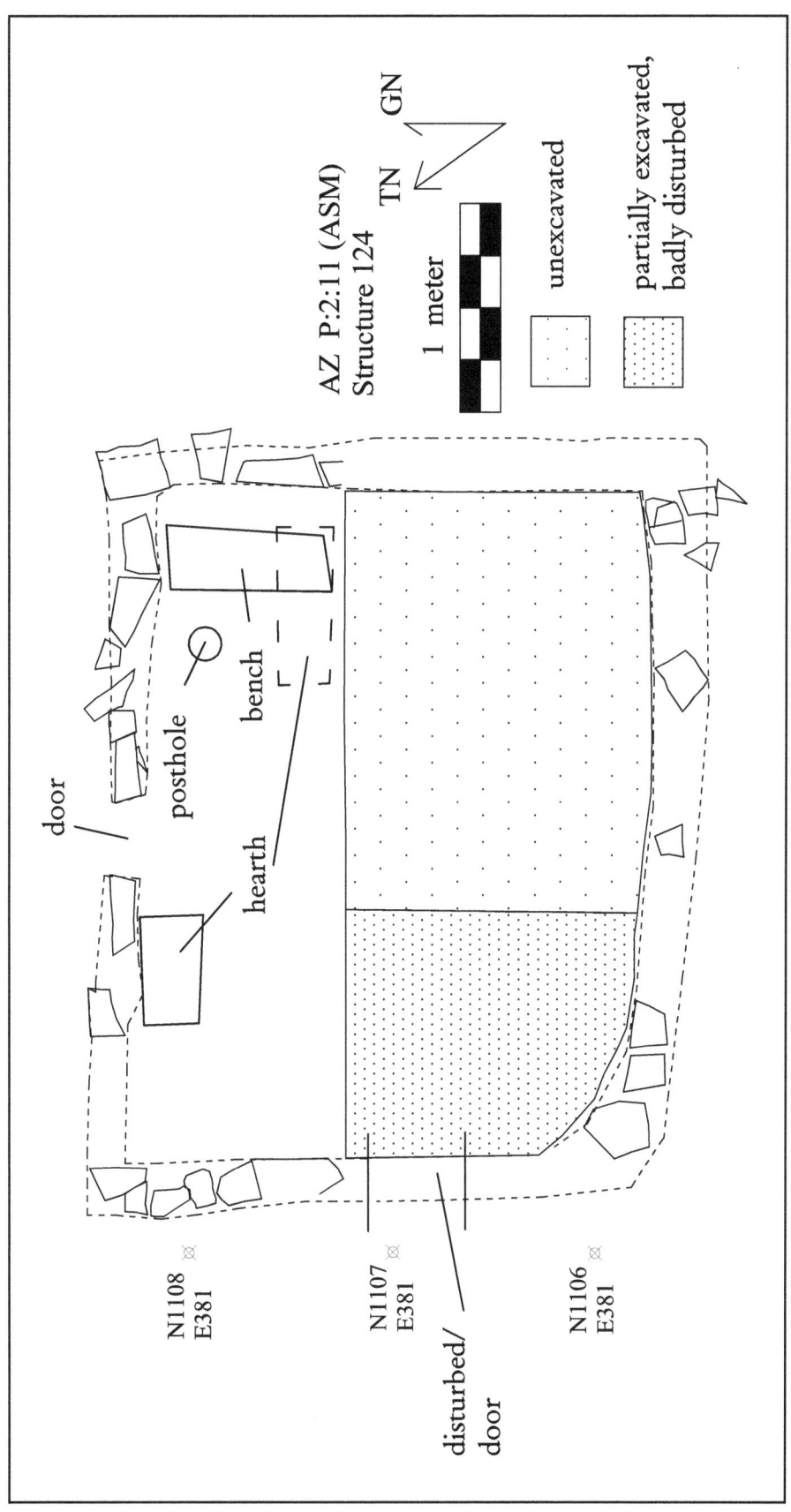

Figure 4.4. Plan view of Structure 124, a habitation room with ritual features.

is connected by an open doorway to a burned corn storage room, S. 158, just like S. 124. It seems likely that the burning of S. 159's roof was caused by the spread of fire from S. 158, similar to the situation with S. 123 and 124. Farther west is an unburned storage room, S. 157, having nothing on its floor, yet still connected by a doorway to the corn storage room. Again, this is identical to the situation with S. 122 through 124. Just like S. 124, S. 159 is distinctive from other habitation rooms in terms of features and floor assemblage.

Floor features include a large, very deep hearth, an adjacent ash pit, a subfloor pit that contained a whole Chavez Pass Polychrome jar in Tonto Polychrome style and a complex bin feature that is interpreted to be a shrine. The hearth is over 40 cm deep and was filled with at least seven distinct layers of ash. The bin feature sits in the northeast corner of the structure and consists of three distinctive sets of upright slabs that enclose a small interior space that is identical in form and size to shrine features found in S. 710, at H2, and on the landscape surrounding H1 and H2. Identical features are still used by Hopi in interior shrines and on the landscape (E.C. Adams 1982; Fewkes 1906; Parsons 1936). Although the soil within the shrine feature was organic, no specific artifacts could be identified. The subfloor feature in the northwest corner of S. 159 is similar to the subfloor feature in S. 120. It is excavated into bedrock and was clearly designed to hold a medium-size jar, just as the one in S. 120 was designed to hold two large jars. In addition to the jar, a small ladle bowl was recovered from the feature beneath the jar. Also, within the jar were the remains of multiple cottontail rabbits. A circular stone that may have been a lid to this jar was on the floor about 50 cm east of the feature.

In addition to the artifacts already mentioned, S. 159 had an extensive floor assemblage. As with many other structures in the room blocks surrounding the south plaza, three whole manos were placed adjacent to the hearth. On the floor against the east wall, and east of the hearth, was the foot of an artiodactyl. Just to the west of the shrine were the remains of an articulated jackrabbit and cottontail. In a small pit, adjacent to the south side of the shrine, was an enormous igneous axe. With the exception of a small chip on its sharpened tip, the axe had no indication of use. It is identical in size (20 cm long), style, and association with a shrine as an axe recovered from the shrine in S. 710, in H2. Finally, a large Sikyatki Polychrome jar was recovered in about 100 pieces in the northwest corner, above the pit feature with the jar. This is just the assemblage in the north half of the structure, as the south half was not excavated.

Ritual Assemblages Within Rooms

Even more so than for S. 124, the S. 159 assemblage appears to be nearly all associated with ritual practices and to be placed rather than a result of being hurriedly abandoned due to fire or other causes. The manos, rabbits, and axes appear to be ritually-associated placements that have been found elsewhere at Chevelon (Table 4.2). As noted above, storage rooms 227 and 286 had comparable floor assemblages (Figure 4.5a). S. 286 had three articulated adult cottontail rabbits placed with their heads toward each other in a clockwise manner (Figure 4.5b). Associated with these rabbits are an igneous axe, two bone awls, and a shaped piece of igneous (a gypsum mineral). Near the rabbit assemblage were two large storage jars. A remarkable aspect to this floor assemblage is that a nearly identical one was recovered from S. 701 in H2, which had two axes and

Table 4.2. Selected Artifacts as Part of Floor Assemblages.

Structure	Manos near or in Features	Articulated Rabbits	Axe	Other
252	On kiva bench	None	One on kiva floor	Large JYW jar sherd
286	None	Three arranged clockwise	One associated with rabbits	Two storage jars; bone awls, selenite
158	Two on floor, not near features	None	None	Two bone awls
159	Three near hearth	Two next to shrine. Two in storage jar	One near shrine	Articulated artiodactyl foot, Sikyatki Poly jar
120	Two near bin	None	None	JYW bowl.
124	Three near/in hearth	None	One on floor	Jeddito Black-on-yellow bowl
603	One in storage bin	None	None	Miniature bowl, ladle bowl
702	One next to storage bin	None	None	
222	Multiple in roof fall & on floor near piki hearths	None	One in wall niche	Several piki stones are also present

Figure 4.5. S. 286 floor assemblage (left). Detailed photo of cottontail rabbits and associated artifacts (right).

three rabbits arranged in a circle (Adams 2002: Figure 6.2).

S. 227 is unique at Chevelon in having a secondary burial of an adult on the floor missing head, hands, and other elements (Appendix C); no associated artifacts were found with the body. It appears the room was in disrepair with the floor partially covered with trash and perhaps even some roof debris. This material was removed from the northern half of the structure to expose the flagstone floor upon which she was placed. It is impossible to know the fate of this individual, but it appears the head and hands were removed postmortem. In the ethnographic literature, similar treatment is usually associated with accusations of witchcraft that lead to the killing of the individual, denial of burial or associated goods, and removal of head and/or hands, but usually perimortem (Walker 1995, 1998).

As Table 4.2 demonstrates, what are usually considered household or subsistence items appear to have been transformed into ritual offerings at the closure of structures, including storage, corn storage, piki house, habitation, and ritual habitation structures. The focus on rabbits is not unique to Chevelon, with articulated rabbits found on room floors and in features in dozens of rooms in the HSC, but most notably in the JYW-associated assemblages at H1 and H2, and Chevelon spanning the period encompassing all three Homol'ovi phases. This suggests a shared ritual heritage involving offerings of rabbits. Although rare in HSC assemblages, axes have a distinctive association with ritual placements as well (Table 4.3). The two instances in S. 701 and 710 at H2 have already been noted. The intersection of rabbits and axes is also noteworthy in S. 286 and 159 at Chevelon and S. 701 at H2. The careful placement of these objects together indicates ritual association.

Both are male gender (Parsons 1939; Tyler 1975). In the piki house, clearly a female gendered structure, an axe was placed into a wall niche.

The manos, on the other hand, seem to be part of a separate ritual assemblage, perhaps associated with female gender. They are placed in numerous rooms either associated with hearths in habitation structures of all types or with bins in storage rooms. None are associated with metates or with grinding bins. All are whole and still have considerable remnant use-life. These manos, then, are being carefully placed in specific locations, depending on room use, as an offering associated with the discontinuation of use of the structure, or sometimes a floor when another is built. Their association with food production features — hearths and storage bins — infers that corn processing is being symbolized. This association is strongly expressed in the room blocks surrounding the south plaza where three of five habitation rooms have manos, including two burned rooms and one unburned. The inference is that mano placement is associated with room closure, not the mode of closure. A similar pattern occurs in storage rooms where two rooms have manos, one from an earlier floor when the roof was not burned, and one from a late floor where the roof was burned. Manos were also found in the floor fill of one of the corn storage rooms. Another link to ritual for these artifacts is their location in kivas. A mano and a stone axe, perhaps representing female and male, were recovered from the bench and floor of K. 252 while an articulated rabbit was found in the fill of K. 279. These will be discussed below with a detailed discussion on ritual and power to be presented later.

Table 4.3. Contexts and Types of Axes Recovered from Homol'ovi Settlement Cluster Villages.

Structure Type[1]	Fill Type	Axe Type and Number	Associated Artifacts	Residues
Kiva	Floor	¾: 2; full: 1	Manos, ochre, whole vessels	2: red hematite
	Bench	¾: 1	Manos, whole vessels	Red hematite
Ritual	Floor	¾: 2; full: 1	Manos, articulated rabbits, projectile points	
	Feature	¾: 3	Manos, rabbit skulls, palette	1: red hematite
	Fill	¾:1; ¾ double bitted: 1; full: 1	Manos, metates	2: red hematite
Ritual Storage	Floor	¾: 3	Manos, pukis	
	Fill	¾: 1	Articulated rabbit	
Piki	Feature	¾: 1	None	
Storage	Floor	¾: 3; spiral: 1	3: Articulated rabbits, ladles, miniature vessels	
	Fill	¾: 1	Whole vessels, manos, figurine	

[1]Ritual structures are defined in E.C. Adams (2002: Table 6.6).

Piki House

S. 222 is the only piki house, so far, discovered at Chevelon. It represents the third piki house identified in the HSC; the other two being S. 209, at H1, and S. 14, at H3. The 25.5 percent frequency of Jeddito Yellow Ware (JYW) places the fill of the piki house in the EHP, which dates 1330 to 1365. The low frequency suggests discontinuation of use of the piki house, at about 1350. Dating of the other two piki houses places them later in time than S. 222, probably after 1365.

S. 222 is a small structure, about 4.5 sq. m, that was part of the original group of structures built at Chevelon, at the junction of two of the original ladder room blocks built about 1290. Initially, it was constructed as a habitation structure with a central hearth. Sometime during its use-life, shortly after the introduction of JYW, the roof of this structure was burned and collapsed with a new floor built over its top. At this time, the hearth was remodeled and a new west wall was constructed. Additionally, a storage bin and two piki hearths were constructed (Figure 4.6). Before use of the structure ended, one of the piki hearths was removed. A piki hearth is quite distinctive from a standard hearth, used for cooking or heating. Instead of having four stones and being generally small, about 30 cm on a side, a piki hearth has stones on only three sides and is rectangular. HSC piki hearths range in length from 50 to 70 cm (E.C. Adams 2001; 2002). The open side of the hearth is necessary because the top is totally covered by the piki stone, making the open side the only option for adding fuel to the fire. In these characteristics, piki hearths are nearly identical to their modern Hopi counterparts, except being smaller (E.C. Adams 1982).

Access to the structure was gained through doors in the north and south walls, and possibly through a roof hatch. It is probable that S. 222 had an upper story that was burned, collapsing both roofs. Floor artifacts were fairly

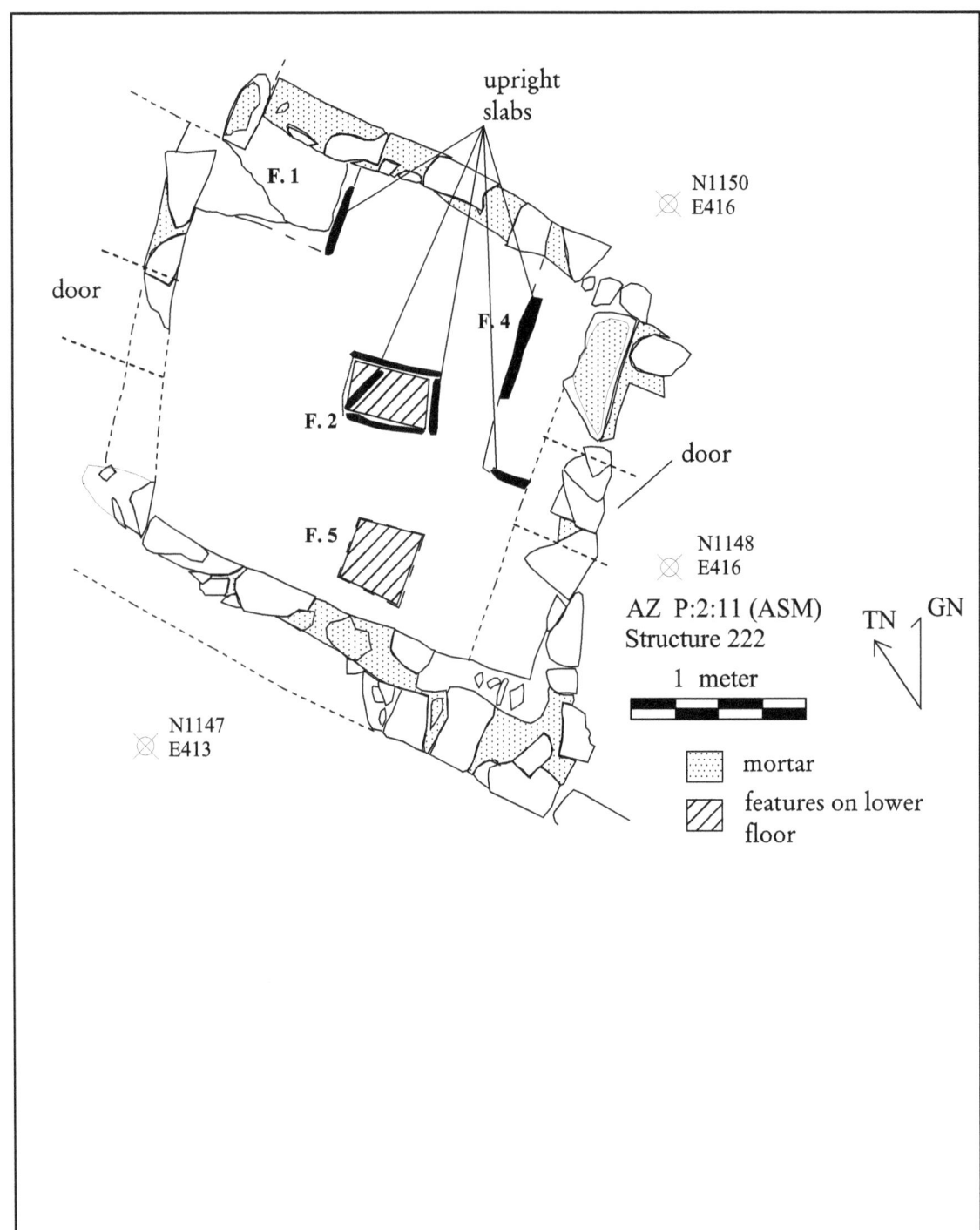

Figure 4.6. Plan view of Structure 222, piki house.

sparse and included a mano, three cores, an abrader, and a few sherds with the stone axe, unusual in that it is made from chert rather than igneous, placed in a niche in the west wall. The assemblage of the unnumbered upper room was much more robust and included griddle/piki stone fragments; mano fragments; a metate fragment; abraders; polishing stones; pecking stones, 2 or 3 with pigment on them; medium to high frequency of sherds, which exhibit a wide range of types from corrugated to White Mountain Red Ware (WMRW) to yellow wares; a few projectile points; some interesting worked bone implements from the south half, including at least two antler tools; quite a bit of yellow clay; and a high frequency of small animal bones, including some fish bones. Unfortunately, the combination of roof/floor collapse and subsequent vandalism have made it difficult to interpret this complex floor assemblage.

Today, piki bread is strongly associated with ceremonies among the Hopi, although this apparently was not always the case (Dedecker 2005, 2006). I have argued that the early piki complex was part of a complex associated with katsina ritual that appeared in the early to mid-1300s (E.C. Adams 1991b). At H1, the piki house is next to an early kiva, two non-kiva structures likely used for religious rituals, and two mealing rooms next to the large south plaza in a complex that was interpreted as a focus of female gender activities associated with plaza-based ritual performances, primarily katsina (E.C. Adams 2002). The remodeling of S. 222, to create the piki house, occurs about the same time as the large south plaza was being built at Chevelon. Could more formal gender roles in Pueblo society be the cause for the remodeling of space at these pueblos (Dedecker 2005; Hegmon et al. 2000)?

Kivas

Kivas at Chevelon fall into two categories: subterranean and surface. Kivas otherwise are characterized by having a ventilation system, usually associated with a bench. Although six kivas are known for certain at Chevelon: K. 901, 905, 248, 279, 252, and 400, only four were sufficiently excavated to offer any meaningful comments (Table 4.4). K. 905 was discovered the last two weeks of the final field season. It is known only from a shallow 1 m-wide trench excavated about 1 m into its fill. It has a burned roof and looks to be completely unvandalized. K. 400 is known only from outlining its walls during the 2002 mapping project at Chevelon. Only its size and the fact that it appears to be completely vandalized are known. The other four kivas will be treated in more depth.

K. 248

This kiva lies in the grid northeast corner of what was once a small plaza in RB200, next to the restricted entryway into the plaza (Figure 4.7). Our interpretation of the construction history of Chevelon indicates that K. 248 is an early kiva built when the village was first established about 1290. It is small and lacks a bench. In this way, it is similar to other early kivas at H3 and H4 (E.C. Adams 2001, 2004b), also dating to the late 1200s. K. 248 was completely vandalized prior to excavation by ASM; however, the walls and wall plaster were mostly intact and, in parts, the fill next to the walls and some floor features were preserved, including a ventilator. The floor was flagstone, but nearly all of the stones had been pulled up and stacked by the vandals. A plastic bag containing trash and a newspaper dating August

Table 4.4. Characteristics of Chevelon Kivas.

Kiva Designation	Location	Size (Sq. m)	Building/Abandonment Date	Mode of Abandonment
248	RB200	7.54	1290-1340	Burned & filled
252	RB200	6.50 (est.)	1350-1390?	Nothing formal
279	RB200	12.00 (est.)	1300/25-1350	Filled
400	RB400/800	16.50	1350-????	Unknown
901	RB300	42.00 (est.)	1300/25-1365	Filled & burned
905	RB300	12.00 (est.)	Unknown	Burned

Figure 4.7. Photograph of east wall of Kiva 248 showing ventilation tunnel.

31, 1978 near the floor suggest the probable period of the vandalism. In addition, the fill from the kiva had been deposited at least in part over the top of S. 227, which was discovered during the excavation of that structure.

K. 248 is 2.6 m by 2.9 m (7.54 sq. m), about 20 percent larger than the average room. Its walls still stood 2.0 m high, nearly full height. These began about 1 m below the present ground surface, probably near the plaza surface during the kiva's use. Unfortunately, the plaza had also been vandalized making it impossible to evaluate its age, length or period of use, and possible features. The walls of the kiva were constructed of tabular to blocky Moenkopi sandstone and covered with 13 layers of plaster, 10 of which were sooted from fires within the kiva. The top layer had faint white handprints on the west wall and the western portions of the south and north walls. Additionally, the imprints of hands were also left in the same locations. Handprints are often used as part of initiation ceremonies among the Hopi and perhaps these had a similar purpose (Parsons 1936).

When use of the kiva came to an end, its roof was burned and collapsed onto the floor; however, during or after the fire, the primary beams were pulled and probably recycled elsewhere in the pueblo (E.C. Adams 2016). After burning, the kiva was filled with trash, apparently to the top of its walls, from indications of fill left in the structure and discoloration of the walls. Much of the fill was ashy and remnants of fill suggest that ash pockets and even layers were typical throughout the structure.

This pattern is common for kivas and some other ritual structures at other Homol'ovi cluster villages and has been described by La Motta (1996), Karunaratne (1997), Walker (1995, 1996b), E.C. Adams (2002, 2016), Walker et al. (2000), E.C. Adams and LaMotta (2006), and E.C. Adams and Fladd (2014). A characteristic of these deposits is the concept of ceremonial trash, first used by Walker (1996b) and later published (Walker 1995, 1996b; Walker et al. 2000), and what more recently have been termed "enriched deposits" (E.C. Adams and LaMotta 2006). Typical of these kiva deposits are a diversity of whole or nearly whole objects (pottery, projectile points), unusual objects (fossils, crystals), parts of articulated animals (usually birds, but also carnivores) (see LaMotta 2006; Strand 1998), and numerous individual deposits of ash or ash layers (Karunaratne 1997). Because K. 248 had been so vandalized, the evidence was somewhat circumstantial, but nevertheless compelling. As indicated, thin layers of the fill deposits still adhered to parts of especially the south and west walls. These indicated numerous ash layers were used to fill the kiva. Second, the fill over S. 227 from K. 248 had numerous whole or nearly whole objects, including a puki made from a Homolovi Polychrome bowl, most of a corrugated jar, and miniature vessels. A quartz crystal and bone awls were also recovered.

The pattern of burning kiva roofs is also quite common in the HSC and seems to be related to closure of the kiva and perhaps purification (LaMotta 1996). Filling of the kiva, as described by Karunaratne (1997), also seems to be part of this pattern of closing and sealing a ceremonial structure. As reported by Hopi (E.C. Adams 1982; Parsons 1936, Titiev 1944), religious activities in kivas can involve rites that could be dangerous to individuals not initiated into these ceremonies. The best way to prevent contamination is to close and burn the structure (E.C. Adams 2016; Walker 1995, 1998). This seems to be the most parsimonious explanation for kiva burning and filling. The objects found in kivas are a continuation of the religious power of the place. Dangerous objects and consecrated objects and even ash would be deposited in such places, as is the case with the handling of ash from hearths in the New Fire ceremony still practiced at Hopi (Fewkes 1900; Parsons 1936).

The pottery recovered from the undisturbed portions of K. 248 fill and from the displaced fill over S. 227 suggests that closure of the kiva occurred during the EHP, 1330 to 1365 (Gavioli 2005). The frequency of 31.5 percent JYW, of total decorated in the kiva fill, puts its discontinuation at about 1340 or slightly later, 50 years after use began. The 10 to 13 layers of plaster, each covered with soot, also suggest a long life for K. 248 (Meyers 2007).

K. 279

K. 279 is a subterranean kiva located in the heart of RB200, in what at the time was a small central plaza that was rapidly filling with rooms (Figure 4.8). Shortly after K. 279 was built, or at the time it was built, two-story rooms were constructed on the north, west, and east sides. All have been mapped and several have been excavated. Details of this complex of structures and an examination of RB200 in terms of history, control of rituals, and power will be addressed later. K. 279 was built while K. 248 was still in use, but certainly afterwards, because several of the structures surrounding K. 279 rest on trash with no JYW, probably dating to the early 1300s. K. 279 is much larger than K. 248, although its length is not known. Location of the surrounding rooms and identification of floor features suggest the kiva is about 4 m long and 3 m wide, or 12 sq. m. The kiva has a bench along its south wall with a standard central ventilator, deflector, and hearth. Although many of the flagstones to the kiva had been removed by Chevelon residents, circular holes in two suggest the presence of at least one vertical loom. Niches for the roofing beams were recovered along the west wall

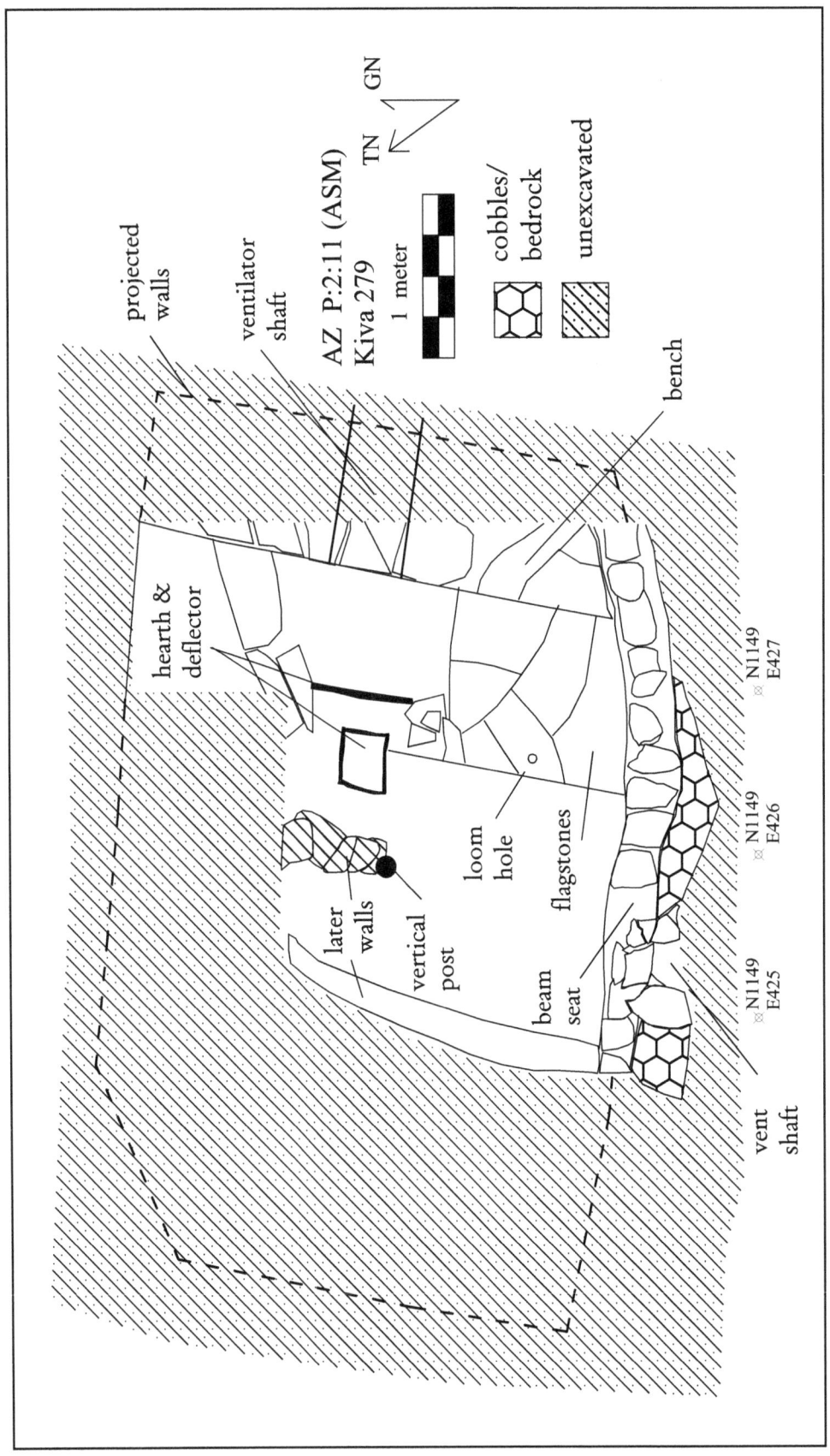

Figure 4.8. Plan view of Kiva 279.

enabling an accurate measurement of the roof height at nearly 2 m. The roof was unburned, although two of its primaries had charring on one side suggesting previous use and recycling, which is typical of large primary beams (E.C. Adams 2016). This seems to have been the case for K. 248 as well.

With the exception of a small portion of the east wall, the west wall was the only one exposed by excavation and revealed 12 plaster layers and 10 sooted layers. This suggests a similar life history to K. 248, which had 13 plaster layers, 10 sooted. No wall decorations were discovered. Apparently, only the upper portions of the walls were constructed of tabular sandstone, which were placed on a ledge cut into the gravelly bedrock surface of the hill. Both the sandstone and bedrock portions were then plastered. Use of the kiva discontinued when the lower portion of the east wall collapsed, probably a result of weakness of the bedrock portion of the wall. The kiva was then rapidly filled with trash, infused with ash layers and individual pockets of ash indicating discrete ash dumps (Figures 4.8, 4.9). The presence of numerous partial to whole pots and articulated animals, including birds, cottontails, and fish, suggest that the deposits are what has been termed ritual trash and qualify as enriched deposits (E.C. Adams and LaMotta 2006; Walker 1996b; Walker et al. 2000). When the kiva was about 75 percent filled, deposition briefly stopped and windblown sand capped these deposits just before the roof collapsed. The roof is completely preserved with casts of the primary and secondary beams, fragments of wood in some of the casts, elements of the closing material of brush and grasses, and the earthen/adobe roof itself. A hearth within the roof-top indicates the roof of the kiva was used by the surrounding room blocks for outside activities while the kiva was in use.

After the roof collapsed or was collapsed, a wall was built over its top to segregate the space into two halves. Only the southern half was excavated and was designated S. 274. Although this space may have been briefly used, it soon was also filled with ash dumps and trash that included more nearly whole pots, articulated animal bones, and many more unusual artifacts, suggesting the area was still being treated as a place for disposal of objects associated with ceremonial activity. At some point, most bottom story rooms surrounding the kiva/plaza space had their doorways sealed and, in some cases, second story rooms also had plaza-facing doorways sealed as well. Both S. 252 and 262, along the west side of the kiva/plaza, had ventilator systems installed beneath the sealed doorways. Less than 1 m of the north half of S. 262 was excavated, revealing a structure filled with animal bone. The excavation of S. 252 revealed it had been converted to an in-room kiva. It will be described below. Creation of K. 252 was likely a response to the loss of K. 279.

The cross-dating of kiva deposits using trade wares and percentage of Jeddito Yellow Ware (%JYW) suggests a beginning date for filling of about 1340 to 1350, continuing to near the end of the MHP, 1385. With construction of K. 279, likely in the early 1300s, its use-life would parallel that of K. 248 at 40 years. The higher %JYW in the fill of K. 279 versus K. 248 suggests its use and filling postdate K. 248 by a decade or more.

K. 252

K. 252 is unlike the previous kivas in that it is not subterranean. It is located in a structure on the west side of the K. 279 plaza. It represents a remodeling of a room into a kiva, probably to replace K. 279 when it was rendered

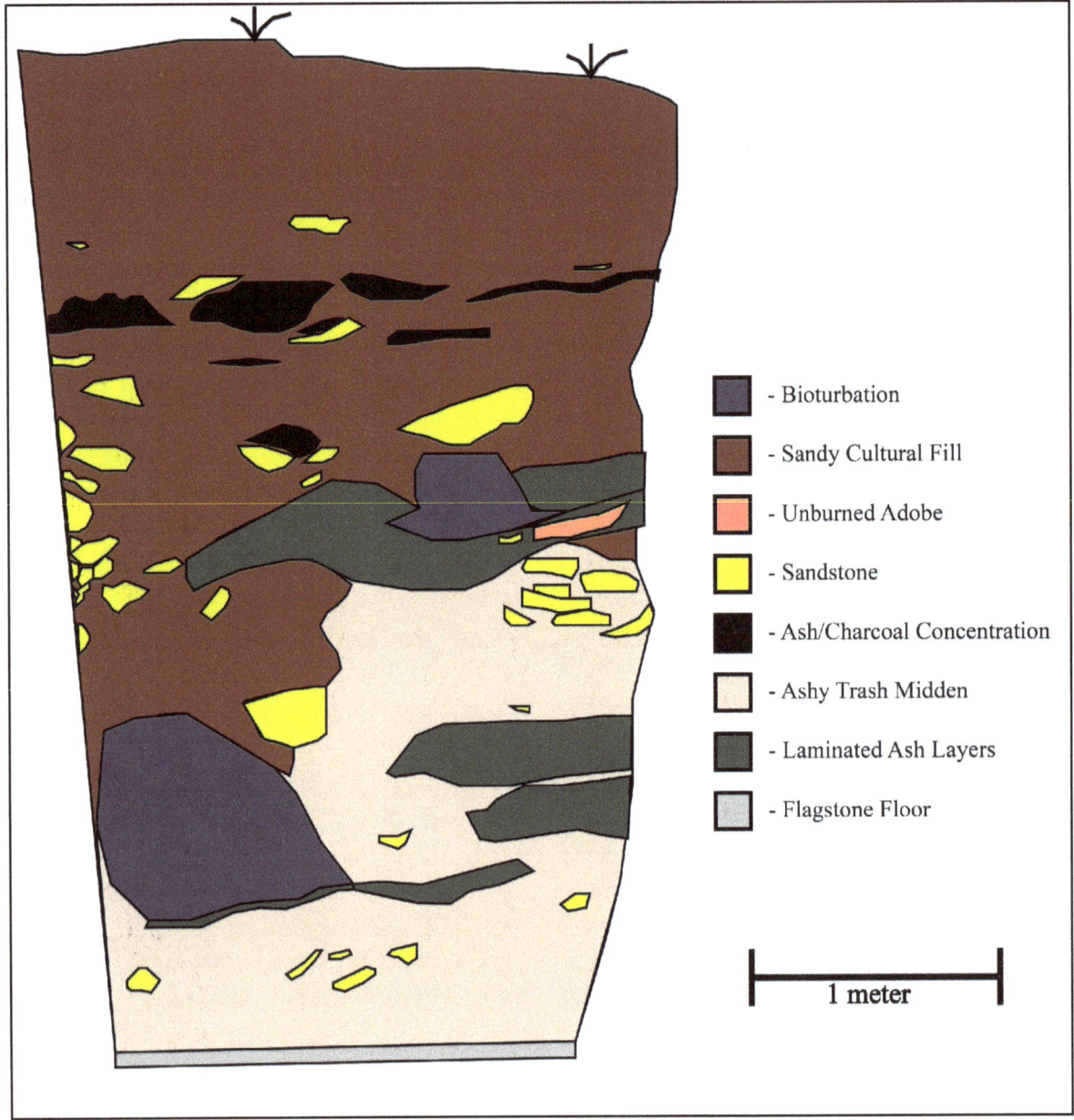

Figure 4.9. Kiva 279 N1152 profile.

unusable due to its collapse. Almost certainly, the structure that was converted to K. 252 was the bottom floor to a two-story set, just like the other rooms surrounding K. 279. To remodel these rooms, the upper room was removed and a bench, ventilator, and new hearth were constructed along with a new roof (Figure 4.10). The room's walls had at least 15 layers of plaster, most sooted. The bench was added over 12 of these layers, signaling a late remodeling of a habitation structure. The bench was constructed using a stone wall facing that was then filled with construction debris and covered with flagstones. The ventilator shaft was off-center in the southern third of the bench. Flagstones were also added to the floor,

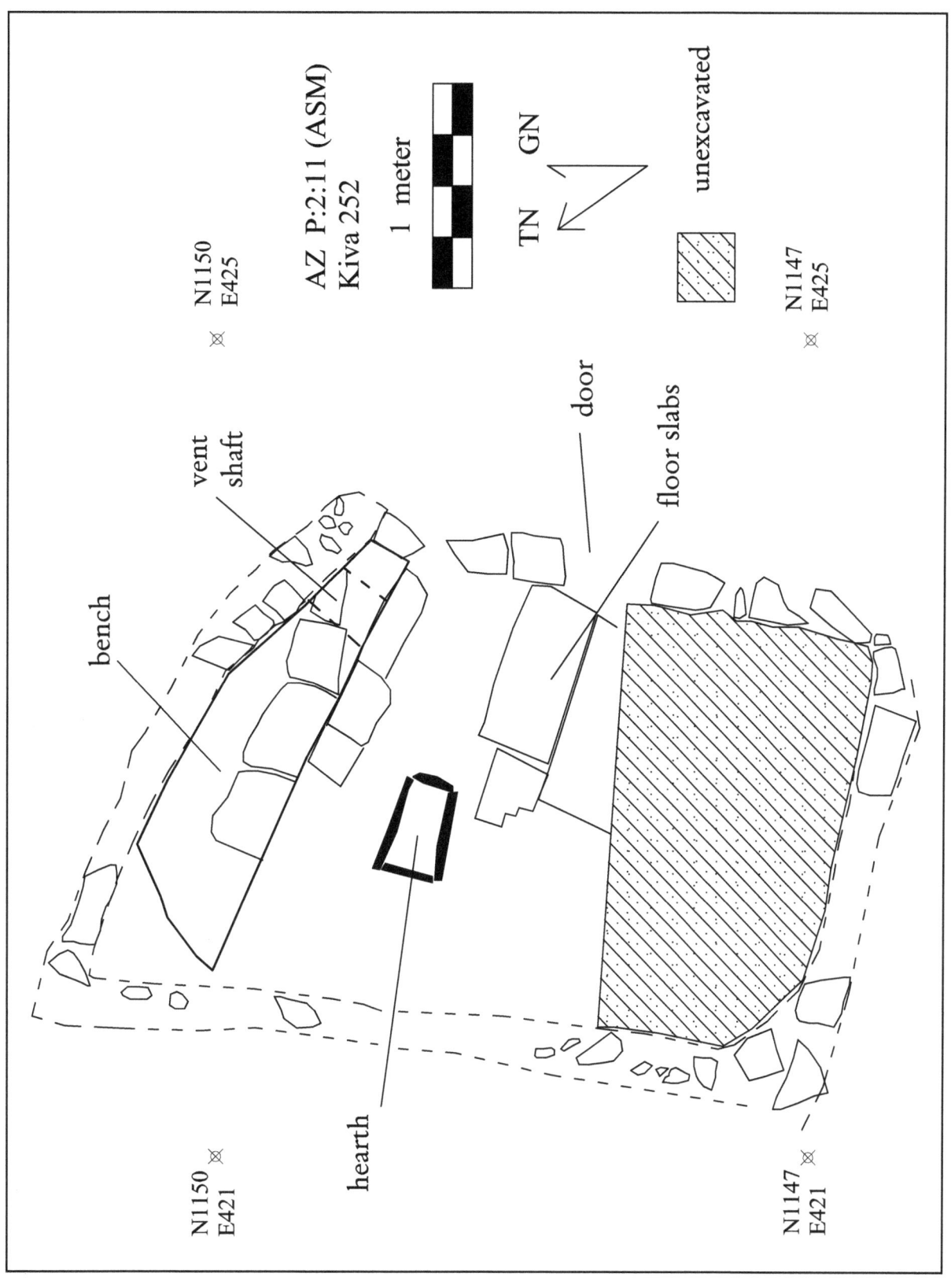

Figure 4.10. Plan view of Structure 252.

possibly removed from K. 279.

Only the eastern half of the kiva was excavated, but wall tracing during excavation suggests it is about 2.5 m by 2.6 m, or 6.50 sq. m, slightly larger than the average Chevelon room and only slightly smaller than K. 248. The only indications of roofing are collapsed, secondary beams mixed in the fill of the room, below wall fall. None of the beams are burned, indicating the roof did not burn. The fact that the roof was not burned suggests use of the kiva ended prior to closure of Chevelon by extensive burning and included removal of its primary beams. Original height of the kiva walls is uncertain, but still stood 1.4 m high at excavation.

Artifacts in K. 252 are scarce. There was no trash fill, supporting other evidence that it was in use to close to the closure of Chevelon. Floor artifacts were scarce, but seem to have been purposefully placed at closure. An intact mano and a large JYW bowl sherd were recovered on the bench and an axe was placed on the floor against the north wall.

As noted in the discussion of K. 279, the construction of K. 252 is clearly much later than K. 279 and seems likely in response to the loss of K. 279, due to the catastrophic failure of its east wall. Given that K. 279 was probably the only functioning kiva in RB200 at the time of the collapse, a replacement kiva was probably essential to the continuity of ceremonial activities for the oldest and probably most powerful groups in Chevelon. The fact that K. 252 was constructed within an existing two-story set of rooms that required their dismantling and refurbishment indicates a late construction and a need for a new ceremonial space. Its apparent use to near the end of the use of RB200, and probably of Chevelon in general, also suggests its time placement.

K. 901

K. 901 is the largest kiva at Chevelon and one of the largest excavated in the HSC (Figure 4.11). It dominates the small, enclosed RB300 plaza, which has been designated RB900 (E.C. Adams 2002: Tables 6.4 & 6.8). Although its exact dimensions are not known because only an estimated 25 percent has been excavated, the location of floor features and two of the four walls suggests it was 6 m wide and 7 m long for a total of 42 sq. m. This makes it the third largest kiva excavated in the cluster behind only K. 708 (58.43 sq. m) at H2 and K. 38 (estimated to be 63.75 sq. m) at H3 (E.C. Adams 2002: Table 6.6). This places it on the small end of what have been termed large kivas in contrast to medium and small kivas (E.C. Adams 2002: Table 6.7). Although it is intermediate in size between medium and large kivas, it is much larger than the largest medium size kiva at 25.78 sq. m, which is K. 901 at H1 (E.C. Adams 2002: Table 6.6). Given the small size of all other kivas at Chevelon and its being more than 15 sq. m larger than any other medium-sized kiva, K. 901 seems better suited to the large kiva than medium kiva category.

As with other subterranean Chevelon kivas, roof height is estimated at close to 2.0 m. At least some of the primaries were supported by vertical posts placed into or in front of the grid north and south walls. The only one of these, excavated as Feature 5, was flanked by columns of mortared stones on each side and it rested on the broad east bench. Given the span of at least 6.5 m to cover the width of the kiva, the primary beams were probably massive and needed additional support beyond the stone wall of the structure. (An intact primary beam recovered from the slightly smaller K. 901 at H1 was a 30-cm diameter Douglas fir and was also supported by vertical posts). The walls of

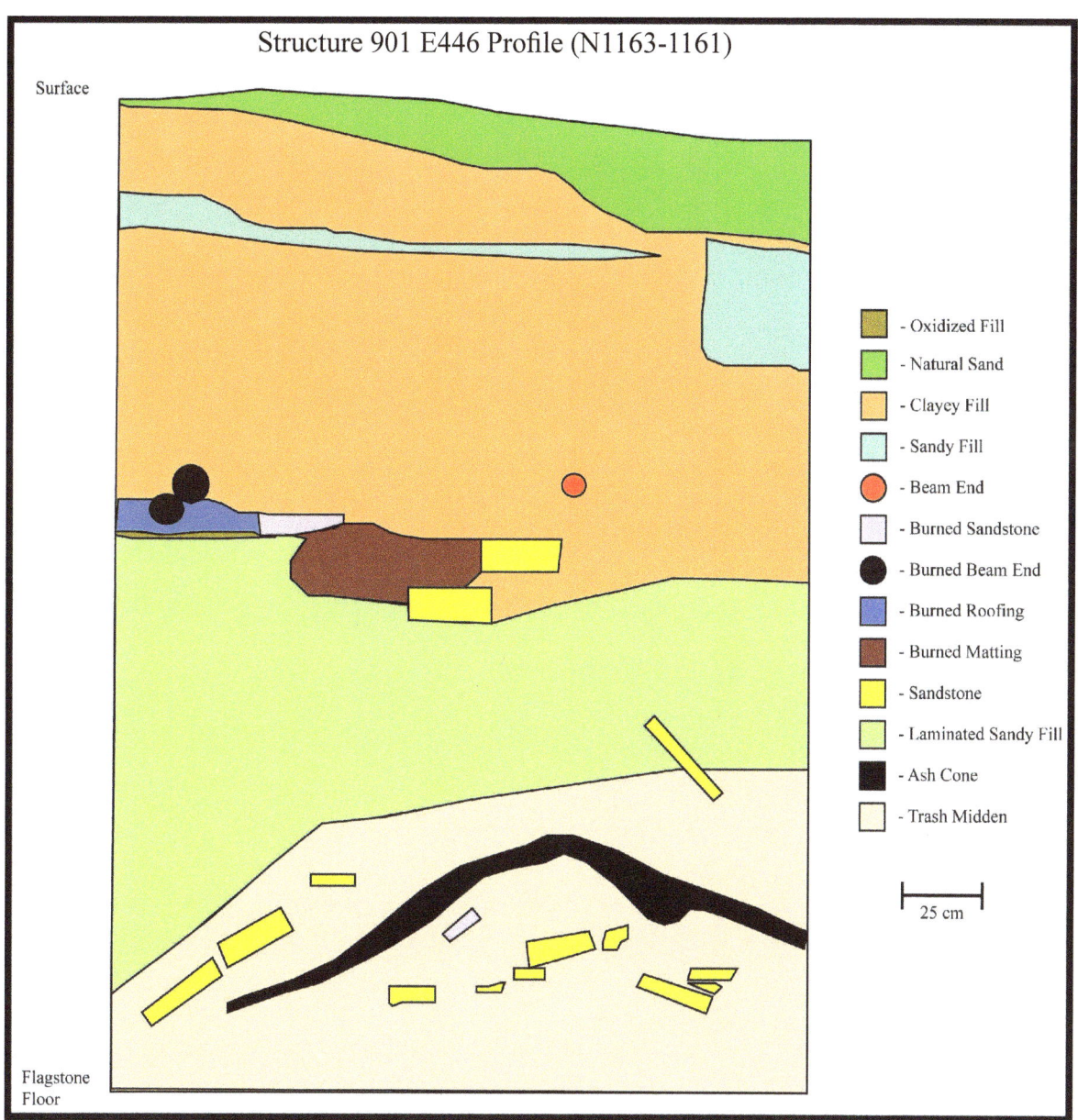

Figure 4.11. Profile view of Kiva 901.

K. 901 are mortared masonry. As is typical of kivas in HSC, the stones are blockier and larger than stones used in household structures.

Wall fall from all but the west wall was recovered in the fill of the structure, suggesting they have mostly collapsed. Part of this collapse was due to the mode of destruction of the kiva, through burning. The floor features are typical of a HSC kiva with a bench (1.5 m wide), ventilator, deflector, and hearth system (Figure 4.12). The deflector is unique among HSC kivas in being a small constructed wall. The floor was covered with flagstones, about 40 percent of which had been removed in the 9 sq. m of floor excavated. Those around the hearth and nearer the walls were still in place. A subfloor pit or cist is present about a meter north of the hearth. Its function and whether

68   E.C. Adams

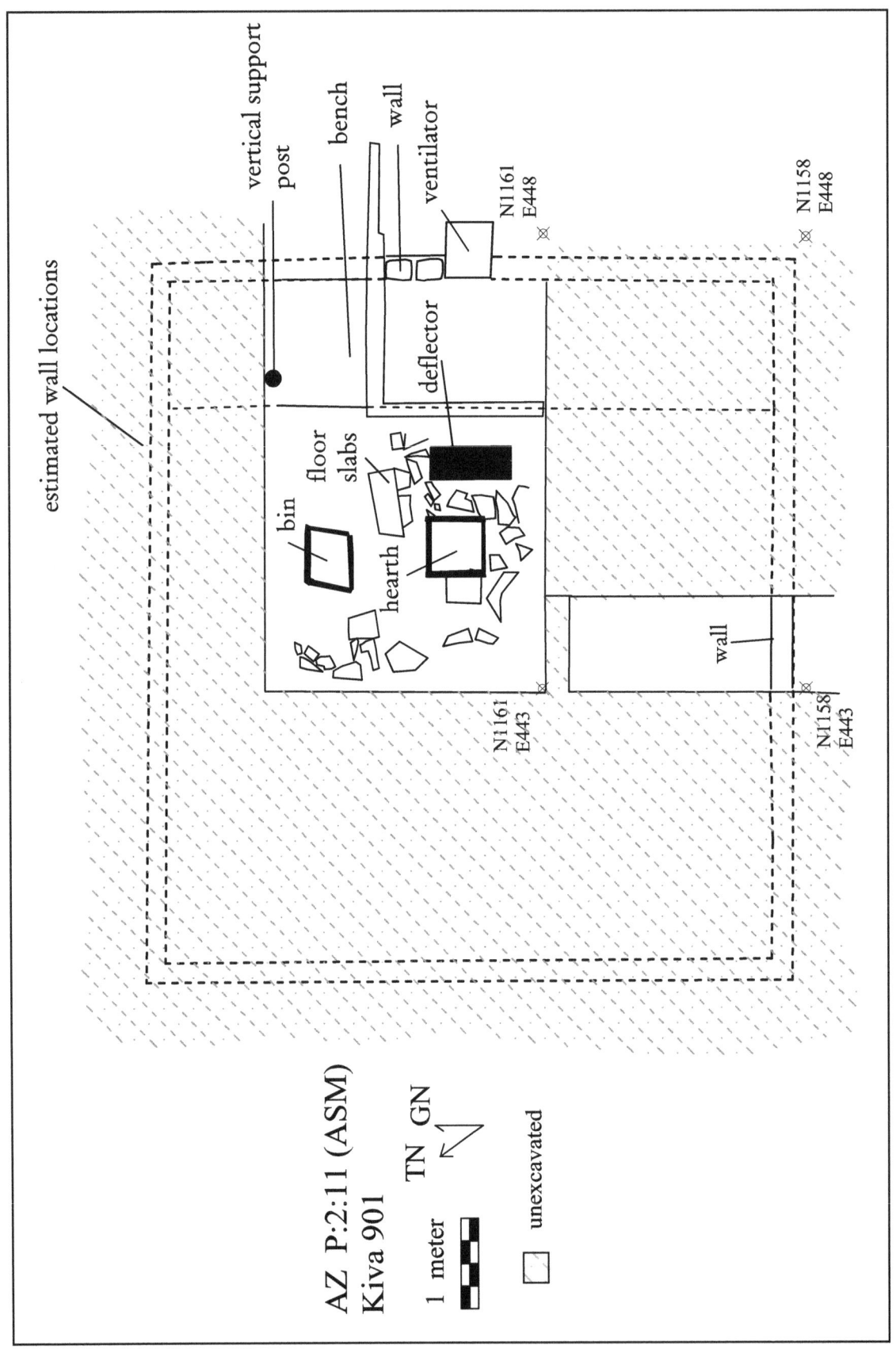

Figure 4.12. Plan view of Kiva 901.

or not it was covered by wood or stone are not known. No artifacts were recovered from its fill. Its location suggests it might have served as a sipapu.

The massiveness of its features and its great size indicate K. 901 had a different community use from the other Chevelon kivas. As discussed elsewhere (E.C. Adams 2002), such kivas are typically community structures intended not only for the private elements of village ceremonies, but also with room for public performances. It could also certainly house larger religious organizations that had formed or were forming in the village (LaMotta 2006). The relationship of K. 901 to the largest group of rooms in Chevelon, RB300, probably played a role in the need for such a large structure. Its date of construction in the early 1300s and discontinuation of use, about 1365, places it intermediate between the other two large HSC kivas, K. 38 at H3, whose construction and use dates roughly 1285/1290 to 1305, and K. 708 at H2, dating 1365 to 1400.

The discontinuation of use and filling/burning of K. 901 are among the most complex in the HSC. The relationships are all based on stratigraphy, with dating of deposits using tree-ring dated ceramics. The reconstructed steps of its filling are enumerated below:

1. When use of K. 901 was discontinued, it was initially filled through its roof hatch, creating a cone of trash on the floor centered over the deflector. This trash cone eventually attained a height of 75 cm, spreading onto the bench and across much of the floor, a distance of more than 2.0 m from its center (Figure 4.13). This midden was filled with large animal bone including deer, antelope and bighorn sheep, articulated birds, several whole or nearly whole pots of all types, unusual pottery forms, *Conus* shell tinklers, projectile points, etc. The cone was then capped with a thick layer of ash. The enriched nature of this deposit is likely due to its being the product of religious ritual practices of kiva closure.

2. The roof of the kiva was then partially burned, causing the collapse of the east wall to near the level of the bench. Many of the wall stones are oxidized on their interior sides from the heat of the fire.

3. Midden material was thrown into the kiva through the collapsed east wall, filling the kiva to about the western extent of the bench and continuing east to outside the kiva walls. Although this deposit is filled with artifacts, the bones are primarily disarticulated rabbit bones and the remaining artifacts are sherds and lithics with no RVs (reconstructible vessels). This midden is more typical of domestic trash.

Figure 4.13. Photograph of trash cone in Kiva 901.

4. The roof of the kiva was evidently breached at some point on its west. Whether on purpose or accidentally, it is not possible to determine, but the roofing beams were found within a few centimeters of the floor. A large midden began to accumulate above the beams, spreading in all directions, until the south wall of the kiva collapsed onto the edge and over this midden. The midden then continued to grow reaching a depth of over 1 m. As with the east midden, the material deposited in the west midden appears to be domestic.

5. The kiva then appears to have sat open with only natural filling by windblown sand in the central and west portions with some midden material continuing to be added through the breach in the east wall. Within the sand are unburned elements of the roof, including grasses, brush, and small secondary beams.

6. The final cultural act in the kiva was the burning of the remainder of the roof. Beams along the north and west walls, and in the center of the kiva, and closing material were completely charred, and the north wall partially collapsed as the roof fell. The sand that had accumulated to that point was oxidized from the heat of the roof, which is estimated to have been about 50 cm above the fill (Figure 4.14). The top 15 cm of the vertical beam support on the kiva bench was also burned and preserved. No cultural filling of the kiva occurred around this event. It is possible the burning took place sometime after Chevelon was depopulated, but it is also just as possible the burning was in conjunction with burning of many other structures in the village upon its depopulation.

7. The kiva then continued to fill with sand and elements of artifacts and burned fill eroding from surrounding rooms, especially on its west and south sides.

Dating of the construction, use, filling, and burning of K. 901 is based on tree-ring dated and seriated ceramics, including JYW, WMRW, Roosevelt Red Ware (RRW), and Zuni Glaze Ware. JYW is the dominant decorated ceramic throughout the cultural filling of the kiva. Based only on observations of excavated sherds, Tonto and Fourmile Polychrome are present in all the fill units. Sikyatki Polychrome (presently dated as post-1385, after LaMotta 2006) is present only in the upper portions of the eastern midden. When this part of the eastern midden was being deposited, the western midden was no longer active. This means that the original midden was deposited sometime between 1340 and 1385 (terminating the use of the kiva) with the intermediate and later middens deposited sometime between 1350 and 1400. Initial burning of the structure (after the early trash cone) would have likely occurred after 1370 and before 1385. It seems unlikely the midden with the Sikyatki Polychrome would have taken longer than 15 years to accumulate. The second burning occurred soon after 1385 because the burned roofing material lies directly on the east midden. It is not possible to tell when the kiva was built, but it likely was constructed when RB300 was built. Based on a midden over which RB300 was built, the kiva would

Figure 4.14. Photograph of oxidized fill with burned roof beams in Kiva 901.

have been constructed before the appearance of JYW, or 1325/30, but after 1300. Given the above fill estimates, it would have ceased use between 1360 and 1370, for a use-life of 30 to 70 years.

There are no physical reasons, visible in the archaeological record, for the cessation of use of K. 901. All of the walls and the roof appear to have been intact at the time its use stopped and it entered the archaeological record. No objects have been discovered placed on the floor, such as occurred at H2, although only 25 percent of the structure has been excavated. Nevertheless, the kiva was both purposefully buried with ceremonial trash and then burned, both features of kivas excavated in the HSC and discussed previously. Perhaps construction of Plaza 000 and movement of some public ceremonial performances into that area contributed to the closure of K. 901. It is also possible that RB300 was being depopulated; however, limited excavation in the room block precludes determining whether or not this was the case.

SUMMARY

In total, 19 generic storage rooms, 14 habitation rooms, a piki house, and six kivas provide enough information to infer use (Table 4.1). These numbers vary from the actual number of rooms excavated (39 with use of 37 known) because some rooms had multiple floors and their use changed through time, usually from habitation to storage. This body of information accounts for about 8 percent of total structures known or estimated to comprise Chevelon. They range in construction and occupation through the full range of what is believed to be Chevelon's occupation, or 1290 to the 1390s. Strong patterns in the organization of space within, and outside, structures are understood. Additionally, much has been recovered to inform on curation, placement, and even symbolism of artifacts recovered in structures and burning of structures. Finally, excavation has revealed patterns of social and household organization and use of space. These will be explored in the sections below.

The Household at Chevelon

The presence of room suites – rooms connected by doorways – is universal in pueblos with contiguous rooms and where such evidence is preserved. These patterns begin in Pueblo I (about 750 C.E.) in the Four Corners and continue into the historic Pueblo period. Discussion of these arguments and the nature of room suites for the HSC is presented in E.C. Adams (2002:127-129). Patterns in the size and composition of room suites also changed through time at the other villages in the settlement cluster with a number of rooms comprising a room suite generally increasing through time. This pattern is attributed to increases in village size necessitating changes in the makeup of households, due to increasing social obligations in large, socially complex villages versus smaller, kinship-sized villages (E.C. Adams 2002:127-129; Dohm 1990).

Excavation in four suites of rooms provides information about households at Chevelon: S. 122 through 124; S. 157 through 159; S. 509/546, 510/547, and S. 268/288/289, 287, and 245 (Table 4.5). These will be discussed individually and patterns will be commented on, in a general sense, at the end of the section. All of these households are associated with the later occupation of the village, although the RB200 room suite was established near the founding of the village. Thus, there is the expectation of larger household size and, therefore, larger size and number of rooms occupied by a household in line with room suites at H1 and H2. In addition to size, the number and type of structures, features, and assemblages are important toward understanding their unique characteristics.

S. 122-124 and 157-159

Some discussion of these clusters of rooms was presented in the description of S. 124 and 159, the two habitation structures with ritual features. Because these two sets of rooms are nearly identical in their makeup, they will be discussed together here. The excavated portions of the suites, for both areas, are identical with an empty storage room on the west, farthest from the plaza, a burned corn storage room next to and east of the storage room, with the ritual/habitation room next to and east of the corn storage room (Figures 4.15-4.18). In both cases, all rooms are connected by open doorways. All structures are one-story. The habitation structures for both room suites appear to be part of more recent additions to RB100 in that their north and south walls abut existing walls, which are the corn storage rooms. There is no indication that either storage structure was ever a habitation structure, so it is unclear how household organization may have shifted, if indeed the habitation rooms were added at a later period. It is also possible that both habitation structures have rooms to their east. These rooms have not been excavated.

S. 124 has a doorway in its north wall that connects it with another room, probably another habitation room, which in turn is almost certainly connected to two other storage rooms similar to the S. 122 through 124 complex. If this is the case, then this room suite has 6 to 8 structures. The jury is still out on the S. 157 to 159 suite in that the absence of a doorway in its north wall does not preclude its having a doorway in its south wall. At present, all one can say is that there were at least 3 to 4 rooms in the household suite.

Domestic Activity

These room suites contain classic elements of domestic activities, which include long-term food storage (corn still on the cob) and cooking. The presence of subfloor and surface storage jars suggests either water or intermediate food storage. The hearth remains reveal cooking for domestic and wild plant resources. Multiple manos on the floor, or the roof in the case of S. 124, suggest corn grinding was part of the household activities, although no mealing bins or rooms were discovered. The presence of articulated rabbits in the subfloor jar and on the floor could be associated with subsistence

Table 4.5. Room Suites at Chevelon.

Suite	Room types	Use span	Abandonment Mode	Other
122-124	Storage, corn storage, ritual habitation	1360-1390	Burned	Habitation room has floor assemblage
157-159	Same as 122-24	1360-1390	Burned	Same as above
509-10, 546-47	Habitation, 2 storage	1360-1390	Burned	Same as above
268, 287-89	Habitation, 3 storage	1300/25-1390	Burned	No floor assemblage

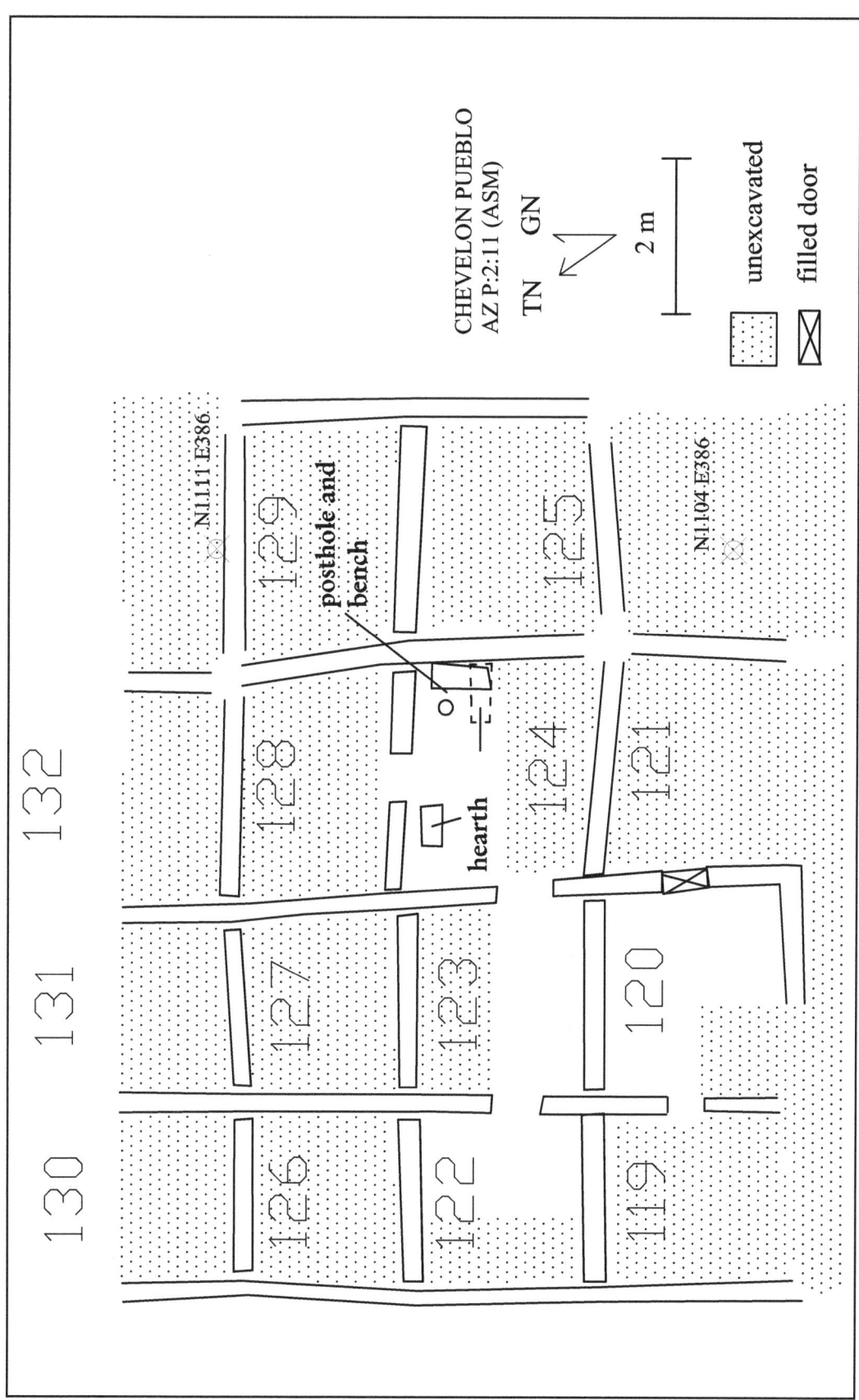

Figure 4.15. Plan view of room suite 122-124.

Figure 4.16. Photograph of Structure 157, storage room.

Figure 4.17. Photograph of Structure 158, burned corn storage room.

Figure 4.18. Photograph of Structure 159, a habitation room with ritual features.

activities, as faunal analysis at Chevelon and other Homol'ovi villages indicate cottontail and jackrabbits were the most common sources of animal protein (Diaz de Valdes 2006; LaMotta 2006; Pierce 2001; Strand 1998; Szuter 1991). Given the corn storage, there is no doubt that both room suites were engaged in domestic activities.

Ritual Versus Ritual Closure

The treatment of S. 124 and 159, as ritual habitation structures, has been discussed earlier. Floor features and artifact assemblages have been argued to support the use of these structures for ritual activities.

Beyond the association of ritual practices with features in these suites based on ethnographic and archaeological inferences, there is the added overlay of ritualized closure. In addition to the burning and sacrificing (sensu Walker 1995) of rooms full of corn stored on the cob, there is the presence of manos and rabbits on the structures' floors. These are not in storage, use, or domestic discard mode, but have been purposely situated on the floor. Thus, the ritual signature of these room suites is enhanced by the floor features in the two habitation rooms, the objects and their placement on the floors of these structures, and the burning of corn and the rooms themselves.

S. 509/546 and 510/547

This suite of rooms consists of one and possibly two, two-story structures. The plaza-facing rooms, S. 509/546, are clearly two stories. The back suite of rooms is vandalized to the degree that the evidence is equivocal as to whether or not there was a second story. Thus, this suite of rooms may only number three. Additionally, only the north half of the structures was excavated, leaving room for the possibility of doors connecting this suite of rooms to others to the south. It should be noted that the southwestern third of S. 509/546 was also totally vandalized. S. 509 is a habitation structure that once contained a hearth and had a limited, but interesting floor assemblage. A reconstructible Chavez Polychrome jar with Tonto Polychrome designs was broken on the floor. Additionally, several lithics and burned corn kernels and corn cobs were present. It appears that the corn was spread over the surface of the floor and ignited. As a result, the surface of the floor was heavily reduced. A similar burning of corn on the cob was recovered from the roof of S. 702. S. 509 had several distinguishable floor layers, indicating a relatively long use-life.

S. 546 is a storage room. No floor features were discovered and the room was totally filled with windblown sand. The roof was relatively intact and completely unburned. S. 510/547 appears to have at least one burned roof; however, there were no floor features nor a floor assemblage recovered in these substantially vandalized structures. Whether one or two structures, they are interpreted to be storage rooms. The first floor rooms were connected by an unsealed doorway.

Interpretation

It appears that this suite of rooms belongs to a single household and that it consisted of three to four rooms, although more cannot be ruled out due to only partial excavation of all structures. It seems that at least one of the rooms was burned at abandonment and that corn was placed on the floor as a means for closing the habitation room and the room suite as a whole. Due to vandalism in the area and only partial excavation, it is not clear whether or not the jar on the floor was whole and whether or not it contained anything, as it was partially burned when the corn was ignited. The absence of burned roof beams suggests this was another form of closure for rooms when there were no plans to continue their use. The sacrifice of corn has been established for the two storage rooms, S. 123 and 158, and this seems to be another example of this closure behavior (E.C. Adams 2016). The use of corn to repeatedly cover surfaces associated with mortuary areas at H1, is another notable example (E.C. Adams 2002, 2016; Miljour 2016).

The form of room suites is decidedly different in RB500 than in RB100, in the limited excavations of these areas. Whereas RB100 households seemed to prefer single-story structures and to expand into the plaza; those in RB500 seem to have adhered to a two-room width, but compensated by adding a second story. There is no obvious reason for such differences other than household or group ideas about how to use space or, perhaps, restrictions of construction within the plaza. Although cultural preferences for how space should look and be organized are well known (Hillier and Hanson 1984), it is difficult to attribute meaning to such patterns at Chevelon with such a low sample size.

S. 268/288/289, 287, 246

This suite of rooms consists of at least five structures and probably a sixth and seventh (Figure 4.19). The lack of clarity stems from the fact that S. 287 was completely vandalized and S. 246 was not excavated, but is probably two stories. Nevertheless, both these structures are connected by doorways to the excavated two-story suite of S. 268/288/289. S. 268 and 289 are habitation structures, whereas S. 287 and 288 are storage structures. Some remodeling of the room suite further complicates interpretation, but still much can be understood as a result of excavations.

Unlike the other room suites, this one was established much earlier. Walls to first-story structures, S. 288 and 289, are sitting on top of trash fill predating the introduction of JYW, thus placing their construction before 1325/30 and after 1290, Chevelon's founding. The depth of the deposits and ceramics suggest construction was closer to 1300. Early in its use, S. 288 was part of the habitation room, S. 289, and separated by only a half wall that was later filled and a doorway was installed. S. 288 was later reduced in size by construction of a new south wall and soon became a household midden. An eight-month neonate was placed in this midden near the end of use of the area.

A unique feature of this room suite is the connection of four first-story rooms by doorways all in a north-south line. S. 288 and 289 were covered by a single room, although this modification was a result of the later remodeling of S. 288. S. 287 was likely a storage room because plaster on its walls was not sooted. It is uncertain whether or not it was once two stories. The south wall to S. 287 rests on bedrock gravel and was probably part of an earlier structure to the south that may have been part of the original suites of rooms constructed at Chevelon. There is no doorway in this wall. S. 246, which lies to the north of S. 268/289, is connected by a doorway to S. 289, but lack of excavation precludes determination of room use. It is not known if the shared wall between S. 289 and 246 sits on early trash or not, as time did not allow excavation to determine this.

Interpretation

This room suite is the earliest documented at Chevelon. It appears that S. 268/289/288 were built as one unit, probably at the same time as S. 246, based on abutment and bonding of walls. This would have involved a minimum of four, and maximum of six, rooms. Later, S. 288 was modified and connected to S. 287 by remodeling its south wall. All of this activity took place before the introduction of JYW about 1325/30. The original construction over a shallow midden, followed by later construction of the S. 288 south wall over much deeper midden, but still predating JYW, suggests considerable activity and growth in RB200 between 1290 and 1325. The household living in this complex must have been fairly sizable from the outset with four to six structures, whose size changed over time. The presence of two habitation structures, and possibly more, indicates a complex household of perhaps two related families or differentiation of use of these structures. Unfortunately, the complete absence of floor artifacts makes interpretation difficult.

The location of the household suite overlooking K. 248 and associated plaza suggests the household was likely one with religious and social authority in the village. Remodeling and expansion of the household area could relate to events in the plaza or to events within the household. It appears that this room suite was built at the same time as adjacent rooms to the west, which were occupied by one or more other households. This is based on abutment and bonding data, and the fact that all were built on the same layer of midden present, in what was once a small plaza in the middle of RB200. It is likely this midden was fill brought in to level the surface to enable construction of numerous new rooms about 1300. These rooms created two distinct plazas, one surrounding K. 248 and the other surrounding K. 279 (Figure 4.20).

Closure, through burning of the S.

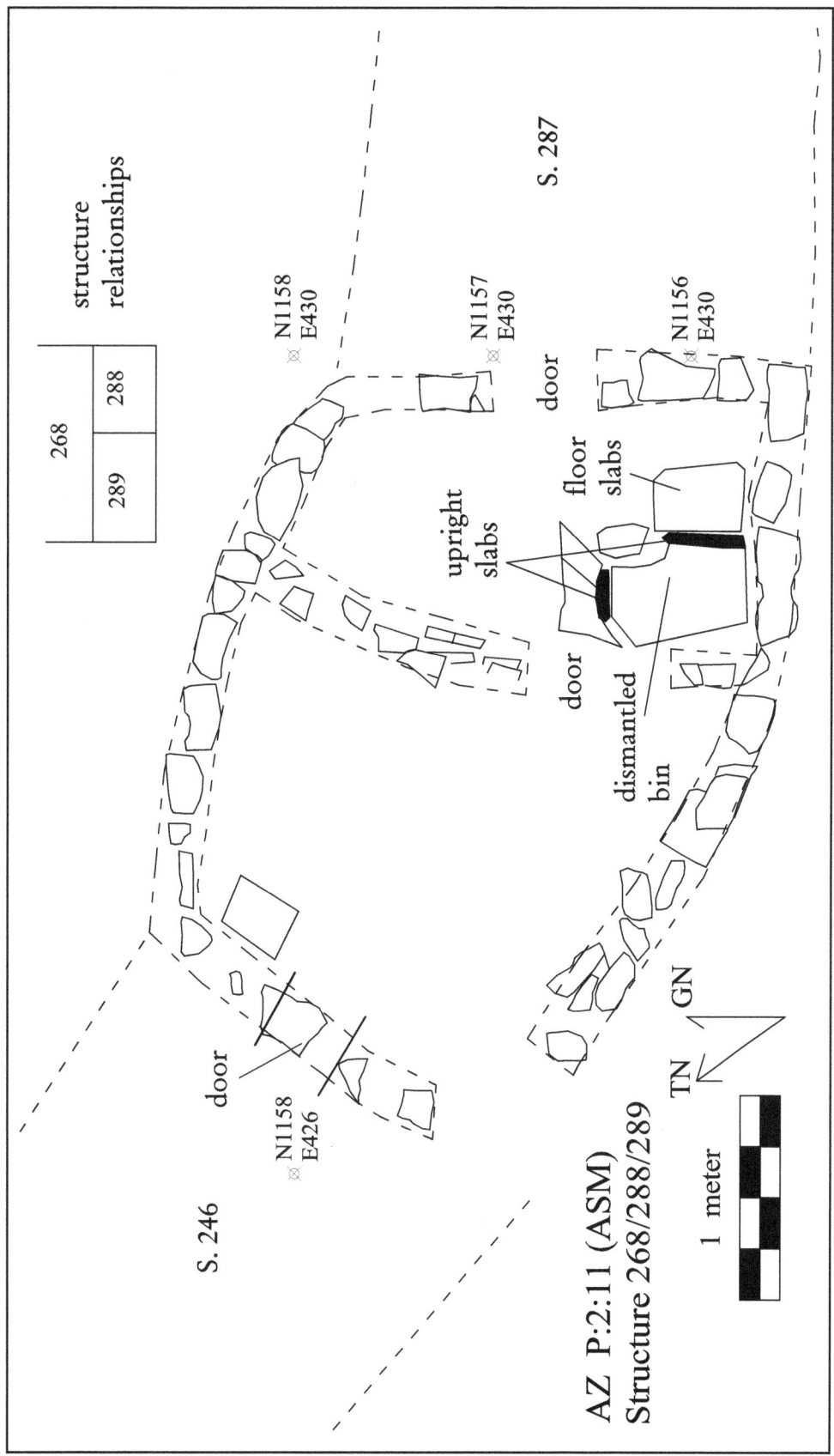

Figure 4.19. Plan of suite 268/289/288.

268/288/289, 246, 287 room suite (Figure 4.21) and the S. 265/269 room suite to its west, was accomplished through a single ignition, as reconstructed with the help of arson investigators (see Chapter 5, which details the forensic evidence for this interpretation). This, at least, indicates the possibility of social relationship between these two households. Such a pattern would follow the ideal lineage affiliation of households in historic Hopi villages, such as Walpi (E.C. Adams 1982). The complete absence of artifacts on the floor of S. 268, when it was burned, and the presence of a light level of secondary trash in S. 289 indicate the household had stopped using the room suite prior to closure. This further supports the likelihood the fire was intentionally set, probably by the occupants.

Summary

The actual size of the four households partially excavated at Chevelon is not entirely clear. At a minimum, they have six, three, three, and five rooms for an average of 4.25 rooms per household. Doorways to unexcavated rooms suggest there are eight, four, four, and six rooms for an average of 5.50 rooms per household. At the historic Hopi village of Orayvi, the average household used 6.5 rooms and had 5.5 individuals (Cameron 1999; Levy 1992; Titiev 1944). This suggests that an average of five rooms per household is reasonable. At 500 rooms, this means Chevelon could have housed up to 100 households. Realistically, because excavations have shown that all rooms were not occupied simultaneously, it is more likely the total number of households was closer to 60. Using Orayvi as an example of household size, a maximum population of 300 or more individuals could have lived at Chevelon in the late 1300s.

A household using an average of five structures is more in line with the expectation of households in aggregated villages. Such an expectation is due to the more complex nature of living in a community, where there are demands on ones time beyond just the needs of subsistence and kinship obligations. In a large village, these obligations expand to include supra-household obligations. Thus, typically, multiple habitation structures and/or structures with special uses, such as piki houses, mealing rooms, and ritual structures, are added to the household room suite, increasing its size and the complexity of the tasks in which the household is involved. To cope with increased communal work parties and social and ceremonial obligations in large villages, typically the household increases in size to include members beyond the nuclear family, usually adult members (Dohm 1990; Pasternak et al. 1976). Therefore, room suites and projected household size at Chevelon are typical of aggregated villages. This suggests that social and religious organization at Chevelon has grown in complexity to meet the needs of a large community.

Spinal Room Blocks

As noted in E.C. Adams (2002:129), the next level of identifiable social relationships in the HSC and in Chevelon in particular is the spinal room block, which is defined as parallel lines of walls, generally three, that are long enough to be subdivided into numerous rooms. This image of ladder-like construction has also fostered the term "ladder construction" for this phenomenon. At least 11 spinal room blocks can be detected at Chevelon. These are listed in Table 4.6, with the two in RB300 not differentiated due to incomplete data. It

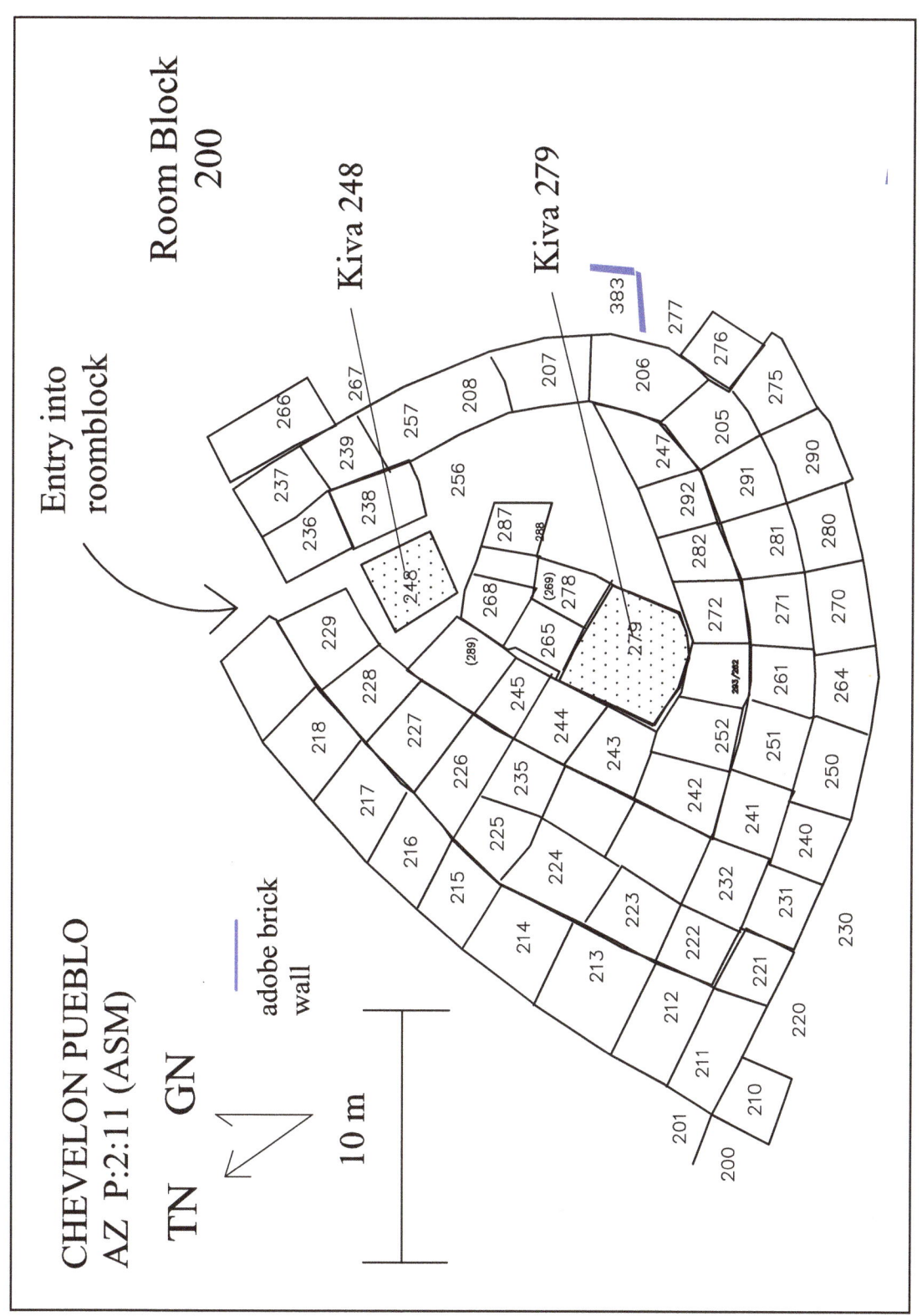

Figure 4.20. Plan view of Room Block 200 plaza with Kivas 248 and 279.

Figure 4.21. Photograph of burned roof to Structure 268, habitation room.

is interesting in looking at Table 4.6 to note that a multiplier effect may be in operation. Ignoring RB400 for the time being, because it is probably different from the others, there seem to be three groupings of spinal room blocks with 10 to 15, 20 to 25, and 40 to 50 rooms. The smaller spinal room blocks appear to be in the earlier parts of the village, whereas, with one exception, the later ones all occur around the south plaza, in the later constructed room blocks. At H1, the four recognizable spinal room blocks had 18, 18, 24, and 24 rooms. The initial construction at H3 had spinal room blocks of 13 rooms. In contrast, the spinal room blocks at H2 were much larger, at least 50 rooms and in some cases up to 200 rooms (E.C. Adams and Hays 1991; Lange 2017). In fact, the consistency of 20 to 25 rooms for four of the building segments around the south plaza and 46 rooms for the other segment at Chevelon follows a wider pattern in the HSC and seems likely more than coincidental.

The planning and construction of multiple rooms suggests cooperation of multiple households. At five rooms/household, the above spinal room blocks would have had two to three households in the small examples, four to five in the medium examples, and eight to 10 in the largest example at Chevelon. It is

Table 4.6. Spinal Room Blocks that have been Identified at Chevelon.

Spinal Block	Number of Rooms[1]	Date of Construction	Dominant Ceramic Assemblage	Comments
200NW	20	1290	Winslow Orange Ware	Part of founding groups
200S	14	1290	Winslow Orange Ware	Part of founding groups
200E	12	1290	Winslow Orange Ware	Part of founding groups
300	20	1300-1325	Winslow Orange Ware	At least two spinal room blocks are present in RB300
400	4	Post-1360	Jeddito Yellow Ware	Associated with kiva
500N	24	Post-1360	Jeddito Yellow Ware	Tonto Polychrome designs common on local pottery
500S	22	Post-1360	Jeddito Yellow Ware	Built after 700 & 500N. Possibly built the same time as 600
100	46	Post-1360	Jeddito Yellow Ware	Tonto Polychrome designs common on local pottery
600	20	Post-1360	Jeddito Yellow Ware	Latest constructed room block
700	25	Post-1360	Jeddito Yellow Ware	Some parts possibly two story

[1]Number of ground floor rooms. Second story rooms are known for RB200, 300, and 500

expected that these households are socially related through kinship by descent, marriage, or social obligations, as was likely the situation in the growth of Hopi communities (Mindeleff 1900). The scalar nature of the spinal room blocks, perhaps doubling from 12 to 24 to 48 to 100 to 200 is in line with the scalar hierarchy model proposed by Gregory Johnson (1989) to explain unit pueblos based on his extensive ethnographic research. Their doubling in size, according to Johnson, was a method of dealing with communication problems encountered when smaller social units get too numerous. The larger units can be based on permanent (simultaneous) or temporary (sequential) hierarchies that are developed to foster communication within these social units. These settlement units may be landholding entities, along the lines proposed by Varien (1999), Adler (1994), and others for Pueblo people living in the Four Corners region.

At Hopi today, landholding units are called clans and are named units holding ceremonial roles within the community defined by their ownership of fetishes or inalienable objects denoting identity and ritual power and authority (Mills 2004). Levy (1992), Bradfield (1971), Whiteley (1988), Cameron (1999) and others have connected social units at Hopi to the control of land and possession of religious authority, although the acceptance of the clan as that unit is in dispute and it is more likely the prime lineage of the clan (the clan matriarch and her brother) that has religious authority and controls access to farmland (Levy 1992).

It is possible, the groups constructing these village segments migrated together to establish or add to existing communities. As noted by Anthony (1990), Cameron (1995), and others, migratory groups are typically rather small and often household size is slightly larger. However, there are numerous examples in the Southwest (Haury 1958), where these groups were considerably larger. Bernardini (2008) suggests that migrating groups may be of virtually any size, as long as they possess a totem or fetish denoting their identity and religious authority when applying to join an existing village. The scalar nature of the spinal units at Chevelon, and generally in the HSC, however, suggests there is an overarching structure to the size and makeup of the social units that build these spinal units, whether they are indigenous to the village or immigrants.

Ritual structures (kivas and surface structures) are associated with RB100, 200, and 300 and perhaps indicate ceremonial hegemony and some authority within the village. The association of ritual structures with spinal room blocks of multiple sizes suggests, as at Hopi, that religious authority is not associated with the number of members within a group, but the possession of important religious objects that denote the owners have the knowledge necessary to perform ceremonies important to the welfare of the entire village. This discussion will be taken up in the sections to follow.

Plaza Spaces

I have discussed plaza space in detail previously (E.C. Adams 2002:144-154) and will use that to contextualize plaza space at Chevelon. In the general discussion of the HSC cluster, I recognized three sizes and two types of plaza. Small plazas or courtyards have less than 250 sq. m, medium plazas between 250 and 750 sq. m, and large plazas have 1000 sq. m or more. These plazas are either bounded (surrounded by rooms on three or four sides) or unbounded with rooms on only one or two sides (E.C. Adams 2002:145). The courtyard-size spaces usually do not have kivas. Typically, the smaller and unbounded plazas are earlier and the larger and bounded plazas are late and associated with the arrival of H2 and the demonstrable presence of katsina rituals.

Chevelon, generally, follows this pattern, but there are notable exceptions. The four plazas at Chevelon are described in Table 4.7. Plaza 200 fits the description of a courtyard or small plaza, but it has two kivas (Figure 4.20). Plaza 900 also fits the description of a small plaza, but it has two and possibly three kivas (Figure 4.22). Plaza 800 is the size of a large plaza, but is unbounded (Figure 1.3). Plaza 000 fits the description of the large late plazas surrounded by rooms found at H1 and H2, yet has no kivas (Figure 1.3). These differences in plazas at Chevelon from other HSC plazas are due to a combination of topography, less settlement density, and the problems with trying to create normative patterns based on typology within a society.

Chevelon is most similar to H1, in length of occupation and size. However, unlike Chevelon, the large late plaza at H1 is built over a floodplain on top of which was added 1 to 2 m of fill. It is relatively easy to build kivas into such fill. The large plaza at Chevelon, on the other hand, is constructed over bedrock or shallow gravels overlying bedrock. There is no place to construct a subterranean kiva. K. 400, which is constructed above the edge of the terrace that topographically separates Plaza 800 from Plaza 000, is placed in the only area possible for building a kiva, yet is not within the plaza. RB200 is quite small due to the adherence of the founders of Chevelon to a small D-shaped knoll at the top of the larger hill on which the village is built. This knoll limited the size of the plaza that could be built inside, Plaza 200.

Plaza 800 is also a result of hill topography. RB100 and 200 are each built on topographic prominences, while Plaza 800 is in a shallow saddle between them. Although partly bound on two and a half sides, Plaza 800 remained odd-shaped and was left partially unbounded even after 1365. Finally, the relatively lower intensity of use of Chevelon versus H1 left more visible the original configuration of the village at its founding; whereas at H1, subsequent remodeling covered over what were probably small plazas with kivas in the original village. The fact that Plaza 000 was constructed even without large, communal kivas, which were present at H1 and H2, indicates the symbolic nature of the plaza itself. For comparison, at the Second Mesa village of Songoòpavi, the primary plaza has no kivas, yet is the focus of public ceremonies.

I have previously discussed the symbolism of the plaza (E.C. Adams 2002: Figure 6.8), relating it to the creation of a super-sized space analogous to the kiva for public religious

Table 4.7. Plaza Spaces at Chevelon.

Plaza	Period of Use	Size (sq. m)	Bounded	No. of Kivas[1]	Other Features
200	1290-1390	135	Yes	2	Hearth, possibly bell-shaped pit
900 (RB300)	1300/25-1390	250	Yes	2+	Roasting pits, hearths, ramadas
800	1300/25-1390	1000	No	2?	Unknown
000 (South)	1360-1390	3400	yes		Firepits?

[1]RB900 might have a third kiva. RB800 has at least two kivas.

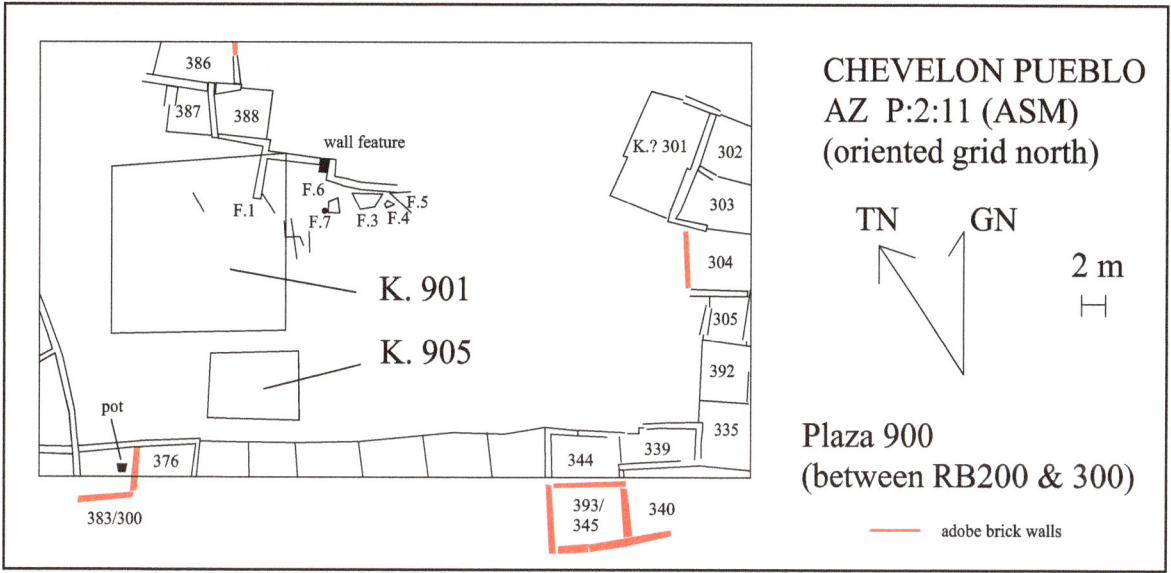

Figure 4.22. Plan view of Plaza 900.

performances. In this space, the sides of the plaza walls, which are bound by one- or two-story rooms, are equivalent to the walls and benches of plaza kivas. The plaza shrine is equivalent to the sipapu of the kiva. Finally, the Hopi perception of sacred and profane during plaza ceremonies, which places the plaza space as sacred and space outside the plaza as profane, fits the concept of the kiva during ceremonies. Thus, Plaza 000, the large plaza space, was built to accommodate the need for a large sacred space, which was separate from kiva space, for the increasing numbers and possible diversity of occupants of Chevelon.

These two spaces — the kiva and the plaza — also symbolize the inclusive and exclusive domains of Pueblo religious rituals, which are primary sources of power in pueblo society. Ownership of inalienable possessions by corporate groups in modern Pueblo societies allows them to maintain their status within the hierarchy of these societies. An essential element to maintaining this power and presence is the performance of private or exclusive religious rituals using structures designed for this purpose (Bernardini 2008; Eggan 1950; Parsons 1939; Titiev 1944). These may be kivas, which typically have multiple users, or ritual structures within room blocks, which are exclusive to these groups.

Today at Hopi, these groups are named clans or supra-kinship organizations called societies or sodalities (Ware 2014). Clan rituals involving use of exclusive fetishes only occur in structures within room blocks, which are always incorporated into the space owned by the clan's prime lineage and home to the clan matriarch (E.C. Adams 1983). Generally, these are not subterranean. Religious societies usually hold their exclusive rituals in plaza kivas, but they can also use spaces within room blocks (E.C. Adams 1982, 1983; Parsons 1936, 1939; Titiev 1944), where many fetishes are placed on altars in order to correctly perform the ceremony. In either case, these spaces are larger than average rooms and have distinctive features. I have described comparable structures in the HSC as kivas and ritual structures (E.C. Adams 2002: Table 6.4).

Plazas, then, serve the other role, the

public or inclusive role, in Pueblo society. Public performances include individuals who are not members of the "secret" societies, but who can recognize the symbolism that is portrayed in these rituals through performance or iconography (Connerton 1989; Mills 2007; Parsons 1939; Potter and Perry 2000; Rappaport 1999). It is this second step, performance, through which the group calls up not only social memory for the observer to react to, but also to legitimize the authority the group has within the community, that explains the role of the plaza. Let us now turn to the individual plaza spaces to understand what role they may have performed at Chevelon through its history. These will be considered in the order of their construction.

Plaza 200

Plaza 200 was created about 1290, at the founding of Chevelon, when groups built three spinal room blocks along the edges of the highest point of the hill to create a D-shaped plaza as described in Chapter 3. Access to Plaza 200 was restricted from the beginning to a small passageway on its north side (Figure 4.20). This restricted access is similar to that for the small plazas at H1; however, Plaza 200 is different in having kivas. The size of Plaza 200 decreased over time until by 1325 it consisted of two small plazas primarily consisting of the roofs of kivas surrounded by rooms including the original K. 248 and a more recently constructed one, K. 279 (Figure 4.20). Access to K. 248 continued to be through the adjacent small passage. It is unclear exactly how K. 279 was accessed as wall clearing and excavations along its south side were incomplete. It is clear the kiva was surrounded on the other three sides by two-story structures making access quite limited.

Other than the kivas, the only other features found within the plaza are a bell-shaped storage pit and a hearth. The pit beneath S. 287; however, is probably from the Basketmaker III occupation and not the later pueblo occupation. The hearth was built into the roof of K. 279 and apparently used while the kiva was in use. The fact that most of the plaza was subsequently covered by rooms and therefore little of it was exposed, suggests there are likely other undiscovered features related to plaza use. No clear plaza surfaces were identified either, except the original plaza surface that was subsequently covered by trash fill, perhaps as leveling so that rooms could be built over the top of it.

Interpretation

Chevelon fits a consistent pattern in the region during the late 1200s and early 1300s in having its earliest occupation on the highest point of the ultimate community. A consistent theme in Hopi ethnographies is that the earliest occupants of a village became the community leaders, having control over the best agricultural land and over who does or does not enter the village and what land they receive to farm (Bradfield 1971, 1995; Levy 1992). These individuals control the most important ceremonies and due to this authority possess the most social power in the community. This power is demonstrated through ownership of fetishes that convey this authority and through ceremonial performance that reinforces this authority. Therefore, if this pattern is true for Chevelon, our expectation is that village leadership was maintained in RB200 and important ceremonial activities took place in the kivas and plaza within this room block. There is strong archaeological evidence to support this perspective.

If our expectation is that power and

authority were concentrated among founders of RB200, then restricting access to Plaza 200 makes sense. Not only did access to the plaza and kivas begin as quite restricted, as other groups joined the Chevelon community, it only grew more so. Additionally, when K. 248 and 279 were closed, they were filled with enriched deposits containing ritually-charged religious objects. Only individuals with appropriate ritual knowledge would deposit these objects, mimicking similar practices within modern faith traditions (Walker 1995).

Plaza 200 began as only about 135 sq. m and by 1325, had been transformed into two plazas each only slightly larger than the kivas within them, or barely 25 sq. m each. The plaza space that is K. 279 is better known. Access to the plaza and kiva, as apparently with K. 248, was possibly restricted to those occupying rooms around them. This is indicated because all rooms west and north of K. 279 had doors facing the plaza. Excavation into two of these rooms indicates a lengthy occupation evidenced by numerous layers of plaster and the conversion of one to a kiva to replace K. 279 when its east wall failed. This further indicates the importance to individuals in this area of maintaining a religious presence and restricting access. Difference in use of this space will become apparent as other plazas are discussed.

Plaza 900 (RB300)

Plaza 900 was built between 1300 and 1325 and was created by the construction of rooms in RB300 on all its sides, although it is possible the east half of the north side was open. Severe erosion on this part of the hill precluded a definitive conclusion. At 250 sq. m, Plaza 900 (Figure 4.22) is about twice the size of Plaza 200 and typical of a small plaza in HSC. Because the plaza was apparently not encroached by later construction, our understanding of its size, features, and use are more complete. In addition to being physically lower than RB200, the fact that rooms on the west side of RB300 abut the eastern rooms to RB200 indicates that Plaza 900 is later than Plaza 200. It also seems to have a larger and probably more diverse population. At about 150 rooms, RB300 is easily the largest room block at Chevelon and its use continued to the end of the occupation of the village.

There are two traits in Plaza 900 that make it unique among Chevelon plazas: the large kiva, K. 901, and multiple large features including a storage unit, ramada, and roasting pit (Figure 4.22). As noted earlier in this chapter, at 42 sq. m, K. 901 is the third largest such structure known in the HSC. Plaza features are common where excavations have been extensive enough to find them. This is especially true at H1, H3, and H4. At these three villages, roasting pits are also present as plaza features, always near kivas. Previously, the presence of corn roasting pits in plaza areas has been suggested as due to their use in community-level activities, especially feasting (E.C. Adams 2001:109; 2002).

The strength of this pattern now at four villages and the lack of corn roasting pits elsewhere in HSC villages indicate this is likely the case for Plaza 900. The interesting closure of the roasting pit with a headless, but otherwise articulated turkey, underscores the probable ritual association of this feature, probably directly tied into activities within K. 901 to which it is adjacent. The slab-lined storage feature in Plaza 900 adjacent to the large roasting pit suggests it could have stored communal corn. The ramada feature had a hearth and was intermediate between K. 901 and the roasting pit suggesting a role for it in these activities; however, less than a square meter of its area was uncovered. In addition to K. 901 there is at least one other kiva, 905, and possibly a third kiva in Plaza 900. Little is known about either one except that K. 905 was burned with no additional cultural activity afterwards.

Interpretation

The complex of features and K. 901 were, apparently, built at the time the plaza was created, between 1300 and 1325. This complex of features, totally or mostly dedicated to ceremonial practices, is unlike anything else recovered in the HSC with the possible exception of H3, which is slightly earlier. Plaza 900 is dramatically different in appearance and use from Plaza 200. Activities are clearly different. Presence of a large kiva able to hold many more individuals is in stark contrast to the small kivas with restricted access in Plaza 200. The more accessible, but still limited access to the plaza with an opening on the north side like Plaza 200, its larger size, and the large kiva suggest the area was used by a larger and more diverse population than was Plaza 200. Use of the plaza and kivas was probably primarily for RB300 occupants, but they could easily have been double the number in RB200. The association of feasting with Plaza 900 activities, as a communal event, is also evidence of a more inclusive social group. It is also possible there was competition between religious leaders of RB200 and 300. Certainly the restricted access to both areas and the ritual closure of all kivas suggests the potential for ceremonial exclusivity.

Plaza 800

Plaza 800 is unique among Chevelon plazas in not being fully bounded by room blocks. Instead, during its pre-1325 form, it was bounded on its northeast, east, and northwest sides by RB200, 300, and 100, respectively (Figure 1.3). At this time, there is evidence of only one kiva, although erosion and extensive vandalism of the plaza's surface could be hiding others. It is even possible the subterranean features, interpreted as pit houses associated with earlier occupations, are, in fact, kivas or were remodeled into kivas. No excavations were completed to evaluate the possibilities, although 108 auger holes spaced at 3 m intervals, plus resistivity and magnetometer assessments, should provide reliable indicators of thermal and non-thermal features. Additionally, no small plaza features, such as roasting pits, hearths, or even surfaces were identified. However, in addition to substantial vandalism of the surface (likely in search of burials), its exposure and slope may have destroyed most of this evidence. At present, its surface is highly eroded and consists mostly of loose cobbles. During this early period, the plaza is defined by topography, consisting of the relatively flat area between RB100 and 200 to RB 300 and south about 20 m from RB200. A recent major erosional channel has begun headward, cutting along its southwest side, as well as on the north side between RB100 and 200, but as yet no features have been exposed.

Sometime after 1365, when the remainder of RB100 was constructed along with the other room blocks used to define Plaza 000, a set of four rooms and a kiva were constructed along the southeast edge of Plaza 800. The four rooms share a common north wall that is exactly aligned with the north wall of the kiva. The kiva was highly disturbed by vandalism so only the walls were revealed for mapping purposes. Testing of one room, S. 403, revealed that the fill and floor had totally eroded away.

Interpretation

Plaza 800 is a large unbounded space with limited information about what activities took place on it. The single unexcavated kiva, within the space, contained JYW, recovered from augering; so it is possible it was not constructed until after 1325. If so, the space could have served for communal activities or hosting public performances of ceremonies involving both RB200 and 300 groups, that were not possible in restricted Plaza 200 and 900 spaces. As the village was transformed with the addition of 150 new rooms around Plaza 000, including construction of RB400, Plaza 800 became better defined spatially. The only information that can be gleaned from RB400 is that it was probably built to define and differentiate space between Plaza 000 and Plaza 800 and to provide a kiva for ceremonial activities. Although it is possible that different groups used the two plaza spaces, for example, those groups surrounding Plaza 000 using it and those adjacent to Plaza 800 using it, there is no way with available data to make this judgment.

Plaza 000

Plaza 000 represents a huge transformation in the concept of space, particularly plaza space in the Chevelon community. Plaza 000 is about 3400 sq. m, making it virtually the same size as the enormous central plaza at H2, which is the largest plaza space in the HSC. The rooms surrounding and creating Plaza 000 were built in two phases, which seem to have been coordinated in their construction. The first phase of building involved the construction of RB100, consisting of 46 rooms, RB700, consisting of 25 rooms, and RB500 (north), consisting of 26 ground floor rooms, probably in the 1360s based on ceramics and abutment/bonding. How the planning and construction of these room blocks to create Plaza 000 was coordinated is not clear, but must have involved leaders in RB200 or perhaps RB300. The second phase of construction, which possibly involved only changes in the original plans for Plaza 000, is the construction of RB600, consisting of 20 ground floor rooms, and RB500 (south), consisting of 22 ground floor rooms. The building of these two room blocks at an angle from the original direction of RB100 and 500, suggests a modification of the original design of the plaza (Figure 1.3).

Interpretation

What could have caused the Chevelon people to construct such an enormous space, especially one that could house no kivas? It is believed the construction of Plaza 000 is an emulation of the concept of large enclosed plazas developing over most of the Pueblo Southwest and introduced to the HSC by the builders of H2, sometime between 1350 and 1365 (E.C. Adams 1991a, 2002). The purpose for these plazas is to create an enormous new communal space for the village, primarily to host public performances of ceremonies, especially katsina performances (E.C. Adams 1991a), in a space that also emulates the sacred domain of the kiva. The construction of such spaces required an organization of labor unparalleled in Pueblo society, at least since Chaco Canyon 250 years earlier. Thus, Plaza 000 was constructed to be different from the other three plazas at Chevelon. It differed from Plazas 200 and 900 in being unrestricted to members of the village. It differed from Plaza 800 in being fully bounded by rooms and formal in layout. Its size and layout suggest formal planning of the space that was perhaps modified partially through construction when RB600 and the southern half of RB500 were built at angles to reduce the quantity of construction and area of enclosure.

The question remains as to who built all of the rooms surrounding Plaza 000. There is no evidence that any of the older room blocks at Chevelon were completely abandoned in favor of a move to the new rooms, although it is possible many moved and limited excavation in the rooms of RB300 leaves open this possibility. Nevertheless, continuous occupation of many of these rooms using pottery contemporary with that in the room blocks around Plaza 000 indicates at least some of the population in RB100, 500, 600, and 700 came from new occupants.

The other questions, who planned the plaza and why, have been touched upon. Presumably, the reason to construct the plaza was to emulate similar plazas at other Homol'ovi villages and at Hopi in order to present public ceremonial performances. Who planned the plaza seems almost certainly to have been leaders already living at Chevelon or, minimally, with their approval. Individuals already occupying Chevelon would certainly have controlled not only who joined the village, but also where they lived. Because only RB200 and 300 had any sizeable population, leadership came from these groups. Power derived from control of religious rituals is represented in both room blocks through the restricted plazas and kivas within them. The desire to add population to the village, the need to absorb these new members into the social fabric of the community, and the need for existing groups to display their authority probably played roles in the decision to allow and probably direct the new migrants to construct Plaza 000 and surrounding rooms.

Social History of Chevelon

RB200

The initial settlement of Chevelon Pueblo, which is estimated to be about 1290, occurred on the highest point of the natural hill and in our parlance is called room block 200. The source of this initial Chevelon population appears to be from Hopi Mesa villages based primarily on color, form, and decoration of the local pottery tradition called Winslow Orange Ware (WOW) by archaeologists (Colton 1956; Lyons 2003; Smith 1971). Room size, room block construction, spatial layout, and kiva form also conform to those in contemporary Hopi Mesa villages, in particular, those on Antelope Mesa where virtually all archaeological work has been done on the mesas (Smith 1971, 1972). These traits are related to the concept of technological style, practice, or habitus (Bourdieu 1977; Clark 2001), wherein migrating groups are expected to reproduce what are their habits or expectations for defining space and especially ritual space at their new home (Connerton 1989).

The fact that RB200 sits at the highest geographic point is typical for the HSC and for villages contemporary and earlier than Chevelon Pueblo. Whether this choice is purely practical because views and breezes are better, or social, symbolizing village hierarchy, is not certain, but evidence suggest social status is most likely. Cross-culturally, societies from Europe to the Middle East to Latin America have chosen the highest point of any natural feature as the starting point for settlements that often reach impressive size. When Hopi elders visit the excavations, they inevitably state that the first occupation by the most important people in the village would be at the highest geographic point.

Ceramics, stratigraphy, and abutment and bonding all support RB200 as being earliest and reveal details of its construction that indicate the probable nature of the founding social groups. Tracing of abutment and bonding relationships in the room block reveals three founding social units, each comprised of two-room wide suites of rooms 5 to 10 rooms long, which created sets of rooms 12, 14, and 20 rooms apiece (Figure 4.23). Thus, as few as 10, or as many as 15, families could have been involved in founding Chevelon. Excavations in RB200 suggest the original rooms were single story, but that second stories were soon added to some rooms before 1325. The construction of these three sets of rooms to form a central plaza indicates their arrival at about the same time and an understanding or agreement on what was spatially appropriate for a settlement at this time. This early planning resulted in rooms focused toward the center, restricting access to the plaza and interior of the room block. The only access was through a 70 cm-wide opening in the northeast corner of the room block. The location of this opening placed it facing a steep, difficult slope with rooms built to the edge of this slope. The slope therefore further restricted any ability to see inside the plaza. Although defensive in appearance, access to RB200 was easily gained from any other direction and at this time, most of the room block was single story. The occupants would not be able to see anyone approaching, which is not an effective defensive strategy.

As rooms were added to RB200, they seem to have been primarily on the inside, restricting the size of the plaza and eventually dividing it into two smaller spaces, each surrounded by two-story rooms (Figure 4.24). This is likely because expansion on the outside would have been possible only by building below the D-shaped pinnacle. Additions to RB200 seem associated with the pre-yellow ware period at Chevelon, or prior to 1325/30, although remodeling was a continuous process within the room block, such as the construction of K. 252 within a former room.

The creation of restricted space in RB200, its continuation, and even increase in exclusivity versus the remainder of the village indicates a strong focus on maintaining power and authority within the community as it expanded in size and population for a century after RB200 was founded. As the founders of the village, the occupants of RB200 evidently maintained their status by restricting participation in the ceremonies they controlled. This is common among social groups at any level of society, as detailed by Connerton (1989); however, exclusivity of religious ritual practices is particularly favored for the maintenance of power and authority in small communities, such as Chevelon (Connerton 1989; Rappaport 1999), continuing today in Hopi and other Pueblo villages (Bradfield 1995; Levy 1992, Parsons 1939).

Each kinship group in Hopi society gains its identity and authority from inalienable objects, such as fetishes, that are used to symbolize their identity and ceremonial power. The importance of these totemic devices is not only in their possession by the group, but also in the recognition of their power by others not in their group. Typically, there are highly guarded and formalized rites associated with religious objects and the knowledge and correct performance of these rites is essential to the continuity of the group and the power of the ceremony (Connerton 1989:44). Connerton (1989:44) goes on to describe another aspect to the performance of religious ritual, which is the importance of connection to the past. The creation and maintenance of space in RB200 for the performance of ceremonies, and especially

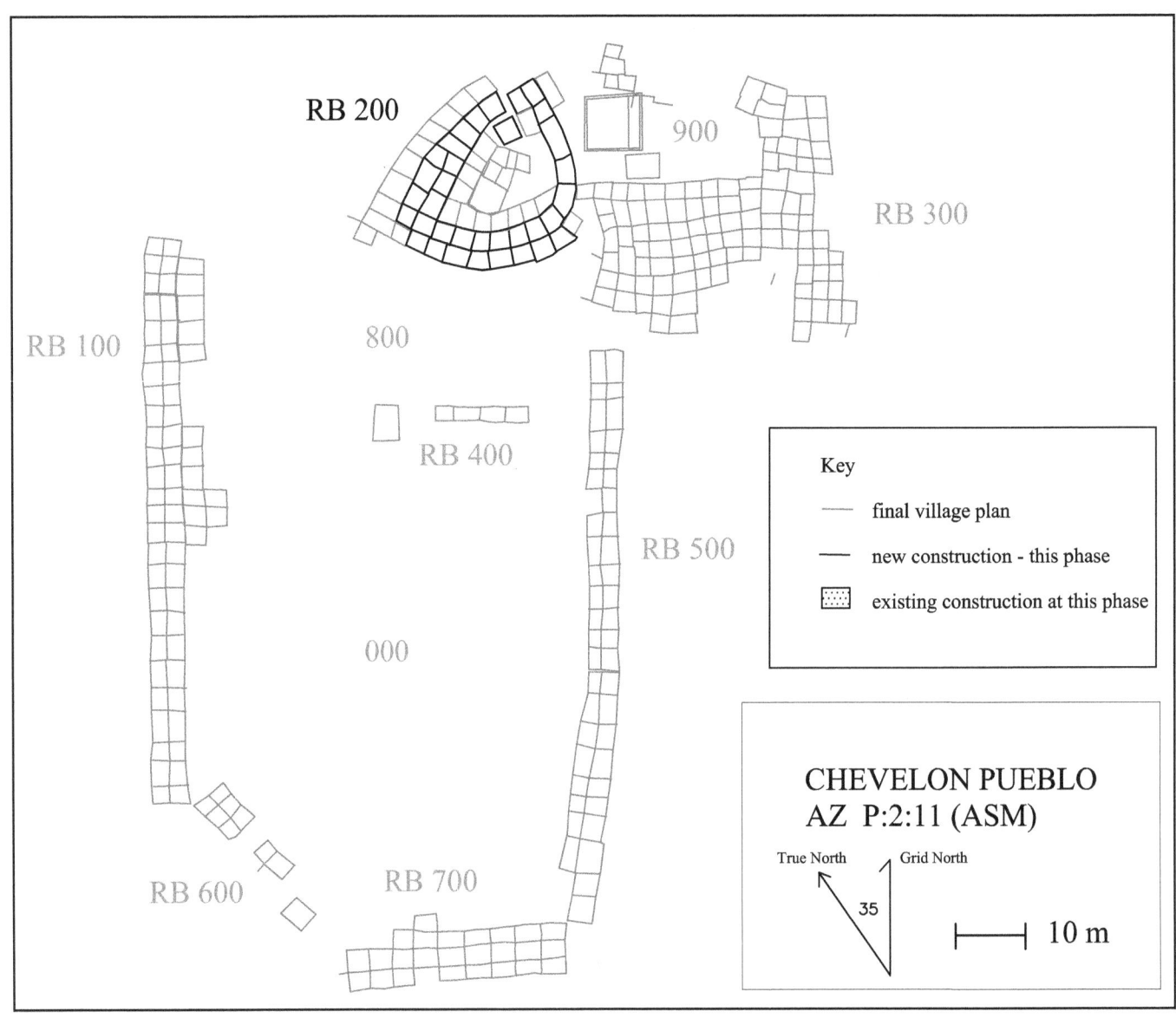

Figure 4.23. Map of Room Block 200 showing initial settlement of Chevelon.

Chapter 4: Architecture 91

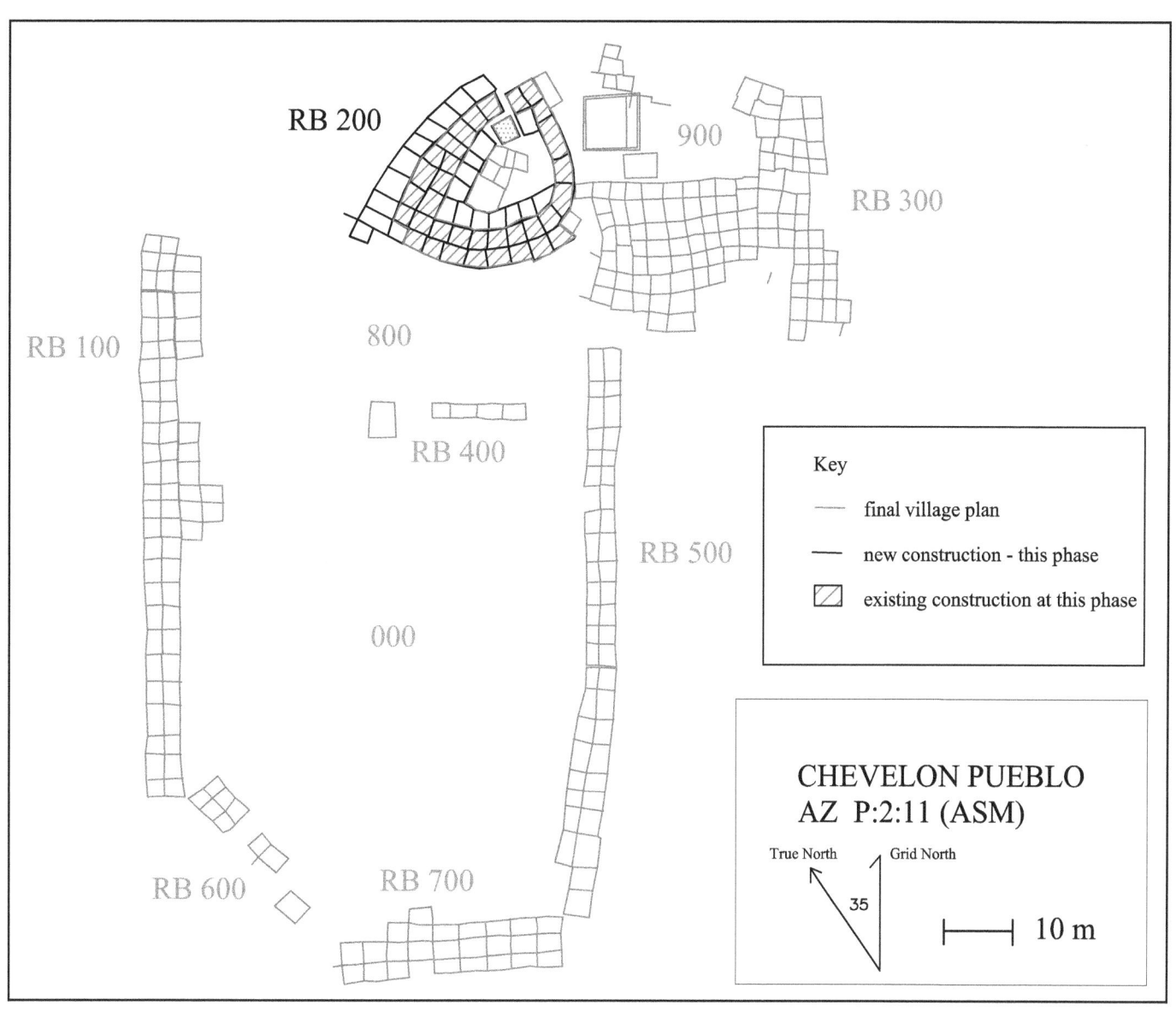

Figure 4.24. Map of Room Block 200 showing pre-1325 additions.

the discard of ceremonial objects into K. 248 and 279, support this interpretation of RB200. Formalized disposal of objects used in these ceremonies is an element of all religious activities, whether Pueblo ceremonies or those of the Abrahamic faith traditions (Connerton 1989; Rappaport 1999; Walker 1995).

The continuous use of RB200 throughout the occupation of Chevelon together with the maintenance of religious facilities indicates the power and authority of the leaders in RB200 was maintained and acknowledged by the later settlers of the village. Use of RB200 continued to the end of village occupation, during the 1390s, when many of the rooms were burned, including S. 264, 265, and 268. Previously, K. 248 and S. 222 had been burned. None of the other rooms, whose use ended early, were burned and S. 222 was remodeled into a piki house. Notably, K. 279 and 252, along with S. 293/262, were not burned. K. 279 was buried and filled with ceremonial trash. K. 252 and S. 293/262 seem to have been used to near the end of occupation of the village, but were not burned. Of the latter three structures, only the kiva was excavated to the floor.

The low number of floor objects and lack of midden suggests that ceremonial objects, used in this kiva, had been removed and were probably transported to their new home, probably on Antelope Mesa, based on sourcing of manufacture of yellow ware pottery traded to Chevelon (Bernardini 2005). Curation of fetishes and objects of ceremonial office as symbols of religious power and authority would be expected for groups migrating into existing villages and hoping to gain entry, according to Hopi oral tradition (Bernardini 2008; Mills 2004). Such objects would carry social or communal memory for the group, known only by the primary family, and are essential to reenact and maintain continuity with the ancestors (Connerton 1989:58-61; Mills 2004).

Thus, RB200 is interpreted as the center of religious power and authority throughout the occupation of Chevelon. This is supported by the continuity of ceremonial structures throughout this period, the lack of accessibility to the interior of the room block, and the disposal of objects involved in religious ritual practices into decommissioned kivas. Such discard behavior is expected when the ritual objects must be kept secret to maintain exclusive control over their use (Connerton 1989; Rappaport 1999). Additionally, to maintain such exclusive use of these objects, they are often imbued with power that makes them dangerous to others in the community who have not been initiated into the esoteric rites of the group (E.C. Adams 2016; Walker 1995, 1996b).

RB300

While RB200 continued to grow, thus shrinking its plaza space, a major expansion of Chevelon occurred with the founding of RB300 and the construction of Plaza 900 (Figure 4.25). The choice of the broad, flat eastern side of the hill, just lower than RB200, is also typical of pueblos in the region during this period (refer to articles in E.C. Adams and Duff 2004b), where early expansion of Pueblo IV villages occurs near the original construction. The builders of this space were certainly new immigrants to Chevelon. Their construction on the west side abuts existing RB200 rooms and overlies midden deposits of at least 70 cm, discarded by RB200 inhabitants as discovered beneath S. 373. Incomplete wall tracing and mapping of RB300, due to severe vandalism of some areas, makes it difficult to discern the specifics of the development of this room block; however,

Chapter 4: Architecture   93

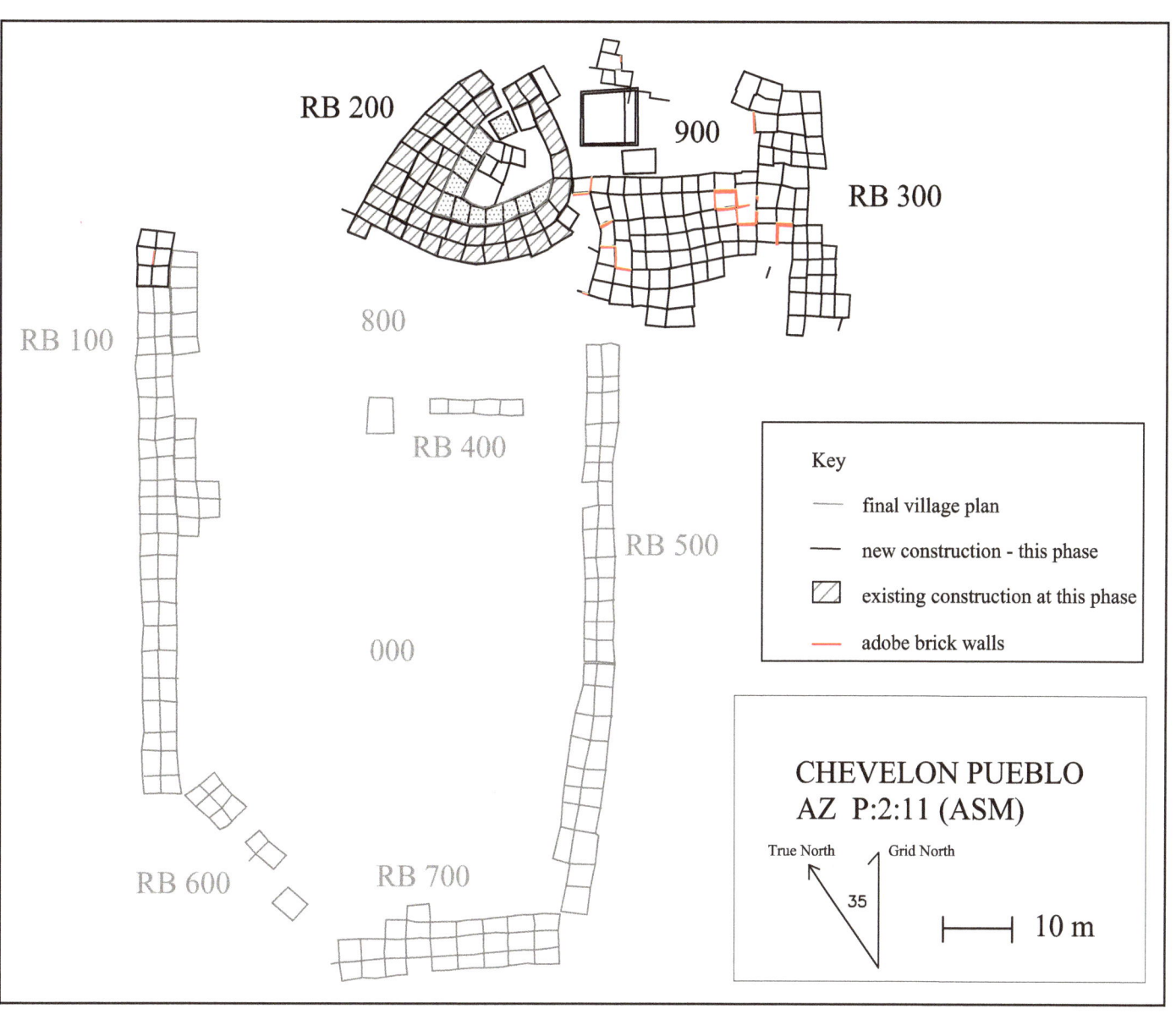

Figure 4.25. Map of Room Block 100, 200, & 300 showing growth prior to 1325 C.E.

there appear to be major spinal room blocks that form the eastern and southern sides of RB300 (Figure 4.26). Rooms along the western side, abutting RB200, also appear to be part of a major addition.

Another unknown is the original size of Plaza 900. In its final configuration, it is about 250 sq. m, but it could have been larger. No rooms abutting the plaza were excavated to determine if they rested on the gravel bedrock or on cultural fill, although extensive augering in the area suggests they mostly rested on the bedrock. Finally, adobe brick architecture was incorporated into RB300 early in its construction, as many interior rooms are built wholly or in part of adobes. Both excavated structures, S. 373 and 393/345, had adobe walls (all four for S. 345) and are built over RB200 midden, in the case of S. 373, or bedrock gravel, in the case of S. 345 (Figure 4.27a,b). This indicates both were built at, or near, the beginning of construction of RB300, or before 1325. Construction in RB300 continued for several years afterward and occupation continued to the end of the Chevelon occupation, in the 1390s; although, use of K. 901 seems to have stopped by 1370.

Yet, with all the unknowns about RB300, much is understood. In terms of ceramics, room size, layout, and plaza space, the builders of RB300 cannot be easily differentiated from their RB200 counterparts. This suggests they, too, migrated from villages on or near the Hopi mesas. Unless under conditions of extreme stress, such as unexpected warfare, groups rarely migrate to unknown areas or join villages with whom they have had no previous contact (Anthony 1990). These factors suggest the founders of RB300 had preexisting relationships with members of RB200. Coming from the same area, these relationships were probably social. Certainly, the plentiful resources of water and arable land would have encouraged others to migrate to Chevelon. Nevertheless, the new migrants also maintained their own ceremonies as indicated by the construction of Plaza 900 and K. 901 and 905.

Why adobes were used in interior construction of RB300 is not fully understood. The adobes had grass and possibly other organics as part of their recipe, unlike at H1 and H3 (Gavioli and Gann 2006). This is similar to adobes found at Awat'ovi and at Fourmile Ruin, both contemporaries of Chevelon (Gann 1996a, 1996b). Analysis of corrugated ceramics reported in Chapter 6 points to a more complex social history than suggested by WOW. Paste recipes and surface treatment (corrugation form, coil width, and obliteration) point to groups who manufactured Puerco Valley Utility and Mogollon Brown Ware being present from near the founding of the village throughout its occupation (Barker 2017; Hays-Gilpin and van Hartesveldt 1998). Given the conservative nature of learning frameworks for manufacturing cooking ware, it seems likely groups east, southeast, and south of Chevelon were present in RB300. Thus, the source of adobe brick technology to Chevelon may be from the southeast where this tradition began in the 1100s (Gann 1996a, 1996b). Migration from an area other than the Hopi mesas using adobes as a basis cannot be demonstrated. Nevertheless, the presence of Pinto Polychrome in the midden beneath S. 373 indicates exchange was taking place with groups in the Silver Creek area prior to 1325 and that region, as a second population source, cannot be ruled out for RB300.

Based on number of rooms and a shorter period of occupation, the population of RB300 was greater than RB200. In comparison to the 10 to 15 families who founded Chevelon and

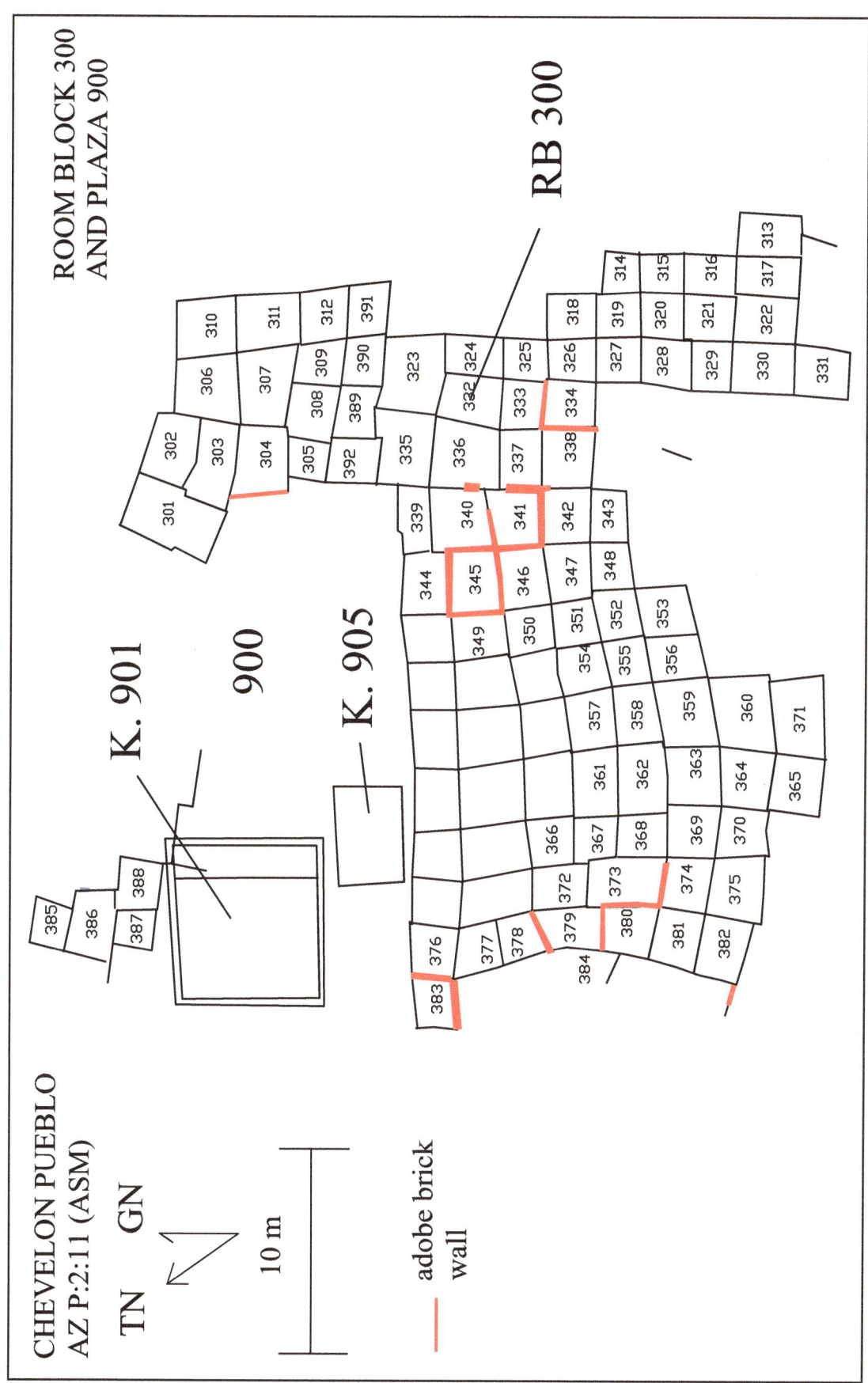

Figure 4.26. Map of Room Block 300 showing layout and Plaza 900.

Figure 4.27. North (left) and west (right) adobe brick walls of Structure 345.

built RB200, at least twice as many founded RB300, which has more than 100 first story rooms with at least half having second-story rooms. To accommodate the larger and possibly more diverse population, RB300 founders did four things. First, they built a plaza nearly twice the size of that in RB200. Second, they apparently did not build into the plaza, thus keeping it the same size. Third, access on the north side seems more open, although still restricted. Finally, a large kiva was constructed. At about 42 sq. m, K. 901 is about 350 percent larger than K. 279. In addition, K. 905 is probably the size of K. 279. It is likely that K. 279 was built at the same time as K. 901, perhaps as a response to religious space being created in Plaza 900. In basic social and ceremonial roles, however, RB300 was probably organized quite similarly to RB200.

The size of K. 901, however, suggests that either the group controlling religious rituals was larger than in RB200 or that more than one religious society used the kiva. Given that K. 901 is comparable in size to plaza kivas in Hopi villages today used by multiple religious societies and that large kivas typically perform that function, K. 901 is seen as an indicator of more ceremonial diversity in RB300 with two or more groups maintaining objects of social and ceremonial authority, using K. 901 to plan and perform the secret parts to their ceremonies. At the same time, K. 901 indicates that either one or more of these religious groups or societies was larger than previous groups or that public performances were conducted in the kiva, much as today with some winter ceremonies at Hopi. There is little room for plaza dances in Plaza 900, just as in Plaza 200. This suggests that neither plaza was designed for public performances by religious groups in their midst, or if performances were conducted, they were quite small. This further suggests K. 901 hosted public performances. An important element of Pueblo ceremonial practice, as villages grew, was to grow membership in the secret societies of the village to ensure the power and authority of the group, but just as importantly, to crosscut kinship units that could be prone to factionalism and migration (E.C. Adams 1991b).

The filling of K. 901 and then its burning further support, as with K. 279 and 248, that closure was accompanied by the disposal of objects used in religious ritual. It is not likely, considering that RB300 continued to be occupied, that these objects represent the major totemic elements of the social groups in the room block, but they likely represent items used in the performance of these rituals (Mills 2004).

When Plaza 000 was constructed sometime later, neither RB200 nor 300 ceremonial groups relinquished the secret rituals that provided the religious authority that they held upon creating or joining the village. In all likelihood, the religious societies and the individuals who controlled them in RB300 were beneath the individuals in RB200 in terms of power and authority by virtue of the members of RB300 gaining entrance, land, and their authority from the religious leaders of RB200.

RB100

The development of RB100 occurred in two phases. The first is related to the small initial construction of about 6 to 10 rooms on the highest and most northern end of a natural ridge that is occupied by RB100 (Figure 4.25). This resulted in the further definition of Plaza 800, which will be discussed in this context. This first construction is contemporary with the founding of RB300, although possibly slightly later. The second building episode in RB100 is construction of the largest spinal room block in the pueblo with the addition of 46 new rooms. This construction is associated with other construction that defined Plaza 000.

Occupants of the initial small construction in RB100 consisted of probably 2 to 3 families. Who this small group was and why they constructed in such a separate location from RB200 and 300 is intriguing. Almost certainly, they represent a separate migratory group from RB300 settlers, either from a different village or at a slightly different time. The presence of a locally made Chavez Pass Polychrome jar with Tonto Polychrome designs in the floor of S. 159 suggests these migrants might have come from either Tonto Basin, to the south, or Silver Creek, to the southeast, where local production of Tonto Polychromes occurred (Crown 1994).

Their construction, separate from the other two clusters of rooms, indicates either the indigenous groups or the migrant group preferred to be physically separated. In order to gain entrance to Chevelon from community leaders based in RB200 and be able to construct a separate set of rooms, it is likely the RB100 group brought with them some form of religious authority that was separate from that already possessed by existing members of the community. S. 159 has been described as a ritual structure whose role was similar to a clan house in modern Hopi society (E.C. Adams 1982; Eggan 1950; Parsons 1936, 1939; Titiev 1944). Such a structure would be expected for a small, separate group with the religious authority necessary to found a separate section of the village. The rich assemblage, recovered from the floor and subfloor of S. 159, likely related to rituals performed in the structure or stored there after public ceremonial performances, and its indirect burning, by igniting a fire in the adjacent corn storage room, indicate these activities were on-going to the end of the occupation of this portion of the room block.

It seems likely that Plaza 800 played a role in the ceremonial life of the adjoining, 100, 200, and 300 room blocks; however, limited testing and no excavations make it difficult to decipher what this role was and whether or not control was exclusive to one room block or was shared. Augering located a kiva with JYW ceramics in its fill suggesting use of this space may have been expanded and formalized with the construction of Plaza 000. If Plaza 800 was actively used before the construction of Plaza 000, it could be the locus of public or inclusive aspects of ceremonies planned within the plazas and kivas of RB200 and 300. Alternatively, Plaza 800 may have been used by occupants of RB100, given members of RB200 and 300 already had plazas and kivas. The informal boundaries of this space, in contrast to Plaza 000, indicate this use would have occurred after RB300 and 100 were built and before the room blocks surrounding Plaza 000 were built, or 1325/30 to 1365. This 35 to 40 year period represents the EHP, at Chevelon and in the HSC, and is a period of relative population stability within the cluster and independence that preceded the major changes accompanying the arrival of H2 (E.C. Adams 2002, 2004a; E.C. Adams et al. 2004).

An important aspect to any religious performance is its public presentation. The audience and the intent of the performance dictate the nature of the ceremony. However, according to Connerton (1989:58-61), there are predictable characteristics that together are called a performative language. These traits include a formalized language, singing, gesture, and dance that include set postures and movements. Typically, (Connerton 1989:65-68) these also include 1) calendrically observed repetition (a sacred time); 2) the repetition of sacred words uttered in language that has an archaic component that triggers the viewing group's social memory and gives the impression that these could be original words; and 3) gestural repetition, that is a sequence of movements and gestures that are essential to the correct performance using the correct words that will please the ancestors. Particularly in archaic rituals, it occurs in the represented presence of the dead or ancestors. Wearing masks is common and is associated with ancestors. Thus, a mythical base and actual ceremony are combined.

The keeping of the esoteric portions of these rituals in the enclosed kivas, combined with public portions that are less esoteric to those not initiated into the ceremonies, is a powerful combination for uniting groups while retaining religious authority. As the village expanded in size and population with multiple groups possessing sacred rituals, the need to share the public portions of these rituals with the broader community could only be performed in larger spaces, such as Plaza 800.

The expansion of RB100 to more than 50 rooms came with the construction of RB400, 500, 600, and 700, involving another 100 rooms (Figure 4.28). As already noted, the construction of all of these room blocks did not occur at the same time, but must have occurred during a short enough time period to coordinate construction to create Plaza 000. Although several rooms around Plaza 000 have been excavated, only in the two suites of rooms where multiple contiguous rooms have been excavated is there enough information to understand the social changes occurring at this time within the village. These groups of rooms, S. 120, 122 to 124 and S. 509/510/546/547, have been previously discussed under household groups. In addition, the individual rooms, in particular, the ritual structure, S. 124, and corn storage structure, S. 123, have been described. As with S. 159, S. 124 appears to be a combination household and ceremonial structure.

The ceremonial practices are represented by floor features and objects discarded in the room previous to and while it was burning. On the basis of a small sample size of two (S. 124 and 159) out of possibly 13, it appears that structures added to the original spinal room block into the plaza space on the east side of RB100 are distinctive habitation structures with religious ritual features (Figure 4.29). The construction of these ceremonial structures, possibly clan houses, is similar to the pattern for the north room block to the central plaza of H2. Here, the entire room block was fronted with small subterranean structures, or kivas. Only one, K. 324, was excavated.

Five of these plaza structures are associated with Plaza 800, then there is a break, and another eight plaza structures are constructed in association with Plaza 000 (Figure 4.29). With the possible exception of one structure on the north or plaza side of RB700, no other structures are built into these plaza spaces after the construction of Plaza 000 and associated room blocks. Thus, it appears that during this expansive phase, the processes outlined in the use of Plaza 800 during the previous phase were formalized during the post-1365 look of Chevelon. Additionally, it appears that new groups with religious authority demonstrated their social power by constructing ritual structures that jutted into the plaza. Additionally, it is possible these groups had more material wealth in that both structures excavated in this set of rooms had adjacent corn storage rooms that were burned (thus, symbolically sacrificing the corn) when the village was depopulated.

Burning, a common practice in closing ceremonial structures, particularly kivas at H2 and H3, seems also to have been practiced at Chevelon with these structures. The strong physical association of the placement of Chevelon ceremonial structures into the plaza space, their burning, abundant floor assemblages, and even the presence of a Sikyatki Polychrome jar on the floor of S. 159, suggest a stronger relationship to H2 religious ritual than noted at H1. The importance of this possible relationship will be explored in Chapter 14.

What is suggested for the late occupation of RB100 is the development of leaders with religious authority in the room blocks surrounding Plaza 000 and in particular in RB100. Although almost certainly less powerful than religious groups in RB200 and 300, it is possible the RB100 ceremonial leaders brought to or developed katsina rituals at Chevelon. This argument is based on evidence I have presented elsewhere (E.C. Adams 1991a, 1994, 2002, 2004a), which looks at the relationship between katsina iconography on pottery, kiva murals, and rock art, and the development of large enclosed plazas within which are placed kivas. This ritual complex is needed for the public and private performance of katsina ceremonies in historic Hopi and evidence strongly suggests this was happening in villages on the Hopi mesas during the fourteenth century and in the Homol'ovi villages following the arrival of H2 (E.C. Adams 2002, 2004a).

As detailed in the discussion above, performance is an essential part of religious ritual in all societies. In traditional societies, according to Connerton (1989) and Rappaport (1999), religious performance is a means for connecting groups to their past and often involves masking, calendrical scheduling of rituals, and a combination of words and gestures in an ordered sequence to make the performance correct. This describes Pueblo and Hopi religion and Hopi katsina rituals in detail. The essence of social memory that is essential in these rituals still plays out in Hopi ceremonies to this day. In terms of RB100, evidence suggests that the correlation of its construction with the construction of other room blocks in order to create a large enclosed plaza, the placement of ceremonial structures on the plaza, the deposition of objects on the floors of these structures, many objects likely used in rituals, and finally the burning of these

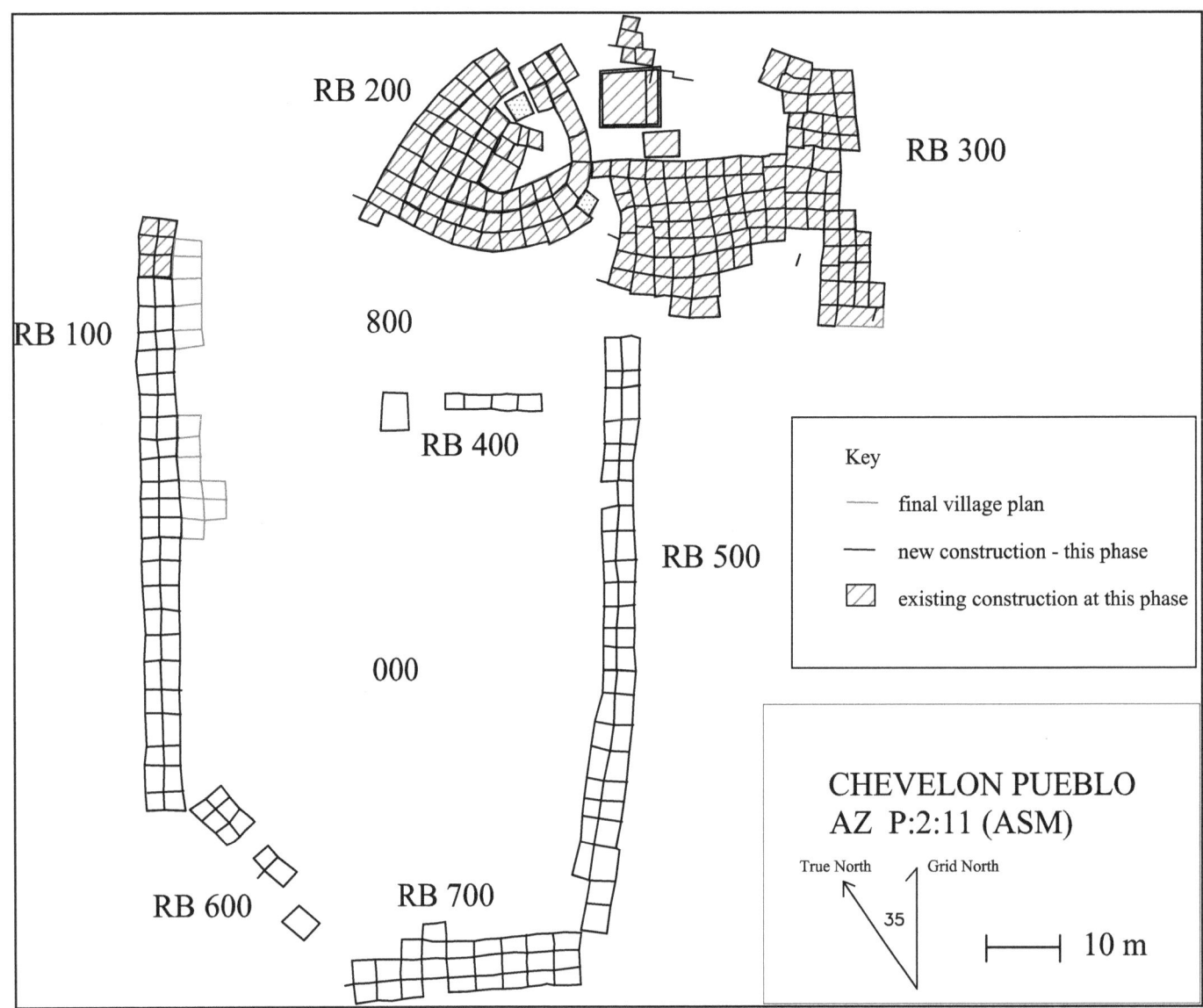

Figure 4.28. Map of room block additions around Plaza 000.

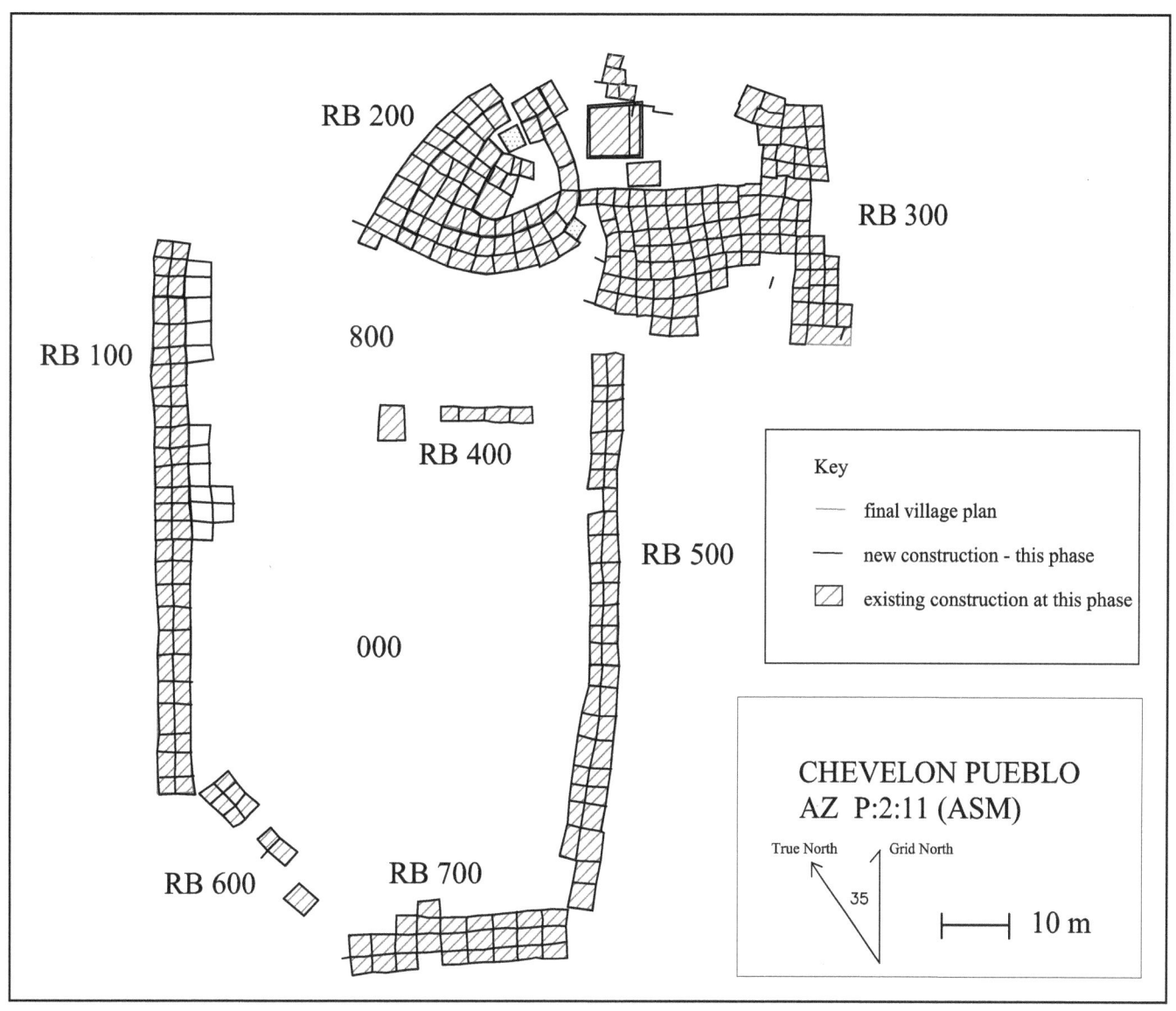

Figure 4.29. Map of Room Block 100 showing added, possibly ritual, structures.

structures upon cessation of their use is strongly connected to H2 religious ritual patterns and the acceptance or emulation of katsina religion at Chevelon.

The pattern described above fits into the Hopi description of religious authority in their villages today (Parsons 1939:210; Titiev 1944), where katsina ceremonies and associated ritual are considered to be a recent introduction to their religious pantheon and within a class of religious ceremonies of much less power than the older ceremonies — Wuwtsim, Flute ceremonies, Snake and Antelope ceremonies, and Women's ceremonies. A consideration of ritual power at Chevelon shows a similar pattern. The oldest portions of the village in RB200 and 300 held exclusive rituals in their respective room block plazas that perhaps had only occasional public performances in Plaza 800. Groups who migrated later and built the room blocks surrounding Plaza 000 were probably not included in these ceremonies or, if they were, never held authority nor had access to the totemic objects that signified the power and authority of their possessors. In contrast, the religious authority of groups surrounding Plaza 000 were involved in major public performances that by their nature were open to the entire community. The lack of kivas in these room blocks could signify either their use of the kiva or kivas in Plaza 800 and RB400, or the basis of ceremonies in non-kiva religious structures. There is certainly precedence for this in other Homol'ovi villages (E.C. Adams 2002) and at Hopi as well, where Flute and other ceremonies are held in rooms within the room blocks (E.C. Adams 1983).

RB 400 Through 700

Little can be said about the remaining room blocks surrounding Plaza 000 because not enough excavation occurred to draw conclusions. As discussed in the RB100 section, no structures with religious use nor any corn storage or piki houses were discovered in the seven rooms excavated in these four room blocks (Figure 1.1). Given that sample size is close to 8 percent, considerably less than the 14 percent in RB100, it is certainly possible these structures were missed. Nevertheless, the layout of the room blocks gives priority in size, age, and rooms intrusive into the plaza to RB100. It is possible that religious authority rested in RB100 because all groups occupying the Plaza 000 room blocks migrated at the same time and individuals with religious authority chose to locate their homes closer to RB200 and 300 as well as physically higher than any other structures surrounding Plaza 000. It is therefore likely, as in Hopi villages today, that these groups have little religious authority and were lower on the social and ceremonial ladder than their counterparts in RB100, 200, and 300. Their relatively late arrival to Chevelon would suggest this from Hopi oral tradition as well.

From the standpoint of material remains, there is nothing excavated from the seven rooms in these room blocks to suggest any wealth garnered through ritual authority or abundance of maize. There were no corn storage rooms, as noted, but in addition, households appear to be smaller with fewer storage rooms than their counterparts in the earlier room blocks. Also, as noted above, the virtual absence of kivas suggests lack of access to religious authority and related rituals within the community. Whether room block ritual structures were present is not known, but it is easy to imagine there are few and more related to household ritual than ritual above the household within which religious authority would need to be demonstrated and performances of some nature would need to be conducted. Nevertheless, at least two of the structures, S. 509 and 702, were closed using the burning of corn on their floor and roof respectively. This form of room closure could be connected to the burning of the corn storage rooms in RB100.

Summary

Limited excavations at Chevelon have been used to assess various levels of village society from households using individual rooms or suites of rooms to room blocks and plaza spaces used by kinship and non-kinship groups. Using the theoretical perspectives of social memory, inalienable objects, Hopi ethnography, and religious ritual theory and applying them to behavioral interpretations of deposits and space, a view of Chevelon as an evolving society has emerged. There is strong archaeological evidence of the creation and maintenance of religious authority or power at Chevelon by manipulating objects and space. The exclusivity of plaza and kiva placement and access in RB200 is particularly noteworthy and in line with the expectations of a community built on the control of religious ritual knowledge, within a limited social group. RB300 was constructed for similar purposes, but with a larger population. Finally, the late addition of room blocks to create Plaza 000 is in accordance with the expectations of the use of this space for village-wide religious ritual performance, probably used by individuals and groups with less authority than those in RB200 and 300, perhaps using katsina ceremonies to gain access through this more limited authority. Examination of ceremonial structures and deposits in kivas, and possible clan rooms, revealed a pattern of disposal and deposition of ritual objects that is expected of groups restricting access to secret knowledge and objects used to perform said rituals.

By studying the size of spinal room block additions, a pattern has emerged of a sequential nature ranging at Chevelon from smaller groups in the 10 to 15 room category, to the most typical groups having 20 to 25 rooms, to the single case of 46 rooms. It appears that groups are not migrating as families, but rather as larger social units comprised of as few as 2 to 3 households, more typically 4 to 5 households, and occasionally as large as 10 households, using 5 rooms as the average used by a household. Whatever the actual size of these groups, it is clear that when the great south plaza was built, several spinal room block groups cooperated to create this space. Too little excavation and too little difference in material culture make it impossible to determine distinctive aspects in these groups. All appear to be consuming JYW; however, some groups probably emigrated from the Silver Creek or Tonto Basin areas, as locally produced, but stylistically accurate examples of Tonto Polychrome are common in the assemblages of households surrounding Plaza 000, often as whole pots. These groups may have followed migration groups involved in settlement of Chevelon, by at least the EHP, and identified through the presence of at least two communities of practice involved in manufacture of utility wares (Barker 2015; also Chapter 6). Thus, the present interpretation is that spinal room blocks are constructed by multiple household groups, likely related by kinship, who migrated to Chevelon together.

Household groups also varied in the size and complexity of the space they used. It appears that older and more powerful groups controlled larger spaces, probably, in part, due to needs to plan and perhaps hold ceremonies within their household space. Additionally, the households occupying the largest spaces in

RB100 also controlled larger spaces including stores of corn unseen in other sections of the village. Whether this relates to sampling or true differences in social power cannot be fully answered. However, the use of corn in these storage rooms as fuel to burn them and the adjacent household ceremonial structures is noteworthy and not accidental. The quantity of corn consumed in the burning of the two corn storage rooms speaks to the access of families in RB100 to good agricultural land and to their willingness to sacrifice this most sacred of food, probably as they left Chevelon to return to one or more Antelope Mesa communities (E.C. Adams 2016). A Sikyatki Polychrome jar on the floor of S. 159, one of these ritual structures, indicates burning of these rooms occurred at the end of the Chevelon occupation and sometime after 1385, when Sikyatki Polychrome was first produced (LaMotta 2006).

Finally, it was noted that the patterns of placement of ceremonial structures, deposits left in these structures, and their burning are similar to those identified at H2. The strong evidence that the arrival of H2 to the HSC brought katsina religion was used to further demonstrate the likelihood these ceremonies were introduced to Chevelon by groups building and living in RB100 and probably groups occupying room blocks surrounding Plaza 000. Perhaps it was access to this religious ritual that enabled these groups to join Chevelon and bring enough ceremonial prestige with them to be accorded access to nearby farming areas by those in RB200 who controlled land and religious ritual at Chevelon.

Another possibility for introduction of katsina ceremonies to Chevelon affords more agency among immigrating groups. E.C. Adams (1991a) and Crown (1994) document katsina iconography on RRW and WMRW ceramics dating 1340 to 1400. Ceramics suggest groups migrating to Chevelon circa 1365 and who established Plaza 000 and surrounding room blocks were partially or mostly derived from groups manufacturing these wares. Thus, groups migrating to Chevelon may already have knowledge of katsina ceremonies when they joined Chevelon. Construction of Plaza 000 in order to perform katsina ceremonies may have been mutually understood between groups migrating from the south and southeast and those migrating from Hopi to H2 and possibly to Chevelon directly. Or, ceremonial knowledge could have been shared between new and old Chevelon occupants or even contested. Combining these scenarios may be most parsimonious with religious leaders in RB200 and 300 obtaining knowledge of katsina ceremonies, which attracted groups with their own knowledge of these ceremonies and who wished to be included in a community where they were being practiced. The following chapters will explore specific artifact assemblages and these will be used to synthesize some of these ideas in the concluding chapters.

Chapter 5
Modeling Prehistoric Structural Fires at Chevelon Pueblo

David J. Icove, J.R. Lally,
A.J. Vonarx, and E. Charles Adams[1]

Interdisciplinary collaboration into complex problems leverages the combined knowledge and experience of researchers and scientists. Such a problem concerns the interpretation of prehistoric fires found at archaeological sites, where the exact origin and cause of these fires are not readily apparent. The standard of care for fire investigation is covered by the peer-reviewed "*NFPA 921 – Guide for Fire and Explosion Investigation*" published by the National Fire Protection Association (NFPA). In this guide, NFPA 921 stresses the use of the *scientific method* to evaluate different hypotheses before arriving at a final conclusion. This approach ensures that preliminary hypotheses are refined and explored before arriving at a final expert conclusion or opinion. It recognizes that, until a cause for the fires can be determined, classifications of accidental, natural, intentionally-set or undetermined are premature.

Traditional evaluations of fire patterns and damage can be used by archaeologists during excavations to develop hypotheses for the origin and cause of a prehistoric fire. However, given the age of these scenes, many patterns will fail to be preserved or go unrecognized by the excavator. As with forensic reconstructions of more recent fires, other sources of information may be utilized in hypothesis development. For prehistoric cultures, these sources include: application of fire dynamics and modeling; professional guidelines and standards; oral histories of descendant populations; material patterns of ancient repeated behavior; forensic science; environmental interactions; fire loss histories; and fire testing using experimental methods.

In 2004, a collaborative project was developed to study prehistoric fires at Chevelon Pueblo, a thirteenth to fourteenth century ancestral Hopi village in Northeastern Arizona. In 2004, fire investigators advised archaeologists in developing modified techniques of *forensic fire scene reconstruction* and fire pattern analysis to be used in excavation. As an outgrowth of hypotheses raised during fieldwork, a series of full-scale compartment tests were completed in 2005 using a reconstructed model that simulated the size and materials used in ancient construction to:

1. replicate a number of scenarios involving intentional human-mediated ignition;

---

[1] Icove – University of Tennessee; Lally – Central New Mexico University, Vonarx and Adams – University of Arizona. This chapter is a revision of the paper originally published by Icove et al. (2008)

2. determine the impact of particular intentional ignition scenarios to architectural materials and room contents and;

3. provide materials and patterns for comparison with prehistoric fire debris.

Data from test compartments were employed in computer fire modeling (with Fire Dynamics Simulator) of accidental ignition scenarios that could have occurred in ancestral Hopi villages such as Chevelon.

Archaeological Study of Ancient Structural Fires: Setting the Stage for Collaboration

Archaeological research into the destructive power of fire, as it relates to architecture, has typically been limited to the study of conflagrations that destroyed cities such as Catal Hüyük in Anatolia (Twiss et al. 2008); Rome; or Paquimé in northwest Mexico (see generally Di Peso 1974). More often than not, archaeologists have used circumstantial evidence to posit causes and motives for expansive fires. Only during the last 20 years have archaeologists begun to look at single fires in single structures. Formal, ongoing collaborations with fire investigators and archaeologists are recent developments.

Until quite recently, archaeologists tended to rely on their understanding of "cultural context" to interpret fires without reference to formal fire investigation. Trends in the attribution of fires as accidental or intentional are readily apparent in the southwestern literature. Up through the 1980s, archaeologists frequently assumed that most prehistoric structural fires were accidental but recognized that some structural fires may have had incendiary origins. Historical period accounts indicate pueblo groups burned perishable roof materials to rid their home of pests, upon the death of an inhabitant, or as a result of conflict (Darling 1998; LeBlanc 1999; Walker 1998). Researchers interpreting earlier sites argued that similar scenarios could account for the presence of burned roofs in the archaeological record (E.C. Adams 2016; Cameron 1990; LeBlanc 1999; R. Lightfoot 1994; Walker 1995).

Prior to formal collaboration with fire investigators, a few archaeologists built model structures and attempted to burn them (Figures 5.1 and 5.2). Based on failed attempts to rapidly ignite an earth and timber structure, Wilshusen (1986) and others assumed that most, if not all structural fires in the prehistoric Southwestern United States were intentionally set. Many archaeologists looked no further for causes of specific events and debated over possible motives for starting these fires. In the 1990s, warfare or ritual became common explanations for structural fires, usually on the basis of circumstantial evidence (Darling 1998; LeBlanc 1999; Walker 1998).

NFPA 921 mandates that researchers must first carefully establish that the cause of a structural fire was incendiary prior to exploring motives for that fire. In the last ten years, archaeologists at several major Southwestern universities have begun to take another look at the cause of individual structural fires and their possibility of spread to abutting architecture. Archaeologists at Southern Methodist University (Adler et al. 2006), the University of New Mexico (Lally 2005), and the University of Arizona (Lally and Vonarx 2011) turned to arson investigators and fire protection engineers to help them explore these ancient mysteries of why so many structures burned so long ago.

Figure. 5.1. A reconstruction of typical pueblo structure or room in preparation for the 2005 fire tests at Homol'ovi State Park in Arizona. Photograph by D.J. Icove.

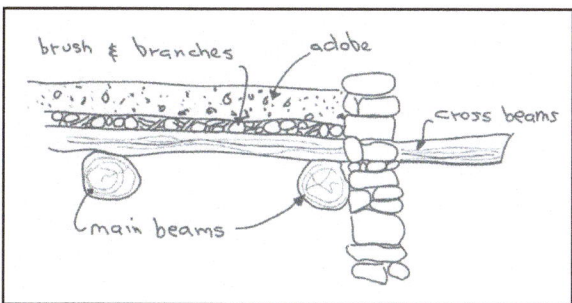

Figures 5.2. A diagram of a typical roof. Drawing by K. Harrison.

Chevelon Pueblo: A Case Study

This study focuses on widespread evidence of structural fires at Chevelon Pueblo. Most structures at Chevelon have stone masonry and mud mortar walls, but adobe brick structures are also present, primarily in RB300. The pueblo contains a variety of room types, defined by their architectural features and assumed functions. Habitation rooms always contained hatches in their roofs for the escape of smoke from hearths built along a wall or in the center of the room. Habitation rooms were closest to or faced the plazas. Storage rooms were positioned behind the habitation room away from the plaza. These were connected to habitation rooms by an open doorway, usually about 70 cm by 40 cm and about 50 cm above the floor. Storage rooms had no roof opening. They had a shared doorway with the habitation room. Rooms with stores of ears of corn also had floor vents, presumably to help with air circulation around the stored corn. The positioning and relative inaccessibility of storage rooms reflects a conscious attempt by villagers to prevent predation on food or other stored items. *Kivas* were constructed like habitation structures, using the same methods, but were built underground and were not connected to other structures. Kivas were usually much larger than other rooms in the pueblo.

Some evidence of structural fire was encountered at other ancestral villages of Homol'ovi Settlement Cluster, but evidence of fire is common and persistent at Chevelon. In other Homol'ovi villages, fire debris from burned roofs is usually encountered only in kivas, which were burned in nearly half the cases (E.C. Adams 2016; E.C. Adams and Fladd 2014). Excavations at Chevelon indicate structural fires occurred in 20 percent, or about 100 rooms. Evidence of burning is found in all room blocks in the village, but concentrated in those surrounding the large plaza. Analysis of ceramic artifacts, collected from the floors of these structures, suggest most were burned at about the same time, with most floors having few to no artifacts, and none were reused after the fire. Evidence of fire includes discoloration of wall plaster or stones, or remains of collapsed burned roofing on the floor. Generally, the recovered burned roofing is missing the largest beams, but the remainder of the burned roof is found in the fill of the structure. Items were left in place in some habitation and storage rooms. In some cases, these items appear to be thermally altered. At times, sections of the floor itself are sintered from brown to bright orange to near black.

Excavations have revealed, burning of contiguous rooms is the rule rather than the exception at Chevelon. Fire debris is scattered on the surface of unexcavated rooms. This suggests that contiguous rooms burned during a fire event, or events that spread between structures. The nature of modern archaeological research makes this hypothesis difficult to verify. In 2005, two rooms were excavated that were half-filled with piles of charred corn on the cob (Figures 1.1, 5.3, and 5.4). The presence of sooted, friable masonry and huge chunks of sintered roofing implies that a high-intensity fire occurred in these rooms with the corn as a primary fuel. It is not hard to imagine that storage rooms, with their high fuel load, could have served as ideal places for a fire to establish itself by natural, accidental, or intentional acts.

Compartment Fires and Southwestern Construction

To establish a fire as intentional or incendiary, researchers must first gain an understanding of the principles of fire, its behavior and dynamics within structures. The excavation methods, employed by modern arson investigators, closely resemble those of archaeologists; both attempt to build a model of past events. The quantity and quality of the evidence collected will determine the completeness and accuracy of that model. Any attempt to model and reconstruct the cause of ancient structural fires should address the following questions:

1. What are the physical dimensions of the compartment?

2. How was the structure used by inhabitants?

3. How was the structure ventilated? Were specific portals open or closed at the time of the fire and how would changes in ventilation influence the fire's growth and behavior?

4. What is the expected fuel load of the compartment?

5. Are the observed thermal alterations consistent or inconsistent with the assumed use and expected fuel load of that room or compartment?

6. What signatures of fire origin and direction of spread exist, if any?

7. What competent sources of ignition were present?

When attempting to reconstruct the nature of a prehistoric structural fire, one must reconstruct the structure (at least conceptually), including all possible ventilation shafts. It is assumed that all structures used for habitation contained an internal hearth. To allow the smoke and soot from an internal hearth to be vented to the outside, a ceiling or near ceiling vent would have been necessary. Still, the presence of a hearth does not dictate the form or nature of openings, nor indicate whether vents were open when the structural fire occurred.

Following *compartment fire theory*, an open diffusion flame, in an enclosed space, creates a buoyant plume of smoke and hot gases. As it rises, it entrains, or draws air from its surroundings. This entrained air cools the buoyant plume as it rises above the fire. When constrained by a roof, the plume is not able to cool as it rises, but spreads out horizontally beneath the ceiling forming a ceiling jet.

During the growth stage of a compartment fire, the walls and ceiling come into play. The upper portions of the room are where the super heated air is contained. A cooler zone exists underneath. As the fire continues, the boundary of this upper hot zone begins to descend toward the floor. As a fire consumes available fuel, the air temperature in the room increases. In specific situations, an impressive event or series of events called *flashover* may occur. Flashover is the short transition period, between growth and fully developed fire, where the room or compartment is totally engulfed in flame. This total room involvement will continue until approximately 80 percent of the fuel is consumed. After the available fuel is consumed, the fire will begin to decay and smolder. It is important to note that not every compartment fire results in flashover. Flashover is controlled by many variables, such as fuel load, heat release rates, room geometry, ceiling height, and ventilation.

In rooms that reach a state of flashover, human survival in the structure is unlikely. Flashover can leave its mark in the archaeological record in the form of *lines of demarcation*. Lines of demarcation are commonly found as bright line boundaries, between the upper hot zone of a room that was fully engulfed in flame, and the cooler areas below. Lines of demarcation indicate how far the hot zone descended toward the floor. The depth to which the hot zone descended provides information concerning the size, intensity, and fuel load of a fire. The presence of lines of demarcation also provides evidence that the roof of the structure was intact at flashover. An intact roof is necessary for flashover to occur. If a roof collapses, or otherwise fails during the growth period of a fire, the upper hot zone will escape to the atmosphere and flashover will normally not occur.

Figure 5.5 is a photograph of a late Pueblo II or early Pueblo III structure on Mesa Portales in Sandoval County, New Mexico, excavated in 2003 by an Eastern New Mexico University Field School. This photograph clearly reveals lines of demarcation approximately 10 cm above the floor. This structure experienced flashover. While fire investigators are often concerned with whether flashover occurred, the process can obliterate subtle fire signatures that researchers can use to point to the area in which a fire began (i.e. an "area of origin").

If researchers cannot identify an area of origin, determining the incendiary nature of the fire may be difficult, at best. When evidence of flashover is encountered, the ever important question of "what was the fuel load?" must be answered. Was the fuel load consistent with the proposed use of the compartment? Is there evidence that the fuel load was bolstered or

Figure 5.3. Burned corn in Structure 123.

Figure 5.4. Burned corn in Structure 158.

specially configured to aid the progression of the fire?

Recent collaborative examinations of these sites, combined with large-scale fire testing and computer modeling, suggest additional hypotheses about prehistoric structural fires were not rigorously pursued. A new taxonomy of scenarios includes a series of accidental explanations: ignition of items near an interior hearth, dust explosions or spontaneous ignition of stored corn, lightning strikes, and exposure from forest fires.

Structural fires can be difficult to investigate because no two structural fires are the same; each fire must be evaluated on its own merits. In the sections that follow, compartment fire testing and mathematical computer models are used as tools to understand the possible scenarios surrounding ancient structural fires at Chevelon. The use of mathematical computer fire modeling programs allow for the rigorous testing of possible fire scenarios. Circumstantial evidence (room contents, evidence of remodeling, post-fire fill of the structure, etc.) are useful for understanding the cultural context of fire events. In the end, suggestions of intentionality should be based on the totality of the evidence collected rather than collecting evidence that may tend to support a particular motive.

Hypothesis Development Using Fire Testing

Over the last few years, the authors of this paper have been involved in two independent research programs, each involving full-scale fire testing on replicated Puebloan structures. Lally constructed an adobe-brick and mud mortar structure with a T-shaped doorway, mimicking the materials in Chihuahua and New Mexico. Vonarx and volunteers built a masonry structure with a window-style

Figure 5.5. Typical fire debris found on interior wall in archeological excavations at Mesa Portales (LA145165). Photo by J. E. Lally.

doorway, reflecting construction techniques at Chevelon Pueblo in Arizona. While the dimensions of each structure were similar (2.5 m by 2.5 m, with a floor to ceiling height of 1.5 m), the thermal properties of walls, roof construction, and ventilation patterns differed in each structure.

As each project hoped to understand ancient fires in a unique cultural context, fuel loads, ventilation patterns, and ignition scenarios tested in each room varied. During her fire tests, Vonarx placed a floor assemblage of ceramic vessels, stone tools, and shell within the structure prior to ignition. In her first trial, no additional fuel was placed within the structure. The roof vent was closed and an open doorway provided ventilation. The ceiling thatching was ignited from inside the structure near a corner (Figure 5.6). The fire spread rapidly across the underside of the ceiling and failure of a primary beam caused the roof to collapse. None of the sandstone, roof sediment, mud plaster, or mortar appeared to be altered thermally. Sooting patterns on walls and artifacts were amazingly subtle and fleeting. Still, the area of the fire's origin could be recognized through patterns of charring to beams. One of the main beams and many cross-beams survived, charred but intact. In a prehistoric structure, partially-charred beams may have been recycled for use, leaving little evidence of fire in the fill.

Vonarx's structure was re-roofed. Dried and husked corn cobs were added as fuel and ignited. The corn smoldered for several hours, but put out only low levels of heat that was survivable by a human. In a third scenario, loosely-packed scrub and local grasses filled half the interior volume of the structure. The pile of corncobs was reignited. The fire flared up, igniting the thatching material and causing the roofing material to collapse on to the floor (Figure 5.7). This fire produced small amounts of fused roofing material that fell into the structure, but these chunks were found only in the two corners closest to the area of ignition. The two primary beams were charred deeply, but did not fail (Figure 5.8). Pyrolysis of roof beams and thatching was "more complete" closer to the source of ventilation than at a distance from ventilation. A piece of wood would be reduced to ash quicker near a vent than at a distance from a vent. If the structure was reroofed, swept out, and re-plastered, only the thermal alterations to sandstone (in corners where the roof met the walls) would have indicated that a fire occurred. Thermal readings were made each minute after ignition, using thermocouples placed at 1.0 m in each wall. An additional thermocouple was placed on a metal post, positioned vertically in the center of the room, which is reproduced in the time/temperature plot in Figure 5.9.

The following year, a second experimental room was constructed contiguous with the first. They were connected by a doorway and the new room had a second doorway in a wall adjacent to the first. The goal of the

Figure 5.6. Roof interior of experimental structure showing smoke and fire ignited by torch.

Figure 5.7. View through doorway of model room engulfed in fire from brush.

Figure 5.8. Burned roof resulting from room intentionally filled with brush.

second room was to conduct experiments to determine if fire could be naturally transferred to an adjacent structure. Both structures were roofed using the same suite of elements as previously. The back, or storage, room was filled with several bushels of ears of corn with husks removed and a small amount of brush to ignite the dried corn. The brush quickly ignited setting some of the corn on fire, but as before, the corn mostly smoldered rather than burned. With the hatch covered, the initial fires did catch the roof on fire and because it was a windy day, the adjoining side of the roof to the second room also caught on fire. The roof of the initial room partially collapsed, but the vigas remained intact. The closing material and the end of several secondary beams partially burned and fell to the floor. Prior to roof collapse, heat built in the first room, but there was no flashover and when the roof collapsed, the heat quickly dissipated. Near the floor, the temperature remained above 150° C for several hours as the corn continued to smolder.

During dissertation research, Lally discovered that fused flooring and plaster are found frequently among remains of burned prehistoric structures. A greater fuel load than present in roofing is required to produce the thermally altered fused adobe fragments observed in the archaeological record at Mesa Portales, Sandoval County, New Mexico.

Testing in New Mexico and Arizona produced similar results and has important repercussions for the interpretation of fire at Chevelon Pueblo and other sites. In all trials, room roofs "failed" within 15 minutes of ignition. The walls, of both structures, remained intact and were structurally sound after multiple fires events. None of the fires would have required abandonment of the structure. Both could have been rehabilitated, re-roofed, and re-occupied with little effort. Considerably less effort would have been required to rehabilitate the structures than was required to build them. Neither structure flashed-over, but this may be related to the small distance between soffit and ceiling. All evidence of fire was located on the inside of the experimental structures. No evidence of fire was located on the exterior of the structure,

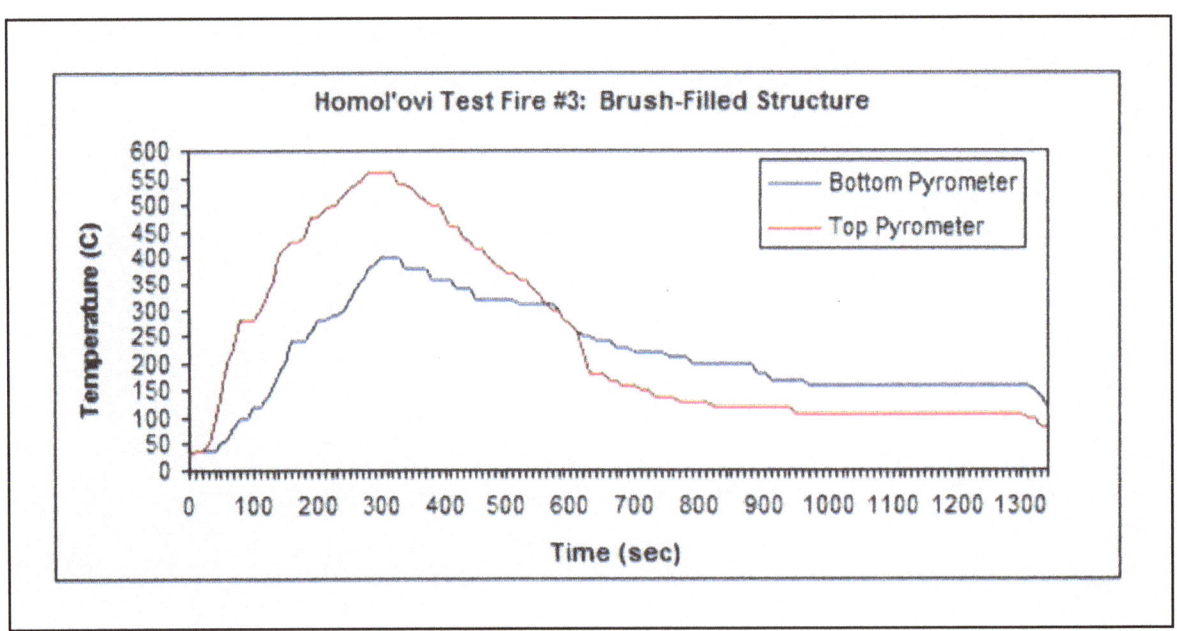

Figure 5.9. Time-temperature plot of heat buildup from brush fire.

except some sooting patterns near the entry and beam sockets on Vonarx's structure that faded quickly with rain.

Hypothesis Development Using Computer Fire Models

Computer simulations, using the National Institute of Standards and Technology's Fire Dynamics Simulator (FDS), examined scenarios for accidental ignition not tested explicitly in live burns. Welhorn and Icove modeled the compartment after Vonarx's test structure in Arizona. The interior of the compartment measured 2.4 m by 2.4 m by 1.5 m. The thickness of the walls was 0.35 m, with a 0.5 m by 0.5 m vent in the center of the ceiling and a 0.5 m wide, 0.7 m tall square opening in a wall for a door. The sill of the door is 0.5 m off the ground. A burner simulating the hearth was situated along the center of the wall opposite the door. Six simulations were run to simulate three separate scenarios. A slice is on the plane x = 1.24 m, the vertical center-line of the room through the door. Each simulation examined temperature, soot density, and oxygen level.

Scenario #1

The first scenario was of a typical cooking fire in the hearth. Cooking in Chevelon's interior hearths probably involved the preparation of maize, beans, and squash often in stews with meat cooked in ceramic jars. Fires would generate just enough heat to boil water, in order to soften and prepare the vegetables. The simulation was run, once with the vent open and once with the vent closed. A 10 kW/m^2 fire was initiated in the hearth. The surface temperature of the hearth increased to 500° C with the air temperature, directly above the hearth, measured around 70° C. In the simulation with the roof hatch open (Figure 5.10), the temperature of the upper layer in the room was between 30° and 40° C or (80° and 100° F), which would not be an unbearable temperature. The oxygen concentration in the room was 21 percent, dropping down to 20 percent just above the hearth. Soot density in the room appeared to be rather low. In the simulation of the typical cooking fire with the hatch closed, the air temperature was roughly 10° C hotter (Figure 5.11) and the soot density was slightly more significant and closer to the floor. It is not expected that a fire would be kept in a room with the roof hatch closed.

Scenario #2

The second scenario involved a larger fuel load with a 20 kW/m2 fire initiating from the burner/hearth. This might reflect a situation in which items sitting close to a hearth ignited accidentally. With the hatch open (Figure 5.12), the air temperature was roughly 40° to 50° C and the soot density was moderate. The oxygen concentration in the room was the same as the previous typical cooking fire scenario. The model suggests that the occupants of the room would have time to make their egress as long as the fire was contained around the hearth. In this scenario with the hatch closed (Figure 5.13), the space is still tenable. The air temperature is around 50° to the mid-60's° C. Soot density is slightly thicker, but the occupants of the room would probably be able to successfully flee from danger.

Scenario #3

The third scenario simulates a room with a large fuel load, presumably a storage room or abandoned room filled with refuse. For this scenario, a 3000 kW/m2 fire was used.

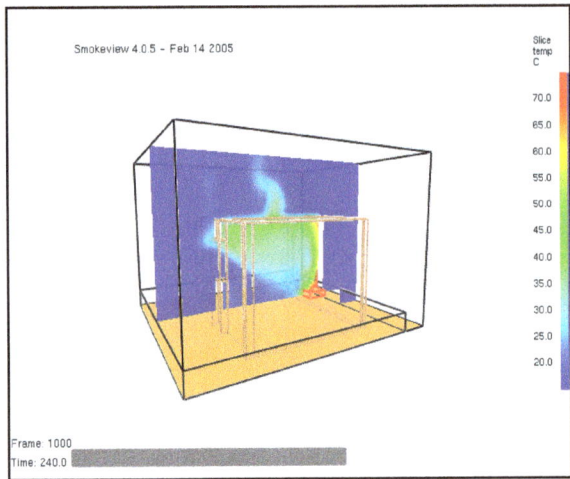

Figure 5.10. Simulation of room fire from hearth with vent open.

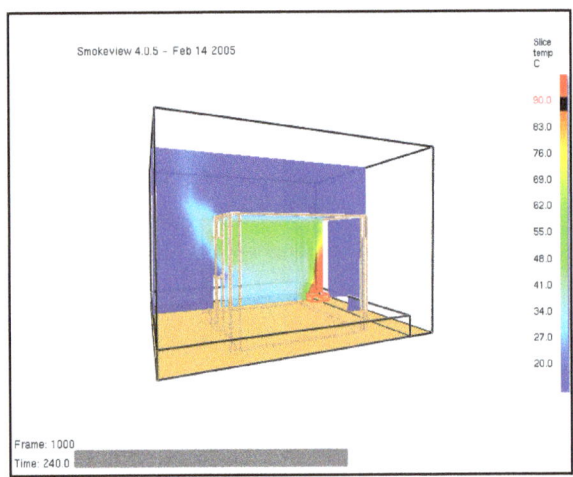

Figure 5.11. Simulation of room fire from hearth with vent closed.

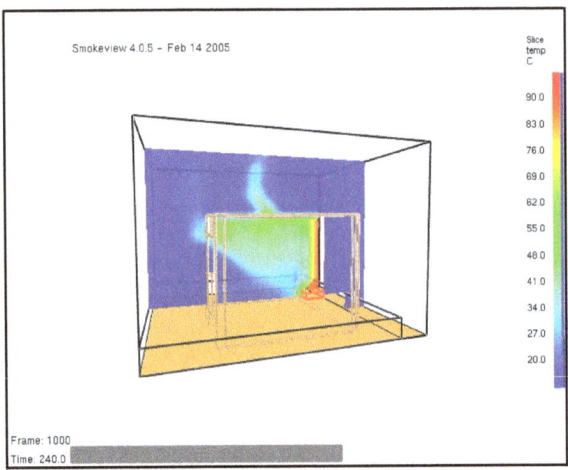

Figure 5.12. Simulation when hearth ignites material on floor with vent open.

Regardless of the simulation being run with the hatch open or closed, the room was untenable soon after ignition. With the hatch open, the room became untenable within six seconds (Figure 5.14), and with the hatch closed, the room became untenable within two seconds (Figure 5.15).

The architecture of habitation rooms at Chevelon included ceiling hatches, creating an environment in which small fires could burn without causing harm to the occupants. The model also demonstrated that, in situations involving a small accidental fire, a room would remain tenable long enough to allow time for escape as the model simulated a four-minute time lapse. However, when a fire is ignited in a room with a large fuel load either by accident or intent, the architecture of the room did not aid in slowing the fire. Regardless of whether the ceiling hatch was open or closed, the fire and heat engulfed the room within seconds, and the room was no longer tenable.

These simulations highlight the potential for applying modern investigative tools to ancient evidence of fire. The authors recognize that the exact parameters of these tests do not necessarily represent what would be expected in the archaeological record. Each of these three scenarios would have produced flame lengths greater than predicted by flame height equations in NFPA 921. As mentioned in discussion of the compartment tests, the distance between soffit and ceiling in prehistoric structures may have inhibited flashover. Modern investigative tools often assume modern construction materials and techniques. Those assumptions cannot be applied to prehistoric structures. The thermal properties of sandstone and adobe construction material have yet to be firmly established. Ancient stone and mud masons did not concern themselves with such things as right angles, standard wall thickness, or uniform roofing

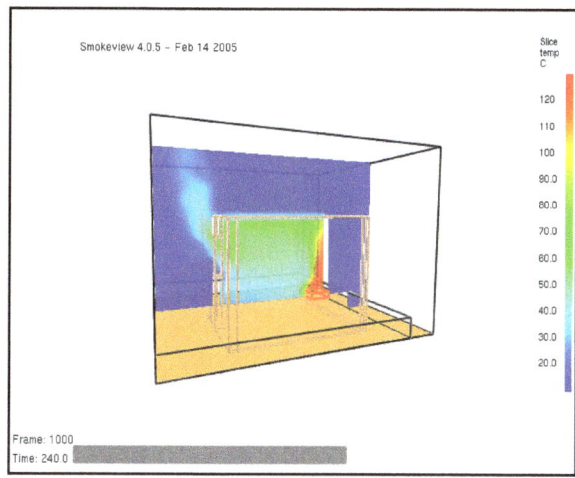

Figure 5.13. Simulation when hearth ignites material on floor with vent closed.

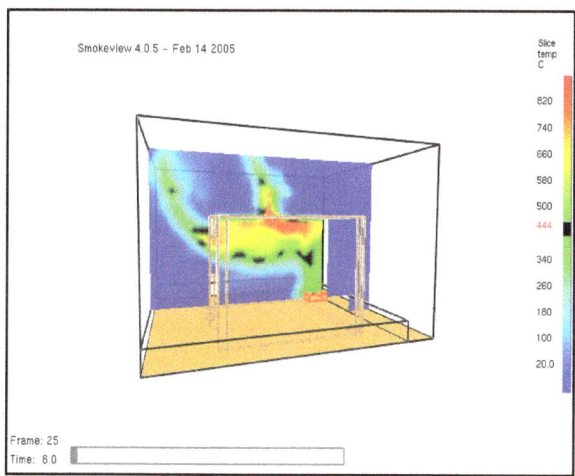

Figure 5.14. Simulation with large fuel load, such as brush, with vent open.

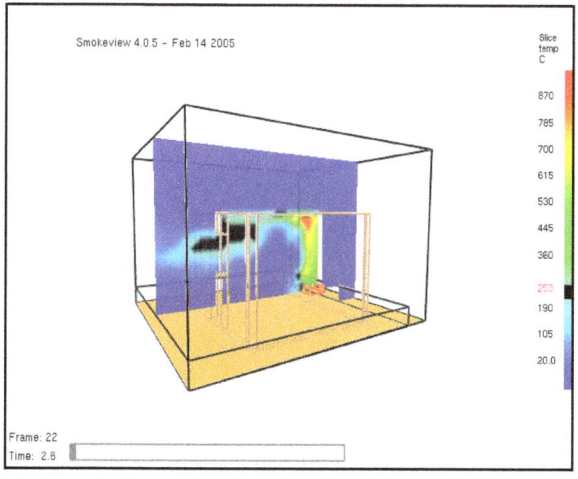

Figure 5.15. Simulation with large fuel load, such as brush, with vent closed.

materials. They used whatever worked. The variability of prehistoric construction is an important consideration for use of computer models and will guide future research.

Conclusions

Given that only a small portion of Chevelon pueblo was excavated, reconstructions of prehistoric events remain incomplete. However, with the help of compartment fire testing and computer modeling, important comparisons to the archaeological record can be made. Fire patterns, documented in excavation, suggest that high intensity fires impacted some rooms. Heavily oxidized wall stones, lines of demarcation close to the floor, and expanses of sintering roofing materials indicate that flashover took place in some prehistoric structures (Figures 5.16 and 5.17). Full-scale compartment tests, meant to simulate some high intensity fires (with added fuels placed on the floor), failed to mimic many of the striking fire patterns found archaeologically.

Clearly, huge amounts of additional fuels must have been present in some of the structures. Computer models reveal that roof hatches, when closed, made prehistoric living quarters untenable and allowed heat from a hearth or other fuel loads to build. Recent discovery of rooms with solid roofs filled with burned corn provide a context in which high intensity fires could have developed. The possibility of fire spread between structures, given the addition of large amounts of corn, was proven to be possible with the aid of wind during experiments in 2006.

Even with multiple lines of evidence, we may never determine the accidental or intentional nature of every fire event that occurred at Chevelon. Each excavated structure must be examined on a case by case basis using the preserved evidence at hand. Great care should be taken when expanding the application of new techniques to ancient evidence. Archaeologists and fire professionals must be aware of the capabilities and limitations of each discipline, but should not be intimidated by the unknown.

Figure 5.16. Heavily oxidized south wall to Structure 123.

Figure 5.17. Sintered roofing material from Structure 123.

Chapter 6
Pottery
Elisabeth Cutright-Smith and Claire S. Barker

The ceramic assemblage from Chevelon Pueblo provides an important body of data that can be utilized to address overarching research questions guiding the excavation and analysis of artifacts recovered from this site and the HSC as a whole. The research questions, set forth for Chevelon by E.C. Adams (2002), coalesce around four major foci including site chronology; ceramic production, use and exchange; the organization of the site; and understanding the structural burning events that occurred at Chevelon Pueblo.

First, the composition of the ceramic assemblage is fundamentally important to refining the chronology of growth and abandonment of the site and placing it within the context of temporal patterns in construction and social organization of other HSC sites. Chronological resolution facilitates the understanding of changes in patterns of ceramic production and exchange as well as interaction between Chevelon residents, inhabitants of other sites within the HSC, and people living in nearby settlement clusters.

Second, the ceramic data allow trends in the production, exchange, and use of ceramics to be examined on both an intra- and inter-site level. Questions about the origins and social identities of residents of different areas of the village can be addressed through analysis of the spatial distribution of key ceramic wares. Additionally, different frequencies of ceramic wares between sites can reveal differences in the demography of sites within the HSC.

Third, excavations over the course of four field seasons have focused on structures that were used for different purposes. Particularly pertinent to ASM's focus on understanding the structure and organization of ritual at Homol'ovi sites, the ceramic assemblage may also be analyzed with attention to differences in the distribution of ceramics between ritual structures and storage/habitation structures at Chevelon. Distinctions between materials recovered from ritual structures and those from structures representing other uses may inform existing knowledge about social interactions maintained by Chevelon residents that facilitated ritual performance.

Finally, the prevalence of structural burning at Chevelon makes the site distinct within the HSC. Burning is identifiable within the ceramic assemblage and analysis of its incidence and appearance on the artifacts can indicate trends in burning across the site, particularly when viewed along temporal and spatial axes.

TOTAL CERAMIC ASSEMBLAGE

Classification

The classification of ceramics in the Chevelon assemblage follows the typology utilized by Hays (1991), Hays-Gilpin et al. (1996), and

Lyons and Hays-Gilpin (2001) for other sites in the HSC. These earlier analyses draw on the ceramic type descriptions proposed by Colton and Hargrave (1937), Colton (1956), Carlson (1970), and Gifford and Smith (1978). Smith's (1971) study of Hopi Yellow Ware types and Triadan's (1994) refinement of White Mountain Red Ware (WMRW) types inform classification of these major decorated wares. Further, Hay's (1991) Jeddito Yellow Ware (JYW) type, Paayu Polychrome, and utility ware, Homol'ovi Gray Ware (HGW), identified in the H2 assemblage, are incorporated into the analysis of ceramics from Chevelon. Hays-Gilpin and van Hartesveldt (1998) redefined and clarified decorated and utility ceramics from the Puerco Valley, east of Chevelon, an important contribution, particularly to the utility ware assemblage at Chevelon. Finally, Barker (2015), as part of her dissertation research, revised and retyped much of the utility ware ceramic assemblage originally typed by Lisa Gavioli and coauthor, Cutright-Smith.

Chevelon Distributions

The distribution of decorated and utility wares in the Chevelon assemblage, presented in Table 6.1, reflects the analysis of a total of 23,718 sherds from excavated contexts between 2003 and 2006. As is evident from the table, four decorated wares — JYW, Winslow Orange Ware (WOW), WMRW, and Roosevelt Red Ware (RRW) — are the most strongly represented in the Chevelon assemblage (Figures 6.1-6.4). Each constitutes at least 2 percent, by sherd count and weight, of the total assemblage. Additionally, three utility wares — Homolovi Orange Ware (HOW) and HGW (lumped together due to the difficulty in establishing consistent criteria for distinguishing burned specimens of these wares (see Lyons and Hays-Gilpin 2001), Tusayan Gray Ware (TGW), and Mogollon Brown Ware (MBW) — are represented in proportions greater than 2 percent, by sherd count and weight, of the total Chevelon assemblage. In fact, they each represent more than 7 percent by count and 13 percent by weight (Table 6.1, Figures 6.5-6.8).

Percentages by ware are reported, both as the percent of total sherd count and percent of total sherd weight. There is an obvious discrepancy between the percent JYW (%JYW), by sherd count and sherd weight. JYW is overrepresented in the sherd count because of the ease of recovering very small indeterminate JYW sherds during excavation. These sherds contribute very minimally to the total sherd weight and, thus, the JYW count is inflated with respect to weight. Where possible, frequencies are given in both percent total sherd count and weight. It should be noted that total ceramics and totals for individual wares do not always match in the tables that follow. This is because each table represents a subset, albeit usually large, of the total assemblage. For example, not every sherd could be assigned to a phase.

Comparisons Within the HSC

These gross distributions of decorated and utility wares in the Chevelon assemblage contrast with distributions evidenced at other sites in the HSC, which are presented in Table 6.2. JYW is the most common ceramic type in the Chevelon assemblage, yet it is found in higher proportions at H2 and in late deposits at H1. By contrast, the proportion of WOW in the Chevelon assemblage is significantly less than all HSC sites *except* H2 and late contexts at H1. As will be discussed further, this pattern is consistent with the findings of Hays-Gilpin

Table 6.1. Number, Weight, and Percentage for Each by Ware from Analyzed Ceramics at Chevelon.

Wares	Count	% total	Weight (g)	% total	Mean Sherd Weight (g)
Hopi White Ware	25	0.11	152	0.08	6.07
Jeddito Yellow Ware	11118	46.88	36996	20.63	3.33
Awatovi Yellow Ware	168	0.71	3676	2.05	21.88
Winslow Orange Ware	2547	10.74	15952	8.89	6.26
Homol'ovi Orange/Gray Ware	1749	7.37	24766	13.81	14.16
Alameda Brown Ware	3	0.01	118	0.07	39.33
White Mountain Red Ware	813	3.43	4952	2.76	6.09
Tusayan White Ware	199	0.84	801	0.45	4.03
Tusayan Gray Ware	1946	8.20	30775	17.16	15.81
Little Colorado White Ware	141	0.59	980	0.55	6.95
Little Colorado Gray Ware	54	0.23	560	0.31	10.37
Tsegi Orange Ware	114	0.48	822	0.46	7.21
Cibola White Ware	311	1.31	2023	1.13	6.50
Roosevelt Red Ware	475	2.00	3408	1.90	7.18
Mogollon Brown Ware	3448	14.54	48981	27.31	14.21
Unknown Plain Ware	101	0.43	1114	0.62	11.03
San Francisco Mountain Gray Ware	2	0.01	16	0.01	8.00
Zuni Types	37	0.16	191	0.11	5.17
Unknown Decorated Ware	143	0.60	466	0.26	3.26
Prescott Gray Ware	1	0.00	4	0.00	4.0
Cibola Gray Ware	6	0.03	54	0.03	9.00
Early Jeddito Yellow Ware	72	0.30	539	0.30	7.49
Puerco Valley Utility Ware	208	0.88	1689	0.94	11.23
Puerco Valley-like Utility Ware	28	0.12	246	0.14	8.12
Puerco Valley-like Decorated Ware	5	0.02	22	0.01	4.40
Other Local Utility Ware	4	0.02	36	0.02	9.00
Total	23718	100.00	179339	100.00	7.56

et al. (1996), Lyons and Hays-Gilpin (2001), Bubemyre (2004) and LaMotta (2006), with respect to temporal trends in the production and use of decorated wares throughout the HSC.

The percentage of WMRW found at Chevelon is significantly greater than the proportion recovered from any other site in the HSC. Particularly revealing is the high incidence of WMRW at Chevelon when compared with contemporaneous deposits at H1; the proportion of WMRW in the Chevelon assemblage is nearly double that in the H1 assemblage. Finally, RRW is four to six times more abundant at Chevelon than at any other Homol'ovi pueblo. The implications of elevated levels of red wares in the Chevelon assemblage for models of exchange, immigration and local ceramic production, will be examined further.

Homol'ovi utility wares (HUW)'s comprise a lower percentage of the total ceramic assemblage than any HSC assemblage except H4 (Table 6.2, Figure 6.5). The founding

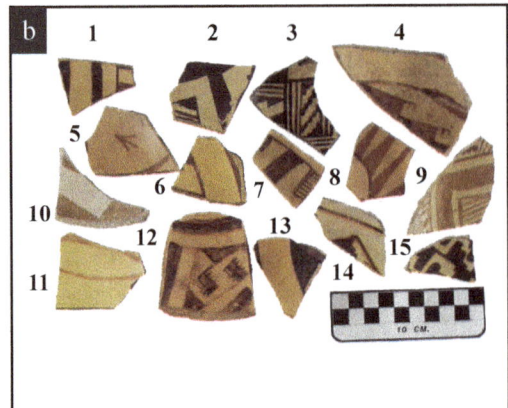
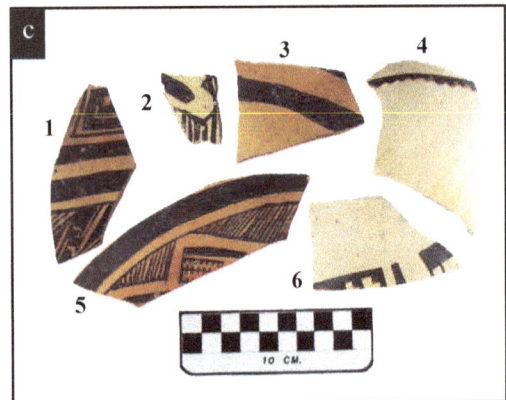
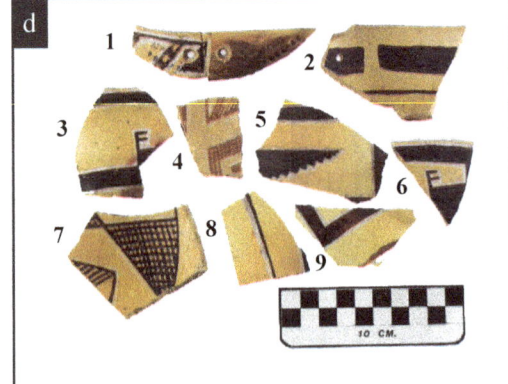

Figure 6.1. Jeddito Yellow Ware sherds: (a) Awatovi and Jeddito Black-on-yellow bowl rims with banding lines; (b) Jeddito Black-on-yellow bowls; (c) Jeddito Black-on-yellow jars; (d) Bidahochi Polychrome, and (e) Jeddito Black-on-yellow Style B (engraved).

Chapter 6: Pottery   121

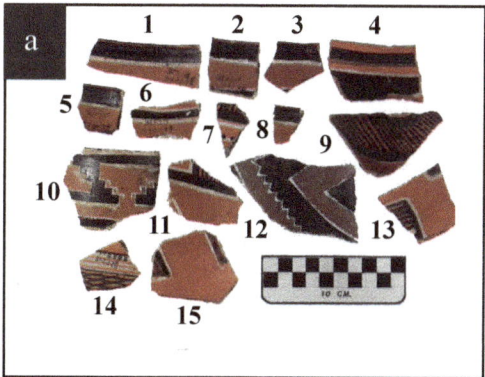

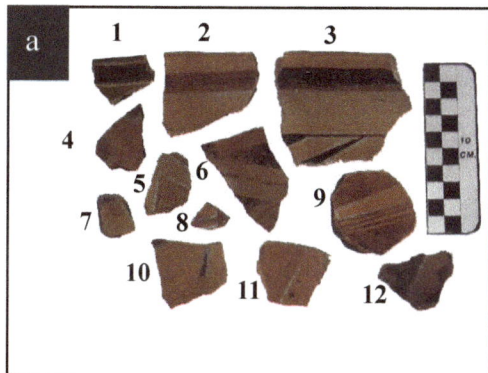

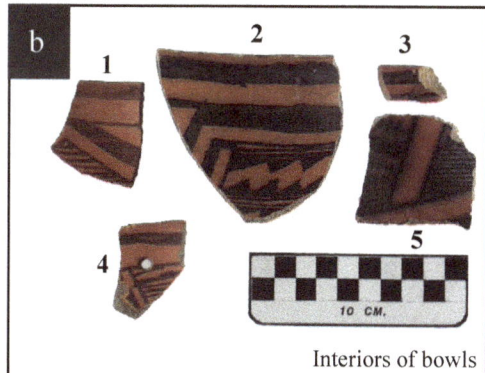

Figure 6.2. Winslow Orange Ware sherds: (a) Homol'ovi Polychrome; (b,c) Chavez Pass Polychrome.

Figure 6.3. White Mountain Red Ware sherds: (a) Fourmile Polychrome; (b,c) Cedar Creek Polychrome; (d) Showlow Polychrome.

  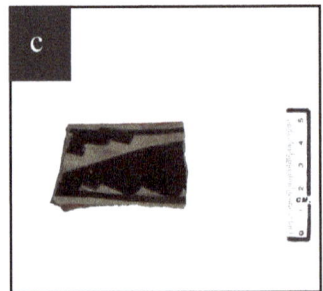

Figure 6.4. Roosevelt Red Ware sherds: (a) Tonto Polychrome; (b,c) Gila Black-on-white and Polychrome

Figure 6.5. Homol'ovi Utility Ware sherds (a) Homolovi Gray and Orange Corrugated sherds. (b) Burned utility ware sherds.

Figure 6.6. Tusayan Gray Corrugated jar sherds.

Figure 6.7. Mogollon Brown Ware sherds: (a,b) Obliterated brown; (c,d) Corrugated gray.

Figure 6.8. Puerco Valley Utility Ware sherds: (a) Corrugated; (b) Plain.

Chapter 6: Pottery   123

Table 6.2. Percentage of Wares from Excavated Homol'ovi Settlement Cluster Villages (E.C. Adams 2002: Table 7.1., unpublished tables for Homol'ovi II).

Ceramic Wares	H4	H3: Early	H3: Late	H2	H1: Early	H1: Late	Chevelon
Jeddito Yellow Ware	0.94	0.98	7.67	49.1	2.51	30.71	46.88
Jeddito Orange Ware	6.85	1.17	0.81	0.4	2.12	0.47	0.30
Winslow Orange Ware	18.19	24.45	21.45	6.8	30.67	13.21	10.74
White Ware	10.37	3.35	3.39	2.6	3.48	3.18	2.85
White Mountain Red Ware	0.44	0.86	1.81	0.3	0.68	1.83	3.43
Roosevelt Red Ware	0.23	0.33	0.56	0.3	0.20	0.30	2.00
Total Decorated	37.67	35.68	38.81	60.0	44.64	49.70	58.07
Total Utility Ware	62.33	64.32	61.19	40.0	55.36	50.30	41.93
Homol'ovi Orange/Gray Ware	3.7	52.44	45.1	20.2	43.69		7.37
Awatovi Yellow Ware			0.46	6.2			0.71
Tusayan Gray Ware	36.42	3.5	2.0	4.3	5.2		8.20
Little Colorado Gray Ware	6.77			0.5	0.19		0.23
Other: Mogollon, Puerco Valley, Cibola, etc.	1.5	5.7	9.75	8.2	2.02		25.41
Alameda Brown Ware	13.95	2.68	2.97	0.6	0.29		0.01
Total Ceramics	16734	18650	22618	28349	1035	28161[1]	23718

[1]Includes only decorated ceramics analyzed by LaMotta (2006).

of H4 corresponds to the beginning of the local ceramic manufacturing tradition. Prior to the local production of pottery, people would have relied on exchange to acquire ceramics, which likely explains the relative scarcity of HUW's in the H4 assemblage. The low frequency of HUW's at Chevelon, however, is a result of higher frequencies of MBW and TGW than at any other HSC pueblo, measured using either count or weight.

This discrepancy was revealed during the reanalysis of Chevelon utility wares by Barker (2015), which resulted in the discovery that many HOW and HGW were more properly identified as MBW, based on characteristics of paste and temper. Reanalysis of other HSC utility wares may result in changes in frequencies presently reported in Table 6.2. Observations by Barker (2015), on the ceramic assemblages of other HSC sites, suggest that the frequency of HUW's at these sites is roughly consistent with the frequencies presented in Table 6.2. TGW is more abundant at Chevelon than at all HSC sites except H4 (Table 6.2, Figure 6.6). However, the differentiation of TGW from HGW was sometimes problematic in the predominantly burned Chevelon assemblage (Gavioli 2005).

Finally, MBW is more common at Chevelon than any other HSC village, as well as being the most common utility ware at Chevelon (Table 6.2, Figures 6.7-6.8). This is likely due, in part, to the more direct access Chevelon had to the Mogollon Rim and contemporary communities residing there than other HSC villages. In addition to proximity, the high frequencies suggest groups moved to Chevelon from these areas. The timing and location of this move within Chevelon pueblo will be treated below.

Interregional Comparisons

Table 6.1 presents the Chevelon data. Table 6.3 presents the distribution of decorated wares in the assemblages from two Pueblo IV (PIV) sites in the upper Silver Creek drainage, one dating 1275 to 1325 and the other 1200 to 1280, that were excavated by the Silver Creek Archaeological Research Program (Mills 1999). Table 6.3 also includes data from Puerco Ruin dating 1250 to 1350 (1988-1989 excavations by NPS [Vint and Burton 1990]), and three PIV sites in the Upper Little Colorado Region, dating 1325 to 1385, analyzed by Duff (1999, 2002). These data underscore regional differences in decorated ware production and circulation. Whereas decorated ceramics imported from the Hopi Mesas to the north (JYW) dominate the Chevelon assemblage along with ceramics produced locally in the Winslow area (WOW); it is clear that ceramics locally produced by Homol'ovi residents did not circulate to sites in either the Silver Creek or ULC regions, nor in the Puerco Valley where most WOW were locally produced (Vint and Burton 1990).

Further, while the Silver Creek sites represent pre-JYW occupations (Mills 1999), and thus the absence of Hopi Yellow Wares is expected at these sites, the differential distribution of JYW across PIV sites in the upper Little Colorado region suggests that residents of Table Rock maintained different interregional formal social relationships than did residents of contemporaneous sites in the region (Duff 2002). In terms of yellow ware, Puerco Ruin is between the frequency at Chevelon and those farther east and south, due to its intermediate location with respect to Hopi Mesa villages and its occupation ending 40 to 50 years earlier than Chevelon, before yellow ware exchange spiked. Interregional

Table 6.3. Number and Percentage of Decorated Wares from Selected Silver Creek and Upper Little Colorado Pueblos.

Wares	Silver Creek Pueblos				Upper Little Colorado Pueblos					
	Pottery Hill		Bailey Ruin		Table Rock		Rattlesnake Point		Hooper Ranch	
	Count	%	Count	%	count	%	count	%	count	%
Cibola White Ware	5461	22.83	12666	16.25	300	1.41	1197	4.63	3175	0.22
Tusayan White Ware	7	0.03	13	0.02						
Little Colorado White Ware	65	0.27	14	0.02						
Puerco Valley Red Ware	1026	4.29	1357	1.74						
Roosevelt Red Ware	95	0.40	4870	6.25	1988	9.38	913	3.53	20	0.00
White Mountain Red Ware	360	1.51	8611	11.05	142	0.67	742	2.87	892	0.06
San Juan Red Ware	3	0.01								
Tsegi Orange Ware	1	0.00	13	0.02						
Winslow Orange Ware	3	0.01	4	0.01						
Jeddito Yellow Ware			4	0.01	803	3.79	24	0.09	4	0.00
Early Zuni Glaze Ware			55	0.07	964	4.55	3399	13.13	635	0.04
Painted Brown Ware	251	1.05	392	0.50						
Undecorated	16541	69.16	48971	62.84	17006	80.21	19605	75.75	10026	68.00
Total	23916	100.00	77928	100.00	21203	100.00	25880	100.00	14752	100.00

social networks and the implications of these networks for expressions of group social identity are explored further below and likely involved utility as well as decorated wares.

Cibola White Ware (CWW) dominates the assemblages from Pottery Hill and Bailey Ruin. Specimens of CWW, analyzed in these assemblages, display a range of variation in paste composition that suggests the use of clays found along the Mogollon Rim as well as the confluence of the LCR and Silver Creek (Mills 1999:245). Local production and consumption of CWW vessels is evidenced in these assemblages. At Chevelon, CWW comprises a mere 1.3 percent by count and 1.1 percent by weight of the total ceramic assemblage, likely because the production of most CWW types predates, or minimally overlaps with, the occupation of Chevelon (Mills et al. 1999: Table 8.4). Similarly, assemblages from the late PIV sites in the Puerco Ruin and upper Little Colorado region, with the exception of Hooper Ranch, also lack significant CWW sherds.

As classically defined (Carlson 1970; Graves 1984), the Silver Creek region has been identified as the primary production center of late WMRW types (Pinedale and later), although subsequent analyses have identified production centers in the Arizona Mountains (Triadan 1997) and in the upper Little Colorado region (Duff 1999, 2002). Compositional analyses, conducted on Fourmile Polychrome samples from several Homol'ovi sites, have indicated the circulation of ceramics to Homol'ovi from two production centers in the Silver Creek region (Duff 2002:142; Triadan 1997).

Furthermore, although local production of WMRW in the upper Little Colorado region has been established, several samples from sites in this area also indicate the movement of WMRW vessels from production centers in the Silver Creek area to the upper Little Colorado region (Duff 2002:112). Therefore, the abundance of WMRW from the Silver Creek area at Chevelon is consistent with a general model of production and distribution. However, the density of WMRW in deposits at Chevelon, compared to upper Little Colorado pueblos, suggests that Chevelon residents maintained stronger ties to the Silver Creek area than did residents of other HSC villages or the upper Little Colorado pueblos, as elaborated below. The specialness of this relationship is underscored by the low frequency of WMRW recovered from Puerco Ruin (Table 6.3), which is the same distance to the production zone as Chevelon.

Lyons (2003) has demonstrated that the production of RRW is closely associated with populations that migrated out of the Kayenta-Tusayan region and into virtually every river drainage in eastern Arizona, between 1260 and 1290. These populations, and their descendants, largely controlled RRW production throughout its developmental sequence (Lyons 2003:74). The strongest evidence for the initial production of RRW types is found at Chodistaas and other pueblos in the Grasshopper region of the Arizona Mountains (Crown 1994; Lyons 2003; Mills et al. 1999; Zedeño 1994).

Thus, the abundance of RRW at Bailey Ruin, in the Silver Creek region and at Table Rock, in the upper Little Colorado region, indicates the immigration of these Kayenta-Tusayan Anasazi populations from the Arizona Mountains (Mills et al. 1999:322). The density of RRW deposits in the Chevelon assemblage most likely denotes the immigration of groups from either the Arizona mountains or Silver Creek region, rather than direct migration of Kayenta-Tusayan RRW producers into the Homol'ovi area. Details of this argument will be presented below.

The production of various corrugated utility wares, at Chevelon and in other HSC pueblos, has typically focused on locally produced HUW's and TGW. It is now clear that Tusayan Corrugated continued to be produced into the late 1300s, as it is common at H2, which was likely not founded until about 1365 (E.C. Adams and Hays 1991; Lange 2017). Alameda Brown Ware, while common at H4 (E.C. Adams 2004a), is generally rare in other HSC pueblos. The redefinition of Puerco Valley ceramics in 1998, which include Showlow Red Ware and Puerco Valley Utility Ware, has added to the diversity of wares now understood to be present in HSC villages, especially at Chevelon. The presence of MBW in HSC villages has, until now, been underappreciated. Many MBW sherds have been mistyped as HOW or HGW. It is also likely that many sherds produced locally in the HSC may have been manufactured in the Mogollon tradition. These groups may have come from villages discovered in recent work 5 to 8 km south of Chevelon where multiple small pueblos have been documented and one tested with radiocarbon dates extending into the mid-1200s (E.C. Adams 2016).

TEMPORAL TRENDS

Building Chronologies — Methodology

Ceramic seriation and cross-dating are the two most powerful chronology-building techniques used at Homol'ovi sites (E.C. Adams 2001, 2002; LaMotta 2006). Whereas tree-ring and radiocarbon dating have been widely applied to obtain absolute dates at sites throughout the Southwest, the efficacy of these dating techniques is compromised by the location and timing of construction in the HSC. Because the HSC is situated within a riparian environment, cottonwood is the predominant wood species utilized in construction at Chevelon, while the availability of driftwood suitable for construction sometimes made it a preferred alternative (Chapter 12; E.C. Adams and Hedberg 2002). Because cottonwood does not display the diagnostic variability in tree-rings necessary to date cutting events (Lyons 2001:126-7), and tree-ring dated driftwood samples produce only a date ante quem for structure construction, neither is suitable for dating construction or deposits (E.C. Adams 2002:59).

Radiocarbon dates have been obtained from contexts at H1 and H2 (see LaMotta 2006 for a summary), yet their precision is compromised by the plateau in the calibration curve corresponding to the fourteenth century, the period during which the majority of construction in the HSC occurs. This plateau often produces an error range for calibrated radiocarbon dates that encompasses virtually the entire century, complicating precise dating within this period (LaMotta 2006). Even multiple targeted samples produce a sigma of about 25 years (LaMotta 2006). Applied together, however, ceramic cross-dating and the careful interpretation of radiocarbon dates obtained from contexts at H1 have verified the assignment of absolute dates to temporal slices reflected in seriation indices at the village (LaMotta 2006). Therefore, ceramic seriation is relied upon for the relative dating of structures and sites in the HSC, while tree-ring dated diagnostic types anchor relative chronologies to absolute dates.

Temporal Phase Scheme

Because WOW is replaced by JYW in the temporal sequence of the HSC (Hays-Gilpin et al. 1996:73), the proportion of these two wares is an important chronological index. At H1, the percent of yellow-hued JYW in the decorated assemblage is considered the primary temporal marker (LaMotta 2006). The use of JYW as a chronological index at H1 is supported by correspondence between the %JYW within the sequence and the actual sequence of stratified deposits. In addition to %JYW, five other attributes of JYW have been determined to be temporally sensitive. These include the rim-to-banding line distance, banding line width (Figure 6.9), rim form, paste color (hue), and temper density (LaMotta 2006). The independent seriation of these attributes that corroborate the percent of JYW seriation confirms its temporal sensitivity.

The phase system devised by LaMotta (2006) using this index is presented in Table 6.4. This chronological model is initially used to date Chevelon deposits on the basis of similarities in layout and development between the villages (E.C. Adams 2002:186-187). Importantly, LaMotta situates the beginning of the Late Homol'ovi Phase (LHP) at the introduction of the late JYW type, Sikyatki Polychrome. At H1, Sikyatki Polychrome first appears in deposits containing 60 %JYW. However, at Chevelon, Sikyatki Polychrome first appears in deposits containing 72 %JYW, which occurs in stratum 4 of S. 373. The %JYW that is applied to Chevelon deposits is revised from that which LaMotta applies to H1 in order to reflect this difference.

Evaluating the Jeddito Yellow Ware Index at Chevelon

In order to simplify the evaluation of the %JYW temporal sensitivity at Chevelon, the distribution of three well-dated WMRW types and two RRW types within strata from K. 279 was evaluated against the start and end dates assigned to those strata on the basis of the %JYW. Table 6.5 presents the results of this analysis. As indicated in the table, the three temporally sensitive WMRW types selected are Pinedale Polychrome (1290 to 1330), Fourmile Polychrome (1330 to 1390), and Showlow Polychrome (1330 to 1390). The two RRW types are Gila and Tonto polychromes (1350 to 1400). Start and end dates for production of these types are based on data presented by Mills and Herr (1999) and E.C. Adams (2002: Table 4.6).

Based on these production dates, it is clear that all WMRW types fall into the correct temporal phase derived from the %JYW, with the exception of the Pinedale Polychrome sherds recovered from Middle Homol'ovi Phase (MHP) deposits, which are from a single vessel in S. 274, stratum 4. While production of Pinedale Polychrome in the Silver Creek region ceases around 1330, these sherds are present in fill dated to 1365 to 1385. The deposit is clearly out-of-phase, that is, the %JYW is at variance with all the other deposits, each of which has at least 350 sherds. The Pinedale Polychrome appears to be an heirloom piece deposited some 30 or more years after its creation. The RRW types complement the information derived from the WMRW types revealing a peak in its deposition in the upper four deposits of S. 279 (below the collapsed roof of the kiva), again ignoring the problematic S. 274, stratum 4. Thus, the dating of the S. 274/279 deposits using WMRW and RRW confirms dates assigned to these deposits using the %JYW derived from LaMotta's (2006) work at H1 and H2 and justifies its application to the deposits at Chevelon. Furthermore, the combination of %JYW and frequency of WMRW and RRW suggests that the filling of S. 274/279 took several decades, from before 1350 to about 1385.

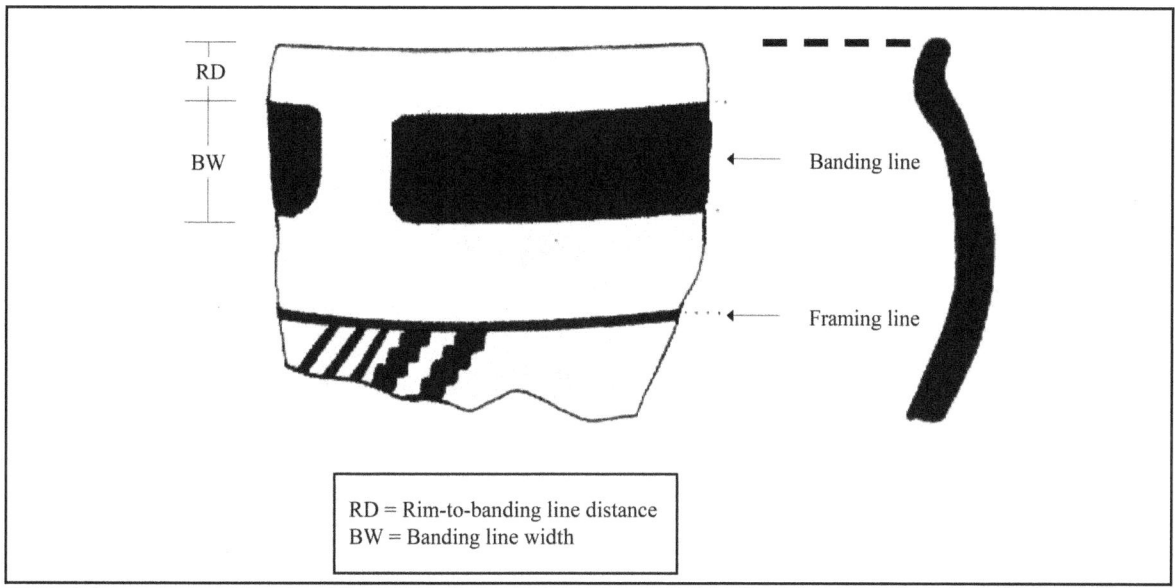

Figure 6.9. Location of measurements on Jeddito Yellow Ware bowls to determine banding line width and rim-to-banding line distance.

Table 6.4. Ceramic Dates for Deposits at Chevelon Based on Percentage of Jeddito Yellow Ware, Adapted from LaMotta (2006).

Ceramic Phase	Approximate Dates (C.E.)	%JYW Seriation used at H1	%JYW (proportion of total decorated) used at Chevelon
Late Homol'ovi Phase	1385-1400	60-100	72-100
Middle Homol'ovi Phase	1365-1385	40.0-59.9	40-71.9
Early Homol'ovi Phase	1325/1330-1365	1-39.9	1-39.9
Tuwiuca Phase	1290-1330		

¹The transition between MHP and LHP is the %JYW present when Sikyatki Polychrome first appears. This accounts for the discrepancy between H1 and Chevelon.

Seriation of Excavated Deposits

The seriation of all analyzed deposits from the 2003 to 2006 excavations is presented in Appendix A. In total, 63 individual strata from excavated structures were assigned phase designations. The decorated sherd counts for the remaining strata identified in the field were of insufficient size (fewer than 30 sherds) to assign phase designations with confidence. A total of 57 of the 63 dated strata (90.5 percent) seriate in the proper depositional sequence. Most of those that are out-of-sequence are considered in appropriate sections below. The situation for S. 274, stratum 4, has already been discussed.

At Chevelon, only four excavated strata were assigned to the Tuwiuca Phase (TP), dated to 1290 to 1330, two of which were excavated from a subfloor unit in RB300. Eleven strata

Table 6.5. Number of White Mountain Red Ware and Roosevelt Red Ware Sherds Within Kiva 274/279 by Stratum.

Structure	Strat	JYW Phase -%JYW	Phase dates	Pinedale Poly count	Fourmile Poly count	Showlow Poly count	Unidentified	Total	Gila & Tonto Polychrome	Date Range from WMRW and RRW
274	3	LHP-75.9	1385-1400				20	20	20	1350-1400
	4	MHP-40.3	1365-1385	35	7		58	100	13	1290-1385
279	1-4	MHP-58.5	1365-1385		6	6	12	24	131	1350-1400
	7	MHP-48.8	1365-1385	3	13	3	107	126	17	1330-1385
	16	EHP-27.1	1325/30-1365		14	4	66	84	2	1330-1350

were assigned to the Early Homol'ovi Phase (EHP) dated 1325/1330 to 1365. EHP deposits are confined to RB200 with the exception of two early dates in RB100, resulting primarily from the presence of what is at least one, and perhaps multiple, reconstructible Tonto Polychrome jars, as well as the incorporation of earlier decorated white wares through curation and from the Basketmaker occupation of the site (Andrews 1982). Sixteen strata were dated to the MHP, 1365 to 1385. Of these strata, twelve were excavated from K. 279 and surrounding structures in the center of RB200. Finally, 32 strata were assigned a LHP designation dated 1385 to 1400. The upper strata in several RB200 and RB100 structures were dated to the LHP, yet the bulk of the LHP ceramic assemblage was recovered from K. 901, the large kiva in RB300. These data indicate the relatively early filling of structures in RB200 and 300 followed by more extensive filling throughout the pueblo during the LHP.

The %JYW is successful in relatively dating stratified deposits at Chevelon, as is indicated by the accurate chronological sequencing of deposits within structures, as well as in the relative sequencing of filling events across the site. These results support its use as a chronological marker. Thus, the phases demarcated by the %JYW provide a viable means of subdividing the ceramic assemblage in order to isolate temporal trends.

Temporal Trends in Jeddito Yellow Ware and Winslow Orange Ware Distribution

Several temporal trends are evident in the distribution by phase of the four major decorated wares recovered from the site — JYW, WOW, WMRW, and RRW — as presented in Table 6.6.

Following the trend articulated by Hays-

Gilpin et al. (1996) for other HSC sites, WOW is the second most ubiquitous decorated ware at Chevelon, but its incidence decreases in frequency through the temporal phases as JYW comes to dominate the decorated assemblage. This waning of WOW and waxing of JYW, in the excavated strata, reflects a restructuring of the means by which decorated ceramics were acquired at Chevelon.

Local production of pottery in the HSC began around 1260 (Lange 1998:50). While research has yet to be conducted on samples from the Chevelon assemblage, ceramic oxidation studies (Lyons 2001; Lyons 2003; Vaitkus 1986), as well as neutron activation analysis (Lyons 2003:45) have indicated that the majority of WOW types were produced using local clay sources. These results are further supported by the recovery of unfired clay coils and patties, as well as artifacts associated with vessel manufacture, from H3 and H4 (Lyons and Hays-Gilpin 2001:226; Lyons 2003).

Local production of pottery at Chevelon is indicated by the recovery of 23 polishing stones from 12 structures, all but four from RB200, RB300, and early rooms in RB100 (see Chapter 7). Because these areas date to the TP and EHP, when local production of pottery is predicted, their distribution supports the probability of local production of decorated and utility wares at Chevelon.

Local decorated production declined in the HSC by approximately 1350 (Hays 1991:131) and was replaced by the import of JYW. The inflection point in the JYW and WOW distributions falls within the MHP. As the bracketing dates for this phase are 1365 to 1385, WOW production likely ceased entirely or was greatly curtailed during this period. Several factors promoting the end of local pottery production have been proposed, including the dearth of wood fuel (E.C. Adams et al. 1993:14; E.C. Adams 2002:58; Hays 1991:47; Hays-Gilpin et al. 1996:74) in conjunction with population growth (E.C. Adams et al. 1993:14) and the increasing involvement of Homol'ovi occupants in a multifaceted exchange network with Hopi Mesa communities. The transition from reliance on locally produced, decorated ceramics to imported, decorated ceramics from Hopi Mesa communities is evidenced in the Chevelon assemblage, as it is in the assemblages from the other HSC pueblos. However, the persistence of local production of utility wares implies that the importation of yellow wares was as much about creating or maintaining social relationships and possibly prestige as it was about resource depletion.

Temporal Trends in Red Ware Distribution

An interesting pattern is revealed in the distribution through time of WMRW in Chevelon deposits. Although WMRW is nearly absent in TP deposits, its proportion in the decorated assemblage peaks during the EHP at 14.5 percent (Table 6.6). This phase begins at the transition from the end of production of Pinedale Polychrome (dated 1290 to 1330) to the beginning of production of Fourmile Polychrome (dated 1330 to 1390) (Mills and Herr 1999). Fourmile Polychrome is the most abundant WMRW type followed by Pinedale Polychrome. The abundance of WMRW decreases in the succeeding MHP and LHP, yet the proportion that it comprises during these periods is nonetheless greater than in the total decorated assemblage from any other HSC site (compare Table 6.2).

When the distribution by phase is analyzed against data from H1 and H3, presented in Tables 6.7 and 6.8 (LaMotta 2006: Table 2.7), roughly similar temporal trends at these sites

Table 6.6. Number and Percentage of Total Decorated of the Four Most
Common Decorated Wares at Chevelon by Ceramic Phase.

Phase	Jeddito Yellow Ware		Winslow Orange Ware		White Mountain Red Ware		Roosevelt Red Ware		Total Decorated
	count	%	count	%	count	%	count	%	count
Tuwuica	3	1.0	185	64.7	2	0.7	33	11.5	286
EHP	342	28.1	394	32.4	176	14.5	73	6.0	1217
MHP	1524	51.8	793	26.9	262	8.9	162	5.5	2943
LHP	7880	84.5	786	8.4	239	2.6	175	1.9	9328
Total	9749	70.8	2158	15.7	679	4.9	443	3.2	13,774

are evident. The ubiquity of WMRW also peaks during the EHP at H3 and then declines in later deposits. At H1, the peak occurs somewhat later, during the MHP, before declining in the LHP. However, the most striking pattern, indicated by a comparison of these three sites, is the elevated level of WMRW at Chevelon as compared with H1 and H3 during each temporal phase following 1330.

The general abundance of WMRW at Chevelon suggests that residents may have participated in different ceramic exchange networks than residents of contemporaneous Homol'ovi sites, or that Chevelon may have been a node in down-the-line exchange of WMRW from the Silver Creek region to other HSC sites. As discussed above, the Silver Creek region is traditionally defined as the core WMRW production area (Carlson 1970; Graves 1984, Mills et al. 1999; Triadan 1997).

While the production, particularly of late WMRW types, has been demonstrated in the Grasshopper (Triadan 1997) and upper Little Colorado (Duff 2002) regions, the results of Triadan's compositional analysis indicate that, as in the upper Little Colorado region, several WMRW samples recovered from Homol'ovi sites were clearly produced using clays from the Silver Creek region (Duff 2002:142). This evidence supports Duff's (2002) inference that occupants of the middle LCR area maintained distinct interregional ties with Silver Creek residents. Whether or not these ties are the product of past migrations into the Homol'ovi area from the Silver Creek region, the consumption of WMRW vessels exemplifies the overt expression of a distinct group identity (or identities) by the Chevelon population as a whole, or a segment of the population versus their nearest neighbors. The relative abundance of MBW, at Chevelon, indicates the decorated wares could be either products of exchange or migration. As considered below, the spatial distribution of WMRW vessels within structures at Chevelon may shed light on the location of participating social groups.

The deposition of WMRW in room fill at Chevelon begins diminishing at roughly the transition from the EHP to the MHP, dated to approximately 1365. This most likely reflects a decrease in the flow of the ware from the Silver Creek region to Chevelon around this time. Importantly, the EHP to MHP transition is also the period during which JYW comes to dominate the decorated assemblage. Therefore,

Table 6.7. Counts and Proportions of Select Temporally-Diagnostic Decorated Ceramic Wares and Types at Homol'ovi I, Organized By Ceramic Phase (LaMotta 2006).

Ware/Type	Phase							
	Tuwuica		Early Homol'ovi		Middle Homol'ovi		Late Homol'ovi	
	N	%	N	%	N	%	N	%
Jeddito Yellow Ware	2	0.3	2399	21.1	2122	46.1	9759	80.2
Bidahochi Poly			108	0.9	133	2.9	77	0.6
Paayu Poly					2	<0.1	14	0.1
Sikyatki Poly							50	0.4
Jeddito Stippled							6	<0.1
Jeddito Engraved							10	<0.1
White Mountain Red Ware	6	0.8	469	4.1	308	6.7	143	1.2
St. Johns Poly								
Pinedale B/r & Poly	2	0.3	8	<0.1	3	<0.1	12	<0.1
Cedar Creek Poly	1	0.1	9	<0.1	6	0.1	2	<0.1
Fourmile Poly			105	0.9	51	1.1	19	0.2
Showlow Poly					1	<0.1	1	<0.1
Zuni Types			16	0.1	19	0.4	25	0.2
Pinnawa G/w			14	0.1	16	0.3	13	0.1
Kechipawan Poly					3	<0.1	5	<0.1
Total decorated pieces	752		11,393		4606		12,162	

Table 6.8. Number and Frequency of White Mountain Red Ware Sherds by Ceramic Phase at Homol'ovi I and Homol'ovi III.

Site	Phase	Total Decorated Ware Sherds	WMRW Percent of Total Decorated Ware Sherds
Homol'ovi I	Tuwiuca	752	0.8
	Early Homol'ovi	11,393	4.1
	Middle Homol'ovi	4606	6.7
	Late Homol'ovi	12,162	1.2
Homol'ovi III	Tuwiuca	7155	2.2
	Early Homol'ovi	2475	5.2
	Middle Homol'ovi	6977	4.0

the distribution of WMRW, at this point in the occupation of Chevelon, may be a proxy for shifts in the focus of interaction from regions to the south and east to the north toward the Hopi Mesas (Lange 1998).

The deposition of WMRW continues to decline precipitously from the MHP to the LHP, when only 2.9 percent of ceramics (by sherd count) are WMRW types. This trend likely reflects the regional depopulation of the Silver

Creek area around 1385, at the beginning of the LHP (Mills and Herr 1999:292).

The distribution of RRW through time is presented in Table 6.6. Although TP deposits appear particularly rich in RRW, these sherds represent most of a reconstructible Pinto Polychrome bowl, which inflates the proportion of the small TP assemblage constituted by RRW. This vessel is important, however, in demonstrating early connections between Chevelon residents and producers of RRW pottery that predate 1330. Similarly, the majority of RRW sherds in the fill assemblage from S. 120 represents several reconstructible jars and causes the assemblage to be classified as EHP, when in fact it probably dates to the LHP (Figure 6.11b). Their appearance in the upper fill from a late-dating structure also inflates the proportion of RRW in the EHP. Other, reconstructible vessels are most notably present in K. 279. Due to large sample sizes and presence of multiple deposits in the kiva, they did not affect temporal assignment.

It appears, therefore, that the MHP was the primary period of RRW deposition at Chevelon, suggesting that RRW vessels were consumed somewhat later in the occupation of the site than were WMRW vessels. As with WMRW, a significant drop-off in RRW deposition is seen during the LHP, perhaps related to depopulation of the Silver Creek, upper Little Colorado River (ULCR), and mountain regions to the south and southeast.

Gavioli (2005) has reported that RRW samples in the Chevelon assemblage display variability in temper that does not follow conventional type descriptions. This was also noted in analysis of material from the 2005 and 2006 field seasons. Prior neutron activation studies of sherds from H1 and H3 have demonstrated that a proportion of RRW at these sites was produced in the Winslow area (Lyons and Hays-Gilpin 2001:156).

These sourcing data are particularly interesting in the context of the strong association between local RRW production and the serial migrations of ancestral Hopi groups. RRW ceramics are interpreted as one of a suite of hallmarks indicating the presence of ancestral Hopi populations originating in the Kayenta-Tusayan region of northeastern Arizona (Lyons 2003). The dating of the earliest RRW types is established on the basis of evidence from Point of Pines and Chodistaas in the Grasshopper region (Zedeño 1994). At these sites, the deposition of RRW is clearly associated with the archaeological signature of immigrants from the Kayenta-Tusayan area (Crown 1994; Zedeño 1994). As demonstrated by Lyons (2003), the production of RRW throughout eastern central and southeastern Arizona and northern Mexico closely tracks the movement of these migrant groups, who maintained control over RRW production throughout its developmental sequence (Lyons 2003:74).

Evidence of local RRW production by northern immigrants is abundant at Silver Creek pueblos as well as in the upper Little Colorado region at Table Rock, which was likely founded by immigrants from the Arizona Mountains after 1325 (Duff 2002:107, 156). Interestingly, residents of Table Rock maintained unique connections to the Hopi mesas that are archaeologically visible in relatively abundant deposits of JYW produced on the Hopi Mesas and not present at any contemporary site in the region. Further, Duff (2002) has suggested that RRW samples in the middle Little Colorado region were likely produced in the upper Little Colorado area—most likely at Table Rock (Duff 2002:156), a pattern also noted by Crown and Bishop (1991) based on sourcing of sherds from H2.

These findings further support the uniqueness of the probable migration of RRW-producing groups to Chevelon, late in its occupation, with its strong association with EHP and MHP deposits suggesting this likely occurred around 1365. Presence of MBW with RRW sherds and reconstructible vessels in K. 279 and RB100 deposits supports this interpretation.

In sum, it is clear that connections between Chevelon residents and RRW producers were established, or at least evidenced, very early in the occupation of the pueblo. Evidence from east-central Arizona indicates the movement of RRW-producing populations into the Arizona Mountains, the Silver Creek and upper Little Colorado regions during the early TP, roughly 1260 to 1290. It is likely, the founders of Chevelon were in contact with these groups during the late TP.

Recent research suggests a reverse migration of sorts after 1350 when Tonto and Gila Polychrome-producing groups migrated from the Arizona Mountains and possibly southeastern Arizona to the Silver Creek, ULCR, and Zuni areas (Clark 2011; D. A. Johnson 1992; Woodbury and Woodbury 1966). Crown and Bishop (1991) and Duff's (2002) analyses suggest that at least some RRW-producing groups in the upper Little Colorado region may have provided vessels to the Homol'ovi area, including Chevelon and H2. By the MHP, RRW appears in Chevelon deposits at higher proportions, including several whole or nearly whole bowls and jars bearing Tonto Polychrome designs than at any other Homol'ovi pueblo. There is evidence to suggest that some degree of local RRW production was conducted at Chevelon, probably representing a move by some of these late migrating groups to Chevelon. MBW is also featured at Chevelon from TP through MHP, peaking about 1365.

The appearance of RRW corresponds with the construction of the large south plaza and surrounding room blocks. Future compositional analyses may more strongly support this inference; however, the data currently available most parsimoniously indicate that groups producing RRW followed pre-existing social ties and migrated to Chevelon from east-central Arizona at the beginning of the MHP. The preponderance of whole and nearly whole vessels of RRW, locally produced and likely produced in Silver Creek or ULCR valley communities, are present in most excavated rooms in RB100 along with very high frequencies of MBW (Figure 6.7).

Temporal Trends in the Distribution of Diagnostic Decorated Types

In the Chevelon assemblage, only WOW, JYW, and WMRW were consistently typed beyond ware, and secure production dates for WOW types have not been determined as a result of the complications inherent in using tree-ring dates from HSC sites, although seriation of deposits at H3 suggest slipped types predate unslipped types (E.C. Adams 2001). Therefore, JYW and WMRW types are the most amenable to temporal analysis of the Chevelon material. Table 6.9 presents a break down by phase of JYW types recovered at Chevelon. By definition, JYW is not present in TP deposits, and the three errant sherds in the Chevelon assemblage were likely due to bioturbation. By looking at the appearance of JYW in villages across the Southwest and the tree-ring dated ceramics that occur in those sites, Benitez (1999) has shown that JYW exchange began at 1325 to 1330.

As is evident from the data, Awatovi/Jeddito Black-on-yellow is the most commonly identified JYW type throughout all phases of occupation. It co-occurs with Awatovi

Black-on-yellow, Jeddito Black-on-yellow, and Bidahochi Polychrome in all phases, but defines the start of EHP at about 1325 to 1330 (Figure 6.1). This overlap is because this artificial type construct represents the majority of sherds that could not be assigned to either yellow ware type due to their small size or lack of distinctive attributes (Hays 1991; LaMotta 2006). The diversity of JYW types deposited in room fill increases through time, reflecting the use and exchange of new types, and the continued use of types with early production start dates.

Particularly interesting is the appearance of Sikyatki Polychrome and Jeddito Engraved specimens in Chevelon deposits (Figure 6.1).

The presence of these two JYW types is used to define the start of the LHP by LaMotta (2006), who has determined production of Sikyatki Polychrome begins at approximately 1385 based on a regional assessment of associated tree-ring dates. Correspondence between relative and absolute chronological measures underscores the internal consistency of the temporal phase scheme at Chevelon. The proportion of Sikyatki Polychrome and Jeddito Engraved at Chevelon is reduced in comparison with H1 (Table 6.7). This is likely due to sampling.

While the vast majority of Sikyatki Polychrome sherds in the Chevelon assemblage were recovered from structure fill, S. 159,

Table 6.9. Number and Percentage of Jeddito Yellow Ware Sherds by Ceramic Phase.

Phase	Types	Count	%	Consensus Dates
Tuwiuca	Awatovi/Jeddito B/Y	2	0.7	1325-1625
	Indeterminate	1	0.3	
Early Homol'ovi	Awatovi B/Y	13	1.1	1325-1375
	Bidahochi Poly	16	1.3	1335-1385
	Jeddito B/Y	14	1.2	1350-1625
	Awatovi/Jeddito B/Y	266	21.9	1325-1425
	Indeterminate	21	1.7	
Middle Homol'ovi	Awatovi B/Y	27	0.9	1325-1375
	Bidahochi Poly	25	0.8	1325-1385
	Jeddito B/Y	6	0.2	1350-1625
	Awatovi/Jeddito B/Y	1115	37.9	1325-1425
	Sikyatki Poly	1		1385-1625
	Indeterminate	156	5.3	
Late Homol'ovi	Awatovi B/Y	248	2.7	1325-1375
	Bidahochi Poly	36	0.4	1325-1385
	Jeddito B/Y	927	9.9	1350-1625
	Awatovi/Jeddito B/Y	2167	23.2	1325-1425
	Sikyatki Poly	20	0.2	1385-1625
	Jeddito Engraved	3		1375-1625
	Paayu Poly	2		1365-1400
	Indeterminate	4538	48.6	

labeled by E.C. Adams (Chapter 4) as a "habitation room with ritual features," produced a large reconstructible Sikyatki Polychrome jar on its floor (Figure 6.10b). This jar was situated above a subfloor pit in the northwest corner of the structure that contained a small ladle bowl overlain by a whole locally manufactured Tonto Polychrome jar (Figure 6.11a, Chapter 4). The Sikyatki Polychrome vessel indicates the closure and burning of Chevelon (the roof of S. 159 was burned) occurs after 1385, in line with the suggested end date of 1390 to 1400 proposed by E.C. Adams (Chapter 4).

Important for interpretations of temporal trends in the deposition of WMRW types, it is evident that indeterminate WMRW constitutes the vast majority of sherds through time at the site. Because WMRW types are defined primarily on the basis of decorative style (Carlson 1970), small sherds generally lack sufficient decorative space to allow for specific types to be assigned. This trend, which has been noted at H2 and H3 (Hays 1991:32; Lyons and Hays-Gilpin 2001: 154), seriously compromises the inferences that may be drawn from the breakdown of WMRW types by temporal phase.

Nevertheless, some patterns are present. Fourmile Polychrome (1330-1390) is the most common of the typed WMRW material in the Chevelon assemblage (Table 6.10). Its distribution through time generally indicates a peak in deposition during the EHP followed by a significantly reduced occurrence in deposits from later periods (Table 6.6). The presence of Pinedale Polychrome and the initial appearance of Fourmile Polychrome, in the EHP, are consistent with the accepted end of production of Pinedale Polychrome and the beginning of production of Fourmile Polychrome in the Silver Creek region, at approximately 1330 (Mills and Herr 1999) and the dating of EHP at 1330 to 1365.

The composition of WMRW types at Chevelon is similar to that reported for H1 (Table 6.7), and is also qualitatively similar to deposits at H2 (Hays 1991) and H3 (Lyons and Hays-Gilpin 2001). Discrepancies in the Chevelon and H1 datasets manifest themselves with a higher proportion of Fourmile Polychrome in EHP strata at Chevelon, a greater percentage of Pinedale Black-on-red and Polychrome in MHP deposits at Chevelon, and the relatively late introduction of Cedar Creek Polychrome into Chevelon deposits in the LHP, as compared with the TP at H1.

The MHP Pinedale Polychrome consists primarily of a large reconstructible bowl recovered from K. 279, which accounts for 35 of the total of 43 sherds. As discussed below, the presence of this vessel in kiva fill that postdates the end of production of Pinedale Polychrome may indicate that the vessel is an heirloom piece that was curated by people with access to K. 279. Because it was most likely produced in the Silver Creek region, the curation of this vessel may further indicate the linkages between this region and the people who used K. 279 for ceremonial purposes, and a possible role for the jar in these ceremonial practices.

The greatest diversity in WMRW types was identified in LHP strata. Although each type is represented by a small number of sherds, LHP deposits contained Cedar Creek Polychrome, St. Johns Polychrome, and Wingate Polychrome sherds. Showlow Polychrome also reappears in LHP strata, having been present during the EHP, but absent in the MHP. While Showlow Polychrome was produced contemporaneously with Fourmile Polychrome (LaMotta 2006), and the production span of Cedar Creek Polychrome overlaps that of Fourmile Polychrome, St.

Figure 6.10. Whole and reconstructible Jeddito Yellow Ware vessels: (a.1-3) Jeddito B/y Style A and B; (b) Sikyatki Polychrome Style B; (c) Jeddito B/y Style A bowl; (d) Bidahochi Polychrome jar; (e) Jeddito B/y Style A jar (f) Jeddito B/y Style A bowl.

Figure 6.11. Whole and reconstructible Roosevelt Red Ware vessels: (a,b) Tonto Polychrome; (c) Whiteriver Polychrome; (d) Gila Polychrome.

Table 6.10. Number and Percentage of White Mountain Red Ware Types by Ceramic Phase.

Phase	Types	Count	%	Consensus Dates
Tuwiuca	Pinedale B/R, Poly	2	0.7	1290-1330
Early Homol'ovi	Indeterminate	107	8.8	
	Pinedale B/R, Poly	2	0.2	1290-1330
	Fourmile Poly	34	2.8	1330-1390
	Showlow Poly	5	0.4	1330-1390
Middle Homol'ovi	Indeterminate	175	5.9	
	Pinedale B/R, Poly	43	1.5	1290-1330
	Fourmile Poly	19	0.6	1290-1330
Late Homol'ovi	Indeterminate	202	2.2	
	St. Johns B/R, Poly	2		1200-1300
	Pinedale B/R, Poly	8	0.1	1290-1330
	Cedar Creek Poly	5	0.1	1300-1350
	Fourmile Poly	21	0.2	1330-1390
	Showlow Poly	6	0.1	1330-1390
	Wingate B/R, Poly	1		1150-1225

Figure 6.12. (a) Homol'ovi Polychrome puki manufactured from a bowl; (b) Red-slipped Jeddito Polychrome bowl; (c) Huckovi Black-on-orange sherd.

Johns Polychrome and Wingate Polychrome were produced early in the WMRW sequence (Mills and Herr 1999), and would be expected in no later than TP deposits. Interestingly, these WMRW types were found exclusively in K. 901. No other LHP deposit produced typable WMRW sherds other than Fourmile Polychrome. This implies that the types found in K. 901 may have been associated with the ceremonial function of the structure as well as with the specific groups who participated in ceremonies in K. 901, likely related to social memory and kiva closure. This is considered in more detail below.

SPATIAL PATTERNS

Spatial Patterns in Ware Distribution among Room Blocks

The spatial distribution of major decorated and utility wares at the site indicates patterns of ceramic use, production, and discard that can shed light on the different origins or social identities of occupants in different regions of the site. For simplicity, the spatial analysis collapses temporal phases in order to understand the distribution of ceramics across space at Chevelon without regard to the influence of time on ceramic deposition. Because room blocks provide a convenient basis for division of the site, Table 6.11 presents the distribution of major decorated and utility wares among excavated room blocks and the RB300 plaza. Implicit in the decision to spatially segregate the data according to room blocks is the developmental scheme for the site elucidated above. Thus, temporal variables in ceramic distribution cannot be completely isolated from spatial variables. Comparisons will be made among room blocks, as well as against the data compiled for the entirety of the site and presented in Table 6.1.

Spatial Patterns in Jeddito Yellow Ware Distribution

As is evident from Table 6.11, the proportion of JYW in RB200 and RB300 falls well below the average for the site, while the percent of JYW in RB400 (represented by a single excavated structure), more closely approximates the Chevelon average. By contrast, JYW is significantly more abundant in the excavated material recovered from RB100, RB900, and the RB300 plaza. As will be discussed below, differences in ceramic distribution as a result of structure use likely contribute to the disparity between the composition of ceramics from the plaza structures and elsewhere at the site.

Spatial Patterns in Local Ceramic Distribution

Table 6.11 indicates that percentages of WOW and HUW below the Chevelon average were recovered from all room blocks except RB200. Of the room blocks producing below average proportions of WOW, the material recovered from RB100 produced the least WOW, with only 1.7 percent of sherds by count. RB400 provides the greatest anomaly with the second highest frequency of WOW but the second lowest HUW. A decrease in frequency of locally-produced utility ware and its replacement with Awatovi Yellow Ware (AYW) is expected for LHP and thus should be apparent in K. 901, which has a high %JYW and sherds of Sikyatki Polychrome. Unexpectedly, AYW is quite rare in K. 901 in contrast to RB300. HUW and MBW are much more common in K. 901, which in reality is dominated by decorated ceramics to the exclusion of all utility ceramics (Table 6.11).

RB300 and RB400 may be more representative of ceramic distribution by ware in the LHP where AYW is nearly double HUW. Surprisingly, both these late room blocks have high frequencies of MBW averaging 23.6 percent, higher than any other room blocks (Table 6.11). This implies local production of MBW, plus exchange with pueblos along the Mogollon Rim, Silver Creek, and ULCR regions while exchange for decorated ware focused with Hopi communities on Antelope Mesa. These data suggest that production of local utility ware, either at Chevelon or at contemporary sites in the HSC, persisted later into the occupation of Chevelon than does the production of local decorated ware (see Hays-Gilpin et al. 1996:74).

These ceramic trends suggest Chevelon had co-residential groups with earlier groups predominantly from the north, or the Hopi mesas, and later groups from the south/southeast by 1365, and possibly earlier. The widespread presence of multiple utility wares, in particular TGW and MBW, in RB200, 300, 400, and to some degree in RB100, along with WOW and later JYW, indicates these co-residential groups cooperated and were likely integrated in many social activities.

Spatial Patterns in Red Ware Distribution

As indicated by Table 6.11, proportions of WMRW, exceeding the Chevelon average, were recovered only from RB200 and RB300—the parts of the site that produce the most EHP and MHP contexts. Given the decline in WMRW frequency following the MHP, these results are likely time-sensitive. In order to evaluate whether differences in the frequency of WMRW between room blocks RB901 are significant when compared to the frequency of WMRW in the entire Chevelon assemblage, chi-square tests were performed on the sherd counts from each room block (Table 6.12). The chi-square values for each room block, when compared to the total, with the exception of RB400, were all statistically significant at a level of $p < 0.05$. These values indicate the relative abundance of WMRW, in RB200 and RB300, and the depressed frequencies of WMRW, in RB100 and RB400 and K. 901, are all statistically significant. Therefore, the clear spatial preference is toward deposition in RB200 and RB300, yet deposition was by no means confined to these room blocks and, in fact, all room blocks produced an elevated proportion of WMRW, with respect to other

Table 6.11. Number and Percentage of Selected Wares by Room Block.

Ware	RB100 count	%	RB200 count	%	RB300 count	%	RB400 count	%	PLAZA 900 count	%	total count	%
Jeddito Yellow Ware	2367	69.2	3178	36.8	266	44.3	271	46.2	5032	70.1	11,114	54.4
Winslow Orange Ware	59	1.7	1592	18.4	61	10.2	40	6.8	666	9.3	2418	11.8
Awatovi Yellow Ware	35	1.0	42	0.5	15	2.5	16	2.7	45	0.6	153	0.7
Homol'ovi Orange/ Gray Ware	88	2.6	825	9.6	8	1.3	9	1.5	288	4.0	1218	6.0
Tusayan Gray Ware	229	6.7	881	10.2	76	12.7	81	13.8	246	3.4	1513	7.4
Mogollon Brown Ware	536	15.7	1392	16.1	135	22.5	145	24.7	559	7.8	2767	13.5
White Mountain Red Ware	29	0.8	507	5.9	35	5.8	16	2.7	214	3.0	801	3.9
Roosevelt Red Ware	76	2.2	221	2.6	4	0.7	8	1.4	130	1.8	439	2.1
Total	3419	100.0	8638	100.0	600	100.0	586	100.0	7180	100.0	20423	100.0

sites in the HSC (see Table 6.2 for comparison).

What these data indicate is that the highest frequencies of WMRW at Chevelon are confined to the oldest portions of the site. This is expected, for the frequency of WMRW in room fill peaks in EHP and MHP deposits, which were overwhelmingly recovered from RB200 and RB300. As was true of the distribution of JYW and local decorated and utility wares, it is likely that spatial patterns in the composition of the ceramic assemblage are indicative of trends in ceramic use and deposition through time. However, as suggested above, the patterning of WMRW (and MBW) across the pueblo may also demonstrate that the occupants of RB200 and RB300 maintained unique social relationships with producers in the Silver Creek region, who supplied these occupants with vessels at greater rates than they did the occupants of the other room blocks. This perhaps facilitated or reinforced what E.C. Adams (Chapter 13) has identified as the consolidation of ritual power and authority in this portion of the site, and particularly in RB200.

Table 6.11 also presents the distribution of RRW across the site. Frequencies of RRW vary significantly with RB100 and 200 having higher frequencies than the site average and RB300 far below the average. Unlike WMRW, these patterns cannot be explained as primarily influenced by time. For example, RB100 has a frequency of 69.2 percent JYW, whereas RB200 has a frequency of only 36.8 percent due to its lengthy occupation in comparison to RB100.

While not indicated in the distribution across room blocks, the RRW recovered from RB100 consists primarily of one, or possible two, large, reconstructible Tonto Polychrome jars recovered in the fill of S. 120. The jars likely postdate the occupation and use of the structure. Although not included in this

Chapter 6: Pottery 143

Table 6.12. Frequency of White Mountain Red Ware Sherds by Room Block and Plaza 900.

Ware	RB100		RB200		RB300		RB400		PLAZA 900		total	proportion of total
	count	%	count	%	count	%	count	%	count	%		
Total Decorated	3934	100	10198	100	661	100	586	100	7906	100	23285	1.00
WMRW Observed	29	0.74	507	4.97	35	5.30	16	2.73	214	0.03	801	0.03
WMRW Expected	135.33		350.81		22.74		20.16		271.97		801	
Chi Square Statistic	83.54		69.54		6.61		0.86		12.35			
Critical value for 1 df at 0.05 prob.	3.841		3.841		3.841		3.841		3.841			

analysis, a reconstructible vessel of a Tonto Polychrome jar on the floor of S. 509 and a whole Tonto Polychrome jar under the floor of S. 159 (both produced of local paste), are also present in rooms around the south plaza. In addition, more than half of utility ware sherds are MBW, representing a diversity of sizes and use for storage and cooking. This suggests groups migrating from the upper Little Colorado region, the Arizona Mountains, or the Silver Creek area settled in RB100, RB500, and likely other parts of room blocks built around the south plaza and possibly participated in its construction,

Conclusions from the Spatial Analysis of Major Ceramic Wares

The spatial data for major decorated and utility wares at Chevelon indicate that the distribution of ceramic use and deposition at the site was conditioned largely by temporal factors affecting the prevalence of JYW, WOW, HUW, AYW, TGW, and WMRW in room block fill across the site.

Interestingly, the frequency distribution of the most common utility ware, MBW, is not chronologically determined. Instead, its frequency is most strongly associated with RRW and WMRW. For example, Table 6.13 reveals that a high frequency of MBW occurs in K. 274/279 where the highest frequency of WMRW and RRW also occurs. At the same time, MBW is also common in RB100, RB300, and RB400 with highly variable frequencies of JYW and variable frequencies of WMRW and RRW. The distribution of MBW suggests it was simply the most popular utility ware for most of the population of Chevelon during much of the EHP through MHP.

Patterns Resulting from Room Use

Distribution in Kiva Versus Non-kiva Structures

Given the interest on the part of researchers affiliated with the HRP in understanding the structure of religious ritual and interactions that facilitated the elaboration of ritual in the HSC, emphasis has been placed on the excavation of structures at all HSC sites, including Chevelon, that were associated with the performance of religious ritual. E.C. Adams (Chapter 4) defines two distinct types of these structures excavated at Chevelon. The first — habitation rooms with ritual features — characterizes two structures on the east side of RB100. Kivas constitute the second class of structures identified at Chevelon, where religious rituals were performed. In total, four kivas were excavated; however, ceramic deposits were analyzed from only three of these structures — K. 248, K. 279, and K. 901. As discussed above in the context of the growth and development of the pueblo, these three kivas (as well as K. 252, which was not analyzed), are all associated with the two oldest room blocks at the site — RB200 and RB300.

As indicated by the seriation of ceramic deposits from these kivas (see Appendix A), K. 248 was filled in the EHP, K. 279 began filling in the EHP and continued to the beginning of the LHP, and K. 901 was filled during the LHP. What these temporal data may indicate is a reorganization of space used for the performance of religious rituals through the increased use of plaza space for large ceremonial performances. This spatial reorganization of performance spaces has been noted at H1 and H2 (E.C. Adams and LaMotta 2006), and is identified as one of the hallmarks of the adoption and elaboration of katsina ceremonialism (E.C. Adams 1991a).

Table 6.13 presents the distribution of ceramic wares recovered from non-kivas, kivas, and the total Chevelon assemblage. For K. 901, ritual deposits are confined to strata 8 through 11. As discussed by E.C. Adams (Chapters 4 and 13), these strata correspond to the fill deposited in the kiva through the roof hatch that forms a cone of ritual trash (sensu Walker 1995). As is evident from the table, proportions of JYW exceeding those found in non-ritual structures were recovered only from K. 901. By contrast, K. 248 and K. 279 contain depressed levels of JYW as compared with the site as a whole, a product of their filling during the EHP and MHP.

The more striking pattern evidenced in the comparison of non-kiva and kiva structures, and comparisons among kivas, is the abundance of WMRW in K. 248 and K. 279. The proportions of WMRW in deposits from these structures exceed those reported for K. 901, non-kiva structures, and the site as a whole by more than 150 percent. As discussed above, the abundance of WMRW in these kiva deposits may indicate that groups utilizing these structures asserted a group identity distinct from other Chevelon residents, characterized by an overt emphasis on ties to producers of WMRW in the Silver Creek region. These social ties may have played a role in reinforcing the power and authority based in religious ritual maintained by the occupants of RB200 (see Chapter 13).

It is interesting that whole or reconstructible RRW vessels were recovered predominantly from non-kiva contexts, with the exception of a reconstructible RRW jar recovered in the upper, MHP, deposits of K. 274/279. Together with the high frequency of MBW, this pattern may suggest the makers of RRW were given access to these exclusive areas after establishing

Table 6.13. Percentage of Types for Chevelon Kivas.

Wares	Non-kiva count	%	248 count	%	274/279 count	%	901 count	%	Site total count	%
Hopi White Ware	8	0.1	3	0.5	14	0.3			25	0.1
Jeddito Yellow Ware	4239	42.3	124	21.0	1764	31.7	4991	66.1	11118	46.5
Awatovi Yellow Ware	95	0.9	7	1.2	23	0.4	43	0.6	168	0.7
Winslow Orange Ware	855	8.5	185	31.4	912	16.4	595	7.9	2547	10.6
Homol'ovi Orange/Gray Ware	718	7.2	56	9.5	695	12.5	280	3.7	1749	7.8
Alameda Brown Ware	2				1				3	
White Mountain Red Ware	184	1.8	36	6.1	392	7.0	201	2.7	813	3.4
Tusayan White Ware	154	1.5	7	1.2	13	0.2	25	0.3	199	0.8
Tusayan Gray Ware	1268	12.7	65	11.0	349	6.3	264	3.5	1946	8.2
Little Colorado White Ware	89	0.9	3	0.5	17	0.3	32	0.4	141	0.6
Little Colorado Gray Ware	24	0.2	1	0.2	19		10	0.1	54	0.2
Tsegi Orange Ware	78	0.8					31	0.4	114	0.6
Cibola White Ware	243	2.4	22	3.7	5	0.1	46	0.6	311	1.3
Roosevelt Red Ware	171	1.7	5	0.8	175	3.1	124	1.6	475	2.0
Mogollon Brown Ware	1869	18.7	60	10.2	1020	18.3	499	6.6	3448	14.5
Unknown Plain Ware	45	0.4	5	0.8	44	0.8	7	0.1	101	0.4
San Francisco Mountain Gray Ware							2		2	
Zuni Types	25	0.2			7	0.1	5	0.1	37	0.2
Unknown Decorated Ware	75	0.7	6	1.0	18	0.3	44	0.6	143	0.7
Prescott Gray Ware	1				1				1	
Cibola Gray Ware	4		1	0.2					6	
Early Jeddito Yellow Ware	55	0.5			11	0.2	6	0.1	72	0.3
Puerco Valley Utility Ware	86	0.9	4	0.7	79	1.4	39	0.5	208	
Puerco Valley-like Utility Ware	21	0.2			6	0.1	1		28	0.1
Puerco Valley-like Decorated Ware	5								5	
Other local utility ware	2		1	0.2	1				4	
Total	10018	100.0	590	100.0	5565	100.0	7545	100.0	23718	100.0

themselves as community members. Their ritual participation is also expressed in S. 120, S. 159, and S. 509, where Tonto Polychrome jars are strongly associated with closure deposits. These practices, likely by immigrants from the south, could also have been to assert ownership and identity.

Material Correlates of Religious Ritual Practice

E.C. Adams and LaMotta (2006) have demonstrated that the ritualized discard of ceremonial objects produces "enriched deposits." These deposits are characterized by a greater proportion of whole or nearly whole objects, rare or unusual objects, and/or non-subsistence fauna than are non-ritual household deposits (E.C. Adams and LaMotta 2006:58). Particularly at the site of H1, enriched deposits contain caches of utilitarian objects, such as reconstructible ceramic vessels, associated with the serving and consumption of food during feasts (E.C. Adams and LaMotta 2006:59). Finally, these enriched deposits are commonly highly structured and often associated with architectural features, such as kiva ventilator shafts, hearths, and roofs. Depositing material in association with these features ritually "closes" or "seals" these features at the termination of their use (E.C. Adams and LaMotta 2006:60; Walker 2005; Walker and Schiffer 2006; Walker et al. 2000).

The results of these studies, which suggest that ceramics were likely incorporated into enriched deposits at Chevelon, are evidence of ritual discard practices. Whole or reconstructible vessels, particularly when deliberately deposited in association with other objects, including rare or unusual objects, provide a strong indication of ritual discard and the formal sealing of architectural features.

Further, the deposition of ceramic artifacts — those with unusual vessel form or decorative style — also suggests the presence of enriched deposits.

Table 6.14 presents a summary of the reconstructible vessels recovered from kiva (some illustrated in Figures 6.10-6.13) and non-kiva deposits at Chevelon (Figures 6.10-6.16). As the data indicate, seven reconstructible vessels, representing a variety of ceramic wares, were recovered from K. 279 (Figure 6.13b). An additional four reconstructible vessels of various wares were recovered from K. 901(Figure 10a-c). Whether or not these vessels were deposited whole remains unclear because neither structure has been fully excavated or analyzed; however, their abundance in these kiva deposits suggests that they were deposited as part of ritualized discard events.

Furthermore, both habitation structures with ritual features contained highly structured deposits with whole or reconstructible vessels that imply ritualized discard (Table 6.14). In S. 159, as discussed above, a subfloor pit was excavated into bedrock in order for a medium-sized Tonto Polychrome jar on local paste to be placed within the pit overlying a small ladle bowl (Figure 6.11a). Within the jar were the remains of several cottontail rabbits (see Chapters 9 and 13). Also in this structure and directly above the Tonto Polychrome jar was a reconstructible Sikyatki Polychrome jar (Figure 6.10b), which was part of an extensive floor assemblage previously described in Chapter 4. The association of ladle, jar, and rabbit remains, along with the floor assemblages, suggests that this constitutes an "enriched deposit."

In S. 124, a reconstructible Tusayan Corrugated jar and whole Jeddito Black-on-yellow bowl were recovered in the vicinity of the hearth. Associated with the hearth and

Table 6.14. Reconstructible Vessels from Chevelon.

Structure	% Whole	Type	Sherd Count	Total Weight
279	<50%	Awatovi/Jeddito B/y bowl	6	247
279	<50%	Pinedale B/r bowl	33	149
279	<50%	Tonto Polychrome jar	17	131
279	<50%	Homol'ovi Corrugated jar	22	473
279	<50%	Tusayan Corrugated jar	34	907
279	<50%	Homol'ovi Corrugated jar	1	529
279	>90%	Puerco Valley Plain ladle	1	46
901	<50%	Homol'ovi Corrugated jar	21	381
901	<50%	Jeddito B/y bowl	9	164
901	<50%	Indet. White Mountain Red Ware bowl	6	226
901	<50%	Awatovi/Jeddito B/y bowl	1	140
120	<50%	Tonto Polychrome jar	25	705
120	<50%	Tonto Polychrome jar	15	445
120	100%	Jeddito B/y bowl style A	1	1022
120	100%	Jeddito B/y jar style A	1	3215
124	>70%	Jeddito B/y bowl style A	1	475
124	>50%	Tusayan Corrugated Jar	6	1139
159	100%	Tonto Polychrome jar	1	1780
159	>90%	Sikyatki Polychrome	>100	3465
159	>75%	Jeddito Yellow Ware ladle bowl	1	111
222	>80%	Tusayan Corrugated jar	1	1536
222	<50%	Homol'ovi Gray Corrugated jar	15	684
222	<50%	Tusayan Corrugated jar	17	817
227	>50%	Homol'ovi Polychrome puki	5	305
264	>80%	Jeddito B/y bowl style A	9	261
264	>90%	Tusayan Corrugated jar	1	465
265	<50%	Jeddito B/y bowl style A	1	35
265	>50%	Jeddito B/y bowl style A	1	244
269	>50%	Jeddito B/y style A rectangular jar	10	144
286	<50%	Homol'ovi Orange Corrugated	>100	1399
286	<50%	Homol'ovi Gray Corrugated	>100	1768
286	>50%	Jeddito B/y Style A	12	205
286	>50%	Bidahochi Polychrome	22	277
286	>90%	Puerco Valley Corrugated	4	926
300	<50%	Gila Polychrome bowl	13	120
373	<50%	Whiteriver Polychrome	5	389
373	<50%	Jeddito Polychrome, red-slipped bowl	5	264
373	<20%	Huckovi B/o bowl	3	129
509	<50%	Tonto Polychrome jar	25	329

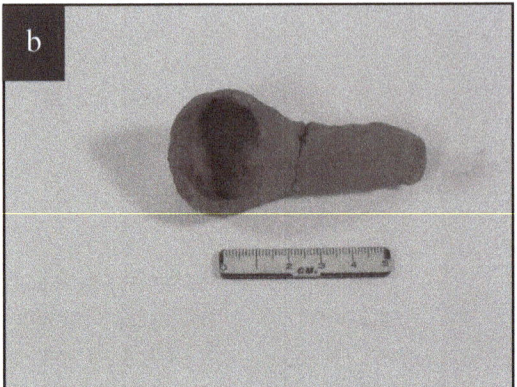

Figure 6.13. (a) Homol'ovi Corrugated jar; (b) Puerco Valley Plain miniature ladle.

Figure 6.14. Tusayan Corrugated jar.   *Figure 6.15. Puerco Valley Corrugated jar.*

these vessels were two manos and a possible piki stone (see Chapter 7). Although not as elaborate as the features identified in S. 159, the association of these objects with the hearth in S. 124 suggests that this is also an enriched deposit. Additionally, the fill deposit in S. 120, which contained multiple reconstructible vessels including two RRW jars, also appears to be an enriched deposit with a diverse assemblage of rare and unusual artifacts (Figures 6.10d,e; 6.11b). The same is likely true in the piki house (S. 222) where multiple ground stone tools and corrugated jars are part of a burned deposit that is obviously enriched (Figure 6.14), and S. 264, S. 265, and S. 268, where a unique "square" seed jar and a sherd with figures in a ceremonial dance line were recovered (Figures 6.16d-f). Certainly, the large storage vessels, and several others in the fill, are associated with the three sacrificed cottontails on the floor of S. 286 and are incorporated into an enriched ritual deposit (Figures 6.10h, 6.15).

Finally, although not associated with a specific architectural feature, three unique JYW sherds were identified in the cone of ritual trash from K. 901 (Figure 6.16b-c). One of these sherds, which likely formed the majority of a large plate, was decorated with an animal motif. The other two sherds were the remnants of two large Jeddito Black-on-yellow bowls, one of which was decorated in the interior with a similar animal motif, while the other was decorated in the interior with an anthropomorphic motif. It is possible that these vessels were utilized in some sort of feasting ritual — an activity that E.C. Adams and LaMotta (2006) suggest results in the formation of enriched deposits in ritual structures. Furthermore, the presence of several large cooking jars may also connect the kiva activities to feasts.

Ceramic Evidence for Structural Burning Classification

As described in Chapters 4 and 5, evidence for structural burning at Chevelon is more prevalent than at any other site in the HSC. Episodes of structural burning are expected to be most visible on decorated ceramics, given the difficulty inherent in differentiating between structural burning and sooting resulting from the use of cooking vessels in the utility ware assemblage (Figure 6.5b). Sooting and paste discoloration on broken edges of decorated sherds is the best indicator of burning after a vessel is broken. The paste of JYW sherds, in particular, often discolors dark green or brown in response to post-depositional burning. However, it is not possible to differentiate burning on JYW sherds resulting from a structural fire or some other cause and it is not even possible to predict that burned edges could result from the collapse of a burned roof onto a whole jar or bowl as discussed in Chapter 5. Rarely are burned JYW sherds in fill actually burned in place. This is suggested by the absence of indications of reduction or oxidation of surrounding soils and fire-damage to other groups of artifacts in the deposit. This is particularly noteworthy in ashy deposits where burned sherds are no more frequent than in non-ashy deposits, indicating burning often took place before deposition. Thus, JYW sherds are typically deposited after being burned elsewhere, possibly by structural fire, but just as likely from other burning events. The only exceptions are sherds on the floors of structures that have burned.

Spatial Trends in Structural Burning

Table 6.15 presents the proportion, by structure, of burned and unburned decorated sherds at

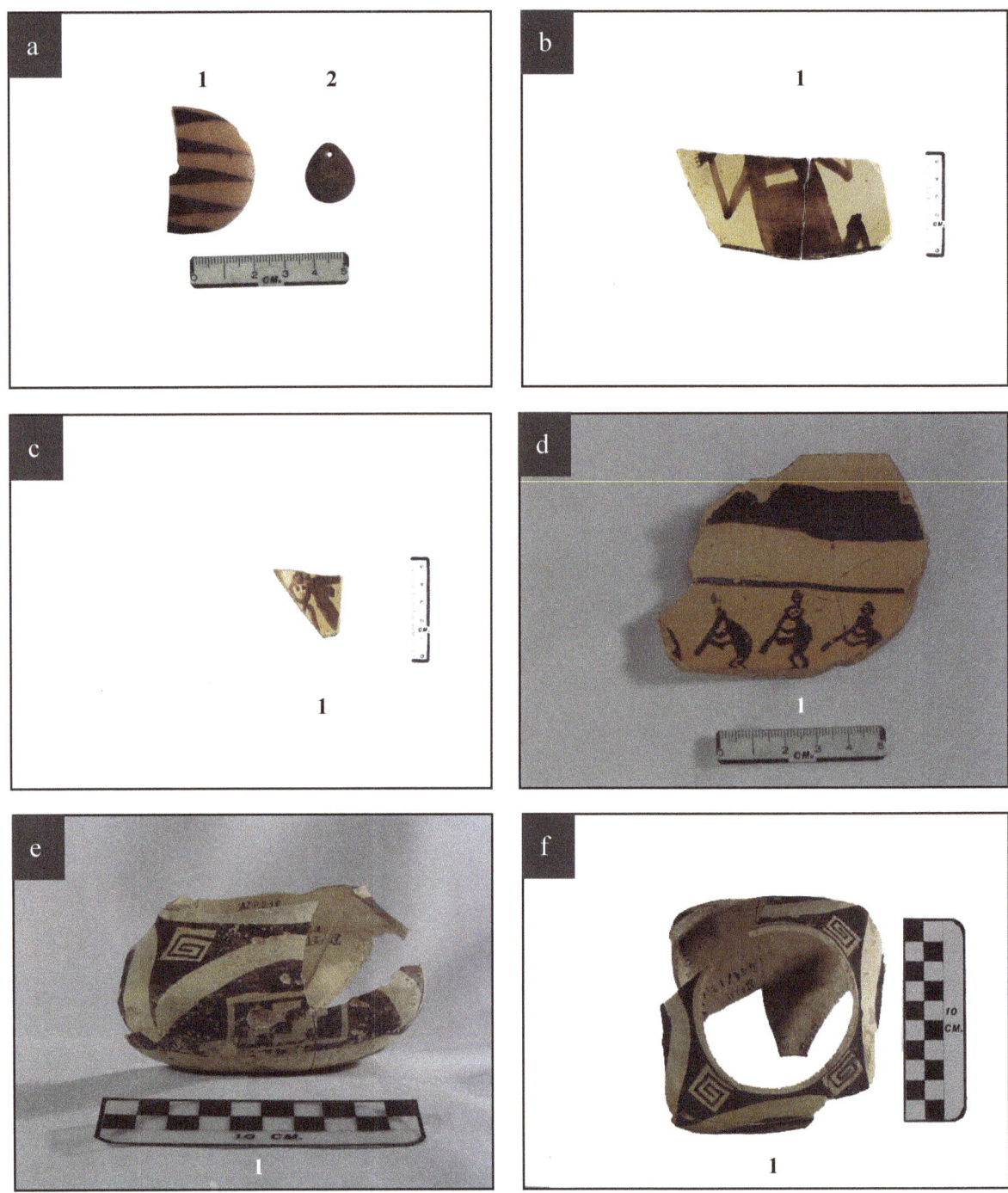

Figure 6.16. Miscellaneous ceramic artifacts: (a) Jeddito Yellow Ware spindle whorl and pendant; (b-d) Jeddito Yellow Ware zoomorph, anthropomorphic head, and dance line; (e, f) side and top view of Jeddito Black-on-yellow rectangular jar.

Chevelon. As is evident from the table, nearly one-fifth of all decorated sherds in room fill at the site display evidence of post-depositional burning. The amount of burning recorded on ceramic material varies widely across the site, from a peak of 78.5 percent burned sherds in the TP subfloor, unit 300, to a low of 2.2 percent burned in the LHP, S. 159. While high levels of burning — 66.3 percent and 56.0 percent sherds burned — are reported for the burned S. 264 and 265, respectively. In fact, two reconstructible vessels from S. 264 are burned (Figures 6.10f), likely from burned roofing collapsing onto them. Structures in RB200 do not display consistently high levels of burning, as compared with structures in other room blocks. This is at least partly attributable to the lower frequency of excavated burned structures in RB200 and the possibility fewer structures had intact roofs in RB200 when Chevelon was burned. Similarly, patterns of burning in contiguous structures — i.e. S. 123 and 124; S. 157, 158, and 159; display a wide range of variability in the frequency of burning. This likely indicates the failure of fire, in rooms where ignition is known to have occurred, to consistently move into adjacent structures, and the small amount of ceramic material present in many of the structures when they were burned. Thus, while structural burning was pervasive, clear spatial patterns to burning episodes on a structure by structure basis are not indicated by the ceramic material.

Temporal Trends in Structural Burning

Because of the abundance of JYW sherds in all structures at Chevelon, temporal patterns in structural burning were assessed by focusing on evidence from the JYW assemblage. Table 6.16 presents the data for the proportion of post-depositional burning seen on JYW sherds across temporal phases at Chevelon. These data indicate a clear decline in the prevalence of burned sherds through time at the site.

These data suggest a pattern of structural burning through the occupation of Chevelon. This is particularly important for arguments that fire has always been a component of Chevelon's history and the final burning is in keeping with this pattern. The low frequency of burned yellow ware in the LHP is likely a result of the preponderance of sherds in burned fill that would be unaffected by structural fire and the general absence of ceramics on floors of burned structures; the exception being S. 264 and S. 159.

Miscellaneous Ceramic Artifacts

A fairly limited array of ceramic artifacts were recovered during excavations at Chevelon (Figure 6.16). These are listed in Table 6.17. Nearly all were recovered from fill deposits, suggesting their deposition was intentional. Miniature vessels and figurines have most commonly been associated with either enriched deposits, or at least ceremonial structures in other HSC pueblos, and this pattern continued at Chevelon with the only figurine recovered from the enriched deposits near the floor of K. 901, and five of the six miniature vessels recovered from the fill of K. 279. The sixth came from the fill of a feature as part of the closure assemblage for S. 603.

Gaming pieces came primarily from storage structures in contrast to shaped sherds of which over half were deposited in kiva fill. Although the puki was recovered from the upper fill of S. 227, this deposit was almost certainly backdirt from the looting of K. 248. Ladle bowls have been found in association with neonatal deposition at H1 and another was found with the neonate in S. 288 in

Table 6.15. Number and Percentage of Burned Jeddito Yellow Ware Sherds by Structure.

Structure	Structure Burned	Burned (post-breakage of vessel) count	%	Unburned count	%	Total Count
120	Yes	73	23.1	243	76.9	316
122	Yes	13	28.3	33	71.7	46
123	Yes	32	24.2	100	75.8	132
124	Yes	29	10.5	247	89.5	276
157	No	2	3.3	58	96.7	60
158	Yes	25	54.3	21	45.7	46
159	Yes	39	2.2	1716	97.8	1755
161	Yes	48	65.8	25	34.2	73
222	Yes-filled later	33	17.4	157	82.6	190
227	No	68	27.8	177	72.2	245
248	Yes-filled later	155	39.6	236	60.4	391
264	Yes	201	66.3	102	33.7	303
265	Yes	61	56.0	48	44.0	109
269	No	64	36.0	114	64.0	178
266/286	No	120	26.9	326	73.1	446
268/289	Yes	83	22.9	279	77.1	362
274/279	No	715	20.9	2699	79.1	3414
288	No	91	30.2	210	69.8	301
300	No-midden	164	78.5	45	21.5	209
373	No	25	19.7	102	80.3	127
345	Yes	25	40.3	37	59.7	62
393	Yes	94	49.7	95	50.3	189
403	No	60	16.9	295	83.1	355
901	Yes-fill earlier	492	9.9	5605	90.1	6097
whole site		2712	17.3	12970	82.7	15682

Table 6.16. Amount and Percentage of Burned Jeddito Yellow Ware Sherds by Phase.

Phase	Unburned count	%	Burned (post-vessel break) count	%	Total Count
Tuwiuca			3	100.0	3
Early Homol'ovi	254	76.0	80	24.0	334
Middle Homol'ovi	1080	79.8	273	20.2	1353
Late Homol'ovi	7294	91.9	635	8.0	7929
Total	8628	89.7	991	10.3	9619

keeping with this pattern. A ladle bowl was also associated with closure of S. 603, while another was placed beneath the Tonto Polychrome jar buried in the floor of S. 159, discussed earlier. Ladle bowls were placed beneath mealing bins at H1 and the one in S. 159 is consistent with their association with cornmeal and perhaps feasting.

CONCLUSIONS

Village growth and occupational history at Chevelon are modeled in this analysis using the same temporal phase scheme devised by LaMotta (2006) for H1. Temporal trends of JYW and WOW deposition at Chevelon follow expected trends identified across pueblos in the HSC. JYW increases dramatically with respect to WOW in the MHP and virtually replaces WOW in the latest dated deposits.

The frequency of WMRW at Chevelon is elevated, with respect to frequencies at all other HSC pueblos. This is particularly striking in K. 248 and K. 279, which contained substantial WMRW sherds and RVs. This evidence indicates that a distinct group identity, characterized by social ties to the Silver Creek region of east-central Arizona, may have been asserted by some occupants of the pueblo or at the very least. WMRW bowls, particularly Fourmile Polychrome, may have added prestige to social groups occupying RB200. Given the abundance of WMRW in the RB200 kivas, these ties to the south may form the basis for the assertion of ritual power and authority by residents of RB200, perhaps vested in early katsina ritual (see Chapter 13).

WMRW is most strongly represented in EHP and MHP deposits, followed by a precipitous decline in the LHP corresponding to the depopulation of the Silver Creek region around 1385, which also corresponds to the end of the MHP. RRW is strongly represented in Chevelon deposits beginning in the MHP and continuing into LHP, in concert with continued local manufacture of this ware. A strong, persistent use of MBW throughout Chevelon's occupation suggests, groups using the decorated wares included migrants from regions of production.

Early connections between Chevelon residents and RRW-producers in east-central Arizona are indicated by the presence of

Table 6.17. Miscellaneous Ceramic Artifacts from Chevelon.

Artifact Type	Structures	Comments
Spindle Whorl	901	Shaped sherd with central hole
Figurine	279	
Gaming Piece	123, 268, 289, 900 (2)	Rectangular pieces
Shaped Sherd	222, 246, 248 (2), 269, 274 (2) 279 (11), 288, 393, 403, 900 (2), 901	Flaked and/or ground. Usually circular or oval
Ladle Bowl	279, 265, 274, 279, 288, 300 (2), 901	
Miniature Vessel	279 (5), 603	
Scoop	901	
Puki	227	Tuwiuca B/o

reconstructible RRW vessels in fill dating to the TP and EHP. Use of local paste recipes suggests local production of RRW at Chevelon. More sophisticated ceramic sourcing is necessary in order to more fully evaluate this observation, but local production of RRW is a strong indicator of immigrant households. These households likely followed pre-existing exchange relationships with Chevelon residents, perhaps represented by the strong presence of WMRW, and established themselves in RB100 and probably elsewhere around the south plaza. Given the consistent association between RRW production and the migrations of itinerant Ancestral Pueblo populations from the Kayenta region of northeastern Arizona, throughout eastern and southern Arizona, it is likely that some of the groups, who first returned to the Silver Creek region between 1350 and 1375, eventually migrated to Chevelon, although immigration from the Tonto Basin or ULCR are also possibilities.

The presence of enriched deposits containing ceramic objects was noted in the fill of a storage room and in two habitation structures with ritual features in RB100 and in K. 279 and K. 901. In the two kivas, these deposits contained several nearly whole reconstructible vessels; while in S. 124 and S. 159, whole ceramic vessels were incorporated into assemblages associated with ritual features and other ritually-discarded objects. High densities of reconstructible vessels, in association with other whole objects, suggest their use in ritual closure of S. 120, 222, 286, and possibly 264 and 265.

Finally, evidence for structural burning is pervasive across time and space at Chevelon. Burning is evident on ceramics from every room block and all temporal phases. However, significant variability is noted in the extent of burning within room blocks, and particularly between contiguous structures. Such variability may demonstrate that fire was not always successfully conducted between contiguous structures at the site. A marked decline in the frequency of burned ceramic material through time at Chevelon likely indicates that only a small amount of pottery remained exposed at the site, at the time of final burning.

Chapter 7
Ground Stone
Melanie Medeiros and E. Charles Adams

Excavations at Chevelon Pueblo yielded a total of 416 ground stone artifacts recovered from undisturbed proveniences. These artifacts were deposited in *primary*, *secondary*, and *de facto* contexts and were recovered from a variety of room types, including kivas, storage structures, habitation structures, a piki house, and some structures of unknown use. This chapter describes the ground stone assemblage while discussing the methodology and interprets spatial and temporal patterns in the assemblage in terms of intra-site and inter-site contexts.

METHODOLOGY

For the purposes of analysis, artifact types are artifacts that have been definitively identified as a type, based on standard attributes, and to those artifacts that are most likely of that type (see J. Adams 2002). All refitted fragments have been considered as one artifact (for example, three refitted pieces were considered as one). Also, all data tables, unless otherwise specified, contain categorizations and statistics pertaining to all 416 ground stone artifacts. Characteristics chosen for inventory and in-depth analysis were defined by synthesizing analyses of ground stone assemblages from other Homol'ovi sites excavated since 1984.

Analysis of the ground stone from Chevelon was conducted in two stages: inventory and in-depth analysis. Each stage was completed for all the ground stone, from disturbed and undisturbed proveniences alike. For inventory purposes, each artifact was identified by type and sub-type, following artifact classifications detailed by both Woodbury (1954) and J. Adams (2002), and its general condition (whole, incomplete, etc) was noted. Basic measurements, including length, width, thickness, use area, and weight were taken, and sketches detailing plan and profile views, and, occasionally, cross-sections were made. Measurements were made with a caliper for artifacts under 14 cm in length/width and were recorded to the nearest hundredth of a centimeter, while those artifacts larger than 14 cm in length/width were measured with a sliding ruler and recorded to the nearest tenth of a centimeter; likewise, smaller artifacts were weighed to the nearest tenth of a gram using a digital scale, while larger artifacts were weighed to the nearest gram using a manual scale.

The in-depth analysis involved more detailed observations concerning specific characteristics often associated with ground stone artifacts. These categories included determination of: the material and cement type, resharpening characteristics (location and timing), presence and type of groove, number of use surfaces, number and timing of uses, grinding motion direction, type and timing of burning, identification of basic residue types and pigment colors, and refit. All artifacts were examined with a hand lens and then, if necessary, under a binocular microscope. Materials and cements were based on types collected and identified by Fratt and M. Biancaniello (1993). Use-wear was characterized based on descriptions by J. Adams (2002) and with photo-micrographs taken by Fratt (1991). Possible quarries from which the ground stone material may have been taken were not considered for this analysis, although evidence about quarries (Fratt and M. Biancaniello 1993; Lange 1998), most likely utilized by members of other Homol'ovi sites, has been documented and may be relevant to the Chevelon ground stone assemblage.

Description of the Chevelon Ground Stone Assemblage

The ground stone assemblage collected from Chevelon consists of 428 individual pieces that were classified as 416 total artifacts. A basic distribution of artifact type is displayed in Table 7.1. As Table 7.1 indicates, manos, miscellaneous ground stone, and piki and griddle stones make up the largest artifact categories. No other artifact categories comprise even 10 percent of the collection. In general, the distribution of artifacts within this assemblage seems average when compared to collections from other pueblo sites from the same time period in the region, perhaps with the exception of the large percentage of piki and griddle stones. (See Fratt 1991: Table 5.2; 2001: Table 9.9; Velado 1999: Table 11.1; Walker 2004: Table 1, for comparisons).

Only 115 (27.6 percent) artifacts are complete, another 104 (25.0 percent) are more than half complete. And another 129 (31.0 percent) are less than half complete (Table 7.2). This percentage fits well with the large number of artifacts recovered from cultural fill deposits (N = 246, 59.1 percent). Over half of ground stone is made from Moenkopi Sandstone, while a third is made from Shinarump Sandstone (Table 7.3). In the H2 and H3 ground stone assemblages, the majority of the artifacts were characterized as Shinarump Sandstone (Fratt 1991, 2001). However, in these assemblages, the number of piki stones and griddle stones were minimal: three of 121 artifacts from H2 (Fratt 1991: Table 5.2); 56 of 1080 from H3 (Fratt 2001: Table 9.2); and only six from H4 (Walker 2004: Table 1). But in the assemblage from Chevelon, the piki and griddle stones combined comprise 8.4 percent of the ground stone. This large percentage of piki and griddle stones at Chevelon, made entirely of Moenkopi Sandstone, may be affecting the distribution of Chevelon material types in favor of Moenkopi Sandstone.

Another possible explanation for the large percentage of Moenkopi Sandstone at Chevelon may be that Moenkopi outcrops are simply more accessible to the inhabitants of Chevelon than are Shinarump. Chevelon Pueblo sits on top of a Moenkopi Sandstone outcrop with numerous exposures used as quarries within 200 m. The nearest Shinarump Sandstone outcrop is on the other side of the LCR floodplain, 4 km north. Walker (2004:6-7) notes that at H4, 66 percent of the ground stone is composed of Moenkopi, while 24 percent is Shinarump, and another 10 percent is composed of miscellaneous materials. He suggests (2004:7) the greater accessibility of Moenkopi, as H4 sits on top of a butte made of this sandstone, as the reason for the dominance of this material in the H4 ground stone assemblage.

As noted in Table 7.1, manos comprise the largest percentage of ground stone artifacts for which definitive use could be determined. Manos generally make up one of the largest artifact categories in the Homol'ovi ground

Table 7.1. Ground Stone Assemblage.

Artifact Type	Number of Artifacts (n)	Percentage of Assemblage (%)
Mano	89	21.39
Metate	12	2.88
Mano/Metate	1	0.24
Mortar	1	0.24
Abrader	25	6.01
Polisher	23	5.53
Axe	8	1.92
Piki stone	17	4.09
Griddle stone	18	4.33
Jewelry	5	1.20
Hoe	2	0.48
Architectural	30	7.21
Miscellaneous	185	44.47
Total	416	100.00

Table 7.2. Completeness of Ground Stone Artifacts.

Artifact Type	Whole	Greater than ½ Complete	Less than ½ Complete	Conjoined Pieces	Reconstruction Complete	Unknown	Total
Mano	22	39	26	1		1	89
Metate	2		6	3		1	12
Mano/Metate						1	1
Mortar	1						1
Abrader	11	6	4			4	25
Polisher	21		2				23
Axe	4	2	1			1	8
Piki stone		1	6	5		5	17
Griddle stone			16	1		1	18
Jewelry	4		1				5
Hoe		2					2
Architectural		6	16	3		5	30
Miscellaneous	49	48	51	5	1	31	185
Total	114	104	129	18	1	50	416

Table 7.3. Ground Stone Material Type.

Artifact Type	Shinarump Sandstone	Moenkopi Sandstone	Coconino Sandstone	Quartzite	Limestone	Unknown/ Other	Argillite	Chert	Basalt	Turquiose	Total
Mano	84	4								1	89
Metate	12										12
Mano/Metate	1										1
Mortar		1									1
Abrader	11	12	1			1					25
Polisher				19		1		3			23
Axe				7				1			8
Piki stone		17									17
Griddle stone		18									18
Jewelry						2		2		1	5
Hoe	1	1									2
Architectural		30									30
Miscelleneous	36	128		9	2	8	1	1			185
Total	145	211	1	35	2	12	1	7	1	1	416

stone assemblages (Fratt 1991, 2001; except see Walker 2004) as well as in other similarly dated Pueblo assemblages (Velado 1999: Table 11.1). As indicated in Table 7.3, artifacts from Chevelon were also composed of quartzite, argillite, and limestone.

Texture is strongly correlated to material source. Shinarump Sandstone ranges from fine to coarse-grained with equally varied cementing material that hold the larger nodules in place during use. Table 7.4 divides artifacts into categories of texture. Those with fine texture were manufactured from Moenkopi and Coconino Sandstones. Categories of medium, coarse, and conglomerate typically derive from Shinarump. Predictably, the greatest diversity in texture occurs in manos, metates, and abraders – all used for reducing other materials in stages, such as wood shafts and corn. Notably, polishers, axes, and jewelry are made of harder conglomerate materials, typically rhyolite, basalt, or Shinarump. Miscellaneous and architectural ground stone, which are typically worked slabs used in features, are made from the local fine-grained Moenkopi Sandstone.

More than half of the artifacts also exhibited evidence of burning, almost half of which was use-related (Table 7.5). Even discounting the use-related burning, 16.3 percent of artifacts were burned, a characterization consistent with the burning of various areas of Chevelon. In fact, excluding artifacts burned from use, architecture, and miscellaneous, nearly half are burned. Many of the burned artifacts were also incomplete and exhibited evidence of burning on at least one broken edge, indicating that they were probably burned after discard. However, only 32 of 224 (14.3 percent) artifacts discovered in floor fill or on contact surfaces were burned; the rest of the undisturbed burned artifacts were recovered from either cultural fill deposits or roof and wall fall contexts (Table 7.6). Although Walker (1995) suggests that burning of discarded artifacts at the Homol'ovi sites, particularly

Table 7.4. Texture of Ground Stone Artifacts.

Artifact Type	Conglomerate	Fine	Medium	Coarse	Variable	Vesicular	Unknown	Total
Mano		24	38	11	4	1	11	89
Metate			7	4	1			12
Mano/Metate			1					1
Mortar		1						1
Abrader		18	5	2				25
Polisher	18	5						23
Axe	7		1					8
Piki stone		17						17
Griddle stone		17	1					18
Jewelry	5							5
Hoe		1	1					2
Architectural		28	2					30
Miscellaneous	6	130	39	5	4	1		185
Total	36	241	95	22	9	2	11	416

Table 7.5. Burned Ground Stone Artifacts by Type.

Artifact Type	Burned	Unburned	Unknown	Total
Mano	44	32	13	89
Metate	4	8		12
Mano/Metate	1			1
Mortar	1			1
Abrader	14	11		25
Polisher	2	21		23
Axe	1	5	2	8
Piki stone	17			17
Griddle stone	18			18
Jewelry		5		5
Hoe	1	1		2
Architectural	21	9		30
Miscellaneous	100	85		185
Total	224	177	15	416

those left on the floor of rooms and kivas, may have ritual significance, it seems that this theory does not explain the majority of the burned artifacts at Chevelon. Rather, most of the burned ground stone at Chevelon appears to have burned when the structures themselves burned, at or after use discontinued. No one room contains a majority of the non-use-related burned artifacts. S. 227, which was not burned, has no non-use-related burned artifacts. The burned artifacts are associated with the various rooms that are closest to the K. 248 (Table 7.7). Although purposeful, discard of used ground stone was occurring at Chevelon, this practice does not include, as a primary action, the ritual burning of these artifacts.

Only 8.2 percent of artifacts had distinguishable reuse — mostly manos and abraders (Table 7.8). Reuse is defined as employing an artifact with a defined purpose in a nontraditional way; for example, a mano reused as a pecking stone. It is expected that numerous miscellaneous artifacts, especially lapstones and handstones, by definition will be repurposed or have multiple intended uses. The small number of reused artifacts may indicate that there was little need to conserve ground stone at Chevelon, a behavior that has been associated with other Homol'ovi assemblages (Fratt 1991, 2001). The lack of ground stone conservation at Chevelon is likely due to easy access to abundant sources of the raw materials needed to produce the ground stone. Nearly six in ten artifacts were recovered from cultural fill or midden deposits (Table 7.9). Another 16.1 percent were recovered from either roof fall or wall fall proveniences, while only about 16.8 percent were recovered from floor fill or contact surfaces.

Manos and Metates

In Pueblo culture, manos and metates are tools used together as food-processing implements, and especially in the production of corn grain (J. Adams 1979, 2002; Fratt 1991). The

Table 7.6. Recovery Context for Burned Ground Stone Artifacts.

Recovery Context	Burned	Unburned	Unknown	Total
Occupation Surface	14	9	2	25
Floor Fill	18	26	1	45
Fill	138	105	3	246
Wall Fall	14	15	1	30
Roof Fall	21	10	6	37
Feature Fill	11	7	2	20
Mixed Wall and Roof Fall	1	1		2
Unknown	7	4		11
Total	224	177	15	416

metate served as the bottom stone upon which materials were ground, while the mano was a hand-held stone that was rubbed in a back-and-forth or circular motion over the metate surface. There are three distinct types of manos and metates: the basin mano and metate, the trough mano and metate, and the flat mano and metate (for descriptions of the characteristics of each, see J. Adams 2002). These various types can generally be identified through either form or an analysis of use-wear. The sequence of basin to trough to flat manos is assumed to be a technological development associated with an increase in grinding intensity and efficiency over time (J. Adams 1993, 2002).

Manos

A total of 89 manos were recovered from Chevelon with more than 80 percent flat (Table 7.1; Table 7.10; Figure 7.1). Given that flat manos are the latest in the technological development of mano/metate forms (Crown 2000:235; J. Adams 1993:332; Lange 1998:101), the dominance of the flat manos in the Chevelon assemblage is expected. All but five of the manos were composed of Shinarump Sandstone (Table 7.3). As Fratt (1991:63) has noted, Shinarump Sandstone has particular qualities, including its variability in texture, durability of cement, and local accessibility, which make it desirable for grinding corn. Although the manos from Chevelon are primarily composed of Shinarump, similar to assemblages from other Homol'ovi sites, there seems to be a focus on medium and fine-grained manos in the Chevelon collection with fewer than 20 percent coarse-grained or variable (Table 7.4). This differs from other Homol'ovi assemblages, which were more evenly distributed over the range of available textures (Fratt 1991:63; 2001:229). One reason for the apparent overrepresentation of medium and fine-grained manos is that these textures may exhaust faster than the coarse-grained manos, especially if finer grained corn is in high demand. This may result in an increased rate of discard. This explanation fits with the recovery of more than half of medium and fine-grained manos from fill. Access to coarser materials may also have been a factor with Shinarump Sandstone sources farther than Moenkopi. Variability in texture of the Shinarump Sandstone outcrops closest to Chevelon has not been assayed to evaluate this explanation.

As shown in Table 7.11, three out of

Table 7.7. Burned Ground Stone Artifacts by Structure.

Structure	Function	Burned	Unburned	Unknown	Total
120	Storage	8	6	1	15
123	Storage		2		2
124	Habitation	8	3		11
158	Storage	5	2	1	8
159	Habitation	5	6	1	12
161	Habitation	1			1
222	Piki House	16	11		27
227	Storage	6	16		22
246	Extramural/Plaza	1			1
248	Kiva	10	1		11
252	Surface Ritual	7	14		21
262	Ritual	2			2
264	Habitation	1			1
265	Storage		3		3
266	Storage			1	1
268	Storage	2	3		5
269	Habitation	7	3	1	11
274	Fill above kiva	3	3		6
279	Kiva	66	51	3	120
286	Storage			1	1
287	Unknown	5	1		6
288	Storage	15	6		21
289	Habitation	5	3		8
293	Surface Ritual	1	2		3
345	Habitation	3	4	1	8
373	Storage	3	3		6
393	Habitation	10	3	1	14
403	Unknown		2		2
603	Habitation	2	2		4
702	Storage	4	1	1	6
704	Storage	2		1	3
705	Unknown		1		1
726	Storage		1		1
900	Plaza/Extramural	5	7		12
901	Kiva	18	14	1	33
0	Extramural	3	3	1	7
Total		224	177	15	416

Table 7.8. Ground Stone Artifact Reuse.

Artifact Type	Single Use	Multiple Indeterminate	Concommitant	Sequential	Concomitant & Sequential	Unused Blank	Indeterminant	Unknown	Total
Mano	66	1	3	2	4	1		12	89
Metate	11					1			12
Mano/Metate	1								1
Mortar	1								1
Abrader	11	1	9	3	1				25
Polisher	18		3	1			1		23
Axe	3		1		1		1	2	8
Piki stone	17								17
Griddle stone	18								18
Jewelry	5								5
Hoe				1		1			2
Architectural	19		1		1		9		30
Miscellaneous	83	3	17	3	11	5	63		185
Total	253	5	34	10	18	8	74	14	416

Table 7.9. Recovery Context for Ground Stone.

Artifact Type	Occupied Surface	Floor Fill	Fill	Wall Fall	Roof Fall	Feature Fill	Mixed Roof/ Wall Fall	Unknown	Total
Mano	6	12	46	5	10	4		6	89
Metate		1	8	2		1			12
Mano/Metate		1							1
Mortar			1						1
Abrader	3	2	17	1	1			1	25
Polisher	3	4	15				1		23
Axe		3	2		1	2			8
Piki Stone	1		10	1	5				17
Griddle Stone		1	16		1				18
Jewelry			3	1	1				5
Hoe			1	1					2
Architectural	1	3	14	3	5	2		2	30
Miscellaneous	11	18	113	16	13	11	1	2	185
Total	25	45	246	30	37	20	2	11	416

Table 7.10. Mano and Metate Subtypes*.

Artifact Type	Percentage of Total Mano/Metate Assemblage	Number of Artifacts
Basin mano		
Trough mano	4.49	4
Flat mano	80.90	72
Indeterminate mano	12.36	11
Blank/unused	2.25	2
Total	100.00	89
Basin metate		
Trough metate	8.33	1
Flat metate	58.33	7
Indeterminate metate	33.33	4
Total	100.00	12
Mano:Metate Ratio	89:12	**7:1
Basin		
Trough	4:8	0.5:1
Flat	73:7	10.5:1
Indet.	11:4	2.75:1

*This table doesn't include the mano/metate fragment, since we couldn't ID whether it's a mano or metate.
**Typical ratio is 4:1; metates being removed from site; trough manos either missing, reused, or metate is overrepresented

four of manos exhibited evidence of multiple use surfaces, mostly having two opposite use surfaces (Figure 7.1). Not surprisingly, flat manos had the most variability. However, trough manos were also represented by multiple surface types (Table 7.11). The high percentage of manos with multiple grinding surfaces suggests high intensity corn grinding was occurring at Chevelon (Fratt 1991:63). Most manos also exhibit evidence of resharpening before their last grinding use, which also indicates high intensity grinding. Manos with resharpening are made of either medium or fine-grained material, indicating that perhaps these manos were extensively used before they were discarded and is consistent with these textures' apparent high discard rate.

Nearly a quarter of manos were whole (Table 7.2). There is a strong correlation with recovery context with whole manos predominantly associated with occupation, floor and floor fill contexts; the exception being kiva fill (Tables 7.9 and 7.12). Broken manos are strongly associated with domestic middens, and roof and wall fall (Table 7.9 and 7.12). Reasons for these relationships will be explored below.

Metates

Twelve metates were recovered from Chevelon (Table 7.1, Figure 7.2). All metates are composed of Shinarump Sandstone (Table 7.3). Seven of the eight metates, identifiable as

Table 7.11. Mano Use Surfaces.

Mano Subtype	One Surface	Two Opposite Surfaces	Two Adjacent Surfaces	Three Surfaces	Four Surfaces	Blank	Indeterminate	Total
Basin mano								
Trough mano		1	1	2				4
Flat mano	9	46		6	2		9	72
Indeterminate mano	3	7		1				11
Blank/unused						2		2
Total	12	54	1	9	2	2	9	89

Table 7.12. Ground Stone Artifact Type by Structure Use.

Artifact Type	Habitation	Storage	Kiva	Extramural/Plaza	Uknown	Piki House	Total
Mano	27	17	33	5	3	4	89
Metate	1	1	7	1	1	1	12
Mano/Metate			1				1
Mortar			1				1
Abrader	4	4	13	1	1	2	25
Polisher	6	5	7	1		4	23
Axe	2	1	3	1		1	8
Piki stone	6	3	5	1		2	17
Griddle stone	3	4	4		1	6	18
Jewelry		3	1		1		5
Hoe	1			1			2
Architectural	3	10	16	1			30
Miscellaneous	32	31	105	8	2	7	185
Total	85	79	196	20	9	27	416

Figure 7.1. One- and two-hand manos with multiple use surfaces: (a) one-hand mano; (b,c) basalt and Shinarump Sandstone two-sided, two-hand manos; (d,e) three-sided, two-hand manos.

to type, are flat with the other trough (Table 7.10). In her analysis of the H3 ground stone, Fratt (2001:230) noted that the ratio of manos to metates was about 6:1. She comments that this appears to be a relatively normal ratio for Western Pueblo sites of this period, citing proportions recorded at Bailey Ruin and also at Pottery Hill (Velado 1999). The ratio of manos to metates at Chevelon is 7.4:1 in line with H3, although the flat mano to metate ratio is a high 10.3:1 (Table 7.10). A third of the metates are burned, a much lower frequency than manos and the general ground stone assemblage (Table 7.5). More than half were recovered from kiva fill and only one was recovered from floor/floor fill (Tables 7.9 & 7.12). Four metates were recovered from the upper fill of K. 279 suggesting they were deposited near or during the final depopulation of the community.

Piki Stones and Griddle Stones

When identifying piki stones versus griddle stones, the definitions provided in J. Adams (2002:229) were utilized (Figure 7.3). In general, griddle stones are tabular stone slabs most often used for cooking tortillas and cakes. They are often expediently designed, but they do exhibit use-related burning, as griddles are placed over hearths for use. Piki stones, on the other hand, are more specialized tabular stones used for cooking piki bread by modern and historic Hopi. The surface is ground very smooth, formally made in a consistent form, and specially prepared with particular oils to help make the surface "non-stick". After much use, piki stones become extensively burned and their surfaces are very unstable due to the multiple use-related burning. Piki stones are usually larger (longer and thicker) than griddle stones, and their surfaces are usually in worse condition when found archaeologically. Piki stones are also associated with "piki hearths", which are three-sided, as opposed to the standard 4-sided hearth (J. Adams 2002:229). For the purposes of the Chevelon ground

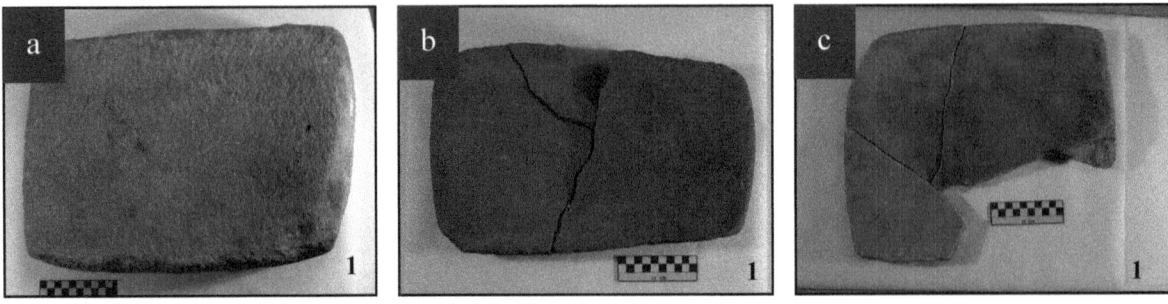

Figure 7.2. Flat metates: (a) medium-grain, flat metate; (b,c) fine-grain, flat metates.

Figure 7.3. Piki stones and griddles: (a) piki stone; (b) piki stone detail; (c) piki stone cross-section; (d,e) griddle stones.

stone assemblage, piki stones were generally identified as separate from griddle stones by the condition of their surface, the visibility of an oil penetration layer, and sometimes thickness of the fragment. While artifacts have been officially classified as either piki stones or griddle stones, further analysis of these artifacts after their surfaces have been cleansed and conserved may reveal characteristics that may affect the current identifications.

A total of 17 piki stones and 18 griddle stones were identified (Table 7.1). All are composed of Moenkopi Sandstone and are fine-grained (Tables 7.3 and 7.4). All exhibit evidence of use-related burning; however, the piki stones show far more extensive burning and surface damage as a result. One piki stone fragment showed evidence of secondary reuse as an abrader; this reuse occurred after the fragment separated from the original stone.

S. 222 is a piki house with two piki hearths (Figure 4.6). Eight of the griddle and piki stone fragments were recovered from the fill of this structure leading to the possibility the highly disturbed surface or floor above S. 222 was also a piki house or similarly specialized food production room (Tables 7.9 and 7.13). S. 227, with nine piki stone and three griddle fragments, and K. 248, with three piki stones and four griddle stones, also contained high proportions of these artifacts. It is unclear, yet, whether the spatial distribution of the piki stones (and griddle stones) is significant in relation to the location of the piki house and the overall structure of the site. Piki houses were identified at H1 (S. 209) and H3 (S. 14) as well as piki stone fragments, including a whole piki stone propped against the outside of the H1 piki house. No piki houses were identified at H2 or H4, although piki-like fragments were recovered from both sites. Based on our current knowledge, piki stones from H4 are earliest in the archaeological record dating between 1260 and 1285 (E.C. Adams 2002, 2004b; Dedecker 2005), becoming more formalized with the appearance of piki houses and hearths at other sites (Adams 2002; Fratt 2001:232). Given that two out of three piki and griddle stones were recovered from RB200 and another 28.6 percent from RB300, totaling 34 of 35 pieces, suggests production of piki and other specialized foods was controlled by the earliest groups at Chevelon, likely helping to bolster their social status in the community. Interestingly, only one fragment (a griddle) was recovered from K. 279, with the majority of contexts associated with earlier uses focused around K. 248 (Table 7.13). This indicates ownership of piki/griddle related cuisine was associated with and possibly controlled by one social group, likely founders of the village.

Abraders

A total of 9 grooved abraders, 15 flat abraders, and 1 indeterminate abrader were recovered (Tables 7.1, 7.14; Figure 7.4). Eleven were complete; another six were more than half complete. All abraders are composed of sandstone (Table 7.3), with fine-grained Moenkopi and Shinarump being nearly equally represented, totaling 23 of 25 artifacts. One abrader was reused. Two abraders have pigment residue on their surfaces: one red, which may be hematite, the other black, which may be pigment or may be heavy carbon residue. Nineteen were recovered from fill or wall and roof fall. Three were recovered from floors and two from floor fill (Table 7.9). Twenty-two abraders were recovered from RB200 from the piki house (S. 222), two kivas (S . 248 and 279), and S. 288 where a neonate was discovered. This distribution is quite similar to the one for piki and griddle stones (Table 7.13).

Polishing Stones

All but two of the 23 polishing stones were whole (Table 7.2, Figure 7.5). All but one were composed of quartzite; the other is made from an unknown material. The majority of the polishing stones were discoid, although at least one was oval-shaped. Only one has multiple use facets often associated with stones used to polish pottery. J. Adams (2002:96-97) suggests that use-wear analysis may help further identify polishing stones as pottery polishers, stone polishers, and floor polishers (Table 7.15). Floor polishers are hand-sized, whereas pottery polishers are much smaller and usually gripped by the fingers. Based on the descriptions by J. Adams (2002), the polishing stones are most likely pottery polishers (N=2) with little sheen and clay caked onto their surfaces or stone polishers (N=9). Only one was identified as a floor polisher with its being purposely shaped and modified for easier grip (Table 7.15). The presence of pottery polishers, some with pottery clay still adhering to them, demonstrates local production of pottery. Seven polishing stones

170 Medeiros and E.C. Adams

Table 7.13. Ground Stone by Structure.

Structure	Function	Mano	Metate	Mano/Metate	Mortar	Abrader	Polisher	Axe	Piki Stone	Griddle Stone	Jewelry
120	Storage	4					3		1		
123	Storage										
124	Habitation	3						1			
158	Storage	2									
159	Habitation	7				1		1			
161	Habitation										
222	Piki House	4	1			2	4	1	2	6	
227	Storage	7	1			1	3		1	3	
246	Extramural/Plaza										
248	Kiva	3				2			3	3	
252	Surface Ritual	2				1	1	1			
262	Ritual										
264	Habitation										
265	Storage						1				1
266	Storage	1									
268	Storage	2									
269	Habitation	4				1				1	
274	Fill above kiva	1	4								
279	Kiva	21	1	1		10	3	1		1	1
286	Storage						1				
287	Unknown	3				1				1	
288	Storage	2				3			1	1	1
289	Habitation	2				1	1			1	
293	Surface Ritual										
345	Habitation	3	1				1		1		
373	Storage						1				1
393	Habitation	2				1			4	1	
403	Unknown										1
603	Habitation	2					1				
702	Storage	1							1		
704	Storage	2									
705	Unknown		1								
726	Storage										
900	Plaza/Extramural	4	1			1	1	1	1		
901	Kiva	6	2		1		3	1	2		
0	Extramural	1									
Total		89	12	1	1	25	23	8	17	18	5

Table 7.14. Abrader Subtypes.

Artifact Type	Percentage of Total Abrader Assemblage	Number of Artifacts
Grooved abrader	36.00	9
Flat abrader	60.00	15
Indeterminate	4.00	1
Total	100.00	25

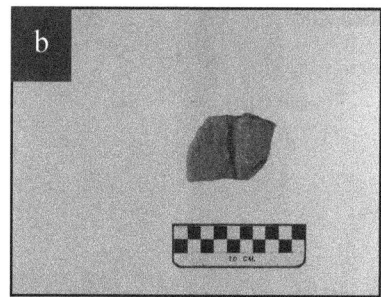

Figure 7.4. Grooved and flat abraders: (a) grooved abrader, burned or heated; (b) grooved abrader; (c) flat abrader; (d) flat abrader from mano; (e) flat abrader with red pigment.

were recovered from floor/floor fill contexts (Table 7.9). Six from habitation structures in association with abraders may indicate loci of pottery manufacture (Tables 7.12 and 7.13).

Axes

Only eight axes, all three-quarter-grooved were recovered from Chevelon; four complete, two nearly complete, one less than half, and one unknown (Tables 7.1, 7.2, 7.16, Figure 7.6). Seven are manufactured of igneous material and one of chert. The igneous axes were manufactured and traded from villages below the Mogollon Rim to the southeast (Table 7.3) One igneous axe appears to be unfinished. One side of the bit is shaped, is relatively smooth, and finishes in a point, while the other side seems to have the beginnings of a point and has been chipped at, but still has portions of the original exterior of the stone present. The axe could be broken or in a resharpening stage, but it seems more likely to be in production, especially because portions of the original exterior are still present on one side of the bit. The axe recovered from a wall niche in S. 222 is made of chert and has a less well-defined groove.

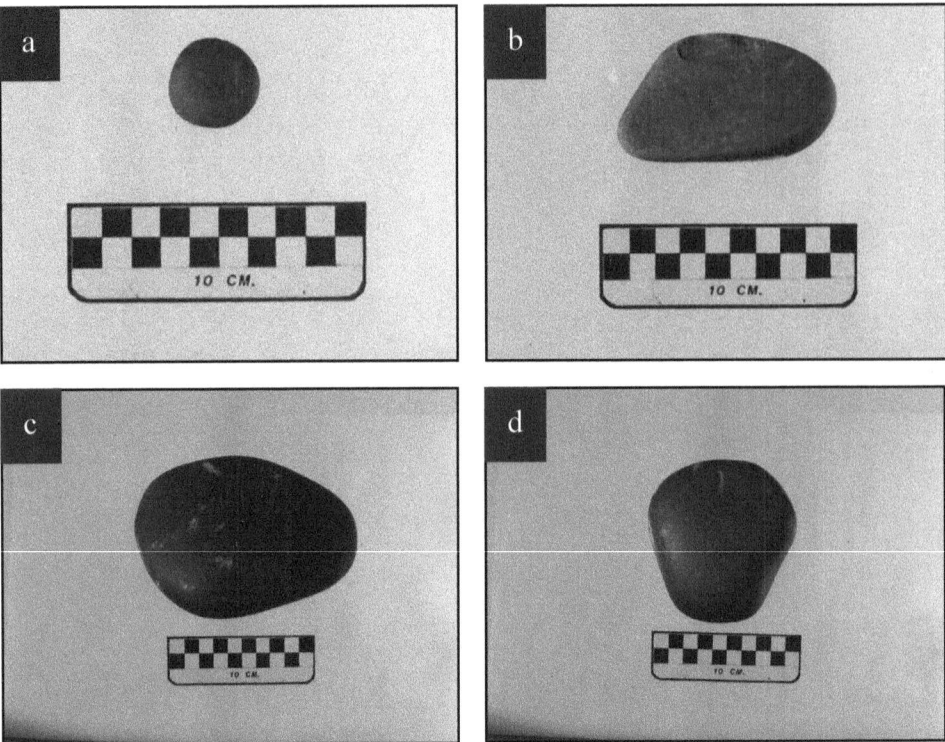

Figure 7.5. Polishing stones: (a) small polishing stone; (b) large polishing stone; (c,d) floor or wall polishing stone.

In terms of type of axe, the Chevelon axes fit into the Homol'ovi context well with 19 of 20 also three-quarter-groove axes. The Chevelon axes composed of igneous, a fine-grained igneous material, occur in the same frequency (88 percent) as from other Homol'ovi cluster sites (85 percent) (Fratt 2001:233). They represent persistent long distance exchange throughout the Cluster's occupation. Many of the other Homol'ovi axes also exhibit extensive resharpening and use, and were often associated with ritual contexts (Fratt 2001:233). This appears to be the case for the axe recovered from the floor of S. 159, which was propped against a shrine feature (Figure 4.5). Three of the eight axes were recovered from fill or roof fall, three from floor fill, and two from features (Table 7.9). Axes were recovered from three of the four excavated kivas, the piki house, from both clan/ritual habitation structures (S. 124 and 159), and from S. 286 floor where it was associated with three sacrificed rabbits arrayed with their heads facing each other (Table 7.12, Figure 7.8). There is no question that axes received special treatment at Chevelon and were strongly associated with structures likely controlled by groups having prestige within the community.

Miscellaneous Artifacts

The miscellaneous artifact category includes 44.5 percent of the total ground stone assemblage (Table 7.1, Figure 7.7). The miscellaneous category includes 15 subtypes, listed in Table 7.17. The largest subcategory is 47 general miscellaneous stones. These artifacts generally have grinding from use or to shape the objects, but the ultimate use of the

Table 7.15. Polishing Stone Subtypes.

Artifact Type	Percentage of Total Polishing Stone Assemblage	Number of Artifacts
Ceramic polisher	8.70	2
Floor polisher	4.35	1
Stone polisher	39.13	9
Burnisher	4.35	1
Indeterminate Polisher	43.48	10
Total	100.00	23

Table 7.16. Axe Statistics.

Structure	Use	Recovery Context	Style	Material	Condition
124	Ritual Habitation	Floor	3/4 groove	Igneous	Whole
159	Ritual Habitation	Feature	3/4 groove	Igneous	Whole
222	Piki	Feature	3/4 groove	Chert	Whole
252	Kiva	Floor	3/4 groove	Igneous	Frag-bit only
279	Kiva	Fill	3/4 groove	Igneous	Frag-head only
286	Storage	Roof Fall	3/4 groove	Igneous	Whole
900	Plaza Feature	Fill	3/4 groove	Igneous	Frag-groove & bit present
901	Kiva	Floor	3/4 groove	Igneous	Nearly whole – missing bit

Figure 7.6. Stone axes and maul: (a) three-quarter groove axes of igneous material; (b) maul.

object remains elusive. Added to this category are four groups of 21 other miscellaneous ground stone objects with one or more distinctive attributes. Together the five groups total 36.8 percent of miscellaneous subtypes (Table 7.17). Forty percent of miscellaneous artifacts are manos/handstones and lapstone slabs. The artifacts included in the manos/handstones category were identified as such primarily because they demonstrated use-wear that was inconclusively associated with either handstones or manos, metates or grinding slabs. The seven grinding stones were likely used for a multitude of tasks, including

Figure 7.7 Miscellaneous ground stone artifacts: (a) mortar; (b) ball; (c) cylinder; (d) notched stone; (e) painted slab; (f) jar lid; (g) hoe fragment; (h) cloud blower side and (i) cloud blower top; (j) petrified wood, lignite, sandstone, shaped sandstone.

food and nonfood grinding. The third largest subcategory of artifacts, at 29, is netherstones, also involved in grinding as the base stone. One artifact, each of a stone ball, eccentric stone, a palette, and a lid cover for a ceramic vessel, were also part of the assemblage. The palette in particular is a curious artifact. It is made of argillite and does not look like other artifacts that have been classified as palettes in other Homol'ovi assemblages (Fratt 1991). However, the Chevelon palette is a small fragment, and as such, prevents us from making more conclusive comments. The stone lid from the floor of S. 159 is adjacent to a large Sikyatki Polychrome jar and was likely used to seal its contents.

SPATIAL DISTRIBUTION

Given the high frequency of several ground stone categories in a select few rooms, it is not surprising that from a total assemblage standpoint, there are strong patterns. RB200 contains 64.9 percent of all ground stone and 56.3 percent of ground stone excluding miscellaneous. Using ceramic counts as a proxy for expected artifact frequency (see Tables 6.1, 6.11, 6.13, and Appendix A), 42.3 percent of ceramics are from RB200, suggesting ground stone is present in an unusually high frequency (Table 7.18). This seems to be due to the high concentration of ground stone in a few kivas and structures: K. 279 and 901 and S. 222, 227, 288, and 252. K. 901 is the only structure in the top six not from RB200 (Table 7.13).

Not surprisingly, the structures with the greatest diversity of ground stone types (K. 279 and 901 and S. 222, 227, 900, and 288) are the same structures having the most total ground stone with the exception of the suite of surface features represented as S. (Plaza) 900, which

are spatially associated with K. 901 (Table 7.12). Two strong patterns emerge: 1) RB200 is the focal point of discard of all types of ground stone with nearly all objects recovered from some form of fill context (Table 7.9). 2) Discard in RB200 and 300/901 is strongly associated with the fill of ceremonial structures (kivas) (Table 7.13). RB200 accounts for 64.9 percent of all ground stone and with the addition of S. 900 and K. 901, it accounts for 75.7 percent of all ground stone, actually lower than the 87.8 percent of ceramics represented by these areas. Thus, the 11 percent of ground stone from S. 900 and K. 901 is actually a depleted assemblage when contrasted with 35 percent of ceramics (Table 7.18). RB200 continues to standout as the locus of many more ground stone objects than ceramics, whereas all other room blocks, except RB400, have fewer than expected versus total ceramics (Tables 7.13, 7.18, 6.11, 6.13, Ceramic Appendix A).

In contrast, objects associated with floors, floor fill and features, which account for only 21.6 percent of total ground stone artifacts, have a higher frequency in RB100 and associated RB600 where 34.1 percent of ground stone artifacts were recovered from these contexts. This is likely because many of these structures were still in use or formally closed and did not include kivas. By comparison, K. 252, which was still in use when Chevelon was depopulated, had five ground stone objects on its floor (Table 7.9). Thus, there is supportive evidence for the use of ground stone, especially whole objects, in structure closure.

Kivas contained 40.4 percent of ceramics and 47.1 percent of ground stone artifacts (Table 7.13). However, when miscellaneous ground stone is removed from the totals, only 39.4 percent came from kivas, exactly as expected from ceramic frequencies. Miscellaneous is especially high in K. 279. Thus, it is the

Table 7.17. Miscellaneous Ground Stone Subtypes.

	Percentage (%) of Total Miscellaneous Artifacts (N=185)	Number of Artifacts
Eccentric stone	0.54	1
General miscellaneous	25.41	47
Grinding slab	3.78	7
Handstone	18.38	34
Lapstone	17.30	32
Lid cover	0.54	1
Mano/Handstone	3.78	7
Metate/Grinding slab	0.54	1
Miscellaneous amorphorous	0.54	1
Miscellaneous burned slab	4.86	9
Miscellaneous slab with worked edge(s)	5.41	10
Miscellaneous slab without worked edge(s)	2.16	4
Netherstone	15.68	29
Palette	0.54	1
Stone ball	0.54	1
Total	100.00	185

influences of non-kiva structures in RB200 which elevates overall frequency of ground stone and suggests that RB200 as a whole is where control of objects was centralized.

Related to object use and discard of ground stone is the frequency and location of burning. Only 10.6 percent of ground stone was burned due to use. This low number should not affect overall patterns in burning of ground stone unrelated to use (Tables 7.5, 7.6 and 7.7). As previously summarized, 53.8 percent of ground stone is burned (Table 7.5) with only 19.2 percent recovered from floor, floor fill, or features while 9.4 percent were recovered from roof deposits, the other context where burning is most likely (Table 7.6). A total of 46.9 percent were recovered from fill, a context unlikely related to primary burning (Table 7.6). Table 7.7 underscores this distribution where 62.5 percent of artifacts from burned structures are also burned versus 52.9 percent in unburned structures. This suggests that structural fires did impact burning of ground stone objects, but that many burned artifacts were also discarded into fill, especially into K. 279, which accounts for 25.0 percent of all burned artifacts and nearly 50 percent of burned ground stone in unburned structures.

Less than a quarter of ground stone was whole (Table 7.2), three-quarters was recovered from fill, and nearly half was burned unrelated to use (Tables 7.2, 7.5, and 7.11). These figures suggest that approximately 75 percent of ground stone was a product of discard after the normal use life of the object was exhausted. However, intentional deposition in RB100 and 200 also suggests that the use lives of many of the objects continued in new contexts related

Chapter 7: Ground Stone 177

to closure and social memory.

The numbers presented above suggest there was a limited need to conserve ground stone at Chevelon. First, a very large percentage of the total assemblage displays discard characteristics. Second, although a relatively small number of artifacts were associated with floor contexts (which might suggest conservation), almost half of these artifacts were whole. If ground stone was not very precious, a large number of whole artifacts should not have been found associated with floor contexts, but instead should have been carried with the inhabitants when they left Chevelon, especially since none of these floor artifacts were large and cumbersome. However, traveling distance taken by emigrants to their new home and available stone there likely played roles in such decisions. Whole artifacts were also found within the secondary deposition contexts, also indicating that wholesale discard or sacrifice of ground stone was not an issue for the occupants of Chevelon.

Temporal Distribution

The temporal distribution of the ground stone assemblage is displayed in Table 7.19. The ground stone artifacts were dated first through provenience and stratigraphy. If no date was specifically associated with an excavation unit, then the structure date was used. If the structure was undated, artifacts were classified as unknown. The 416 artifacts from dated deposits are distributed as 5.3 percent during the Tuwiuca Phase (TP), 9.4 percent during Early Homol'ovi Phase (EHP), 30.3 percent druing Middle Homol'ovi Phase (MHP), and 50.5 percent during Late Homol'ovi Phase (LHP); 4.6 percent of the artifacts could not be classified as to a phase. Due to small sample

Table 7.18. Frequency of Ground Stone versus Ceramics by Room Block.

Room Block	100	200	300	400	600	700	900	Other	Total
Ceramics > 1.0%	3419 = 16.7%	8638 = 42.3%	600 = 2.9%	586 = 2.9%	Not analyzed	Not analyzed	7180 = 35.2%	N/A	20,423
Ground Stone	49 = 12.4%	270 = 68.5%	28 = 7.1%	2 = 0.5%	4 (NIT*)	11 (NIT*)	45 = 11.4%	7 (NIT*)	394
Ratio: GS/CER x 100	1.43	3.12	4.67	0.34			0.63		1.93

*NIT= Not Included in Total

size, the TP and the EHP are considered together.

If we compare percentage of ground stone by time period to percentage of ceramics by time period (Table 6.6 and 7.19), there are small, but notable, differences. Percentage of ground stone for TP and EHP is 14.7 percent compared to 10.9 percent ceramics. For MHP, this disparity is greatest with 30.3 percent of ground stone versus only 21.4 percent ceramics. The LHP has fewer than predicted ground stone artifacts at 50.55 versus 67.65 of ceramics (Tables 6.6 and 7.19). The higher frequency of ground stone in TP/EHP, and MHP in particular, reflect the high frequency of ground stone in RB200, which is dominated by MHP deposits and secondarily by EHP deposits. The low percentage of LHP is a product of these deposits being focused in K. 901 and structures surrounding the south plaza, where fewer ground stone objects have been discarded because many of these structures were still in use to or nearly to depopulation of the pueblo.

Some interesting patterns in artifact percentage by time are notable in Table 7.19. Higher than expected percentages of polishers, piki stones, and griddles occur in TP/EHP deposits, due to their strong association with S. 222 and 227, and K. 248. As discussed previously, this pattern suggests control of specific feasting practices in RB200 from its founding. The only notable anomalies in MHP artifacts are the higher than expected frequencies of metates and abraders. All the metates come from K. 274/279 with four from the latest fill deposits of the kiva, suggesting their deposition is related to closure rituals for the kiva and possibly the oldest parts of RB200.

LHP also has an unexpectedly high frequency of piki stones concentrated in habitation S. 345 and 393 (N=3) in RB300. RB300 is the second oldest room block in Chevelon and continuity, or shared control of piki bread-making with RB200, is indicated. Of particular note is the temporal distribution of axes in the assemblage with six of eight from LHP and one each from MHP and EHP. All axes are associated with ceremonial deposits. There are one each in three of the four kivas (252, 279 and 901; keep in mind K. 248, the fourth kiva, was 99 percent vandalized). There were also axes recovered from structures associated with kivas (S. 900); from a ritual deposit in S. 286 associated with three sacrificed rabbits; from ritual (clan house) S. 124 and 159; and piki house, S. 222, where it had been placed in a wall feature. The spatial and temporal distribution of axes suggests a continuity of their use for closure of structures used in religious activities through time and space (Table 7.16). Although axes have been associated with warfare (LeBlanc 1999), it is unlikely their use in these structures is associated with warfare, although their exact meaning is unclear.

Conclusions

Overall, the Chevelon ground stone assemblage is typical of Pueblo cultures of the same time period and region, although the large number of piki and griddle stones recovered from this site and from several other Homol'ovi sites suggests that the inhabitants of these sites were involved in new types of cuisine that at Chevelon is associated with prestige and likely control of feasting associated with ceremonies controlled by village founders and early occupants of the pueblo. The large number of burned artifacts and the large number of artifacts recovered from cultural fill/midden deposits indicates that three-quarters of ground

	Tuwiuca Phase 1290–1325 C.E.	Early Homol'ovi Phase 1325–1365 C.E.	Middle Homol'ovi Phase 1365–1385 C.E.	Late Homol'ovi Phase 1385–1400 C.E.	Unknown	Total
Mano	7	8	22	48	4	89
Metate	1	1	5	5		12
Mano/Metate			1			1
Mortar				1		1
Abrader	1	4	10	9	1	25
Polisher	3	4	3	13		23
Axe		1	1	6		8
Piki stone	1	5		11		17
Griddle stone	3	9	1	4	1	18
Jewelry			1	4		5
Hoe				1	1	2
Architectural	2		10	17	1	30
Miscellaneous	4	7	72	91	11	185
Total	22	39	126	210	19	416

Table 7.19. Temporal Distribution of Ground Stone.

stone artifacts were products of discard.

It is clear that ground stone artifacts played an important role in everyday practices of manufacture and cooking of cornmeal and production of pottery. However, the archeological record for some ground stone at Chevelon has less to do with everyday use and more to do with their role in structure retirement and settlement closure. Prominent in these activities are manos and axes. Whole manos are strongly associated with closure of habitation structures in the late occupied rooms surrounding the south plaza. Axes, on the other hand, are 100 percent correlated with closure of spaces devoted to religious ritual activities.

Discard of broken, or used up, ground stone objects into the fill of ceremonial structures (kivas and others) underscores the important contribution that ground stone makes to ceremonial trash (Walker 1995, 1996a; Walker et al. 2000). After all, Chevelon occupants had many choices in where to discard these objects including general community middens or in the fill of discontinued domestic structures, yet these spaces have purposely depleted ground stone assemblages (sensu Schiffer 1987), indicating disposal of ground stone was intentional. The association of ground stone with preparation of corn, the ultimate sustenance of a pueblo person (with which their life is intimately tied [Loftin 2003; Parsons 1939]) and their community. In addition, the incredible longevity of most ground stone objects, used in food preparation, where manos, metates, and piki stones are passed on to descendent women in their lineages, suggests ground stone involved in corn cuisine is the ultimate symbol and object to be sacrificed when a room, area, or community is being closed.

Chapter 8
Raw Material Procurement, Technological Organization, and Ritual Use: Contextualizing Flaked Stone Production and Use at Chevelon

Melanie Medeiros

Since the beginning of HRP, analysis of flaked stone has played an important role in contributing to the determination of individual village social and technological organization, and in facilitating our understanding of the inhabitants' knowledge of, and relationships with, the surrounding cultural and geological landscapes. The same is true of the Chevelon flaked stone analysis and, although the Chevelon assemblage is significantly smaller than those from H1, H2 (Lyons and Pitablo 1996; Sullivan and Madsen 1991), or H3 (Young 2001), analysis of this assemblage has resulted in informative conclusions and interpretations regarding the production, use, and social significance of flaked stone artifacts at Chevelon. To that end, this discussion presents a description of the Chevelon flaked stone assemblage, addresses questions relating to raw material procurement and technological organization, and contextualizes what we know about the flaked stone assemblage from Chevelon, within the greater body of Homol'ovi flaked stone research.

Specifically, this chapter imparts a qualitative, quantitative, and a theoretical analysis of the Chevelon flaked stone assemblage, organized into three broad sections. First, the Chevelon assemblage is described in terms of its overall characteristics. Second, questions concerning raw material procurement, technological organization, and tool use are considered, particularly through possible exchange relationships in relation to the flaked stone assemblages from H2 and H3, and as important components of ritual action and social memory. Third, the Chevelon assemblage is contextualized both spatially and temporally in order to reveal broader patterns pertaining to technological and social organization within the village itself.

Of note and importance to the analyses presented in this chapter is the (unintentional) sampling bias in favor of ritual structures/deposits over domestic structures/deposits. Just over 71 percent (N=5,624) of the Chevelon flaked stone assemblage was recovered from three kivas (K. 248, 274/279 and, 901), two storage rooms with ritual deposits (S. 266/286), and one plaza area (Plaza 900) in the oldest areas — RB200 and RB300 — of the site. Overall, these structures also had higher ratios of flaked stone by volume than other non-ritual structures at the site. This distribution in favor of ritual structures/deposits has two important consequences for our understanding of flaked stone use at the site. First, because a significant portion of the flaked stone assemblage was recovered from midden deposits in these areas, we are seeing the later stages — recycling and discard — of flaked stone use more than any other stages, which include procurement, production, and (domestic) use. Second, because so many of the midden deposits in these areas are enriched deposits (Adams and LaMotta 2006), the importance of flaked stone, and especially projectile points, in ritual behavior at Chevelon is much clearer than is the use of flaked stone in domestic contexts. As a result, we do not have a very good handle on the use of flaked stone in everyday, domestic contexts, and we have not been able to clearly identify activity areas in which flaked stone manufacture or use took place, with the possible exception of S. 161 and certain areas of Plaza 900. These consequences heavily weight the discussion of flaked stone at Chevelon towards both ritual uses and room blocks RB200 and RB300.

Terminology

The artifact classifications to type utilized in this chapter are based on definitions, attributes, and characteristics (Table 8.1) initially outlined by Sullivan and Rozen (1985) and subsequently employed in other flaked stone analyses conducted by the HRP (e.g., Krebs 1999; Lyons and Pitblado 1996; Sullivan and Madsen 1991; Young 2001). Consistent implementation of artifact classifications throughout the Homol'ovi flaked stone assemblages makes comparison between these assemblages a viable exercise.

Methodology

Analysis of the flaked stone assemblage from Chevelon was conducted in two phases, following established HRP protocols. Only flaked stone from undisturbed and defined contexts was included in the analysis. The first phase, called inventory, documents the assemblage based on artifact type, raw material, cortex presence or absence, platform type, size classification, and quantity. In this initial phase, Sullivan and Rozen's (1985) debitage classification scheme, which categorizes flakes based on their completeness, was utilized to provide specific artifact types for all debitage. However, following numerous critiques (e.g., Amick and Maudlin 1989; Ensor and Roemer 1989; Prentiss 1998; Prentiss and Romanski 1989; also see Lyons and Pitblado 1996), the Sullivan and Rozen system is not used as an indicator of technological organization. In addition, individual tools, whether expedient or formal, were recorded and then separated from the general assemblage for additional, in-depth analysis in phase two.

Phase two of the analysis focused on further documentation of identified tools and utilized or retouched flakes. Cores, as well as retouched and manufacturing tools, underwent more intensive analysis, which considered production and use as well as morphological attributes in order to comprehensively consider theoretical and interpretive issues. Tools were examined with a 10x hand lens and selected artifacts were documented photographically. Projectile points and bifaces were further classified, both typologically and chronologically, following Tagg (1994) and Justice (2002). Approximately

Table 8.1. Definition of Artifact Types Used for the Chevelon Flaked Stone Analysis*.

DEBITAGE TYPES

Complete Flake: contains a bulb of percussion and a platform, and the flake margins are intact.

Broken Flake: contains a bulb of percussion and a platform, but the flaked margins are not intact (e.g., the proximal end of a flake)

Split Flake: contains a bulb of percussion and a platform, but the flake is broken and this break begins at the bulb of percussion. Often the break is along the striking axis and only one half of the flake is present.

Flake Fragment: contains an interior surface created by percussion but the bulb and platform are not present (e.g., the distal portion of a flake).

Debris: does not contain a bulb of percussion, platform, or discernible interior surface (i.e., cannot be oriented according to where it was struck).

Burned (Fire-cracked rock): does not contain a bulb of percussion, platform, or discernible interior surface but does contain signs of heating such as spalls or cracks.

Spall: a flake or piece of debris that contains evidence of battering, as if it had spalled off of a hammerstone or pecking stone. Pieces of debitage in which the platform was prepared by battering are not considered spalls.

TOOL TYPES

Edge-damaged Piece: exhibits regular contiguous flake scars (less than 2 mm in length) which cover at least 1 cm of an edge.

Scraper: exhibits steep, even, unifacial retouch (i.e., flake scars that are contiguous and over 2 mm in length) along one or more edges creating a fairly formally shaped edge.

Retouched Piece: exhibits contiguous flake scars (over 2 mm in length) which form a usable edge at least 1 cm in length. The retouch can be unifacial or bifacial.

Chopper: pebbles, cobbles, or small rocks that have been modified through unifacial or bifacial flaking to produce a sharp edge.

Projectile Point: bifacially worked piece with evidence of a pointed end and a hafting element.

Biface: a bifacially worked piece in which flake scars have been intentionally removed from all edges as a means of shaping the artifact. Triangular projectile points (points without notches to demarcate a haft element) are classified as bifaces.

Drill: an artifact with a projection which shows signs of utilization. Drills can be formally or informally shaped.

Wedge: an artifact that is usually rectangular and exhibits retouch or battering along opposite sides of the piece. The retouch and battering appear to be the result of the artifact being struck on the end with some force. The Homol'ovi wedges are very similar in morphology to artifacts that have been called *pièces esquillées* (Brezillon 1971).

CORE TOOLS

Flake Core: contains a bulb of percussion and/or the interior surface of a flake and has at least two negative scars, which do not form an edge that was used (i.e., a retouched piece).

Core: has at least two negative flake scars and no bulb of percussion.

Other: this category is comprised of 1) pieces of raw material that have been tested, but only one piece has been removed; and 2) pieces of raw material that have been struck, as evidenced by concentric circles produced by a blow, but no flakes have been removed.

MANUFACTURING TOOLS

Pecking Stone: an artifact with a step-like battering on one or more edges. The edges may be shaped by flaking or may be unmodified, except for battering.

Hammerstone: an artifact with battering on one or more edges, but does not exhibit the characteristics of a core or a pecking stone. The battering is usually finer than that on a pecking stone.

*Note: Reproduced from Young (2001).

43 percent (N=261) of tools from the analyzed Chevelon assemblage were subjected to in-depth analysis.

THE ASSEMBLAGE

The analyzed Chevelon flaked stone assemblage consists of 7,894 pieces of debitage, tools, and cores recovered during excavations conducted between 2003 and 2005 (Table 8.2). The analyzed assemblage represents flaked stone from 26 different structures and extramural areas within the site; all four chronological occupation periods at Chevelon (see Chapter 3) are also represented.

As is characteristic of other Homol'ovi flaked stone assemblages (E.C. Adams 2004c; Lyons and Pitblado 1996; Sullivan and Madsen 1991; Young 2001), debitage dominates the Chevelon flaked stone, comprising 90.82 percent of the total assemblage (Table 8.2). Tools represent another 5.94 percent of the flaked stone. This flaked stone class can be further subdivided into expedient tools (edge-damaged and retouched flakes, scrapers, choppers, and wedges) (Figures 8.1-8.2), formal tools (projectile points, bifaces, and drills) (Figures 8.3-8.5), and manufacturing tools (pecking and hammerstones) (Figure 8.6), representing 3.37 percent, 1.93 percent, and 0.65 percent of the assemblage, respectively. Cores occur in a relatively low percentage (2.09 percent), while artifacts classified as "other", tested and unidentified pieces, and fire-cracked rock (FCR) also comprise a minor portion of the assemblage (1.15 percent).

The basic distribution of flaked stone classes within the Chevelon assemblage is similar to those at H2 (Lyons and Pitblado 1996) and H3 (Young 2001). However, debitage comprises a higher proportion of the assemblage at Chevelon and H3 (92.01 percent) compared to H2 (81.85 percent), while tools (11.34 percent) and cores (5.05 percent) comprise higher proportions of the H2 assemblage when compared to Chevelon and H3 (5.32 percent [tools] and 2.66 percent [cores]). The implications of these differences in technological organization are discussed in further detail below.

Raw Material

Eight types of raw material, identified by geologic morphology, were distinguished in the Chevelon flaked stone assemblage. Chert, in many different colors and textures, is the most common raw material used to produce flaked stone at Chevelon (Table 8.2). Petrified wood is the second most common raw material from which flaked stone was produced. Both chert and petrified wood, which generally have performance characteristics desirable for producing flaked stone (Odell 2004; Whittaker 1994:66, Figure 4.1), are locally available from the exposed gravel terraces surrounding Chevelon and other Homol'ovi villages, and from the Petrified Forest National Park (PEFO) and throughout the middle LCR Valley. In fact, high quality chert and quartzite are present on the small outcrop on which Chevelon is built. The high quality and wide availability of both chert and petrified wood, in part, explains their large-scale ubiquitous use to produce flaked stone in the Homol'ovi area.

Adams (2002:43–44, 214) has indicated that the Petrified Forest member of the Chinle Formation outcrops on a mesa west of H3 and H4, and that there are petrified wood sources near the HSC that likely were exploited by the inhabitants of the Homol'ovi villages for the manufacture of flaked stone. In addition, a day-trip along I-40, east of Chevelon Ruin,

Table 8.2. Summary of Chevelon Flaked Stone Assemblage.

	Chert		Chalcedony		Quartzite		Igneous		Petrified Wood		Obsidian		Other		Sandstone		Total
	%	N	%	N	%	N	%	N	%	N	%	N	%	N	%	N	
Debitage																	
Complete Flake	81.90	2964	0.55	20	4.51	163	0.08	3	9.34	338	3.54	128	0.03	1	0.06	2	3619
Broken Flake	78.51	179	1.75	4	6.14	14			10.09	23	3.51	8					228
Split Flake	81.94	59			5.56	4			5.56	4	5.56	4	1.39	1			72
Flake Fragment	81.45	1458	1.17	21	3.58	64	0.06	1	7.82	140	5.59	100			0.34	6	1790
Debris	88.74	1269	0.14	2	4.13	59			4.89	70	1.96	28			0.14	2	1430
Spall	56.66	17			43.33	13											30
Subtotal	82.94	5946	0.66	47	4.42	317	0.056	4	8.02	575	3.74	268	0.028	2	0.14	10	7169
Tools																	
Edge-damaged	75.76	125	1.21	2	1.82	3			18.18	30	3.03	5					165
Scraper	47.06	8							52.94	9							17
Retouched	67.95	53	3.85	3					23.07	18	5.13	4					78
Chopper	50	1			50	1											2
Projectile Point	62.5	80	1.56	2			1.56	2	16.79	22	16.79	22					128
Biface	50	11							40.9	9	9.09	2					22
Drill	50	1							50	1							2
Wedge	25	1							25	1	50	2					4
Peckingstone	38.71	12			61.29	19											31
Hammerstone	40.0	8			60.0	12											20
Subtotal	63.97	300	1.49	7	7.46	35	0.43	2	19.19	90	7.46	35					469
Cores																	
Flake Core	81.25	13			6.25	1			6.25	1	6.25	1					16
Core	85.31	122			10.49	15			3.50	5	0.7	1					143
Core-Tool	83.33	5							16.67	1							6
Subtotal	84.85	140			9.70	16			4.24	7	1.21	2					165
Other																	
Other	66.6	4			33.3	2											6
Fire-cracked Rock	97.65	83			1.18	1			1.18	1							85
Subtotal	95.6	87			3.30	3			1.10	1							91
Total	82.0	6473	0.68	54	4.70	371	0.08	6	8.53	673	3.87	305	0.03	2	0.13	10	7894

Figure 8.1. Edge-damaged flakes and other expedient flaked tools: all chert except upper right, which is petrified wood.

Figure 8.2. Bifaces and drills: (1,2) chalcedony and petrified wood bifaces; (3,4) drill and drill point; (5) hafted blade; (6-8) chert, petrified wood, obsidian bifaces.

Figure 8.3. Pre-pueblo projectile points: top row: (1,2) San Jose; (3,4) Northern Side-Notched; (5,6) datil; middle row: (7-9) San Pedro; (10) Black Mesa; (11) Gypsum; bottom row: (12) Gypsum; (13-15) Lake Mojave; (16) Clovis.

Chapter 8: Flaked Stone 187

Figure 8.4. Early Pueblo projectile points: (a) Corner-notched points and (b) Western Triangular.

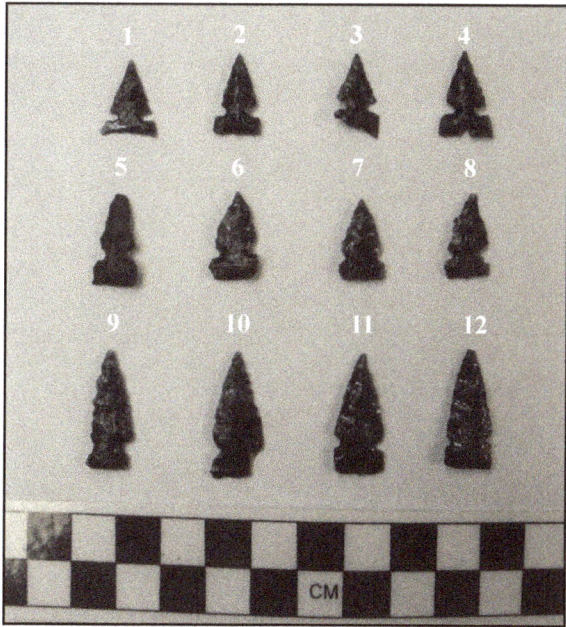

Figure 8.5. Late Pueblo arrow points of obsidian

Figure 8.6. Hammerstones and pecking stones: (1, 2, 4-7) quartzite peckingstones, central row with red ochre; (3) chert chopper; (8) quartzite hammer stone.

undertaken by the author, Chuck Adams, and Rich Lange in the summer of 2005 discovered petrified wood deposits eroding from gravel terraces north of the LCR and west of Jackrabbit Ruin, less than 8 km (5 miles) from Chevelon Ruin, and well within a day's round-trip walk (20 km [Varien 1999]).

Quartzite, another locally available raw material derived from the Shinarump Conglomerate, also represents a considerable proportion of the Chevelon assemblage. Other locally available raw materials, including chalcedony (likely from translucent pieces of petrified wood), non-specific igneous materials, sandstone, and unidentified or other materials, each comprise less than 1 percent of the total assemblage.

The only non-local raw material in the Chevelon flaked stone assemblage is obsidian, a volcanic glass, which composes 3.74 percent of the total assemblage. Just as with obsidian assemblages from H1, H2, and H3, all of which were occupied more-or-less contemporaneously with Chevelon (E.C. Adams 2002), Chevelon's projectile point assemblage is dominated by obsidian from the Government Mountain source (Table 8.3; see Harry 1987, 1989; Shackley 1997, 2010; Young 2001), located in the San Francisco Volcanic Fields near Flagstaff, approximately 125 km west of the Homol'ovi region. Comparisons to sourced projectile points from Homol'ovi and other sites are discussed later.

Raw Material Utilization

As is evidenced in Table 8.2, chert dominates all flaked stone artifact classes within the Chevelon flaked stone assemblage. There are, however, other patterns apparent in the type of raw material preferred for the production of specific artifact types. Fine-grained materials (chert, chalcedony, petrified wood, and obsidian) were overwhelmingly preferred for the manufacture of both expedient and formal tools. Most tools were made from chert, although both petrified wood and obsidian also comprise a significant proportion of the tool assemblage (Table 8.2). Although it was hypothesized that obsidian, and perhaps petrified wood, would be the preferred materials for the manufacture of bifaces and projectile points, typically valued artifacts. This was not the case with the Chevelon assemblage in which chert was utilized 3.57:1 over petrified wood and 3.72:1 over obsidian for the production of projectile points and bifaces. These ratios are similar to those found at H3, where chert was preferred 3.5:1 over petrified wood and 2.8:1 over obsidian (Young 2001), as well as those at H2, where chert was preferred 4.3:1 over petrified wood and 2.5:1 over obsidian (Lyons and Pitblado 1996).

Although the ratios of chert to petrified wood and chert to obsidian use are similar among all three sites, it should be noted that obsidian use for valued artifacts at Chevelon is more limited than at either H2 or H3, which are closer to the Government Mountain source, while both H2 and H3 have more limited use of petrified wood for valued artifacts than does Chevelon, which is closest to the PEFO, a possible source of petrified wood for the Homol'ovi area (see discussion below). It is yet to be determined whether these small differences in raw material use ratios, between chert and petrified wood and obsidian, are meaningful or not; sourcing of the petrified wood from all three sites would need to be undertaken first. However, more intensive study of these ratios could highlight possible differences in raw material procurement strategies and participation in exchange networks among Homol'ovi villages.

Table 8.3. Sources of Obsidian from Homol'ovi and Puerco Valley Villages.

		Homol'ovi Sites				
Source		Homol'ovi I* AZ J:14:3	Homol'ovi II* AZ J:14:15	Homol'ovi III** AZ J:14:14	Homol'ovi IV* AZ J:14:13	Chevelon* AZ P:2:11
Black Tank	Count	1				
	% within Source	100.0				
	% within Site/Sample	1.3				
	% of Total	0.4				
Government Mountain	Count	71	41	35	2	44
	% within Source	35.0	20.0	17.0	1.0	21.0
	% within Site/Sample	92.2	91.1	97.2	100.0	91.7
	% of Total	30.9	17.8	15.2	0.9	19.1
Patridge Creek	Count	1	1			
	% within Source	50.0	50.0			
	% within Site/Sample	1.3	2.2			
	% of Total	0.4	0.4			
RS Hill/ Sitegreaves Peak	Count	3	1			
	% within Source	75.0	25.0			
	% within Site/Sample	3.9	2.2			
	% of Total	1.9	0.4			
Slate Mountain (Wallace Tank)	Count					1
	% within Source					100.0
	% within Site/Sample					2.1
	% of Total					0.4
Topaz Basin	Count		1			
	% within Source		100.0			
	% within Site/Sample		2.2			
	% of Total		0.4			
Mount Taylor/ Grants Ridge	Count					
	% within Source					
	% within Site/Sample					
	% of Total					
Mule Creek	Count					
	% within Source					
	% within Site/Sample					
	% of Total					

Table 8.3. Sources of Obsidian from Homol'ovi and Puerco Valley Villages, cont'd.

Source		Homol'ovi Sites				
		Homol'ovi I* AZ J:14:3	Homol'ovi II* AZ J:14:15	Homol'ovi III** AZ J:14:14	Homol'ovi IV* AZ J:14:13	Chevelon* AZ P:2:11
Valle Grande Rhyolite (Cerro del Medio)	Count					
	% within Source					
	% within Site/Sample					
	% of Total					
unknown	Count	1	1	1		3
	% within Source	16.6	16.6	16.6		50.0
	% within Site/Sample	1.3	2.2	2.8		6.3
	% of Total	0.4	0.4	0.4		1.3
TOTAL	Count	77	45	36		48
	% of Total	33.4	19.6	15.7		20.9

Source		Puerco Valley/Petrified Forest Villages			
		Stone Axe***	Black Axe***	Wallace Tank	Puerco Ruin
Black Tank	Count				
	% within Source				
	% within Site/Sample				
	% of Total				
Government Mountain	Count	4		2	7
	% within Source	2.0		1.0	3.0
	% within Site/Sample	40.0		66.6	77.7
	% of Total	1.7		0.9	
Partridge Creek	Count				
	% within Source				
	% within Site/Sample				
	% of Total				
RS Hill/Sitgreaves Peak	Count				
	% within Source				
	% within Site/Sample				
	% of Total				
Slate Mountain (Wallace Tank)	Count				
	% within Source				
	% within Site/Sample				
	% of Total				
Topaz Basin	Count				

Table 8.3. Sources of Obsidian from Homol'ovi and Puerco Valley Villages, cont'd.

Source		Puerco Valley/Petrified Forest Villages			
		Stone Axe***	Black Axe***	Wallace Tank	Puerco Ruin
Mount Taylor/Grants Ridge	% within Source				
	% within Site/Sample				
	% of Total				
	Count	4	1	1	2
	% within Source	50.0	12.5	12.5	25.0
	% within Site/Sample	40.0	50.0	33.3	22.2
	% of Total	1.7	0.4	0.4	0.9
Mule Creek	Count	1			
	% within Source	100.0			
	% within Site/Sample	10.0			
	% of Total	0.4			
Valle Grande Rhyolite (Cerro del Medio)	Count	1	1		
	% within Source	50.0	50.0		
	% within Site/Sample	10.0	50.0		
	% of Total	0.4	0.4		
unknown	Count				
	% within Source				
	% within Site/Sample				
	% of Total				
TOTAL	Count	10	2	3	9
	% of Total	4.3	0.9	1.3	3.9

*Shackley 2010 (XRF: x-ray florescence).
**Harry 1989 (BSE:back-scattered electron imaging): 12 of the Homol'ovi II samples (11 Gov't Mtn & 1 unk.) and 36 of the Homol'ovi III samples (35 Gov't Mtn. and 1 unk).
***Personal communication from G. Schachner 2010.

Quartzite, which comprised less than 1 percent of the retouched tool assemblage (Table 8.2), was favored 3:2 over chert, for use as manufacturing tools, and neither petrified wood nor obsidian was used in the manufacture of other flaked stone. Chert and quartzite cobbles are equally locally available. The preference for quartzite over chert, obsidian, and petrified wood is likely related to each material's performance characteristics rather than distance to resources (Odell 2004; Whittaker 1994:66, Figure 4.1). Manufacturing (percussive) tools require that the raw material be durable and maintain an edge through repeated battering, while characteristics generally desirable for the manufacture of flake stone tools—brittleness, fine granularity, isotropism, and conchoidal fracture—may actually be detrimental in manufacturing tools (Odell 2004:18, 21).

Petrified wood (NPS 2007) and obsidian

are too brittle to withstand use as a hard-percussion tool. Chert is an ideal raw material for the manufacture of stone tools, because chert is "generally isotropic and produce[s] firm, thin margins, making [it] ideal [for] sharp-edge tools" (Odell 2004:19). Chert is also valued for its hardness (a seven on the Mohs scale of hardness) and toughness, qualities valued in manufacturing (percussive) tools and which led to its occasional use as such. However, its preferred use was as a raw material for flaked stone tools. Quartzite, on the other hand, is a very hard (also a seven on the Mohs scale of hardness) metamorphic rock derived from sandstone that is both "durable and has the capacity to hold an edge through incessant pounding," but which only "sometimes possesses qualities of isotropism and conchoidal fracture favorable for tool production" (Odell 2004:21). These characteristics make quartzite more valued as a manufacturing (percussive) tool than as a raw material for the manufacture of flaked stone tools.

Chert and quartzite cores represent the majority of the core assemblage, while few cores of petrified wood or obsidian were recovered from Chevelon (Table 8.2). However, quartzite represents the lowest flake to core ratio (15.3:1), whereas chert (33.3:1), petrified wood (72.1:1), and obsidian (120:1) have higher flake to core ratios. This suggests that quartzite cores were used less intensively than were cores of other fine-grained material, and in particular for material that was difficult to acquire (i.e., rarer). Quartzite cores also may have been less intensively used than chert cores, even though both are locally available, because quartzite has less desirable performance characteristics for use as flaked stone than chert (see discussion above; also see Odell 2004; Whittaker 1994:66, Figure 4.1).

Raw Material Procurement

There are two issues to be addressed when considering strategies for raw material procurement at Chevelon. First, although petrified wood is considered a local raw material, questions have arisen regarding 1) whether Chevelon may have obtained its petrified wood from what is today PEFO as, geographically, it is one of the closest Homol'ovi sites to the PEFO; 2) whether Chevelon might have higher proportions of petrified wood in its flaked stone assemblage because of its proximity to the PEFO; and 3) whether Chevelon may have traded petrified wood to other Homol'ovi sites. The second issue relates to the method of procurement of obsidian from Government Mountain by Chevelon inhabitants.

Petrified Wood

At this point, the three questions relating to the procurement and possible exchange of petrified wood by the Chevelon inhabitants can only be partially addressed. While large amounts of petrified wood are available from the PEFO, about 70 km east of the Homol'ovi area, petrified wood is also locally available in Chinle Formation exposures that occur throughout the Homol'ovi area (Lange 1998). Variation between the locally available petrified wood and that from the PEFO is poorly understood and therefore, to date, knowledge concerning differences that could source petrified wood to specific outcrops is unavailable (Wells 1994). At this time, therefore, we cannot determine from where, specifically, the Chevelon inhabitants obtained their petrified wood. However, the size, morphological characteristics, and color of the Chevelon flaked stone is generally consistent with locally available (8 to 10 km) petrified wood and it is therefore possible that most of the petrified wood utilized at Chevelon was locally obtained.

Although our inability to source petrified wood prohibits full understanding of the procurement of this raw material by Chevelon inhabitants, we can use other data to address questions related to the percentage of petrified wood at Chevelon and its possible use as a trade item between Chevelon and the other Homol'ovi sites. Despite Chevelon's closer proximity to what is today known as the PEFO, the proportion of petrified wood is consistent among the H2 (8.54 percent), H3 (7.49 percent), and Chevelon (8.02 percent) flaked stone assemblages. These similar percentages indicate that Chevelon did not have greater access to petrified wood and, as a result, Chevelon did not have more petrified wood in its assemblage than the other Homol'ovi sites because of its proximity to the PEFO. However, what is interesting is that petrified wood comprises approximately 10 percent of the tool assemblages from both H2 and H3, whereas it comprises approximately 19 percent of the tool assemblage at Chevelon. These data suggest that Chevelon inhabitants may have preferred petrified wood to produce expedient and informal tools for reasons beyond raw material availability and performance characteristics.

It should also be noted that the overwhelming majority (89.9 percent) of petrified wood at Chevelon was recovered from two distinct areas of the site: various structures within RB100, although specifically from S. 120, and Plaza 900 and K. 901 in RB300; K. 279 also contained a fair amount of petrified wood (6.39%) (Table 8.4). The frequency for petrified wood in RB100 is an astounding 27.5 percent of all raw material and 14.0 percent in S. 900/901, much higher than other areas of the village, especially RB200 where it is a minute 1.7 percent of all raw materials. Using a best-fit chi-squared test (Shennan 1988), the distributions of petrified wood in RB100, RB300 (including Plaza 900 and K. 901), and K. 279 and its low frequency in RB200, are all statistically significant at $p < .001$. In addition, most of the petrified wood came from deposits dating to the Late Homol'ovi phase (LHP).

The apparent preference for petrified wood for tool-making at Chevelon, as well as the spatial and temporal distribution of petrified wood discussed above, suggests two things: that there may be a social connection between RB100 and S. 900/901, and that the preferential use of petrified wood for tools at Chevelon may in fact be for social reasons (rather than as a result of raw material availability and/or more desirable performance characteristics), perhaps related to increased trade with groups to the east and settlement by immigrant communities from the Silver Creek, Upper Little Colorado River (ULCR) Valley, and/or PEFO areas (Chapters 4 and 6; also see E.C. Adams 2002; Duff 1999, 2002). Based on the occupational chronology of Chevelon, similarities in the ceramic assemblages with PEFO villages, and the preference for petrified wood as a raw material evident at the PEFO sites shared with occupants of RB 100 and deposits in K. 901, E.C. Adams (2009, personal communication) has suggested that inhabitants from Puerco Ruin and other Pueblo IV (PIV) settlements, such as Stone Axe, in the PEFO, rather than groups from Silver Creek or the ULCR Valley, may have immigrated to Chevelon during the LHP. According to Jennings (1967, 1980) and others who have worked at Puerco Ruin (Burton 1990), the site was likely depopulated around 1350 C.E. Stone Axe was also likely depopulated late in the 1300s, as it contained late-dating ceramics including Sikyatki

194 Medeiros

Table 8.4. Distribution of Flaked Stone Raw Materials by Structure.

Structure	Chert %	Chert N	Chalcedony %	Chalcedony N	Quartzite %	Quartzite N	Igneous %	Igneous N	Petrified Wood %	Petrified Wood N	Obsidian %	Obsidian N	Other %	Other N	Sandstone %	Sandstone N	TOTAL
120	61.59	202	0.30	1	5.18	17			32.01	105	0.91	3					328
123	62.38	63			4.95	5			29.70	30	2.97	3					101
158	75.86	88	1.72	2	4.31	5			17.24	20					0.86	1	116
159											100.00	1					1
161	76.84	73							22.11	21	1.05	1					95
222	90.73	274	0.33	1	5.96	18			1.32	4	1.66	5					302
227	78.57	154	2.04	4	11.74	23			2.04	4	5.10	10			0.51	1	196
246	100.0	8															8
248	100.0	1															1
264	95.83	23							4.17	1							24
265	92.86	13			7.14	1											14
266	89.93	125			1.44	2	0.72	1	1.44	2	6.47	9					139
268	89.72	96	0.93	1	3.74	4					5.61	6					107
269	87.58	134	1.96	3	5.23	8			0.65	1	4.58	7					153
274	89.05	439	0.41	2	5.27	26	0.20	1	0.41	2	4.67	23					493
279	87.55	1371	0.64	10	4.73	74	0.13	2	2.75	43	4.15	65			0.06	1	1566
286	84.68	304			0.28	1			0.84	3	14.20	51					359
287	33.33	1									66.67	2					3
288	91.43	224	0.82	2	3.67	9			1.22	3	2.86	7					245
289	100.00	4															4
293	100.00	1															1
300	93.30	209			5.80	13			0.89	2							224
345	87.50	7			12.50	1											8
373	92.54	124			5.22	7			0.75	1	1.49	2					134

Table 8.4. Distribution of Flaked Stone Raw Materials by Structure, cont'd.

Structure	Chert %	Chert N	Chalcedony %	Chalcedony N	Quartzite %	Quartzite N	Igneous %	Igneous N	Petrified Wood %	Petrified Wood N	Obsidian %	Obsidian N	Other %	Other N	Sandstone %	Sandstone N	TOTAL
393	96.77	180	0.54	1	0.54	1					2.15	4					186
403	50.00	1									50.00	1					2
603	25.00	1							50.00	2	25.00	1					4
702	100.00	1															1
704	91.67	11			8.33	1											12
726											100.00	1					1
900	85.86	874	0.69	7	2.75	28			7.07	72	3.63	37					1018
901	71.63	1467	0.98	20	6.20	127	0.10	2	17.43	357	3.22	66	0.10	2	0.34	7	2048
TOTAL	82.00	6473	0.68	54	4.70	371	0.08	6	8.53	673	3.86	305	0.03	2	0.13	10	7894

Polychrome and some Zuni Glaze Wares (Greg Schachner 2009, personal communication to E. C. Adams). These dates correspond with use of RB100 and others around the south plaza as well as filling of K. 901 and associated features in Plaza 900 (see Chapter 3).

The PEFO sites also contain large quantities of Roosevelt Red Ware, Jeddito Yellow Ware (JYW), Winslow Orange Ware, and Zuni Ware, with all but the JYW appearing locally made. This ceramic distribution is more similar to the distribution of ceramics at Chevelon than other Homol'ovi pueblos (see Chapter 6). In addition, petrified wood served as the primary raw material for flaked stone manufacture, likely because of its local availability and performance characteristics, for the inhabitants of the PEFO sites, and large quantities of this raw material showing substantial quarrying effects are visible on the ground surface adjacent to these sites (Burton 1990; E.C. Adams 2010, personal communication). If inhabitants of these sites did migrate to Chevelon and, as seems assured based on the clear dominance of petrified wood as a flaked stone raw material at these sites, were accustomed to using petrified wood, it makes sense they would prefer it over local chert, especially given its availability in the general vicinity of Chevelon.

Obsidian

Geochemical sourcing, conducted via Energy Dispersive X-ray Fluorescence analysis, of 48 obsidian samples from the Chevelon assemblage indicate that like the other Homol'ovi sites, more than 90 percent of the assemblage is from the Government Mountain source (Shackley 2010; Table 8.3). Of the remaining four samples, one, a projectile point, was sourced to the Slate Mountain/Wallace Tank source, also part of the San Francisco Volcanic Fields near Flagstaff. According to Shackley (2010), this source is rarely seen in archaeological contexts, having been documented at only one other archaeological site, Fourmile Ruin (discussed further below). The remaining three specimens, one of which was a projectile point, could not be chemically linked to any known North American obsidian source.

In comparison, very little obsidian has been recovered from the Pueblo III (PIII) sites in the Silver Creek area (Kaldahl 1999). More obsidian is present at sites in the ULCR Valley (Scott Van Keuren 2010, personal communication to E. C. Adams), and obsidian from Government Mountain dominates the obsidian assemblage at three PIV sites — Fourmile Ruin, Pinedale Ruin, and Shumway — recently investigated in the area, although approximately 9 percent of the obsidian sourced from these three sites is from sources in western New Mexico, including the Mount Taylor and Mule Creek sources (Shackley 2009). Like those in the Silver Creek area, sites in the PEFO, except perhaps from Stone Axe which has a sizable quantity of obsidian compared to other sites in its immediate area (Greg Schachner 2009, personal communication), also have relatively little obsidian. However, several small samples of obsidian from four PIV sites — Stone Axe, Black Axe, Wallace Tank, and Puerco Ruin — show greater diversity in their composition, with more obsidian from eastern sources (Table 8.3), such as Mount Taylor-Grants Ridge, Mule Creek, and Valle Grande (Cerro del Medio), all of which are in western New Mexico (Burton and Hughes 1990; Schachner 2009, personal communication); A total of 54 percent of the obsidian sourced from these sites is from Government Mountain (Table 8.3).

Interestingly, as documented through an extensive database of archaeological obsidian sourcing, compiled as part of the Southwest Social Networks in Late Prehistory project, the obsidian assemblages from these PEFO sites are the only ones containing an extensive mix of sources from northern Arizona and western New Mexico (Jeff Clark 2010, personal communication to E. C. Adams; Borck et al. 2015). Based on the composition of obsidian assemblages from the various settlement communities located near Homol'ovi, Chevelon's obsidian assemblage more closely resembles those documented in the Silver Creek and ULCR Valley sites than those recovered from the PEFO sites.

Therefore, how obsidian was procured for use in the manufacture of flaked stone at Chevelon is more straightforward than petrified wood. As has been suggested by Young (2001) and Harry (1989) regarding the H3 flaked stone assemblage, Chevelon inhabitants most likely obtained obsidian through exchange maintained at the household level rather than through centralized exchange. While most obsidian recovered from Chevelon was concentrated in ritual and domestic trash deposits within K. 274/279 and K. 901, smaller quantities of obsidian were also found in multiple deposit contexts throughout the site, in structures of varying functions. In addition, the proportion of obsidian present within the kivas is not statistically significant, at the 95 percent confidence level, when compared to the distribution of other raw materials in these structures versus other structures and deposit contexts, further supporting the interpretation that obsidian was obtained at the household level at Chevelon.

The general distribution of obsidian throughout the site indicates that no particular household controlled access to obsidian at Chevelon (Table 8.4), and that the use and distribution of obsidian at Chevelon is not tied to a specific phase of the site's occupation. However, while no single household controlled access to obsidian, 60.7 percent of all obsidian recovered from Chevelon came from structures located within RB200 (see Table 8.4), the oldest and most prestigious part of the site (see Chapter 4); another 21.6 percent was recovered from K. 901. By volume, K. 274/279 had the most obsidian (4.39 pieces of obsidian/m3), followed by all the ritual structures (S. 248. 266/286, and 274/279) in RB200 (3.57 pieces of obsidian/m^3), RB200 in general (2.99 pieces of obsidian/m^3), and RB900 (2.89 pieces of obsidian/m^3); all other room blocks of the site had less than 1.2 pieces of obsidian/m^3. As discussed in more detail later in this chapter, the concentration of obsidian in RB200 and its concentration in ritual structures and deposits suggest that obsidian held significant value for the inhabitants of Chevelon, and was likely deposited in this area due to its value and its association with ritual, protection, and power (Parsons 1939).

At the same time, the Chevelon assemblage contains only two obsidian cores, and relatively small percentages of obsidian debitage and obsidian tools having cortex on them (8.96 percent and 14.29 percent, respectively) (Table 8.2). Even if wedges, which have been hypothesized to be exhausted obsidian cores (see R. Nelson 1989; Young 2001), are included in these calculations as cores rather than tools, only four obsidian cores, all of which have cortex, have been recovered. On the other hand, a large proportion of the obsidian assemblage has no cortex (90.16 percent), and most of the non-cortical specimens are debitage (88.73 percent).

These data, along with the high obsidian debitage to core ratio (60:1, if there are four obsidian cores, 120:1 if only two obsidian cores), indicate that it is likely that obsidian was transported to Chevelon in an already reduced form rather than as whole or virtually whole nodules, and that once at Chevelon, pieces of obsidian were intensively utilized. It may even be that Chevelon households received obsidian secondhand through established trade relationships with the larger and more prominent Homol'ovi villages (Lange 2006, personal communication) or from other source communities (e.g., Chavez Pass, Anderson Mesa, Flagstaff area; see G. Brown 1990, 1991; Vierra 1993a, 1993b for a fuller discussion of the obsidian exchange networks in northern Arizona).

Young (2001) has suggested that Homol'ovi inhabitants may have provided yellow ware pottery or cotton to Anderson Mesa in exchange for Government Mountain obsidian. While this explanation makes sense for both H1, where cotton was produced on a massive scale, and H2, which functioned to bring significant quantities of yellow ware pottery from the Hopi Mesas to the Homol'ovi area (E.C. Adams 2002), this explanation is not as plausible for explaining the obsidian exchange relationship for Chevelon, especially if Chevelon was receiving the majority of its obsidian secondhand through other Homol'ovi villages. Instead, it may be that Chevelon, given its geographic proximity to the rich estuary environment created by Chevelon Creek, provided the other Homol'ovi sites and Anderson Mesa, if in fact a more direct exchange relationship existed, with water-based faunal resources, including fish, turtles, and waterfowl, for use in domestic and/or ritual contexts. Thus, it seems likely that residents of other Homol'ovi villages would have established and maintained an exchange relationship with the residents of Chevelon in order to gain access to domestic and ceremonial resources available near Chevelon Creek (see Chapters 9 and 11 for additional discussion).

TECHNOLOGICAL ORGANIZATION

Overall, the production of flaked stone at Chevelon reflects reliance on expedient core reduction technology and tool manufacture rather than on developed curated technologies (see Bamforth 1986; Binford 1973, 1979; M. Nelson 1991; and Young 2001). Following Binford, Bamforth (1986:38) states that "technologies based on curation comprise tools that are effective for a variety of tasks, are manufactured in anticipation of use, are maintained through a number of uses, are transported from locality to locality for these uses, and are recycled to other tasks when no longer useful for their primary purposes," while expedient technologies "comprise tools that are manufactured, used, and discarded according to the needs of the moment" (Bamforth 1986:38). The focus of the Chevelon assemblage was determined by an analysis of the proportion of the assemblage reflecting tool production, the ratio of prepared platforms to total platforms, and the ratio of bifaces to cores in the Chevelon assemblage.

Formal versus Informal Tools

The proportion of formal tools within a tool assemblage is considered an indicator of curated versus expedient technologies. Expedient and informal tools are those tools that are often used "as is" without further modification, while formal tools require more preparation, skill, and time and typically reflect standardized production techniques. Higher percentages of informal tools indicate expedient technologies, whereas higher percentages of formal tools indicate more reliance on curated technologies (Andrefsky 1994; Bamforth 1986; Odell 2004).

The Chevelon tool assemblage is primarily composed of informal tools (edge-damaged and retouched pieces, scrapers, choppers, and wedges), which represent 64.56 percent of the retouched tools (Table 8.2). Approximately one-third of the retouched tool assemblage was formally prepared (projectile points, bifaces, and drills). It should be noted, however, that approximately one-fifth of the projectile points recovered from Chevelon actually predate the occupation of the site and therefore were not manufactured by, but instead were collected and curated by, the inhabitants of Chevelon (Table 8.5; see discussion below).

In addition, nearly half of the projectile points assigned a temporal designation cannot be definitively attributed to the PIV period and may in fact date to earlier periods, Pueblo II (PII) or PIII (see Table 8.5), in which case the curation of projectile points at Chevelon would be even more noteworthy. Despite the earlier dates of some formally manufactured tools, the significant percentage of informal tools indicates that, although formal tools were incorporated into the Chevelon assemblage through collection and manufacture, the primary means of tool production was expedient. The use of a primarily expedient technology by Chevelon's inhabitants is not surprising given the availability of high quality raw materials near the village as well as the low level of residential mobility practiced by the village's population (Andrefsky 1994; Kelly 2001; Parry and Kelly 1987).

Platform Preparation

Expedient technologies generally do not prepare platforms before core reduction. Curated technologies, on the other hand, utilize

Table 8.5. Distribution of Projectile Points by Structure.

Structure	Early Archaic	Middle Archaic	Middle Archaic/ Basketmaker III	Late Archaic	Late Archaic/ Basketmaker	Basketmaker III	Pueblo I	Pueblo II/IV	Pueblo III/IV	Unk.	Total
120						1				1	2
123								2			2
159								1			1
222								1		2	3
227							1				1
246								1			1
264					1						1
265							1	1			2
266				1		1		1		1	4
269								1		3	4
274			1						2		3
286			1					1		1	3
287								3			3
288								1	1		2
289						1		1			2
293								1			1
300								1			1
345								1			1
373								1		1	2
393				1				2	1		4
403								1		1	2
603										2	2
702								1			1
726								1			1
900				1			1	3	1	1	7
Kiva											
248								1			1
279	1	1		3		5	2	29	8	11	60
901					1	3		7		1	12
TOTAL	1	1	2	6	2	11	5	62	13	25	128

platform preparation to ensure that flakes are removed in predictable shapes from precise locations on the core, again indicative of more standardized manufacture techniques.

Plain, unprepared platforms dominate the Chevelon assemblage, while prepared platforms represent a miniscule proportion (2.80 percent) of the assemblage, further supporting the interpretation that the production of flaked stone at Chevelon relied on expedient technologies (Table 8.6).

Biface to Core Ratios

Comparison of biface to core ratios is a third indicator of whether an assemblage reflects an expedient or curated technology. Bifaces and artifacts identified as cores are compared because these two artifact types represent standardized (curated) and unstandardized (expedient) reduction techniques. Larger biface to core ratios indicate curated technologies, while lower ratios indicate expedient technologies.

Unexpectedly, the Chevelon assemblage has a very high biface to core ratio: 0.91 (Table 8.7), suggesting that in fact the inhabitants of Chevelon may have utilized a curated technology. However, there are additional factors that must be taken into consideration when interpreting this unusually high ratio.

While the flaked stone technologies at H2, H3, and Chevelon have all been characterized as expedient, there are some significant differences in technological organization among these three assemblages that have implications for our understanding of the relationship between flaked stone technologies and social organization.

As mentioned previously, the percentages of debitage at both H3 and Chevelon are approximately equivalent and higher than at H2, while the percentages of tools and cores at H2 are almost double those at H3 and at Chevelon. At first glance, these variations in the proportions of tools and cores between sites suggest that H2 may have been using cores less intensively and producing more tools from debitage than either H3 or Chevelon. On closer inspection, however, we find that the proportion of edge-damaged pieces at H2 accounts for 73.35 percent of the tool assemblage whereas, at H3 (13.29 percent) and Chevelon (35.64 percent), edge-damaged pieces account for significantly smaller percentages of the tool assemblage.

While these differences may indeed reflect heightened use of these informal tools at H2, they may also signify inconsistencies in the identification of edge-damaged flakes. This second option seems particularly plausible, given the extreme differences in the percentages of edge-damaged flakes between all three sites. The differences in the proportions of cores between H2 and, H3, and Chevelon, however, seem to represent an actual difference in the utilization of cores between the three sites.

Significant differences in technological organization between H2 and H3, on the one hand, and Chevelon, on the other hand, become clear when Young's (2001) temporal comparisons of these ratios are taken into consideration.

First, in considering platform preparation ratios between H2 and Chevelon, the ratios are similar. At both these sites plain, unprepared platforms comprise the majority of the assemblage, while prepared platforms account for a minor percentage (Table 8.6). These similarities suggest that at these sites, platforms were not usually prepared before striking.

The differences arise in comparison of the biface to core ratios among the three sites. As indicated above, Chevelon has a high biface

Table 8.6. Distribution of Platform Type by Flake Category.

Flake Category	Absent %	N	Cortical %	N	Plain %	N	Dihedral %	N	Facetted %	N	Crushed %	N	Indeterminate %	N	Total N
Complete Flake	0.17	6	13.04	472	82.43	2983			0.39	14	2.95	107	1.02	37	3619
Broken Flake	1.75	4	9.65	22	80.70	184			0.44	1	7.02	16	0.44	1	228
Split Flake	1.39	1	9.72	7	70.83	51	1.39	1			8.33	6	8.33	6	72
Flake Fragment													100.0	1790	1790
TOTAL	0.19	11	8.78	501	56.37	3218	0.02	1	0.26	15	2.26	129	32.12	1834	5709

to core ratio at 0.91. H2 (0.08) and H3 (0.29) have significantly lower biface to core ratios (see Table 8.7). The differences in these three ratios indicate that Chevelon had a significantly more curated flaked stone technology. At the same time, when the Chevelon biface to core ratio is compared to those calculated for the Basketmaker II (BMII), Basketmaker III, and PIII periods reported by Young (2001:244), Chevelon's is most comparable to the BMII ratio (0.50). In fact, Chevelon's ratio is even significantly higher than the BMII ratio, again suggesting a curated technology for Chevelon. However, based on all other available flaked stone data as previously discussed, it is clear that Chevelon did not have a curated technology, but in fact overwhelmingly relied upon expedient flaked stone technologies. As a result, there must be another factor influencing the biface to core ratio calculated for Chevelon.

When considering the biface to core ratio, the issue is reflected in the number of bifaces, which include projectile points, rather than in the number of cores recovered from Chevelon. A disproportionate number of projectile points (N=128, 27.65 percent) are included in the Chevelon tool assemblage when compared to either the H2 (N=88, 5.36 percent) or the H3 (N=136, 8.89 percent) tool assemblages. And, while projectile points were often recycled due to the time and effort required to produce them (e.g., see Young 2001:246), this activity still does not explain the relative overabundance of projectile points in the Chevelon assemblage.

According to analyses of the projectile points conducted by Thompsen (2005) and Vonarx (2006, 2008), 23 projectile points in the Chevelon assemblage actually date to preceramic periods (Table 8.5, Figure 8.3). Another five are morphologically closest to Pueblo I (PI) and definitely predate the occupation of Chevelon (Figure 8.4). Vonarx

Table 8.7. Biface to Core Ratios by Raw Material and Temporal Phase at Chevelon, Homol'ovi II, and Homol'ovi III.

Biface to Core Ratio: Raw Material Type

	All Material Types	Chert	Petrified Wood	Obsidian
Chevelon	0.91	0.65	4.4	12.0[a]
Homol'ovi II[b]	0.08	0.05	0.11	1.5[c]
Homol'ovi III	0.29	0.24	0.63	3.08[d]

Biface to Core Ratio: Phase

	Tuwuica Phase/Founder Phase	Early Homol'ovi Phase	Middle Homol'ovi Phase	Late Homol'ovi Phase	Unknown.
Chevelon	0.13	0.44	1.84[e]	0.7	
Homol'ovi II[f]	—	—	—	0.08	
Homol'ovi III	0.2	0.56	0.08	0.29	

[a]If wedges are considered as exhausted obsidian cores, the biface:core ratio is 6.0.
[b]Includes counts as published in Lyons and Pitblado (1996); i.e., not the total projectile point count from Krebs, which is 88.
[c]If wedges are considered as exhausted obsidian cores, the biface:core ratio is 0.71.
[d]If wedges are considered as exhausted obsidian cores, the biface:core ratio is 0.69.
[e]Driven by low number of structures with deposits associated with this phase and the high number of projectile points (~47 percent of total) in one of the two structures
[f]Homol'ovi II was only occupied during the Late Phase.
Note: Following Young (2001), bifaces include bifaces and projectile points, and cores include cores and flake cores.
Note: For HIII, if the Founder (1280s C.E.) and Early (1290s–1300 C.E.) phases are combined as the Early Phase, then the biface to core ratio is 0.34.

(2006:9) has suggested that these older (Archaic and Basketmaker/PI) style points may have been purposefully collected and curated by the inhabitants of Chevelon "as crucial points of access to ongoing memory work," in which recognition of the antiquity of the projectile points, whether explicit or implicit, would have facilitated their collection, curation, and use in ritual activities (see discussion below) as a means of creating and maintaining the village's social memory through a connection and commemoration of the past (Chapters 4 and 13; see Connerton 1989; Mills and Walker 2008). In fact, research at Rock Art Ranch only 6 km south of Chevelon Pueblo has recorded 80 preceramic sites and recovered over 141 preceramic projectile points. Therefore, sources for the Chevelon points are nearby (Lange et al. 2015).

Purposeful collection, curation, and disposal of older projectile points at Chevelon would have inflated the biface to core ratio. If these earlier points, as well as any points that were not identified to any specific time period, are removed from the calculations, the Chevelon biface to core ratio drops significantly, from 0.91 to 0.625. However, this ratio is still significantly higher than that for the other two Homol'ovi sites. It may be that other points dating to earlier Pueblo periods (i.e., PI–PIII, at least five points, and possibly totaling as high as 67; Table 8.5, Figure 8.5) have also been curated at Chevelon and these points are contributing to the inflated biface to core ratio. Unfortunately, because 62 of these points date to between the PII and PIV periods, and further temporal resolution is not possible at this time, the effect of these points on the biface to core ratio at Chevelon cannot be further evaluated.

Spatial Patterns in the Chevelon Flaked Stone Assemblage

In this section, the spatial distribution of flaked stone by raw material and flaked stone class will be discussed in terms of depositional context and variability between structures. Although data have been calculated for all recorded depositional contexts, particular attention will be paid to assemblages recovered from occupational surfaces, feature fill, and general fill, as these contexts in particular are assumed to represent distinct prehistoric behavior.

Depositional Context

Raw Material and Depositional Context

The distribution of raw materials by depositional context was generally consistent across the site (Table 8.8). Chert represented the highest percentages (70.21–87.21 percent) in all deposit contexts, followed by petrified wood (5.52–15.54 percent); both quartzite and obsidian occurred in consistent, but lower, percentages. However, petrified wood was recovered in much higher proportions from occupational surfaces and general fill than from any other context; this distribution was confirmed as significant at $p < .001$, using a best-fit chi-squared test. In addition, chalcedony, obsidian, and quartzite also occur in relatively high frequencies in floor fill. Interestingly, all the petrified wood recovered from an occupation surface came from two structures in RB100 — S. 120 and 161. At the same time, although obsidian was fairly evenly distributed across depositional contexts, no obsidian was recovered from an occupational surface. Rather than suggesting flaked tool manufacture, these patterns suggest placement of high-valued flaked stone materials was part of closure practices, especially in RB100. This pattern is amplified by the relationship of flaked stone classes to depopulation context below.

Flaked Stone Classes and Depositional Context

Similar to the distribution of raw materials, flaked stone classes are fairly evenly distributed by depositional context (Table 8.9). Debitage is evenly distributed across all contexts and, not surprisingly, debitage also accounts for the greatest percentage of artifacts recovered from all contexts. Cores occur in slightly higher proportions in floor fill and on occupational surfaces, but overall, their distribution is fairly even. Tools also occur in higher proportions in floor fill and on occupational surfaces, and in significantly smaller proportions in other contexts. Interestingly, the only tool types recovered from occupational surfaces and floor fill contexts are projectile points, bifaces, and edge-damaged and retouched flakes.

While the distribution of debitage is ubiquitous across the site and likely does not represent any noteworthy behavior, it is significant that the distribution of cores and tools on structure floors and in floor fill (N = 64) is restricted almost exclusively to structures located in RB200 (N = 41) and K. 901 (N = 14), with a few found in S. 161 (N = 5), RB300 (N = 3), and RB600 (N = 1). More significantly, 28 of these cores and tools were recovered from structures with ritual deposits and/or functions, including K. 279 and 901, storage structures 266/286, and S. 603. Twenty-four of the 28 are tools and 4 are cores. Seven of the tools are projectile points, two bifaces, 12 edge-damaged flakes, and three manufacturing tools.

The distribution pattern of cores and tools on occupational surfaces and in floor fill is likely attributable to a combination of manufacturing, curation (storage), and ritual behavior. As discussed in more detail in the next section, the cores on the floor of S. 161 are probably representative of flaked stone manufacturing activities. This may also be the case with the cores recovered from the floor of S. 222, the piki house. However, most of the cores and tools from occupational surfaces and floor fill were recovered from storage structures, and generally represent curation behavior. In addition, most were not recovered from structures with identified ritual deposits on their floors (see E.C. Adams, Chapter 4). Exceptions are a biface and an edge-damaged flake recovered from the floor of S. 286; a storage structure that contained a ritual burial of three articulated rabbits, along with several other artifacts; and a petrified wood projectile point recovered from the floor fill of S. 603, a habitation structure, that may represent part of an enriched or closing deposit (see Footnote 6).

Six projectile points, two of which are early projectile points (see discussion in subsequent section, Projectile Points), and one biface, all made of petrified wood, were also recovered from the floor fill of K. 279, and likely represent ritual behavior. Combining deposition of raw material categories, tools, and cores on floors and floor fill provides a convincing argument that these patterns were intentional and representational. It appears that objects of petrified wood and, to a lesser extent, obsidian are being selected for placement in structures over much of Chevelon during their decommissioning from the living world into the afterlife of the structures and community. The selected objects likely also involved social memory and pieces of places, which are clearly represented by petrified wood and obsidian. Petrified wood, as noted above, likely

Chapter 8: Flaked Stone 205

Table 8.8. Distribution of Flaked Stone Raw Materials by Depositional Context.

Context	Chert %	Chert N	Chalcedony %	Chalcedony N	Quartzite %	Quartzite N	Igneous %	Igneous N	Petrified Wood %	Petrified Wood N	Obsidian %	Obsidian N	Other %	Other N	Sandstone %	Sandstone N	Total
Occupational Surface	80.4	119	0.68	1	3.38	5			15.54	23							148
Floor Fill	79.82	273	1.46	5	7.02	24	0.29	1	5.56	19	5.56	19	0.29	1			342
General Fill	80.56	4119	0.7	36	4.99	255	0.08	4	9.39	480	4.09	209	0.02	1	0.18	9	5113
Feature Fill	86.32	808	0.75	7	4.06	38			5.98	56	2.89	27					936
Roof Fall	87.21	600	0.44	3	3.63	25			5.52	38	3.2	22					688
Wall Fall	85.17	488	0.35	2	3.14	18	0.17	1	6.81	39	4.19	24			0.17	1	573
Other*	70.21	66			6.38	6			19.15	18	4.26	4					94
Total	82.0	6473	0.68	54	4.70	371	0.08	6	8.53	673	3.86	305	0.03	2	0.13	10	7894

*Other represents any deposit context that does fall into the other categories, which, most often, is wall cleaning. As a result, the "other" category is not included in discussions of depositional context.

connects some residents to their villages of origin whereas obsidian likely represents the San Francisco Mountains, home of katsinas and often capped with snow.

Variability Across Structures

Flaked stone assemblages were recovered from 31 structures, representing six different uses — habitation, storage, piki house, kiva, non-kiva ritual, and unknown — as well as from three extramural or plaza surfaces (Table 8.10). Variability between structures within flaked stone classes and raw material distributions was observed when the assemblages from these structures were compared. Patterns that were observed are detailed below.

Flaked Stone Classes

Every excavated structure contained flaked stone debitage (Table 8.11a). However, the majority of tools, both formal and expedient, recovered from Chevelon were concentrated in the two kivas, K. 279 and 901, and in the related fill above and/or adjacent to the kivas (S. 274 and Plaza 900) (Table 8.11b). S. 704 is the only structure that did not contain any tools in its flaked stone assemblage.

Flaked stone assemblages were absent from occupation surfaces of 20 structures; no kiva contained any flaked stone on its occupation surface. All of the extramural/plaza areas were also lacking flaked stone on use surfaces. Eighty-two percent of the flaked stone assemblage, including tools and cores, from S. 161 was recovered from its occupation surface, suggesting that the manufacture of flaked stone may have occurred in this structure. Eight structures and two extramural areas contained flaked stone within feature fill. Structures of every function, except non-kiva

Table 8.9. Distribution of Flaked Stone Classes by Depositional Context.

Context	Debitage %	Debitage N	Tools %	Tools N	Cores %	Cores N	Other Artifacts %	Other Artifacts N	TOTAL
Occupational Surface	86.49	128	8.11	12	3.38	5	2.02	3	148
Floor Fill	83.63	286	11.40	39	4.09	14	0.88	3	342
General Fill	90.89	4647	6.43	329	2.01	103	0.66	34	5113
Feature Fill	94.12	881	3.10	29	2.14	20	0.64	6	936
Roof Fall	86.48	595	5.09	35	2.03	14	6.4	44	688
Wall Fall	95.11	545	3.67	21	1.22	7			573
Other	92.55	87	4.26	4	2.13	2	1.06	1	94
Total	90.82	7169	5.94	469	2.09	165	1.15	91	7894

ritual, contained artifacts within feature fill. However, while all eight structures and both extramural areas contained tools in features, only one extramural area, Plaza 900, contained more than three tools in its feature fill.

In addition, only two structures and two extramural areas contained cores within feature fill; again, only one extramural area, Plaza 900, contained more than three cores (Table 8.11c). There are several possible explanations for the presence of numerous tools and cores in the feature fill in Plaza 900. First, it is possible that this extramural area underwent unique abandonment processes related to ritual practices, as has been suggested for unusual assemblage depositional contexts at several other Homol'ovi sites (Lyons and Pitblado 1996; LaMotta 1996; Strand 1998; see Walker 1995 for a full discussion). Second, Plaza 900 contained many features, including several large roasting pits, a ramada, and a storage unit. It is possible that the unique flaked stone assemblages associated with these features are representative of the activities that occurred within these features and on the plaza surface. For example, the presence of 23 cores, as well as a large amount of debitage in Plaza 900,

could indicate that lithic reduction and/or tool manufacture was occurring in the plaza area. No manufacturing tools (i.e., hammerstones and pecking stones), the presence of which would bolster this interpretation, were recovered from the excavated plaza area. However, only a small sample of Plaza 900 was excavated, and it is possible that hammerstones and pecking stones used in lithic reduction activities are located in the unexcavated portions of this outside area; they also could have been stored or disposed of in other contexts. At other Homol'ovi sites, cores were often recycled in roasting pits, similar to worn out ground stone (Young 2001). Of the 23 cores recovered from Plaza 900, five came directly from a roasting pit in the plaza area, while an additional 16 came from ashy midden deposits, possibly representing episodes of hearth or roasting pit cleanings. It seems likely, therefore, that at Chevelon, cores were also recycled for use in roasting pits.

Hammerstones and pecking stones, which are used in the manufacture and maintenance, respectively, of ground stone and flaked stone artifacts, were widely distributed based on structure use, although two structure types

Table 8.10. Distribution of Flaked Stone by Structure and Depositional Context.

Structure	Function	Occupational Surface %	N	General Fill %	N	Feature Fill %	N	Wall Fall %	N	Roof Fall %	N	Floor Fill %	N	Other %	N	TOTAL
120	Habitation	4.88	16	29.57	97	25.61	84	9.45	31	20.12	66	5.94		10.37	34	328
123	Storage			46.53	47			14.85	15				6	32.67	33	101
158	Storage			29.31	34			56.03	65	8.62	10	6.03	7			116
159	Habitation			100.0	1											1
161	Habitation	82.11	78	4.21	4	1.05	1					12.63	12			95
222	Piki House	1.66	5	51.99	157	3.31	10	17.55	53	25.49	77					302
227	Storage			40.82	80	23.47	46	1.02	2	2.04	4	32.65	64			196
246	Extramural/Plaza	100.0													8	1
248	Kiva	25.0		100.0	1											1
264	Habitation		6					7.14	1	12.5	3	62.5	15			24
265	Storage			71.43	10					21.43	3					14
266	Storage	2.16	3	46.73	50			53.96	75	31.65	44	12.23	17			139
268	Storage							9.35	10	43.93	47					107
269	Habitation	3.27	5	73.86	113	5.23	8			2.61	4	4.58	7	10.45	16	153
274	Fill above kiva	57.0			281	43.0		212						493		
279	Kiva	1.67		98.85	1548	0.06	1	0.64	10			0.45	7			1566
286	Storage		6	53.76	193	1.12	4			32.31	116	11.14	40			359
287	Unknown	33.33	1	66.7	2											3
288	Storage	2.86	7	77.14	189							20.0	49			245
289	Habitation			25.0	1					50.0	2			25.0	1	4
293	Surface Ritual	100.0													1	1
300	Extramural/Trash	79.91		20.09	45										224	
345	Storage	12.5	1	12.5	1							75.0	6			8
373	Storage	2.24	3	35.82	48			7.46	10	41.79	56	5.97	8	6.72	9	134
393	Habitation	9.14	17	10.22	19			32.26	60	48.38	90					186
403	Unknown			10.53	2											2
603	Habitation			75.0	3							25.0	1			4
702	Storage													100	1	1
704	Storage			100.0	12											12
726	Storage							100.0	1							1
900	Plaza/Extramural	26.92		85.84	1758	1.90	39	1.37	28	5.86	120	5.03	103		1018	2048
901	Kiva															
TOTAL		1.87	148	64.77	5113	11.86	936	7.26	573	8.72	688	4.33	342	1.19	94	7894

Chapter 8: Flaked Stone 207

Table 8.11a. Distribution of Flake Categories by Structure.

Structure	Complete Flake %	N	Broken Flake %	N	Split Flake %	N	Flake Fragment %	N	Debris %	N	Spalls %	N	TOTAL %	N
120	43.0	129	2.67	8	0.33	1	20.67	62	33.33	100			4.18	300
123	42.7	38	4.49	4	1.12	1	21.35	19	30.34	27			1.24	89
158	32.1	36	5.36	6			29.46	33	33.04	37			1.56	112
161	46.51	40	2.33	2			32.56	28	18.6	16			1.20	86
222	66.30	179	0.74	2	2.22	6	22.22	60	7.78	21	0.74	2	3.77	270
227	44.97	76	6.51	11	4.14	7	20.12	34	21.3	36	2.96	5	2.36	169
246	28.57	2	14.29	1	28.57	2	28.57	2					0.10	7
264	34.78	8	8.7	2			30.43	7	26.09	6			0.32	23
265	45.45	5					9.1	1	45.45	5			0.15	11
266	40.31	52			2.33	3	31.78	41	24.81	32	0.78	1	1.80	129
268	47.06	48	0.98	1	0.98	1	8.82	9	42.16	43			1.42	102
269	50.0	72	1.39	2	1.39	2	20.14	29	26.39	38	0.69	1	2.01	144
274	53.29	251			0.21	1	29.30	138	15.92	75	1.27	6	6.57	471
279	55.51	797	1.81	26	1.26	18	26.43	379	14.23	204	0.77	11	20.02	1435
286	47.97	165	2.62	9	2.03	7	29.36	101	18.02	62			4.80	344
288	52.85	111	0.48	1	1.43	3	25.71	54	18.1	38	1.43	3	2.93	210
300	52.36	111	0.94	2			14.62	31	32.08	68			2.96	212
345	33.33	2							66.67	4			0.08	6
373	71.32	92					17.83	23	10.08	13	0.78	1	1.80	129
393	46.07	82	1.12	2	0.56	1	29.21	52	23.03	41			2.48	178
704	72.72	8							27.27	3			0.15	11
900	51.0	480	3.40	32	0.64	6	25.4	239	19.55	184			13.13	941
901	46.64	835	6.54	117	0.73	13	25.03	448	21.06	377			24.97	1790
TOTAL	50.48	3619	3.18	228	1.00	72	24.97	1790	19.95	1430	0.42	30	100.0	7169

contained over 78 percent of the manufacturing tool assemblage (Table 8.11b, Figure 8.6). Half were recovered from the general fill of K. 274/279 and 901, while another third were recovered from within five storage structures. The remaining pecking and hammerstones were recovered from the piki house, from extramural areas, and from two habitation structures. The pecking stones and hammerstones recovered from the two kivas were collected almost exclusively from enriched midden deposits (E.C. Adams and LaMotta 2006; Chapter 13). They were not recovered from contexts reflecting their original function. The majority of the pecking and hammerstones recovered from the piki house were found in roof fall, among numerous ground stone artifacts, suggesting that ground stone manufacture and maintenance may have occurred on the floor of the structure above the piki house. It is also possible that the hammerstones, pecking stones, and ground stone assemblage recovered from within S. 222 (the piki house) represents another enriched deposit (see Chapter 7),

Chapter 8: Flaked Stone   209

Table 8.11b. Distribution of Flaked Stone Tools by Structure.

Str.	Edge-Damaged %	N	Scraper %	N	Retouched %	N	Chopper %	N	Projectile Point %	N	Biface %	N	Drill %	N	Wedge %	N	Pecking stone %	N	Hammer stone %	N	TOTAL
120	50.0	7			28.57	4			14.29	2					7.14	1					14
123	28.57	2			42.86	3			28.57	2											7
158	33.33	1	33.33	1	33.33	1															3
159									100.0	1											1
161	50.0	2			25.0	1					25.0	1									4
222	14.29	2			7.14	1			21.43	3							42.86	6	14.29	2	14
227	46.15	6			15.38	2			7.69	1							15.38	2	15.38	2	13
246									100.0	1											1
248									100.0	1											1
264									100.0	1											1
265	33.33	1							66.67	2											3
266	44.44	4							44.44	4									1.11	1	9
268	100.0	2																			2
269	28.57	2			14.29	1			57.14	4											7
274	30.77	4			15.38	2			23.08	3			7.69	1			23.08	3			13
279	16.67	17			6.86	7			59.8	60	3.92	5					4.9	5	7.84	8	102
286	15.38	2			15.38	2			23.08	3	15.38	2					7.69	1	23.1	3	13
287									100.0	3											3
288	33.33	5							13.33	2	6.67	1					33.33	5	13.33	2	15
289									66.67	2									33.33	1	3
293									100.0	1											1
300	33.33	1							33.33	1							33.33	1			3
345									50.0	1							50.0	1			2
373	60.0	3							40.0	2											5
393	42.86	3							57.14	4											7
403									100.0	2											2
603									50.0	2	50.0	2									4
702											100.0	1									1
726									100.0	1											1
900	46.15	24			28.85	15			13.46	7	11.54	6									52
901	47.53	77	9.88	16	24.07	39	1.23	2	7.41	12	2.47	4	0.62	1	1.85	3	4.32	7	0.62	1	162
TOTAL	35.18	165	3.63	17	16.63	78	0.43	2	27.29	128	4.69	22	0.43	2	0.9	4	6.61	31	4.26	20	469

Table 8.11c. Distribution of Cores by Structure.

Structure	Flake Core %	N	Core %	N	Core-Tool %	N	TOTAL %	N
120	16.67	1	50.0	3	33.33	2	3.64	6
123						1	0.61	1
158			100.0	1			0.61	1
161			100.0	2			1.21	2
222	5.88	1	94.1	16			10.30	17
227	33.33	2	66.7	4			3.64	6
266			100.0	1			0.61	1
268			100.0	3			1.82	3
269			100.0	2			1.21	2
274			100.0	9			5.45	9
279	3.45	1	96.55	28			17.58	29
286	40.0	2	60.0	3			3.03	5
288	5.0	1	95.0	19			12.12	20
289			100.0	1			0.61	1
300			100.0	9			5.45	9
393			100.0	1			0.61	1
704	100	1					0.61	1
900	8.7	2	82.60	19	8.7	2	13.94	23
901	17.86	5	78.57	22	3.57	1	16.97	28
TOTAL	9.70	16	86.67	143	3.64	6	100.0	165

similar to that found in S. 120, 124, and 159.

Cores were recovered from 16 structures of all uses and from three extramural areas (Figure 8.7). However, K. 274 and 901, the piki house, a storage structure (S. 288), and Plaza 900 contained an overwhelming majority of the cores, ranging from 10.30 percent to 17.58 percent (Table 8.11c). As mentioned previously, the high number of cores recovered from the Plaza 900 area is likely because they were recycled in the roasting pits in this area. Interestingly, although S. 161 has been identified as an area where lithic reduction may have occurred, only two cores (and no manufacturing tools) were recovered from the structure. Only half of S. 161 was excavated, so it is entirely possible that additional cores, as well as manufacturing tools, are located in the unexcavated portion. It is also possible that only the later stages of lithic reduction—the production of tools from existing flakes—occurred in S. 161; these later stages do not utilize cores, pecking stones, or hammerstones, which would explain their virtual absence from the structure. Approximately 37 percent of the debitage from S. 161 does not contain cortex, suggesting these flakes may be from later reduction stages; however, they could also simply have come from cores without cortex. In order to more thoroughly evaluate the possibility that the later stages of lithic reduction were occurring in S. 161, a more detailed examination of the flakes from this structure would need to be conducted in order to determine the stage of manufacture of the flakes.

Projectile Points

One hundred and twenty-eight projectile points were recovered from all structure types at Chevelon. All but three structures contained at least one projectile point and 18 structures contained two or more (Table 8.5). K. 279, however, contained just under half of all projectile points; 10 of the 23 (43.48 percent) Archaic and Basketmaker projectile points were also recovered from K. 279 (Figure 8.8a-c). In addition, three projectile points were recovered from S. 274, fill located directly over K. 279. Another four, early projectile points were recovered from K. 901, which also contained the second largest number of projectile points in one structure. No other structure excavated at Chevelon contained more than one Archaic or Basketmaker projectile point, and the majority of structures contained none of these points.

Given the value and uses historically ascribed to projectile points by Pueblo groups (Parsons 1939; Beaglehole 1936; Sedig 2007; also see discussion, below), the large number of projectile points recovered from Chevelon is clearly meaningful and representative of activities above and beyond hunting and war-related activities, those most often associated with such artifacts (LeBlanc 1999). In particular, the large number of preceramic projectile points is an unusual finding because there are no published reports indicating the recovery of more than four preceramic points from undisturbed Pueblo fill (Vonarx 2006:5), at sites outside of the Homol'ovi area, although

Figure 8.7. Cores: (1-4) chert; (5) quartzite; (6) basalt.

this may be a result of how projectile points are described in the literature.

Krebs (1999) also looked at the distribution of preceramic points in the Homol'ovi assemblages. In her report, she indicates that preceramic points may often have been referred to as "un-notched projectile points". She, however, does not provide a discussion of the number of un-notched projectile points described in the literature.

In addition, over 80 percent of the early (Archaic through PI) points at Chevelon were recovered from enriched deposits (see Chapters 4 and 13; E.C. Adams and LaMotta 2006; Walker 1995) within domestic or ritual structures, especially from K. 274/279; and RB200. In conjunction with the ethnographic evidence, the large number of preceramic points and their deposit contexts indicate these points held significant value for the inhabitants of the site and should be considered ritually charged objects related to power, memory, and prestige (Vonarx 2006; also see discussion, below).

While the quantity and spatial distribution of preceramic projectile points at Chevelon

(a). Upper strata: (1) San Jose; (2) Dolores; (3) Biface; (4-5) Western Triangular; (6) Northern Side-Notched; (7-8) Pueblo Side-Notched, Pueblo III/IV style; (9) Pueblo Side-Notched, Pueblo II style; (10) Great Basin Stemmed base.

(b). Middle strata: (1-6, 8, 10-11, 13-14, 16-17) Pueblo Side-Notched, Pueblo III/IV style; (7, 9, 15) Western Triangular; (12) Basketmaker II style biface.

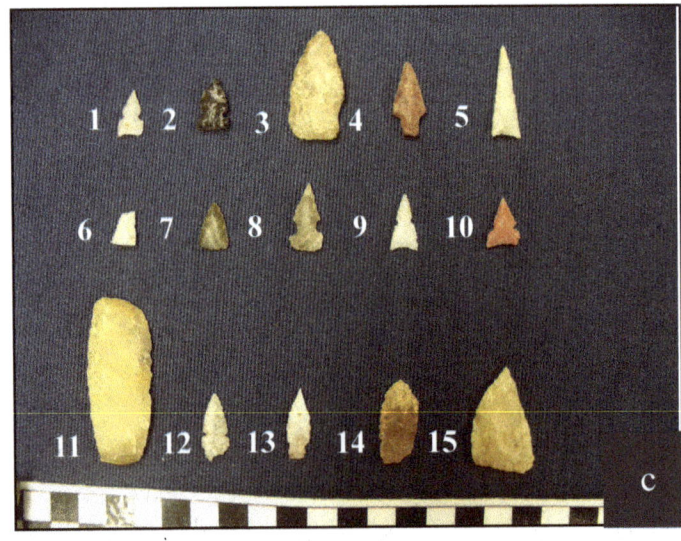

(c). Lower strata: (1-2, 8-10, 12) Pueblo Side-Notched, Pueblo III/IV style; (3,13) Datil; (4) Gypsum; (5-6) Western Side-Notched; (7) Unknown tip; (11) Paleoindian style biface; (14-15) Basketmaker II style bifaces.

Figure 8.8. Projectile points and bifaces from Kiva 279.

clearly indicates they were important to the inhabitants of the site, overall, the disproportionate distribution of all projectile points (both early and PIV period points) in K. 279 and 901, which is statistically significant at the p <.001 level using the best-fit chi-squared test, indicates the disposal of projectile points was conducted as an important component of some ritual activities. Parsons (1939) provides the best explanation of ritual practices involving projectile points among ethnographic Pueblo groups.

General Distribution

Except for the unique assemblage of tools and cores found in feature fill in the Plaza 900 area and the concentration of projectile points in K. 279 and 901, the disproportionate number of flaked stone of all classes in these kivas as well as in the plaza is related to the large amount of prehistoric trash — ritual and domestic — contained within their fill. For example, the ratio of tools to total flaked stone categories is 5.94 percent, and is only significantly exceeded in K. 901 at 9.05. None of the three structures contained flaked stone assemblages associated with their occupation surfaces; instead, 98.85 percent of the flaked stone in K. 279, 57.0 percent of the flaked stone in S. 274, and 85.84 percent of the flaked stone within K. 901 was recovered from midden. In K. 274/279, the midden layers were almost all enriched deposits and ritual in nature (Diaz de Valdes 2006, Chapter 9); as a result, virtually all of the flaked stone material recovered from K. 274/279 was contained in ritual midden deposits. K. 901, on the other hand, contained both enriched midden layers and domestic trash layers; while debitage, tools, and cores were found in both types of deposits, with more tools, especially projectile points, recovered from enriched deposits.

Approximately 27 percent of the flaked stone assemblage was recovered from the general fill of Plaza 900 with 69 percent of that recovered from feature fill. Although initially, these were characterized as domestic middens, given their adjacency to K. 901, it is likely some deposits and features were associated with ritual practices.

Raw Materials

Although the distribution of chert is ubiquitous, further consideration of the spatial distribution of raw materials at Chevelon revealed several interesting patterns, particularly in terms of the distribution of petrified wood and obsidian between room blocks and within specific structures.

In the following discussions, the percentages of petrified wood and obsidian in S. 403 and 603 have not been addressed. Both these structures have high proportions of these materials; however, these high percentages are misleading as both these structures have very low flaked stone counts (N=2, N=3, respectively). So, even though S. 403's flaked stone assemblage is 50 percent obsidian, this represents only one artifact; a similar situation occurs with S. 603. However, especially in the case of S. 603, which was primarily intact, or undisturbed, the fact that only three pieces of flaked stone, all of which were projectile points or bifaces and all of which were either petrified wood or obsidian, probably represents significant behavior, perhaps in the form of an enriched deposit or a closing deposit.

Petrified Wood

Thirteen structures did not contain any petrified wood, despite its local availability

(Table 8.4). These thirteen structures include five storage, three habitation, two unknown function, one kiva, one extramural/plaza area, and one surface ritual structure. Also, although two of the three extramural areas contained petrified wood, one of these areas (Extramural Area 300) contained only two pieces, which comprises less than 1 percent of the area's total flaked stone assemblage. Significantly, high concentrations of petrified wood (between 17 percent and 32 percent of each structure's flaked stone assemblage) were recovered from habitation and storage structures in the RB100 and from K. 901. The next highest percentage of petrified wood occurred in Plaza 900. All other structures and extramural areas contained substantially less petrified wood.

This uneven distribution of petrified wood, in favor of the RB100 and K. 901/Plaza 900, could reflect restricted access to petrified wood as a raw material source. However, given the local availability of this resource, this explanation seems unlikely. Instead, it is possible that the high percentages of petrified wood in the RB100 and in K. 901 may reflect ties between occupants of those structures with communities east of Chevelon, most likely in the PEFO area, where petrified wood is abundant. This interpretation is reinforced by the significant increase in Tonto Polychrome jars and bowls both locally made and imported from the east (see Chapter 6). E.C. Adams (see Chapter 4 and Chapter 13) has suggested that a social connection may exist between the inhabitants of the RB300, and users of K. 901, which contains significant quantities of petrified wood, and RB100. In particular, he argues that some occupants of the RB300 may have constructed and moved to RB100 during the Middle Homol'ovi Phase (MHP) or LHP.

If this is the case, the large percentages of petrified wood seen in K. 901 and the RB100 may be related to a specific group of people living at Chevelon, perhaps immigrants from Puerco Ruin or other pueblos in the PEFO or points farther east. High frequencies of White Mountain Red Ware at Chevelon during the Early Homol'ovi Phase (EHP) and MHP suggest longstanding relationships between the two areas that would create social relationships conducive to migration (Anthony 1990).

Obsidian

Historically, the color black — the color of obsidian — is a powerful and ritually important color for Hopi and other Pueblo groups: it is associated with the nadir (underworld) and the zenith (heavens/clouds) and with katsinas and death (Parsons 1939:99, 175, 200). Perhaps not coincidentally, the vast majority of the obsidian recovered from Chevelon and other Homol'ovi sites was sourced to Government Mountain, located in the San Francisco Volcanic Field, near Flagstaff. In Hopi traditions, the San Francisco Peaks are the home of the katsinas and the entrance to the underworld (Parsons 1939:175, 200). This connection between the importance of the color black, the ritual significance of the San Francisco Peaks, and the geographic origin of more than 90 percent of the obsidian from the HSC, including Chevelon, suggests that obsidian may have played an important role in the religious structure and the control of power at Chevelon. This helps explain the presence of six PIV style obsidian points in K. 901 that appear to be made by three flintknappers (Figure 8.9). This inference is supported by the spatial distribution of obsidian at Chevelon, which unlike the distribution of petrified wood, is related to ritual structures and powerful areas of the village.

Ten structures, representing every structure type except unknown, as well as two extramural areas, were devoid of any obsidian artifacts (Table 8.4). Similar to the distribution of petrified wood, obsidian, although found throughout the site, is concentrated in RB200 with 63 percent and, in particular, in ritual structures and enriched deposits. Within RB200, two structures — K. 279 and S. 286 — contain significant quantities of obsidian (Table 8.4). While this is expected from K. 279, the high concentration of obsidian in S. 286 (14.2 percent of the structure assemblage, 16.7 percent of the total obsidian assemblage), a storage structure, seems unusual. However, S. 286 contained a ritual floor assemblage – an axe, bone awls, and three cottontails, presumably sacrificed-, were arranged on an otherwise clean floor. Interestingly, none of the obsidian from S. 286 was recovered in direct association with the ritual assemblage, but rather was recovered from general fill, roof fall, and floor fill contexts. Perhaps the inclusion of a large amount of obsidian in the post-abandonment fill of S. 286 was meant to commemorate the ritual assemblage preserved on the floor as an act of social memory.

The three other structures/areas at Chevelon containing high proportions of the total obsidian assemblage are K. 279 and 901 and Plaza 900. These three structures contained 28.85 percent, 21.64 percent, and 12.13 percent, respectively, of the total obsidian assemblage, even though the recovered obsidian represented only between 3 and 5 percent of the flaked stone assemblages from these units (see Table 8.4). These percentages are expected given the high proportion of excavated cultural material coming from this area. Statistically, the proportions of obsidian in K. 279 and Plaza 900 were not significant using a best-fit chi-squared test. While the proportion of obsidian in K. 901 was significant at the $0.0.5 > p > 0.02$ level, this still appears to be largely driven by the sheer number of artifacts recovered from K. 901, based on a low (0.04) Cramer's V value.

Projectile Point Raw Material

Over 60 percent of projectile points recovered from Chevelon are made from chert, although projectile points made from both petrified wood and obsidian are also common in the Chevelon assemblage (Table 8.12; also see Table 8.2). This pattern — chert as the dominant raw material type, followed by petrified wood and obsidian — also holds true when the projectile point assemblage is considered from a temporal perspective. Chert represents approximately 64 and 58 percent of the preceramic and PIV projectile point assemblage, respectively, while petrified wood accounts for about 14 percent and 20 percent, respectively, and obsidian for about 14 percent and 19 percent, respectively. Projectile points manufactured from chalcedony or igneous materials represent small proportions of the assemblages. Obsidian and petrified wood occur at much higher frequencies in the

Figure 8.9. Obsidian projectile points from Plaza 900/Kiva 901 showing three styles with 1 and 2 being shorter and 3 and 4 having different notching patterns tthan 5 and 6.

Table 8.12. Distribution of Projectile Points by Raw Material.

Phase	Chert	Chalcedony	Igneous	Petrified Wood	Obsidian	Total
Early Archaic			1			1
Middle Archaic	1					1
Middle Archaic/Basketmaker II	2					2
Late Archaic	3	1		1	1	6
Late Archaic/Basketmaker	1			1		2
Basketmaker III	6			2	3	11
Pueblo I	5					5
Pueblo II/IV	35	1	1	12	13	62
Pueblo III/IV	9			3	1	13
Unknown	18			3	4	25
Total	80	2	2	22	22	128

projectile point assemblage than they do in the general flaked stone assemblage (see Table 8.2 and 8.12), suggesting these material types were preferred for the manufacture of projectile points. While the performance characteristics of obsidian are somewhat superior to that of petrified wood and chert, they do not fully explain this discrepancy. Rather, obsidian was also chosen for use in the manufacture of projectile points for other reasons, including for its local scarcity, due to distance to source, and its association with the San Francisco Peaks, as discussed elsewhere in this chapter.

This strikingly similar distribution of raw material for the entire projectile point assemblage as well as when considered between temporal periods suggests two things: 1) projectile points recovered from Chevelon were most often manufactured from easily obtainable, high quality raw materials, primarily chert; and, 2) the decision to collect older projectile points was likely more strongly tied to other attributes of the point, rather than the material.

Research at Rock Art Ranch 6 km south of Chevelon Pueblo has recovered 216 points of which 59 (27.3 percent) are petrified wood and only one (0.5 percent) is obsidian. Eight (3.7 percent) igneous points are also present. This suggests the frequency of preceramic points, in terms of material, likely affected the assemblage recovered from Chevelon. Early projectile points made from obsidian or petrified wood were only recovered from K. 279 (N=6) and 901 (N=2), with the exception of one Late Archaic/ Basketmaker petrified wood point recovered from S. 264, a habitation structure dating to the LHP (Table 8.13). It appears that the combination of these two raw materials, including early projectile points, was restricted to the older and more ritually powerful portions of the site, whereas PIV projectile points, made from these two raw materials, while concentrated in K. 279 and 901, were also recovered from other areas of the site (Tables 8.5, 8.12, and 8.13).

Table 8.13. Distribution of Projectile Point Raw Materials by Structure.

S.	Chert	Chalcedony	Igneous	Petrified Wood	Obsidian	Total
120	1				1	2
123	1				1	2
159					1	1
222	3					3
227	1					1
246	1					1
248	1					1
264				1		1
265	2					2
266	3				1	4
269	3				1	4
274	3					3
279	35		1	14	10	60
286	3					3
287	1				2	3
288	1			1		2
289	2					2
293	1					1
300	1					1
345	1					1
373	2					2
393	3	1				4
403	1				1	2
603				1	1	2
726					1	1
900	3	1		2	1	7
901	7		1	3	1	12
TOTAL	80	2	2	22	22	128

TEMPORAL VARIATION IN THE CHEVELON FLAKED STONE ASSEMBLAGE

Temporal Variation in Flaked Stone Classes

A breakdown of structures by chronological period is presented in Table 8.14. Flaked stone class proportions in the Chevelon assemblage remain relatively stable throughout all four occupation periods (Table 8.15). Debitage consistently accounts for between 90 percent and 93 percent of the total assemblage, while tools represent approximately 4 percent to 6 percent, and cores comprise approximately 2 percent to 4 percent.

There are two patterns in the temporal

Table 8.14. Chronological Distribution of Structures at Chevelon.

Tuwuica Phase	Early Homol'ovi Phase	Middle Homol'ovi Phase	Late Homol'ovi Phase	Unknown.
1290–1330 C.E.	1325/1330–1365 C.E.	1365–1385 C.E.	1385–1400 C.E.	
S. 227	S. 222	S. 274	S. 120	S. 246
S. 300	S. 248	K. 279	S. 122	S. 287
	S. 266		S. 123	S. 293
			S. 124	
			S. 157	
			S. 158	
			S. 159	
			S. 161	
			S. 264	
			S. 265	
			S. 268	
			S. 269	
			S. 286	
			S. 288	
			S. 289	
			S. 345	
			S. 373	
			S. 393	
			S. 403	
			S. 603	
			S. 704	
			S. 729	
			Plaza 900	
			K. 901	

distribution of flaked stone classes worth mentioning. First, the proportion of tools in the total assemblage steadily increases over time, from 3.88 percent, in the Tuwuica Phase (TP), to 6.28 percent, in the LHP. Second, the percentage of cores contained within the assemblage decreases by half, going from about 4 percent to about 2 percent, between the TP and EHP, and the MHP and LHP. These trends suggest that as time passed, raw material resources were being used more intensively.

Debitage to core and debitage to retouched tool ratios confirm this finding (Table 8.16). Between the two early periods and the two later periods, the number of flakes produced from a single core almost doubles. At the same time, approximately 1.5 to 2 times the number of tools is being produced from debitage during the Middle and Late phases versus during the TP and Early phases.

At this point, it is unclear why raw materials, in general, may have been used more intensively over time. Although the population of Chevelon appears to have grown significantly between the village's founding and its eventual closure, most of the raw material types in the assemblage are abundant even today, and many are locally available. However, the increase

Table 8.15. Temporal Distribution of Flaked Stone Classes.

Time Period	Debitage		Tools		Cores		
	%	N	%	N	%	N	TOTAL
Tuwuica Phase	92.48	381	3.88	16	3.64	15	412
Early Homol'ovi Phase	90.48	399	5.44	24	4.08	18	441
Middle Homol'ovi Phase	92.57	1906	5.59	115	1.85	38	2059
Late Homol'ovi Phase	91.74	4476	6.33	309	1.93	94	4879
Unknown	58.33	7	41.66	5			12
TOTAL	91.87	7169	6.01	469	2.11	165	7803

Table 8.16. Temporal Distribution of Flaked Stone Class Ratios.

Time Period	Debitage to Cores	Debitage to Retouched Tools	Debitage to Manufacturing Tools
Tuwiuca Phase	25.4:1	34.64:1	76.2:1
Early Homol'ovi Phase	22.17:1	26.6:1	44.33:1
Middle Homol'ovi Phase	50.16:1	16.57:1	119.13:1
Late Homol'ovi Phase	47.62:1	14.49:1	213.14:1
Unknown	n/a	1.4:1	n/a

in population likely also led to an increase in the time devoted to domestic/economic and perhaps ritual tasks, and may simply have left less time to collect raw materials for stone tool manufacture, leading to more intensive use of those already collected. It may also be that the reorganization of settlement systems that took place across the region in the late 1300s disrupted exchange networks, causing some raw materials — obsidian, and perhaps petrified wood — to be more intensively utilized.

Temporal Variation in Raw Material Use

In all four periods, chert is the dominant raw material (Table 8.17). Both quartzite and obsidian comprise significantly smaller proportions of the assemblages, but their percentages remain fairly consistent. The exception is that percentage of quartzite during the TP, is double the three subsequent phases. The real change is reflected in the use of chert and petrified wood during the LHP. During the three earlier occupation periods, petrified wood represented between 1 percent and 2 percent of the flaked stone assemblages. By the Late phase, petrified wood accounts for 12.42 percent of the assemblage. Although chert remains the dominant raw material during the LHP, its percentage drops. These trends are reflected in the spatial concentration of petrified wood in the RB100 and in K. 901, which date to the LHP. While this change in raw material use could be attributed to availability, this seems highly unlikely given the abundance of both chert and petrified wood easily accessible in the Chevelon area today. Instead, the change is probably related to preference for petrified wood over chert by the inhabitants of the RB100 households and may be related to social connections between the inhabitants of the RB100, who may have been using K. 901, and communities to the east of Chevelon.

THE RITUAL SIGNIFICANCE OF FLAKED STONE IN THE CHEVELON ASSEMBLAGE: THEORIZING SOCIAL MEMORY

Melanie Medeiros and A.J. Vonarx

Thus far, this chapter has focused on examining general artifact characteristics, as well as identifying raw material procurement strategies for, and discussing the technological organization of, the Chevelon flaked stone assemblage. However, the recovery of so many preceramic projectile points from Chevelon, and specifically from enriched deposits in two kivas located in RB200, suggests that all flaked stone at Chevelon was not manufactured in and used for only domestic purposes. Rather, flaked stone — most notably projectile points — played an important role in the ritual lives of the people living at Chevelon.

Historically, projectile points were considered to be powerful objects by Hopi, and by Pueblo groups in general (Beaglehole 1936; Parsons 1939). Although archaeologists generally assume projectile points were used in hunting and war-related activities, ethnographic research indicates they were also used in a variety of personal and communal ritual activities to afford protection and health benefits and to confer (ritual) power, as well as outside of ritual action, as a defense against negative spiritual influences. According to Parsons (1939:332), projectile points were believed to have been "dropped by the fingers of Lightning", and hence are referred to as

Table 8.17. Temporal Distribution of Raw Materials.

Time Period	Chert %	Chert N	Chalcedony %	Chalcedony N	Quartzite %	Quartzite N	Igneous %	Igneous N	Petrified Wood %	Petrified Wood N	Obsidian %	Obsidian N	Other %	Other N	Sandstone %	Sandstone N	TOTAL
Tuwuica	86.43	363	0.95	4	8.57	36					2.38	10			0.24	1	420
EHP	90.49	400	0.23	1	4.52	20	0.23	1	1.43	6	3.17	14					442
MHP	87.91	1810	0.58	12	4.86	100	0.15	3	1.36	6	4.27	88			0.05	1	2059
LHP	78.41	3890	0.75	37	4.33	215	0.04	2	2.19	45	3.85	191	0.04	2	0.16	8	4961
Unknown	83.33	10							12.42	616	16.67	2					12
TOTAL	82.0	6473	0.68	54	4.70	371	0.08	6	8.53	673	3.87	305	0.03	2	0.13	10	7894

lightening stones by many Pueblo groups, including the Hopi.

Ethnographically documented uses of projectile points by Pueblo groups, outside of hunting and war-related activities, include, as medicinal or life-giving objects, talismans in death rituals, charms or amulets, mythical objects, and tokens in games or competitions (Beaglehole 1936; Parsons 1939; Sedig 2007). As a safeguard against danger or other negative spiritual influences, and particularly to protect against harm from witchcraft, supernatural or otherwise potentially treacherous beings (e.g., the Spanish), and hazardous periods of time or events (e.g., nighttime, "the dangerous moon", etc.), projectile points were often used in conjunction with ash (Parsons 1939:106–107) and were given as gifts, placed in one's mouth, and worn as necklaces or hair pieces, or otherwise carried about one's person (Parsons 1939:332). Several studies (Dittert 1959; Parsons 1939; Simpson 1953) also indicate that the collection or gathering of projectile points from ruins for ritual use was practiced by Pueblo groups, notably the Hopi, Zuni, Laguna, and Acoma. Early projectile points, in particular, were considered the most powerful and were highly valued (Dittert 1959:363; Sedig 2007:71–72). Such projectile points were sometimes included in shaman's bundles for use in ritual activities (Parsons 1939), an activity documented archaeologically at H1, where a shaman's bundle, consisting of a projectile point with other colored stones: a quartz crystal, and a shell frog covered with turquoise mosaic, was recovered from S. 418 (E. C. Adams 2009, personal communication).

There are two components to understanding the ritual character of projectile points and their role in the creation and maintenance of social memory at Chevelon: 1) the deposit contexts from which the points have been recovered and 2) the types of projectile points that have been identified.

Enriched Deposits

In turning to the first component, as defined by E.C. Adams and LaMotta (2006), the term "enriched deposit" generally refers to those deposits made under the guise of ritual activities that include deposits with unusual types, or more complete artifacts than other deposits; deposits containing items expected to be "curated, despite abandonment, or scavenged afterward"; deposits that are offertory or sacrificial in nature; deposits containing ceremonial trash (sensu Walker 1995); or deposits or caches with mundane artifacts that are "probably residues from ceremonial support activities such as feasts" (E.C. Adams and LaMotta 2006:59).

E.C. Adams and LaMotta (2006:59) also note artifacts that can serve as weapons, and projectile points, in particular, tend to occur in enriched deposits within the Homol'ovi villages. For example, at H1, seven projectile points, two of which dated to the preceramic period, were recovered from an enriched deposit between 65 cm and 96 cm above the floor of a ritual structure, S. 729. Artifacts recovered from this enriched deposit include whole manos and a metate, a pot break, a rabbit jaw, a bifacially flaked obsidian knife dating to the BMII period, several pieces of selenite, human ribs, a pigment-mixing slab, polishers, worked bone, and a slab with pigment, among other items.

At Chevelon, over half of the projectile points were recovered from enriched deposits, primarily from within kiva fill, especially from within K. 279 and the fill above it labeled S. 274, but also from other structure types and deposit contexts (Tables 8.12 and 8.13). The majority of the projectile points were recovered singly; however, several deposits contained three or more projectile points, although none contained more than five. Deposits with multiple projectile points tended to occur in K. 279 and 901, rather than in other structure types; such deposits also tended to contain a significant number of "exotic" items, such as articulated animal remains, artifacts made from non-local shell, whole or reconstructible ceramic vessels, and pigmented and/or painted slabs, and were associated with ash (E.C. Adams and Fladd 2014). For example, over one-third of the projectile points recovered from K. 279 were found with articulated animal remains, generally bird, but also rabbit and fish. Preceramic points in particular were often found in enriched deposits. For example, the 10 preceramic points recovered from K. 279 (Figure 8.8a-c) "tended to be accompanied by at least one Pueblo era point (86 percent of cases), and were slightly more likely to be in a deposit with shell (67 percent), minerals (46 percent), miniature vessels (51 percent), or partially reconstructible vessels (69 percent) when compared to later points and their associated kiva deposits" (Vonarx 2006:8).

The deposition of projectile points in enriched deposits, especially those concentrated in K. 279, highlights the importance of these artifacts in on-going ritual activities at Chevelon.

Preceramic Projectile Points and Social Memory

Of the 128 projectile points recovered during excavations at Chevelon, 28 definitively pre-date the occupation of Chevelon (Figures 8.1 and 8.2), while another 62 were identified as dating between the PII and PIV periods, and therefore could also pre-date the occupation of the site. Even if only the definitive pre-PIV points are considered, the projectile point assemblage from Chevelon includes an unusual number of early points. In comparison, of the 203 projectile points recovered from H1, only 13 were preceramic, while of the 88 projectile points recovered from H2, only 11 were preceramic (Krebs 1999).

Given that the majority of these points were recovered from enriched deposits within ritual structures, it seems clear that they should be considered ritually charged objects that held significant value and power to the people of Chevelon. E.C. Adams (Chapters 4 and 13) and Vonarx (2006) have further suggested that these early points, in particular, may have been important objects in the creation and maintenance of social memory at Chevelon, invoking, through their use in ritual events, recognition of and reverence for the past. However, as Vonarx (2006:8) has also noted, the reasons why these early projectile points were collected from the landscape and ritually deposited at Chevelon are not fully understood, at this time.

It seems clear that preceramic points, which tend to be much larger and made of distinctive materials, were recognized as "different" by the inhabitants of Chevelon. As discussed above, ethnographic study of historic Pueblo groups indicates that several Western Pueblo tribes, including the Hopi, ascribed particular value to projectile points from earlier time periods, and specifically collected these from ruins to be used in a variety of ceremonial functions, including in medicinal and hunting rituals (Dittert 1959:363; Parsons 1939; Sedig 2007:71–72; Simpson 1953). Whether their unique appearance, when compared to typical PIV projectile points, or whether recognition (implicit or explicit) of their antiquity and/or specific ties to past persons, places, or events resulted in their curation and eventual ritual deposition, however, is something that cannot be proven with the current archaeological data, but the contexts of their deposition are suggestive of practices similar to those described in the ethnographic literature.

Summary and Conclusions

In summary, analysis of the flaked stone assemblage from Chevelon has provided a number of interesting insights into the social and technological organization of the village. In particular, the Chevelon flaked stone assemblage is typologically similar to other contemporary Homol'ovi assemblages. Technological production is organized around expedient techniques centered on core reduction and tool production. Debitage accounts for approximately 90 percent of the overall assemblage; informal retouched tools are ubiquitous, and projectile points and bifaces are the most commonly recovered formal tools. Raw material use in the Chevelon assemblage is also consistent with other Homol'ovi assemblages in that chert dominates, but quartzite and petrified wood, both locally available, and obsidian, a non-local material, also were important raw materials.

However, spatial and temporal variation, within the Chevelon assemblage, indicates that some characteristics of its flaked stone assemblage may be unrelated to either technological organization or raw material procurement and use. The flaked stone assemblage also highlights the importance of social networks within Chevelon, between Chevelon and other Homol'ovi villages, and other PIV settlements, as well as the significance of artifact type and raw material in the control of power and enactment of ritual. In particular, the dominance of petrified wood in RB100 and K. 901/Plaza 900 suggests a social connection between the two areas of the pueblo and possible migration to Chevelon by populations located to the east of Chevelon; more generally, it indicates a preference for the use of petrified wood over chert that is likely more social in nature than explicitly related to raw material performance characteristics.

The concentration of obsidian in ritual structures and in RB200, the oldest area of the pueblo, in conjunction with ethnohistoric evidence, indicates that the use, control, and deposition of this non-local raw material was important in the control of resources, power, and prestige at Chevelon. Finally, the significant number of Archaic and Basketmaker projectile points recovered from Chevelon, most of which were recovered from kivas and/or enriched deposits in RB200 and 300, emphasizes the role these points played in ritual activities and the development of social memory at the site. Further investigation of curation may reveal that other artifact types are also important facets in the construction of social memory at Chevelon.

Chapter 9
Faunal Remains from Chevelon
Rachel Diaz de Valdes and E. Charles Adams

In prehispanic times, animals played an important economic (Bayham 1982; R. Dean 2003) and ceremonial (Roler 1999; Strand 1998) role in the lives of the people throughout the Southwest. Historically, animals were used, not only for food, but for ritual and manufacturing purposes (Beaglehole 1936; Tyler 1979, 1991). This chapter will focus on use of animals at Chevelon for subsistence and will also explore the role of animals in ceremonial and ritual contexts.

Methodology

Vertebrate remains were identified using standard zooarchaeological methods. All identifications of the materials reported here were made by the author using the comparative skeletal collection of the Stanley J. Olsen Zooarchaeology Laboratory, housed in the ASM, the University of Arizona. A number of primary data classes are recorded. All specimens were identified to the most specific taxonomic level possible. The "cf." designation is used when a specimen is considered to be closest to the taxa listed, but the identification cannot be made with the same certainty as other identifications. The "sp." suffix is used when the specimen could have come from more than one species within a given genus. Specimens are also identified in terms of the skeletal elements represented, the portion recovered, and symmetry. Those specimens that cross-mended (re-fit) are counted as a single specimen. Indicators for sex, age, and modifications were noted where observed. Modifications are classified as burned, gnawed, and cut. Burned specimens may result from exposure to fire during cooking. Burns may also occur if specimens are burned intentionally or unintentionally after discard (Gilchrist and Mytum 1986). Whether the bone was carbonized or calcined was recorded as well as to what degree each element exhibited this burning. *Carbonized* signifies that the bone turned to carbon as a result of partial burning. *Calcined* indicates that the bone burned at a high temperature, but below the point of fusion. This causes the loss of moisture and the reduction, or oxidation, of carbonates and other compounds within the bone (Stiner et al. 1995). Any evidence of animal gnawing, either rodent or carnivore, was also documented. Both have individual diagnostic characteristics that make them identifiable. Cultural modifications, such as cut marks, are described according to location, quantity, and directionality.

The main quantification index used is NISP or the number of identified specimens of bone. NISP avoids the problems often encountered with other derived quantification units such as MNE, MAU and MNI (Grayson 1984; McCracken 2003). Theoretically, this analytical unit should be reproducible by subsequent analysts. However, the "tenacity and identification skills of the analyst may influence NISP measures." (Lyman 1994a: 51). Although reproducible, NISP contains an inherent bias, due to variability in the fragmentation of elements from different species. Larger animals, such as cattle, are more susceptible to an inflated NISP, due to intense processing for food (Marshall and Pilgram 1991). Also, fragments of bone from larger animals are less likely to contain identifiable characteristics then fragments from smaller animals (Pavao 1994). This counting measure is used as the primary analytic technique for comparing inter-site variability within the Chevelon faunal material since it is dominated by lagomorphs and less likely to be prone to inflation.

General Faunal Composition

Due to the excellent preservation of faunal material at Chevelon, as at other Homol'ovi pueblos, only a portion of the entire faunal assemblage recovered from Chevelon has been analyzed (Diaz de Valdes 2007). As a result, 24 structures have been analyzed resulting in 16,068 identified specimens (Tables 9.1 and 9.2).

These structures include five kivas, one piki room, six habitation structures, seven storage rooms, one habitation room converted to storage, and four plaza areas (S. 246, 200, 300, and 900). The vast majority (N =13,624, 84.79 percent), of the identified specimens is contributed by rabbits, rodents, unidentified small mammals (essentially rabbits or rodents), and unidentifiable specimens. Birds, carnivores (including unidentified medium mammals), artiodactyls (including unidentified large mammals), reptiles, amphibians and fish, together, account for 15.21 percent of the total NISP of the sample (Table 9.3). Appendix B lists unusual or rare taxa by structure.

Modern Environment

The modern environmental landscape around Chevelon (see Chapter 2 for a more in-depth discussion) is arid and dominated by low bushes, scrub brush, and grasses characterized by the Upper Sonoran Life Zone (Lowe 1964b). The fauna is notable for its lack of variety with lagomorphs dominating the landscape. Several perennial streams run through the area, creating riparian habitats that prehistorically dominated by willows and cottonwoods. The watercourses also attract migrating birds and larger game. Paleoenvironmental reconstruction based on archaeological floral and faunal evidence, as well as historical accounts of the environment, tell us that little has changed in the last several hundred years (E.C. Adams 2002). Putting the archaeological faunal assemblage in this environmental context is important to understanding prehistoric subsistence strategies and even ritual use.

The Assemblage

Lagomorphs

Lagomorphs (cottontails and jack rabbits) are a ubiquitous and rapidly reproducing species. They can withstand heavy hunting pressure without greatly reducing their numbers. Their remains constitute a large percentage of almost every archaeological assemblage from the Southwest. At Chevelon, 52.25 percent (8395 NISP) of the identified remains are lagomorphs. They are found in the fill of every structure.

Human consumption leaves a distinct

Table 9.1. General Taxonomic Composition of the Chevelon Pueblo Faunal Dataset.

Taxon	NISP	Burning[1]	%NISP
Class Osteichthyes, Order Unknown	72	4b	0.45
Order Cypriniformes (Minnow-like Fishes)	4		0.02
Family Cyprinidae (Minnows)	66		0.41
Family Catostomidae	27	1b	0.17
Xyrauchen texanus (Razorback Sucker)	12		0.07
Total Fish	**181**	-	**1.13**
Class Amphibia, Order Salientia (Frogs and Toads)	3		0.02
Order Squamata, Suborder Serpentes (Snakes)	98		0.60
Family Colubridae (Colubrid Snakes)	64		0.40
Family Elapidae, Subfamily Crotalidae (Pit Viper)	1		0.01
Suborder Sauria (Lizards)	1		0.01
Crotaphytus sp. (Collared/Leopard Lizard)	3		0.02
Total Reptiles	**170**	-	**1.11**
Class Aves, Order Unknown, Body Size Unknown	69	1b	0.43
Class Aves, Order Unknown, Small Bird	71	1b	0.44
Class Aves, Order Unknown, Medium Bird	71	3b	0.44
Class Aves, Order Unknown, Large Bird	22		0.14
Podiceps caspicus (Eared Grebe)	1		0.01
Podilymbus podiceps (Pied-billed Grebe)	18		0.11
Ardea herodias (Great Blue Heron)	2		0.01
Butorides vivescens (Green Heron)	1		0.01
Order Falconiformes (Birds of Prey)	12		0.07
Buteo sp. (Buteonine Hawks)	6		0.04
Buteo jamaicensis (Red-tailed Hawk)	2		0.01
Aquila chrysaetos (Golden Eagle)	13		0.08
Circus cyaneus (Marsh Hawk)	3		0.02
Falco sp. (Falcon/Kestrel/Merlin)	5		0.03
Family Anatidae (Ducks, Geese, and Swans)	84	1b	0.05
Anas platyrhynchos (Mallard)	3		0.02
Anas sp., duck-sized	22		0.14
Anas acuta (Pintail)	1		0.01
Aythya valisineria (Canvasback)	1		0.01
Mergus merganser (Common Merganser)	2		0.01
Family Phasianidae (Quails)	6		0.04
Callipepla sp. (Scaled Quail/Gambel's Quail)	2		0.01
Meleagris gallopavo (Turkey)	74		0.04
Grus canadensis (Sandhill Crane)	9		0.06
Family Rallidae (Rails, Gallinules, and Coots)	4		0.02
Fulica americana (American Coot)	13		0.08

Table 9.1. General Taxonomic Composition of the Chevelon Pueblo Faunal Dataset, cont'd.

Taxon	NISP	Burning		%NISP
Family Scolopacidae/ Charadriidae (Sandpipers / Plovers)	5			0.03
Family Columbidae (Pigeons, Doves)	5			0.03
Zenaidura macroura (Morning Dove)	1			0.01
Charadrius vociferus (Killdeer)	1			0.01
Family Strigidae (Owls)	5			0.03
Family Caprimulgidae (Nighthawks and Whip-poor-wills)	1			0.01
Order Passeriformes (Perching Birds)	12			0.07
Family Corvidae (Ravens, Crows, Magpies, Jays)	62			0.39
Corvus corax (Common Raven)	34			0.21
Family Icteridae (Blackbirds, Meadowlarks, Orioles)	5			0.03
Sialia sp. (Bluebirds)	11			0.07
Total Birds	**512**	**3b**		**3.19**
Order Lagomorpha (Hares and Rabbits)	31			0.19
Family Leporidae (Hares and Rabbits)	185			1.15
Sylvilagus sp. (Cottontails)	7116	175b	95c	44.29
Lepus sp. (Hares and Jackrabbits)	332	7b		2.07
Lepus californicus (Black-tailed Jackrabbit)	690	30b	17c	4.29
Lepus alleni (Antelope Jackrabbit)	41			0.26
Total Rabbits	**8395**	**212b**	**112c**	**52.25**
Order Rodentia (Rodents)	1643	6b		1.01
Family Sciuridae (Squirrels)	36	1c		0.22
Ammospermophilus sp. (Antelope Squirrels)	22			0.14
Ammospermophilus leucurus (White-tailed Antelope Squirrel)	4			0.02
Spermophilus sp. (Ground Squirrels)	7			0.04
Spermophilus variegatus (Rock Squirrel)	40			0.25
Cynomys sp. (Prairie Dogs)	98	3b		0.61
Cynomys gunnisoni (Gunnison's Prairie Dog)	4			0.02
Thomomys sp. (Pocket Gophers)	98	1b		0.61
Perognathus sp. (Pocket Mice)	25			0.16
Dipodomys sp. (Kangaroo Rats)	22	1b		0.14
Subfamily Cricetinae (New World Rats and Mice)	101			0.69
Peromyscus sp. (White-footed Mice)	29			0.18
Onychomys sp. (Grasshopper Mice)	86			0.54
Neotoma sp. (Woodrats)	250			1.56
Neotoma albigula (White-throated Woodrat)	11			0.07
Ondatra zibethicus (Muskrat)	17			0.11
Castor canadensis (Beaver)	6	1b		0.04

Table 9.1. General Taxonomic Composition of the Chevelon Pueblo Faunal Dataset, cont'd.

Taxon	NISP	Burning		%NISP
Rodents	**1029**	**124b**	**1c**	**6.40**
Family Canidae (Coyotes, Dogs, Wolves, and Foxes)	9			0.06
Canis latrans (Coyote)	20			0.12
Canis sp. (Coyote/Domestic Dog/Wolf)	20			0.12
Canis latrans/ Canis familiaris (Coyote/Domestic Dog)	6			0.04
Vulpes vulpes (Red Fox)	1			0.01
Taxidea taxus (Badger)	1			0.01
Felis rufus (Bobcat)	8			0.05
Felis concolor (Mountain Lion)	4			0.02
Carnivores	**69**	**-**		**0.43**
Order Artiodactyla (Even-toed Ungulates)	153	21b		0.95
Family Cervidae (Deer)	8			0.05
Odocoileus hemionus (Mule Deer)	15	2b		0.09
Odocoileus sp. (Mule Deer/White-tailed Deer)	45			0.28
Family Antilocapridae (Pronghorns)	9			0.06
Antilocapra americana (Pronghorn)	15	1b		0.09
Ovis canadensis (Bighorn Sheep)	41			0.26
Artiodactyls	**286**	**24b**		**1.78**
Unid. Sm. Mammals	2068	196b	155c	12.87
Unid. Med. Mammals	259	31b	7c	1.61
Unid. Lg. Mammals	530	13844b	114c	3.30
Unid. Mammals	1206	209b	19c	7.50
Unclassifiable	1363	28b	10c	8.49
Total Analyzed Specimens	**16,068**	**861b**	**316c**	**100.00**

[1] "b" indicates burned or carbonized specimens and "c" indicates calcined specimens.

Table 9.2. Use of Excavated Rooms.

Structure Number	Room Use
222	Piki/ Habitation
227	Storage
246	Plaza
248	Kiva
252	Kiva
274	Fill above Kiva
279	Kiva
265	Habitation
269	Storage/ Habitation
286	Storage
287	Unknown
288	Storage
293	Surface
120	Storage
268/289	Storage/ Habitation
373/300	Storage
345	Storage/ Habitation
393	Habitation
509	Habitation
546	Storage
547	Storage
900	Plaza
901	Kiva

Table 9.3. General Taxonomic Composition of the Chevelon Pueblo Faunal Dataset.

Taxon	NISP	%NISP
Fish	181	0.90
Reptiles	170	0.20
Amphibians		
Birds	512	3.19
Bats		
Rabbits	8395	52.25
Rodents	1029	6.40
Carnivores	69	0.43
Artiodactyls	286	1.78
Unidentified Small Mammals	2068	12.87
Unidentified Medium Mammals	259	1.61
Unidentified Large Mammals	530	3.30
Unidentified. Mammals	1206	7.50
Unclassifiable	1363	8.49
Total Analyzed Specimens	16,068	100.00

taphonomic signature (Hockett and Haws 2002). There tends to be a reliably complete element representation, since rabbits are small and are often butchered and consumed in the same place. Breaking, or snapping, of long bone shafts is common for marrow extraction and offer a unique human taphonomic signature that then can be observed in the archaeological record. There can also be cut marks on the bone to indicate butchering. Also, burning of bones can indicate cooking and consumption (Hockett and Haws 2002). Of all the specimens, 3.9 percent NISP (324 NISP) of lagomorphs were burned or calcined. Although a small package of meat, rabbit supplied a significant and consistent portion of the diet.

Not only were rabbits an important source of food, but they also served ceremonial and social roles. For the Hopi, communal rabbit hunts were important social events (Beaglehole 1936). There were numerous fully articulated rabbit interments found in the depositional fill of rooms at Chevelon, as well as in several different locations throughout the HSC (LaMotta 2006; Strand 1998). The rabbit burials include a number of single rabbit interments at H2 and H1 (LaMotta 1996, 2006). Excavations at Chevelon uncovered two single rabbit interments (Table 9.4; Figure 9.1). One was found in the fill of K. 279 and was surrounded by corn impressions. The rabbit was also missing its hind feet. The second rabbit was complete and found in the fill of S. 120 with no associated artifacts. Also, at both H2 (E.C. Adams 2002) and Chevelon, three articulated rabbits were found on the floor of a structure,

Table 9.4. *Lepus/Sylvilagus* Ratio and Artiodactyl Index for Homol'ovi II, Homol'ovi III, Homol'ovi IV and Chevelon.

Site[1]	*Lepus/Sylvilagus* Ratio	Artiodactyl Index (including size class specimens)
H2	0.706	0.084
H3	0.492	0.020
H4	n/a	0.139
Chevelon	0.780	0.072

[1] Data from H2, H3 and H4 are from Strand and McKim (1996).

Figure 9.1. Articulated rabbits (cottontail): (a) Kiva 279; (b) Structure 120.

purposefully laid out on their sides in a circle (Figure 9.2). That the same arrangement and number of individuals was found at both sites is striking. There were also objects on the floor of each room in association with the rabbits. Two axes and a loom anchor block were found near the three rabbits on the floor at H2. At Chevelon, the rabbits were found with two reconstructible gray ware jars, a flaked stone chopper, an igneous axe, two awls, a piece of selenite, and two miscellaneous pieces of ground stone. Also, with the exception of a kiva in the Marsh Pass region (LaMotta 1996) and the kiva at Chevelon, most of the rabbit burials occur in surface rooms. E.C. Adams (Chapter 13) suggests that this ritual offering of rabbits indicates a shared ritual heritage among Chevelon, H1, and H2 residents. Historically, the Hopi performed ritual killing and burial of rabbits as part of the 'killing *Masau'wuh*' ritual (Parsons 1936). *Masau'wuh* is a germination deity as well as a death deity. Rabbits are also important components to feasting (LaMotta 2006; Strand 1998). For example, Strand (1998) counted more than 4,200 rabbit bones in S. 210 at H1, likely deposited from feasting events that took place in nearby plaza and kiva spaces. Articulated rabbit feet are common at Chevelon and likely indicators of rabbit pelts. The presence of several rabbit feet, near the floor along the east wall of K. 279, likely represent rabbit pelts deposited or left soon after the kiva's north wall collapsed. Rabbit feet were also part of the ritual assemblage left on the floor of clan house S. 159 (Table 9.4).

Because rabbits are everywhere, people do not have to go far in order to procure them. By looking at the relative frequency

Figure 9.2. Three articulated cottontails from the floor of Structure 286.

of cottontails (*Sylvilagus* sp.) within the assemblage, we can deduce something about the past environment. This relationship is known as the lagomorph index (Strand and McKim 1996; Szuter 1991) and is calculated by dividing the NISP for cottontails by the NISP of all the lagomorphs. The closer the result is to 1.0 the greater the number of cottontails present in the assemblage. Cottontails favor a more dense vegetation in order to hide in and avoid predators, while jackrabbits generally inhabit open grasslands and employ a flight strategy (Strand and McKim 1996: 202). The lagomorph index for Chevelon is 0.78, which indicates presence of a brushier landscape (Table 9.5). Also, agriculturalists probably utilized species of flora and fauna that were drawn to these anthropogenically modified landscapes (Fish and Nabhan 1991:44). The presence of weedy species of plants and lagomorphs in the assemblage supports this theory (K. Adams, Chapter 11).

Rodents

Rodents can be a problematic segment of the assemblage. Due to their burrowing nature, many may be intrusive. Also, rodents tend to live in human dwellings and could represent prehistoric pests, especially as predators of stored foods. As a result, rodents were eaten occasionally because they were readily available and relatively easy to capture (Sobolik 1992). Rodents comprise 6.40 percent NISP of the assemblage (1029 NISP). Of that, 1.3 percent did exhibit some evidence of burning, indicating cooking and consumption.

The beaver (*Castor canadensis*) and muskrat (*Ondatra zibethicus*) remains are two noteworthy rodent species. Both inhabit permanent streams and river systems (Lowe 1964b: 254-255). These riparian species are probably not intrusive. The beaver humerus from K. 901 exhibits modification including obvious cut marks along with some possible

Table 9.5. Contextual Data for Turkey and Sandhill Crane Remains from Chevelon.

Taxon	NISP	Element	Structure	Provenience	Description
EARLY					
Meleagris gallopavo (Turkey)	1	scapula	279	520	ashy deposit
Meleagris gallopavo (Turkey)	1	humerus	279	344	red clay deposit
Meleagris gallopavo (Turkey)	2	vertebra, type unknown	279	519	midden right above the bench
Grus canadensis (Sandhill Crane)	1	humerus	300	480	early midden under floor of S. 373
Grus canadensis (Sandhill Crane)	1	humerus	274	596	fill above roof of K. 279
LATE					
Grus canadensis (Sandhill Crane)	1	coracoid	901	931	kiva midden
Grus canadensis (Sandhill Crane)	1	cranium	900	828	vent shaft
Grus canadensis (Sandhill Crane)	3	thoracic	900	834	Occupational surface next to vent shaft

polishing (Figure 9.3). A muskrat incisor was recovered from K. 279 and a mandible plus five teeth from S. 288. The clear association of both animals, along with fish, birds, frogs/toads (discussed below), was likely symbolically important to the Chevelon people as metaphors for water or moisture. In addition, their pelts may have been favored in ceremonial attire. The association of beaver and muskrat remains with kiva deposits and a neonate burial in S. 288, reinforce the impression they had ritual importance to Chevelon inhabitants.

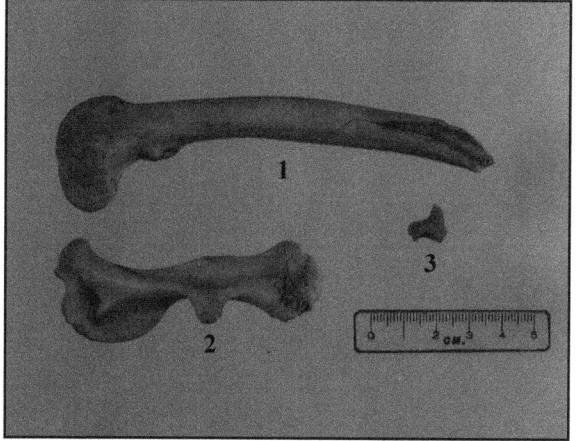

Figure 9.3. Bones of Rodents: Beaver (Castor canadensis).

Carnivores

The major carnivore taxa in the assemblage are coyote (*Canis latrans*) or domestic dog (*Canis familiaris*) and bobcat (*Felis rufus*), but badger (*Taxidea taxus*), mountain lion (*Felis concolor*), and red fox (*Vulpes vulpes*) are also present (Figure 9.4.2-9.4.6). The total remains account for 0.43 percent NISP (69 NISP) of the entire assemblage. There is no archaeological

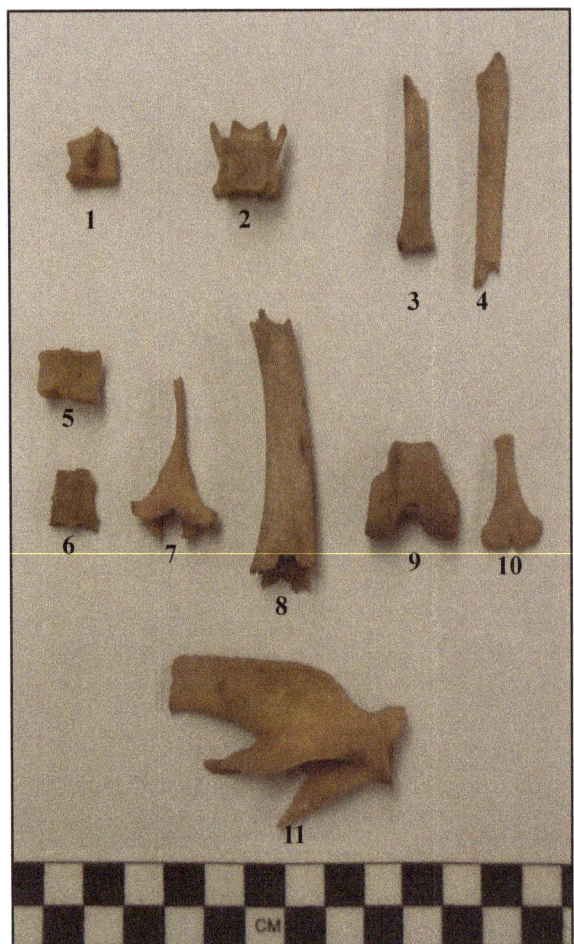

Figure 9.4. Bones of carnivores: Carnivora (1, 3, 4); Canidae (2); Canis latrans (coyote) – second row (5-10); Felis rufus (bobcat, Kiva 279, stratum 1, level 1) – bottom row (11).

or ethnographic evidence that carnivores were eaten and this is supported by the complete absence of burning in the assemblage.

There is evidence for ritualized use of coyote/dog remains, especially crania, as far back as Basketmaker times in the Western Pueblo sequence (Hill 2000). There are indications that coyotes were linked conceptually with witches and witchcraft power among the Hopi (Parsons 1936:281). Coyote/dog remains (*Canis* sp.) were recovered from seven Chevelon structures—K. 248, 279, and 901, S. 268/289, 373, 393, and 120—three

habitation and one storage structure, and Plaza 900. Disposal of coyotes/dogs in kivas, at H1 and H2, (LaMotta 1996, 2006; Strand 1998) suggest these patterns are meaningful cluster-wide. Badger, represented by a humerus in K. 279, is associated with medicine and curing among the Western Pueblos, generally. In reference to Hopi, Eggan (1950:84) reports that badger is "the medicine animal par excellence, and through his digging ability controls all roots." Prehispanic support for this perspective comes from their portrayal underground in murals found on fifteenth to seventeenth century Hopi kivas in villages on Antelope Mesa (Smith 1952). Badger Clan is also responsible for the katsina season and katsina initiation on First Mesa (Parsons 1936).

It is noteworthy that felids are particularly well represented in the Chevelon assemblage, including mountain lion, in comparison to other Homol'ovi assemblages (LaMotta 2006; Pierce 2001; Strand 1998; Strand and McKim 1996). On the Hopi mesas, the mountain lion is known for its role as a warrior and is associated with power, much like the bear (Tyler 1975:235). Bobcat elements were found in storage S. 227 (calcaneus), K. 279 (third phalanx), two in K. 248 (mandibles), one in S. 287 (third phalanx), and Plaza 900 (metatarsal). A mountain lion calcaneus was found in the piki house, S. 222, and an accessory and metacarpal, in S. 287. (Because, S. 287 was completely vandalized, it has not been included in Appendix B.) The red fox metacarpal came from K. 279. These elements, which were found in room fill, may be the remains of pelts or ritual paraphernalia (Walker 1995).

Artiodactyls

The artiodactyl assemblages from the Homol'ovi sites are fairly uncomplicated, taxonomically, and represent 1.78 percent NISP (286 NISP) of the Chevelon assemblage. The major taxa are bighorn sheep (*Ovis canadenis*), pronghorn (*Antilocapra americana*), and mule deer (*Odocoileus hemionus*) (Figure 9.5a,b). Logically, one would expect that locally-available pronghorn and deer would be the most prevalent taxa at Chevelon, but in actuality, bighorn sheep is the most common, although if *Odocoileus* sp. is included, deer are most numerous, at 60, followed by 41 bighorn sheep and 15 pronghorn (Table 9.1). If the ancient distribution of bighorn mirrored that of today, then the local inhabitants of Chevelon would have had to travel over 100 km (one way) in order to find bighorn, which would be in the Grand Canyon area (D. Brown 1994). At this point, one can do little more than speculate, but one plausible explanation, put forth by LaMotta (2006), is that the hunting of bighorn was part of an ancestral socio-ceremonial complex that had been brought to Chevelon and other Homol'ovi villages by immigrants from northern Arizona, where bighorn sheep were locally available. The bighorn may also have been obtained through trade. But either way, inhabitants of Chevelon were going out of their way to procure these animals. A single humerus of bighorn sheep was recovered from K. 248, while eight elements, from leg and back-bones, were recovered from the surface of the south bench of K. 901. In contrast, 34 remains of deer were recovered from the fill of K. 279 and another 11 from K. 901.

Artiodactyls, undoubtedly, contributed to diet as 24 (8.4 percent) are burned; however, no bighorn, and only one pronghorn, are burned (Table 9.1). The relative importance of artiodactyls, compared to lagomorphs in diet, can be demonstrated using the artiodactyl index (Bayham 1982; Szuter 1989; Strand and McKim 1996; Table 9.5). This is calculated

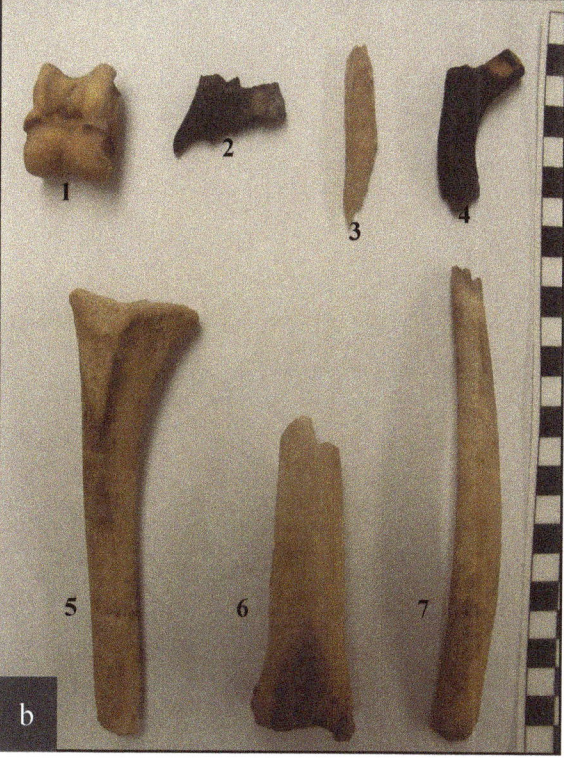

Figure 9.5. Artiodactyla bone : Odocoileus hemionus (mule deer): (a) vertebrae; (b) long bones. Kiva 279, stratum 1, level 1.

by dividing the NISP of artiodactyls by the sum of the NISP for both artiodactyls and lagomorphs. Strand and McKim (1996:205) advocate including small and large mammal remains to the count, since artiodactyl remains can be highly fragmented and are sometimes difficult to identify. This inclusion offsets the under-representation that may occur when only identified remains are counted. For the traditional count, an index of .034 was obtained. For the count including small and large mammal remains, the index was .072. These indices are similar to those calculated for H2 (Strand and McKim 1996:205), H3, and H4 (Pierce 2001), showing that artiodactyl did not contribute significantly to diet (Table 9.4).

Intra-site analysis, of the Chevelon remains, reveals an interesting distributional pattern for artiodactyl remains. K. 901 and 279 have almost identical numbers of artiodactyl remains at 67 and 63 respectively totaling 45.5 percent of all artiodactyl remains; however, the larger sample size from K. 279 means frequency of artiodactyl remains in K. 901 is, in fact, higher. Bighorn are much more highly concentrated in K. 901 and absent in K. 279, where identified remains are all deer. Statistically and logically, these preferences are not accidental and could relate to choices relating to identity or social memory, such as those described earlier by LaMotta (2006). In either case, artiodactyl are important contributors to the ritual deposits in both kivas. K. 248 has one bighorn sheep and one pronghorn, both humeri. There is also historical evidence for the ritualized use of artiodactyl elements by the Hopi. The Hopi attached hoofs, including the phalanges, to costumes and also used scapulas to construct rattles and musical instruments (Parsons 1936:652).

Aves

The bird remains from Chevelon are the most taxonomically diverse of all the faunal groups discussed in this chapter. It is a moderate-sized sample with 512 elements representing 3.19 percent of the total assemblage from 14 families of birds. Of the 512, a total of 279 are identified specimens and 233 unidentified specimens. Chevelon is the most diverse of the Homol'ovi villages possibly because it sits at the confluence of the permanent Chevelon Creek that flows into and creates a permanent flow downstream in the LCR, creating rich and varied habitats. In addition, seeps, one kilometer upstream from the pueblo, create permanent marshlands attractive to many bird species. In fact, Arizona Game and Fish created a bird sanctuary across Chevelon Creek from the pueblo more than a century ago in recognition of this diversity. Upstream, Chevelon Creek creates a unique habitat, with groves of black walnut and hackberry, which provide additional variety in bird habitat. Fish and amphibians in the river provide food for some raptors and exotic species, including blue heron.

Raven (*Corvas corax*) is common with 62 family-level and 34 species-level remains. Turkey (*Meleagris gallopavo*) is rare, with only six bones and one headless, but otherwise articulated, bird from the fill of a feature in Plaza 900 (Table 9.6). Birds of prey (Falconiformes) include red-tail hawk, marsh hawk, golden eagle, falcons, and kestrels or sparrow hawks (Figure 9.6), while owls (Strigidae) are relatively rare represented by only five bones (Figure 9.7).

As expected, Chevelon has a considerable number of water birds that includes grebes (Podicepidae), rails and coots (Rallidae), shorebirds (Charadriiformes), herons

Table 9.6. List of Taxa Defined as Rare/Unusual.

Birds	NISP	Carnivores	NISP
Anas acuta (Pintail)	1	Canidae (Coyotes, Dogs, Wolves, and Foxes)	9
Aythya valisineria (Canvasback)	1	*Taxidea taxus* (Badger)	1
Phasianidae (Quails)	6	*Felis concolor* (Mountain Lion)	4
Callipepla sp. (Scaled Quail/Gambel's Quail)	2	*Castor canadensis* (Beaver)	6
Rallidae (Rails, Gallinules, and Coots)	4	*Canis latrans/Canis familiaris* (Coyote/Domestic Dog)	6
Scolopacidae/Charadriidae (Sandpipers/Plovers)	5	*Vulpes vulpes* (Red Fox)	1
Charadrius vociferus (Killdeer)	1	*Felis rufus* (Bobcat)	8
Caprimulgidae (Nighthawks and Whippoor-wills)	1	*Ondatra zibethicus* (Muskrat)	17
Buteo jamaicensis (Red-tailed Hawk)	2	*Canis latrans* (Coyote)	20
Podilymbus podiceps (Pied-billed Grebe)	18	*Canis* sp. (Coyote/Domestic Dog/Wolf)	20
Falconiformes (Birds of Prey)	12	**Artiodactyls**	
Circus cyaneus (Marsh Hawk)	3	Cervidae (Deer)	8
Anas platyrhynchos (Mallard)	3	Antilocapridae (Pronghorns)	9
Anatidae (Ducks, Geese, and Swans)	8	*Odocoileus* sp. (Mule deer/White-tailed Deer)	45
Meleagris gallopavo (Turkey)	74	*Odocoileus hemionus* (Mule Deer)	15
Buteo sp. (Buteonine Hawks)	6	*Antilocapra americana* (Pronghorn)	15
Grus canadensis (Sandhill Crane)	9	*Ovis canadensis* (Bighorn Sheep)	41
Fulica americana (American Coot)	13	Artiodactyla (Even-toed Ungulates)	153
Passeriformes (Perching Birds)	12	**Herpetofauna**	
Sialia sp. (Bluebirds)	11	*Crotaphytus* sp. (Collared/Leopard Lizard)	3
Corvidae (Ravens, Crows, Magpies, Jays)		Cypriniformes (Minnow-like Fishes)	4
Corvus corax (Common Raven)	26	*Xyrauchen texanus* (Razorback Sucker)	2
Anas sp., duck-sized	22	Catostomidae	27
Aquila chrysaetos (Golden Eagle)	13	Osteichthyes	72
		Cyprinidae (Minnows)	66

238 Diaz de Valdes

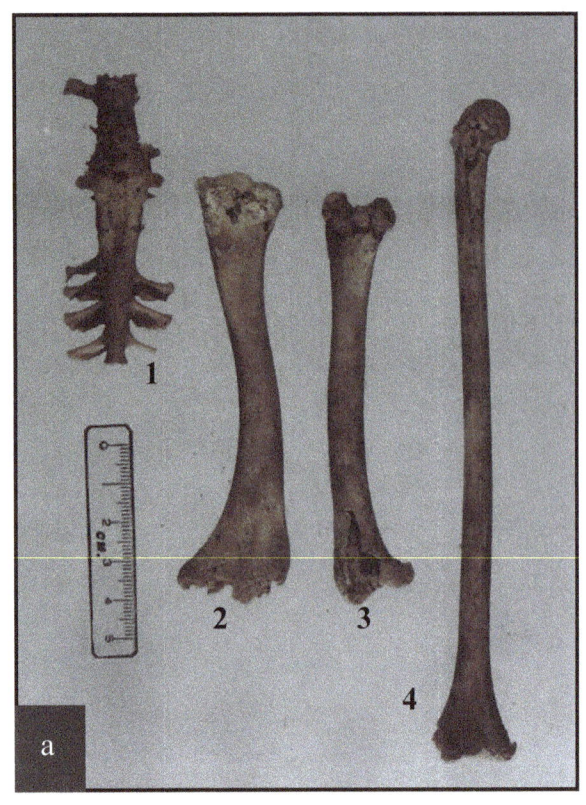

a. Raven.

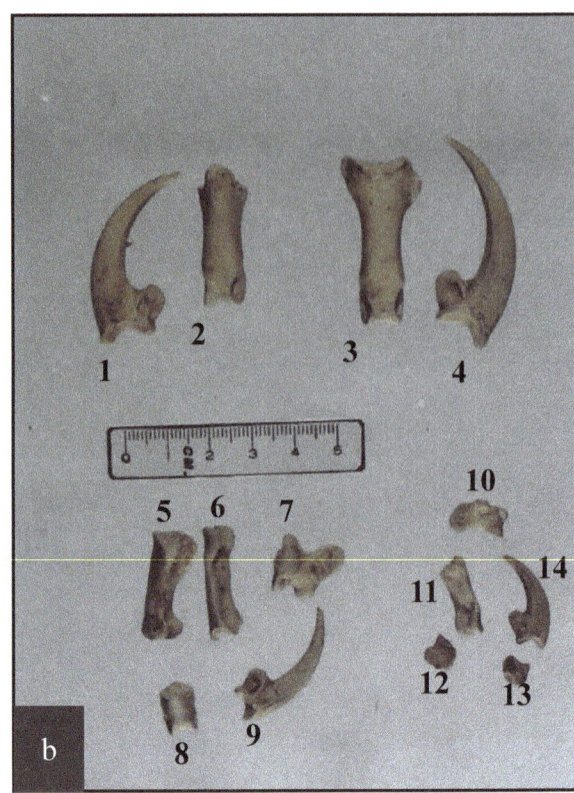

b. Raptor talons.

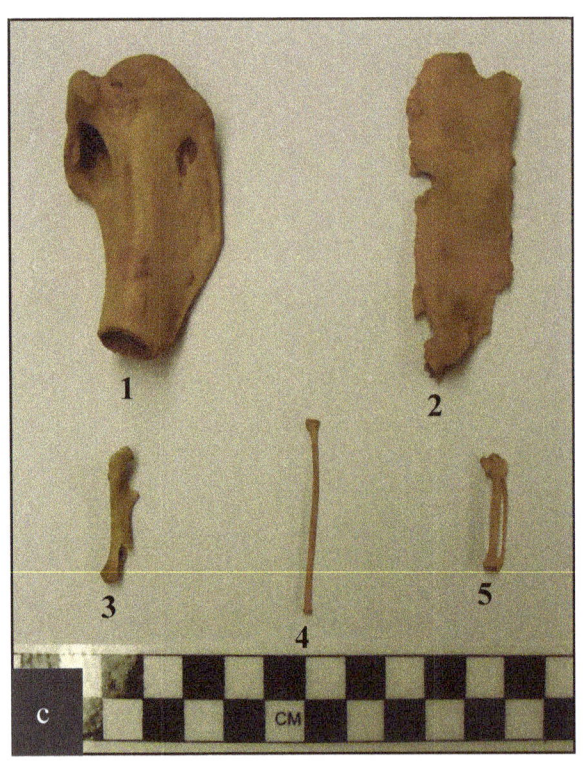

(c.1) Aquila chrysactos (golden eagle – cut); (c.2) Accipitridae (hawks and eagles); (c.3,4) Circus cyaneus (marsh hawk); (c.5) Falco sparverius (sparrow hawk/kestrel). Kiva 279, stratum 1, level 1.

Figure 9.6a-c. Bones of ravens and birds of prey.

Figure 9.7. Articulated raven wing from Kiva 901.

(Ardiedae), gulls/terns (Lanidae), and geese and ducks (Anatidae) (Figure 9.8). Grassland birds, including quails (Phasianidae), meadowlarks/ black birds (Icteridae), and doves (Columbidae), plus insect eaters (Caprimulgidae) are all present in low numbers. Over time, at the cluster as a whole, others (LaMotta 2006; Strand 1998) have observed that turkey decreases in abundance, while sandhill crane increases. Turkey (McKusick 1986) and sandhill crane (Perkins 1981) are physically similar in many respects — both are large, terrestrial birds and cranes are locally, seasonally available (Figure 9.9). Attempts at turkey domestication, at H3, suggest such attempts were not always successful (Senior and Pierce 1989). Turkeys were likely raised primarily for their feathers and not for consumption, as they are usually found articulated and rarely in domestic refuse where rabbit bone is ubiquitous (1989:249).

It is therefore possible, as Strand (1998) has suggested, that sandhill crane was used as a substitute for turkey, due to accessibility. But is the increase in use of sandhill crane related to reduced use of turkey? For example, LaMotta (2006) has suggested that sandhill crane may have been part of a distinctive ritual complex that emerged first at H1, and developed into something of more widespread significance among the later villages. If so, then sandhill crane and turkey would not necessarily have been treated alike in either time period, and might, therefore, exhibit different archaeological patterns.

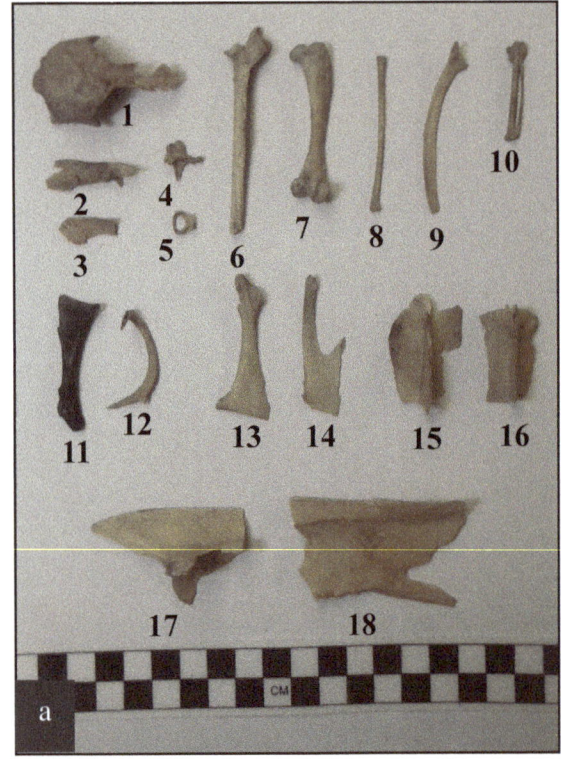
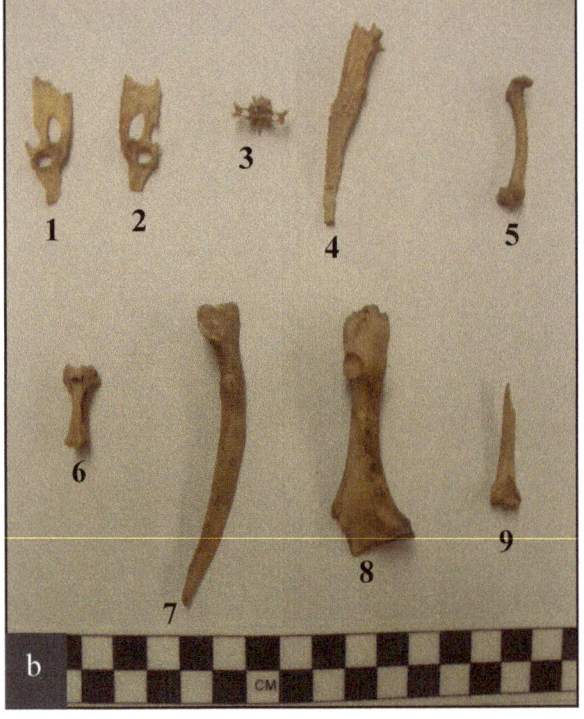

a. Ducks: Family Anatidae (ducks, geese, swans): (top row): Family Anatidae; (middle row): Anas acuta *(pintail);* Anas americana *(american wigeon);* Aythya valisimeria *(canvasback); (bottom row):* Mergus merganser *(common merganser). Kiva 279, stratum 1, level 1.*

b. Grebes and Herons: (Family and Order Ciconiifores): (1-3) Podilymbus podiceps *(pied-billed grebe) (4)* Podiceps caspicus *(eared grebe); (5) Ardeidae; (6-7)* Ardea herodias *(great blue heron); (8)* Butorides virescens *(green heron). Kiva 279, stratum 1, level 1.*

Figure 9.8. Bones of water birds.

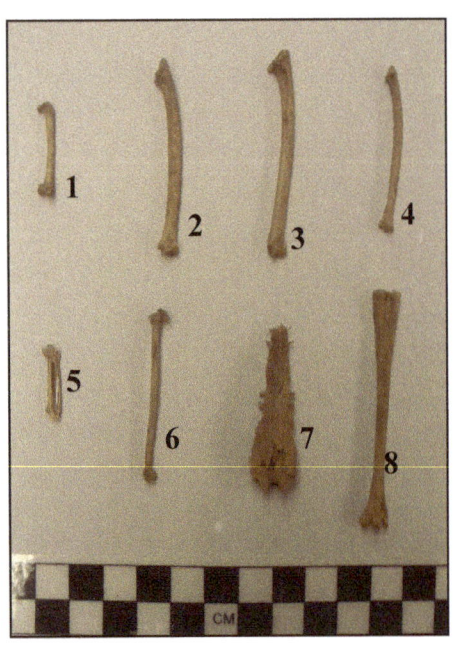

Figure 9.9. Bones of land birds: (1) Zenaidura macroura *(mourning dove); (2-4)* Columbidae *(pigeons, doves); (5)* Ieteridae *(meadowlark); (6)* Phasianidae *(quail); (7)* Strigidae *(owl); (8)* Corvus corax *(raven). Kiva 279, stratum 1 level 1.*

The contextual data from Chevelon (Table 9.5) offers a basis for evaluating these different hypotheses. Admittedly, the sample size for each taxon is limited; however, assemblages are robust. By comparing the specific context for the early and late material, it is possible to determine which scenario is most supported. The early material from Chevelon includes the Tuwiuca, Early and Middle Homol'ovi Phases, and the late material includes the Late Homol'ovi Phase (LHP). This temporal division was made due to the limitation of the sample size.

For the early period, four turkey elements were all recovered from the midden of K. 279. There are also two sandhill crane elements; one was from the fill under S. 373 and the other from S. 274, which is the fill above K. 279. The early assemblage also contained a headless turkey burial in the large circular roasting pit in Plaza 900.

For the late period, most of the individual elements recovered are sandhill crane. One element was found in the midden and another in the vent shaft of K. 901. Nearby, were four elements located on the occupational surface next to the vent shaft for K. 901. Also, there was a first phalanx of a sandhill crane in the subfloor of a storage feature in S. 120. However, turkey elements were recovered from late contexts in the fill of K. 252 and 901.

The early turkey elements are found in a kiva, as are all but one of the late sandhill crane and turkey elements. The non-kiva element is from an enriched deposit associated with two Roosevelt Red Ware jars in S. 120. Also in the early material, none of the sandhill crane was found in K. 279. This contextual information points to a partial replacement of turkey by sandhill crane, in the LHP, and to association of both birds with ritual practices. It also reinforces the social relationship between K. 901/Plaza 900 and RB100, noted in the flaked stone by Medeiros.

Amphibians and Reptiles

The only herpetofauna taxa found at Chevelon are collared lizard, common harmless snake, and frog/toad elements. Frogs and toads are associated with water and moisture in Pueblo culture. Their presence in K. 252 and 901 and Plaza 900 adjacent to K. 901 support their ritual use at Chevelon. Lizards, toads, and common harmless snakes are often omitted, in part, because the bulk of the remains are clearly intrusive (e.g., whole or partial skeletons found in natural, post-abandonment deposits). This may have been the case in S. 293 where more than 150 snake bones were recovered. Thus, the 170 NISP, 1.11 percent, for reptile, is inflated by this single individual. However, snakes do have important ceremonial functions, so their presence must be noted. What is important here is not what is present, but what is absent. This assemblage is notable for its lack of turtle remains. The absence of turtle remains at Chevelon is particularly striking because, as Strand (1998:152) notes, "Fewkes (1898:525) recorded that the Hopi collected turtles in Chevelon and Clear Creek". The turtle remains were found by Fewkes in some of the graves at Chevelon (Fewkes 1904). At H2, turtle shell was also completely absent, but a minimum of turtle remains were found at H1 (LaMotta 2006), and at H3, a turtle carapace was used to hold red pigment (Pierce 2001).

Fish

Fish bones, found at H1, indicate that fish were exploited, not as a staple food, but rather on a seasonal basis, "when they were locally available and easiest to catch" (McCracken

2003:55). Fish comprise 1.13 percent of the assemblage (181 NISP) (Figure 9.10). None of the fish remains exhibited burning, but fish were probably utilized at Chevelon to augment the diet, similar to H1.

In K. 279, an articulated fish and a rabbit's foot were discovered just above the hearth, and under the fallen hatch slab. There are no ethnographic correlates to explain the presence of the fish, but it fits the spatial pattern of previously documented animal skulls or articulated animal remains placed in the center of kivas just above the hearth, such as the headless articulated dog on the hearth to K. 901 at H1 (Hill 2000; LaMotta 2006).

But, why did this kiva contain a fish instead of a skull? Perhaps, the fish interment symbolizes the riparian habitat, or water itself, and, in addition to food, played a role in the ceremonial practices of the community. E.C. Adams (2002) has speculated that Chevelon Pueblo's location and access to riparian taxa, such as fish, was used to enhance exchange. He also states that, "this could explain the apparently higher frequency of exchanged artifacts at Chevelon than at other Homol'ovi villages and could offer the opportunity for increased power and prestige" (E.C. Adams 2002:14). The relative abundance of fish at Chevelon is similar to H1. But the number and diversity of water birds at Chevelon is higher than at any other village in the cluster. This grouping of aquatic taxa, including frogs/toads, beaver, and muskrat likely reflect the importance and value of the river's resources to the people of Chevelon.

Rare/Unusual Taxa

As stated previously, rare and unusual taxa were determined by identifying all of the taxa that represented less than 1 percent NISP of

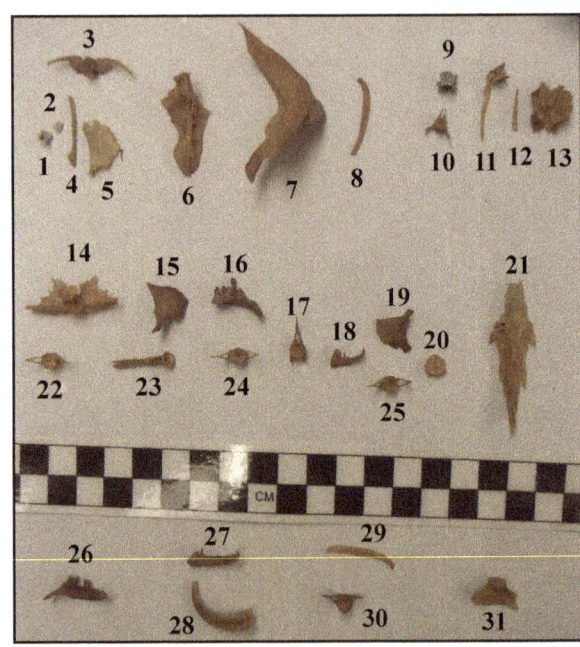

Figure 9.10. Fish bones: (top row) Osteichthyes, order unknown (fish); (middle row) Family Catostomidae (suckers); (bottom row, left five) Xyrauchen texanus (Razorback sucker); (bottom row, far right) Cyprinidae (minnow).

the entire assemblage (Table 9.6, Appendix B). Only taxa identified to the level of Order (or Family and below) were included. The total NISP of rare/unusual taxa was 755. Reliable interpretations, in general, need a sample of 200 individuals or 1400 specimens (Reitz and Wing 1999). Since the total is well below that mark, any interpretations will not be definitive, but rather suggestive.

All of the articulated animals found at Chevelon, except lagomorphs, also appear in the list of taxa defined as rare/unusual (Tables 9.6, 9.7, and 9.8). Since the rare/unusual definition for this model was not dependent on whether the remains were found articulated, this is an intriguing relationship. Another interesting observation is that all of the rare/unusual taxa identified for this model were also recognized by LaMotta (2006) as 'ritually sensitive,' with the exception of the fish remains. Historically, ethnographers

Table 9.7. List of Cranial Elements Found at Chevelon.

S.	Taxa	Element
222	Order Artiodactyla (Even-toed Ungulates) cranial fragment	Cranial fragment
	Family Anatidae (Ducks, Geese, and Swans) cranial fragment	Cranial fragment
	Family Cervidae (Deer)	Mandible
288	*Corvus corax* (Common Raven)	Crania
279	*Antilocapra americana* (Pronghorn)	Cranial fragment
	Buteo sp. (Buteonine Hawks)	Crania
	Order Artiodactyla (Even-toed Ungulates)	Cranial fragment
	Order Artiodactyla (Even-toed Ungulates)	Cranial fragment
	Ovis canadensis (Bighorn Sheep)	Cranial fragment
900	*Grus canadensis* (Sandhill Crane)	Crania
901	*Odocoileus hemionus* (Mule Deer) cranial	Cranial fragment
	Order Artiodactyla (Even-toed Ungulates)	Cranial fragment
	Order Artiodactyla (Even-toed Ungulates)	Cranial fragment
	Canis latrans (Coyote)	Mandible
	Canis latrans (Coyote)	Mandible
	Corvus corax (Common Raven)	Crania
	Order Artiodactyla (Even-toed Ungulates)	Cranial fragment

identified specific groups of animals as having ritual significance. Raptors, turkeys, and ravens figure prominently in historical Western Pueblo religious practices and beliefs (Tyler 1979). They are important for their feathers, which are used in making prayer sticks, standards, masks, and other elements of ceremonial costumes. They are also important for their skins, wings, and claws, which are fashioned into a variety of ritual paraphernalia. There is evidence for ritualized use of coyote/dog remains, especially crania (Table 9.7), as far back as Basketmaker times in the Western Pueblo sequence (Hill 2000). There are indications that coyotes were linked conceptually with witches and witchcraft power among the Hopi (Parsons 1936:281). Badger is associated with medicine and curing among the Western Pueblos, generally. As described earlier, for Hopi, badger is an important medicine animal (Eggan 1950:84)

Hoofs of artiodactyl, which include phalanges, are used as rattles within turtle shells by performers in Hopi ceremonies, while scapulas are used with gourds and rasps as musical instruments during ceremonies (Parsons 1936:652). Specific elements also can be defined as "enriched", such as animal skulls (Table 9.7). This element may represent a sacrificial or offertory deposit (E.C. Adams and LaMotta 2006:59).

The cranial elements, found at Chevelon, were found in a variety of contexts (Table 9.7; Figure 9.11). The raven skulls were found in K. 901 and S. 288, a storage room with a human neonate in its fill. The coyote mandibles were found in K. 901, and the sandhill crane skull was found in the fill above K. 901. All of the artiodactyl skulls were fragments. What is interesting is that all of the skulls are associated

Table 9.8. Articulated Animal Remains Found at Chevelon.

Taxa	Location	Portion	Age	Comments
Meleagris gallapavo (turkey)	Found at the top of a roasting pit in the plaza of RB900	Complete except for the head	Adult	
Corvus corax (common raven)	Fill of K. 901	portion of bird complete	Adult	
Sylvilagus sp. (cottontail)	On the floor of S. 286, a storage room	Three complete skeletons	Adult	Found laid out on their sides in a circle with a igneous axe, two bone awls, two large storage jars, and a piece of shaped selenite
cf. *Sialia* sp. (Blue bird)	Found in the fill from the floor of S. 345	Complete except for the head	Adult	Not identified in the field as an articulated bird probably due to the head
Aquila chrysaetos (Golden Eagle)	Found in the fill from a bin feature in S. 345	Complete left foot	Adult	A sherd was also found in the fill of the bin
Sylvilagus sp. (cottontail)	Found in the fill of S. 120	Complete unburned skeleton	Adult	No associated objects
Corvus corax (common raven)	Found in the fill of K. 279	Wing	Immature	Found in a cluster that included disarticulated *Sylvilagus* sp. bones
Corvus corax (common raven)	Found directly in front of the ventilator shaft opening for K. 279	Wing	Immature	Found in a cluster that included disarticulated *Sylvilagus* sp. bones
Sylvilagus sp. (cottontail)	Found in the fill of K. 279	Complete except for hind feet	Adult	Unburned corncobs appear to have been laid out around the rabbit
cf. Cyprinidae (Minnow)	Found just above the hearth and under the fallen hatch slab of K. 279	Complete	Unknown	Found next to an articulated *Sylvilagus* sp. foot
Ovis canadensis (Bighorn sheep)	Found on the bench of K. 901	Lumbar vertebral section	Adult	Found next to a articulated *Corvus corax*
Corvus corax (common raven)	Found on the bench of K. 901	Hind section	Adult	Found next to articulated *Ovis canadensis*

with ritual structures, K. 279 and 901, and enriched deposits from a piki house, and a room with a neonate.

Interpretations

Deposits, enriched with faunal remains, are found in ritual, habitation, and storage structures. The ritual structures are identified based on architectural evidence (E.C. Adams 2002; Karunaratne 1997). At Chevelon, this includes K. 901 and 279 and S. 222, a piki room. E.C. Adams (2002:130) defines piki houses as social activity structures, rather than domestic structures and they are grouped with kivas in terms of ritual practices (E.C. Adams 2002:130). In order to determine if enriched deposits occur at the same or greater frequency in ritual vs. non-ritual structures, the chi-square test of goodness of fit was used (Table 9.9) with the Yates' correction, since the matrix was a 2 by 2 (Milton 1999). This analysis shows that the enriched deposits occur at the same frequency in ritual and non-ritual structures.

Walker (1996b) has suggested that the disposal of ritual objects is more likely to occur in abandoned ritual places. While ritual classification for these structures was based solely on architectural evidence, it should be noted that the inclusion of human remains can create a strong ritual signature in the

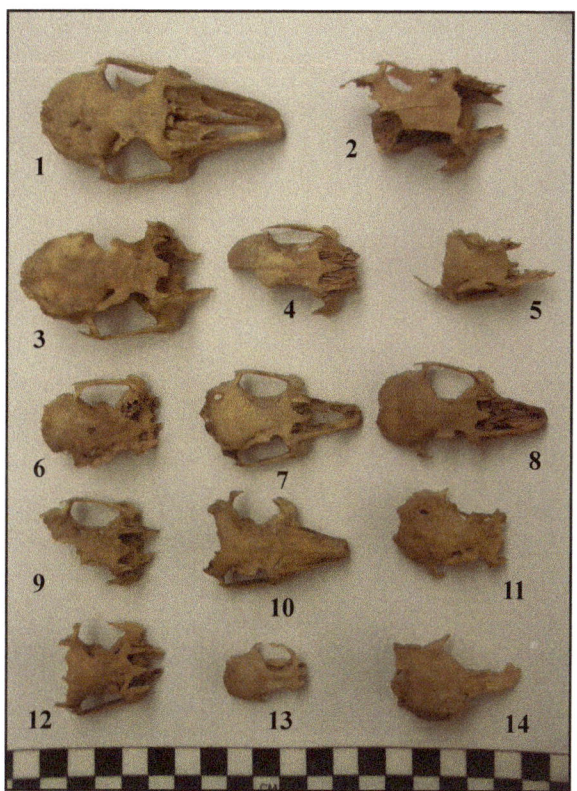

Figure 9.11. Animal skulls: (1-3) Lepus californicus; *(4-12)* Sylvilagus sp.; *(13)* Neotoma albigula *(white-throated woodrat); and (14)* Anatidae *(Kiva 279, Stratum 1, Level 1).*

depositional history of a non-ritual structure (Walker 1995; LaMotta 1996). This ritual signature can involve, not only faunal remains, but other aspects of material culture, such as fossils, crystals, and miniature vessels (LaMotta 1996). So, do these enriched deposits, in fact,

Table 9.9. Chi-square Goodness of Fit Test for Ritual vs. Non-ritual Structures.

Fauna	Ritual	Non-Ritual	Total
Enriched fauna	514	387	901
Non-enriched fauna	9191	5976	15167
Total	9705	6363	16068

df = 1
Significance Level of .05 at 1df = 7.88
Yates Chi-Square = 0.027 < Sig Level
Variable Relationship: Independent

represent activities associated with ritual as suggested by E.C. Adams and LaMotta (2006)? There are other site formation processes, such as accidental inclusions, resulting in articulated animals that could account for the presence of some patterns. However, the enriched deposits are not defined solely by articulated faunal remains. Their association with other objects and ash indicate most were purposely placed. The rabbit, in K. 279, was purposely placed with corn around it and a similar arrangement of three rabbits, recovered from S. 286 was found at H2, both involving multiple other classes of artifacts (LaMotta 2006). Also, the ethnographic evidence (Tyler 1975, 1979; Parsons 1936; Eggan 1950; Titiev 1944) and previous archaeological research (Strand 1998; LaMotta 2006; Walker 1995; Hill 2000) support the ritual association of deposits having articulated fauna and rare taxa.

Because enriched deposits are associated with ritual activity, how do we explain this distribution? The ethnographic and archaeological record does demonstrate that ritual practice is not necessarily limited to kivas/ritual structures. These ritual activities may not be related to structures, but related to social practices. Walker et al. (2000:353) argued that ritual can be used to negotiate and structure social relations, usually hierarchical, and can have a material expression.

Mills (2004) uses Annette Weiner's (1992) concept of inalienable objects for understanding and evaluating the role of these "social valuables." She defines these inalienable objects as "repositories of knowledge because they materialize histories of social relations" (Mills 2004:240) and suggests that this concept can be used as an alternative to that of prestige goods. These objects are often singularities, rarely circulate, and are used in ceremonies of authentication and commemoration (Mills 2004:240). Mills also notes that inalienable objects can either be collectively or individually owned. For example, animal parts placed on an altar may represent collective ownership, but animal parts may also be part of an individual society member's dance costume (Mills 2004:241). These individually owned animal remains, from a costume, would likely be buried with the individual, while collectively owned remains would likely end up within room fill. Using this interpretive tool, it appears that these enriched deposits are collectively owned, but may represent both collective and individual ritual activities. So, the expectation is that deposits in ritual structures will more commonly correspond to collective ritual activities and those in habitation and storage rooms will represent individual ritual activities.

Can we see a difference between types of enriched deposits present in ritual vs. nonritual structures? Cranial elements from rare or unusual animals were found only in locations defined as ritual, with the exception of S. 288, which did contain ritualized fill, due to the burial of a neonate in its fill. These elements may correspond to collective ritual activities. But, do cranial elements occur at the same, or greater, frequency at the site than other elements from rare taxa? To determine this, a chi-square test was applied to the data (Table 9.10). This analysis shows that the cranial elements occur at the same frequency as other elements from rare and unusual taxa. Because they occur at the same frequency as other elements and are concentrated in ritual structures, they support the hypothesis that they are associated with collective ritual activities. Beaver, badger, red fox, bobcat, and mountain lion were only found in ritual structures. It is likely, these animals were tied to collective rituals.

While skulls and certain taxa are associated with collective rituals, rabbits may be associated with individual ritual. Two of the three rabbit burials were located in non-ritual structures, as were most of the rabbits found at the other sites in the cluster (LaMotta 2006; Strand 1998). The rabbit in K. 279 is the exception.

Participation in the ritual activities associated with this kiva may have been more restricted and, thus, the activities might resemble individual, as well as collective, rituals. Given the location and the fact that all the other rabbits within the cluster were found in non-ritual contexts, the rabbit in K. 279 is interpreted as representing an individual ritual activity.

The inclusion of human remains impacts the depositional history of a room. S. 288 and 227 are storage rooms that contain human remains. S. 288 had a neonate placed in its fill and S. 227 had an articulated young woman on the floor (Appendix C). LaMotta (1996) found a strong correlation between the distribution of disarticulated and partially articulated human remains and the distribution of structures identified as ritual. He proposes that these human remains were differentially deposited in such rooms as part of an abandonment or closure ritual (LaMotta 1996:62). Neonates were given special treatment at H3 by inclusion in a burial area also used for burial of turkeys and parrots (E.C. Adams 2001; 2002). In addition, neonates at H1 also stimulate burial of numerous rare and unusual artifacts (LaMotta 2006). Given this strong association, the inclusion of human remains in S. 227 and 288 likely altered the deposition in these rooms from non-ritual to ritual, although the structures themselves may never have been ritual structures.

For this analysis, the afterlife (filling) of these structures was not included as ritual. However, the inclusion of human remains in this ritual context is interpreted as another example of collective ritual activities (Mills 2004).

Table 9.10. Chi-square Goodness of Fit Test for Cranial vs. Other Rare Elements.

Structure	Cranial Elements (NISP)	Other Rare Elements (NISP)	Total
222	3	12	15
227		6	6
274		3	3
279	5	86	91
265			
288		3	3
120	1	18	19
268/289		16	16
373/300		8	8
345		7	7
393		3	3
900		7	7
901	1	14	15
Total	7	21	28

df = 13
Significance Level of .05 at 13 df = 22.4
Sum chi^2 = 4.217 < Sig Level
Variable Relationship: Independent

COMPARISONS TO OTHER FAUNAL ASSEMBLAGES IN THE HSC

Lagomorphs and artiodactyls appear to be the greatest contributor to the diet of the people at Chevelon and other villages within the cluster (Strand and McKim 1996:216). In order to examine the relationship of this utilization, the *Lepus/Sylvilagus* Ratio and artiodactyl index for H2, H3 and H4 were compared to Chevelon (Table 9.4). The *Lepus/Sylvilagus* ratio is obtained by dividing the total NISP of *Sylvilagus* by the total NISP of lagomorphs. The index shows a marked difference between the relative abundance of species within each assemblage. Although relatively close in proximity, H2 shows a preference for *Lepus*, H3 shows almost an equal number of both lagomorphs and, at Chevelon, *Sylvilagus* dominates the assemblage. The index for Chevelon is nearly identical to H2, both considerably higher than H3. This suggests a brushier landscape around Chevelon, which favors cottontails.

The artiodactyl indexes are more comparable (Table 9.4). All four sites show that lagomorphs were the dominate source of meat. Although, H4 does show a slightly higher ratio that favors artiodactyls, this may be due to changing subsistence patterns or resource availability, since H4 is the earliest of the sites, but its smaller sample size could also be a factor.

Chevelon does share broad patterns of animal use in ritual practices including animal sacrifice, production of pelts, and use of aquatic, riparian, and carnivorous taxa in ceremonial activities. Remains of these activities tend to accrue in ritual deposits of mostly ceremonial trash (sensu Walker 1995), in structures having many uses prior to their filling. Associations of animal remains with other artifact classes, creating enriched deposits, will be summarized in chapter 13.

Worked Bone

Table 9.11 lists the 123 worked bone artifacts by the structure from which they were recovered from Chevelon during excavations (Figure 9.12). The most common categories are awls and miscellaneous bone tools. The latter are primarily fragments of bone with polishing, grinding, or other indications of alteration. Detailed analysis of wear on awls was not done to differentiate the many uses to which awls are put in Pueblo society (Jones in Andronescu and Glinsky 2004; Klandrud 2002). The only awls associated with a floor assemblage were in S. 286, in association with the three sacrificed cottontails discussed above.

Not surprisingly, the highest frequency of bone artifacts came from K. 279, followed by the piki house, S. 222, and K. 901. A dozen awls were recovered from K. 279 fill, suggesting their association with ceremonial practices either as ornaments or used in the manufacture of garments (Parsons 1936, 1939). The high diversity of worked bone types and in total frequency, in S. 222, suggests it was a locus of storage or disposal of these items. The high frequency of ground stone in S. 222, including piki stones, indicate this structure may have been a focal point for women's activities in RB200, much like S. 311 and 312 in the women's ritual precinct at H1, also the locus of a piki house (E.C. Adams 2002:130-131, Figure 6.3). Just as interesting is the broad distribution of bone artifacts occurring in 25 structures, 19 containing bone awls. Unlike H1, where bone awls were associated with roof fall, where they were likely being stored, deposition of the Chevelon awls does not seem to correlate with roof deposits (Klandrud 2002). The broad presence of workhorse tools, such as awls, fleshers, reamers, drills, and antler tines, indicates primarily household-level activities are being represented in bone tools with only limited production of bone artifacts into ornaments. Fewkes (1898, 1904) noted the presence of a variety of bone artifacts associated with burials he exhumed at Chevelon in 1896. No doubt the diversity and quantity of the worked bone assemblage at Chevelon was much larger than that represented in the abandoned rooms that are the focus of this analysis.

Table 9.11. Bone Tools from Chevelon by Type and Structure Number.

Str./tool type	Awl	Needle	Weaving tool	Tube	Pendant	Cylinder	Gaming piece	Antler tine	Antler tool	Drill/ punch	Hair pin	Reamer	Flesher	Misc.	Total
120	2														2
123														3	3
158	2														2
161	3														3
222	1			1			1		2					12	17
227														1	1
248	1													5	6
264	1								1						2
266							1								1
268	1														1
269											1				1
274	1														1
279	12			2	1	1				1				25	42
286	2		1										1		4
287	1													1	2
288												1			1
289	1			2											3
300	1			1							1		1		4
345	1						1								2
373		1					1							1	3
393	1													1	2
603	1													1	2
702	1												1		2
900	3					1					1			2	7
901	1		1			1		2			1			2	9
Total	37	1	2	6	1	3	4	2	3	1	4	1	3	55	123

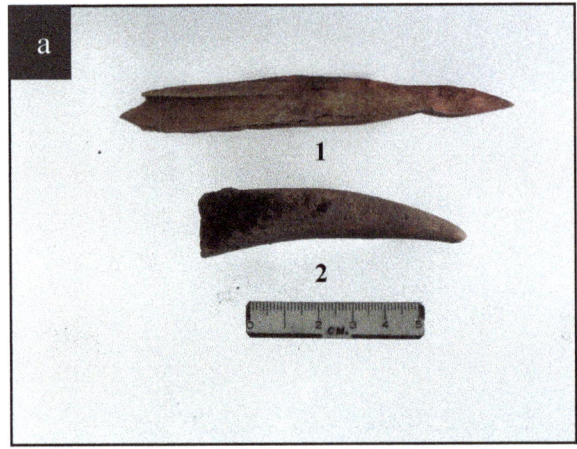

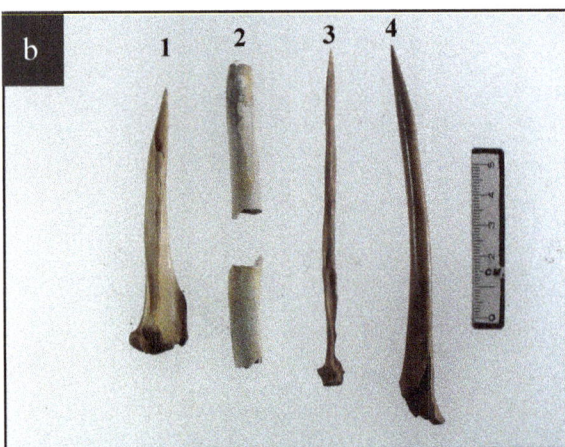

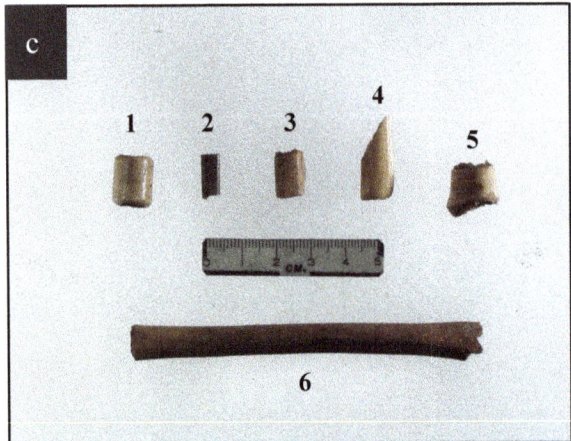

Figure 9.12. Worked bone: (a.1) bone awl with red pigment; (a.2) burned antler tine; (b.1) bone awl; (b.2,3) bone tube raw material; (b.4) hair pin; (c.1-5) bone tubes; (c.6) bone tube raw material.

Summary

The subsistence strategies of the people of Chevelon included a wide variety of taxa. As expected, the majority of the diet was supplied by the readily available lagomorphs. Rodents may also have contributed, minimally, to the diet and most likely were taken as available. There is also evidence in the form of sacrifice of whole or articulated specimens of cottontails, various birds, a fish, and numerous phalanges, likely representing hides, and their placement in kivas and rooms with enriched deposits, that these species were ritually important to the inhabitants. Carnivorous mammals, with the possible exception of domesticated dogs, are present purely as ritual or special-use species. Artiodactyl did add to the diet, but may also have been killed opportunistically, as mule deer and pronghorn still visit the LCR for water and forage during the fall and winter. The presence of the non-local bighorn is an interesting pattern and may be explained as a socio-ceremonial complex where Chevelon's inhabitants directly obtained animals in long-distance hunts or through trade. In all Homol'ovi cluster villages, their association with ceremonial structures, or deposits enriched with multiple other articulated animals and rare and unusual objects, indicates their exclusive use in ceremonial practices.

The lack of turtle remains is puzzling, given their presence in graves at Chevelon, the use of Chevelon Creek as a historic turtle hunting ground by Hopi, and the presence of turtles at other HSC sites. Fish also augmented the village's nutritional regime and, along with aquatic birds, frogs/toads, and mammals, were procured as a major source of social and ceremonial prestige for Chevelon's inhabitants.

Chapter 10
Shell
Marycruz Magaña Hernández

The excavations at Chevelon Ruin (AZ P:2:11[ASM]) resulted in the recovery of 1,207 pieces of shell from 21 of 39 excavated structures. The assemblage is dominated by freshwater mussel with some marine ornaments. This chapter discusses the analysis criteria, the shell species and origins, the artifact classes, the evidence of manufacturing, the provenience and the similarities or differences with excavated assemblages from other villages in the HSC.

METHODOLOGY OF ANALYSIS

Prior to analysis, the material was divided into unworked and worked material. From the 1,207 pieces of the total assemblage, 1,130 are unworked and 77 are worked; the unworked category is comprised of miscellaneous shell (and includes pieces of broken shell and full valves as raw materials that do not seem to be cut or ground, or have any evidence of manufacture), debitage, and unfinished artifacts. The species of unworked shell are mostly *Anodonta californiensis*, some terrestrial gastropods of the genus *Sonorella*, an unidentified species of terrestrial gastropods, and three marine species: *Pecten vogdesi*, *Argopecten circularis*, and *Glycymeris gigantea*.

The biological terms and identification follow terms and nomenclatures used by Keen (1971) and Abbott (1996) with the assistance of local specialists, Arthur Vokes, ASM, and Dr. Adrián Velázquez, curator of archaeology in Templo Mayor, Mexico.

The classification for worked material used in this analysis follows Suárez (1989), Fenner (1971), and Velázquez (1999). Following Suárez (1989:46), the artifacts from Chevelon are all ornamental. The specific uses of the shell ornaments are determined from the morphological characteristics and the archaeological context where the artifacts were found. Within each category, shells are divided into two groups or families: *automorphic* or whole shell, which includes all the artifacts that keep the natural form of the shell, and *xenomorphic*, where the shapes of the artifacts are different from the original shell (Velázquez 1999:32).

The families are divided into subfamilies, with the automorphic form divided into gastropod and pelecypod, in agreement with the biological class of the mollusk from which they were manufactured. The xenomorphic family is divided into geometric or not geometric forms, which includes all geometric, anthropomorphic, and zoomorphic artifacts. The subfamilies are subdivided into types according to formal aspects based on more specific characteristics (Suárez 1989:46).

Genus, Species, and Provenience of the Assemblage

The artifacts studied in this research are manufactured on shells belonging to the phyllum *Mollusca*, which is comprised of five classes: gastropoda (snails), pelecypoda (clams or bivalves), cephalopoda (squids), amphineura (quitons) and scaphopoda (tusk shells) (Keen 1971:13). Chevelon's assemblage is represented only by the gastropoda and pelecypoda classes with marine, freshwater, and terrestrial species. A total of nine genera and twelve species have been identified and consist of six gastropods (Table 10.1) and six pelecypods (Table 10.2).

The species come from three sources: the Gulf of California, the LCR and streams and canyons of the region, and the terrestrial snails that inhabit the area. The marine pieces include *Glycymeris* sp., *Laevicardium elatum*, *Pecten vogdesi*, *Argopecten circularis*, *Olivella dama*, *Nassarius tiarula*, and *Conus* sp. The *Glycymeris* were mostly used for bracelets, and other species of the *Glycymeridae* family (*Glycymeris maculata*) were preferable for rings. Only one fragment of *Laevicardium elatum* was found in the assemblage. These are often used as arm bands. Although these species can be found on the Coast of California and the Gulf of California, it seems that most were likely recovered from the Gulf of California because the other marine species found at Chevelon and in the Hohokam area originated in the Gulf of California (Vokes 2006:1).

There are two fragments of the family Pectinidae: *Pecten* and *Argopecten*. Neither was modified, although, because both were fragments, other portions could have been worked. Typically, these species were worked into whole shell pendants with a perforation on the top. These ornaments were commonly used in north Mexico and the American Southwest (Braniff 1989; Fenner 1971; Haury 1976). *Olivella dama* was mainly used for the manufacture of beads with the apex or spire removed. Sometimes the outer lip was modified and the base was ground. *Conus* were used as shell tinklers. The snail was cut in half, drilled on the base (these could be conic or cylindrical), and hung on a cord. *Nassarius tiarula* are small snails used in necklaces needing only slight modification. They are quite rare in the U.S. Southwest (LaMotta 1996).

The freshwater mussel *Anodonta californiensis* had a wide distribution in rivers and streams of Arizona. The inhabitants of Chevelon could have gotten them from the LCR or Chevelon Creek. According to Bequaert and Miller (1973), the *Anodonta* was completely extinguished in the area by 1956. Today, *Anodonta* is only found in Arizona in remote places, such as the Apache reservations (Arizona Game and Fish Department 2001:1). Also present in the assemblage is the terrestrial gastropod, *Sonorella* sp. Some species of this genus are also already extinct (U.S. Fish and Wildlife Service 1998:1).

The Use of Shell at Chevelon

The following shell artifacts types were found: beads; discoidal beads; tinklers; rectangular, quadrangular, circular and triangular pendants; bracelets and armlets; and a ring-pendant (Table 10.3).

Beads

All, except the discoidal beads, which were not possible to identify to species, are made

Table 10.1. Identification of Gastropods by Family, Genus, and Species.

Family	Genus	Species	Source	Complete	Fragments
Olividae	Olivella	dama	GULF OF CALIFORNIA	30	
CONIDAE	sp.			1
	Conus	fergusoni			3
		regularis			1
		ximenes			2
Nassaridae	Nassarius	tirula			1
Helminthoglyptidae	Sonorella	sp.	Terrestrial		17
Not identifiable				1	
			TOTAL	31	25

Table 10.2. Identification of Pelecypods by Family, Genus, and Species.

Family	Genus	Species	Source	Complete	Fragments
Unionidae	Anodonta	californiensis	Freshwater	4	1129
Nonidentifiable			Freshwater	1	
Pectinidae	Pecten	vogdesi			1
	Argopecten	circularis	GULF OF CALIFORNIA		1
Glycymerididae	Glycymeris	gigantea			3
		maculata		1	
Cardidae	Laevicardium	elatum			1
			TOTAL		1135

of *Olivella dama*.

Whole Shell Beads

The whole shell beads include all of those pieces that show the natural shape of the shell and have only been modifed with a perforation or a removal of a part of the shell (Figure 10.1). The beads were classified into four different types: a) Without apex, b) Without spire, c) Transversal section of the snail and, d) Without half spire, with a variant without exterior lip.

Table 10.3. Distribution of Shell Artifacts by Structure.

Structure	Use	Unworked shell	Debitage	Ornamental unknown	Pendants	Beads	Tinklers	Bracelets	Rings	Total	%
Unknown			1							1	0.1
200	Plaza	15	2	2						19	1.6
222	Piki room	82	6			3	1			92	7.6
227	Storage	58	5		1	2				66	5.5
246	Plaza	13								13	1.1
248	Kiva	116	9	1		3				129	10.7
260	Habitation	1								1	0.1
265	Habitation	38	4	1		1				44	3.6
266	Storage	37	5		1					43	3.6
268	Habitation	31	1						1	33	2.7
269	Storage	8	2		1					11	0.9
274	Kiva fill-279	33	4	1	1		1	1		41	3.4
279	Kiva	101	19	2	2	8	3	1		136	11.3
286	Storage	29	2		2	1				32	2.7
287	Storage	113	36			7		1		157	13.0
288	Storage	45	21	2	3		2			73	6.0
289	Habitation	3				1				4	0.3
345	Habitation	2			1		1			4	0.3
373	Storage	34	14	2	3					53	4.4
393	Habitation	9	2		1					12	1.0
403	Storage	5	4							9	0.7
900	Plaza	60	42	2	2	2		1		109	9.0
901	Kiva	20	13	3	6	1	1			44	3.6
900 F.2	Trash deposit	37	17	6	2	1				63	5.2
900 F.3	Roasting pit	2								2	0.2
900 F.5	Storage	7	9							16	1.3
TOTAL		899	216	22	26	30	9	4	1	1207	100.0

The edge shown on the artifacts lets us infer the manufacturing techniques used to remove the parts of the snail. Just one piece has a perforation, which is irregular and possibly made by a percussion technique producing an unexpected fracture (Suárez 1989:30). This perforation is located on the basal dorsal portion of the gastropod. The whole beads come from S. 222, 227, 248, 265, 274, 279, 287, and 289 and Plaza 900, Feature 2 (Table 10.3).

Discoidal Beads

Discoidal beads are those pieces that are perforated, but keep a radial symmetry with the perforation (Figure 10.1). These sometimes appear grouped on a string (Velázquez 1999:81). Due to extensive modification, no genus or species were able to be identified. They were collected from S. 286 and Plaza 900 (Table 10.3).

Pendants

The pendants are divided into those that keep the natural shape of the shell and geometrics. Within the whole shell, pendants are the half snail pendants better known in southwestern archaeology as tinklers, which are often manufactured on *Conus* sp. Three species were identified in the Chevelon assemblage: *C. fergusoni*, *C. ximenes* and *C. regularis*, totaling seven pieces (Figure 10.2; Table 10.1). The perforations on them are conical, cylindrical, and concave with divergent walls. The pieces come from S. 222, 248, 265, 279, 287, 288, 345 and Plaza 900 (Table 10.3). There are two complete pendants. One is a *Nassarius tiarula* artifact with a perforation on the exterior lip from S. 345; the other is a highly modified circular pendant of *Glycymeris gigantus* with

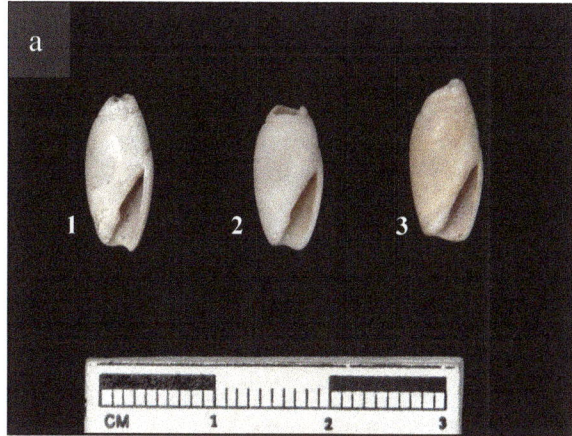

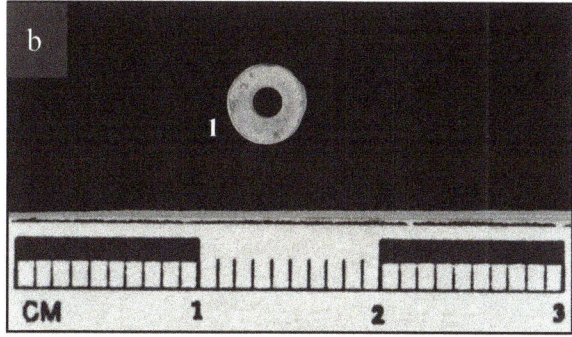

Figure 10.1. Whole shell beads of Olivella dama *and unknown shell.*

a central hole (Figure 10.2), found in S. 345.

The geometric pendants are circular, rectangular, quadrangular, and triangular (Figure 10.3). All are made on *Anodonta californiensis*, totaling 26 artifacts. The perforations are mostly cylindrical. All of these objects are fragmentary, preserved due to the beneficial location of the shell in the deposits. The pendants were found in S. 227, 266, 269, 274, 279, 286, 288, 373, and 393 and Plaza 900 (Table 10.3).

Ring Pendant

The ring pendant is from *Glycymeris maculata* (Figure 10.4). Its general form is circular. The umbo is present and the hinge is ground with an irregular shaped perforation in the middle. The band section is plain. Vokes (2006:9) mentions

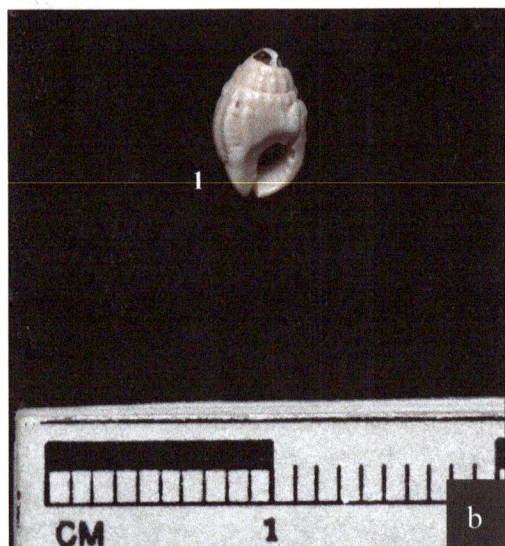

Figure 10.2. Shell pendants of Conus *sp.,* Nassarius *sp.,* Laevicardium elatum.

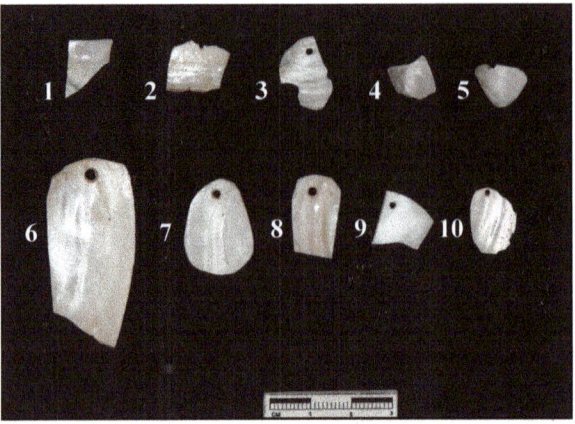

Figure 10.3. Shell pendants of Anodonta californiensis.

that these types of artifacts are multifunctional because they were used as rings, pendants, or earrings. This ring-pendant comes from the floor of S. 268 (Table 10.3).

Bracelets and Armlets

A fragment of a possible armlet of *Laevicardium elatum* was recovered from Plaza 900. Generally, armlets have a greater diameter than bracelets and were used on forearms. Bracelets having a smaller diameter were used on wrists or ankles. *Glycymeris* sp. is generally the species used for the manufacture of bracelets in northwest Mexico and the U.S. Southwest. Three broken pieces of bracelets are present; none are decorated and all are missing the umbo (Figure 10.5). The bracelets came from S. 274, 279, and 287 (Table 10.3). In two cases, *Glycymeris* sp. bracelet fragments were sharpened into awls (Figure 10.6).

EVIDENCE FOR MANUFACTURING

The analysis of the material provides evidence of three stages of manufacture of ornaments in Chevelon. These are artifacts in the process of being manufactured, manufacturing debris, and raw materials, all of them on *Anodonta californiensis*. The only evidence of manufacture on seashells was modification of two broken *Glycymeris* sp. bracelets.

Artifacts in the Process of Being Manufactured

Seventeen objects from *Anodonta* and two pieces of *Glycymeris gigantus* seem to be

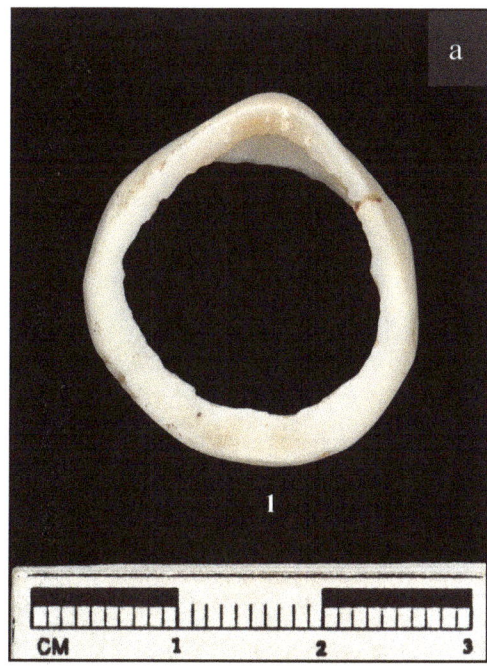

Figure 10.4. Glycymeris maculata *shell ring and fragment of* Glycymeris gigantus *showing modification.*

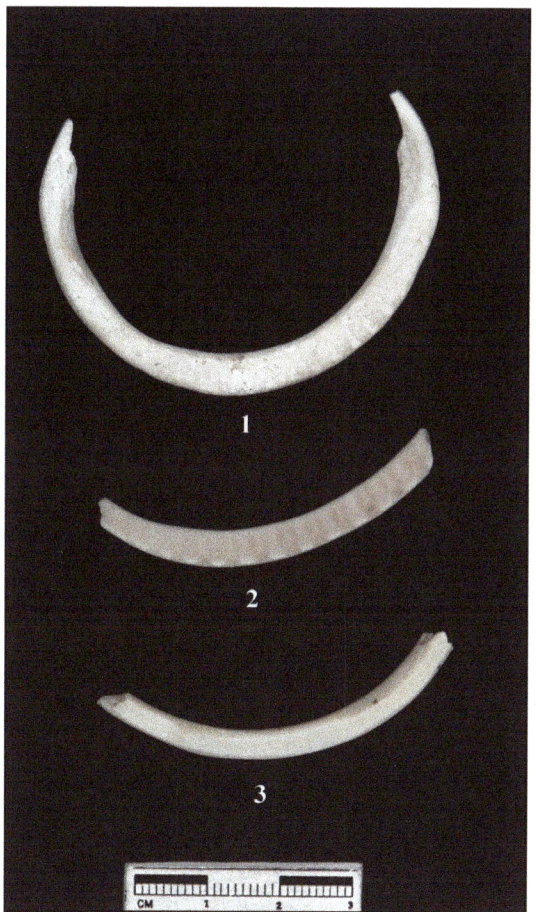

Figure 10.5. Glycymeris *sp. shell bracelets.*

artifacts in the process of being manufactured (Figures 10.3, 10.6). For the *Glycymeris*, the final product seems to be awls. *Anodonta* all appear to be pendants in different stages of production. Some show one or several edges finished to varying degrees, possibly by cutting and/or grinding to create triangular, circular, quadrangular, and rectangular pendants. These artifacts were recovered from S. 265, 279, 288, and 373 and Plaza 900 (Table 10.3).

Manufacturing Debris

Manufacturing debris results from the process of manufacturing artifacts. In Chevelon's assemblage, all manufacturing debris resulted

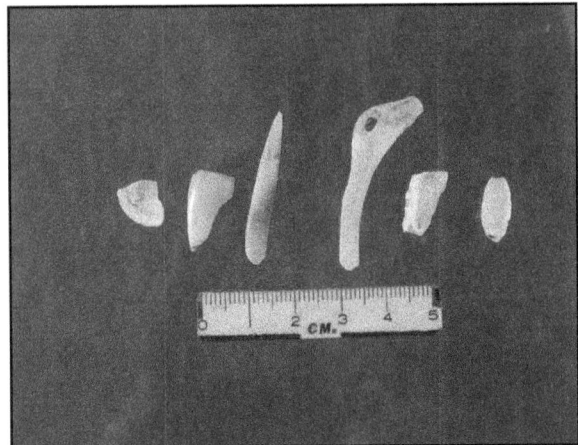

Figure 10.6. Miscellaneous reworked shell: (a,b) unknown; (c,d) Glycymeris *sp. (e) unknown; (f)* Olivella dama.

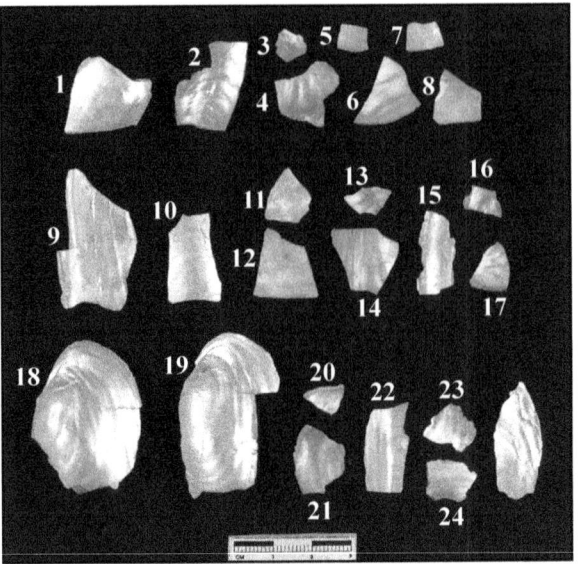

Figure 10.7. Manufacturing debris from Anodonta californiensis *ornament production.*

from carving on *Anodonta californiensis*. Debris was recovered from 14 structures: S. 222, 227, 248, 265, 266, 268, 274, 279, 287, 288, 373, and 393 and Plazas 200 and 900 (Table 10.3; Figure 10.7).

Raw Material

Two left valves of *Anodonta* were recovered from S. 287. Some shells of the terrestrial gastropod, *Sonorella* sp., were recovered, but do not seem to be culturally modified.

Anodonta Manufacture and Use

There is abundant evidence for the manufacture of artifacts at Chevelon using *Anodonta californiensis*. This is probably because this mollusk could be easily obtained from nearby, LCR and Chevelon Creek.

The best way to work *Anodonta* is when it is still fresh because it is more malleable and easier to cut and finish the piece (Vokes 2006:9). The tools used to cut the valves were probably unmodified flakes from chert and petrified wood, which are materials found in abundance in the area (Figure 10.8; Chapter 8; Thompson 2005:4). This could be inferred by samples taken from some pendants and manufacturing debris (on *Anodonta*) that were analyzed for evidence of manufacturing techniques and the materials used for these purposes. These samples were analyzed with Electronic Microscopy and the preliminary results show chert artifacts were used for cutting with sandstone used to finish the piece.

Grinding was probably done using the locally abundant sandstone, either as a formal or informal tool. These were used to remove imperfections resulting from the cutting and to give a finish to the piece. The perforation was made with a wood, bone, or stone drill applied by rotary movements with both hands (Suárez 1989:29).

Given the abundance of unmodified *Anodonta* shell, mostly from the fill of a majority of analyzed structures, it is likely Chevelon inhabitants utilized *Anodonta* as a food source. There is evidence in other southwestern sites along the Salt and Santa Cruz rivers that this mussel was eaten and the shell used as raw material (Vokes 2006:4, citing Haury 1976; and Vokes 1989). At Chevelon, evidence for consumption is that 83.9 percent of the fragments show no evidence of manufacture.

Spatial and Temporal Patterns

The shell artifacts are from room blocks 200, 300, 400 and 900 (the plaza space for RB300). The greatest concentration of shell materials are in RB200 and RB900 with 74 percent and 19 percent of the assemblage respectively (Table 10.3). These frequencies parallel the extent of excavation in these areas.

The shell materials are distributed in habitation and storage structures, kivas, a piki house, Plazas 200 and 900, and structures with unknown use. The rooms with the most shell are storage rooms, kivas, and Plazas 200 and 900 (Table 10.4). Storage rooms are the structures with the most unworked shell and manufacturing debris followed by the kivas. Kivas and storage rooms together account for two-thirds of ornamental artifacts. The habitation rooms and the piki house have fewer ornaments. This distribution is partly accounted for by the nature of sampling; however, ornaments are significantly under-represented in habitation rooms when sampling by structure is taken into account.

In terms of stratigraphy, 88 percent of the artifacts from the total assemblage come from fill and 12.1 percent of the artifacts come from features and floor fill. The feature fill is from S. 227, 265, 269, 287, 373, and 900 and F.2, F.3, and F.5, and includes unworked shell, manufacturing debris and some ornaments. The assemblage from floor fill comes from S. 227, 265, 269, 286, 288 and 345. Most of the artifacts are unworked shell with just one ornament and some fragments of debitage. This distribution suggests the assemblage is basically derived of material discarded into middens, in decommissioned storage rooms and kivas.

About 38 percent of the material can be temporally placed. These deposits are divided into four phases: Tuwiuca Phase (TP), Early Homol'ovi Phase (EHP), Middle Homol'ovi Phase (MHP), and Late Homol'ovi Phase (LHP) (see Chapters 4 and 6). According to the data, RB200 has temporal continuity in the shell material during the four phases (see Table 10.5), while it is not until the LHP when materials from the other room blocks appear (RB300, RB400 and K. 901). This distribution is a result of the dating of the sampled structures and has no implications of shell use through time.

The most shell is present in the LHP followed by the MHP, EHP, and the TP (Table 10.5). The unworked shell and manufacturing debris are present during all four phases, but mainly in the LHP. Beads and pendants are present during the three Homol'ovi phases, but

Figure 10.8. Petrified wood flakes possibly used in the manufacture of freshwater shell artifacts.

tinklers and bracelets do not appear until the MHP. The only other assemblage comparable in time is H3 and shows similar trends with more ornaments present in what are essentially MHP deposits versus earlier ones (Urban 2001). Given the adequate sample sizes from the time periods, this trend appears to be a product of behavior, rather than sampling biased by time period.

COMPARISONS TO ASSEMBLAGES FROM OTHER CLUSTER SITES AND BEYOND

The shell materials from the other Homol'ovi sites have several things in common with Chevelon's assemblage. In all cases, the use of the shell is ornamental, but at H2, Urban (1991:112) created the category called "utilitarian," which consists of shell fragments transformed and utilized as tools. The two bracelet fragments of *Glycymeris gigantea* shaped into awls would fit into her utilitarian category. The artifact types are similar from one site to another having beads, pendants, bracelets, armlets, and rings in almost all the sites using the same species of *Anodonta californiensis*, *Olivella dama*, *Pecten vogdesi*, *Sonorella* sp., *Glycymeris gigantea*, *Conus* sp., *Laevicardium elatum*, and *Nassarius* sp. The principal sources of the shell materials for the HSC were the same as Chevelon — the Gulf of California for marine species, the LCR for the freshwater mussel, and some terrestrial species that inhabit the region.

In comparison with the other villages, the quantity of shell recovered at Chevelon is larger than the other assemblages with 1,207 artifacts. At H4, the total is 144 (Harper 2004:111), at H3, there are 428 (Urban, 2001), and at H2, only 14 (Urban 1991); however, this is only from the 1984 excavations of five rooms and an exterior work space. Within the assemblages of all the sites, there is a strong presence of freshwater mussel, *Anodonta californiensis*. At H4, this accounts for about 30 percent of the artifacts, for H3, about 40 percent (Harper 2004:112) and for H2, about 14 percent. In contrast, Chevelon has 93.5 percent, with fewer seashells and less variety of species.

It should be noted that the excavation of burials at Chevelon in 1896 by Jesse Walter Fewkes produced numerous marine shells, such as bracelets and armlets, made from *Glycymeris gigantea*, and other artifacts like a piece of wood with incrustations in shell, probably *Haliotis* sp. (Fewkes 1898:362). Other artifacts include an object from *Turitella tigrina*, with

Table 10.4. Shell Distribution by Room Use and Artifact Type.

Room use	Unworked shell	Debitage	Artifacts in process	Ornamental Unknown	Pendant	Bead	Tinkler	Bracelet	Ring	Total
Habitation	84	7	1	1	2	2	1		1	99
Storage	336	96	4		11	10	2	1		460
Kiva	270	45	3	4	9	12	4	2		349
Piki house	82	6				3	1			92
Unknown		1								1
Plaza (includes Plaza 200 and 900)	127	59	9	3	4	3	1	1		207
TOTAL	899	214	17	7	26	30	9	4	1	1207

Table 10.5. Distribution of Datable Shell Artifacts by Phase and Structure.

Phase	Structure	Artifact Type	Genus and species from the ornaments	Quantity	%
Tuwiuca Phase 1290-1325 C.E..	227	Unworked shell		16	1.3
		Debitage		1	0.1
Total Tuwiuca				17	1.4
Early Homol'ovi Phase 1325-1365 C.E.	222	Unworked shell		18	1.5
		Debitage		1	0.1
		Beads	*Olivella dama*	1	0.1
	248	Unworked shell		52	4.3
		Debitage		5	0.4
		Beads	*Olivella dama*	2	0.2
		Ornamental Unknown		1	0.1
	279	Unworked shell		30	2.5
		Beads	*Olivella dama*	6	0.5
		Pendant	*Anodonta californiensis*	1	0.1
	288	Debitage		19	1.6
Total Early				136	11.4
Middle Homol'ovi Phase 1365-1385 C.E.	268	Unworked shell		17	1.4
	274	Bracelet	*Glycymeris gigantea*	1	0.1
		Unworked shell		21	1.7
		Ornamental Unknown		1	0.1
	279	Unworked shell		69	5.7
		Debitage		18	1.5
		Tinkler	*Conus fergusoni*	3	0.2
		Pendant	*Anodonta californiensis*	1	0.1
		Ornamental Unknown		1	0.1
		Beads	*Olivella dama*	2	0.2
	288	Debitage		7	0.6
Total Middle				141	11.7

Table 10.5. Distribution of Datable Shell Artifacts by Phase and Structure, cont'd.

Phase	Structure	Artifact Type	Genus and species from the ornaments	Quantity	%
Late Homol'ovi Phase 1385-1390/1400 C.E.	227	Unworked shell		21	1.7
		Debitage		4	0.3
	265	Debitage		2	0.2
		Unworked shell		21	1.7
		Beads	*Olivella dama*	1	0.1
	268	Unworked shell		2	0.2
	269	Unworked shell		7	0.6
		Debitage		2	0.2
		Pendant	*Anodonta californiensis*	1	0.1
	274	Debitage		2	0.2
		Unworked shell		11	0.9
		Pendant	*Anodonta californiensis*	1	0.1
	286	Unworked shell		28	2.3
		Bead	*Olivella dama*	1	0.1
	288	Unworked shell		2	0.2
		Tinkler	*Conus ximenes*	1	0.1
		Pendant	*Anodonta californiensis*	1	0.1
	373	Debitage		1	0.1
	393	Pendant	*Anodonta californiensis*	1	0.1
		Debitage		2	0.2
		Unworked shell		3	0.2
	403	Unworked shell		5	0.4
		Debitage		4	0.3
	900	Tinkler	*Conus regularis*		
	901	Pendant	*Anodonta californiensis*	6	0.5
		Debitage		13	1.1
		Unworked shell		22	1.8
		Beads	*Olivella dama*	1	0.1
Total Late				167	14.0
Grand Total				461	38.2

a perforation on the exterior lip, probably a whole shell pendant; a complete shell on *Laevicardium elatum*, decorated with painted lines in black; an artifact in *Melongena patula*, without a spire; and an artifact on *Strombus galeatus*, also without a spire.

At Homol'ovi sites, the manufacture of artifacts on *Anodonta* is remarkable, but expected, given that the villages are far from the source of marine specimens and have an abundant local supply of shell (Urban 1991:113).

The assemblage of H1 is different from the rest of the assemblages of the HSC because manufacturing debris and complete valves of marine specimens are present in the materials. The assemblage from H1 has not yet been analyzed, but the collection could be more extensive than Chevelon's with a wider variety of artifacts and species.

The materials of Chevelon and other HSC villages are similar to the artifacts found in other sites from the fourteenth century in the Southwest and northwest Mexico. The Hohokam developed a specialized industry in the manufacture of shell ornaments, probably as a result of being close to the source of raw materials in the Gulf of California (Haury 1965:135). The Hohokam traded shell ornaments to groups to the north in the Pueblo area (Haury 1965:136). The influence of these groups is evident on the materials recovered by Fewkes including *Laevicardium*, with painted decorations, or the trumpet of *Strombus gigas* (Fewkes 1898:362), similar to the trumpet reported by Haury for Snaketown (Haury 1965:161). For H1, LaMotta (2006) reported a *Glycymeris* sp. shell frog with turquoise mosaic, similar to the ones recovered by Fewkes at Chevelon and to ones recovered in the Hohokam region (Haury 1965).

Individuals in the HSC were not the only ones to manufacture ornaments on freshwater mussels. Snaketown and Río Nuevo in the Central Tucson Basin have evidence of this work (Haury 1965:136; Vokes 2006:4). For Snaketown, Haury (1965:136) noted that the freshwater mussel is more fragile than the seashells, making it less suitable for manufacture. This fragility is also evident in the debris from Chevelon.

CONCLUSIONS

The shell material comes from three sources: the Gulf of California, the LCR drainage system, and terrestrial species. The freshwater mussel, *Anodonta californiensis*, and the terrestrial snails were locally obtained, but the marine species came to Chevelon through exchange with other groups to the south as finished artifacts from the Hohokam or intermediary groups (Harper 2004:114; Urban 2001). This can be deduced because no evidence of manufacture on these species was found at Chevelon. Haury (1965:135) proposed that the Hohokam exchanged shell artifacts with groups inside the Pueblo area through the Verde, Tonto, and Salt River valleys. The artifacts recovered by Fewkes (1898, 1904), at Chevelon, are very similar to the artifacts reported by Haury (1965) for Snaketown. The presence of Jeddito Yellow Ware, in the Hohokam area, indicates at least one item that could have been exchanged from the HSC to groups possessing shell ornaments. Citing the use of shell at Hopi as personal adornments, as well as in numerous rituals invoking water, Fewkes (1898, 1904) speculated that shell recovered from burials at Chevelon and H1 had similar uses.

The inhabitants of Chevelon developed a shell industry to manufacture objects for personal adornment using the local freshwater mussel *A. californiensis*. However, *Anodonta* was not a substitute for ornaments made of seashells. The quantity of unworked shell from *Anodonta* at Chevelon is about 74 percent of the total assemblage, which suggests that the inhabitants of Chevelon were exploiting this mollusk as a food source and not just as raw material for ornaments. The ornaments on *Anodonta* were manufactured with locally available material, probably using chert flakes for cutting and sandstone for grinding the ornaments into their final forms. The manufacture of artifacts made of *A. californiensis* is not exclusive to Chevelon. The other Homol'ovi sites also developed a shell industry from this mollusk creating artifacts similar to Chevelon's, but each site had its own forms. Other sites in the Southwest, where freshwater mussels were used to manufacture ornamental artifacts, include the Hohokam, where Haury (1965) reports some ornaments from a freshwater mollusk. Another example is the Río Nuevo site in the central Tucson Basin where *A. californiensis* was used as a food source and as raw material to manufacture ornamental artifacts (Vokes 2006:4).

Shell materials are present at Chevelon since the TP continuing until the LHP. The shell is concentrated in K. 248, 279, and 901, storage, S. 287, and features in Plaza 900. At H4, the materials related to shell manufacture are concentrated in the plaza area suggesting this was a primary locus of manufacture (Harper 2004:111). This could be the same case at Chevelon in Plaza 900, where the materials are mostly unworked shell and manufacturing debris, and in S. 287 where unworked shell, manufacturing debris, and some artifacts in the process of being manufactured into ornaments were found.

Shell was an important material for the inhabitants of Chevelon who brought it from far distances through exchange for personal adornment and possibly for rituals. This could account, in part, for its concentration in kiva fill. The manufacture of shell ornaments on local species is more predominant at Chevelon than any other site within the HSC. A possible explanation is its unique location along the Chevelon Creek with its permanent flow of water.

Chapter 11
Charred Plant Remains
Karen R. Adams

SETTING THE SCENE: THE MODERN PLANT ENVIRONMENT

The modern local vegetation surrounding Chevelon Pueblo consists of sparsely distributed grasses, shrubs dominated by more than one species of saltbush (*Atriplex*), and introduced aggressive plants, such as camel thorn (*Alhagi camelorum*) and tumbleweed (*Salsola pestifer*), from other continents. The nearby streambanks of Chevelon Creek are currently dominated by dense stands of introduced saltcedar or tamarix (*Tamarix pentandra*), with numerous native plants struggling to compete. The LCR edges are also dominated by tamarix, along with cottonwood (*Populus fremontii*), willow (*Salix*), and New Mexican privet (*Forestiera neomexicana*). Efforts to assess modern vegetation in the area have included informal plant surveys during mid-summer visits in 2003, 2004, and 2005, accompanied by collection and verification of plant herbarium specimens.

On the broad floodplain and in the nearby low upland area surrounding Chevelon Pueblo, a variety of plants were observed (Table 11.1). The dominant plants include a number of species of saltbush (*Atriplex*), along with many herbaceous (non-woody) perennials and annuals. Although the region has felt the effects of domestic animal grazing during the historic period, many plants of interest to human groups still grow in this area, many of them likely in reduced proportions and populations, relative to the thirteenth and fourteenth centuries. Among these are a number of weedy annuals capable of producing abundant quantities of edible seeds or fruit (amaranth, sunflower, tansy mustard, spectacle pod, goosefoot, woolly-wheat, stickleaf) or parts useful for other needs (tobacco). Important perennial resources include various grasses (dropseed and Indian rice grass), cacti (prickly pear and cholla), saltbush plants, seep-weed, coyote gourd, Mormon tea, narrow-leaf yucca, globemallow, and thorn-apple. Although rare within 8 km of Chevelon Pueblo today, scattered juniper trees offer construction elements, fuel, and edible fruit. Records of travelers from the nineteenth century report a heavier grass cover, including grama grass (*Bouteloua*), on the low hills above the LCR floodplains (K. Adams 1996; Colton 1937; Miksicek 1991).

Reconstructing the nature of native riparian vegetation, adjacent to and within Chevelon Creek (Figure 11.1) and the LCR, requires use of historic documents and access to a protected stretch of the river (upper "Chevelon Creek") to understand the extent of historic changes to the region's riparian plant communities. Both drainages are now lined with introduced tamarix plants so thick they generally out-compete indigenous vegetation. However, Colton (1937) has summarized some of the early written records of LCR explorers, who reported seeing groves of cottonwoods

Table 11.1. Plants Observed on the Wide Foodplain and in the Drier Upland Area Immediately Surrounding Chevelon Pueblo.

Common Name	Species	Family
Amaranth, pigweed	*Amaranthus* spp.	Amaranthaceae
Rabbitbrush	*Chrysothamnus* sp.	Asteraceae
Daisy flea bane	*Erigeron* sp.	Asteraceae
Pearly everlasting	*Gnaphalium luteo-album* Linnaeus*	Asteraceae
Sunflower	*Helianthus annuus*	Asteraceae
Crown-beard	*Verbesina* sp.	Asteraceae
Tansy mustard	*Descurainia pinnata*	Brassicaceae
Spectacle pod	*Dithyrea wislizenii*	Brassicaceae
Prickly pear	*Opuntia* spp.	Cactaceae
Cholla	*Opuntia* spp.	Cactaceae
Sand-spurry	*Spergularia marina* (Linnaeus) Grisebach*	Caryophyllaceae
4-wing saltbush	*Atriplex canescens*	Chenopodiaceae
Saltbush	*Atriplex* sp.	Chenopodiaceae
Goosefoot	*Chenopodium* spp.	Chenopodiaceae
Tumbleweed	*Salsola pestifer***	Chenopodiaceae
Greasewood	*Sarcobatus* sp.	Chenopodiaceae
Seep-weed	*Suaeda* sp.	Chenopodiaceae
Rocky Mt. beeweed	*Cleome serrulata* Pursh	Cleomaceae
Coyote gourd	*Cucurbita foetidissima*	Cucurbitaceae
Juniper	*Juniperus* sp.	Cupressaceae
Mormon tea	*Ephedra* sp.	Ephedraceae
Camelthorn	*Alhagi camelorum***	Fabaceae
Narrow-leaf yucca	*Yucca* sp.	Liliaceae
Flax	*Linum* sp.	Linaceae
Stickleaf	*Mentzelia multiflora* (Nuttall) A. Gray*	Loasaceae
Stickleaf	*Mentzelia pumila*	Loasaceae
Globemallow	*Sphaeralcea* sp.	Malvaceae
Evening primrose	*Oenothera* sp.	Onagraceae
Woolly-wheat	*Plantago* sp. (native)	Plantaginaceae
Dropseed grass	*Sporobolus* sp.	Poaceae
Indian rice grass	*Stipa hymenoides*	Poaceae
Thorn-apple	*Datura* sp.	Solanaceae
Wild tobacco	*Nicotiana attenuata*	Solanaceae
White horse nettle	*Solanum elaegnifolium*	Solanaceae

Plants with an * are represented by herbarium specimens verified by Kathryn Mauz in the University of Arizona herbarium.
Plants with ** are considered historically introduced from another continent. Terminology follows Kearney and Peebles (1960), Correll and Correll (1975), and Christy (1998). Plants arranged by family.

*Figure 11.1. Chevelon Creek near Chevelon Pueblo, dominated by introduced tamarisk (*Tamarix pentandra*) plants.*

and willows lining the region's rivers and creeks and who occasionally bogged down in extensive swamps in the vicinity of nearby Winslow, Arizona. Observations, between the sixteenth and nineteenth centuries, reveal a nearly permanent and relatively narrow LCR that regularly shifted within its channel, was hemmed in by fairly shallow banks, and occupied by beaver colonies. Heavy sheep and cattle grazing in the 1870s through the 1880s, coupled with drought conditions, shifted the balance of vegetation significantly and altered the character of the river so that it became much broader, impermanent, and began carrying high quantities of silt during flooding that regularly spread out over the landscape.

Riparian plant resources, available to Chevelon Pueblo occupants, likely included a wide variety of native species (Table 11.2). Reconnaissance, along Chevelon Creek near the pueblo, revealed a limited number of the same native plant taxa observed in the protected "upper Chevelon Creek" site, approximately 5.5 km south of the pueblo (Figure 11.2). Along the creek near the pueblo today, one can still find species of bulrush, cattail, rocky mountain beeweed, and a few native grasses. However, the upper Chevelon Creek locale has protected a much longer list of native plant resources useful to human groups because a constricted Chevelon Creek channel and a dam near the pueblo has flooded the canyon so that it is naturally secluded from grazing. Introduced tamarix has not been able to flourish in this healthy and diverse native plant community (Table 11.2). Many of these same native plants would likely have grown along Chevelon Creek nearer to Chevelon Pueblo during the late thirteenth through late fourteenth centuries. Cottonwood, willow, walnut, netleaf hackberry, New Mexican privet, and box elder trees are all large woody trees or shrubs that provide edible fruit and wood for many household uses. In addition, various species of bulrush and rush, reedgrass and other grasses, sagebrush, horsetail, wild roses, spiderwort, and wild grapes offer both subsistence and raw materials for daily needs. Numerous other plants, among them thorn-apple, Indian tea, and desert 4-O'clock, provide additional medicinal/ceremonial and/or ritual resources. The ethnographic literature of Native American groups in the Southwestern U.S. lists historic uses of many of these plants, or their close relatives, and it is reasonable to assume that the knowledge about, and use of, these plants has been carried down through time.

Methodology of Analysis

Over the four-year Chevelon Pueblo project, archaeologists collected visible plant parts (macrobotanical samples) during excavation, and routinely acquired sediment samples (flotation samples) to recover tiny plant remains by use of a water flotation technique. Archaeologists systematically collected

Table 11.2. Plants Observed Within and Adjacent to Chevelon Creek in the Vicinity of Chevelon Pueblo, and in the Protected Riparian Location Known As Upper Chevelon Creek, Approximately 5.5 km South of Chevelon Pueblo.

Common Name	Species	Family
Box-elder	*Acer negundo* L.*	Aceraceae
Milkweed	*Asclepias* sp.	Asclepiadaceae
Ragweed	*Ambrosia* sp.	Asteraceae
Sagebrush	*Artemisia carruthii* Wood*	Asteraceae
Sagebrush	*Artemisia ludoviciana*	Asteraceae
Brickellia	*Brickellia* sp.	Asteraceae
Winterfat	*Eurotia lanata*	Asteraceae
Telegraph plant	*Heterotheca villosa* (Pursh) Shinners*	Asteraceae
Goldon-rod	*Solidago missouriensis* Nutt.*	Asteraceae
Indian tea	*Thelesperma megapotamicum* (Spreng.) Kuntze*	Asteraceae
Cocklebur	*Xanthium* sp.	Asteraceae
Rocky Mt. beeweed	*Cleome serrulata* Pursh*	Cleomaceae
Spiderwort	*Tradescantia* sp.	Commelinaceae
Bulrush	*Scirpus acutus* Muhlenberg*	Cyperaceae
Bulrush	*Scirpus americanus* Persoon*	Cyperaceae
Bulrush	*Scirpus maritimus* Linnaeus*	Cyperaceae
Bulrush	*Scirpus pungens* Vahl*	Cyperaceae
Horsetail	*Equisetum* sp.	Equisetaceae
False-indigo	*Amorpha fruticosa* L.*	Fabaceae
White clover	*Melilotus albus***	Fabaceae
Walnut	*Juglans major* (Torr.) Heller*	Juglandaceae
Rush	*Juncus ensifolius* Wikstr.*	Juncaceae
Rush	*Juncus tenuis* Willd.*	Juncaceae
Rush	*Juncus torreyi* Coville*	Juncaceae
Hop	*Humulus americanus* Nutt.*	Moraceae
Desert 4-O'clock	*Mirabilis linearis* (Pursh) Heimerl*	Nyctaginaceae
New Mexican privet	*Forestiera neomexicana*	Oleaceae
Common plantain	*Plantago major* L.*, **	Plantaginaceae
Bent grass	*Agrostis stolonifera* L.*	Poaceae
Cheatgrass	*Bromus tectorum***	Poaceae
Reedgrass	*Phragmites australis* (Cav.) Trin. Ex Steudel*	Poaceae
Rabbit's foot grass	*Polypogon monspeliensis* (Linnaeus) Desfontaine*	Poaceae
Water-pimpernel	*Samolus floribundus* HBK.*	Primulaceae
Wild rose	*Rosa* sp.	Rosaceae
Cottonwood	*Populus* sp.	Salicaceae
Willow	*Salix exigua* Nutt.*	Salicaceae

Table 11.2. Plants Observed Within and Adjacent to Chevelon Creek in the Vicinity of Chevelon Pueblo, and in the Protected Riparian Location Known As Upper Chevelon Creek, Approximately 5.5 km South of Chevelon Pueblo, cont'd.

Common Name	Species	Family
Willow	*Salix monticola* Bebb ex Coult.*	Salicaceae
Thorn-apple	*Datura* sp.	Solanaceae
Tamarix	*Tamarix pentandra***	Tamaricaceae
Cattail	*Typha latifolia* L.*	Typhaceae
Netleaf hackberry	*Celtis reticulata*	Ulmaceae
Wild grape	*Vitis* sp.	Vitaceae

Plants with an * are represented by herbarium specimens verified by Kathryn Mauz in the University of Arizona herbarium.
Plants with ** are considered historically introduced from another continent. Terminology follows Kearney and Peebles (1960), Correll and Correll (1975), and Welsh (1993). Plants arranged by family.

Figure 11.2. The protected "Chevelon Uplands" approximately 5.5 miles south of Chevelon Pueblo, dominated by willows (Salix) *and a wide variety of native plants.*

flotation samples from a standard list of loci, whether plant remains were visible or not. Macrobotanical samples represent a more discretionary sample type, dependent on recognition of larger plant parts in site sediment, time available, and other excavation constraints. Together, these two sample types provide perspective on a range of microscopic (flotation samples) and larger plant remains (macrobotanical samples), resulting from daily activities of puebloan groups. A total of 100 macrobotanical samples and 95 flotation samples have been analyzed, representing numerous puebloan structures serving a variety of functions, and dating to different time periods within the century of Chevelon Pueblo occupation (Table 11.3).

The flotation samples were processed by a simple bucket system that resulted in collection of a buoyant light fraction. Light fractions, ranging from 5 to 535 ml in volume, were divided into a series of particle sizes (>4.0 mm, 2.0 to 4.0 mm, 1.0 to 2.0 mm, 0.5 to 1.0 mm, and <0.5 mm) for ease of examination. Materials, in each particle size, were then examined for seeds and other reproductive

Table 11.3. Archaeobotanical Samples Analyzed for this Report, Arranged by Structure.

Structure	Time Period	Time Period Code	Structure Function	Flotation Samples N =	Macrobotanical Samples N =
120	LHP 1385-1400	4	storage with bin features	1	
123	LHP 1385-1400	4	corn storage	1	
124	LHP 1385-1400	4	habitation with ritual features	1	
158	LHP 1385-1400	4	corn storage	1	
159	LHP 1385-1400	4	habitation with ritual features	6	
161	LHP 1385-1400	4	habitation	4	
222	EHP 1325-1365	2	piki house	7	12
227	LHP 1385-1400	4	storage with bin features	6	9
246	EHP 1325-1365		midden near K. 248		1
248	EHP 1325-1365	2	kiva		2
252	LHP 1385-1400	4	kiva	1	
260	LHP 1385-1400		fill of S. 264		1
262	LHP 1385-1400	4	habitation	1	
264	LHP 1385-1400	4	habitation	6	1
265	LHP 1385-1400	4	habitation	6	3
266	MHP 1365-1385	3	storage with no bin features	2	2
268	LHP-MHP	4-3	habitation	3	1
269	LHP 1385-1400	4	habitation		1
274	MHP-LHP 1365-1400	3-4	fill above kiva	1	5
279	MHP 1365-1385	3	kiva	11	13
286	EHP-LHP 1325-1400	2-4	storage with bin features, for ritual items	2	8
287		UNK	unknown		1
288	LHP 1385-1400 (contexts considered here)	4	storage with bin features	3	4
289	LHP 1385-1400	4	habitation	3	2
300	Tuwiuca 1290-1325	1	midden beneath S. 373	2	4
345	MHP 1365-1385	3	habitation	7	4
373	LHP 1385-1400	4	storage with bin features	3	3
393	LHP 1385-1400	4	habitation		6
403	LHP 1385-1400		storage		1
603	MHP-LHP 1365–1400	3-4	habitation	3	
702	LHP 1385-1400	4	storage with bin features	2	
900	LHP 1385-1400	4	plaza to RB300	8	16
901	LHP 1385-1400	4	kiva	4	

parts, with the exception of the smallest particle size with items less than 0.5 mm in broadest dimension, which were not examined. These tiny specimens are usually broken pieces of larger items that have already been identified on the basis of more complete specimens.

For macrobotanical samples, materials were spread out and examined, first for charred non-wood specimens and then, for wood fragments. Up to 20 pieces of charred wood were identified from both macrobotanical and flotation samples, or as many fragments as were available with a broad enough cross-section surface to view anatomical details. All items were identified at magnifications ranging from 8x to 50x, using a Zeiss binocular microscope, and in comparison to an extensive modern collection of regional charred and uncharred plant materials backed by herbarium specimens deposited in the University of Arizona herbarium (ARIZ).

DESCRIPTION OF THE ARCHAEOBOTANICAL ASSEMBLAGE

A minimum of 42 separate plant taxa, many of them represented by more than one plant part, were preserved in all flotation and macrobotanical samples examined (Table 11.4). Nearly all of these specimens are charred and are assumed to have burned in some way due to the actions of humans in the past. Most uncharred specimens present in the samples are assumed to be more recent in age and will not be further discussed. However, a small number of seeds and seed fragments of two species of domesticated squash (*Cucurbita moschata* and *Cucurbita pepo*) were recovered in uncharred condition, and are considered representative of domesticates utilized by the Chevelon Pueblo occupants.

In the discussions that follow, emphasis will be placed on the interpretation of the systematically acquired flotation samples. The non-systematically acquired macrobotanical samples confirm the patterning of many of the plant remains within the flotation samples, and will be highlighted only when they offer independent information on plant use in the past. The criteria of identification of the majority of taxa/parts recovered in these samples have been previously reported (K. Adams 1994a; K. Adams and Murray 2004).

Domesticated Plants

Maize/Corn

Evidence of maize (*Zea mays*) was recovered in many flotation samples from a diversity of Chevelon Pueblo structures (Table 11.5). Charred ear (Figure 11.3), cob, and/or kernel specimens preserved in 59 of 95 (62.1 percent) flotation samples, making it the most ubiquitous domesticate present in the deposits. Maize was recovered in storage structures with and without bin features, in habitations, in a piki house, in kivas, and in two corn storage rooms (S. 123 and 158).

A small number of the well-preserved kernels within flotation samples were complete enough to determine endosperm type. They appeared to represent pop and/or flint endosperm, both of which are harder than flour kernels, and would require more grinding effort. Pop and flint kernels are also insect-resistant and store well.

The fact that some of these kernels were aligned and attached to one another in ranks suggests they burned while still on their cobs, most likely as ears in storage. Maize kernels with extruded contents burned shortly after harvest, prior to complete drying, as moisture

Table 11.4. List of Plant Taxa and Parts Recovered in all Flotation and
Macrobotanical Samples Analyzed from Chevelon Pueblo.

Taxon	Common Name	Part
Acer	box elder	wood
Allenrolfea	pickleweed	seed
Allenrolfea	pickleweed	wood
Allenrolfea/ Sarcobatus	pickleweed/greasewood	wood
Arctostaphylos	manzanita	seed
Artemisia	sagebrush	wood
Atriplex	saltbush	seed
Atriplex	saltbush	twig
Atriplex	saltbush	wood
Atriplex canescens	4-wing saltbush	fruit core
Cercocarpus	mountain mahogany	wood
Cheno-am	Cheno-am	seed
Chrysothamnus	rabbitbrush	wood
Cleome	beeweed	seed
Compositae	sunflower family	stem fragment
Corispermum	bugseed	seed
Cucurbita	squash	rind fragment
Cucurbita	squash	seed fragment
Cucurbita moschata	butternut squash	seed
Cucurbita pepo	pumpkin squash	seed, seed fragment
Cycloloma	winged pigweed	seed
Echinocereus	hedgehog cactus	seed
Ephedra	Mormon tea	wood
Eragrostis	love grass	caryopsis
Forestiera	privet	wood
Gossypium	cotton (domesticated)	seed, seed fragment
Juglans	walnut	wood
Juniperus	juniper	bark fragment
Juniperus	juniper	berry
Juniperus	juniper	leaf scale
Juniperus	juniper	seed
Juniperus	juniper	twig
Juniperus	juniper	wood
Monocotyledon	monocotyledon	fibers, tissue
Opuntia (p. pear)	prickly pear	seed, seed fragment
Phragmites	reedgrass	stem fragment, stem segment
Physalis	ground cherry	seed fragment

Table 11.4. List of Plant Taxa and Parts Recovered in all Flotation and
Macrobotanical Samples Analyzed from Chevelon Pueblo, cont'd.

Taxon	Common Name	Part
Pinus	pine	bark scale
Pinus	pine	wood
Pinus edulis	pinyon pine	wood
Pinus ponderosa	ponderosa pine	needle fragment
Pinus ponderosa	ponderosa pine	wood
Poaceae	grass	caryopsis
Poaceae	grass	culm base
Poaceae	grass	stem fragment
Populus/Salix	cottonwood/willow	twig
Populus/Salix	cottonwood/willow	wood
Portulaca	purslane	seed
Pseudotsuga	Douglas fir	wood
Purshia/Cowania	bitterbrush/cliff-rose	wood
Quercus	oak	wood
Rhus aromatica	lemonade berry	fruit
Rhus aromatica	lemonade berry	wood
Rosaceae	rose family	wood
Salvia reflexa	chia	seed
Sarcobatus	greasewood	wood
Scirpus	bulrush	achene
Sphaeralcea	globemallow	seed
Stipa hymenoides	Indian rice grass	caryopsis, floret
Vitis	wild grape	wood
Yucca	yucca	leaf fragment
Yucca baccata	broad-leaf yucca	seed, seed fragment
Zea mays	maize/corn	cob fragment, cob segment, cupule
Zea mays	maize/corn	cob/kernel mass
Zea mays	maize/corn	ear fragment, ear segment
Zea mays	maize/corn	embryo
Zea mays	maize/corn	fused kernel mass
Zea mays	maize/corn	kernel, kernel fragment
Zea mays	maize/corn	stem fragment

Note: All Specimens are Charred, with the exception of a few squash (*Cucurbita moschata* and *Cucurbita pepo*) seeds and seed fragments.

Table 11.5. Presence of Charred Maize (*Zea mays*) Remains in Flotation Samples from Chevelon Pueblo Structures, Arranged by Time Period.

Structure	Structure Function	Time Period	Comments
288	storage with bin features	1	
300	midden beneath S. 373	1	
222	piki house	2	
227	storage with bin features	2	
274	fill above kiva	3-4	
266	storage with no bin features	3	
279	kiva	3	
345	habitation	3	
603	habitation	3-4	flint or pop endosperm
123	corn storage	4	some aligned; pop endosperm; some with extruded contents
124	habitation with ritual features	4	
158	corn storage	4	
159	habitation with ritual features	4	
161	habitation	4	
227	storage with bin features	4	
252	kiva	4	
262	habitation	4	
264	habitation	4	
265	habitation	4	
289	habitation	4	
373	storage with bin features	4	
702	storage with bin features	4	pop endosperm; some aligned; some with extruded contents
900	plaza to RB300	4	
901	kiva	4	

Time periods: 1 = Tuwiuca, 1290-1325 C.E.; 2 = Early Homol'ovi Phase, 1325-1365 C.E.; 3 = Middle Homol'ovi Phase, 1365-1385 C.E.; 4 = Late Homol'ovi Phase, 1385-1400 C.E.

turned to steam and expanded the interior contents of the kernels outward (Figure 11.4). This was particularly noticeable in kernels excavated from corn storage S. 123 and from storage S. 702.

No flotation samples from undisturbed floor or floor feature contexts were available from two corn storage rooms (S. 123 and 158). Yet, the charred maize ear remains preserved within them, along with grass and reed grass stems that perhaps provided cushioning for the maize harvest, together confirm the specialized storage function of these two locations. Although maize was also recovered within other structure types (Table 11.12), it was usually associated with cooking features such

*Figure 11.3. A maize (*Zea mays*) ear, with kernels aligned along a cob, that burned in storage Structure 702 (PD851 FS2).*

*Figure 11.4. Maize (*Zea mays*) kernels from storage Structure 702. Note the kernel on the left has extruded interior contents, indicating it likely burned while still moist, shortly after harvest. Normal kernel on the right is not extruded.*

as hearths and roasting pits. In addition, the two corn storage rooms contained virtually no other potential plant foods, with the exception of Indian rice grass grains, which may have incidentally entered the room on the grass stems.

In addition to the extensive record of maize in flotation samples, maize cob fragments, cob/kernel masses, ear fragments, fused masses of kernels, and single kernels or kernel fragments were routinely recovered as macrobotanical samples during excavation. A sample of these charred specimens was selected by R. Emerson Howell (Table 11.6). Howell examined a total of 182 fairly intact kernels and 84 cob segments (each one complete around the circumference for at least a portion of its length). Kernel dimensions (Table 11.7) and cob segment traits (Table 11.8) display some variability among the specimens examined, and some of this variability may be due to the effects of charring. Casual observations indicate that cobs shrink notably as they burn, so the original Chevelon cobs were likely larger than indicated in Table 11.8. Kernels can shrink or swell, depending on their moisture content. The extent of alteration of maize parts due to burning is currently under study.

Type of Maize Grown at Chevelon Pueblo

Based on the sample of Chevelon Pueblo maize kernels and cob segments examined to date, farmers grew a flint/pop maize with rectangular kernels that, on average, were nearly twice as wide as thick. 'Cob row' number averaged 10.3 rows of kernels, and cupules (a cupule is a pocket that holds two kernels) were wide and shallow, likely making it relatively easy to remove the kernels. Chevelon farmers may also have grown maize with flour kernels, although a larger sample of kernels should be examined to confirm this. This is based on the relatively low average number of kernel rows per ear (10.3) and on general kernel shape. In the Mogollon Highlands region at Tularosa Cave, a low average ear row number was noted at the end of the Georgetown (500-700 C.E.) phase (Cutler 1952), when an 8-rowed flour maize (Maís de Ocho) appears to have been introduced from Mexico, and quickly adopted by farmers. Maís de Ocho is an 8-rowed maize with large, floury kernels that are wide and

Table 11.6. Maize (*Zea mays*) Kernels and Cob Segments Collected as Macrofossils by Excavators, and Examined by R. Emerson Howell.

Structure	Number of Kernels	Number of Cob Segments
117		1
123	54	9
161	15	7
200		1
227	1	5
264	36	21
265		1
279		10
287		2
288		1
289		4
373		5
702	59	16
900	17	1
Totals	182	84

Table 11.7. Basic Measurements of 182 Charred Maize Kernels Collected as Macrofossils, and Examined by R. Emerson Howell

	Length (mm)	Thickness (mm)	Width (mm)	Volume (mm^2)
Mean	8.1	4.1	7.4	244.2
Standard Deviation	0.92	0.78	0.92	74.63
Range	5.5-10.8	5.0-7.0	5.0-10.0	120.5-325.6

Table 11.8. Basic Observations and Measurements of 182 Charred Maize Cob Segments Collected as Macrofossils, and Examined by R. Emerson Howell.

	Cob Row Number	Cob Diameter (mm)	Cupule Width (mm)	Cupule Length (mm)	Cupule Depth (mm)	Rachis Segment Length (mm)	Rachis Diameter (mm)	Pith Diameter (mm)
Mean	10.3	11.9	6.0	1.5	1.0	3.2	8.5	4.7
Standard Deviation	1.8	5.1	1.4	0.8	0.4	0.4	2.3	1.5
Range	6.0-16.0	5.4-35.0	1.3-8.9	0.7-3.0	0.2-2.0	2.3-4.8	3.0-19.0	1.6-9.5

flat (K. Adams 1994b), in comparison to other Southwestern maize types.

Whether the variability in Chevelon maize represents more than one maize landrace is currently unknown. A landrace is essentially a "cultivated variety" or "cutivar" of maize having specific growth, vegetative, and reproductive traits, and environmental tolerances that allow it to be distinguished from other maize landraces (K. Adams et al. 2006). Some modern-day examples include large-eared blue flour maize from the Rio Grande region of New Mexico, and small-eared yellow flint maize grown in the Sonoran Desert of southern Arizona. It is assumed that maize landraces develop locally or regionally as they are grown in and adapt to a geographical/ecological location over time, and as farmers continually apply selection pressure by annually choosing kernels for planting that match their mental template of the ideal maize ear.

The problem with recognizing ancient landraces of maize is complicated by the level of normal variability potentially existing within and between landraces. A carefully controlled modern experimental grow-out of a single landrace of indigenous Southwestern U. S. maize (Tohono O'odham flour) exposed to varying moisture conditions revealed statistically significant differences in maize ear, cob, and kernel traits that correlated with irrigation and rainfall amounts and timing (K. Adams et al. 1999). Such environmental affects on morphological traits may well have operated in the past, and the variability in Chevelon Pueblo maize morphology, documented by Howell, may fall within the realm of that due to differences between and among growing seasons. In addition, until the normal variability of maize kernel and cob traits of numerous indigenous Southwestern U. S. maize landraces grown under identical environmental conditions is well documented (K. Adams et al. 2006), the normal range of variability in these traits between and among maize landraces remains unknown.

Maize Use Through time

When examining a subset of 86 flotation samples that are securely dated to a single phase of occupation, maize was grown and eaten in all time periods (Table 11.9). However, maize presence in Chevelon deposits declines in ubiquity from a high of 81.8 percent, in the Early Homol'ovi Phase (EHP), to 75 percent, in the Middle Homol'ovi Phase (MHP), and reaches a low of 56.8 percent in the Late Homol'ovi Phase (LHP). The last two phases have good sample

Table 11.9. Distribution of Evidence of Domesticates in 86 Flotation Samples of Secure Time Period.

Time period	Total Samples	Samples with *Zea*		Samples with *Cucurbita*		Samples with *Gossypium*	
	N	N	%	N	%	N	%
1	4	3	75.0	2	50.0		
2	11	9	81.8			1	9.1
3	20	15	75.0	2	10.0	1	5.0
4	51	29	56.8	4	7.8	5	9.8

Time periods: 1 = Tuwiuca, 1290-1325 C.E.; 2 = Early Homol'ovi Phase, 1325-1365 C.E.; 3 = Middle Homol'ovi Phase, 1365-1385 C.E.; 4 = Late Homol'ovi Phase, 1385-1400 C.E. All remains were charred, with the exception of a few Cucurbita specimens.

representation, so this decline suggests that growing maize became more difficult as the century of Chevelon Pueblo occupation progressed. Perhaps the temperature and precipitation requirements of maize were not being met, or the floodplain fields were exposed to increasing inundation that could damage crops and reduce productivity. Clearly, other circumstances may also have been operating that caused an overall decrease in the maize harvests and a reduction in the role of maize in subsistence from the EHP through the LHP.

This apparent decline appears to contrast with the fact that a number of rooms, including S. 123 and 158 (discussed below), were filled with maize ears that burned at the end of the Pueblo's occupation, indicating that maize was in storage for the future. Yet, the flotation record suggests that, by the LHP, maize was not being prepared as often, and accidents of preparation were not being incorporated into structure fill and midden debris as often as earlier in time. The basic question boils down to how much maize is needed to be a regularly eaten food source, with debris from preparation and left-over cobs routinely being utilized for fuel timber or discarded into fires and then into middens, and is the flotation record a good indicator of this? It is possible that all the maize in storage at Chevelon Pueblo upon abandonment represents less maize than what people desired for daily consumption, despite what appears to be an abundance. Historic records indicate that farmers aimed to have 160 kg of maize kernels in storage per person per year (Van West 1994:125) and possibly, the final maize harvests were not producing enough to satisfy the daily maize needs of all the individuals living in the Pueblo. However, this issue is equivocal, and if the flotation record is not an accurate reflection of daily maize use through time, then the LHP occupants may have had access to maize in amounts similar to earlier phases.

Other Domesicates

Other domesticates that preserved in Chevelon Pueblo flotation samples include two species of squash (*Cucurbita moschata*, *Cucurbita pepo*), along with unidentified squash seed and rind fragments, and cotton (*Gossypium*) seeds and seed fragments (Table 11.10). Archaeologists also recovered a limited number of squash seeds and seed fragments as macrobotanical specimens in two locations (habitation S. 345 and storage S. 288). Squash evidence occurs as early as the Tuwiuca Phase (TP), and in both the MHP and LHP, and cotton spans the EHP through the LHP. Although these data reveal use of these two domesticates through time, it was not nearly to the extent of reliance on maize (Table 11.9), although preparation and preservation factors may mask the role of squash in subsistence. Although there is no clear trend to decreasing or increasing use of these two crops, small sample size makes it difficult to assess change through time.

Remains of squash (*Cucurbita*) were recovered within habitations, but not within storage rooms. The preservation potential of squash in archaeological sites is low, relative to maize, so the possibility exists that this pattern is unrelated to ancient storage habits. However, squash is much more likely to decay if not cut up and dried properly, so if squash fruit were stored whole, perhaps they were kept within habitations where they could be regularly checked for signs of spoilage.

Notably missing from the extensive flotation record from Chevelon Pueblo are beans. Up to three varieties of beans are

Table 11.10. Presence of Charred and Uncharred Squash (*Cucurbita*) Seed and Rind Specimens, and Charred Cotton (*Gossypium*) Seeds in Flotation Samples from Chevelon Structures, Arranged by Time Period.

Structure	Structure Function	Time Period	Taxon	Part
300	midden beneath STR 373	1	*Cucurbita*	rind fragment
300	midden beneath STR 373	1	*Cucurbita moschata*	seed
300	midden beneath STR 373	1	*Cucurbita pepo*	seed fragment
222	piki house	2	*Gossypium*	seed
279	kiva	3	*Cucurbita*	seed fragment
345	habitation	3	*Cucurbita*	seed fragment
345	habitation	3	*Gossypium*	seed
159	habitation with ritual features	4	*Cucurbita*	rind fragment
901	kiva	4	*Cucurbita*	rind fragment
124	habitation with ritual features	4	*Cucurbita pepo*	seed
901	kiva	4	*Cucurbita pepo*	seed fragment
264	habitation	4	*Gossypium*	seed
702	storage with bin features	4	*Gossypium*	seed
901	kiva	4	*Gossypium*	seed fragment

Time periods: 1 = Tuwiuca, 1290-1325 C.E.; 2 = Early Homol'ovi Phase, 1325-1365 C.E.; 3 = Middle Homol'ovi Phase,. 1365-1385 C.E.; 4 = Late Homol'ovi Phase, 1385-1400 C.E..

present in all four of the Homol'ovi villages averaging 10 percent ubiquity. It is hard to imagine Chevelon inhabitants not growing beans, which have been a staple of Ancestral Pueblo and Hopi diet for centuries; therefore, their absence from the botanical record cannot be explained.

For these domesticated plants, the evidence at Chevelon Pueblo suggests that maize was stored in specific corn storage structures and prepared in habitations, in storage rooms with thermal features, and in at least one kiva. Squash appear to have been stored in habitations where they could be closely watched for signs of decay.

Wild Plants

Subsistence Resources

A diversity of reproductive parts of native wild plants preserved within flotation samples suggests that many local resources provided foods for inhabitants of Chevelon Pueblo during its century of use (Table 11.11). Macrobotanical samples add broad-leaf yucca (*Yucca baccata*) seeds (fill in plaza to RB 300), and a ground cherry (*Physalis*) seed fragment (midden associated with K. 279) to this list. People could have easily gathered quantities of seeds of annual plants, many of which likely grew on the nearby floodplains and in active and fallow agricultural fields. This group includes species in the Cheno-am (*Chenopodium* and/or *Amaranthus*) group, winged pigweed (*Cycloloma*), bugseed

Table 11.11. Distribution of Reproductive Parts of Wild Plants in 86 Flotation Samples of Secure Time Period. All Remains were Charred.

Taxon	Part	Time Period			
		1	2	3	4
	Flotation Sample Number	4	11	20	51
		ubiquity of taxon/part			
		%	%	%	%
Cheno-am	seed	25	54.5	10.0	9.8
Eragrostis	caryopsis	25	27.3	5.0	19.6
Cycloloma	seed	25	27.3	5.0	13.7
Opuntia (p. pear)	seed	25	18.2	15.0	11.8
Corispermum	seed	50	18.2		9.8
Portulaca	seed		36.4	5.0	2.0
Stipa hymenoides	caryopsis, floret		27.3	5.0	3.9
Scirpus	achene		9.1	10.0	7.8
Sphaeralcea	seed		9.1	5.0	2.0
Yucca baccata	seed, seed fragment		18.2		2.0
Cleome	seed		9.1		2.0
Juniperus	berry, seed			5.0	3.9
Allenrolfea	seed	25			
Rhus aromatica	fruit		18.2		
Arctostaphylos	seed		9.1		
Echinocereus	seed		9.1		
Salvia reflexa	seed		9.1		
Poaceae	caryopsis			5.0	
Atriplex canescens	fruit core				2.0
Atriplex	seed				2.0
Unknown	seed(s)				5.9
	Total Taxa	6	15	10	15

Time periods: 1 = Tuwiuca, 1290-1325 C.E.; 2 = EHP, 1325-1365 C.E.; 3 = MHP, 1365-1385 C.E.; 4 = LHP, 1385-1400 C.E..

(*Corispermum*), purslane (*Portulaca*), beeweed (*Cleome*), and chia (*Salvia reflexa*). Three of these plants are absent from the local area today, and may have succumbed to heavy historic grazing pressures (winged pigweed, bugseed), and/or possibly grew best in higher elevations (chia). Perennial plants growing in the area also provided foods, among them: lovegrass (*Eragrostis*) grains, whose appearance is so similar to dropseed grass (*Sporobolus*) that it is possible some/all are actually dropseed; prickly pear cactus (*Opuntia*) fruit; Indian rice grass (*Stipa hymenoides*) grains; bulrush (*Scirpus*) achenes; globemallow (*Sphaeralcea*) seeds; broad-leaf yucca (*Yucca baccata*) fruit; pickleweed (*Allenrolfea*) seeds; hedgehog cactus (*Echinocereus*) fruit; and saltbush

(*Atriplex*, including *Atriplex canescens*) seeds and fruit. A few additional perennials may not have grown in the immediate vicinity of the pueblo. Juniper (*Juniperus*) and lemonade berry (*Rhus aromatica*) are abundant in, and adjacent to, side canyons to Chevelon, within 4 to 6 km south of the pueblo. Manzanita (*Arctostaphylos*) is not locally available and, likely, is present as part of flood debris from higher elevations.

Many of the native plants harvested for food in the EHP were the same ones harvested in the MHP and LHP. The diversity of taxa is fairly similar across the three phases, indicating a broad knowledge and utilization of a suite of wild plants for over a century. Three rare taxa (lemonade berry, manzanita, chia), that may have required travel to uplands for harvest, are unique to the EHP, suggesting occupants of that time period either gathered non-local resources, or possibly that floods naturally carried upland species closer to the Pueblo and people took advantage of this. MHP and LHP occupants relied heavily on wild plants that could all have easily grown nearby, with the exception of juniper trees.

For most wild plants, there are no strong indications of differences in subsistence resources between habitations, storage rooms, a kiva, and the plaza (Table 11.12). When

Table 11.12. Presence of Taxa with Charred Reproductive Parts (e.g. seeds, fruit) in Undisturbed Floor or Floor Feature Contexts of Different Structure Types and a Plaza Area.

	Habitations		Storage Rooms		Kiva	Plaza
	Normal	W/ Ritual Features	Piki House	Normal		
Number of Structures	4	1	1	4	1	1
Taxon						
Atriplex				x		
Atriplex canescens				x		
Cheno-am	x		x	x		x
Cucurbita		x				
Cycloloma	x		x	x		
Eragrostis	x		x			
Gossypium	x					
Opuntia (p. pear)	x			x		
Portulaca						x
Rhus aromatica				x		
Sphaeralcea		x		x		
Stipa hymenoides	x	x				
Yucca baccata		x	x			
Zea mays	x	x	x	x	x	

Habitations are: normal (S. 161, S. 264, S. 265, and S. 268), and one with ritual features (S. 159). Storage rooms include: a piki house (S. 222) and four storage rooms with bin features (S. 120, S. 227, S. 288, S. 373). K. 279 is the kiva. S. 900 is the plaza to the RB300.

considering a limited range of structure contexts that include clearly-associated floor assemblages and hearths or other thermal features, many of the same wild foods recovered in habitations are those recovered in storage rooms, suggesting that plants, routinely prepared inside family dwellings, were often stored nearby. One habitation with ritual features preserved a slightly different subset of foods, which could be due to a smaller sample size or possibly to a different set of food-related activities that took place there. The piki house also contained a subset of food resources, all of them held in common with other structure types. Surprisingly, only maize was recovered in a kiva hearth, suggesting limited food preparation there. Finally, the plant remains preserved within Plaza 900 is the only example of *Portulaca* and is the only area without maize. This may indicate preparation of foods distinctive for ceremonies practiced in adjacent K. 901 or the limited sample size.

Non-Subsistence Resources

Chevelon Pueblo families had many needs for wood and other non-edible parts of plants (Table 11.13). Based on flotation samples, they regularly carried in cottonwood or willow wood for construction (see also Chapter 12) and for regular use as fuel and other daily needs. After kernels had been removed from maize cobs, the cobs provided a nice tinder and fuel source. Parts of locally available saltbush shrubs, privet trees, and grasses were often gathered and carried into the pueblo, as were stems and branches of greasewood, rabbitbrush, pickleweed, Mormon tea, reedgrass, and yucca leaves. A number of upland trees/shrubs were available as driftwood along both Chevelon Creek and the LCR (see Chapter 12), and occupants of the pueblo often took advantage of this circumstance. High and mid-elevation species, such as ponderosa pine, mountain mahogany, pinyon pine, oak, and manzanita, were probably regularly deposited along banks of the region's creeks and rivers, along with wood of riparian trees such as box elder and walnut. Of course, people may also have traveled to nearby upland locales for some of their specific wood needs, including cliff rose and lemonade berry. Although pinyon pine wood clearly provided Chevelon Pueblo with construction elements (Chapter 12), its low presence in other contexts suggests people considered it primarily a building material, or avoided it as fuel due to excessive smokiness caused by pine resin. The macrobotanical record essentially confirms the use of many of these woody plants, and adds Douglas fir (*Pseudotsuga*) from undisturbed fill in Plaza 900.

As with subsistence resources, many of the wood types and other plant parts useful in material culture were recovered in habitations, storage rooms, a kiva, and the plaza (Table 11.14). When considering a limited range of structure contexts that include clearly-associated floor assemblages and hearths or other thermal features, many of the same wood types recovered in habitations are those recovered in other structure types. The list of taxa is quite long, revealing a broad knowledge of many vegetative plant resources and their useful qualities for construction, fuel, tools, and other daily purposes. People utilized wood outdoors in plazas, as well as indoors. Materials recovered in undisturbed trashy fill within two corn storage rooms include evidence of grass and reedgrass stems, which possibly served as layers upon which maize ears could be stacked and/or cushioned.

Table 11.13. Distribution of Non-Reproductive Parts of Wild Plants in 86 Flotation Samples of Secure Time Period. All Remains were Charred.

		Time Period			
		1	2	3	4
	Flotation Sample Number	4	11	20	51
		ubiquity of taxon/part			
Taxon	Part	%	%	%	%
Populus/Salix	wood	100	90.9	65.0	70.6
Zea mays	cob fragment, cupule, stem fragment	75	72.7	80.0	51.0
Atriplex	twig, wood	75	27.3	45.0	43.1
Forestiera	wood	25	27.3	35.0	9.8
Poaceae	culm base, stem fragment	25	18.2	25.0	39.2
Pinus ponderosa	wood, needle fragment	25	36.4	10.0	9.8
Juniperus	leaf scale, twig, wood		63.6	85.0	64.7
Sarcobatus	wood	100		35.0	5.9
Cercocarpus	wood	50		35.0	19.6
Acer	wood	50		35.0	11.8
Chrysothamnus	wood	50		25.0	2.0
Phragmites	stem fragment		45.5	15.0	21.6
Allenrolfea/ Sarcobatus	wood		45.5	20.0	7.8
Purshia/Cowainia	wood		36.4	5.0	5.9
Rosaceae	wood	25		15.0	5.9
Juglans	wood		9.1	10.0	5.9
Quercus	wood		45.5	5.0	
Allenrolfea	wood	25			5.9
Unknown	leaf, root fragment, twig, wood			10.0	9.8
Ephedra	wood			10.0	3.9
Pinus	bark scale, wood		9.1		2.0
Monocotyledon	tissue			5.0	2.0
Yucca	leaf fragment			5.0	
Pinus edulis	wood				2.0
Rhus aromatica	wood				2.0
	Total Taxa	12	13	21	23

Time periods: 1 = Tuwiuca,. 1290-1325 C.E.; 2 = Early Homol'ovi Phase, 1325-1365 C.E.; 3 = Middle Homol'ovi Phase, 1365-1385 C.E.; 4 = Late Homol'ovi Phase, 1385-1400 C.E.

Table 11.14. Distribution of Taxa with Charred Vegetative Parts (e.g., wood, stems, leaves) in Undisturbed Floor or Floor Feature Contexts of Different Structure Types and a Plaza Area.

	Habitations		Storage Rooms		Kiva	Plaza
	Normal	W/ Ritual Features	Piki House	Normal		
Number of Structures	6	1	1	4	1	1
Taxon						
Acer	x			x		x
Allenrolfea						
Allenrolfea/Sarcobatus	x		x		x	
Atriplex	x	x	x	x	x	
Cercocarpus	x			x		
Chrysothamnus	x			x		
Compositae		x				
Ephedra		x				
Forestiera	x	x	x		x	
Juglans	x			x		
Juniperus	x	x	x	x	x	x
Monocotyledon				x		
Phragmites	x	x	x	x	x	
Poaceae	x			x	x	
Pinus	x					
Pinus ponderosa	x		x			x
Populus/Salix	x	x	x	x		x
Purshia/Cowania	x		x			
Quercus			x	x		
Rosaceae	x	x		x		
Sarcobatus				x		

Habitations are: normal (S. 161, S. 264, S. 265, and S. 268), and one with ritual features (S. 159). Storage rooms include: a piki house (S. 222) and four storage rooms with bin features (S. 120, S. 227, S. 288, S. 373). K. 279 is the kiva. S. 900 is the plaza to the RB300.

Comparison to Other Homol'ovi Settlement Cluster Assemblages

The archaeobotanical record of Chevelon Pueblo can be compared to those of four HSC villages (H1, H2, H3, and H4) farther down the LCR. Reports on archaeobotanical remains from these sites include published (K. Adams 1996, 2001; Miksicek 1991) and unpublished documents (K. Adams 1992, 1994a, 1999, 2000; Miksicek 1988). K. Adams and LaMotta (2001) then synthesized subsistence and plant use through time at these sites.

All HSC pueblos share common utilization of a wide range of wild plants for both subsistence and non-subsistence needs. All groups gathered seeds of annual plants as food, such as goosefoot, pigweed, bugseed, winged pigweed, purslane, Rocky Mountain beeweed, and others. They also harvested grass grains and cactus fruit, along with bulrush achenes, saltbush fruit, lemonade berry fruit, juniper berries, and yucca fruit. The major wood choice appears to have consistently been cottonwood and/or willow wood, along with juniper, pickleweed/greasewood, saltbush, sagebrush, and a number of non-local trees and shrubs from higher elevations, such as ponderosa pine, pinyon pine, oak, manzanita, Douglas fir, box elder, and ash. Some of their wood arrived as driftwood transported by creeks and rivers, especially during flooding (E.C. Adams and Hedberg 2002). Occupants of Chevelon Pueblo clearly utilized many of the same woods and non-subsistence resources, as did the occupants of the Homol'ovi Pueblos located down the LCR.

Maize and cotton evidence from flotation samples within thermal features at the other pueblos reveals some interesting patterns (Table 11.15). Maize use during the TP (about 1260 C.E. to about 1325 C.E.) varied among the Homol'ovi sites, ranging between 44.4 percent and 72.4 percent ubiquity within flotation samples. At Chevelon Pueblo, the presence of maize, within 75 percent of TP flotation samples, suggests an early focus on maize, similar to the other sites. In contrast, as the end of the occupation sequence approached, maize presence in flotation samples from the LHP at H2 dropped to 50 percent, quite similar to a low of 56.8 percent in the Chevelon Pueblo LHP samples. One interpretation could be that reliance on maize lessened for Puebloans as the occupation of the region came to an end. However, the presence of burned maize in numerous storage rooms at the end of Chevelon Pueblo's occupation contradicts this interpretation, and the issue remains of how many people could be fed with the stored maize, and how the quantity in storage compared with that of earlier occupations. Because none of the other pueblos were extensively burned when depopulated, it is difficult to compare the assemblages and to know if storage of maize at Chevelon was any different from its counterparts downstream.

The archaeobotanical record suggests a different story for cotton. The presence of cotton seeds and seed fragments in flotation samples climbed steadily among the Homol'ovi Pueblos, reaching a high of 33.3 percent at H2 (Table 11.15), indicative of production for exchange with other communities. In sharp contrast, the presence of cotton evidence at Chevelon Pueblo reaches only 9.8 percent by the LHP, implying cotton crops were not a major focus of farming efforts near the end of the occupation. It is possible that the floodplain surrounding Chevelon Pueblo, composed of a mixture of sediments from both Chevelon Creek and the LCR, was not the best location to raise cotton plants. If this were true, perhaps Chevelon occupants acquired cotton lint, cloth,

Table 11.15. Comparative Data on Maize (*Zea mays*) and Cotton (*Gossypium*) Remains from Four Homol'ovi Settlement Cluster Villages Farther Down the Little Colorado River.

Site	Number of samples	Ubiquity of maize (%)	Ubiquity of cotton (%)
Tuwiuca Phase (ca 1260 C.E. - ca. 1325 C.E.)			
Homol'ovi IV	18	44.4	5.6
Homol'ovi III	30	72.4	17.2
Homol'ovi II	5	60.0	20.0
Homol'ovi Phase (ca. 1325 C.E. – ca. 1400 C.E.)			
Homol'ovi IV	54	75.9	27.8
Homol'ovi III	21	90.5	28.6
Homol'ovi II	18	50.0	33.3

Note: Flotation samples represent only thermal features (hearths, ash pits, firepits, roasting pits). Data originally reported by E.C. Adams and LaMotta (2001). Sites listed in chronological order within phases.

or garments from their Homol'ovi pueblo neighbors or just grew enough for personal use rather than for exchange (E.C. Adams 2002).

A number of additional domesticates were grown at pueblos H1, H2, H3 and H4 (K. Adams 1992, 1994a, 1996, 1999, 2000, 2001; K. Adams and LaMotta 2001; Miksicek 1988, 1991). These included three species of squash (*Cucurbita moschata*, *C. pepo*, and *C. mixta*), bottle gourd (*Lagenaria siceraria*), and three species of beans including common beans (*Phaseolus vulgaris*), tepary beans (*P. acutifolius*), and lima beans (*P. lunatus*). Of this list, only limited evidence of two species of squash (*C. moschata* and *C. pepo*) has been identified at Chevelon Pueblo. As with cotton, possibly some soil or environmental factor restricted the number of crops easily grown on the floodplain adjacent to the pueblo. As noted earlier, the absence of beans at Chevelon is unique among the five villages and is likely a product of either sampling or preservation in the botanical record of Chevelon Pueblo.

SUMMARY AND CONCLUSIONS

Subsistence

During the fourteenth century, the Chevelon Pueblo occupants were farmers who successfully grew maize with pop and/or flint type kernels, and possibly with flour kernels as well. They also cultivated limited amounts of two species of squash and cotton. However, as the end of the fourteenth century approached, growing maize may have become more difficult, as maize declined in ubiquity within flotation samples associated with the final Puebloan occupation. Perhaps this decline can be attributed, in part, to the combination of extreme flood events in the early 1380s damaging farming infrastructure in the floodplain, followed by a decade-long drought in the 1390s (Van West 1996). It is clear that some maize was in storage, however, as numerous storage rooms with maize burned near the end of Pueblo occupation. As maize declined, efforts did not appear to shift to growing more cotton. The reasons for these patterns may be linked to soil characteristics or other environmental traits associated with the Chevelon.

Through time, families also gathered a broad range of wild plants from a diversity of habitats, including from the uplands. Numerous weedy annual plants that prefer disturbed habitats such as agricultural fields, trash middens, and path edges offered abundant seeds for harvest. Other perennial plants, among them grasses and cacti, provided dependable edible resources. Some of these plant species missing from the modern local area today may have succumbed to historic grazing pressures and/or other environmental shifts.

Non-Subsistence Needs

Chevelon Pueblo groups gathered a range of wood types, including cottonwood and willow trees of riparian habitats, and juniper trees and saltbush shrubs of drier terraces, for fuel and roofing. Many other locally available woody plants provided additional resources. In addition, upland trees/shrubs transported as driftwood by both Chevelon Creek and the LCR were regularly collected as both fuel and the raw materials for construction and tool making. Left-over maize cobs were abundant enough to be regularly added to fires as a tinder or fuel source.

Spatial Patterns in the Assemblage

Wild foods routinely prepared in family dwellings were also stored in storage rooms. One habitation with ritual features contained a sub-set of the long list of subsistence resources, either due to small sample size or possibly to some differences in the activities in these specialized locations. Domesticated plants display more distinct patterning. Corn storage rooms were, clearly, the locations where maize ears were kept, yet maize preparation and consumption took place in other structure types including habitations and kivas. Although corn was prepared in the piki house, other foods were as well. A range of foods were also prepared outdoors in a plaza setting, likely during the warmer months of the calendar year. Although the sample size is low, squash fruit appear to have been stored primarily within habitations, perhaps because people could watch them closely for signs of spoilage.

Temporal Patterns in the Assemblage

The diversity of wild plants gathered through time seems remarkably stable. For over a century, the Chevelon Pueblo occupants harvested and prepared many of the same foods from a range of annual and perennial plants in the vicinity of the pueblo. They also traveled to upland locales for some rarer items, especially during the EHP. Their knowledge of wild plants and animals was critical to buffering poor maize crops, especially when maize productivity was low or absent for more than one year in a row. The lowered ubiquity of maize parts in LHP contexts, near the end of the occupation, is discussed above.

Seasonality of Chevelon Pueblo Occupation

The majority of wild taxa-providing foods ripen during the summer through fall months, with the exception of late spring ripening Indian rice grass. Agricultural activities associated with field preparation, planting, field tending, harvesting, and drying of the maize crop required farmers to be in the area from at least mid-spring through mid to late fall. The fact that maize was stored in corn storage rooms suggests families also lived in the pueblo through the winter months, drawing on stored maize as needed.

Chevelon Pueblo and Other Homol'ovi Settlement Cluster Pueblos

The history of plant use at Chevelon Pueblo parallels that of other HSC pueblos. Based on presence of maize remains within flotation samples, maize was heavily relied upon for much of the century of occupation, but declined toward the end, possibly due to the environmental conditions noted above. Environmental factors such as temperature and/or precipitation, coupled with decline in productivity of fields farmed for many decades, may in part explain the increasing difficulties related to growing maize. Chevelon Pueblo had access to squash and cotton, but neither played a major role over time. It seems reasonable to assume that cotton was supplied to Chevelon Pueblo from others within the HSC or the small amount produced at Chevelon met local needs. A wide range of the same wild plants provided food and wood for daily needs for all groups living in this region.

Changes in Vegetation Between Then and Now

The archaeobotanical record of Chevelon Pueblo suggests the fourteenth century plant communities of the area were more like those described in the mid to late 1800s than those present today. Historic nineteenth century travelers report a diverse native riparian flora along rivers and their tributaries. This is unlike the modern streambanks of Chevelon Creek and the LCR, today, dominated by non-native tamarix; rather, these descriptions more accurately describe the protected upper Chevelon Creek approximately 6 km south of the pueblo. Those early travelers also recorded a heavier grass cover on low hills and terraces above the floodplains, today, occupied by a variety of shrubs resistant to grazing. For land managers interested in restoring landscapes to a former composition and appearance, the archaeobotanical and historic records together provide a multi-century perspective useful in such endeavors.

Chapter 12
Wood Use Behavior, Resource Procurements, and Construction Technologies at Chevelon

Margaret Shaw, A.J. Vonarx, and R. Emerson Howell

In many southwestern sites, tree rings provide a precise, accurate, and valuable dating method for archaeologists interested in ancestral Puebloan prehistory. However, dendroarchaeological samples must also be interpreted with regard to the environmental and behavioral contexts in which wood was harvested and used (Ahlstrom 1985; J. Dean 1988a; J. Dean et al. 1985; English et al. 2001). Although almost all wood recovered at Chevelon is not useful for chronology, good preservation provides an excellent opportunity for examining trends in wood use, construction techniques, and resource management.

Our study summarizes results from analyses of 450 archaeological wood species samples collected during the first three seasons of excavation at Chevelon Pueblo. We expect that distant tree species will be more common in later constructions (following E.C. Adams and Hedberg 2002), reflecting increased dependence on driftwood as the quality and/or quantity of local wood resources was expended. We also hypothesize that, while wood species diversity will vary by individual structure, the greatest diversity will be associated with ritual structures and large-sized rooms, as the environmentally close species of wood are ill-suited for the roofs in large rooms.

ENVIRONMENTAL CONTEXT

The LCR stretches over 400 km from its headwaters in the White Mountains to its junction with the Colorado River. While the diversity of live tree species is very low in the Homol'ovi area, a large variety of species grow upstream. Thirty kilometers to the south of Chevelon, the landscape at lower elevations is dominated by piñon (*Pinus edulis*) and juniper (*Juniperus*) forests. At the higher elevations and farther away (in some cases, 100 km away), oak (*Quercus*), Ponderosa pine (*Pinus ponderosa*), spruce (*Picea*), and Douglas fir (*Pseudotsuga menziesii*) are dominate (E.C. Adams and Hedberg 2002). We believe that much of the diversity in wood species present in the archaeological remains of Homol'ovi sites is linked directly to the prehistory of the Little Colorado, its tributaries, and episodic availability of driftwood.

METHODOLOGY

A total of 450 archaeological wood samples from Chevelon Pueblo were analyzed and identified to the highest taxonomical order possible through microscopic analysis of the exposed macroscopic cellular structure of transverse view. The varying nature of cellular structure between species found in the region allowed for rather reliable identification. If cellular structure was not well–preserved or easily viewed, we attempted to place the specimen in "conifer" or "non-conifer" categories. If identification was possible, but could not be classified, the samples were assigned "UNID." Samples were assigned "NOID" if no identification at all was possible because cell structure was not preserved sufficiently. For some pine samples, we could not distinguish between *Pinus ponderosa* and *Pinus edulis*, and assigned them to the broader category of cf. *Pinus*.

Our wood species identification utilized a variety of keys (Minnis 1987) and comparative photographs of archaeological wood samples made by K. Adams (1996). We also consulted comparative collections housed at the University of Arizona Tree-Ring Laboratory and the ASM's Borderlands Laboratory. Jeffrey Dean, Rex Adams, David Street, and Dick Warren at the Laboratory of Tree-Ring Research consulted with us on especially problematic samples.

Species Diversity at Chevelon Compared to Modern Driftwood

E.C. Adams and Hedberg (2002) suggest that episodic floods, and not people, transported distant wood species to the vicinity of Homol'ovi villages. To evaluate this possibility, the variability of archaeological wood species at Chevelon was compared to the diversity in a modern driftwood pile deposited near H1 in 1993 (Table 12.1). The comparison reveals that the amount of cottonwood in the Chevelon samples (70 percent, of total) is significantly higher than that found in the driftwood sample (21 percent, of total). In contrast, the percentage of distant tree species (Douglas fir and Ponderosa pine) at Chevelon is considerably less than from the driftwood pile. Nevertheless, given their ubiquity in driftwood, exotic timbers used for construction at Chevelon were probably harvested from driftwood in antiquity. Interestingly, environmentally near-wood species, such as oak and juniper at Chevelon, also do not match those of the driftwood pile, with juniper over-represented at Chevelon and oak under-represented. Juniper is clearly under-represented in the driftwood pile in comparison to its regional ubiquity. More than likely, the oak at Chevelon was transported by water, while the juniper could have been harvested either from the landscape of preferentially selected from driftwood.

Species Diversity Related to Structure Use and Size

As demonstrated in Table 12.2, wood species diversity varies greatly between individual rooms at Chevelon. To address additional trends, data on the assumed uses of 28 rooms at Chevelon were compiled with respect to their length, width, and internal area (Tables 12.3 and 12.4). Six types of structural uses were recognized: kiva, habitation, storage, piki house/habitation, kiva fill, and plaza feature. Room size was divided into categories of Large (>6m^2), Medium (4.0m^2 to 5.5m^2), and Small (<3.5m^2). To facilitate this discussion, only rooms with known area data were considered.

Species Diversity Versus Room Use

A comparison of the wood species diversity by room use revealed that 57 percent to 60 percent

Table 12.1. Chevelon Species vs. Modern Driftwood.

Species	Juniper	Non-conifer	Pine	Ponderosa Pine	Populus	Douglas fir	Quercus
Chevelon							
Number	38	16	32	15	260	6	3
Percent	10.3	4.3	8.6	4.1	70.3	1.6	0.8
Driftwood							
Number	1	110	13	34	54	24	22
Percent	0.4	42.6	4.0	13.2	20.9	9.3	8.5

of species present in habitation and storage rooms were cottonwood, with most other species falling into ranges of around 1 percent to 8 percent (Table 12.4 and Figure 12.1). However, juniper appears in concentrations of almost 20 percent in storage rooms, compared to only 3 percent in habitation rooms. Juniper is more resistant to insect infestation than pine or cottonwood and may have been preferred in rooms filled with maize or other foods vulnerable to insect predation. Only 49 percent of the wood present in kivas was cottonwood (Figure 12.2) and the fill above K. 279 contained no cottonwood at all (Figure 12.3). Almost half of all the samples found in the fill above K. 279 were piñon. Alternatively, 5 percent of specimens found in kivas and 13 percent found in the fill above K. 279 could be considered exotics or 'distant species' (e.g., Ponderosa pine and Douglas fir), slightly higher than site average. It should be noted that, while the distribution of species found within the piki house/habitation room (S. 222) correlated fairly well with ranges found in other habitation rooms, there was less cottonwood (only about 10 percent). Of interest is that oak, often used for fuel, was present only in the piki house/habitation room. In addition, this analysis supports one of the original stated hypotheses that ritual structures contain a wider variety of species than habitation or storage rooms.

Species Diversity Versus Room Size

Given the small number of rooms and limited samples of small and large structures, perceived differences are just as likely due to sampling, as real preferences by Chevelon inhabitants. As a result, no statistical comparisons were attempted. A comparison of the wood species diversity by room size revealed that medium-sized rooms contained higher percentages of cottonwood (56 percent) and juniper (9 percent) than large-sized rooms, which contained only 46 percent and 4 percent respectively (Table 12.3). Medium-sized rooms also exhibited a high, overall, species diversity, likely due to its larger sample size.

Species Diversity Related to Structure Roof

In the analyses above, a wood sample was attributed to a structure if it was found within the bounds of four surviving wall segments. We recognized, early on, that not all samples removed from a structure's fill were part of that structure's roof in antiquity. As one of this study's main foci is the use of different wood and plant species for construction, a subset of data from only roof deposits was compiled.

The minimum number of wood and other plant species present in each roof varies greatly (Table 12.5) Roofs with the fewest samples

Table 12.2. Wood Species Diversity by Structure.

Room	Douglas Fir	Ponderosa Pine	*Pinus* spp.	Piñon	Juniper	Cottonwood	Walnut	Oak	Non-Conifer	Atriplex	Cerc	Cac	Phragmites	Roseceae	Unidentified	No Identity	Total
120			1		4	34				2	1	1		2		1	46
158				4	10	22									2		38
222		1		4	1	11		1	2							5	25
227				1		5										2	8
248		1		2													3
260						5										1	6
264				1		11			1							1	14
265		5		2	2	32									2	8	51
266		1				3			1							4	9
268				1		21			2							1	25
269	1			2		3	1		1						1		9
274	1			4					1							2	8
276			1														1
279					1	5										1	7
280																1	1
286	3	5		5		2										2	17
287	1			1	1			1								1	5
289						1			2								3
300		2															2
345					3	9			2	1					2		17
365						1											1
373				1	5	3			2	1				2	3		17
393				3		1											4
403									1								1
465						1											1
576						1											1
603					1	4		1		1							7
702						10									1		11
704					1	1											2
900			2	2	2	14			1								21
901					1	8									7		16
902						1											1
Total	6	15	4	33	32	209	1	3	16	5	1	1	3	2	17	30	378

Table 12.3. Wood Species Diversity at Chevelon: Room Size.

Structure	Use	Douglas Fir	Ponderosa Pine	*Pinus* spp.	Piñon	Juniper	Cottonwood	Walnut	Oak	Non-Conifer	Atriplex	Cerc	Cac	Phragmites	Roseceae	Unidentified	No Identity	Total
Large																		
248	Kiva		1		2													3
279	Kiva					1	5										1	5
269	Storage/ Habitation			2		3	1		1							1		9
227	Storage				1		5										2	8
Total		1	1		5	1	13	1		1	1						1	3	27
Medium																		
264	Habitation				1		11			1							1	14
265	Habitation	1	5		2	2	32									2	8	51
268	Habitation				1		21			2							1	25
289	Habitation						1			2								3
393	Habitation				3		1											4
603	Habitation					1	4		1	1								7
274	Kiva	1			4					1							2	8
222	Piki/ Habitation		1		4	1	11		1	2							5	25
300	Plaza		2															2
345	Storage/ Habitation					3	9			2	1					2		17
120	Storage			1		4	34				2	1	1		2		1	46
158	Storage				4	10	22									2		38
286	Storage	3	5		5		2										2	17
272	Storage				1	5	3			2	1			2		3		17
702	Storage						10							1				11
Total		4	13	1	25	26	161		2	12	5	1	1	3	2	9	20	285
Small																		
403	Storage									1								1
Total		5	14	1	30	27	174	1	2	14	5	1	1	3	2	10	23	314

Table 12.4. Wood Species Diversity at Chevelon: Use.

Structure	Douglas Fir	Ponderosa Pine	*Pinus* spp.	Piñon	Juniper	Cottonwood	Walnut	Oak	Non-Conifer	Atriplex	Cerc	Cac	Phragmites	Roseceae	Unidentified	No Identity	Total
Kiva																	
248		1		2													3
279					1	5										1	7
Total		1		2	1	5										1	10
Habitation																	
264				1		11			1							1	14
265		5		2	2	32									2	8	51
268				1		21			2							1	25
289						1			2								3
393				3		1											4
603					1	4		1	1								7
Total		5		7	3	70		1	5	1					2	10	104
Storage/ Habitation																	
269	1			2		3	1		1						1		9
Storage																	
227				1		5										2	8
120			1		4	34				2	1	1		2		1	46
158				2	10	22									2		38
286	3	5		5		2										2	17
373				1	5	3			2	1			2		3	9	17
702						10							1				11
Total	3	5	1	11	19	76			2	3	1	1	3	2	5	5	137
Other																	
222		1		4	1	11		1	2							5	25
274	1			4					1							2	8
300		2															2
Total	1	3	0	8	1	11	0	1	3	0	0	0	0	0	0	7	35

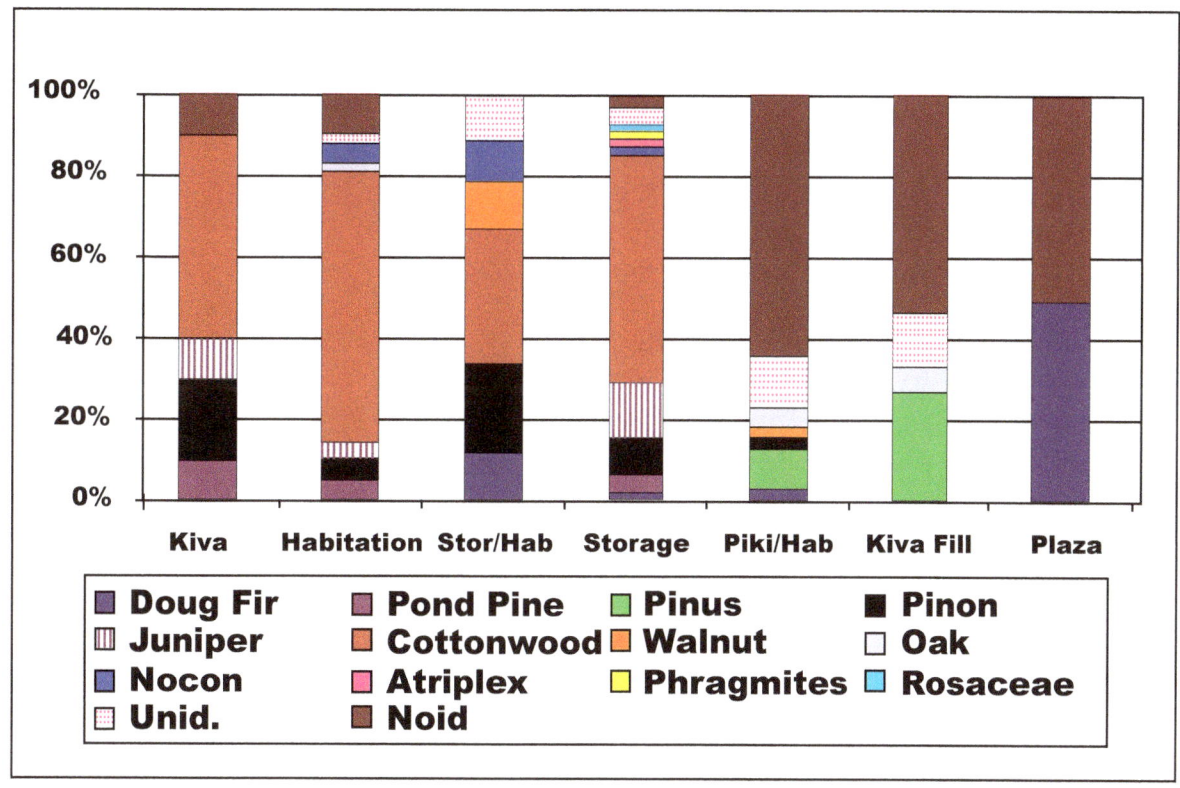

Figure 12.1. Wood species diversity at Chevelon: wood use.

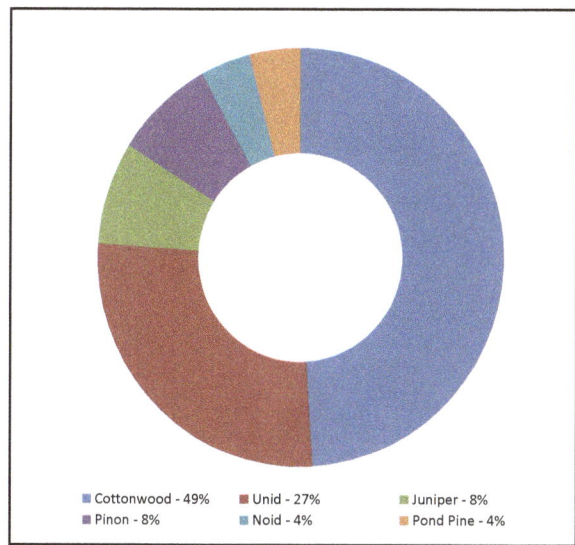

Figure 12.2. Percentage of wood species found in kivas at Chevelon.

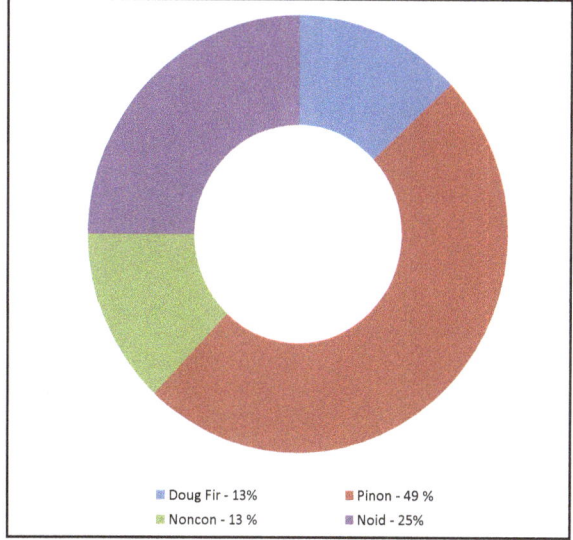

Figure 12.3. Percentage of wood species found in Structure 274 (Kiva 279 fill) at Chevelon.

typically had the least diversity with S. 120, 222, and 269 being the exceptions with high diversity relative to sample size. One well-preserved, burned roof (S. 120) hosted six different species. The fact that the most diverse rooms were from two different room blocks and three room uses suggests wood was likely being selected as much by appropriate size as species.

E.C. Adams (2002:77) noted that the largest circumference beams, or primaries, are often missing from collapsed roofing debris and may have been recycled for newer roofs. At Chevelon, samples from nine possible primary beams were recovered and identified to species (Table 12.6). All samples were heavily charred and may have exited the "recycling circuit" as a result of intense fire and beam failure. We expected that timbers of mountain species from driftwood piles would dominate the collection of primaries because many large cottonwood segments have crooks and curves greatly diminishing their load-bearing capacity. However, cottonwood primaries were represented by five of the nine beams. What cottonwood timbers lack in tensile strength, they make up for in circumference and length. In fact, the largest diameter beam discovered at Chevelon was a cottonwood primary removed from the large kiva, K. 901. As Hough (1898) mentions, cottonwood was preferred for use in kiva roofs at Hopi in the nineteenth century and ritual significance is attached to the roots, even today, in their use as katsina dolls.

Secondary beams show great species diversity, overall, and account for much of the variability in species use between rooms (Table 12.2). During an attempt to build a replica pueblo roof in 2005, one of the authors (Vonarx) noted that modern driftwood piles were richest in timbers measuring 0.8 to 1.4 m long and 5 to 9 cm in diameter. Two to three secondary timbers could be overlapped to span a room length of 2.5 m. During archaeological excavations, at least two rooms at Chevelon appeared to contain slats or natural planks of wood as part of secondary or tertiary wood layers. Natural planks of cottonwood and Ponderosa pine were discovered in driftwood piles in 2005 and lend credence to the idea that driftwood in prehistory provided and altered

Table 12.5. Roof Samples and Minimum Number of Species.

Structure	Total Roof Samples	Minimum No. of Species
120	29	6
158	33	3
222	18	5
227	4	2
248	1	1
264	11	2
265	54	4
266	9	2
268	24	2
269	9	4
274	8	2
276		
279		
280		
286	14	3
287		
289	2	1
300		
345	15	3
373	7	3
393	2	1
403		
603		
702	6	2
204		
900		
901	14	3
902		

Table 12.6. Primary Beams from Chevelon Structures.

Structure	Use	Species	Max Circ (cm)	Note
227	Storage	Populus	15	
264	Habitation	Populus	13	
268	Storage	Not Identified	12	
268	Storage	Ponderosa Pine	10	Paired Primary
268	Storage	Piñon	10	Paired Primary
269	Storage/habitation	Douglas Fir	12	
289	Habitation	Populus	12	
900	Plaza/kiva	Populus	14	
901	Kiva	Populus	24	

important construction materials useful for both secondary and tertiary beams.

Species Diversity Related to Time

At present, only the broadest view of wood use and diversity can be stated in terms of time and space. RB200 and RB300 were the first constructed at Chevelon, while RBs 100, 400, 500, 600, and 700 came later. As we cannot be sure if and when particular rooms were in use, re-roofed, or renovated, a more detailed discussion of wood use through time is inappropriate.

Figure 12.4 compares the species composition of roofs in the two early room blocks compared with roofs from the five later room blocks. There is a definite difference in the range of species used over time. In the early room blocks, at least seven species of wood were used in each roof. In the later room blocks, only two species — juniper and cottonwood — were common. This suggests that driftwood piles, with their diversity of species and sizes of wood, were used extensively in the earlier construction of rooms. When these were exhausted, Chevelon inhabitants resorted to the two locally available species of roofing size, cottonwood, and juniper. This finding might be somewhat skewed because only three rooms from later room blocks have been excavated, while a dozen structures were excavated in RB200 and RB300.

FUTURE/POTENTIAL LINES OF RESEARCH

As noted, there are numerous possibilities for examining patterns of wood use at Chevelon Pueblo, given the large data set.

While several two-story structures were excavated, preservation of individual roofs within these pairs differed significantly. In a number of two-story areas, roofs burned almost completely (preserving the beams), while many of the unburned roofs did not survive. This situation currently makes the study of species preference by structure-story impossible. How a wood beam has burned and whether or not is has been reused are also important considerations for analyses conducted on wood beam use in construction. For example, full-scale testing of fire scenarios in the summer 2005 demonstrated that a primary beam having two-thirds the width of its diameter burned may remain intact and be suitable for recycling. A

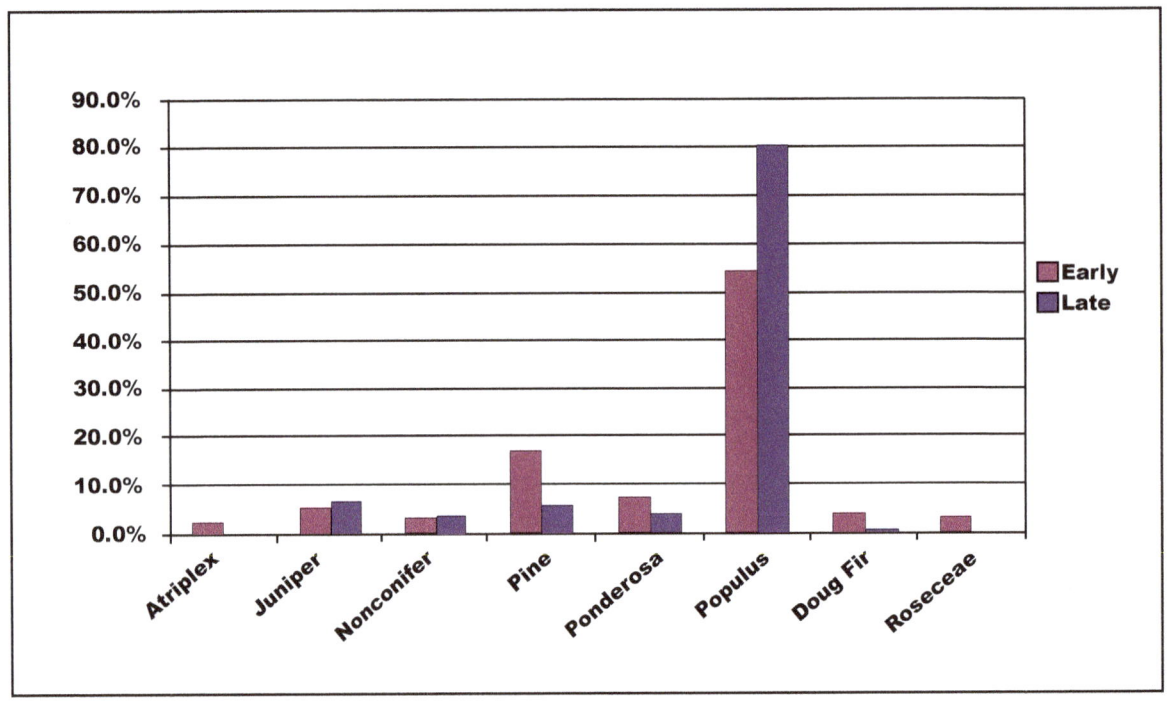

Figure 12.4. Species diversity in early and late room blocks.

comparison of material found in hearths versus that found in roofs would also be insightful and demonstrate if there was preference for fuel wood or construction wood.

There are also two distinct methods of pueblo construction present at Chevelon: adobe and stone. The difference in construction technologies leads to the natural question "Are different types or ratios of wood being used for roof construction purposes in the two distinct construction techniques?" But, as only two adobe structures have been excavated to date and only one yielded roofing beams, more data are necessary to conduct a reasonably informed analysis.

At present, we have little sense of just how quickly local cottonwood stands would have been regenerated although there is a reference in Hough's (1898) ethnobotanical study that the Hopi were planting/propagating cottonwood for use in construction and as material used for ceremonial purposes. We suggest that stand dynamics of cottonwood along nearby Chevelon Creek, within which native botanical species have not been forced to compete with invasive species, also be examined as part of future research. This information would be useful to the current study of wood behavior as well as to larger studies of estuary resource use by Chevelon villagers.

Samuels and Betancourt (1982) and Allen et al. (1998) have suggested that piñon-juniper expansion, since the late nineteenth century, may represent recovery from heavy prehistoric harvesting (Figure 12.5). These types of land-use studies could provide additional contextual frameworks within which wood species were harvested and used at Chevelon, and have the potential to add considerably to lines of evidence regarding early fourteenth century intensification of trade and kinship ties. It may also inform the abandonment of the site in the late fourteenth/early fifteenth century, due, in part, to a lack of localized, reliable wood resources that could be used for building, heating, cooking, and ceramic firing being depleted. In this sense, the concentration on cottonwood and juniper for late construction at Chevelon Pueblo is suggestive that wood resources were being depleted. Although floods can replenish wood resources, this is not indicated at Chevelon.

Conclusions

At the beginning of our analysis, we posited that a diverse number of tree species will be more common in later constructions as local resources were depleted and that the greatest diversity of species will be associated with ritual structures. Our analysis did not support our first claim as the comparison between early and late constructed room blocks demonstrated. It appears instead that Chevelon residents relied on driftwood as its principal source for construction wood until it was depleted before using local stands of cottonwood and juniper. The second hypothesis also was not supported, likely because Chevelon residents chose wood not by its species, but by its suitability for the structure needing roofing.

Our examination of wood species distribution stresses that both local timbers (cottonwood) and exotic species (as driftwood) were heavily relied upon to meet construction and fuel needs. Room size appears to be influential for which conifer species were preferentially utilized, especially in the construction of earlier large rooms. However, this may have been the exception rather than the rule. We found that locally available

Figure 12.5. 1899 (top, photographer: William Henry Jackson) and 2012 (bottom from Beyond by Ken) photos of juniper expansion between Acoma and Enchanted Mesa.

cottonwood dominated construction relative to overall room usage, which correlates with Hough's (1898) assertion that cottonwood was the material of choice among late nineteenth century Hopi. As suggested by the driftwood pile examined near H1 (E.C. Adams and Hedberg 2002), cottonwood was the dominant species in driftwood as well as populating the local floodplain. Therefore, it should not be a surprise that it is the most common species at Chevelon throughout its history.

Chapter 13
What We Have Learned
E. Charles Adams

There are many aspects of what we have learned from our research at Chevelon. In this chapter, I will present the major features of our new understanding that have the most relevance to topics of anthropological and archaeological interest within the present paradigms. Most of these topics will be constructed on the earlier foundations established within the ASM record of fieldwork and publications, reports, theses, and dissertations (E.C. Adams 1996, 2001, 2002, 2004a,b; Gann 2003; Meyers 2007; LaMotta 2006; Lange 1998; Lyons 2001; Strand 1998; Walker 1995; Young 1996).

Spatial Patterns at Chevelon

The lengthy occupation that Chevelon shares with H1 proved problematic when trying to understand how H1 developed and looked at any point in time, even with the excavation of 70 structures. The smaller size and lower population of Chevelon has provided glimpses into these processes of growth that now can be used to better understand the development of H1. The earliest room blocks at Chevelon, RB200 and RB300, although they continued to be used throughout the occupation of the village, nevertheless were able to maintain much of their original character and remained physically separate from each other. Such was not the case at H1 where massive remodeling obscured, not only the Tuwiuca Phase (TP) settlement, but also much of the Early Homol'ovi Phase (EHP) and Middle Homol'ovi Phase (MHP) manifestations. Being able to recover not only intact deposits from these earlier phases at Chevelon, but also rooms that were either built, used, or remodeled during all of these phases has been critical to reconstructing how the village looked, how large it was, and how power was constituted in its layout and location.

The singular spatial patterns identified at Chevelon that seem to predominate in the HSC and other contemporary villages in the region are:

1. Initial construction involving multiple groups each building a linear set of rooms using ladder construction on the highest point of a geographic prominence surrounding a small plaza.

2. Expansion that results in an agglomerated grouping of rooms that cover and reduce the open space as new construction is added to existing rooms.

3. The addition of separate blocks of rooms near, but separate from the original rooms and room block. These also use ladder construction to create a room block plan that includes a small plaza space. The number of these will vary by village. These early additions seem to be built mostly by immigrants from the same area as the founder settlers, a process Anthony (1990) refers to as migration streams.

4. At some point later in the life of the village, open space becomes the priority. This space

will be variable in size, but become the largest space in the village. It is created by construction of multiple room blocks to surround the space creating a plaza. This shift in spatial priorities comes with a reorganization of the village, but not a replacement of the social order. At Chevelon this construction and reorganization is accompanied by immigration of substantial numbers of households or possibly larger social groupings. In the HSC, including Chevelon, this innovation is associated with the arrival of katsina rituals and ceremonies, but likely involved other forms of sodality type social institutions consecrated through control of religious rituals.

Temporal Patterns at Chevelon

The successful application of the Jeddito Yellow Ware Index (%JYW) (E.C. Adams 2001, 2002; LaMotta 2006) to Chevelon has allowed detailed understanding of the chronological relationships of rooms and room blocks to each other and of Chevelon to other members of the cluster. As a result, the ability to divide the Chevelon occupation into four time periods of variable length using attributes of Jeddito Yellow Ware (JYW) and the appearance and frequency of ceramics exchanged to Chevelon, has made dating of Chevelon the most precise yet within the HSC.

Somewhat surprisingly, Cutright-Smith and Barker (Chapter 6) determined that the relationship of %JYW to various exchanged types, used by LaMotta to relatively date his deposits, fit almost exactly at Chevelon. For example, Sikyatki Polychrome appears at Chevelon when %JYW is at 72 percent while it appears at H1 and H2 at 60 percent. The ability to correctly seriate over 95 percent of deposits in these three villages using ceramic percentages has allowed detailed understanding of change and continuity at Chevelon and within the HSC. It has provided the added advantage of recognizing "out-of-phase" deposits that upon more detailed investigation usually reveal a different formation process was involved, such as inclusion of one or more broken whole or partial decorated vessels.

Chevelon Social History

Here the highlights of this history and its implications for not only Chevelon and other HSC villages, but also contemporary villages in the region will be presented. This will be managed in an effort to avoid recapitulating the detailed history of the village described in Chapter 4.

Founders

The three groups who established Chevelon migrated from the Hopi Mesas about 1290 based on ceramics found in the earliest midden beneath RB300 and from the decorative and technological canons with which the pottery was manufactured, as outlined by Lyons (2001, 2003). As noted previously, these groups settled on the three edges of the triangular or D-shaped hill that was the highest point, creating a small plaza within which they built two small kivas. Entry to this plaza was restricted to a small opening on the north side facing the LCR. The resulting exclusiveness of access into RB200 has been interpreted as a means for the most powerful groups at Chevelon to restrict access to rituals and, possibly, performances within the plaza and kivas to other community members as the village grew. When, after 50 or more years, both kivas were closed and began to be filled, a small third kiva was crafted from one of the original rooms in the room block presumably to provide continuity to these ritual practices.

All original growth at Chevelon occurred within the confines of RB200. Rooms were added to both the interior and the exterior. The interior additions covered portions of the original plaza and in fact divided it into two small courtyard spaces each focused on a kiva. The exterior additions were mostly along the south and west edges. In addition, second story rooms were added to many originally single-story rooms, such as the adobe brick structure added as a second story to S. 227. The scope of this growth, probably more than doubling the original size of the three small spinal room blocks, was too great to be due to natural growth alone and must have involved additional immigrants. Their incorporation into RB200 suggests they were socially related to the founders.

First Expansion

The first major expansion of Chevelon occurred about 1300 when RB300 was begun. The groups who designed RB300 appear to have also migrated from the Hopi area based on similarities in ceramics, kiva design, and planning of space. This expansion, still before the arrival of JYW, about 1325 to 1330, is associated with the first appearance of adobe bricks. Adobes are the result either of groups arriving with the technological know-how to build rooms using adobe bricks or diffusion of this knowledge from the upper Little Colorado River (ULCR) area, where it is much earlier (Gann 1996a, 1996b). As discussed in Chapter 4, the widespread use of this technology in the region, including at H1 and H3, and later at Fourmile Pueblo, suggests the use of adobe bricks is more likely the result of the spread of the technology rather than groups who insisted on using it for their dwellings. This argument is supported by the persistent presence of White Mountain Red Ware (WMRW), primarily Fourmile Polychrome, and rare occurrences of Pinto Polychrome and later Gila and Tonto polychromes that suggest contact with groups from the Puerco Valley (Petrified Forest National Park) to Silver Creek. However, no local manufacture of these ceramic technologies has been detected in TP or EHP deposits when RB200 and RB300 were established and grew.

Although the footprint of both RB200 and 300 expanded, RB300 eventually grew to be the largest room block in Chevelon with approximately 150 rooms during the EHP. As with RB200, the opening to the RB300 plaza (RB900) was to the north facing the LCR and restricted access to its interior. Although excavations in RB300 were limited, compared to RB200 and 100, extensive excavation in the large kiva, 901, provides a material perspective on the residents of the area. The differences and similarities between K. 901, 248, and 279 are instructive.

1. At 42 sq m, K. 901 is more than double the area of the combined K. 248 and 279.

2. K. 901 was in use to 1375-85, whereas K. 248's use stopped between 1335-40 and K. 279, between 1345-50.

3. The roof of K. 248 was burned when use discontinued. The roof to K. 901 was also burned soon after use discontinued, but was burned a second time a decade or more later.

4. Ceremonial trash (Walker 1995, 1996a), characterized by enriched artifact assemblages having articulated animals, rare/unusual artifacts, and infusions or cappings of ash (E.C. Adams and LaMotta 2006), was used only as initial fill in K. 901 to cover the central floor features and bench. In contrast, K. 248 and 279 were continuously filled with ceremonial trash.

a. K. 901 ceremonial trash had numerous articulated segments to animals, in particular artiodactyls, especially bighorn sheep, and ravens. It was also filled with ground stone, an axe, and ceramic vessels with eccentric shapes. *Conus* shell tinklers and a fossil were present, although projectile points were relatively scarce (see Table 13.1). Finally, the ceremonial trash deposit was capped with a thick layer of ash (E.C. Adams and Fladd 2014). The kiva was later used for numerous massive dumps of domestic trash that probably accumulated over many years.

b. K. 248 and 279 had dozens of individual ash dumps and numerous ash layers extending from top to bottom of the structures' space (E.C. Adams and Fladd 2014). Whole vessels, articulated animals, especially birds and rabbits, dozens of projectile points (many pre-Chevelon in age), axes, fossils, and many miniature pots and ladles were also present. Although artiodactyls were present, they were mostly mule deer and more dispersed through the fill of the kivas. No domestic trash was deposited in either kiva.

The differences in intensity, duration, and details of ceremonial trash deposition between K. 901 and the RB200 kivas represent not only different histories of use, but different perspectives on what can and cannot be discarded into a kiva after its systemic use-life is terminated. In K. 901, the occupants of RB300 (and possibly RB100) buried the kiva's floor features and bench with material containing large quantities of bighorn sheep, raven wings, and other objects that were significant actors in rituals performed by users of the kiva (Figure 4.11). When this rapid accumulation of material was completed, it was capped with a thick layer of ash to close the ceremonial history of this kiva. It was then available for non-religious uses, especially disposal of routine domestic trash filled with disarticulated rabbit bone, charcoal, sherds, and flaked stone. The contrast in the types of artifacts within the two categories of deposits could not be starker.

In contrast for the occupants of RB200, the systemic use-life of the kiva and the religious power with which it imbued its users

Table 13.1. Chevelon Structures with Five or More Unusual/Rare Artifacts Frequently Found in Ritual Structures or Enriched Deposits in Other HSC Villages.

Structure	Phase	Bead	Fossil	Worked Stone – ornamental	Axe	Limonite	Hematite	Crystal	Tabular Petrified Wood	Total
222	EHP	1		1	1	1			2	6
227	EHP	1						1	4	6
248	EHP	2	1	1		1		1	4	10
279	EHP-MHP	1	2	4	1			3	26	37
286	LHP				1	1	2	1	1	2	8
900	LHP				1	1		2	1	27	32
901	LHP	1	1		1				32	35
Total		6	4	8	5	4	3	7	97	134

and performers was continued throughout its filling until it was literally level with the ground (Figure 13.1). The restricted filling of the kivas is in keeping with the view here that RB200 kept its ceremonies tightly controlled in terms of who owned the knowledge and who could participate. In keeping with this, to continue to control this knowledge, the religious objects owned by the group or groups in RB200 could only be discarded within space they could control. A corollary to this behavior could be, as at Hopi today, that objects used in some of the rituals performed in such spaces in fact were so powerful that in the wrong hands, they could hurt or even kill the individual. Therefore, the belief in the power of these sacred spaces and related objects could be protected and even enhanced not only during its active use, but even after the end of its active use-life.

Figure 13.1. Profile of Kiva 279 showing numerous ash dumps.

Second Expansion

The second major expansion of Chevelon occurred between 1360 and 1375 when the south plaza was formed by the construction of major spinal room blocks on three of its sides with a fourth, smaller set of spinal rooms and a kiva separating the south plaza from the earlier and informal RB800 plaza. This expansion did not necessarily involve members of the existing room blocks, but was certainly controlled by them. It could very well be that groups performing or controlling the knowledge of katsina rituals were invited to join the existing Chevelon residents. It is also possible, but deemed less likely, that construction of these room blocks and the south plaza was a prerequisite to the katsina religion even being allowed to be performed or introduced to a community. As I have argued elsewhere (E.C. Adams 2002, 2004a), the archaeological record at H2 speaks loudly to its having katsina ceremonies and its members probably introduced them to the existing members of the HSC, which would have been H1, Chevelon, and probably Jackrabbit and Cottonwood Creek. However, this distinctive Hopi-style katsina ritual could have been preceded by the introduction of an older katsina religion to Chevelon from groups south who manufactured Fourmile Polychrome and various Salado polychromes (E.C. Adams 1991a; Crown 1994).

The south plaza provided a counterbalance to the exclusionary ceremonies that apparently were being performed at Chevelon up to the time of its construction. Conceivably, the groups that occupied the two principal room blocks each conducted their own ceremonies creating physical barriers to the participation of members from the other group. Given this situation, what would have prompted the village leaders to promote or support construction of a large plaza surrounded by rooms presumably containing at least some new residents? The explanation is probably one or more of the following:

1. The competition between the existing room block groups was threatening the continuity of the village and the plaza space provided the facilities to promote mutual cooperation, perhaps in a new ceremony or ceremonies.

2. The new room blocks were constructed by new immigrants who brought with them religious practices that promoted continuity of the village.

3. The new immigrants provided much needed labor and/or marriage partners to the community.

How many people are we talking about? The limited excavations in these room blocks recovered estimates of the size of three households, one in RB500 and two in RB100. These households have minimally 4, 8, and 4 rooms, but could easily be 8, 8, and 8 rooms. Given the available data, average number of rooms per household is minimally 5.33. With 137 ground floor rooms and evidence for a few second story rooms, 160 rooms would accommodate 30 households. A minimum population of 150 is reasonable, using Hopi censuses between 1890 and 1940 that indicate 5 to 6 individuals per household (Levy 1992; Titiev 1944). Given the probable rapid construction and contemporary use of these rooms, 150 people is a viable estimate.

So, who were the new immigrants? The continuity in ceramic types used and architectural technology indicate possible sources of the population surrounding the south plaza were other members of the HSC or groups from Hopi Mesa villages, perhaps the same sources of population for the first two migrations. However, all villages in the HSC that were still occupied also constructed large plazas surrounded by room blocks. Homol'ovi Research Program (HRP) excavations suggest they too were expanding rather than contracting or emigrating to the larger villages, including Chevelon at this time. They would have been competing for immigrants from within the cluster and outside it. Physical proximity and prior social relationships with members of Jackrabbit and Cottonwood Creek pueblos, along with their depopulation between 1350 and 1385, make them prime candidates for new community members at Chevelon toward the end of the MHP or beginning of the Late Homol'ovi Phase (LHP).

However, there is another explanation for who built the south plaza room blocks and why. This population source is the individuals living in RB200 and 300. As noted, K. 248 and 279 were both discontinued in the EHP and use of K. 901 discontinued about 1375, during the MHP. In the only area where excavation provides ample evidence, it appears that many of the rooms facing K. 279 continued use past the end of the use-life of the kiva, which ended about 1345-50 with the construction of K. 252, extending use to the LHP, or past 1385. Many of the rooms in the interior of RB200, such as S. 265 and 268 room suites, were not in use when their upper story rooms were burned. Their floors were devoid of artifacts or had shallow trash deposits. %JYW in this trash indicates these middens date to the LHP, meaning their used ended after 1385, but, prior to depopulation of the entire village, before 1400.

Excavations suggest burned rooms were in use or roofed at the time of the fire, indicating which areas of Chevelon were still occupied at 1390 to 1400. The most extensive burning occurs in the room blocks surrounding the south plaza plus rooms along the south and west of RB200. With the exception of K. 901, there appears to be less burning in RB300 and the remainder of RB200 also is less burned or burning involves structures no longer in use.

Could this all be evidence that RB200 and RB300 were much reduced in population at the time the large plaza and surrounding room blocks were built? The estimated population of 150 people for RB200, 300, and the northern suites of RB100 is identical to the estimate for the newly constructed rooms.

Therefore, the most parsimonious explanation for who initiated construction in the south plaza room blocks and subsequent occupation seems to be members of RB200 and 300. Many of the structures in these room blocks were already quite old at 50 or so years, when the south plaza expansion occurred. This may be why the roofing materials in many of these rooms were not recycled in the later rooms. If a majority of the construction and occupation was by Chevelon occupants, it is easier to accommodate migration by fewer outside individuals into Chevelon following its second expansion. These groups could have come from Cottonwood Creek and Jackrabbit pueblos, both depopulated before Chevelon, and groups producing Tonto Polychrome using their own recipes applied to local clays. These other likely sources for the population who occupied the south plaza room blocks will be discussed in the following section.

Why would the occupants or RB200 and 300 construct the large spinal room blocks that created the south plaza?

1. One possibility is competitive emulation. If other villages were constructing these large attached plazas, then to remain competitive in attracting new populations or retaining existing populations, leadership must provide a quality of life comparable to its neighbors. These plaza spaces were new community spaces that were less exclusionary to village residents, especially newcomers.

2. A second possibility related to the first is that large plaza spaces were viewed as essential religious architecture for the performance of community ceremonies by contemporary communities across the Pueblo Southwest (E.C. Adams and Duff 2004a), including katsina ceremonies, which were being performed at H2 and in Hopi Mesa villages at the time.

3. Related to the first two is the desire of village leaders to remain in control or to maintain social power and religious authority within their communities. In order to do so, change was sometimes necessary. This change could be controlled by the religious hierarchy through the construction of the large south plaza and occupation of structures in positions of power, such as those fronting the plaza in RB100.

There is no indication that RB200 and 300 were ever completely depopulated; however, many parts of these older segments of Chevelon were either no longer used or used only sporadically in the later years of Chevelon's occupation. The continuity of filling of K. 248 and later, K. 279, even after its roof collapsed, and the fact that rooms surrounding K. 279 had their doorways sealed and many had their floors partly covered with trash, indicates RB200 was still an important sacred space, even if sparsely occupied. Much like modern Walpi with more than 200 rooms, which today is occupied by fewer than five families, all with vital religious responsibilities, the older parts of Chevelon evoked the physical connection to and memory of Chevelon's roots and its religious heritage. The rooms that are believed to still be occupied in RB200 to the end of its occupation face south toward Plaza 800 and the south plaza. These rooms have floor assemblages, burned roofs, and burned corn, hallmarks of rooms used to the end in RBs 100, 500, and 700.

MIGRATION AND CHEVELON'S ROLE IN THE HOMOL'OVI SETTLEMENT CLUSTER

Migration is a central theme in the creation and growth of the HSC and so it is with Chevelon. There are three major growth periods in the history of the pueblo that exceed anything that could be produced through natural growth. These are the founding of the village (RB200) around 1290 and its growth over the next 10 years. The founding of RB300 and its in-filling from about 1300 to 1350, and the expansion using spinal room blocks to create the south plaza sometime between 1360 and 1375. The initial founding and early growth of RB200 totaled perhaps 75 rooms and 15 families. RB300 may have involved as many as 25 families using 125 rooms at its maximum. As just noted, the combined room blocks around the south plaza total another 150 rooms and perhaps 30 families.

The founders of Homol'ovi originated from Hopi Mesa villages with INAA evidence on JYW suggesting they may have come from Antelope Mesa villages (Bernardini 2005). Certainly, with seven villages that were occupied in the late 1200s on Antelope Mesa (E.C. Adams et al. 2004; Bernardini 2005), it was easily the most populous of the four Hopi mesas and the most logical to be able to afford to shed population to settle the various HSC villages, including Chevelon. The ubiquitous Winslow Orange Ware (WOW) decorated pottery is technologically and stylistically indistinguishable from its Hopi Mesa counterparts of Jeddito Black-on-orange and related types and wares as described by Lyons (2003), which comprised the Hopi pottery tradition of the 1275 to 1325 period.

WOW comprises 10.8 percent of total ceramics at Chevelon (Table 6.1). Similarity in kiva and room architecture and layout also reinforce the Hopi mesas as the source of Chevelon's initial occupation (E.C. Adams 2013a; Smith 1971).

Nevertheless, there is evidence from the outset of connections to the Silver Creek and ULCR areas through possibly locally-produced Pinto Polychrome in the RB200 midden beneath RB300 and Mogollon Brown Ware in pre-yellow ware deposits in RB200, indicating some residents were probably from the south as well. These southern migrants may have been among the first wave of settlers who augmented the initial RB200 construction by the social groups who built the three spinal room blocks that defined its initial configuration.

I have argued that the initial migration to settle the Homol'ovi portion of the LCR valley was for Hopi Mesa communities to lay claim to this area during a period of considerable population movement and migration associated with the emptying of the regions around the modern Four Corners area beginning in the 1260s and climaxing about 1285 (E.C. Adams 2002; E.C. Adams and Duff 2004a; Kohler et al. 2010; Varien et al. 2007). The eventual spread of five villages over a distance of 32 km along the LCR where water flow is certain, the floodplain is wide, and riparian habitats had been exploited for generations fit well into this model. In this context, Chevelon is strategically located to not only take advantage of these resources, but to effectively control them as well by being stationed at the headwaters to a permanent flow of water into the LCR from Chevelon Creek. If we accept this model, then it makes sense that all of the villages would come from the same cluster of settlements in the Hopi region, those on Antelope Mesa.

Only more detailed analyses of the material record of both regions will shed light on who these groups might have been. Certainly, it seems likely that the founders of H4 were also the founders of H1 who also absorbed the residents of the small community of H3 by 1300 to 1305 (E.C. Adams 2001). Chevelon also was growing during this period, but it is not clear that either Cottonwood Creek or Jackrabbit were as well. Surface collections and mapping of Cottonwood Creek and limited excavations at Jackrabbit by New Mexico State University suggest neither village was large in the early 1300s and, in fact, Jackrabbit may not even have been inhabited from 1325 to 1375.

The first major expansion of Chevelon occurred during this period of consolidation in the rest of the HSC. It is possible, but not presently provable, that RB300 was founded not by new migrants from the Hopi area, but from residents in the HSC leaving other communities, in particular Jackrabbit. Without access to a permanent flow of water (see Figure 2.1) Jackrabbit's inhabitants were at a competitive disadvantage to Chevelon. The apparently strong leadership at Chevelon might also have attracted Jackrabbit's and even Cottonwood Creek's residents. Based on INAA data discussed below, it is likely that social relationships between the three villages took place during the first decade or two after their founding and these relationships might have even existed at the Hopi mesas, prior to their migration along the LCR (but see Bernardini 2005).

Although only 40 JYW sherds were sampled as to locus of production using INAA by Bernardini (2005: Table 5.7) from each of the six HSC villages occupied after yellow ware was introduced, the results are intriguing for the present discussion. Chevelon, Jackrabbit, and Cottonwood Creek each have strong associations with Awat'ovi and Kawayka'a, with Jackrabbit and Chevelon having 31 to 41 percent from the Awat'ovi reference group and Cottonwood Creek with 25 percent, but having 42 percent from the Kawayka'a reference group, with the other two having 22 to 24 percent. In contrast, H1 and H2 each have over 50 percent referenced to Awat'ovi, lower percentages from Kawayka'a and substantial percentages from Second Mesa reference groups, which are absent at Cottonwood Creek and Chevelon and account for only 7 percent at Jackrabbit. Statistically, there is strong evidence that groups from either Jackrabbit or Cottonwood Creek were likely affiliated with the same communities on Antelope Mesa and that these relationships stem from their founding populations. Therefore, groups from either or both Cottonwood Creek and Jackrabbit could have contributed to Chevelon's growth either during the RB300 expansion or the following south plaza room block expansion.

The last migrant groups to join Chevelon have left substantial evidence in the form of local variants of Tonto Polychrome and other varieties of Roosevelt Red Ware (RRW), as previously described. Some RRW at Chevelon has light paste identical to WMRW, which is manufactured only in the Silver Creek area (Duff 2002; Triadan 1997). RRW, with light paste identical to that recovered from Chevelon, was recovered from a room block using form-molded bricks at Fourmile Ruin near the end of its occupation, which ended about 1385 (D. A. Johnson 1992). Duff (2002:154) also reports Gila and Tonto polychromes were manufactured at Table Rock pueblo on the ULCR. The manufacture of RRW (Salado Polychromes) was also present before 1325 at Bailey Ruin (Mills et al. 1999), a potential source for people who produced the Pinto Polychrome found in the RB200 midden. Finally, Crown and Bishop (1991) sourced RRW recovered from H2 to the Silver

Creek area. The Tonto Basin and numerous communities in the Arizona Mountains (Triadan and Zedeño 2004) are other loci of production for RRW during this period, but the lack of a history of contact along with paste color and INAA data suggest the likely source of the migrants making this pottery lies in the Silver Creek or, possibly, ULCR areas.

Another population source for Chevelon could be Puerco Valley communities, which were centrally located between Silver Creek and Chevelon. Ceramics from Wallace Tank and Stone Axe include JYW, WMRW, and RRW and locally produced WOW and Homol'ovi Utility Ware (HUW). These shared ceramic traditions suggest enduring relationships between the two areas. Using INAA, Barker (2017) has sourced HUW at Chevelon as coming from villages in the Puerco Valley. In addition, these groups had ready access to petrified wood (see Chapter 8). The high frequency of petrified wood in the four sampled RB100 rooms and in K. 901 may point to some migrants to Chevelon having their homes in communities occupying Puerco Valley. Local production of RRW in Puerco Valley, however, has not yet been documented.

Puerco Valley Utility Ware is also present at Chevelon throughout its occupation with some of it locally produced as HUW (Barker 2017). The groups most likely manufacturing this utility ware occupied the pueblos in the Puerco River valley. Finally, the earliest documented manufacture of adobe bricks in the LCR valley was in small Pueblo III communities in the ULCR valley who manufactured Cibola White and Gray wares (Westfall 19820; D.A. Johnson 1992). Stone Axe pueblo is constructed almost entirely of form-molded adobes. The presence of adobe bricks in RB200 and 300 no later than EHP also supports contact and immigration from the ULCR/Puerco Valley area.

EXPLOITATION OF PLANT AND ANIMAL RESOURCES

The chapters by Karen Adams; Margaret Shaw, A.J. Vonarx and Ryan Howell; and Rachel Diaz de Valdes suggest that generally local resources were used for subsistence, architectural, fuel, and ritual needs. A wide range of local native plants and animals were relied upon for subsistence. The combination of wild plants and animals augmented the basic reliance on maize agriculture.

What is distinctive about the Chevelon ethnobotanical record versus other excavated members of the HSC is the evidence of maize storage, the relative lack of cotton agriculture, and the strong evidence of room use left in the botanical record. The record of maize is covered in detail by Karen Adams; however, what is intriguing about the Chevelon record of maize is that a dozen or more burned corn storage rooms were documented from surface evidence with details of their contents provided by excavations in two of them. Evidence of their location across the village is easily detected because so many have been disturbed by vandalism, which leaves abundant remains of burned corn kernels and cobs on the surface. Careful mapping of these locations indicates they are concentrated in the room blocks surrounding the south plaza and along the south and west edge of RB200.

My interpretation of this evidence is that all were burned in a single event associated with the depopulation of Chevelon as the occupants moved (back in most cases) to Hopi Mesa villages. Attempts to map these storage rooms using a magnetometer, which tends to reveal areas of burning from the resultant magnetic anomalies, proved unproductive. This seemed to be a result of the high remanent magnetism from the iron-rich soils of the area, which made it difficult to distinguish fire-caused magnetic properties from background noise. The surface evidence of burning provides the best record.

The two sampled burned corn storage rooms, S. 123 and 158, preserved an almost complete record of the contents of these rooms (Figure 4.15). What was lost was due to heating to the point of converting some of the contents to ash, not because of incomplete combustion. The two storage rooms suggest that their only storage use was for maize. No other plants, except grasses and reeds, are present, and Karen Adams interprets these as probably related to augmenting the storage of the corn or possibly remnants from the burned roof, rather than as also being stored. In contrast, storage and habitation rooms on each side of the corn storage rooms revealed remains of wide varieties of plants stored or consumed. These include domestic plants, such as various squashes, as well as a diversity of wild plants. Also, in both cases, the corn storage was adjacent to the habitation rooms, in the middle of room suites, that limited access by others and facilitated access and monitoring by the inhabitants.

The strong record of burning and preservation at Chevelon versus other HSC villages, yet the relatively weak record of cotton, indicates it was simply not grown to the extent it was at H1, H2, and even H3 (Table 11.15). As discussed earlier, this could be related to there being less landscape diversity and fewer options for upland farming around Chevelon than with the other villages thus forcing groups from Chevelon to use the floodplain for maize farming, rather than the uplands as was the case for H1 and H2 (E.C. Adams 2002). The 10 percent ubiquity of cotton from flotation samples also can be interpreted as adequate for local consumption with no exchange. It could also relate to Chevelon having other items available for exchange, including riparian plants and animals, versus the other HSC communities, and these were used to acquire the cotton needed for the village's needs.

Architectural and fuel needs were met, as elsewhere in the HSC (E.C. Adams and Hedberg 2002), through reliance on driftwood, although Chevelon differs from the other settlements in continuing strong reliance on cottonwood for roofing, in fact increasing in intensity in the later room blocks. The greater diversity of wood species in earlier construction seems related to construction of kivas, which required larger timbers that could be best met by large driftwood species of fir and pine, and the availability of a large supply of driftwood. As found elsewhere in the HSC, kivas have the most diversity in wood species attributable both to their larger size and their special use.

The later reliance on cottonwood and juniper in construction may indicate the driftwood resources were exhausted and local materials were sought. E.C. Adams and Hedberg (2002) note the lack of tree-ring dates from driftwood after the early 1300s, which they cite as evidence for the absence of later floods in the area. Cottonwood would be available on the LCR floodplain and small stands of juniper occur within 5 km south of Chevelon with substantial stands 10 to 15 km south. Additionally, the rapid and large-scale construction needed for the south plaza room blocks would have required extensive wood resources that could probably only be met by harvesting locally available species complemented with occasional pieces of driftwood or wood recycled from earlier structures in RB200 and 300.

Among animals only the bighorn sheep would have to be collected a long distance from Chevelon. The historic distribution of the desert bighorn sheep brings it no closer than the Grand Canyon, which is more than 175 km northwest of Chevelon. The fact that it is the most abundant of the three artiodactyl species with the other two (mule deer and pronghorn antelope) locally available, indicates considerable effort went into its acquisition. It is also common at H1, where LaMotta (2006) suggests its importance may relate to the origins of some of the H1 populations from the Kayenta Anasazi region near the Utah/Arizona border, where desert bighorn were locally available, heavily hunted, and apparently important to prestige within the local communities (Chapter 9). According to LaMotta (2006), the presence of desert bighorn in localized portions of H1, including male skulls with horns, would make its acquisition a priority for such immigrant populations.

Although desert bighorn is concentrated in K. 901 with several articulated pieces on the bench within the initial trash cone enriched with ceremonial trash, it also occurs in K. 279 with several pieces in S. 289 and 269, both storage rooms between K. 248 and 279, S. 345, which also had an articulated golden eagle talon and blue bird skull, and several in the fill of S. 120. The concentration in RB200 and 300 support LaMotta's expectation that desert bighorn sheep might be associated with the early groups in the HSC originating or descendent from Kayenta "Anasazi." The concentration in S. 120 is associated with an enriched deposit that will be treated below. However, in the previous discussion on migration and the history of the village, a connection between the earlier room blocks and construction of the south plaza room blocks was made and use of bighorn sheep could indicate such a relationship. In this context, desert bighorn sheep present an excellent example of the importance of evoking social memory in ceremonial performances; in this case, harkening back to ancestors who migrated long ago to the Hopi mesas and later to H1 and Chevelon. Given the association of makers of RRW with descendent Kayenta groups (Clark 2001; Lyons 2003) and recovery of Tonto Polychrome vessels from S. 120 and elsewhere around Plaza 000, deposition of bighorn sheep in K. 901 and S. 120 may be linked to arrival in Chevelon of direct descendents of ancient Kayenta groups. Maintaining such linkages to a distant past and distant land are viewed as products of diasporic behavior linked to the Kayenta (Lyons 2013).

WEALTH, RITUAL, POWER, AND SOCIAL MEMORY

A fair amount of space in Chapter 4 was devoted to discussions of ritual deposits, wealth, power, and social memory. These will be revisited with a fuller array of material culture to consider. As discussed above and in Chapter 4, there are strong patterns of use and deposition in the oldest parts of the village and in the ritual structures within these parts. Here, we shall explore the spatial, temporal, and material patterns throughout the village to underscore the strength of the patterns within Chevelon that point to ritual practices as the primary component of deposition on floors not only within Chevelon, but probably also in much of the archaeological record of the Pueblo Southwest.

First, some definitions are needed. According to E.C. Adams and LaMotta (2006:59), enriched deposits have "a higher frequency of complete objects, exotic goods, or nonsubsistence fauna than domestic secondary trash." They go on to note that "Some enriched deposits represent sacrificial or offertory deposits of fauna or artifacts. Others consist of residues from the making of ceremonial paraphernalia or no longer usable ritual items. Still others are probably residues from ceremonial support activities such as feasts" (2006:59). Examples cited include canid and raptor skeletons, ceremonial trash (Walker 1996b), pigment-grinding residues, dense ash deposits from hearths (E.C. Adams and Fladd 2014; Miljour 2016), fetishes, fossils, bighorn sheep, and so forth.

Mills (2004:238-39) describes the source of prestige in the Pueblo Southwest as ritual and ideology. She uses the concept of inalienable objects, which "are used to construct social identities and communicate differences between individuals and groups" (see also Myers 2001:3). She describes two classes of inalienable possessions, collective and individual. "Some objects are owned by particular groups, but because of the importance of these groups and the rituals that they maintain, they are considered to be the most valuable and are owned collectively by these societies. They bring prestige to group leaders, kachina impersonators, and those responsible for caring for them" (Mills 2004:247). Inalienable possessions are not always made of materials from long distances or exotics. Contextual data are needed for their recognition and interpretation. Depositional contexts, the formal structuring of these deposits, and biographies are essential to understanding their purpose (2004:247). Mills (2004:239) also notes the importance of agency and social memory in structuring the ethnographic and archaeological record.

The argument presented in Chapter 4 and previously in this chapter is that the earliest parts of the village had the most power within Chevelon society due to their being the first occupants of the village. This pattern is seen in Hopi oral tradition, where power, prestige, and authority are allocated to groups who founded the various Hopi villages, traditionally the Bear Clan (Eggan 1950; Levy 1992; Titiev 1944). The archaeological record at Chevelon strongly supports the central religious authority of the occupants of RB200 throughout the occupation of the village, followed by those who occupied RB300 and thirdly by those occupying the northern third of RB100. Noteworthy is the concentration of objects used in rituals in the form of enriched deposits in nearly every structure of RB200 and in the limited areas excavated in RB300. Together, they paint a pattern of accumulation of wealth and prestige in RB200 through the control of objects used in ceremonial activities involving rituals and performances. The maintenance of the ritual record throughout the occupation of RB200 is further support for the centrality and continuity of these activities and their acceptance by others who joined the community during its 100 years of occupation. It is the ability of the religious authorities at Chevelon to continue to use RB200 and to a lesser degree, RB300, as central places for commemorating the ritual history of the village and to their authority as religious leaders that is invoked using social memory.

Distribution of Rare/Unusual Objects

Tables 13.1 and 13.2 illustrate the distribution of material remains that historically have been noted within the HSC as associated with ritual structures and ritual activities. As noted earlier, enriched deposits are not limited to ritual structures and their distribution within the village provides a better understanding of the meaning of these deposits. Table 13.1 lists only those structures having five or more artifacts from the set of nine categories. Although the size of the excavated sample clearly plays a role in the higher frequencies of petrified wood in particular, this does not explain the complete absence of significant frequencies of these rare and unusual objects anywhere outside RB200 and the kiva/plaza area in RB300.

Table 13.2 shows a similar distribution of structures having rare and unusual shell, animal remains, axes, and flaked lithic materials (Appendix B). The list of structures is again dominated by RB200 and the kiva/plaza complex in RB300. Plaza 300 is a small sample of the early RB200 midden prior to the construction of RB300. Only an interesting deposit in the fill of Str. 120 and the floor assemblage of ritual S. 159, join the RB200 group. K. 248 and 252 have not been fully analyzed and thus could certainly join this small list of structures. Additionally, only the articulated fauna from S. 159 and 286 have been analyzed. To get a sense of the concentration of these classes of materials in these structures, the percentage of total remains for all excavations at Chevelon of those included in this short list of structures is included in the last row. Roughly a third of structures are represented in Table 13.2.

Three significant aspects to the structures represented in these tables are their range of time, the broad array of structure uses involved, and the presence of both floor assemblages and fill assemblages. As the tables illustrate, enriched deposits begin in the TP with Plaza 300, are widespread during the EHP, then concentrate in K. 279 throughout the MHP continuing in the habitation/storage suites represented by S. 268/289/288 and 265/269 during the LHP. These suites of rooms separate K. 248 and 279. In other words, there is continuous deposition of ritually-charged, enriched deposits in RB200 from the founding of the village almost to its depopulation. I will return to this point after looking at the spatial distributions.

Structures represented in the tables include a piki house, four storage rooms, two habitation rooms, and two kivas in RB200. Enriched assemblages occur on the floor of S. 286, a storage room; in the floor fill of S. 222, the piki house; storage S. 227, associated with the adult female on its floor; and the floor fill of habitation S. 289, 268, and storage S. 269. In other words, these deposits occurred immediately after use of the structure stopped. Only S. 248, 288, and K. 279 have deeper enriched fill deposits; however, S. 288 is unique in having a human neonate inserted into its fill, thus changing the nature of the assemblage, which was then enriched with numerous birds and whole or nearly whole pots. Continuous deposition of enriched deposits, then, is unique to the RB200 kivas.

What does this all mean? Unlike elsewhere in the village where storage rooms and habitation rooms have been excavated, the deposits used to close numerous structures in RB200 are filled with more objects obtained from a long-distance, such as obsidian, bighorn sheep, axes, and *Conus* tinklers, and rare objects, such as fossils and ancient projectile points, that could confer more prestige and wealth on these individuals than anywhere else in the village. Additionally, many items associated with rituals, including faunal remains, fossils, pigments, and projectile points, are common, especially in the kivas (Table 13.1 and 13.2). Thus, these enriched deposits represent the remains of discarded items used in religious performances and differential access to rare and distant items. This clearly shows that wealth and status are closely intertwined with ownership of objects used in the performance of ceremonies at Chevelon.

Similarly, the continuous use of ceremonial structures as private and restricted depositories of remains from ritual practices is evident in the 2.0 m of deposits in K. 248 and over 3.0 m of deposits in K. 279. Ceramics suggest these deposits accumulated over a period of perhaps 50 years, from 1335 to 1385. It is noteworthy that the individual structures did not receive additional deposits once a shallow midden of enriched material covered their floors. Instead, the supra-household religious structures received these deposits. The evidence presented above indicates that during the LHP, substantial portions of RB200 were no longer occupied at all or only seasonally. Nevertheless, individuals and groups whose roots lay in this room block, returned to deposit objects in one or the other kivas, then covered the deposit with ash, or emptied the contents of their hearth into the kiva. It is likely that two groups, each represented by a kiva, were involved in making these deposits, since filling of the kivas overlapped for a decade or more.

There are subtle differences between K. 248 and 279, which may relate to social identity and ceremonial practices between groups using them. First, different wood was used to construct the kiva roofs. The roof of K. 248 was constructed using ponderosa pine and pinyon, neither locally available but probably present as driftwood. When its 40 to 50 year use came to an end, the roof of K. 248 was burned. In contrast, the roof of K. 279 was constructed using five vigas of cottonwood and one of juniper, all locally available. When the north wall of K. 279 collapsed after 50 years of use, the roof was left in place and not burned. The meaning of the choices for wood cannot truly be deciphered, but cottonwood is preferred in Hopi kivas today in part due to its association with water. In contrast, the pine trees in K. 248 are associated with higher elevation areas south of Chevelon where snow and moisture from clouds is much higher. The pine trees could also symbolize regions to the south from which some residents of Chevelon migrated.

Closure of the kivas other than treatment of the roof had numerous similarities — deposits (often ashy) with abundant birds, canids, and artiodactyla. Some differences do stand out, despite almost ten times as much undisturbed fill in K. 279 versus K. 248. K. 248 has three piki and three griddle stones versus one in K. 279. It has four ravens versus one in K. 279. It has bones from one pronghorn and one bighorn sheep; K. 279 has neither but does have 39 deer bones. Ash deposition in K. 248 was more concentrated in thicker deposits suggestive of groups or multi-household participation. Although these are occasionally present in K. 279, predominantly its ash dumps are smaller, suggesting a single hearth was involved.

It is not possible to "read" or interpret the meaning of these subtle differences, but together they suggest different beliefs. These in turn resulted in different ceremonial practices beginning with how to build the kiva, then how to close the kiva, and finally who is permitted and what is permitted to contribute to the 30 to 40 year filling of each kiva. Differences in aves and artiodactyla no doubt relate to social identity in ceremonial knowledge and participation.

In all of the deposits represented in Tables 13.1 and 13.2, there is no clear indication of the deposition of inalienable possessions belonging to individuals. It may be that these are represented in the fill of some of the individual structures. However, the deposits in the fill and floor of household structures may represent household or small group deposits rather than that of individuals. Typically, these deposits are fairly large and complex in terms of the objects within them and appear to represent household rather than individual deposition, possibly households vested with

Table 13.2. Chevelon Structures with Rare/Unusual Artifacts from Shell, Plant, and Animal Remains.

Structure	Phase	Birds	*Bighorn Sheep & Artiodactyl	Canid Felids	Articulated Animals	Projectile Points	Obsidian	*Conus* Tinklers
120	LHP	4	7	4C	1 rabbit	2	3	
159	LHP	NA	NA	NA	4 rabbits, 1 artiodactyl	1	NA	NA
222	EHP	4	9A	1F		3	5	1
227	EHP	3	1+7A	1F	Human adult female	1	9	
268/289	LHP	2	1	1F		2	6	
269	LHP		3			2	8	
274/279	EHP-MHP	62	10+32A	5F, 2C	1 rabbit, 1 fish, 2 crows	63	87	3
286	LHP	NA	NA	NA	3 rabbits	3	52	
288	EHP	10	2A		Human neonate	2	7	1
300	TP	2	3A	4C		1		
900	LHP	6	3A	1F, 1C	1 turkey	7	37	1
901	LHP	8	8+14A	3C	1 bighorn sheep, 2 crows	12	65	
Site (%)		49	88	70	83	77	93	67

*No letter is Bighorn Sheep, A is Artiodactyl

religious authority, much as those described in Hopi ethnographies (Levy 1992). This was the interpretation presented in Chapter 4 for S. 124 and 159.

It may be that small discrete deposits in kivas are from individuals and need to be examined individually rather than in bulk as presented in Tables 13.1 and 13.2. It is possible that in many cases artifacts related to individual ritual practices are perishable or too few to distinguish in the archaeological record. It may also be that individuals were more likely to take their possessions with them when they left Chevelon or they were interred with them when deceased. Finally, until a household stopped use of their rooms, it may have been inappropriate for individuals to dispose of inalienable objects in spaces subject to everyday use. The next best place would be in ritual structures with which the individual is affiliated.

One important element to religious performances is feasting (Mills 2007; Potter and Perry 2000). S. 210 in H1 is an excellent example of a likely depository for rabbits used in feasts (Strand 1998; LaMotta 2006). Another example is S. 262, adjacent to K. 279 and 252. Only preliminary testing of the structure was possible at the end of the last field season, but the density and array of bone was nearly identical to those in S. 210. Numerous roasting pits in Plaza 900 associated with K. 901 and the remains of a dismantled roasting pit in Plaza

900 indicate these activities were integrated into ceremonial practices at Chevelon, similar to H1 and H3 (E.C. Adams 2001, 2002).

Social Memory

All societies use devices, usually involving objects, to emulate and commemorate past events (E.C. Adams 2016; Connerton 1989; Mills and Walker 2008; Van Dyke and Alcock 2003). These can be political, social, or religious, but the key elements are the use of objects in conjunction with performances or rituals to remind community members of these events. Nowhere is there more use of such objects to maintain social memory than in religious performances. These occur in every culture, including those of modern Western states in Europe and the United States involving all religious faiths. For Southwest Pueblo groups today as Mills (2004) and others have noted, prestige and power are inextricably tied to the control of ceremonies and ceremonial objects, such as totems, altar pieces, and the like.

For Chevelon, there is compelling evidence that RB200 in particular played this pivotal role in the history of the village. The predominance of rare, unusual, and long-distance objects in deposits in many structures in RB200 in contrast to the remainder of the village underscores the prestige, power and, ultimately, authority that individuals living in RB200 had within the Chevelon community. The fact that RB200 is the oldest and least accessible area in Chevelon accounts for not only the reason why this room block has the most power, but also why it was able to maintain this authority seemingly through the entire occupation of Chevelon. The situation of these items of wealth in religious structures connects them to the religious authority that the RB200 groups had within the community. Continuation of these depositional practices in habitation and storage rooms into LHP, after the kivas were filled, likely is associated with final closure of the entire room block associated with burning (E.C. Adams 2016). The centrality of households and the structures they use to the lives of Pueblo people, for example Whiteley (2015), is also illustrated in the closure of household units centered on S. 124 and 159 at Chevelon and has recently been associated with house society models (Heitman 2015; Miller 2010; Mills 2015).

There is evidence that this authority may have been shared during the MHP with groups from RB300 and the northern third of rooms in RB100. This is further suggested with the construction of the south plaza room blocks and the continued use of K. 901 for perhaps 20 years, during the MHP, after K. 279 collapsed. Similarities in use of artiodactyla in kiva closure between K. 248 and 901 may indicate when groups using K. 248 closed their kiva in the 1330s, they were allowed to use K. 901 to practice their ceremonies. However, the favored explanation for the reduced occupation and activity in RB200 during the LHP is because most of its members relocated to rooms surrounding the south plaza, particularly the upper third of RB100.

This occurred during the MHP and it is likely that at least the deposits above the roof of K. 279, designated as S. 274, were created after the south plaza room blocks were constructed. There is a substantial increase in the number of RRW vessels in these upper deposits that suggest either involvement by immigrants in creating these deposits or higher prestige conferred by the Tonto Polychrome jars that made them desirable as objects to be disposed in the kiva. Some deposits in S. 274 have assemblages more similar to domestic trash than those below the kiva roof, which could also account for the increase in Tonto Polychrome jars.

The situation in RB300 is not as easily understood because only three rooms within the room block have been excavated. Ceramics from all of these rooms indicate their continued use to the end of the Chevelon occupation, but there is no way to determine how typical this was. Given that there are about 150 rooms in RB300, most founded before 1325, it is likely that many were no longer used by the LHP. Additional evidence for this argument is provided by K. 901, which was closed at the beginning of the LHP. This limited evidence suggests many of the rooms surrounding the south plaza were in fact occupied by residents of RB200 and 300 rather than by new migrants. The continued use of partially abandoned areas of a village is still practiced in modern Hopi society with use of kivas and other ritual structures at Walpi and Orayvi though both villages had minimal occupations. Both Walpi and Orayvi continue to host ceremonial performances reaffirming ritual authority of leaders who no longer reside in the villages, a distinct possibility for RB200 and 300 where some houses continued to be used until the entire community was depopulated.

Community Ritual and Katsina Religion

If the construction of the south plaza room blocks was intended to create a space with unrestricted access by all members of the village and in particular to religious ceremonies, is there any evidence of this in the archaeological record at Chevelon? LaMotta (2006) and Mills (2004) both address the issue of finding evidence for sodalities or religious societies in the archaeological record and in particular evidence for the appearance of katsina religion in the fourteenth century. Elsewhere (E.C. Adams 1991b), I proposed that katsina religion appeared at the same time as plaza spaces and plaza kivas. I postulated some of the relationships of iconography in rock art, pottery and kiva murals, and some associations of objects. E.C. Adams and LaMotta (2006) developed the concept of enriched deposits as one approach to identifying better material correlates of the effect of katsina religion on the archaeological record. Definitions for the E.C. Adams and LaMotta (2006) and Mills (2004) approaches have been presented in previous sections. So what does the material record at Chevelon tell us about katsina religion and other broader-based religious societies? First, as Mills (2004) points out, katsina religion is not the first supra-household religious society among the Hopi according to their traditions and to the archeological record (Parsons 1936; Titiev 1944).

LaMotta (2006) and E.C. Adams (2002, 2004a) argue that elaborated, Hopi Mesa-style katsina rituals can only be clearly identified with the arrival of H2 in the HSC. Using the frequency of JYW in deposits at H1 and H2, LaMotta dates the earliest structures and fill deposits excavated at H2 as occurring during the MHP, which he dates as spanning 1365 to 1385. The frequency of JYW in these deposits averages 58.3 percent. Comparable frequencies of JYW at Chevelon occur in the upper four strata of K. 279 and therefore also includes all the S. 274 strata that overlie the kiva's roof. The frequency of JYW in K. 248 is in the 35 percent range, certainly predating this period whereas the earliest deposits in K 901 are in the 70 to 75 percent range at the beginning of the LHP, clearly postdating the filling of K. 279 and the probable construction of the south plaza and associated room blocks. It may not be coincidental that the frequency of JYW in the last deposit in S. 274 is 75.9 %JYW, while the first deposit in K. 901 is 74.9 %JYW.

The filling of K. 279, which begins during the EHP should be a bellwether of any distinctive change in intensity of ritual practices and disposal of related objects, if one occurred in conjunction with the construction of the south plaza area. None can be detected. It is as if nothing changed at all with respect to how the sacred K. 279 space was to be filled. It seems that the members of RB200 maintained their original rituals from start to finish, covering perhaps 40 years, based on JYW frequencies that range from 27.1 percent at the bottom of the kiva to 75.9 percent at the top. This supports the perspective that the religious societies that were in existence when Chevelon was founded, which did not involve katsinas, continued throughout its history. This is not unlike Hopi religion today, which views katsina religion as a late overlay to the foundational religious structure of Hopi society and includes the many fall and winter ceremonials involving men's and women's societies (Parsons 1936; Titiev 1944).

The different method of filling K. 901 that includes covering only the floor of the kiva, the much higher artifact density, an even greater focus on articulated animals within the deposit, and the capping with a solid, complete, and deep layer of ash, may be hallmarks of different ceremonies and related ritual practices. The presence of Sikyatki Polychrome throughout the deposits of K. 901, although in very low frequencies, may also be more closely allied with katsina rituals as the only two bowls with katsina faces painted on their interiors were polychromes from H2 (E.C. Adams 2002, Walker 1996b). Regardless of these differences, they are mostly subtle and do not signal a major change in ritual practices or performances. As with RB200, however, it may be that the occupants of RB300, who were the primary users of K. 901, were similarly tradition bound and katsina ceremonies were not performed in the small plaza nor planned in the large kiva.

K. 400 is the single kiva associated with the south plaza and it was completely vandalized. The absence of other kivas within the south plaza may mean that katsina rituals were not central to the use of this space or that the secretive parts of its planning and performance took place either in K. 901 or in non-kiva spaces, such as the two excavated ritual structures, 159 and 124. Regardless of whether or not K. 901 was initially used in katsina rituals, the discontinuation of its use 10 to 20 years before the rest of Chevelon was no longer used indicates ceremonial organization took place elsewhere in the village and performance probably focused in the south plaza.

Thus, the patterns in ritual practices in the south plaza room blocks also bear investigation. These include the following:

1. Use of rooms within room blocks as foci of ritual planning and storage.

2. Burning/sacrifice of maize on use surfaces as closure.
   a. Burning of corn storage rooms at closure.

3. Placement of whole manos with considerable remnant use-life in or adjacent to bins in storage and habitation rooms with secondary placement next to hearths in habitation rooms.

4. Sacrifice of whole pots through breakage.

5. Sacrifice of rabbits.

Of these five patterns that occur in the south plaza room blocks, (5) is shared with K. 279, where an individual rabbit is interred.

Multiple rabbit sacrifice occurs in S. 286 at Chevelon and S. 701 at H2 (E.C. Adams 2002: Fig. 6.2) as well as S. 159, although not in such a formal layout as the other two. In general, rabbit sacrifice seems to predate the construction of the south plaza room blocks. The other early pattern is (1), the use of ritual structures other than kivas for planning and probably performance of rituals. These are common at H1 throughout its occupation and also occur in the other villages. A complete list is provided in E.C. Adams (2002: Table 6.6). In fact such structures were probably always common in aggregated communities where many ceremonies involving small groups of people were common. Even the rows of small kivas that are along the northern room blocks in the central and western plazas at H2 probably played a similar role. K. 714 in the west plaza has paintings of the landscape that Hopi religious leaders interpreted as used by the village's "Sun Chief" (E.C. Adams 2002: Figure 6.9).

The other three ritual activities – burning maize, placement of manos, and purposeful breakage of pottery seem to be either unique to Chevelon, as in the first two, or associated with later periods, such as pot breakage. Patterns of purposeful breakage of bowls have been found in at least two structures at H1. Laboratory experiments suggest a rock was used to strike the exterior bottom of the bowl after it was placed in the upper fill of the structures. Numerous whole jars in the fill of S. 120, the Sikyatki Polychrome jar on the floor of S. 159, and the Tonto Polychrome jar on the floor of S. 509 are good examples of probably purposeful breakage in three of the 13 rooms tested around the south plaza. The breakage seems most related to the actual closure of not only the individual structures but possibly also the entire village. Purposeful breakage is probably not associated with communal ritual introduced with the construction of the south plaza and associated room blocks.

Modern and historic Hopi katsina religion is focused on the growth and production of maize using symbols representing maize in its many forms, fertility, and rain — all necessary for the growth and maturation of maize plants (E.C. Adams 2016; Loftin 2003). Certainly, similar foci are associated with other Hopi ceremonies, but most have more complex roles in Hopi society. Thus, the interaction of rituals involving maize through its sacrifice by burning and the object most associated with its processing, the mano, may very well be rituals introduced late in the history of Chevelon. Their recovery only from rooms surrounding and facing the large late plazas are noteworthy as is their complete absence in the interior rooms in RB200 and 300. Manos in and around hearths/bins occur in S. 159, 120, 124, 603, and 702 (Table 4.2). Manos also occur in burned corn storage room 158. Empty storage rooms 122, 157, 546, and 547 did not contain manos. Flotation samples suggest these rooms were not used to store maize (Chapter 11).

The association of whole manos with rooms where corn was stored, processed and eaten is clear. Both patterns are related to room closure, not just site depopulation, such as S. 603 whose roof beams were pulled and recycled and the room was not burned. A striking and important element to katsina ceremonialism is intensive corn grinding within specialized rooms by groups of women. Sets of corn grinding rooms, one with six grinding bins, and a piki house were uncovered at H1 and associated with construction of the south plaza and ceremonial performances in the plaza. Limited excavations at Chevelon did not uncover corn grinding rooms, although they certainly exist, but a piki house was discovered in RB200. Placement of manos in so many rooms most likely symbolizes not only household but also communal corn grinding for feasts associated with public performances in Chevelon's south plaza.

Thus, the room with the strongest signature for its use in conjunction with late plaza-based rituals, possibly katsina rituals, is S. 159 (Figure 4.16). This is followed by S. 124. In S. 159 are sacrificed rabbits (four or more), three whole manos, an axe, and a broken jar. As noted in Chapter 4 and Table 4.2, the constellation of sacrificed rabbits, axe, manos, and other objects is also present and perhaps associated with early Chevelon rituals that continued throughout the village's occupation, although ceramics from S. 286, where the assemblage of three rabbits, an axe, two awls, selenite, and two grinding stones is LHP. Thus, multiple rabbit sacrifices with axes and other objects may be exclusively LHP.

The irony of the increasing focus on maize in Chevelon ritual is the apparent decrease of maize in flotation samples at Chevelon, as well as H2 (K. Adams, Chapter 11). Perhaps this is due to increased commitment to cotton production, but although this is indicated at H1 and H2, the production of cotton by Chevelon occupants never seems to have been high. Its increase in ubiquity to 10 percent of flotation samples from practically nothing, however, might help explain some of the drop in maize. The other peculiarity with the decrease in maize in LHP flotation samples in the HSC is the obvious huge commitment of storage to maize at Chevelon with two excavated storage rooms having at least 60 cm of freshly harvested maize and many others exposed from being vandalized by pothunters. Perhaps, because the maize is burned and preserved, we are impressed by its seeming bounty, when in fact the harvest was meager for the village's needs, thus finally convincing the occupants to leave after the harvest was completed. Rough estimates of burned corn storage rooms number 10 to 15 out of more than 100 storage rooms, many burned with no stored maize. Which perception is more correct cannot be resolved on present evidence.

Ritual Placement

From the previous discussions in this chapter and Chapter 4, it seems that every floor assemblage uncovered in our small sample of rooms in Chevelon was more than likely placed by the inhabitants rather than simply left, the distinction between curation of objects and primary trash (LaMotta and Schiffer 1999; Schiffer 1987). In most, if not all of these cases, this placement has ritual overtones rather than objects just being placed in storage, or curated for future planned use. Floor assemblages were recovered from S. 286, 124, 159, 120, 603, 345, and 264 (Table 13.3, Figures 4.5 and 13.2-13.3). All structures have multiple pieces of whole pottery, except 345. All, but S. 264 and 286, have one or more whole manos. Three have multiple articulated animals or animal parts. Extensive previous discussions have implicated the placement of articulated animals and parts as strongly connected to ritual practice.

The manos are also clearly placed. It could be argued that these are simply in storage, but these are whole manos in rooms whose use has discontinued at various times during Chevelon's occupation, including S. 603, 159, 120, and 124. Whole manos are highly valued by Pueblo and Navajo people due to the expense in finding good stone for their manufacture, then the investment in time to manufacture the object, and the time it takes in use to become most efficient with a metate. Both groups still need them for some traditional corn grinding in conjunction with rituals associated with community ceremonies and household practices. Manos with remnant use-life are being sacrificed in these rooms as most found in middens are broken or completely used (Chapter 7). The pots in S. 159 and 286 are certainly being left behind in association with floor assemblages stemming from household rituals. A Tonto Polychrome jar beneath the floor of S. 159 is filled with animal bone, including at least two partially articulated rabbits.

The implication is that most of the objects left on floors at Chevelon are the result of purposeful placement, not in storage – curated for later use, but as offerings or sacrifices. LaMotta and Schiffer (1999) have carefully evaluated such assemblages and relate remnant use-life of multiple objects as associated with sacrifice and ritual activity rather than curation of items with an expectation of returning to use them. This is underscored by the burning of many of these structures over the floor assemblages, including S. 264, 345, 159, and 124. Montgomery (1992) came to the same conclusion with respect to the floor assemblages recovered from the burned rooms at Chodistaas, a small village near Grasshopper Pueblo in the Mogollon Rim country. Given these strong patterns in multiple villages, I encourage archaeologists to carefully think about the assemblages of objects on their floors.

Summary – The Meaning of Assemblages of Ritual Objects

The record of religious ritual practices at Chevelon has been shown to be broad and diverse. The assemblages can be ascribed to group ritual practices at the household and supra-household levels, and individual ritual practices. Assemblages can also be divided into those involving placement of artifacts, which is typically on the floors of structures, versus those as a result of discard. Table 13.4 summarizes the structures at Chevelon with assemblages believed to be related to rituals or ceremonies, which include totemic-like objects, skins used in performance, sacrifice of whole objects, and disposal of broken ritual objects, i.e., ceremonial trash.

Discard assemblages in household space are probably related to single or short-term events and involve single deposits, multiple categories of artifacts, mixtures of domestic and rare or unusual artifacts, and do not typically involve ash. The rare or unusual objects may be used in individual rituals in service to communal or individual needs. Floor assemblages are argued to be primarily purposeful placement following ritualized proscriptions. As noted, these are thought to be closure practices used by households because they involve living or habitation spaces rather than storage spaces.

The artifacts themselves suggest household closure as they include domestic or everyday whole objects. Typically, these objects are placed next to and within features. The fact that these involve whole objects with substantial remnant use-life, especially pots and manos, mixed with articulated animals, usually whole rabbits, and rare and valued artifacts, such as axes or unusual vessel forms, indicates the floor assemblage has been ritualized rather than curated. The final indication that these floor assemblages consist of objects being sacrificed is that many of the pots are purposely broken and the roofs are ignited with the resulting burned roofs lying directly on the floors. The fact that similar assemblages occur in burned and unburned structures whose use stopped before the village was depopulated indicates the assemblages are related to household closure practices rather than site-wide catastrophic depopulation.

Multiple household spaces may include S. 124 and 159 room suites, but if so, these are different from kiva spaces in that they involve a more limited participation in closure of the structure than do kiva spaces. It is likely that a single, primary lineage owned these household spaces and was responsible for their closure, much as at Hopi today, where the primary lineage possesses the totems of the clan or migration group, and is privy to the use, location, and activation of these religious objects. So, even though S. 124 and 159 room suites may have included multiple families as participants in the ceremonies owned by these households, the disposal of the objects was at the single household level. This is reinforced by the additional sacrifice of storerooms of maize by each of these households. Maize was almost certainly owned by the household, as evidenced in S. 158 and 123, both of which were accessible only by going through the S. 124 and 159 habitation spaces.

K. 248, 279, and 901 have unique and distinctive life histories from any other structure at Chevelon and their filling fits a broad pattern in the HSC (E.C. Adams 2016; E.C. Adams and Fladd 2014). The enriched deposits that partially or totally fill these structures are quantitatively and to some degree qualitatively different from all other structures. Most distinctive about kivas are the length of time generally used to fill them, the uniqueness of many fill units, and the use of ash in their filling.

The time factor is related to the apparent use of kivas to store a community's social memory by connecting present activities to the past through their deposition in former religious structures. As noted, this is particularly true for both RB200 kivas. Originally, these kivas were the staging areas for the performance of secret ceremonies that commemorated the religious authority and power of participants over the other members of the community. When these kivas could no longer be used to stage these events, they were essential in commemorating these older ritual activities, probably through performance, followed by deposition of objects into the group's kivas, (Connerton 1989; Rappaport 1999). This continued use of mostly

Table 13.3. Chevelon Structures with Floor Assemblages.

Structure	Pottery	Ground Stone	Articulated Animals	Other
120	Two whole vessels, one under floor	Two	None	None
124	Two whole vessels	Three	None	Piki/ griddle stone
159	Two whole vessels, one under floor	Three	Two rabbits, 1 artiodactyl foot	Axe
264	Two whole vessels	None	None	Basket
286	Two whole vessels	None	Three rabbits	Axe, bone awls
345	One whole vessel	Large piki stone fragment, mano	Golden eagle foot, blue bird head	
603	Ladle, miniature vessel	One	None	None

Figure 13.2. Structure 286 floor assemblage.

Figure 13.3. Structure 124 floor assemblage.

abandoned areas of a village is still practiced in modern Hopi society with use of kivas and other ritual structures at Walpi and Orayvi, though both villages are sparsely or seasonally occupied.

At the same time, the dozens of individual dumps visible as ash deposits and placements of articulated animals, for example the articulated rabbit surrounded by ears of corn in K. 279, reveal the actions of individuals in creating this archaeological record. Although the meaning of these individual actions may not be known, their patterning across Chevelon and the HSC provides insights into the ability of individuals and small groups to affect the history of villages. The continuity of RB200 in all religious activities in Chevelon from its founding to at least 1385, for about 95 years, is clearly one of group agency. Similarly, the small, enriched deposits in individual structures on their floors and in their floor fill or fill, are similar examples of community practice in the service of individual agents. The most lasting and ubiquitous example of human agency at Chevelon is the burning of individual or small groups of structures. In many cases, this involved the sacrifice of maize, but whole objects from many categories were involved.

In the end, it seems likely that burning and ash belong to the same category of symbolism in the Chevelon belief system (E.C. Adams 2016; E.C. Adams and Fladd 2014). During the Hopi New Fire Ceremony (Fewkes 1900), households clean out their hearths, whose ash is deposited in specific areas, in order to start a new fire in the family hearth that harkens the start of a new year. This renewal is symbolized by ash removal. In the same way, fire is used to cleanse and purify, to create renewal in the household and community. Fire and ash are symbols and media used to end one chapter and begin a new one in the life-history of a hearth, a building, or a community. Burning is transformative from one state to another. Ash symbolizes this altered and used-up state. The ubiquity of ash deposits in religious structures at Chevelon and other HSC villages, the careful disposal in appropriate areas of kiva ash and ash from the New Fire Ceremony at Hopi, and documentation of ethnographers of these practices Pueblo-wide (Parsons 1939), suggest that ash can be transformed into a sacred element.

In this light, then, it is suggested that the burning of structures at Chevelon culminating with the burning of the village through many individually-set fires, was an act of purification and closure. Why the inhabitants felt compelled to perform this act is not yet known. Nevertheless, the orderliness of the burning from the emptying out of some structures prior to burning to the careful placement of objects on the floors of structures that were then burned, clearly point to a planned closure of Chevelon, rather than a forced one. The ritual practices associated with the planning and execution of this event point to the use of fire as the closing of one chapter of the lives of the individuals, households, and groups occupying the village with a known opening of another chapter in their new migrant homes. The chemistry of the ceramic pastes of the imported JYW pottery points to Antelope Mesa as this new home (Bernardini 2015; Bishop et al. 1988). The resulting long distance migration contributed to the inventory of objects left behind (LaMotta and Schiffer 1999; Schiffer 1987; Stevenson 1982). Antelope Mesa communities are 100 km north. It simply is not practical to bring all of your belongings with you. Priorities would include seed corn, a few personal belongings that could be carried, and personal, household, and community-based religious objects or inalienable possessions

(Bernardini 2008; Mills 2004; Weiner 1992). The general absence of inalienable objects in Chevelon deposits also points to a planned rather than forced departure.

Table 13.4. Structure Deposits Grouped According to Interpretation of Ritual or Ceremonial Activities.

	Individual (pots, manos, partially articulated faunal remains)	Household (broken pots, manos, articulated faunal remains)	Multiple Household	Human Remains
Placement – Floor	120, 264, 509, 603	124, 159, 222, 286	252 (bench & floor), 901 bench	227
Placement – Other	702 (burned maize on roof)		279 (ash deposits, articulated animals)	
Discard – Floor fill				227
Discard – Fill		120, 222, 300 (all involving purposeful breakage)	248, 279, 901	288

Chapter 14
Future Directions
E. Charles Adams

Although much about life at Chevelon is better understood through ASM's research, there is still much that is incompletely understood. This chapter will focus more on what future research might profitably pursue rather than on summarizing what we do know, which was the focus of Chapter 13.

What We Do Not Yet Understand

Why They Left

There were storerooms with newly harvested maize. Water flowed down Chevelon Creek into the LCR, exchange with remaining members of the HSC and Hopi Mesa communities continued, yet amidst all this, the occupants of Chevelon migrated. Although we know that some storerooms had maize, we do not know whether a stack of maize 60 cm high was a good harvest or a poor one. We do not know if some storerooms had maize while others did not. In other words, it is hard to interpret the evidence. The impression is one of abundance of food freshly placed into storage. Nevertheless, the archaebotanical evidence points to less maize during the Late Homol'ovi Phase (LHP) than at any other period in Chevelon's history. This was also the case for H1 and H2. It is not likely that members of the HSC were voluntarily eating less maize in their diet. Also, the extensive deposits of LHP ceramics and middens at Chevelon, H1, and H2 point to more people rather than fewer within the cluster. It is quite possible the environmental uncertainty of the period 1380 to 1400 was tangibly affecting food security at the three remaining members of HSC and the combination of less food and more people forced the final decision to move.

Previously, I (E.C. Adams 2002) suggested that the HSC was increasingly converting the floodplain fields to cotton production while moving maize to upland area fields (also see Lange 1998). This is suggested in the increase in upland farm areas associated with the arrival of H2 as well as a spike in cotton ubiquity in flotation samples from H1 and H2. At Chevelon, cotton was never plentiful in the botanical record, although its presence did rise to 10 percent of flotation samples in the LHP.

I have suggested that this was perhaps due in large part to the lack of options for upland farming in the vicinity of Chevelon versus H1 and H2. Instead, Chevelon's populace may have exchanged its unique riparian resources and access to White Mountain Red Ware (WMRW) and Roosevelt Red Ware (RRW) for cotton grown by its neighbors. In this context, the increase in cotton production at Chevelon may reveal a decision or need to start growing its own during the LHP. Perhaps the demand among Hopi villages for H1 and H2 cotton diminished the supply to Chevelon. Regardless of the exact cause or causes, the decision of HSC farmers to move some maize production to upland areas and for Chevelon farmers to convert some of their maize fields to cotton fields bore a subsistence risk. The tree-ring record points to the possibility of a series of major floods on the LCR, in the early 1380s, that could have disrupted farming on the floodplain. This was followed by a severe drought lasting at least 10 years that extended to the end of the fourteenth century (E.C. Adams 2002; E.C. Adams and Hedberg 2002; Lange 1998; Van West 1996). Historic flood events in Chevelon Creek recorded on gauges dwarf those along the LCR due to the narrowness of the canyon and its high walls (E.C. Adams and Hedberg 2002). Such flood events could have catastrophic effects on the Chevelon farms through a combination of flooding, erosion, and migration of the LCR's stream channel away from existing fields. These combined factors could create a situation that warranted rapid depopulation of the settlement cluster and of Chevelon in particular. Perhaps it is within this context that maize production dropped during LHP.

As noted by Duff (1998, 2002) and Adams and Duff (2004a), many of the nearest settlement clusters to HSC were being depopulated about 1385. The latest tree-ring dates in both the Anderson Mesa cluster and Silver Creek cluster are the mid-1380s, which corresponds with the beginning of LHP and when some migrants from Silver Creek appear to have settled in Chevelon. The smaller Bidahochi and Puerco River clusters were probably depopulated about the same time or a little earlier, although Stone Axe Pueblo may have been an exception to this trend. This means that by 1385 or slightly later, the only remaining settlement clusters near Homol'ovi were the Hopi Mesa villages at 80 to 90 km and the Zuni villages at 135 to 150 km. Whatever the cause of this demographic collapse, its impact on the HSC and Chevelon were bound to be profound in terms of exchange partners, security, and perhaps even need to exist.

If a major reason for the establishment of the HSC in the late 1200s was to secure traditional ancestral Hopi lands before migrating groups from the Four Corners region began to settle and lay claim to the then unoccupied area (E.C. Adams 2002), then, by the late 1300s, this need was gone. If, as proposed by LeBlanc (1999), warfare was endemic in the region at this time, alliances with nearby clusters that may have helped mitigate conflict would have disappeared along with the clusters themselves. Certainly, these alliances were based on the exchange of many materials as well as the movement of people. The loss of these exchange partners would also have had a dampening effect on the wealth within the HSC villages as well as their continued need to exist. Even demand for cotton production could have declined in the end for Chevelon whose population was most closely connected to communities east and south.

Whatever the ultimate cause of the depopulation of Chevelon, it is likely related as much to the situation in other villages in the HSC and those in nearby clusters as to subsistence or environmental stress. Chevelon did not exist in isolation, as the archaeological record of exchange attests, and the disappearance of most of its neighbors did affect its inhabitants. Whether or not this would cause people to move is not certain, but it almost certainly contributed to the final decision to do so. As among Pueblo people today, social relationships are the core to their society. Disruption of these relationships could only have a negative impact on the remaining communities.

Thus, the reasons behind why Chevelon and the HSC were ultimately depopulated in favor of Hopi villages is complex and in need of additional study. The factors involved are possibly environmental and certainly social. Both influences can be gleaned from the archaeological record, but the weight of their effects cannot as yet. The possibility that direct warfare on Chevelon was the cause has circumstantial evidence, including extensive burning and involving stores of food. LeBlanc (1999), among many, cites this as evidence of warfare. Certainly, warfare is one possible explanation, but as noted extensively throughout this volume, there are other cultural causes for burning that do not include conflict.

It is what is missing from the archaeological record at Chevelon that argues against conflict as the explanation for its depopulation. These include an absence of victims that would include numerous unburied bodies showing evidence of trauma within and outside rooms (Kuckelman 20023; Potter and Chuipka 2013), the lack of evidence for hurried and unplanned closure of households that leaves extensive floor assemblages in modes of use rather than curation, or ritual arrangement, and the lack of weapons recovered from Chevelon. Weapons include arrow points and axes and objects that would not preserve in the archaeological record. Axes are extremely rare and always associated with ritual deposits or ceremonial trash, and the primary location of projectile points is in kiva fill, with many of the points dating from Basketmaker III as far back as Paleoindian. The archaeological record does not favor conflict, but it cannot be completely ruled out either.

Just as important a question that cannot be answered, is who would attack Chevelon and why? There are no clues in the archaeological record of Chevelon or in the remainder of the cluster. There is no archaeological evidence for conflict between villages in the HSC, although there is strong evidence for witchcraft persecution at H2 (Walker 1995, 1998). At H2, there is virtually no burning (see chapter 4), except the kivas, some of which contain bodies of adults and children. The massive size of H2, the open landscape that makes any approach easily seen, and the highly restricted access to the plaza kivas in which the bodies were found, makes their death by outside groups highly unlikely. Also, the lack of any substantial burning at other HSC villages and none associated with their depopulation, makes Chevelon's burning even more unique and suggests that neither groups outside the cluster nor within the cluster are very viable candidates. It is unusual in warfare for there to be only one attack. Again, conflict cannot be ruled out, but there is a lack of evidence to explain or understand warfare as the cause of burning and closure of Chevelon, and, there are stronger explanations.

Why They Burned Their Structures

This topic has been discussed at length in several chapters, but the explanation is still not fully determined. As noted in Chapter 5, determining the cause of a fire is far different than determining the reasons behind the cause. The evidence associated with burning structures is the following:

1. Burned structures include those with floor assemblages, those without floor assemblages but no post-abandonment fill, those with some secondary trash, and those with abundant post-abandonment natural and cultural fill.

2. Burning of structures dates from several periods during Chevelon's occupation, not just at its depopulation.

3. Not every structure with a roof was burned.

4. Multiple fires were set to burn the rooms

ignited at the closure of Chevelon.

5. Most of the structural fires were the last cultural acts associated with the involved structures.

6. The burning of numerous corn storage rooms involving evidence that the corn had been recently harvested due to high moisture content suggests the fires were set at the same time.

These data have been argued to point to the burning as ritual closure of Chevelon. As argued in the previous chapter, fire is associated with purification, including the Greeks, within the Old and New Testaments, Mesoamerican states, and the historic Pueblos (E.C. Adams 2016; Parsons 1939:364, 464). It is possible that Chevelon was burned in order to purify it. Purification can be for renewal or for the destruction of objects and areas that are either contaminated or pose a danger to others (often from witches) who have not been initiated and thus don't know how to protect themselves.

Some Hopi societies are involved with journeys to the after-life and can come into contact with the dead (Titiev 1944). Individuals not initiated into these societies can become sick or die from contact with objects or spaces used by these groups in their rites. Witches also pose continuous threats to Pueblo groups and burning of witches or their households and belongings is a method of purification (Walker 1998). Similarly, most Pueblo societies use ashes to ward off witches (Parsons 1939:464). In all cases, protection from spiritual contamination is the goal.

Burning could also simply be to deny access to objects and spaces at Chevelon by other groups. Rather than denying access to the sacred, such burning would deny access to the secular realm of the village as well. The burning of corn storage rooms, for example, would prevent others in the area from using the stores for their own uses. This could be a defensive strategy to keep groups perceived as enemies from having food stores even though no attack ever took place. Given that all other settlement clusters other than Hopi and Zuni had been depopulated by the 1390s (E.C. Adams and Duff 2004a), the only alternatives are non-pueblo groups or other members of the cluster. There is yet no evidence to support either scenario. The explanation favored here is purification through ritual practices for whatever the reason, but much more work needs to be done.

Jeddito Yellow Ware, Cotton, *Anodonta*, Turtle Shell, and Roosevelt Red Ware

Although some ideas have been presented, there is still not an adequate understanding of why so little cotton was grown at Chevelon at all times during its history, why *Anodonta californiensis* was so dominant in the shell assemblage, why there was a total absence of turtle shell at Chevelon, and how Jeddito Yellow Ware (JYW) arrived at Chevelon. Each of these is a question because other information suggests there are other possibilities.

With respect to cotton, the archaeological record from the other HSC villages, as summarized in Chapter 11, suggests that cotton seeds were commonly found in flotation samples many times at Chevelon, including the LHP when cotton ubiquity was about 10 percent, yet, was three times higher at H1 and H2. Various explanations for this difference have already been posited, including limited access to upland areas for growing maize that was available to H1, H2, and H3, which would allow space to grow cotton in the floodplain, or the preference of Chevelon's inhabitants to exchange for their cotton using other rare items, or, the amount produced met Chevelon's needs and none was exchanged.

In the case of turtle shells, Fewkes (1904) reports Hopi visits to Chevelon in particular to collect turtle shells for use in their rituals. Additionally, turtle bone and shell has been recovered from the other Homol'ovi villages, as reported in Chapter 9. Their association with ritual practice in historic Hopi communities, their recovery from kiva contexts at H3, and the extensive excavations in kivas at Chevelon makes their absence particularly puzzling. One possible explanation is that turtles and turtle shell were buried in distinctive areas outside the pueblo walls, similar to the bird burial ground found at H3 and to ones used for golden eagles and red-tailed hawks by Hopi today (Pierce 2001; Titiev 1944). Another possibility is that turtle shells were so valued by Chevelon occupants and/or were rare and valued objects for exchange to community members in their new homes, that they were taken with the immigrants.

Anodonta represents 93.5 percent of the Chevelon shell assemblage, as detailed in Chapter 10. This high frequency is unexpected because in other villages excavated in the HSC, its frequency, although high, was typically less than 50 percent. In addition, Fewkes (1898, 1904) recovered a broad array of Pacific Coast and Gulf of California seashells associated with Chevelon burials. The minimal reworking of seashell by Chevelon's inhabitants and its almost exclusive use with human burials indicate seashell was a highly valued object that belonged primarily to the individual. The exception is *Conus*, which is typically used in ritual performance as tinklers on costumes among the modern Hopi and was found in kivas at Chevelon (Fewkes 1898) The working of *Anodonta* into occasional ornaments was probably to complement the valued seashell, which appears to be in shorter supply than previously, probably due to fewer communities in the Salt and Gila river valleys and general declines in exchange of shell region-wide. *Anodonta*'s highly friable nature may have resulted in much more breakage and debitage in the archaeological record. There is also strong evidence that *Anodonta* was used as a food source with the shells recovered primarily in the fill of structures, likely refuse from these activities. This is represented by the categories of unworked shell and shell debris in Magaña's Table 10.3.

The distribution of shell at Chevelon is concentrated in RB200 with 74.2 percent followed by RB900 and K. 901 with 19.4 percent. Only 6.4 percent occurs elsewhere in the sample analyzed by Magaña. Unlike other material classes, only 18.3 percent of the shell is from K. 248, 274/279, and 901. The number of shell remains is steady from Early Homol'ovi Phase (EHP) through LHP, although the sample is dominated by Middle Homol'ovi Phase (MHP) and LHP deposits. This suggests that *Anodonta* was used more in EHP than other periods.

All of these facts suggest that *Anodonta* was an important food source throughout the Chevelon occupation and that its shell was valued as a necessary ornamental complement to the relatively rare seashells. The preponderance of *Anodonta* shell in RB200 and the fact that it comes from water may indicate a tertiary importance, its use as a mnemonic device associated with water. Its absence in kivas, but wide distribution in storage and habitation rooms in RB200 indicates it might relate more to household or individual, rather than group, ritual. It does not seem strongly related to any enriched deposits. This leaves open the possibility that the concentrations of shell in RB200 are primarily due to refuse from subsistence needs and ornament manufacture. This relationship needs further exploration as larger samples from Chevelon are examined.

The nature of the exchange relationship with Hopi Mesa villages has yet to be resolved. Three models of exchange have been proposed by various authors (E.C. Adams 2002; E.C. Adams et al. 1993; Bernardini 2005). Is JYW being exchanged to the HSC by groups wanting ties with Hopi Mesa villages, as proposed by Bernardini (2005)? In this case, groups from existing off-mesa villages are initiating the contact in anticipation of migration. ASM researchers view JYW exchange as resulting from the HSC being settled by migrants from Hopi Mesa villages, but have not yet resolved just how this relationship evolved. E.C. Adams et al. (1993) noted that the percentage of JYW (%JYW) in HSC villages declined in frequency with distance from H2, suggesting that direct exchange with Hopi Mesa villages that manufactured JYW was with H2, which then exchanged it to the other HSC villages. With more information on sources of JYW using neutron activation analysis and on the chronology of exchange and frequency of JYW in late deposits at H1 and Chevelon, it now appears more likely that exchange with Hopi Mesa villages was independent with each member of the HSC. However, a promising approach of looking at exterior design motifs on JYW bowls that may represent pottery-making groups, could clarify details of these relationships (E.C. Adams 2013b; LeBlanc and Henderson 2009).

Finally, the relationship of Chevelon Pueblo to groups to the south and southeast where WMRW, RRW, Mogollon Brown Ware (MBW), and Puerco Valley Utility Ware were manufactured and exchanged into Chevelon needs more exploration. Initial ceramic analysis focused on decorated ceramics, which discovered extensive exchange of WMRW in the EHP and MHP followed by exchange and eventual local production of RRW in MHP and LHP. This suggests migration of RRW-producing groups to Chevelon during MHP when the community was constructing the south plaza and associated room blocks. With more extensive analysis of utility wares, it has become apparent that exchange and local production of MBW was extensive perhaps beginning in the Tuwiuca Phase and certainly by EHP. This suggests some MBW-producing groups either helped settle Chevelon or were early immigrants and present in RB200 and 300. Additional analysis and some targeted excavation are needed to better understand the co-residency of groups from the north and the south.

Chevelon's Role within the Homol'ovi Settlement Cluster

From 19 years of fieldwork in the HSC, including four at Chevelon, it is clear that the HSC is not a monolithic entity comprised of redundant elements. Each village has a distinct history and played a unique and important role in the evolution of the HSC. The villages are more like interlocking pieces to a puzzle. Our perspective changes as we gain more information not just from individual villages, but also from villages that differ significantly with each other in size, length of occupation, period of occupation, and so forth. This has certainly been the case with Chevelon. It is clear from the work at Chevelon in concert with previous research on five other villages, that each village is more-or-less autonomous from the others in terms of subsistence. Their distribution across the landscape and along the LCR, spaced an average of 5 km apart, was to provide a subsistence base for each village, much like the Hohokam communities along a canal system, although the dependency relationships are much less for the members of the HSC because the flow of water is beyond any village's control (E.C. Adams 2002). This means that although Chevelon was situated at the point where the permanent flow of Chevelon Creek entered the LCR, it was not technologically feasible or necessary to capture or divert all the flow of water. Even if this could have been accomplished, the equally productive flow of Clear Creek, 11 km downstream, would have met the water needs of the other pueblos.

Chevelon provides a perspective from the eastern edge of the HSC, unlike the predominance of work in H1 through H4, all in the west. From Chevelon's perspective, relationships with settlement clusters to the south and east are much more important. This is one of the unique roles played by Chevelon and was integral to the important role that the HSC played in regional exchange. This ultimately led, apparently, to an immigration of groups from the south to settle in Chevelon. The growth of Chevelon over its 100-year history is parallel to the other large, long-lived village in the cluster, H1. The strong parallels in how the villages grew physically, their chronology, and their social and religious organizations are important to understanding these trends in the HSC and to applying the refined chronology based on %JYW in deposits to the remaining members of the cluster. This will help in unifying our ability to understand relationships between individual villages at points in time.

Nevertheless, the arrival of H2, although more profound in its effect on H1, still affected Chevelon in a big way. JYW increased to nearly the same levels at Chevelon as at H1 and H2 in the LHP. A large plaza was constructed at the same time and to the virtually exact dimensions of the central plaza at H2. This is presumably in emulation of H2 and to incorporate katsina and other community-based religious practices into Chevelon society, perhaps decentralizing religious authority. Finally, the source of JYW pottery is the same at Chevelon as for H2 (and H1), from Awat'ovi and Kawayka'a. However, this conclusion is drawn from a very small sample of pottery, 40 sherds from each village analyzed by Bernardini (2005). It is essential to understand if there are trends in the source of JYW at the villages. It is unknown whether Bernardini's samples represent EHP, MHP, or LHP ceramics equally or if they are biased toward LHP. Thus, the preponderance of JYW from the large Antelope Mesa villages could be a late development in the history of the HSC, affected by the arrival of H2. However, if the source of the JYW is consistent through time, it would suggest groups from Antelope Mesa likely settled all HSC villages and continued to interact with individual villages rather than primarily H2. As noted above, the analysis of the temporal and spatial trends in exchange of JYW using exterior design motifs might further enlighten understanding of JYW exchange and the relationships between individual Hopi Mesa villages and individual members of the HSC.

The Homol'ovi Settlement Cluster and the History of the Region

Given the lengthy history of the cluster and the distinctive roles played by each of the villages within the cluster with respect to contacts outside, several roles can be better understood from the analysis of the Chevelon material. These outside relationships were with Anderson Mesa villages, Hopi Mesa villages, Silver Creek villages, Puerco of the

West villages, and the Bidahochi villages (E.C. Adams 2002). Exchange with upper Little Colorado River (ULCR) villages and villages below the Mogollon Rim may also have taken place (Mills et al. 2013). Each of these five clusters lies within 50 to 80 km of the HSC and exchange can be documented with Hopi, Anderson Mesa, Silver Creek, and Puerco Valley.

From this information, the following conclusions can be drawn:

1. The HSC is very important in the extensive exchange of goods that was taking place throughout the region.
    a. Each village played a distinct role in this exchange and in most cases with adjacent clusters. Ignoring H2 for the time being, Chevelon had connections to the south and east with Silver Creek and possibly Mogollon Rim, Puerco Valley, and ULCR communities. H1, H3, and H4 had connections to Hopi and Anderson Mesa and perhaps to Verde Valley communities (see Mills et al. 2013).
    b. Products in this exchange are pottery, cotton, obsidian and probably riparian fauna, agave, axes made of various igneous rocks, and petrified wood.
        i. The aquatic birds at Awat'ovi (Olsen and Wheeler 1978) could easily have been obtained from HSC villages initially and later, after HSC was no longer occupied, by travel to the area (E.C. Adams et al. 2015).

2. The major engine in this exchange was cotton grown in the LCR by several of the HSC villages. H1 and H2 seem to have played a larger role in this exchange than did Chevelon.

3. The unique relationship with Hopi Mesa villages is also evident. The primary occupants of HSC are Hopi who migrated from Hopi Mesa villages. Neutron Activation Analysis, all aspects of decorated pottery manufacture, including design layout, show strong and continuous ties to and influence from Hopi Mesa village occupants on HSC occupants (E.C. Adams 2013a).

4. There is evidence in utility wares that throughout the occupation of HSC, and especially at its end, significant numbers of inhabitants had come from communities to the south. This evidence is strongest at Chevelon where MBW is the most common utility ware, but is also evident throughout the HSC after 1300 in the production of Homolovi Utility Ware (HUW) where 25 to 30 percent show technological characteristics consistent with individuals trained in the MBW tradition (Barker 2017).

Recently, Wes Bernardini (2005) has questioned the model of migration from Hopi Mesa villages to settle HSC villages on the basis of the size of the populations involved. Initial settlement of the HSC involving H4 involved perhaps 200 individuals, not all arriving at the same time (E.C. Adams 2004b). Later settlement of five villages involved the migration of H4 to H1. H3, comprising at most 75 individuals, probably also moved to H1. Similarly, the settlement of Chevelon and its subsequent early growth involved perhaps 150 people. Neither Cottonwood Creek nor Jackrabbit Ruin had occupations of more than 100 people at any point in time and certainly not when they were founded in the late 1200s.

Therefore, we are talking about a population of fewer than 500 people to establish the HSC (See E.C. Adams 2004a: Table 12.1). This amounts to less than 20 percent of the estimated Hopi Mesa population about 1300 (E.C. Adams et al. 2004: Table 13.4). By 1400, Hopi population had climbed to more than double its 1300 population due to the influx of groups from Homol'ovi and other settlement clusters. This is reflected especially at Awat'ovi and Kawayka'a, which together increase by 1900 rooms, enough to absorb huge numbers of immigrants, including the entire population of Chevelon, H2, and H1 (E.C. Adams 2002: Table 1.1).

But the room counts and population figures are hard to interpret and easy to fudge. The strong similarity in technological style in ceramics, kiva design, room design, and village layout between the two areas suggests more than just contact (see Clark 2001). It implies immigration with the direction from Hopi to Homol'ovi, since no villages in the HSC predate 1260 and dozens on the Hopi mesas do (E.C. Adams et al. 2004). The complete absence of settlements in the area requires a major migration. As just described, locally produced decorated pottery follows Hopi Mesa pottery design conventions and a majority of utility wares also derive from the Hopi Mesa region (Barker 2017; Lyons 2003).

Of equal significance is the preponderance of JYW in HSC decorated pottery collections at H1, H2, and Chevelon, which all approach 90 percent by the end of the occupation and comprise about 50 percent of total ceramics. Unlike most other clusters where JYW never exceeds 5 to 10 percent of total ceramics, the HSC stands out (Bernardini and Brown 2004; Duff 2004). This suggests lengthy, enmeshed exchange between the two areas due to a common ancestry. By combining chemical paste analysis with the study of exterior "glyphs," we hope to further define the structure of JYW exchange from the production end at Hopi to the consumption end at Homol'ovi. In addition an extensive reanalysis of locally produced HUW from all HSC villages is underway that will better represent populations who did not have a tradition of decorated pottery. It is likely the results of these analyses will support parts of Bernardini's (2005) and E.C. Adams (2002) claims and clarify in richer detail the ethnically diverse groups who occupied each HSC pueblo.

FINAL THOUGHTS

After 19 years of excavations, five at H3, one at H4 (which overlapped with H3), six at H2 (which overlapped with H1), six at H1, and four at Chevelon, our understanding of the rich and complex life of those people who occupied the various HSC villages for about 150 years is greatly enriched. This research and its many publications add to our understanding and appreciation of Hopi history during an important period of transition when much of the Western Pueblo region was depopulated and major reorganization of community life was taking place. This report on Chevelon research highlights our thorough understanding of the chronology of the cluster, our evolving understanding of the sources of its populations, the relationships between villages within the cluster, and the relationships with nearby settlement clusters. It also examines the important role of ritual and ceremony in the lives of its people that formed a substantial portion of the archaeological record and the dramatic end to the occupation of the village.

References

Abbott, Tucker
    1996 *Seashells of North America: A Guide to Field Identification*. Golden Field Guides, St. Martin's Press, New York.

Abruzzi, William S.
    1981 Ecological Succession and Mormon Colonization in the Little Colorado River Basin. Unpublished Ph.D. dissertation, Department of Anthropology, State University of New York, Binghamton.

    1989 Ecology, Resource Redistribution, and Mormon Settlement in Northeastern Arizona. *American Anthropologist* 91:642-655.

Adams, E. Charles
    1982 *Walpi Archaeological Project: Synthesis and Interpretation*. Ms. on file, Arizona State Museum, University of Arizona, Tucson.

    1983 The Architectural Analogue to Hopi Social Organization and Room Use and Implications for Prehistoric Southwestern Culture. *American Antiquity* 48:44-61.

    1991a Homol'ovi in the 14th Century. In *Homol'ovi II: Archaeology of an Ancestral Hopi Village, Arizona*, edited by E. Charles Adams and Kelley Ann Hays, pp. 116-21. Anthropological Papers No. 55. University of Arizona Press, Tucson.

    1991b *The Origin and Development of the Pueblo Katsina Cult*. University of Arizona Press, Tucson.

    1994 The Katsina Cult: A Western Pueblo Perspective. In *Kachinas in the Pueblo World*, edited by Polly Schaafsma, pp. 35-46. University of New Mexico Press, Albuquerque.

    1996 Understanding Aggregation in the Homol'ovi Pueblos: Scalar Stress and Social Power. In *River of Change: Prehistory of the Middle Little Colorado River Valley, Arizona*, edited by E. Charles Adams, pp. 1-14. Arizona State Museum Archaeological Series No. 155. University of Arizona, Tucson.

    2001 *Homol'ovi III: A Pueblo Hamlet in the Middle Little Colorado River Valley*. Arizona State Museum Archaeological Series No. 193. University of Arizona, Tucson.

    2002 *Homol'ovi: An Ancient Hopi Settlement Cluster*. University of Arizona Press, Tucson.

    2004a Homol'ovi: A 13th and 14th Century Settlement Cluster in Northeastern Arizona. In *The Protohistoric Pueblo World: A.D. 1275-1600*, edited by E. Charles Adams and Andrew I. Duff, pp. 119-127. University of Arizona Press, Tucson.

    2004b *Homol'ovi IV: The First Village*. Arizona State Museum Occasional Electronic Publication, No. 1. University of Arizona, Tucson.

Adams, E. Charles, *cont'd*
  2004c Flaked Stone. In *Homol'ovi IV: The First Village*. Arizona State Museum Occasional Electronic Publication, No. 1, edited by E. Charles Adams, pp. 89-94. University of Arizona, Tucson.

  2013a Relations with Neighbors to the South – Tusayan. *Archaeology Southwest* 27(3):16-18.

  2013b Relationships among Design, Time, Source, and Glyphs on Prehispanic Jeddito Yellow Ware. *Kiva* 79:125-146.

  2016 Closure and Dedication Practices in the Homol'ovi Settlement Cluster, Northeastern Arizona. *American Antiquity* 81:42-57.

Adams, E. Charles, and Andrew I. Duff
  2004a Settlement Clusters and the Pueblo IV Period. In *The Protohistoric Pueblo World: A.D. 1275-1600*, edited by E. Charles Adams and Andrew I. Duff, pp. 3-16. University of Arizona Press, Tucson.

Adams, E. Charles, and Andrew I. Duff, editors
  2004b *The Protohistoric Pueblo World: A.D. 1275-1600*. University of Arizona Press, Tucson.

Adams, E. Charles, and Samantha G. Fladd
  2014 Composition and Interpretation of Stratified Deposits in Ancestral Hopi Villages at Homol'ovi. *Journal of Archaeological and Anthropological Science* 7:1-14.

Adams, E. Charles Adams, Samantha G. Fladd, Richard C. Lange, and Claire S. Barker
  2015 Back in Time: Research at Rock Art Ranch in Northeastern Arizona. Paper presented in the symposium: Homol'ovi: A Gathering Place. Presented at the 80th Annual Meeting of the Society for American Archaeology, San Francisco.

Adams, E. Charles, and Kelley A. Hays, editors
  1991 *Homol'ovi II: Archaeology of an Ancestral Hopi Village, Arizona*. Anthropological Papers No. 55. University of Arizona Press, Tucson.

Adams, E. Charles, and Charla Hedberg
  2002 Driftwood Use at Homol'ovi and Implications for Interpreting the Archaeological Record. *Kiva* 67:363-384.

Adams, E. Charles, and Vincent M. LaMotta
  2006 New Perspectives on an Ancient Religion: Katsina Ritual and the Archaeological Record. In *Religion in the Prehispanic Southwest*, edited by Christine S. VanPool, Todd L. VanPool, and David A. Phillips, Jr., pp. 53-66. Altamira Press, Lanham, Maryland.

Adams, E. Charles, Vincent M. LaMotta, and Kurt Dongoske
  2004 Hopi Settlement Clusters Past and Present. In *The Protohistoric Pueblo World: A.D. 1275-1600*, edited by E. Charles Adams and Andrew I. Duff, pp. 128-136. University of Arizona Press, Tucson.

Adams, E. Charles, Miriam T. Stark, and Deborah Dosh
  1993 Ceramic Distribution and Exchange: Jeddito Yellow Ware and Implications for Social Complexity. *Journal of Field Archaeology* 20:3-21.

Adams, Jenny L.
   1979   Stone Artifacts from Walpi, Part 1: Ground Stone. Walpi Archaeological Project, Phase II, Volume 4. Manuscript on file, Arizona State Museum, University of Arizona, Tucson.

   1993   Toward Understanding the Technological Development of Manos and Metates on the Hopi Mesas. *Kiva* 58:331-344.

   2002   *Ground Stone Analysis: A Technological Approach.* University of Utah Press, Salt Lake City.

Adams, Karen R.
   1992   Charred Plant Remains from HP-36 (AZ J:14:36) and Homol'ovi III (AZ J:14:14) in North-Central Arizona. Manuscript on file, Homol'ovi Research Program, Arizona State Museum, University of Arizona, Tucson.

   1994a   Carbonized Plant Remains from Structure 708, A Great Kiva at Homol'ovi II (AZ J:14:15), Little Colorado River. On file, Arizona State Museum, Tucson.

   1994b   A Regional Synthesis of *Zea mays* in the Prehistoric American Southwest, pp. 273-302. In *Corn and Culture in the Prehistoric New World*, edited by Sissel Johannessen and Christine A. Hastorf. Westview Press, Boulder, Colorado.

   1996   Archaeobotany of the Middle Little Colorado River. In *River of Change: Prehistory of the Middle Little Colorado River Valley, Arizona*, edited by E. Charles Adams, pp. 163-186. Arizona State Museum Archaeological Series No. 185. University of Arizona, Tucson.

   1999   Charred Plant Remains from Thermal Features and Other Ash-Laden Deposits at Homol'ovi I. Manuscript on file, Homol'ovi Research Program, Arizona State Museum, University of Arizona, Tucson.

   2000   Charred Plant Remains from Thermal Features and Ash Deposits at Homol'ovi I (AZ:J:14:3) and Homol'ovi II (AZ:J:14:15). Manuscript on file, Arizona State Museum, University of Arizona, Tucson.

   2001   Charred Plant Remains. In *Homol'ovi III: A Pueblo Hamlet in the Middle Little Colorado River Valley*, edited by E. Charles Adams, pp. 313-320. Arizona State Museum Archaeological Series No. 193. University of Arizona, Tucson.

   2004   Charred Plant Remains. In *Homol'ovi IV: The First Pueblo.* Arizona State Museum Occasional Electronic Publication, No. 1, edited by E. Charles Adams, pp. 105-109. University of Arizona, Tucson.

Adams, Karen R., and Vincent M. LaMotta
   2001   Settlement Clusters as Units for Macrobotanical Analysis: A View from the Middle Little Colorado Region. Paper presented at the 66th Annual Meeting of the Society for American Archaeology, New Orleans, Louisiana.

Adams, Karen R., Cathryn M. Meegan, Scott G. Ortman, R. Emerson Howell, Lindsay C. Werth, Deborah A. Muenchrath, Michael K. O'Neill, and Candice A.C. Gardner
   2006   MAÍS (Maize of American Indigenous Societies) Southwest: Ear Descriptions and Traits that Distinguish 27 Morphologically Distinct Groups of 123 Historic USDA Maize (*Zea mays* L. ssp. *mays*) Accessions and Data Relevant to Archaeological Subsistence Models. Manuscript on file: *http://farmingtonsc.nmsu.edu*

Adams, Karen R., Deborah A. Muenchrath, and Dylan M. Schwindt
1999 Moisture Effects on the Morphology of Ears, Cobs and Kernels of a North American Maize (*Zea mays* L.) Cultivar, and Implications for the Interpretation of Archaeological Maize. In *Journal of Archaeological Science* 26:483-496.

Adams, Karen R., and Shawn S. Murray
2004 Identification Criteria for Plant Remains Recovered from Archaeological Sites in the Central Mesa Verde Region. Available: *http:/www.crowcanyon.org/plantID*.

Adler, Michael
1994 Population Aggregation and the Anasazi Social Landscape. In *The Ancient Southwest Community: Models and Methods for the Study of Prehistoric Social Organization*, edited by W. H. Wills and Robert D. Leonard, pp. 85-101. University of New Mexico Press, Albuquerque.

Adler, Michael A., D.K. Ezekoye, and Timothy Klatt
2006 Arson of the Ancestors? Interdisciplinary Research into Ancient Structural Fires in the American Southwest. Paper presented at the 10th Biennial Southwest Symposium, Las Cruces, New Mexico.

Ahlstrom, Richard V. N.
1985 The Interpretation of Archaeological Tree Rings. Unpublished Ph.D. dissertation, Department of Antrhopology, University of Arizona, Tucson.

Allen, C. D., Julio L. Betancourt, and Tom W. Swetnam
1998 Landscape Changes in the Southwestern United States: Techniques, Long-term Data Sets, and Trends. In *Perspectives on the Land Use History of North America: A Context for Understanding our Changing Environment*. U.S. Geological Survey, Biological Resources Division, Biological Science Report USGS/BRD/BSR 1998-0003 (Revised September 1999).

Amick, Daniel S., and Raymond P. Maudlin
1989 Comments on Sullivan and Rozen's "Debitage Analysis and Archaeological Interpretation." *American Antiquity* 54:166–168.

Andrefsky, William
1994 Raw Material Availability and the Organization of Technology. *American Antiquity* 59:21-34.

Andrews, Michael J.
1982 An Archaeological Assessment of Homol'ovi III and Chevelon Ruin, Northern Arizona. Manuscript prepared for the Arizona State Land Department, Phoenix, by Northern Arizona University, Flagstaff.

Andronescu, Lucia, and Karin Glinsky
2004 Faunal Analysis. In *Homol'ovi IV: The First Village*. ASM Occasional Electronic Publication, No. 1, edited by E. Charles Adams, pp. 95-99. Arizona State Museum, University of Arizona, Tucson.

Anthony, David W.
1990 Migration in Archaeology: The Baby and the Bathwater. *American Anthropologist* 92:885-914.

Appadurai, Arjun, editor
1986 *The Social Life of Things: Commodities inn Cultural Perspective*. Cambridge University Press, Cambridge.

Arizona Game and Fish Department
   2001   Unpublished abstract compiled and edited by the Heritage Data Management System, Arizona Game and Fish Department, Phoenix, Arizona.

Bamforth, Douglas B.
   1986   Technological Efficiency and Tool Curation. *American Antiquity* 51:38–50.

Barker, Claire S.
   2017   Inconspicuous Identity: Using Everyday Objects to Explore Social Identity Within the Homol'ovi Settlement Cluster, A.D. 1260-1400. Ph.D. dissertation, School of Anthropology, University of Arizona, Tucson.

Bayham, Frank
   1982   A Diachronic Analysis of Prehistoric Animal Exploitation at Ventana Cave. Ph.D. dissertation, Arizona State University, Tempe.

Beaglehole, Ernest
   1936   *Hopi Hunting and Hunting Ritual*. Yale University Publications in Anthropology 4:1-26.

Bell, Catherine
   1997   *Ritual: Perspectives and Dimensions*. Oxford University Press, New York.

Benitez, Alexander
   1999   Refining 14th Century Jeddito Yellow Ware Chronology and Its Distribution in Central Arizona. Unpublished Master's Thesis, Department of Anthropology, University of Texas, Austin.

Bequaert, Joseph C. and Walter B. Miller
   1973   *The Mollusk of the Arid Southwest: With an Arizona Check List*. University of Arizona Press, Tucson.

Bernardini, Wesley
   2005   *Hopi Oral Tradition and the Archaeology of Identity*. University of Arizona Press, Tucson.

   2008   Identity as History: Hopi Clans and the Curation of Oral Tradition. *Journal of Anthropological Research* 65:483-509.

Bernardini, Wesley, and Gary M. Brown
   2004   The Formation of Settlement Clusters on Antelope Mesa. In *The Protohistoric Pueblo World: A.D. 1275-1600*, edited by E. Charles Adams and Andrew I. Duff, pp. 108-118. University of Arizona Press, Tucson.

Binford, Lewis R.
   1973   Interassemblage Variability—The Mousterian and the "Functional" Argument. In *The Explanation of Culture Change: Models in Prehistory,* edited by Colin Renfrew, pp. 227–253. G. Duckworth, London.

   1979 Organization and Formation Processes: Looking at Curated Technologies. *Journal of Anthropological Research* 35:255-273.

Bishop, Ronald, Veletta Canouts, Suzanne De Atley, Alfred Qoyawayma, and C. W. Aikens
   1988   The Formation of Ceramic Analytical Groups: Hopi Pottery Production and Exchange, A.D. 1300-1600. *Journal of Field Archaeology* 15:317-337.

Borck, Lewis, Barbara J. Mills, Matthew A. Peeples, Jeffery J Clark
   2015   Are Social Networks Survival Networks: An Example from the Late Pre-Hispanic US Southwest. Journal of Archaeological Method and Theory 22:33-57.

Bourdieu, Pierre
   1977   *Outline of a Theory of Practice*. Translated by N. Nice, Cambridge Studies in Social Anthropology, No. 16. Cambridge University Press, Cambridge.

Bradfield, Maitland
   1971   Changing Patterns of Hopi Agriculture. In *Journal of the Royal Anthropological Institute*, Occasional Paper, No. 30.

   1995   *An Interpretation of Hopi Culture*. Duffield, Derbyshire: M.A. Bradfield.

Brandt, Elizabeth
   1984   Egalitarianism, Hierarchy, and Centralization in the Pueblos. In *The Ancient Southwestern Community: Models and Methods for the Study of Prehistoric Social Organization*, edited by W.H.Wills and Robert D. Leonard, pp. 9-23. University of New Mexico Press, Albuquerque.

Braniff, Beatriz.
   1989   *Arqueomoluscos de Sonora, Noroeste y Occidente de Mesoamérica*. Cuadernos de trabajo No. 9. ENAH-INAH. México.

Brew, John Otis
   1949   The History of Awatovi. In *Franciscan Awatovi: The Excavation and Conjectural Reconstruction of a 17th-Century Spanish Mission Establishment at a Hopi Indian Town in Northeastern Arizona*, edited by Ross G. Montgomery, Watson Smith, and J.O. Brew, pp. 2-43. Papers of the Peabody Museum of American Archaeology and Ethnology, Vol. 36. Harvard University, Cambridge, Massachusetts.

Brown, David E., editor
   1994   *Biotic Communities: Southwestern United States and Northwestern Mexico*. University of Utah Press, Salt Lake City.

Brown, Gary M.
   1990 Specialized Lithic Exchange and Production on Anderson Mesa. In *Technological Change in the Chavez Pass Region, North-Central Arizona*, edited by Gary M. Brown, pp. 173-206. Anthropological Research Papers No. 41. Arizona State University, Tempe.

   1991   Embedded and Direct Lithic Resource Procurement Strategies on Anderson Mesa. *Kiva* 56:359-384.

Bubemyre, Trixi
   2004   Ceramics. In *Homol'ovi IV: The First Village*, edited by E. Charles Adams, pp. 55-76. Arizona State Musuem Occasional Electronic Publication, No. 1. University of Arizona, Tucson.

Buikstra, Jane E., and Douglas H. Ubelaker, editors
   1994   *Standards for Data Collection from Human Skeletal Remains*. Arkansas Archaeological Survey Research Series No. 44. Fayetteville, Arkansas.

Burton, Jeffrey F.
  1990 *Archaeological Investigations at Puerco Ruin, Petrified Forest National Park, Arizona.* Publications in Anthropology No. 54. Western Archaeological and Conservation Center, National Park Service, U.S. Department of the Interior, Tucson.

Burton, Jeffrey F., and Richard Hughes E.
  1990 Obsidian Source Analysis. In *Archaeological Investigations at Puerco Ruin, Petrified Forest National Park, Arizona,* pp. 283–288. Publications in Anthropology No. 64. Western Archaeological and Conservation Center, National Park Service, U.S. Department of the Interior, Tucson.

Cameron, Catherine
  1990 Pit Structure Abandonment in the Four Corners Region of the American Southwest: Late Basketmaker III and Pueblo I Periods. *Journal of Field Archaeology* 17:27-37.

  1995 Migration and Movement of Southwestern Peoples. *Journal of Anthropological Archaeology* 14:104-124.

  1999 *Hopi Dwellings: Architecture at Orayvi.* University of Arizona Press, Tucson.

Carlson, Roy L.
  1970 *White Mountain Red Ware: A Pottery Tradition of East-central Arizona and Western New Mexico.* Anthropological Papers No. 19. University of Arizona Press, Tucson.

Clark, Jeffrey J.
  2001 *Tracking Prehistoric Migrations: Pueblo Settlers among the Tonto Basin Hohokam.* Anthropological Papers of the University of Arizona, No. 65. University of Arizona Press, Tucson.

  2011 Disappearance and Diaspora: Contrasting Two Migrations in the Southern U.S. Southwest. In *Rethinking Anthropological Perspectives on Migration*, edited by Graciela S. Cabana and Jeffery S. Clark, pp. 84-108, University Press of Florida, Gainesville.

Colton, Harold S.
  1937 Some Notes on the Original Condition of the Little Colorado River: A Side Light on the Problems of Erosion. *Museum Notes* 10(6):17-20. Museum of Northern Arizona, Flagstaff.

  1956 *Pottery Types of the Southwest, Wares 5A, 5B, 6A, 6B, 7A, 7B, 7C: San Juan Red Ware, Tsegi Orange Ware, Homolovi Orange Ware, Winslow Orange Ware, Awatovi Yellow Ware, Jeddito Yellow Ware, Sichomovi Red Ware.* Ceramic Series, No. 3C. Museum of Northern Arizona, Flagstaff.

Colton, Harold H., and Lyndon L. Hargrave
  1937 *Handbook of Northern Arizona Pottery Wares.* Museum of Northern Arizona, Bulletin 11. Flagstaff.

Connerton, Paul
  1989 *How Societies Remember.* Cambridge University Press, Cambridge.

Courlander, Harold
  1971 *The Fourth World of the Hopis.* Crown Publishers, New York.

Crown, Patricia
    1994   *Ceramics and Ideology: Salado Polychrome Pottery*. University of New Mexico Press, Albuquerque.

    2000   Women's Role in Changing Cuisine. In *Women and Men in the Prehispanic Southwest: Labor, Power, and Prestige*, edited by Patricia L. Crown, pp. 221-266. School of American Research Press, Santa Fe.

Crown, Patricia, and Ronald Bishop
    1991   Manufacture of Gila Polychrome in the Greater American Southwest: An Instrumental Neutron Activation Analysis. In *Homol'ovi II: Archaeology of an Ancestral Hopi Village, Arizona,* edited by E. Charles Adams and Kelley Ann Hays, pp. 49-56. Anthropological Papers No. 55. University of Arizona Press, Tucson.

Cutler, Hugh
    1952   A Preliminary Survey of Plant Remains of Tularosa Cave. In *Mogollon Cultural Continuity and Change. The Stratigraphic Analysis of Tularosa and Cordova Caves*, by Paul S. Martin, pp. 461-479. Fieldiana: Anthropology, No. 40. Field Museum of Natural History, Chicago.

Darling, Andrew
    1998   Mass Inhumation and the Execution of Witches in the American Southwest. *American Anthropologist* 100:732-752.

Dean, Jeffrey S.
    1988a   A Model of Anasazi Behavioral Adaptation. In *The Anasazi in a Changing Environment*, edited by George J. Gumerman, pp. 25-44. Cambridge University Press, Cambridge.

Dean, Jeffrey S., Robert C. Euler, George J. Gumerman, Fred Plog, Richard H. Hevley, and Thor N. V. Karlstrom
    1985   Human Behavior, Demography, and Paleoenvironment on the Colorado Plateaus. *American Antiquity* 50:537–554.

Dean, Rebecca
    2003   People, Pests and Prey: The Emergence of Agricultural Economics in the Desert Southwest. Unpublished Ph.D. Dissertation, Department of Anthropology, University of Arizona, Tucson.

Dedecker, Melanie
    2005   Piki Bread. Unpublished Master's Thesis, Department of Anthropology, University of Arizona, Tucson.

    2006   The Role of Ground Stone Exchange in the Homol'ovi Settlement Cluster. Paper presented in *Recent Research at Chevelon Ruin, an Ancient Hopi Village in Northeastern Arizona*, presented at the 71st Annual Meeting of the Society for American Archaeology, San Juan, Puerto Rico.

Diaz de Valdes, Rachel E.
    2006   Paper presented in the symposium: *Recent Research at Chevelon Ruin, an Ancient Hopi Village in Northeastern Arizona*, presented at the 71st Annual Meeting of the Society for American Archaeology, San Juan, Puerto Rico.

    2007   Ritual Use of Fauna at Chevelon Ruin. Master's thesis, Department of Anthropology, University of Arizona, Tucson.

Di Peso, Charles
    1974   *Casas Grandes. A Fallen Trading Center of the Gran Chichimeca*. Vol. 6. Northland Press, Flagstaff, Arizona.

Dittert, Alfred E.
    1959   *Culture Change in the Cebolleta Mesa Region, Central Western New Mexico*. Ph.D. dissertation. Department of Anthropology, University of Arizona, Tucson.

Dohm, Karen
    1990   Effect of Population Nucelation on House Size for Pueblos in the American Southwest. *Journal of Anthropological Archaeology* 9:201-239.

Duff, Andrew I.
    1998   The Process of Migration in the Late Prehistoric Southwest. In *Migration and Reorganization: The Pueblo IV Period in the American Southwest*, edited by Katherine Spielmann, pp. 31-52. Anthropological Research Papers, No. 51. Arizona State University, Tempe.

    1999   *Regional Interaction and the Transformation of Western Pueblo Identities, A.D. 1275–1400*. Ph.D. dissertation, Department of Anthropology, Arizona State University, Tempe.

    2002   *Western Pueblo Identities: Regional Interaction, Migration, and Transformation*. University of Arizona Press, Tucson.

    2004   Settlement Clustering and Village Interaction in the Upper Little Colorado Region. In *The Protohistoric Pueblo World: A.D. 1275-1600*, edited by E. Charles Adams and Andrew I. Duff, pp. 75-85. University of Arizona Press, Tucson.

Eggan, Fred
    1950   *Social Organization of the Western Pueblos*. University of Chicago Press, Chicago.

English, N. B., Julio L. Betancourt, Jeffrey S. Dean, and J. Quade
    2001   Strontium Isotopes Reveal Distant Sources of Architectural Timber in Chaco Canyon, New Mexico. *Proceedings of the National Academy of Sciences* 98(21): 111891-111896.

Ensor, H. Blaine, and Erwin Roemer, Jr.
    1989   Comments on Sullivan and Rozen's Debitage Analysis and Archaeological Interpretation. *American Antiquity* 54:175–178.

Fenner, Gloria J.
    1971   Introduction to Casas Grandes Shell. In *Casas Grandes: A Fallen Trading Center of the Gran Chichimeca*, Volume 6, Ceramics and Shell, edited by Charles C. Di Peso, John B. Rinaldo, and Gloria J. Fenner, pp. 385-389. Northland Press, Flagstaff.

Fewkes, Jesse Walter
    1898   Preliminary Account of An Expedition to the Pueblo Ruins Near Winslow, Arizona, in 1896. In *Annual Report of the Smithsonian Institution for 1896*, pp. 517-540. Smithsonian Institution, Washinton, D.C.

    1900   New Fire Ceremony at Walpi. *American Anthropologist* 2:79-138.

Fewkes, Jesse Walter, *cont'd*
  1904   Two Summer's Work in Pueblo Ruins. In *Twenty-second Annual Report of the Bureau of American Ethnology for 1899-1900*, pp. 3-196. Smithsonian Institution, Washington, D.C.

  1906   Hopi Shrines near the East Mesa, Arizona. *American Anthropologist* 8:346-375.

Fish, Suzanne
  1991   Pollen. In *Homol'ovi II: Archaeology of an Ancestral Hopi Village, Arizona*, edited by E. Charles Adams and Kelley Ann Hays, pp. 84-87. Anthropological Papers No. 55. University of Arizona Press, Tucson.

  2001   Pollen Results. In *Homol'ovi III: A Pueblo Hamlet in the Middle Little Colorado River Valley*, edited by E. Charles Adams, pp. 321-334. Arizona State Museum Archaeological Series No. 193. University of Arizona, Tucson.

Fish, Suzanne K., and Gary P. Nabhan
  1991   Desert as Context: The Hohokam Environment. *Exploring the Hohokam, Prehistoric Desert Peoples of the American Southwest*, edited by George J. Gumerman, pp. 29-60. University of New Mexico Press, Albuquerque.

Forde, C. Daryll
  1929   Hopi Agriculture and Land Ownership. *Journal of the Royal Anthropological Institute* 41:357-405.

Fowles, Severin
  2013   *An Archaeology of Doings: Secularism and the Study of Pueblo Religion*. School of Advanced Research, Santa Fe, New Mexico.

Fratt, Lee
  1991   Ground Stone. In *Homol'ovi II: The Archaeology of an Ancestral Hopi Village*, edited by E. Charles Adams and Kelley Ann Hays, pp. 57-74. Anthropological Papers No. 55. University of Arizona Press, Tucson.

  2001   Homol'ovi III Ground Stone. In *Homol'ovi III: A Pueblo Hamlet in the Middle Little Colorado River Valley*, edited by E. Charles Adams, pp. 227-238. Arizona State Museum Archaeological Series No. 193. University of Arizona, Tucson.

Fratt, Lee, and Maggie Biancaniello
  1993   Homol'ovi III Ground Stone in the Raw: A Study of Local Sandstone Used to Make Ground Stone Artifacts. *Kiva* 48:373-91.

Gann, Douglas
  1996a The Adobe Brick Site: Investigations in Pre-Hispanic Adobe Brick Architecture. Master's thesis, Department of Anthropology, University of Arizona, Tucson.

  1996b The Use of Adobe Brick Architecture in the Homol'ovi Region. In *River of Change: Prehistory of the Middle Little Colorado River Valley, Arizona*, edited by E. Charles Adams, pp. 93-105. Arizona State Museum Archaeological Series No. 155. University of Arizona, Tucson.

  2003   Spatial Integration: A Space Syntax Analysis of the Villages of the Homol'ovi Cluster. Unpublished PhD Dissertation, Department of Anthropology, University of Arizona, Tucson.

Gavioli, Lisa
   2005   Chevelon Ceramic Analysis for the 2003 and 2004 Field Seasons. Ms. on file, Homol'ovi Lab, Arizona State Museum, University of Arizona, Tucson.

Gavioli, Lisa, and Douglas Gann
   2006   Prehispanic Adobe Brick Architecture: Evidence from Chevelon Ruin, Northern Arizona. Paper presented in the symposium: *Recent Research at Chevelon Ruin, an Ancient Hopi Village in Northeastern Arizona*, presented at the 71st Annual Meeting of the Society for American Archaeology, San Juan, Puerto Rico.

Giddens, Anthony
   1979   *Central Problems in Social Theory: Action, Structure, and Contradiction in Social Analysis*. University of California Press, Berkeley.

   1981   *Power, Property, and the State*. University of California Press, Berkeley.

Gifford, James C., and Watson Smith
   1978   *Gray Corrugated Pottery from Awatovi and Other Jeddito Sites in Northeastern Arizona*. Papers of the Peabody Museum of Archaeology and Ethnology, Vol. 69. Harvard University, Cambridge, Massachusetts.

Gilchrist, Roberta, and Harold Mytum
   1986   Experimental Archaeological and Burnt Animal Bone from Archaeological Sites. In *Circaea* 4:29-38.

Godsen, Chris
   2005   What Do Objects Want? *Journal of Archaeological Method and Theory* 12:193-211.

Godsen, Chris, and Yvonne Marshall
   1999   The Cultural Biography of Objects. *World Archaeology* 31:169-178.

Graves, Michael W.
   1984   Temporal Variation among White Mountain Redware Design Styles. *Kiva* 50:3-24.

Grayson, D. K.
   1984   *Quantitative Zooarchaeology: Topics in the Analysis of Archaeological Faunas*. Academic Press, Inc., New York.

Hack, John T.
   1942   *The Changing Physical Environment of the Hopi Indians of Arizona*. Papers of the Peabody Museum of American Archaeology and Ethnology, Vol. 35, No. 1. Harvard University, Cambridge, Massachusetts.

Harper, Barbara
   2004   Shell. In *Homol'ovi IV: The First Village*. Arizona State Museum Occasional Electronic Publication, No. 1, edited by E. Charles Adams, pp. 111-115. University of Arizona, Tucson.

Harry, Karen
   1987   An Analysis of the Obsidian Assemblage at Homol'ovi III. Manuscript on file, Homol'ovi Research Program, Arizona State Museum, University of Arizona, Tucson.

   1989   The Obsidian Assemblage from Homol'ovi III: Social and Economic Implications. *Kiva* 54:285-296.

Haury, Emil W.
    1958   Evidence at Point of Pines for a Prehistoric Migration from Northern Arizona. In *Migrations in New World Culture History*, edited by Raymond H. Thompson, pp. 1-7. University of Arizona Press, Tucson.

    1965   Shell. In *Excavations at Snaketown: Material Culture*, edited by Harold S. Gladwin, Emil W. Haury, E. B. Sayles, and Nora Gladwin, pp. 135-153. Medallion Papers, No. 25. Gila Pueblo, Globe, Arizona.

    1976   *The Hohokam, Desert Farmers and Craftsmen: Excavations at Snaketown*, 1964-1965. University of Arizona Press, Tucson.

Hays, Kelley A.
    1991   Ceramics. In *Homol'ovi II: Archaeology of an Ancestral Hopi Village, Arizona*, edited by E. Charles Adams and Kelley A. Hays, pp. 23-48. Anthropological Papers No. 55. University of Arizona Press, Tucson.

Hays-Gilpin, Kelley A., Trixi Bubemyre, and Louise Senior
    1996   The Rise and Demise of Winslow Orange Ware. In *River of Change: Prehistory of the Middle Little Colorado River Valley, Arizona*, edited by E. Charles Adams, pp. 36-92. Arizona State Museum Archaeological Series No. 155. University of Arizona, Tucson.

Hays-Gilpin, Kelley, and Eric van Hartesveldt
    1998   *Prehistoric Ceramics of the Puerco Valley: The Chambers-Sanders Trust Lands Ceramic Conference*. Ceramic Series, No. 7. Museum of Northern Arizona, Flagstaff.

Hegmon, Michelle, Scott G. Ortman, and Jeannette L. Mobley-Tanaka
    2000   Women, Men, and the Organization of Space. In *Women and Men in the Prehispanic Southwest*, edited by Patricia L. Crown, pp. 43-90. School of American Research Press, Santa Fe, New Mexico.

Heitman, Carrie
    2015   The House of Our Ancestors: New Research on the Prehistory of Chaco Canyon. In *Chaco Revisited: New Research on the Prehistory of Chaco Canyon*, edited by Carrie C. Heitman and Stephen Plog, pp. 215-248. University of Arizona Press, Tucson.

Hill, Erica
    2000   The Contextual Analysis of Animal Interments and Ritual Practices in Southwestern North America. *Kiva* 65:361-398.

Hillier, Bill, and Julienne Hanson
    1984   *The Social Logic of Space*. Cambridge University Press, New York.

Hockett, Bryan, and Jonathan A. Haws
    2002   Taphonomic and Methodological Perspectives of Leporid Hunting during the Upper Paleolithic of the Western Mediterranean Basin. *Journal of Archaeological Method and Theory* 9:269-302.

Hodder, Ian, and Scott Hutson
    2003   *Reading the Past: Current Approaches to Interpretation in Archaeology*, Third Edition. Cambridge University Press, Cambridge.

Hough, Walter
    1898   Environmental Interrelations in Arizona. *American Anthropologist*. 11(5):133-155.

Huckell, Bruce
    1999   Report of Excavations at God's Pocket. Manuscript on file, Homol'ovi Research Program, Arizona State Museum, University of Arizona, Tucson.

Icove, David J., H.E. Welborn, A.J. Vonarx, E. Charles Adams, James R. Lally, Timothy G. Huff
    2008   Scientific Investigation and Modeling of Prehistoric Structural Fires at Chevelon Pueblo. In *Proceedings of the 2006 International Symposium on Fire Investigation Science and Technology*, pp. 457-467. National Association of Arson Investigators, Sarasota, Florida.

Jennings, Calvin H.
    1967   Excavations at the Puerco Site; Preliminary Report. Manuscript on file, Western Archaeological and Conservation Center, National Park Service, Tucson.

    1980   Further Investigations at the Puerco Site, Petrified National Forest Park. Arizona. Manuscript on file, Western Archaeological and Conservation Center, National Park Service, Tucson.

Johnson, Duane L., and Mitra N. Jha
    1993   Blue Corn. In *New Crops*, edited by J. Janick and J.E. Simon, pp. 228-230. Wiley, New York.

Johnson, Douglas A.
    1992   Adobe Brick Architecture and Salado Ceramics at Fourmile Ruin. In *Proceedings of the Second Salado Conference, Globe, Arizona*, edited by Richard C. Lange and Stephen Germick, pp. 131-138. Arizona Archaeological Society, Phoenix.

Johnson, Gregory
    1989   Dynamics of Southwestern Prehistory: Far Outside – Looking In. In *Dynamics of Southwestern Prehistory*, edited by Linda S. Cordell and George J. Gumerman, pp. 371-389. Washington, D.C.: Smithsonian Institution.

Justice, Noel D.
    2002   Stone Age Spear and Arrow Points of the Southwestern United States. Indiana University Press, Bloomington.

Kaldahl, Eric
    1999   Chipped Stone. In *Living on the Edge of the Rim: Excavations and Analysis of the Silver Creek Archaeological Research Project, 1993-1998*, edited by Barbara J. Mills, Sarah A. Herr, and Scott van Keuren, pp. 325–372. Arizona State Museum Archaeological Series No. 192. University of Arizona, Tucson.

Karunaratne, Priyantha
    1997   Variability of Ritual Space and Abandonment Deposits as Expressed in the Archaeological Record: A Study on Pueblo IV Villages in the Homol'ovi Region, Northeastern Arizona. Master's thesis, Department of Anthropology, University of Arizona, Tucson.

Keen, Myra A.
    1971   *Sea Shells of Tropical West America: Marine Mollusks from Baja California to Peru*. Second edition. Stanford University Press, Stanford.

Kelly, Robert L.
    2001   *Prehistory of the Carson Desert and Stillwater Mountains: Environment, Mobility, and Subsistence in a Great Basin Wetland*. University of Utah Anthropological Papers, No. 123. Salt Lake City, Utah.

Klandrud, Sarah
    2002   Bone Tools and Roof Deposits at Homol'ovi Villages. Poster presented at the 67th Annual Meeting of the Society for American Archaeology, Denver, Colorado.

Kohler, Timothy A., Mark D. Varien, and Aaron M. Wright, editors
    2010   *Leaving Mesa Verde: Peril and Change in the Thirteenth-Century Southwest.* The University of Arizona Press, Tucson.

Kolbe, Thomas
    1991   The Geomorphology and Alluvial Chronology of the Middle Little Colorado River Valley. Master's Thesis, Department of Quaternary Studies, Northern Arizona University, Flagstaff.

Krebs, Billie
    1999   An Analysis of the Projectile Point Assemblage from Homol'ovi I and II. Honor's Thesis, Department of Anthropology, University of Arizona, Tucson. On file.

Kuckelman, Kristin
    2002   The Bioarchaeology and Taphonomy of Violence at Castle Rock and Sand Canyon Pueblos, Southwestern Colorado. *American Antiquity* 67:486-513.

Lally, J.R.
    2005   Reconstructing the Cause and Origin of Structural Fires in the Archaeological Record of the Greater Southwest. Unpublished Ph.D. dissertation, Department of Anthropology, University of New Mexico, Albuquerque.

Lally, J.R., and A. J. Vonarx
    2011   Fire: Accidental or Intentional? An Archaeological Toolkit for Evaluating Accident and Intent in Ancient Structural Fires. In *Contemporary Archaeologies of the Southwest*, edited by William H. Walker and Kathryn R. Venzor, pp. 157-171. University Press of Colorado, Boulder.

LaMotta, Vincent M.
    1996   The Use of Disarticulated Human Remains in Abandonment Ritual at Homol'ovi. Master's Thesis, Department of Anthropology, University of Arizona, Tucson.

    2006   Zooarchaeology and Chronology of Homol'ovi I and Other Pueblo IV Period Sites in the Central Little Colorado River Valley, Northern Arizona. Unpublished Ph.D. dissertation. Department of Anthropology, University of Arizona, Tucson.

LaMotta, Vincent M., and Michael B. Schiffer
    1999   Formation Processes of House Floor Assemblages. In *The Archaeology of Household Activities*, edited by Penelope M. Allison, pp. 19-29. Routledge, New York.

Lange, Richard C.
    1996   The Little Colorado River, Farming, and Prehistory in the Homol'ovi Area. In *River of Change: Prehistory of the Middle Little Colorado River Valley, Arizona*, edited by E. Charles Adams, pp. 239-258. Arizona State Museum Archaeological Series No. 185. University of Arizona, Tucson.

    1998   *Prehistoric Land-Use and Settlement of the Middle Little Colorado River Valley: The Survey of Homolovi Ruins State Park, Winslow, Arizona.* Arizona State Museum Archaeological Series No. 189. University of Arizona, Tucson.

Lange, Richard C., *cont'd*
  2017 Homol'ovi II Final Report. Homol'ovi Research Program, Arizona State Museum, University of Arizona, Tucson.

Lange, Richard C., E. Charles Adams, Samantha G. Fladd
  2015 Rock Art Ranch Survey Report for 2014 Field Season. Unpublished manuscript, Homol'ovi Research Program, Arizona State Museum, University of Arizona, Tucson.

LeBlanc, Steven A.,
  1999 *Prehistoric Warfare in the American Southwest.* University of Utah Press, Salt Lake City, Utah.

LeBlanc, Steven A., and Lucinda Henderson
  2009 *Marks of the Maker: Seeking Artists' Identities in Hopi Yellow Ware Bowls.* Papers of the Peabody Museum of Archaeology and Ethnology, No. 84, Harvard University, Cambridge, Massachusetts.

Levy, Jerrold
  1992 *Old Orayvi Revisited.* University of Arizona Press, Tucson.

Lightfoot, Kent G.
  1984 *Prehistoric Political Dynamics: A Case Study from the American Southwest.* Northern Illinois University Press, DeKalb, Illinois.

Lightfoot, Ricky
  1994 *The Duckfoot Site, Vol. 2: Archaeology of the House and Household.* Occasional Papers, No. 4. Crow Canyon Archaeological Center, Cortez, Colorado.

Loftin, John D.
  2003 *Religion and Hopi Life.* University of Indiana Press, Bloomington, Indiana. Second edition.

Lowe, Charles H.
  1964a *Arizona's Natural Environment.* University of Arizona Press, Tucson.

Lowe, Charles H., editor
  1964b *The Vertebrates of Arizona with a Major Section on Arizona Habitats.* University of Arizona Press, Tucson.

Lyman, R. Lee
  1994a Quantitative Units and Terminology in Zooarchaeology. *American Antiquity* 59: 36-71.

  1994b *Vertebrate Taphonomy.* Cambridge University Press, Cambridge, U.K.

Lyons, Patrick D.
  2001 Winslow Orange Ware and the Ancestral Hopi Migration Horizon. Unpublished Ph.D. dissertation, Department of Anthropology, University of Arizona, Tucson.

  2003 *Ancestral Hopi Migrations.* Anthropological Papers No. 68. University of Arizona Press, Tucson.

  2013 Jeddito Yellow Ware, Migration, and the Kayenta Diaspora. *Kiva* 79:147-174.

Lyons, Patrick D., and Kelley A. Hays-Gilpin
    2001   Homol'ovi III Ceramics. In *Homol'ovi III: A Pueblo Hamlet in the Middle Little Colorado River Valley*, edited by E. Charles Adams, pp. 137-226. Arizona State Museum Archaeological Series No. 193. University of Arizona, Tucson.

Lyons, Patrick D. and Bonnie L. Pitblado
    1996   Chipped Stone Research in the Middle Little Colorado River Valley, Past and Present. In *River of Change: Prehistory of the Middle Little Colorado River Valley, Arizona*, edited by E. Charles Adams, pp. 219-239. Arizona State Museum Archaeological Series No. 185. University of Arizona, Tucson.

Marshall, Fiona, and Tom Pilgram
    1991   NISP vs. MNI in Quantification of Body-Part Representation. *American Antiquity* 58:261-269.

McCracken, Erin
    2003   Fish Remains from the Homol'ovi Villages. Master's thesis, Department of Anthropology, University of Arizona, Tucson.

McKusick, Charmion
    1986   *Southwest Indian Turkeys: Prehistory and Comparative Osteology*. Southwest Bird Laboratory, Globe, Arizona.

Meyers, Julia
    2007   Prehistoric Wall Decoration in the American Southwest: A Behavioral Approach. Unpublished Ph.D. dissertation, Department of Anthropology, University of Arizona, Tucson.

Miksicek, Charles
    1988   Plant Remains Recovered by Flotation from Homol'ovi III. Portion of letter report dated Sept. 20, 1988 on file, Homol'ovi Research Program, Arizona State Museum, Tucson.

    1991   Paleoethnobotany. In *Homol'ovi II; Archaeology of an Ancestral Hopi Village, Arizona*, edited by E. Charles Adams, pp. 88-102. Anthropological Papers, No. 55. University of Arizona Press, Tucson.

Miljour, Heather J.
    2016   Homol'ovi I Pueblo: An Examination of Plant Remains within Ash Closure, Renewal, and Dedication Deposits. Unpublished Master's Thesis. School of Anthropology, University of Arizona, Tucson.

Miller, Myles
    2010   Dust to Dust: Ritual Termination of Jornada Mogollon Pueblos in South-Central New Mexico. Paper presented at the 75th Annual Meeting of the Society for American Archaeology, St. Louis, Missouri.

Mills, Barbara J.
    1999   The Reorganization of Silver Creek Communities from the 11th to 14th Centuries. In *Living on the Edge of the Rim: Excavations and Analysis of the Silver Creek Archaeological Research Project 1993-1998*, edited by Barbara J. Mills, Sarah A. Herr, and Scott Van Keuren, pp. 505-512. Arizona State Museum Archaeological Series No. 192, Vol. 2. University of Arizona Press, Tucson.

    2004   The Establishment and Defeat of Hierarchy: Inalienable Possessions and the History of Collective Prestige Structures in the Pueblo Southwest. *American Anthropologist* 106:238-251.

Mills, Barbara J., *cont'd*
    2007   Performing the Feast: Visual Display and Suprahousehold Commensalism in the Puebloan Southwest. *American Antiquity* 72:210-239.

    2015   Unpacking the House: Ritual Practice and Social Networks at Chaco. In *Chaco Revisited: New Research on the Prehistory of Chaco Canyon*, edited by Carrie C. Heitman and Stephen Plog, pp. 249-271. University of Arizona Press, Tucson.

Mills, Barbara J., Jeffery J. Clark, Matthew A. Peeples, William R, Haas, Jr., John M. Roberts, Jr, Brent Hill, Deborah L. Huntley, Lewis Borck, Ronald L. Breiger, Aaron Clauset, and M. Steven Shackley.
    2013   The Transformation of Social Networks in the Late Prehispanic U.S. Southwest. *Proceedings of the National Academy of Sciences* 110:5785-5790.

Mills, Barbara J., and Sarah H. Herr
    1999   Chronology of the Mogollon Rim Region. In *Living on the Edge of the Rim: Excavations and Analysis of the Silver Creek Archaeological Research Project 1993-1998*, edited by Barbara J. Mills, Sarah A. Herr, and Scott Van Keuren, pp. 269-293. Arizona State Museum Archaeological Series, no. 192, vol. 1. University of Arizona Press, Tucson.

Mills, Barbara J., Sarah A. Herr, Susan L. Stinson, and Daniela Triadan
    1999   Ceramic Production and Distribution. In *Living on the Edge of the Rim: Excavations and Analysis of the Silver Creek Archaeological Research Project 1993-1998*, edited by Barbara J. Mills, Sarah A. Herr, and Scott Van Keuren, pp. 295-324. Arizona State Museum Archaeological Series No. 192, Vol. 2. University of Arizona Press, Tucson.

Mills, Barbara J., and William H. Walker
    2008   Introduction: Memory, Materiality, and Depositional Practice. In *Memory Work: Archaeologies of Material Practices*, edited by Barbara J. Mills and William H. Walker, pp. 3-23. School for Advanced Research Press, Santa Fe, New Mexico.

Milton, Susan J.
    1999   *Statistical Methods in the Biological and Health Sciences.* McGraw-Hill, Boston.

Mindeleff, Cosmos
    1900   Localization of Tusayan Clans. In *Nineteenth Annual Report of the Bureau of American Ethnology for the Years 1897-1898,* pp. 635-653. U.S. Government Printing Office, Washington, D.C.

Minnis, Paul E.
    1987   Identification of Wood from Archaeological Sites in the American Southwest, I. Keys for Gymnosperms. *Journal of Archaeological Science* 14:121-131.

Montgomery, Barbara K.
    1992   Understanding the Formation of the Archaeological Record: Ceramic Variability at Chodistaas Pueblo, Arizona. Unpublished Ph.D. dissertation, Department of Anthropology, University of Arizona, Tucson.

Myers, Fred R.
    2001   Introduction. In *The Empire of Things: Regimes of Value and Material Culture*, edited by Fred R. Myers, pp. 3-61. School of American Research Press, Santa Fe, New Mexico.

Nelson, Margaret C.
1991 The Study of Technological Organization. In *Archaeological Method and Theory*, edited by Michael B. Schiffer, pp. 57-100. University of Arizona Press, Tucson.

Nelson, Russell
1989 Wedges at Homol'ovi III. Manuscript on file, Homol'ovi Research Program, Arizona State Museum, University of Arizona, Tucson.

Nequatewa, Edmund
1936 *Truth of a Hopi*. Bulletin 8. Museum of Northern Arizona, Flagstaff.

Odell, George
2004 *Lithic Analysis*. Manuals in Archaeological Method, Theory, and Technique. Springer Science + Business Media, New York.

Olsen, Stanley J., and Richard Page Wheeler
1978 *Bones from Awatovi, Northeastern Arizona*. Papers of the Peabody Museum of Archaeology and Ethnology, Vol. 78, No. 1 and 2. Harvard University, Cambridge.

Ortiz, Alfonso A.
1969 *The Tewa World*. University of Chicago Press, Illinois.

Page, Gordon
1940 Hopi Agricultural Notes. U.S. Department of Agriculture, Soil Conservation Service, Washington, D.C.

Parry, William J. and Robert L. Kelly
1987 Expedient Core Technology and Sedentism. In *The Organization of Core Technology*, edited by Jay K. Johnson and Carol A. Morrow, pp. 51-77. Westview Press, Boulder.

Parsons, Elsie Clews, editor
1936 *The Journals of Alexander M. Stephen*. 2 vols. Columbian University Press, New York.

1939 *Pueblo Indian Religion*. 2 vols. University of Chicago Press, Illinois..

Pasternek, Burton, Carol Ember, and Melvin Ember
1976 On the Conditions Favoring Extended Family Households. *Journal of Anthropological Research* 32:109-123.

Pavao, Barnet
1994 *Toward a Taphonomy of Leporid Skeletons: Photondensitometry Assays*. Unpublished honors thesis. State University of New York at Binghamton, Binghamton.

Perkins, Dwight Lee
1981 The Sandhill Crane in Arizona. Unpublished Master's Thesis, Department of Anthropology, The University of Arizona, Tucson.

Pierce, Linda
2001 Faunal Remains. In *Homol'ovi III: A Pueblo Hamlet in the Middle Little Colorado River Valley*, edited by E. Charles Adams, pp. 273-284. Arizona State Museum Archaeological Series No. 193. University of Arizona, Tucson

Potter, James M., and Jason P. Chuipka
   2013   Perimortem Mutilation of Human Remains in an Early Village in the American Southwest: A Case for Ethnic Violence. *Journal of Anthropological Archaeology* 29:507-523.

Potter, James M., and Elizabeth M. Perry
   2000   Ritual as a Power Source in the American Southwest. In *Alternative Leadership Strategies in the Prehispanic Southwest*, edited by Barbara J. Mills, pp. 60-78. University of Arizona Press, Tucson.

Prentiss, William C.
   1998   The Reliability and Validity of a Lithic Debitage Typology: Implications for Archaeological Interpretation. *American Antiquity* 63:635-650.

Prentiss, William C., and E. J. Romanski
   1989   Experimental Evaluation of Sullivan and Rozen's Debitage Typology. In *Experiments in Lithic Technology*, edited by Daniel S. Amick and Raymond P. Maudlin, pp. 89–100. BAR International Series 528. BAR, Oxford, England.

Rappaport, Roy A.
   1979   *Ecology, Meaning, and Religion*. Richmond, North Atlantic Books, California.

   1999   *Ritual and Religion in the Making of Humanity*. Cambridge University Press, Cambridge.

Reitz, Elizabeth J., and Elizabeth S. Wing
   1999   *Zooarchaeology*. Cambridge University Press, Cambridge.

Roler, Kathy Lynne
   1999   The Chaco Phenomenon: A Faunal Perspective from the Peripheries. Unpublished Ph.D. dissertation, Department of Anthropology, Arizona State University, Tempe.

Samuels, Michael L., and Julio L. Betancourt
   1982   Modeling the Long-term Effects of Fuelwood Harvests on Pinyon-Juniper Woodlands. *Environmental Management* 6:505-515.

Schiffer, Michael B.
   1987   *Behavioral Archaeology*. Academic Press, New York.

Sedig, Jakob W.
   2007   Getting to the Point: An Examination of Projectile Point Use in the Northern American Southwest, A.D. 900-1300. Unpublished Master's thesis, Department of Anthropology, University of Colorado, Boulder.

Senior, Louise M., and Linda Pierce
   1989   Turkeys and Domestication in the Southwest: Implications from Homol'ovi III. *Kiva* 54:245-259.

Shackley, M. Steven
   1997   An Energy Dispersive X-Ray Fluorescence (EDXRF) Analysis of Obsidian Artifacts from Five Ancestral Hopi Sites: Awat'ovi, Kawaika'a, Bidahochi, Fourmile Ruin, and Homol'ovi II in Northern Arizona. Manuscript on file, Homol'ovi Research Program Laboratory, Arizona State Museum, University of Arizona, Tucson.

Shackley, M. Steven, *cont'd*
  2009 Source Provenance of Obsidian Artifacts from Fourmile Ruin (AZ P:12:4 ASM), Shumway Ruin (AZ P:12:127), and Pinedale Ruin (AZ P:12:2), Silver Creek Area, Northern Arizona. Manuscript on file, Homol'ovi Research Program Laboratory, Arizona State Museum, University of Arizona, Tucson.

  2010 Source Provenance of Obsidian Artifacts from the Late Classic Sites of Chevelon, Homol'ovi I, and Homol'ovi II in Northern Arizona. Manuscript on file, Homol'ovi Research Program Laboratory, Arizona State Museum, University of Arizona, Tucson.

Shaw, Margaret, A.J. Vonarx, and R. Emerson Howell
  2006 Wood Use Behavior, Resource Recycling, and Construction Technologies at Chevelon Pueblo. Paper presented in the symposium: *Recent Research at Chevelon Ruin, an Ancient Hopi Village in Northeastern Arizona*, presented at the 71st Annual Meeting of the Society for American Archaeology, San Juan, Puerto Rico.

Shennan, Stephen
  1988 *Quantifying Archaeology*. Edinburgh University Press, Edinburgh, Scotland.

Simpson, Ruth DeEtte
  1953 *The Hopi Indians*. Southwest Museum Leaflets No. 25. Southwest Museum, Los Angeles.

Smith, Watson
  1952 *Kiva Mural Decorations at Awsatovi and Kawaika-a, with a Survey of Other Wall Paintings in the Pueblo Southwest*. Papers of the Peabody Museum of American Archaeology and Ethnology, Vol. 37. Harvard University, Cambridge.

  1971 *Painted Ceramics of the Western Mound at Awatovi*. Papers of the Peabody Museum of Archaeology and Ethnology, Vol. 38. Harvard University, Cambridge, Massachusetts.

  1972 *Prehistoric Kivas as of Antelope Mesa, Northeastern Arizona*. Papers of the Peabody Museum of Archaeology and Ethnology, Vol. 39, No. 1. Harvard University, Cambridge, Massachusetts.

Sobolik, Kristin D.
  1992 Direct Evidence for the Importance of Small Animals to Prehistoric Diets: A Review of Coprolite Studies. *North American Archaeologist* 14:227-244.

Stevenson, Mark G.
  1982 Toward an Understanding of Site Abandonment Behavior: Evidence from Historic Mining Camps in the Southwest Yukon. *Journal of Anthropological Archaeology* 1:237-265.

Stiner, Mary C., Steven Kuhn, Stephen Weiner, and Ofer Bar-Yosef.
  1995 Differential Burning, Recrystallization, and Fragmentation of Archaeological Bone. *Journal of Archaeological Science* 22:223-237.

Strand, Jennifer
  1998 An Analysis of Homol'ovi Fauna with Emphasis on Ritual Behavior. Ph.D. dissertation, Department of Anthropology, University of Arizona, Tucson.

Strand, Jennifer, and Rebecca McKim
 1996 Analysis of the Fauna from Homol'ovi II. In *River of Change: Prehistory of the Middle Little Colorado River Valley, Arizona*, edited by E. Charles Adams, pp. 187-217. Arizona State Museum Archaeological Papers, No. 185. University of Arizona, Tucson.

Suárez, Diez Lourdes.
 1989 *Conchas Prehispanicas en México*. BAR International Series, No. 514. Oxford, England.

Sullivan, Alan P., III, and John H. Madsen
 1991 Chipped Stone. In *Homol'ovi II: Archaeology of an Ancestral Hopi Village, Arizona*, edited by E. Charles Adams and Kelly Ann Hays, pp. 75-83. Anthropological Papers No. 55. University of Arizona Press, Tucson.

Sullivan, Alan P., III, and Kenneth C. Rozen
 1985 Debitage Analysis and Archaeological Interpretation. *American Antiquity* 50:755-779.

Szuter, Christine R.
 1989 Hunting by Prehistoric Horticulturalists in the American Southwest. Unpublished Ph.D. dissertation, Department of Anthropology, University of Arizona, Tucson.

 1991 Faunal Remains. In *Homol'ovi II: Archaeology of an Ancestral Hopi Village, Arizona*, edited by E. Charles Adams and Kelly Ann Hays, pp. 103-111. Anthropological Papers No. 55. University of Arizona Press, Tucson.

Tagg, Martyn D.
 1994 Projectile Points of East-Central Arizona: Forms and Chronology. In *Middle Little Colorado River Archaeology: From the Parks to the People*, edited by Anne Trinkle Jones and Martyn D. Tagg, pp. 87-115. Arizona Archaeological Society, Phoenix.

Thompson, Kerry F.
 2005 Analysis of the Lithic Assemblage from the 2003 and 2004 Homol'ovi Research Program Excavations at Chevelon Ruin (AZ P 2:11). Manuscript on file, Homol'ovi Laboratory, Arizona State Museum, University of Arizona, Tucson.

Titiev, Mischa
 1944 *Old Oraibi: A Study of the Hopi Indians of Third Mesa*. Papers of the Peabody Museum of American Archaeology and Ethnology, Vol. 22. Harvard University, Cambridge, Massachusetts.

Triadan, Daniela
 1994 White Mountain Redware: Expensive Trade Goods or Local Commodity? A Study of the Production, Distribution and Function of White Mountain Redware During the 14th Century in the Grasshopper Region, East-Central Arizona. Unpublished Ph.D. dissertation, Freie Universität Berlin, Germany. University Microfilms, Ann Arbor, Michigan.

 1997 *Ceramic Commodities and Common Containers: Production and Distribution of White Mountain Red Ware in the Grasshopper Region, Arizona*. Anthropological Papers, No. 61. University of Arizona Press, Tucson.

Triadan, Daniela, and M. Nieves Zedeño
  2004 The Political Geography and Territoriality of 14th-Century Settlements in the Mogollon Mountains of East-Central Arizona. In *The Protohistoric Pueblo World, A.D. 1275-1600*, edited by E. Charles Adams and Andrew I. Duff, pp. 95-107. University of Arizona Press, Tucson.

Twiss, Katheryn C., Amy Bogaard, Doru Bogdan, Tristan Carter, Michael P. Charles, Shahina Farid, Nerissa Russell, Mirjana Stevanović, E. Nurcan Yalman, and Lisa Yeomans
  2008 Arson or accident? The burning of a Neolithic house at Çatalhöyük. *Journal of Field Archaeology* 33:41–57.

Tyler, Hamilton A.
  1975 *Pueblo Animals and Myths*. University of Oklahoma Press, Norman.

  1979 *Pueblo Birds and Myths*. University of Oklahoma Press, Norman.

  1991 *Pueblo Birds and Myths*. Northland Press, Flagstaff, Arizona.

U.S. Fish and Wildlife Service
  1998 Endangered and threatened wildlife and plants: withdrawal of proposed rule to list the San Xavier talus snail (*Sonorella eremita*) as endangered.

Urban, Sharon
  1991 Shell. In *Homol'ovi II: Archaeology of an Ancestral Hopi Village, Arizona*, edited by E. Charles Adams and Kelley Ann Hays, pp. 112-115. Anthropological Papers No. 55. University of Arizona Press, Tucson.

  2001 By Land, By Stream, By Sea: Shell from Homol'ovi III. In *Homol'ovi III: A Pueblo Hamlet in the Middle Little Colorado River Valley*, edited by E. Charles Adams, pp. 299-312. Arizona State Museum Archaeological Series No. 193. University of Arizona, Tucson.

Vaitkus, Robert
  1986 Experimental Replication of Winslow Orange Wares: A Prehistoric Assemblage at Homol'ovi II and Homol'ovi III. MS on file, Homol'ovi Research Program, Arizona State Museum, University of Arizona, Tucson.

Van Dyke, Ruth M., and Susan E. Alcock, editors
  2003 *Archaeologies of Memory*. Blackwell Publishers, Malden. Massachusetts.

Van West, Carla
  1994 *River, Rain, or Ruin: Intermittent Prehistoric Land Use along the Middle Little Colorado River*. Statistical Research Technical Series, No. 53. Tucson, Arizona.

  1996 Modeling Prehistoric Agricultural Strategies and Human Settlement in the Middle Little Colorado River Valley. In *River of Change: Prehistory of the Middle Little Colorado River Valley, Arizona*, edited by E. Charles Adams, pp. 15-35. Arizona State Museum Archaeological Papers, No. 185. University of Arizona, Tucson.

Varien, Mark
  1999 *Sedentism and Mobility in a Social Landscape: Mesa Verde and Beyond*. University of Arizona Press, Tucson.

Varien, Mark D., Scott G. Ortman, Timothy A. Kohler, Donna M. Glowacki, and C. David Johnson
   2007   Historical Ecology in the Mesa Verde Region: Results from the Village Ecodynamics Project. *American Antiquity* 72:273-299.

Velado, Martha Trenna
   1999   Ground Stone Technology. In *Living on the Edge of the Rim: Excavations and Analysis of the Silver Creek Archaeological Research Project 1993-1998*, edited by Barbara J. Mills, Sarah A. Herr, and Scott Van Keuren, pp. 373-403. Arizona State Museum, Archaeological Series, no. 192, University of Arizona, Tucson.

Velázquez, Castro Adrián
   1999   *Tipología de los objetos de concha del Templo Mayor de Tenochtitlan*. Col. Científica No. 392. Serie historia. INAH. México.

Vierra, Bradley J.
   1993a   Examining Long-Term Changes in Lithic Procurement and Reduction Strategies. In *Across the Colorado Plateau: Anthropological Studies for the Transwestern Pipeline Expansion Project*, edited by Bradley J. Vierra, Tim W. Burchett, Kenneth L. Brown, Marie E. Brown, Paul T. Kay, and Carl J. Phagan, pp. 139-352. Office of Contract Archaeology and Maxwell Museum of Anthropology, Albuquerque, New Mexico.

   1993b   Lithic Synthesis and Conclusions. In *Across the Colorado Plateau: Anthropological Studies for the Transwestern Pipeline Expansion Project,* edited by Bradley J. Vierra, Tim W. Burchett, Kenneth L. Brown, Marie E. Brown, Paul T. Kay, and Carl J. Phagan, pp. 353-382. Office of Contract Archaeology and Maxwell Museum of Anthropology, Albuquerque, New Mexico.

Vint, James, and Jeffery Burton
   1990   Ceramics. In *Archaeological Investigations at Puerco Ruin, Petrified Forest National Park, Arizona*, edited by Jeffery F. Burton, pp. 97-126. Western Archaeological and Conservation Center, Publications in Anthropology, No. 54. Tucson, Arizona.

Vokes, Arthur W.
   1989   Shell Artifacts. In The *1982-1984 Excavations at Las Colinas: Special Studies and Data Tables*. Arizona State Museum Archaeological Series, No. 162. University of Arizona, Tucson.

   2006   Shell artifacts. In *Rio Nuevo Archaeology Program, 2000-2003: Investigations at the San Agustin Mission and Mission Gardens, Tucson Presidio, Tucson Pressed Brick Company, and Clearwater Site,* edited by J. Homer Thiel and Jonathan B. Mabry. Technical Report, No. 2004-11. Center for Desert Archaeology, Tucson, Arizona.

Vonarx, A. J.
   2006   Preceramic Points in Pueblo Places: A Case Study in Heirlooming at Chevelon Pueblo. Paper presented at the 71st Annual Meeting of the Society for American Archaeology, San Juan, Puerto Rico.

   2008   Analysis of Projectile Points from Chevelon Ruin, 2003–2006 excavations. Unpublished database. On file at the Homol'ovi Research Program Laboratory, Arizona State Museum, University of Arizona, Tucson.

Walker, William H.
   1995   Ritual Prehistory: A Pueblo Case Study. Unpublished Ph.D. dissertation. Department of Anthropology, University of Arizona, Tucson.

   1996a   *Homol'ovi: A Cultural Crossroads*. Arizona Archaeological Society, Winslow.

Walker, William H., *cont'd*

    1996b   Ritual Deposits: Another Perspective. In *River of Change: Prehistory of the Middle Little Colorado River Valley, Arizona,* edited by E. Charles Adams, pp. 75-91. Arizona State Museum Archaeological Series, No. 185. University of Arizona, Tucson.

    1998   Where are the Witches of Prehistory? *Journal of Archaeological Method and Theory* 5:245-308.

    1999   Ritual Life History and the Afterlife of People and Things. *Journal of the Southwest* 41:383-405.

    2002   Stratigraphy and Practical Reason. *American Anthropologist* 101:159-177.

    2004   Ground Stone: A Behavioral Perspective. In *Homol'ovi IV: The First Village. Arizona State Museum Occasional Electronic Publication*, No. 1, edited by E. Charles Adams, pp. 77-88. University of Arizona, Tucson.

    2005   Witches, Practice, and the Context of Pueblo Cannabilism. In *Social Violence in the Prehispanic American Southwest,* edited by Patricia Crown and Deborah Nichols, pp. 143-183. University of Arizona Press, Tucson.

Walker, William H., Vincent M. LaMotta, and E. Charles Adams

    2000   Katsinas and Kiva Abandonment at Homol'ovi: A Deposit-oriented Perspective on Religion in Southwest Prehistory. In *The Archaeology of Regional Interaction: Religion, Warfare, and Exchange across the American Southwest and Beyond*, edited by Michelle Hegmon, pp. 341-360. University Press of Colorado, Boulder.

Walker, William H., and Michael Brian Schiffer

    2006   The Materiality of Social Power: The Artifact Acquisition Perspective. J*ournal of Archaeological Method and Theory* 13:67-88.

Ware, John A.

    2014   *A Pueblo Social History: Kinship, Sodality, and Community in the Northern Southwest*. School for Advanced Research Press, Santa Fe, New Mexico.

Weiner, Annette

    1992   *Inalienable Possessions: The Paradox of Keeping-While-Giving*. University of California Press, Berkeley.

Wells, Susan J.

    1994   Settlement and Environment at Petrified Forest National Park, Homol'ovi State Park, and the Southwest Hopi Buttes: A Comparison. In *Middle Colorado River Archaeology: From the Parks to the People*, edited by Anne Trinkle Jones and Martyn D. Tagg, pp. 69–86. The Arizona Archaeologist No. 27. Arizona Archaeological Society, Phoenix.

Westfall, Deborah

    1982   *Prehistory of the St. Johns Area, East Central Arizona: The TEP St. Johns Project*. Arizona State Museum Archaeological Series No. 153. University of Arizona, Tucson.

Whiteley, Peter

    1988   *Deliberate Acts: Changing Hopi Culture through the Oraibi Split*. University of Arizona Press, Tucson.

    2015   Chacoan Kinship. In *Chaco Revisited: New Research on the Prehistory of Chaco Canyon*, edited by Carrie C. Heitman and Stephen Plog, pp. 272-304. University of Arizona Press, Tucson.

Whittaker, John C.
　1994　*Flintknapping: Making & Understanding Stone Tools*. University of Texas Press, Austin.

Wilshusen, Richard H.
　1986　The Relationship between Abandonment Mode and Ritual Use in Pueblo I Anasazi Protokivas. *Journal of Field Archaeology* 13:245-254.

Woodbury, Richard B.
　1954　*Prehistoric Stone Implements of Northeastern Arizona*. Papers of the Peabody Museum of American Archaeology and Ethnology, No. 34. Harvard University, Cambridge.

Woodbury, Richard B., and Natalie F.S. Woodbury
　1966　Decorated Pottery of the Zuni Area. In *The Excavation of Hawikuh by Frederick Webb Hodge: Report of the Hendricks-Hodge Expedition,* edited by Watson Smith, Richard B. Woodbury, and Natalie F.S. Woodbury, Appenix II. Contributions from the Museum of the American Indian, Heye Foundation, Vol. 20, pp. 302-336. Museum of the American Indian, Heye Foundation, New York.

Young, Lisa A.
　1996　Mobility and Farmers: The Pithouse-to-Pueblo Transition in Northeastern Arizona. Ph.D. dissertation, Department of Anthropology, University of Arizona, Tucson.

　2001　Flaked Stone: Technology and Raw Material Procurement. In *Homol'ovi III: A Pueblo Hamlet in the Middle Little Colorado River Valley*, edited by E. Charles Adams, pp. 239-272. Arizona State Museum Archaeological Series No. 193. University of Arizona, Tucson.

Young, Lisa, and Karen G. Harry
　1989　A Prelimnary Analysis of Temporal Changes in the Homol'ovi III Chipped Stone Assemblage. *Kiva* 54:273-284.

Zedeño, María Nieves
　1994　*Sourcing Prehistoric Ceramics at Chodistaas Pueblo, Arizona: The Circulation of People and Pots in the Grasshopper Region*. Anthropological Papers No. 58. University of Arizona Press, Tucson.

APPENDIX A

Seriation by Stratum Based on Jeddito Yellow Ware Index (%JYW) for all Structures Excavated at Chevelon Pueblo

Abbreviations Used in Appendix A	
%JYW	Jeddito Yellow Ware Index
JYW	Jeddito Yellow Ware
WOW	Winslow Orange Ware
WMRW	White Mountain Red Ware
RRW	Roosevelt Red Ware
TP	Tuwiuca Phase
EHP	Early Homol'ovi Phase
MHP	Middle Homol'ovi Phase
LHP	Late Homol'ovi Phase

364 Appendix A

Structure	Year Excavated	Stratum	JYW count	%JYW	WOW count	%	WMRW count	%	RRW count	%	Total Decorated Sherd Count	Phase
222	2003	3	3	17.6	4	23.5	6	35.3			17	
		5	36	31.9	31	27.4	32	28.3	1	0.9	113	EHP
		6			3							
		8	7	14.3	8	16.3	9	18.4			49	EHP
		11	1	50.0	1	50.0					2	
227	2003	1	4	26.7	5	33.3			5	33.3	15	
		2	1	11.1	3	33.3					9	
		3	40	70.2	7	12.3			1	1.8	57	MHP
		4	14	25.5	20	36.4	1	1.8			55	EHP
		5	2	2.5	78	97.5					80	TP
		6	2	9.5	13	61.9	1	4.8	1	4.8	21	
248	2003	1	49	32.2	71	46.7	13	8.6	2	1.3	152	EHP
		2	5	15.6	14	43.8	7	21.9	1	3.1	32	
		6	53	34.0	71	45.5	13	8.3			156	EHP
		7	10	27.8	20	55.6	3	8.3	2	5.6	36	
		8	6	40.0	9	60.0					15	
264	2003	3	191	95.5	3	1.5			2	1.0	200	LHP
		5	52	92.9	3	5.4					56	LHP
		6	22	88.0	2	8.0	1	4.0			25	
		7	19	95.0	1	5.0					20	
		8	2	100.0							2	
266	2003	2	4	66.7							6	

Structure	Year Excavated	Stratum	JYW count	%JYW	WOW count	%	WMRW count	%	RRW count	%	Total Decorated	Phase
266, Cont'd	2003, Cont'd	3	5	55.6							9	
		6	3	37.5							8	
		7	2	20.0							10	
286	2003	1	55	80.9	6	8.8			6	8.8	68	LHP
		2	206	78.3	24	9.1	2	0.8	8	3.0	263	LHP
		3	15	23.1	49	75.4	1	1.5			65	EHP
		5	1	100.0							1	
		F1-1	1	100.0							1	
265	2003-04	1	5	71.4							7	
		2	6	50.0							12	
		3	1	25.0							4	
		3	3	75.0							4	
		4	41	82.0	3	6.0			1	2.0	50	LHP
		5	6	50.0	3	25.0	1	8.3			12	
		7	1	25.0	3	75.0					4	
		8	2	50.0							4	
		9	13	76.5							17	
269	2003-04	1	5	62.5	2	25.0	1	12.5			8	LHP
		2	43	89.6	2	4.2	1	2.1			48	LHP
		2	50	75.8	7	10.6	2	3.0			66	LHP
		3	1	100.0							1	
		4	27	77.1	2	5.7	1	2.9			35	LHP
		6	2	33.3	3	50.0					6	

366 Appendix A

Structure	Year Excavated	Stratum	JYW count	%JYW	WOW count	%	WMRW count	%	RRW count	%	Total Decorated	Phase
269, cont'd	2003-04, cont'd	7	2	66.7							3	
		8	3	50.0	1	16.7					6	
		10	2	100.0							2	
		11	4	100.0							4	
		12	13	100.0							13	
		13	5	100.0							5	
268	2004	1	22	47.8	16	34.8	2	4.3	2	4.3	46	MHP
		2	57	73.1	12	15.4	3	3.8	6	7.7	78	LHP
		3	81	84.4	7	7.4	1	1.1	4	4.2	95	LHP
		4	9	56.3	7	43.7					16	
		5	64	77.1	12	14.5	3	3.6	1	1.2	83	LHP
289	2004	1	1	33.3					1	33.3	3	
		2	19	70.4	8	29.6					27	
		3	23	95.8			1	4.2			24	
		4	5	62.5	2	25.0	1	12.5			8	
		5	2	66.7							3	
		6	5	100.0							5	
		7	2	50.0	5	71.4					7	
274	2003-04	1	8	40.0	5	25.0	4	20.0	3	15.0	20	
		2			4	4	100				100	
		3	315	75.9	65	15.7	11	2.7	20	4.8	415	LHP
		4	243	40.3	173	28.7	100	16.6	12	2.0	603	MHP
		7	6	85.7							7	

Structure	Year Excavated	Stratum	JYW count	%JYW	WOW count	%	WMRW count	%	RRW count	%	Total Decorated	Phase
274, cont'd	2003-04, cont'd	15	4	100.0							4	
		16	3	9.1	8	24.2	19	57.6			33	EHP
279	2003-04	1	33	55.0	15	25.0	1	1.7	7	11.7	60	MHP
		2	119	57.8	63	30.6	2	1.0	18	8.7	206	MHP
		3	386	58.8	174	26.5	4	0.6	78	11.9	657	MHP
		4	257	59.1	119	27.4	17	3.9	28	6.4	435	MHP
		5	13	44.8	8	27.6	2	0.7	4	13.8	29	
		6			3	37.5	5	62.5			8	
		7	382	48.8	204	26.1	126	16.1	17	2.2	783	MHP
		8	3	23.1	4	30.8	3	23.1	1	7.7	13	
		9	3	50.0	2	33.3	1	16.7			6	
		10	3	100.0							3	
		12	3	37.5			3	37.5			8	
		14	2	40.0	2	40.0	1	20.0			5	
		15	2	40.0			1	20.0			5	
		16	95	27.1	112	31.9	84	23.9	2	0.6	351	EHP
		17	1	11.1	2	22.2	5	55.6			9	
		18	26	52.0	5	10.0	8	16.0			50	MHP
288	2004	1	38	70.4	8	14.8	2	3.7	1	1.9	54	MHP
		2	12	100.0							12	
		3	21	63.6	12	36.4					33	MHP
		4	15	55.6	14	51.9					27	
		5	10	47.6	4	19.0					21	MHP
		6	16	50.0	12	37.5	2	6.3	6	28.6	32	MHP
		7	7	17.9	3	7.7					39	EHP

368 Appendix A

Structure	Year Excavated	Stratum	JYW count	%JYW	WOW count	%	WMRW count	%	RRW count	%	Total Decorated	Phase
288, cont'd	2004, cont'd	8	1	100.0							1	
		9	4	44.4							9	
		11	1	50.0			1	50.0			2	
		13			21	77.8					27	
		14	2	6.7	14	46.7					30	TP*
		15			3	42.9					7	
		16			7	87.5					8	
300	2004	1			64	48.1	2	1.5	24	18.0	133	TP
		2	1	1.4	43	58.9			9	12.3	73	TP
		3			1	50.0			1	50.0	2	
373	2004	1	5	55.6	3	33.3			3	33.3	9	
			5	41.7			1	8.3			12	
		3	2	66.7			1	33.3			3	
		4	54	72.0	11	14.7	5	6.7			75	LHP
		8			3	100.0					3	
345	2004	1	9	56.3	3	18.8	3	18.8			16	
		2	6	75.0			2	25.0			8	
		4	11	50.0	5	22.7	4	18.2	1	4.5	22	
		5			1	100.0					1	
		6	8	47.1	3	17.6	2	11.8			17	

Structure	Year Excavated	Stratum	JYW count	%JYW	WOW count	%	WMRW count	%	RRW count	%	Total Decorated	Phase
345, cont'd	2004, cont'd	7			2	100.0					2	
393	2004	2	2	66.7							3	
		3	4	44.4	1	11.1	2	22.2			9	
		4	108	81.8	17	12.9	8	6.1	1	0.8	132	LHP
		5	9	69.2	2	15.4	2	15.4			13	
		6									33	
		7	1	100							1	
403	2004	2	257	79.1	35	10.8	12	3.7	8	2.5	325	LHP
		3	12	85.7	1	7.1	1	7.1			14	
		5	2	18.2	3	27.3	3	27.3			11	
120	2005	1	5	83.3							6	
		2	2	100.0							2	
		3	8	27.6					2	6.9	29	
		4	19	50.0							38	MHP
		5	31	93.9							33	LHP
		6	45	35.4	4	3.1	3	2.4	62	48.8	127	EHP
		7							3	100.0	3	
		8	3	60.0							5	
		9	2	66.7							3	
		10	16	34.0	3	6.4	1	2.1	6	12.8	47	EHP
		11					1	100.0			1	
		12			2	50.0					4	
		13	2	14.3	5	35.7					14	

370 Appendix A

Structure	Year Excavated	Stratum	JYW count	%JYW	WOW count	%	WMRW count	%	RRW count	%	Total Decorated	Phase
120, cont'd	2005, cont'd	15										
122	2006	1	5	83.3							6	
		2	16	66.7	7	29.2					24	
		3	13	86.7	1	6.7					15	
		4										
		5	1	100.0							1	
123	2005	1	70	81.4	4	4.7	1	1.2			86	LHP
		2	6	100.0							6	
		3	14	77.8							18	
		4	1	100.0							1	
		5	10	52.6							19	
		6										
		8										
		15										
124	2006	1	11	68.8							16	
		2	102	94.4	2	1.9	1	0.9			108	LHP
		3	22	62.9	5	14.3					35	MHP
		4	36	85.7	4	9.5					42	LHP
		5	5	41.7	3	25.0			1	8.3	12	
		7	12	75.0	1	6.3					16	
		8	12	75.0	1	6.3					16	
		9			1	100.0					1	

Structure	Year Excavated	Stratum	JYW count	%JYW	WOW count	%	WMRW count	%	RRW count	%	Total Decorated	Phase
124, cont'd	2006, cont'd	10									1	
		11	7	100.0							7	
157	2006	1	31	100.0							31	LHP
		2	23	92.0	1	4.0	2	8.0			25	
		6										
		8	1	50.0							2	
158	2005	1			1	33.3					3	
		3	1	100.0							1	
		4	1	100.0							1	
		5	5	45.5	4	36.4					11	
		9	1	6.3	1	6.3	14	87.5			16	
		12									2	
		14			2	33.3					6	
159	2006	2	94	100.0							94	LHP
		3	576	99.7			1	0.2			578	LHP
		4	92	100.0							92	LHP
		5	45	97.8							46	LHP
		7	355	99.4	1	0.3					357	LHP
		8	24	100.0							24	
		9	36	100.0							36	LHP
		12	16	100.0							16	
		13	2	100.0							2	

372 Appendix A

Structure	Year Excavated	Stratum	JYW count	%JYW	WOW count	%	WMRW count	%	RRW count	%	Total Decorated	Phase
159, cont'd	2006, cont'd	18	3	100.0							3	LHP
161	2005	1	39	92.9							42	
		2	14	60.9	1	4.3	2	8.7	1	4.3	23	
		3										
		5			2	40.0					5	
		6			1	100						
901	2005	2	242	95.3	4	1.6	2	0.8	4	1.6	254	LHP
	2006	3	543	67.1	226	27.9	15	1.9	11	1.4	809	MHP
	2005	4	371	97.9	3	0.8	1	0.3			379	LHP
	2005	5	95	87.2	9	8.3	2	1.8			109	LHP
	2005-06	6	398	95.2	9	2.2	1	0.2	6	1.4	418	LHP
	2005	7	442	70.8	81	13.0	42	6.7	24	3.8	624	MHP
	2005	8	274	74.9	28	7.7	23	6.3	17	4.6	366	LHP
	2005	11	290	74.9	32	8.3	21	5.4	12	3.1	387	LHP

*Jeddito Yellow Ware sherds recovered in this stratum are intrusive

APPENDIX B

*Distribution of Rare/Unusual Animal
Taxa at Chevelon by Structure*

Structure	Taxon	Element
120	*Anas* sp., (Duck-sized)	ulna
	Canis latrans (Coyote)	astragalus
		calcaneum
	Aves (Birds)	metatarsal/tarsometatarsus
		metatarsal/tarsometatarsus
	Corvus corax (Common Raven)	metatarsal/tarsometatarsus
	Anatidae (Ducks, Geese, and Swans)	femur
	Cyprinidae (Minnows)	vertebra, type unknown
	Grus Canadensis (Sandhill Crane)	1st phalanx
	Artiodactyla (Even-toed Ungulates)	molar/premolar, dental position unknown
	Ovis canadensis (Bighorn Sheep)	radius/radioulna
		humerus
	Aves (Birds)	metatarsal/tarsometatarsus
		phalanx
		phalanx
		innominate
		sacrum/synsacrum
222	*Corvus corax* (Common Raven)	metacarpal/carpometacarpus
	Anatidae (Ducks, Geese, and Swans)	cranium
		coracoid
	Antilocapridae (Pronghorns)	ulna
		ulna
	Cervidae (Deer)	mandible
		mandible
	Cyprinidae (Minnows)	cranium
		cranium
		deciduous molar from lower jaw, type unknown
		vertebra, type unknown
		vertebra, type unknown
		2 misc. fish frag.
	Phasianidae (Quails)	tibia/tibiofibula/tibiotarsus
	Felis concolor (Mountain Lion)	calcaneum
	Aves (Birds)	metatarsal/tarsometatarsus
	Artiodactyla (Even-toed Ungulates)	tooth, dental position unknown

Structure	Taxon	Element
222, cont'd		femur
		cranium
		lumbar
	Felis rufus (Bobcat)	calcaneum
	Artiodactyla (Even-toed Ungulates)	femur
		tooth, dental position unknown
		premolar, dental position unknown
		humerus
		premolar, dental position unknown
		humerus
		scapula
	Cypriniformes (Minnow-like Fishes)	indeterminate bone
	Passeriformes (Perching Birds)	clavicle/furculum
		coracoid
		ulnar (cuneiform)
	Ovis canadensis (Bighorn Sheep)	1st phalanx
268/269	*Anas* sp., (Duck-sized)	metacarpal/carpometacarpus
	Buteo sp. (Buteonine Hawks)	cervical
	Canis sp. (Coyote/Domestic Dog/Wolf)	caudal
	Catostomidae (Suckers)	cleithrum
		cleithrum
		hyomandibular
	Ovis canadensis (Bighorn Sheep)	phalanx
		rib
269	Aves (Birds)	tibia/tibiofibula/tibiotarsus
		tibia/tibiofibula/tibiotarsus
		tibia/tibiofibula/tibiotarsus
274	*Fulica americana* (American Coot)	metacarpal/carpometacarpus
		metacarpal/carpometacarpus
	Falconiformes (Birds of Prey)	metatarsal/tarsometatarsus
279	*Anas acuta* (Pintail)	humerus
	Anas platyrhynchos (Mallard)	humerus
		radius/radioulna

Structure	Taxon	Element
279, *cont'd*		ulna
	Anas sp., (Duck-sized)	humerus
	Antilocapra americana (Pronghorn)	scapula
		cranium
		innominate
		rib
		rib
		rib
		second phalanx
	Aves (Birds)	metacarpal/carpometacarpus
	Aythya valisineria (Canvasback)	femur
	Buteo jamaicensis (Red-tailed Hawk)	digit
		femur
	Buteo sp. (Buteonine Hawks)	metacarpal/carpometacarpus
		quadrate
		cranium
	Callipepla sp. (Scaled Quail/Gambel's Quail)	sternabra/sternum
	Canis latrans (Coyote)	femur
	Canis sp. (Coyote/Domestic Dog/Wolf)	lumbar
	Castor canadensis (Beaver)	clavicle/furculum
	Circus cyaneus (Marsh Hawk)	sacrum/synsacrum
		sternabra/sternum
		sternabra/sternum
	Corvus corax (Common Raven)	phalanx-rear
		phalanx-rear
		first phalanx
		second phalanx
		femur
		metatarsal/tarsometatarsus
		tibia/tibiofibula/tibiotarsus
		femur
		clavicle/ furculum
		metatarsal/tarsometatarsus
	Catostomidae (Suckers)	basioccipital
		brachiostegels

Structure	Taxon	Element
279, *cont'd*	Cyprinidae (Minnows)	Scapula
	Rallidae (Rails, Gallinules, and Coots)	metatarsal/tarsometatarsus
	Scolopacidae/Charadriidae (Sandpipers/Plovers)	humerus
	Felis concolor (Mountain Lion)	sternabra/sternum
	Felis rufus (Bobcat)	third phalanx
		femur
		2 atlas
		3 rib
	Fulica americana (American Coot)	coracoids
		humerus
		metacarpal/carpometacarpus
		metacarpal/carpometacarpus
		radius/radioulna
		ulna
		ulna
	Grus canadensis (Sandhill Crane)	humerus
	Meleagris gallopavo (Turkey)	humerus
		scapula
		2 vertebra type unknown
	Odocoileus hemionus (Mule Deer)	scapula
		rib
	Ondatra zibethicus (Muskrat)	second incisor from lower jaw
	Artiodactyla (Even-toed Ungulates)	thoracic
		thoracic
		deciduous molar dental position unknown
		deciduous molar from lower jaw
		innominate
		scapula
		cervical
		deciduous incisor, type unknown
		dental position unknown
		rib
		rib

Structure	Taxon	Element
279, *cont'd*		cranium
		metapodial
		rib
		scapula
		thoracic
		thoracic
		ulna
		innominate
	Aves (Birds)	metacarpal/carpometacarpus
		thoracic
		3 lumbar
		Cranium
	Cypriniformes (Minnow-like Fishes)	Caudal
	Ovis canadensis (Bighorn Sheep)	second molar from upper jaw
		third molar from upper jaw
		Cranium
		first phalanxs
		second phalanx
		cervical
		thoracic
		thoracic
	Aves (Birds)	2 metacarpal/carpometacarpus
	Podilymbus podiceps (Pied-billed Grebe)	radius/radioulna
		ulna
	Taxidea taxus (Badger)	humerus
	Xyrauchen texanus (Razorback Sucker)	maxilla
		vomer
288	*Antilocapra americana* (Pronghorn)	humerus
	Corvus corax (Common Raven)	coracoid
		digit
		metatarsal/tarsometatarsus
		scapula
		cranium
		femur

Structure	Taxon	Element
288, *cont'd*		femur
		sternabra/sternum
	Aves (Birds)	2 tibia/tibiofibula/tibiotarsus
	Catostomidae (Suckers)	vertebra, type unknown
	Ondatra zibethicus (Muskrat)	mandible
		5 tooth dental position unknown
	Artiodactyla (Even-toed Ungulates)	podial
	Podilymbus podiceps (Pied-billed Grebe)	femur
345	*Anas* sp., (Duck-sized)	femur
		tibia/tibiofibula/tibiotarsus
	Odocoileus sp. (Mule Deer/Whitetailed Deer)	thoracic
373/300	*Canis latrans/Canis familiaris* (Coyote/Domestic Dog)	humerus
		vertebra, type unknown
		vertebra, type unknown
	Crotaphytus sp. (Collared/Leopard Lizard)	vertebra, type unknown
	Fulica americana (American Coot)	coracoid
	Grus canadensis (Sandhill Crane)	humerus
	Aves (Birds)	metatarsal/tarsometatarsus
	Odocoileus hemionus (Mule Deer)	unknown
	Artiodactyla (Even-toed Ungulates)	podial
		thoracic
		thoracic
393	*Canis* sp.(Coyote/Domestic Dog/Wolf)	femur
		6 ribs
	Artiodactyla (Even-toed Ungulates)	podial
	Aves (Birds)	metatarsal/tarsometatarsus
900	*Anas* sp., (Duck-sized)	ulna
	Corvus corax (Common Raven)	lumbar
	Aves (birds)	digit

Structure	Taxon	Element
900, *cont'd*	*Crotaphytus* sp. (Collared/Leopard Lizard)	cranium
	Canidae (Coyotes, Dogs, Wolves, and Foxes)	humerus
	Felis rufus (Bobcat)	cervical
	Grus canadensis (Sandhill Crane)	cranium
		rib
		thoracic
	Odocoileus hemionus (Mule Deer)	femur
		phalanx
		thoracic
901	*Antilocapra americana* (Pronghorn)	femur
		thoracic
	Buteo sp. (Buteonine Hawks)	coracoid
		scapula
	Canis latrans (Coyote)	mandible
		first molar from lower jaw
		mandible
	Castor canadensis (Beaver)	humerus
	Charadrius vociferus (killdeer)	metacarpal/carpometacarpus
	Corvus corax (Common Raven)	carapace/plastron
		cranium
		femur
	Caprimulgidae (Nighthawks and Whip-poor-wills)	metacarpal/carpometacarpus
	Catostomidae (Suckers)	rib
	Grus canadensis (Sandhill Crane)	coracoid
	Odocoileus hemionus (Mule Deer)	innominate
		second premolar from lower jaw
	Aves (Birds)	metatarsal/tarsometatarsus
		cranium
	Catostomidae (Suckers)	preoperculum
	Artiodactyla (Even-toed Ungulates)	antler
		cranium
		cranium

Structure	Taxon	Element
901, *cont'd*		thoracic
		molar/premolar dental position
		unknown
		sternabra/sternum
		rib
	Aves (Birds)	metatarsal/tarsometatarsus
	Ovis canadensis (Bighorn Sheep)	femur
		radius/radioulna
		lumbar
		rib
		rib
		rib
		thoracic
		thoracic

APPENDIX C

Summary of In-field Observations on Human Skeletal Remains (Burial #1) Encountered in Structure 227, Chevelon Ruin (AZ P:2:11 [ASM])

Vincent M. LaMotta
Department of Anthropology
University of Illinois, Chicago

BACKGROUND

I visited the Homol'ovi Research Program's on-going excavations at the Chevelon Ruin near Winslow, Arizona on Monday, July 7, 2003. A collection of human skeletal remains had been encountered near the floor of Structure (S.) 227 on June 20. Dr. Barnet Pavao-Zuckerman examined the partly-exposed remains on June 25 and tentatively identified traces of carnivore activity on some of the bones. When I arrived at the site on July 7 the human remains were still only partially exposed. I was asked to expose the bones and to document them as fully as possible during my brief one-day visit. I spent much of the day exposing the articulated spinal column and feet, drafting a detailed map, compiling a catalogue of elements present, examining the bones for taphonomic indicators that would explain the depositional history of the assemblage, and attempting to determine the age and sex of the individual. I was assisted by Ryan Howell, the crew chief in charge of S. 227. Burial forms and other HRP paperwork related to the human remains were completed by Ryan Howell. In accordance with the wishes of the Hopi tribe, the skeletal remains were left in situ and reburied at the end of the 2003 field season. Consequently, this brief report is based solely on my field notes and observations while on site.

SPATIAL & STRATIGRAPHIC CONTEXT OF THE SKELETON

The partially-articulated skeleton of an adult of indeterminate sex was discovered within a few centimeters of the flagstone floor of S. 227. The bones were mostly concentrated within a 1 by 1 meter area in the northern portion of the room. The remains were found directly below a deposit comprised of roof decay products, according to the excavator. All of the bones I exposed were lying within a natural deposit of fine water-lain clay and laminated wind-blown sand. There was no evidence for a burial pit, nor were there any directly-associated artifacts or "grave goods." A thin lense of white powdery material was observed in direct contact with the floor in the area of the articulated vertebral column, but it is unclear what this deposit represents. The proximity of the skeletal remains to the floor surface indicates they were deposited in the room around the time the structure was abandoned. There was no evidence of recent vandalism in the immediate vicinity of the skeleton.

SEX

The sex of the individual could not be determined since most of the key elements (pubic symphysis, cranium, proximal femur) were either absent or poorly preserved. The greater sciatic notch of the left innominate was sufficiently preserved to assign it a score according to the system published by Buikstra and Ubelaker (1994:18). The notch is broad in females, but is more constricted in males. This individual was scored a "three" on a scale of one to five (one being "female" and five being "male"), an equivocal result.

AGE

The individual was clearly an adult at the time of death, although an exact age cannot be ascertained. Again, many skeletal elements and portions that are critical for assessing age were absent or poorly preserved. The individual was clearly into the adult range because the proximal humerus was fully fused, and it appeared that the clavicles and sacrum were also fused (see Buikstra and Ubelaker 1994:figure 20). Additionally, the single permanent molar/premolar that was found in the assemblage showed significant occlusal wear.

ELEMENTS REPRESENTED & STATE OF ARTICULATION

Much of the skeleton was represented in the assemblage, but several elements were conspicuously absent. The cranium and mandible were both absent, although at least one loose adult tooth was present. The first four cervical vertebrae (atlas, axis, C3, C4) were also missing. It is possible that the entire head and upper neck was dissociated from the torso as a unit when soft tissues were still present to hold these elements together. The rest of the cervical vertebrae (C5-7), all of the thoracic vertebrae, all of the lumbar vertebrae, and the sacrum were present and fully articulated with each other. The articulated spinal column was oriented east-west with its ventral (belly) side downward (the head, if present, would have been pointed to the east). Portions of at least five ribs were still articulated with the thoracic vertebrae, but at least 16 other rib fragments were scattered in and amongst the skeleton and even into the southern portion of the room where no other human remains were found. No manubrium (breast bone) was present. The right innominate was missing but the left side was present, completely dissociated from the sacrum.

Neither scapula was found, but both clavicles and both humerii were present. These upper arm and shoulder girdle elements were in correct anatomical position relative to each other and relative to the articulated spinal column. The left clavicle was articulated with the left humerus, and both bones were found on the left side of the spine. Likewise, the right clavicle and humerus were articulated, and both were found to the right of the spinal column. On both sides, however, the clavicle-humerus pair was found at some distance from the spinal column, indicating that both of the upper arms/shoulders were at some point dissociated from the torso. The lower arms appear to have been more completely disarticulated. The bones of the left forearm (radius and ulna) were still articulated with each other, but the pair was found 75 cm away from the left humerus and on the right side of the spinal column. The right radius was absent. The right ulna was found on the right side near the cranial end of the spinal column. Both hands and wrists were missing in their entirety, with the exception of two carpal (wrist) bones that were still articulated with the left radius/ulna pair. A single loose distal phalanx was also observed, but it was not determined if this element was from a hand or foot.

The lower limbs were also disarticulated and extremely jumbled. Both femora were present, but neither was in correct anatomical position relative to the spinal column or pelvis. The left femur was found on the right side of the spine. The left patella was also present but not articulated with the femur. The right femur was found underneath the articulated spinal column, suggesting that the right leg was completely dissociated from the torso before the skeleton was deposited in the room. Both lower legs (tibia and fibula) were missing but, remarkably, portions of both feet were found. The articulated partial left foot was located approximately 35 cm west of the sacrum. All seven tarsal (ankle) bones were present and articulated, along with the proximal ends of three metatarsals. The partly-articulated right ankle (consisting of four loosely associated tarsal bones) was found in the general area where the skull would have been if it were present and articulated with the spinal column. There was no duplication of elements, so it is unlikely that more than one individual was present in the assemblage.

Taphonomic Indicators

Many of the skeletal elements present had suffered significant damage, at least some of which was clearly caused by carnivore gnawing. One of the most striking aspects of this assemblage is the fact that most of the long bones were missing the epiphyses. In many cases, the preserved ends of the diaphyses (shafts) were fragmented in a ragged fashion. It is probable that some or all of this damage is due to carnivore activities since the spongy bone housed in the epiphyses is often targeted for consumption by carnivores. Clear evidence of carnivore damage was found on the left forearm: Several unequivocal examples of cone-shaped punctures were observed on the paired left radius and ulna, near the epiphyses. These punctures occur "when the bone collapses under the pressures of teeth, leaving a clear, more or less oval depression in the bone, often with flakes of the outer wall of the bone pressed into the puncture," (Lyman 1994:206). The size of these depressions suggests a coyote or like-sized carnivore could have been the agent. The damage pattern observed on the ribs may also be attributable to carnivore damage. It was noted that many of the ribs exhibited ragged fractures toward the costal ends, and that no manubrium was found. Such damage could be inflicted by carnivores intent on consuming the soft tissues of the chest cavity. Finally, the ragged fractures on the distal ends of the left metatarsals, along with the absence of most extremities, is suggestive of carnivore damage. Unfortunately, it was not possible to examine the remains in a controlled laboratory setting where microscopic damage patterns could be discerned. Nonetheless, the macroscopic data indicate that carnivores did play some role in the taphonomic history of this skeleton.

It was not possible to ascertain a cause of death for this individual from the osteological evidence that was preserved, nor does the depositional context offer any clues in this regard. There was no observable evidence of pathology. No traces of perimortem trauma or post-mortem 'processing' of the remains (such as cutmarks or burning) were observed. Again, it is not possible to state definitively that such traces are absent without examining the remains under a microscope and without the proper lighting and comparative materials. In general, the bones were very well preserved. No evidence of surface weathering or root damage was observed.

Inferred Depositional History

Several tentative inferences can be made regarding the depositional history of the skeleton found in S. 227. These remains probably entered the structure as a secondary burial—meaning the body was initially deposited elsewhere, allowed to decay for some period of time, and then gathered up and re-deposited in its present location. This sequence of events is suggested by the extremely jumbled nature of the bones, indicating the body could have been already partly disarticulated when it was deposited in the room. The fact that many of the smallest elements are missing also hints at redeposition: These elements are the most likely to be left at the initial deposition locale or lost in transit during the re-deposition process. All of the articulations that are still present represent portions of the anatomy held together by extremely strong tissues that would be among the last to decay. If this sequence of events is correct, it is possible that the carnivore damage occurred during the interval prior to re-deposition, especially if the body were lying on the surface somewhere away from the site. If so, it did not remain exposed for very long since there are almost no indications of surface weathering.

The pattern of missing elements is somewhat puzzling and may be attributable, in part, to cultural activities. For instance, the fact that both tibia and fibulae are absent, but portions of both feet are present, is not easily explained by natural processes. The absence of head and hands is also curious. If this individual met a violent death, it is possible that the hands and head were removed as trophies—this scenario, however, is purely speculative and is not directly supported by any other lines of osteological evidence.

In summary, the condition of the human skeletal remains found in S. 227 is probably due to several different depositional and taphonomic processes, including (but probably not limited to) carnivore activity and secondary burial. This assemblage of human skeletal remains is unlike any other I have examined from the other Homol'ovi sites. As far as I am aware, this is the only confirmed evidence for carnivore damage on human skeletal remains from any of these sites.

Table C.1. Inventory of Elements Present.

Skull + Dentition

Cranium	absent
Mandible	absent
Dentition	one loose tooth present, molar/premolar, significant occlusal wear

Vertebrae + Pelvis

Cervical vertebrae	atlas, axis, c3, c4 missing; c5-7 present, articulated
Thoracic vertebrae	all present, articulated
Lumbar vertebrae	all present, articulated
Sacrum	present, articulated with vertebrae
R innominate	absent
L innominate	present (ilium/ischium only)

Ribs

21 fragments present (unsided); at least five R ribs were still articulated with thoracic vertebrae

Manubrium	absent

Shoulder Girdle, Arms + Hands

R + L scapula	both apparently absent, but there may have been at least one loose fragment of a glenoid fossa
R clavicle	present, articulated w/ R humerus
L clavicle	present, articulated w/ L humerus
R humerus	present, articulated w/ R clavicle
L humerus	present, articulated w/ L clavicle
R radius	absent
L radius	present, articulated w/ L ulna
R ulna	present
L ulna	present, articulated w/ L radius
Carpals	all absent, except for two associated with the articulated L radius/L ulna
Metacarpals	all absent
Phalanges	all absent, with the possible exception of one loose distal phalanx (which may have been a foot phalanx)

Legs + Feet

R femur	present
L femur	present
R patella	absent
L patella	present
R + L tibia	both absent
R + L fibula	both absent

Table C.1. Inventory of Elements Present, cont'd.

Legs + Feet, cont'd	
R tarsals	at least four present, articulated
L tarsals	all seven present, articulated
R metatarsals	absent
L metatarsals	three present, articulated w/ L tarsals
Phalanges	all absent, with the possible exception of one loose distal phalanx (which may have been a hand phalanx)

390   *Appendix C: LaMotta*

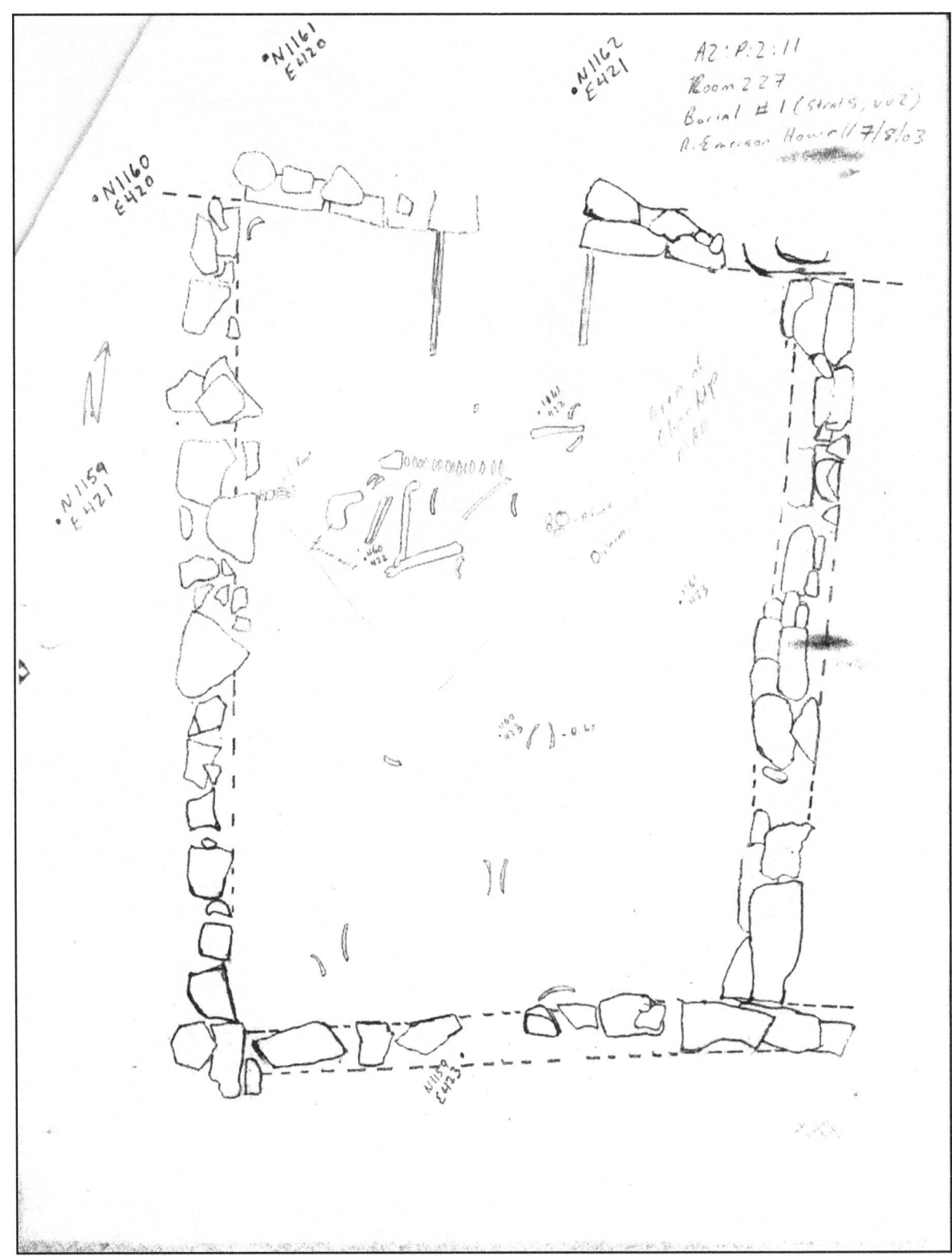

Figure C.1. Field Sketch of structure and location of human remains.

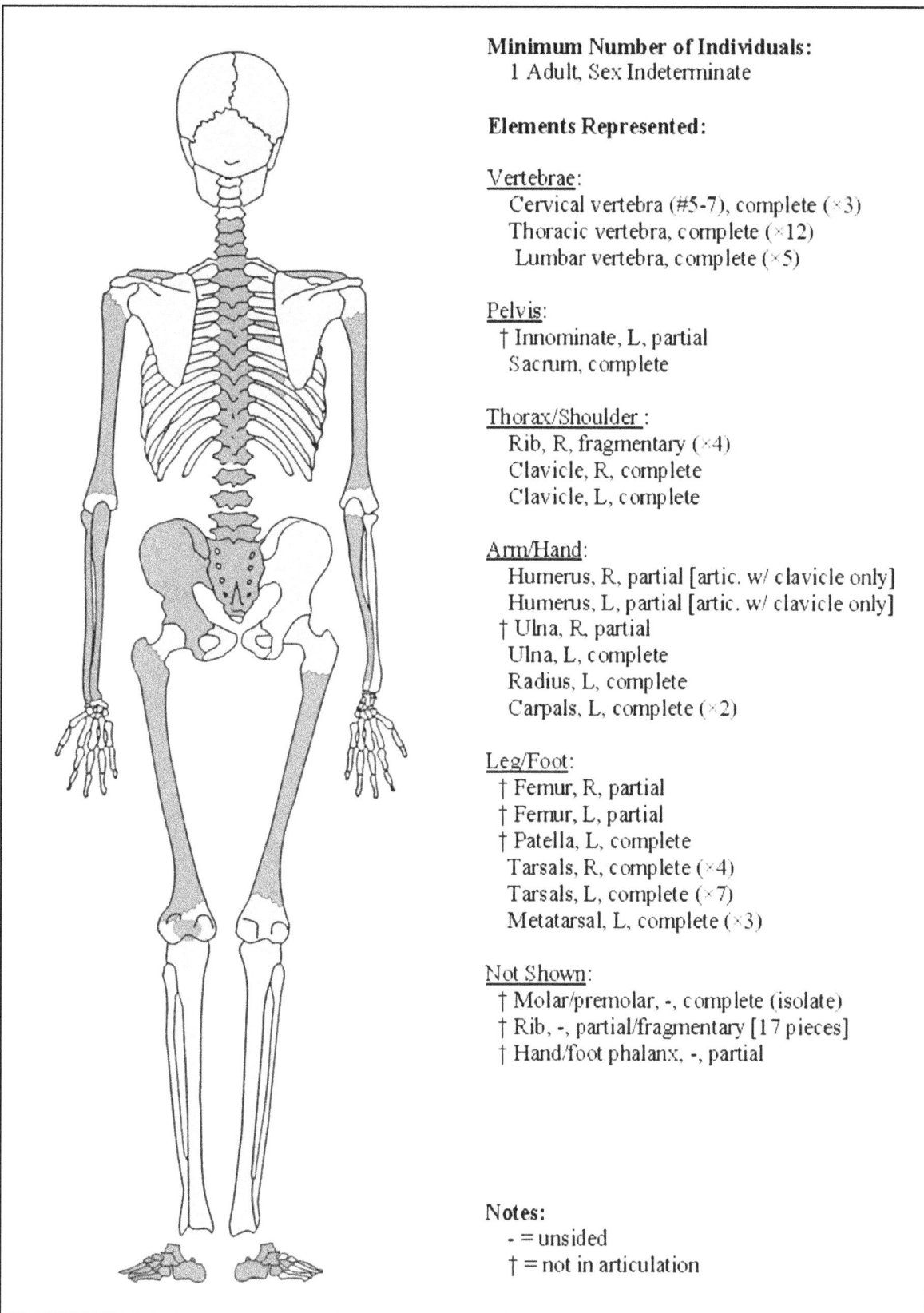

Minimum Number of Individuals:
1 Adult, Sex Indeterminate

Elements Represented:

Vertebrae:
  Cervical vertebra (#5-7), complete (×3)
  Thoracic vertebra, complete (×12)
  Lumbar vertebra, complete (×5)

Pelvis:
  † Innominate, L, partial
  Sacrum, complete

Thorax/Shoulder:
  Rib, R, fragmentary (×4)
  Clavicle, R, complete
  Clavicle, L, complete

Arm/Hand:
  Humerus, R, partial [artic. w/ clavicle only]
  Humerus, L, partial [artic. w/ clavicle only]
  † Ulna, R, partial
  Ulna, L, complete
  Radius, L, complete
  Carpals, L, complete (×2)

Leg/Foot:
  † Femur, R, partial
  † Femur, L, partial
  † Patella, L, complete
  Tarsals, R, complete (×4)
  Tarsals, L, complete (×7)
  Metatarsal, L, complete (×3)

Not Shown:
  † Molar/premolar, -, complete (isolate)
  † Rib, -, partial/fragmentary [17 pieces]
  † Hand/foot phalanx, -, partial

Notes:
  - = unsided
  † = not in articulation

Figure C.2. Skeletal elements represented (shaded).

APPENDIX D

Provenience Details for Illustrated Artifacts and Objects

Chapter 6

Figure Number	Object	Material Code*	Structure	PD	FS
6.1a	1	0	279	516	1
	2	0	279	516	1
	3	0	279	516	1
	4	0	279	516	1
	5	0	279	516	1
	6	0	279	516	1
	7	0	279	516	1
	8	0	279	516	1
	9	0	279	516	1
	10	0	279	516	1
	11	0	279	516	1
6.1b	1	0	279	516	1
	2	0	279	516	1
	3	0	279	516	1
	4	0	279	516	1
	5	0	279	516	1
	6	0	279	516	1
	7	0	279	516	1
	8	0	279	516	1
	9	0	279	516	1
	10	0	279	516	1
	11	0	279	516	1
	12	0	279	516	1
	13	0	279	516	1
	14	0	279	516	1
	15	0	279	516	1
6.1c	1	0	279	516	1
	2	0	279	516	1
	3	0	279	516	1
	4	0	279	516	1
	5	0	279	516	1
	6	0	279	516	1
6.1d	1	0	279	516	1
	2	0	279	516	1
	3	0	279	516	1
	4	0	279	516	1
	5	0	279	516	1

* Material Codes: 0 = Ceramics, 1 = Ground Stone, 2 = Flaked Stone, 4 = Shell, 6 = Animal Bone

Figure Number	Object	Material Code	Structure	PD	FS
6.1d, *cont'd*	6	0	279	516	1
	7	0	279	516	1
	8	0	279	516	1
	9	0	279	516	1
6.1e	1	0	279	516	1
	2	0	279	516	1
	3	0	279	516	1
6.2a	1	0	279	516	1
	2	0	279	516	1
	3	0	279	516	1
	4	0	279	516	1
	5	0	279	516	1
	6	0	279	516	1
	7	0	279	516	1
	8	0	279	516	1
	9	0	279	516	1
	10	0	279	516	1
	11	0	279	516	1
	12	0	279	516	1
6.2b	1	0	279	516	1
	2	0	279	516	1
	3	0	279	516	1
	4	0	279	516	1
	5	0	279	516	1
	6	0	279	516	1
	7	0	279	516	1
6.2c	1	0	279	516	1
6.3a	1	0	279	516	1
	2	0	279	516	1
	3	0	279	516	1
	4	0	279	516	1
	5	0	279	516	1
	6	0	279	516	1
	7	0	279	516	1
	8	0	279	516	1
	9	0	279	516	1
	10	0	279	516	1
	11	0	279	516	1

* Material Codes: 0 = Ceramics, 1 = Ground Stone, 2 = Flaked Stone, 4 = Shell, 6 = Animal Bone

396   *Appendix D*

Figure Number	Object	Material Code	Structure	PD	FS
6.3a, *cont'd*	12	0	279	516	1
	13	0	279	516	1
	14	0	279	516	1
	15	0	279	516	1
6.3b	1	0	279	516	1
	2	0	279	516	1
	3	0	279	516	1
	4	0	279	516	1
	5	0	279	516	1
6.3c	1	0	279	516	1
	2	0	279	516	1
	3	0	279	516	1
	4	0	279	516	1
	5	0	279	516	1
6.3d	1	0	279	516	1
	2	0	279	516	1
	3	0	279	516	1
	4	0	279	516	1
	5	0	279	516	1
6.4a	1	0	279	516	1
	2	0	279	516	1
	3	0	279	516	1
	4	0	279	516	1
	5	0	279	516	1
	6	0	279	516	1
	7	0	279	516	1
	8	0	279	516	1
	9	0	279	516	1
	10	0	279	516	1
6.4b	1	0	279	516	1
	2	0	279	516	1
	3	0	279	516	1
	4	0	279	516	1
	5	0	279	516	1
	6	0	279	516	1
6.4c	1	0	901	933	1
6.5a	1	0	279	516	1
	2	0	279	516	1

* Material Codes: 0 = Ceramics, 1 = Ground Stone, 2 = Flaked Stone, 4 = Shell, 6 = Animal Bone

Figure Number	Object	Material Code	Structure	PD	FS
6.5a, *cont'd*	3	0	279	516	1
	4	0	279	516	1
	5	0	279	516	1
	6	0	279	516	1
	7	0	279	516	1
	8	0	279	516	1
	9	0	279	516	1
	10	0	279	516	1
	11	0	279	516	1
	12	0	279	516	1
	13	0	279	516	1
6.5b	1	0	279	516	1
	2	0	279	516	1
	3	0	279	516	1
	4	0	279	516	1
	5	0	279	516	1
	6	0	279	516	1
	7	0	279	516	1
	8	0	279	516	1
	9	0	279	516	1
	10	0	279	516	1
	11	0	279	516	1
	12	0	279	516	1
	13	0	279	516	1
	14	0	279	516	1
	15	0	279	516	1
6.6	1	0	123	997	1
	2	0	123	997	1
	3	0	123	997	1
6.7	1	0	124	1320	13
	2	0	124	1316	1
	3	0	222	62	1
	4	0	124	320	13
	5	0	124	1316	1
	6	0	279	523	1
	7	0	279	523	1
	8	0	279	523	1
	9	0	279	523	1

* Material Codes: 0 = Ceramics, 1 = Ground Stone, 2 = Flaked Stone, 4 = Shell, 6 = Animal Bone

398 *Appendix D*

Figure Number	Object	Material Code	Structure	PD	FS
6.7, *cont'd*	10	0	279	523	1
6.8a	1	0	901	835	1
	2	0	901	835	1
6.8b	1	0	279	576	1
	2	0	279	576	1
	3	0	279	576	1
	4	0	279	576	1
	5	0	279	576	1
	6	0	279	576	1
	7	0	279	576	1
	8	0	279	576	1
	9	0	279	576	1
	10	0	279	576	1
6.10a	1	0	900	827	14
	2	0	901	1036	14
	3	0	900	828	22
6.10b	1	0	159	1387	15
6.10c	1	0	120	794	26
6.10d	1	0	286	155	13
6.10e	1	0	120	989	13
6.10f	1	0	264	96	25
6.11a	1	0	159	1387	15
6.11b	1	0	120	1105	13
6.11c	1	0	373	481	13
6.11d	1	0	227	227	13
6.12a	1	0	227	39	14
6.12b	1	0	373	481	15
6.12c	1	0	373	481	14
6.13a	1	0	264	102	21
6.13b	1	0	279	341	13
6.14	1	0	222	194	14
6.15	1	0	286	158	24
6.16a	1	0	901	943	19
	2	0	279	1058	14
6.16b	1	0	901	1042	1
6.16c	1	0	901	943	1
6.16d	1	0	269	364	13
6.16e	1	0	269	644	13
6.16f	1	0	269	644	13

* Material Codes: 0 = Ceramics, 1 = Ground Stone, 2 = Flaked Stone, 4 = Shell, 6 = Animal Bone

Chapter 7

Figure Number	Object	Material Code*	Structure	PD	FS
7.1a	1	1	269	361	13
7.1b	1	1	274	522	15
7.1c	1	1	227	134	13
7.1d	1	1	227	135	40
7.1e	1	1	269	445	15
7.2a	1	1	901	1047	14
7.2b	1	1	274	591	14
7.2c	1	1	227	133	15
7.3a	1	1	393	304	13
7.3b	1	1	269	363	16
7.3c	1	1	345	314	18
7.3d	1	1	269	363	16
7.3e	1	1	345	314	17
7.4a	1	1	279	1053	31
7.4b	1	1	900	411	14
7.4c	1	1	289	566	14
7.4d	1	1	279	510	16
7.4e	1	1	269	645	13
7.5a	1	1	279	595	14
7.5b	1	1	269	120	21
7.5c	1	1	345	314	21
7.5d	1	1	289	565	15
7.6a	1	1	159	1389	13
	2	1	124	1319	13
	3	1	286	152	17
7.6b	1	1	900	924	13
7.7a	1	1	901	1035	16
7.7b	1	1	269	361	13
7.7c	1	1	279	966	15
7.7d	1	1	120	785	21
7.7e	1	1	279	763	16
7.7f	1	1	159	1333	17
7.7g	1	1	268	0	17
7.7h	1	1	248	111	13
7.7i	1	1	248	111	13
7.7j	1	1	248	117	17
	2	1	227	33	15

* Material Codes: 0 = Ceramics, 1 = Ground Stone, 2 = Flaked Stone, 4 = Shell, 6 = Animal Bone

Figure Number	Object	Material Code	Structure	PD	FS
7.7j, *cont'd*	3	1	222	47	18
	4	1	403	277	13
	5	1	222	95	16
	6	1	227	47	18

* Material Codes: 0 = Ceramics, 1 = Ground Stone, 2 = Flaked Stone, 4 = Shell, 6 = Animal Bone

Chapter 8

Figure Number	Object	Material Code*	Structure	PD	FS
8.1	1	2	901	933	25
	2	2	901	821	24
	3	2	901	821	25
	4	2	901	830	18
	5	2	901	835	25
	6	2	901	943	28
	7	2	901	938	23
	8	2	901	830	16
	9	2	901	933	24
	10	2	901	931	18
	11	2	901	928	15
	12	2	901	822	18
8.2	1	2	901	1031	22
	2	2	279	880	16
	3	2	248	17	18
	4	2	279	773	13
	5	2	279	1054	15
	6	2	288	553	14
	7	2	248	168	17
	8	2	293	1144	13
8.3	1	2	266	77	14
	2	2	274	594	18
	3	2	901	1130	14
	4	2	279	516	15
	5	2	900	837	16
	6	2	286	236	14
	7	2	120	991	15
	8	2	264	98	14
	9	2	345	295	15
	10	2	900	619	14
	11	2	279	983	18
	12	2	227	22	13
	13	2	279	983	34
	14	2	279	1058	32
	15	2	248	168	15
	16	2		surface	
8.4a	1	2	900	411	13

* Material Codes: 0 = Ceramics, 1 = Ground Stone, 2 = Flaked Stone, 4 = Shell, 6 = Animal Bone

402 Appendix D

Figure Number	Object	Material Code	Structure	PD	FS
8.4a, cont'd	2	2	279	877	16
	3	2	248	172	18
	4	2	265	447	14
	5	2	227	139	13
8.4b	1	2	269	128	13
	2	2	279	978	16
	3	2	279	984	14
	4	2	274	522	16
	5	2	279	344	16
	6	2	400	1	15
	7	2	393	530	16
	8	2	279	1058	14
	9	2	288	255	24
	10	2	900	721	15
8.5	1	2	269	638	13
	2	2	279	519	13
	3	2	159	1323	15
	4	2	726	224	24
	5	2	901	943	15
	6	2	123	987	13
	7	2	287	19	16
	8	2	287	19	17
	9	2	287	107	16
	10	2	287	107	15
	11	2	287	107	21
	12	2	287	107	14
8.6	1	2	222	47	17
	2	2	222	195	15
	3	2	222	49	15
	4	2	222	198	14
	5	2	222	59	16
	6	2	222	194	22
	7	2	222	59	15
	8	2	222	194	34
8.7	1	2	222	59	13
	2	2	222	53	24
	3	2	222	56	23
	4	2	222	193	31

* Material Codes: 0 = Ceramics, 1 = Ground Stone, 2 = Flaked Stone, 4 = Shell, 6 = Animal Bone

Figure Number	Object	Material Code	Structure	PD	FS
8.7, *cont'd*	5	2	222	194	27
	6	2	222	55	14
8.8a	1	2	279	594	18
	2	2	279	877	16
	3	2	279	880	16
	4	2	279	344	16
	5	2	279	510	15
	6	2	279	516	15
	7	2	279	518	17
	8	2	279	970	13
	9	2	279	973	18
	10	2	279	520	25
8.8b	1	2	279	520	16
	2	2	279	520	22
	3	2	279	589	13
	4	2	279	590	15
	5	2	279	595	13
	6	2	279	577	16
	7	2	279	978	17
	8	2	279	978	13
	9	2	279	978	16
	10	2	279	981	31
	11	2	279	987	17
	12	2	279	981	14
	13	2	279	984	17
	14	2	279	984	28
	15	2	279	984	14
	16	2	279	1050	13
	17	2	279	1050	14
8.8c	1	2	279	979	14
	2	2	279	983	30
	3	2	279	983	34
	4	2	279	983	18
	5	2	279	983	23
	6	2	279	1051	15
	7	2	279	1051	16
	8	2	279	1051	18
	9	2	279	1052	15

* Material Codes: 0 = Ceramics, 1 = Ground Stone, 2 = Flaked Stone, 4 = Shell, 6 = Animal Bone

Figure Number	Object	Material Code	Structure	PD	FS
8.8c, *cont'd*	10	2	279	1053	29
	11	2	279	1054	15
	12	2	279	1056	16
	13	2	279	1056	17
	14	2	279	1056	27
	15	2	279	1056	24
8.9	1	2	900	19	16
	2	2	900	19	17
	3	2	900	107	16
	4	2	900	107	15
	5	2	900	107	21
	6	2	900	107	14

* Material Codes: 0 = Ceramics, 1 = Ground Stone, 2 = Flaked Stone, 4 = Shell, 6 = Animal Bone

Chapter 9

Figure Number	Object	Material Code*	Structure	PD	FS
9.1a	1	6	279	966	5
9.1b	1	6	120	1096	15
9.2	1	6	286	158	16-18
9.3	1	6	345	542	5
	2	6	279	598	5
	3	6	279	599	5
9.4	1	6	279	1058	5
	2	6	279	1058	5
	3	6	279	1058	5
	4	6	279	1058	5
	5	6	279	1058	5
	6	6	279	1058	5
	7	6	279	1058	5
	8	6	279	1058	5
	9	6	279	1058	5
	10	6	279	1058	5
	11	6	279	1058	5
9.5a	1	6	279	1080	5
	2	6	279	1080	5
	3	6	279	1080	5
	4	6	279	1080	5
	5	6	279	1080	5
	6	6	279	1080	5
	7	6	279	1080	5
	8	6	279	1080	5
9.5b	1	6	279	1080	5
	2	6	279	1080	5
	3	6	279	1080	5
	4	6	279	1080	5
	5	6	279	1080	5
	6	6	279	1080	5
	7	6	279	1080	5
9.6a	1	6	279	1058	5
	2	6	279	1058	5
	3	6	279	1058	5
	4	6	279	1058	5
9.6b	1	6	279	1058	5

* Material Codes: 0 = Ceramics, 1 = Ground Stone, 2 = Flaked Stone, 4 = Shell, 6 = Animal Bone

Figure Number	Object	Material Code	Structure	PD	FS
9.6b, *cont'd*	2	6	279	1058	5
	3	6	279	1058	5
	4	6	279	1058	5
	5	6	279	1058	5
	6	6	279	1058	5
	7	6	279	1058	5
	8	6	279	1058	5
	9	6	279	1058	5
	10	6	279	1058	5
	11	6	279	1058	5
	12	6	279	1058	5
	13	6	279	1058	5
	14	6	279	1058	5
9.6c	1	6	279	1058	5
	2	6	279	1058	5
	3	6	279	1058	5
	4	6	279	1058	5
	5	6	279	1058	5
9.7	1	6	901	1042	15
9.8a	1	6	279	1058	5
	2	6	279	1058	5
	3	6	279	1058	5
	4	6	279	1058	5
	5	6	279	1058	5
	6	6	279	1058	5
	7	6	279	1058	5
	8	6	279	1058	5
	9	6	279	1058	5
	10	6	279	1058	5
	11	6	279	1058	5
	12	6	279	1058	5
	13	6	279	1058	5
	14	6	279	1058	5
	15	6	279	1058	5
	16	6	279	1058	5
	17	6	279	1058	5
	18	6	279	1058	5
9.8b	1	6	279	1058	5

* Material Codes: 0 = Ceramics, 1 = Ground Stone, 2 = Flaked Stone, 4 = Shell, 6 = Animal Bone

Figure Number	Object	Material Code	Structure	PD	FS
9.8b, *cont'd*	2	6	279	1058	5
	3	6	279	1058	5
	4	6	279	1058	5
	5	6	279	1058	5
	6	6	279	1058	5
	7	6	279	1058	5
	8	6	279	1058	5
	9	6	279	1058	5
9.9	1	6	279	1058	5
	2	6	279	1058	5
	3	6	279	1058	5
	4	6	279	1058	5
	5	6	279	1058	5
	6	6	279	1058	5
	7	6	279	1058	5
	8	6	279	1058	5
9.10	1	6	279	1058	5
	2	6	279	1058	5
	3	6	279	1058	5
	4	6	279	1058	5
	5	6	279	1058	5
	6	6	279	1058	5
	7	6	279	1058	5
	8	6	279	1058	5
	9	6	279	1058	5
	10	6	279	1058	5
	11	6	279	1058	5
	12	6	279	1058	5
	13	6	279	1058	5
	14	6	279	1058	5
	15	6	279	1058	5
	16	6	279	1058	5
	17	6	279	1058	5
	18	6	279	1058	5
	19	6	279	1058	5
	20	6	279	1058	5
	21	6	279	1058	5
	22	6	279	1058	5

* Material Codes: 0 = Ceramics, 1 = Ground Stone, 2 = Flaked Stone, 4 = Shell, 6 = Animal Bone

Figure Number	Object	Material Code	Structure	PD	FS
9.10, *cont'd*	23	6	279	1058	5
	24	6	279	1058	5
	25	6	279	1058	5
	26	6	279	1058	5
	27	6	279	1058	5
	28	6	279	1058	5
	29	6	279	1058	5
	30	6	279	1058	5
	31	6	279	1058	5
9.11	1	6	279	1058	5
	2	6	279	1058	5
	3	6	279	1058	5
	4	6	279	1058	5
	5	6	279	1058	5
	6	6	279	1058	5
	7	6	279	1058	5
	8	6	279	1058	5
	9	6	279	1058	5
	10	6	279	1058	5
	11	6	279	1058	5
	12	6	279	1058	5
	13	6	279	1058	5
	14	6	279	1058	5
9.12a	1	6	901	1036	26
	2	6	901	943	22
9.12b	1	6	279	770	13
	2	6	123	1006	21
	3	6	900	939	13
	4	6	158	1072	22
9.12c	1	6	279	983	29
	2	6	123	997	16
	3	6	279	764	23
	4	6	279	774	21
	5	6	279	763	27
	6	6	900	828	17

* Material Codes: 0 = Ceramics, 1 = Ground Stone, 2 = Flaked Stone, 4 = Shell, 6 = Animal Bone

Chapter 10

Figure Number	Object	Material Code*	Structure	PD	FS
10.1a	1	4	248	172	16
	2	4	900	421	13
	3	4	279	520	21
10.1b	1	4	300	482	23
10.2a	1	4	287	118	15
	2	4	279	524	15
	3	4	279	878	13
10.2b	1	4	345	539	13
10.2c	1	4	900	393	13
10.3	1	4	286	150	14
	2	4	286	150	15
	3	4	393	530	15
	4	4	345	539	17
	5	4	269	637	19
	6	4	227	26	15
	7	4	300	479	13
	8	4	279	510	29
	9	4	901	821	17
	10	4	279	868	14
10.4	1	4	287	114	21
	2	4	279	506	14
	3	4	279	594	17
10.5a	1	4	268	259	14
10.5b	1	4	900	486	16
10.6	1	4	279	518	19
	2	4	279	518	19
	3	4	279	518	19
	4	4	279	518	19
	5	4	279	518	19
	6	4	279	518	19
	7	4	279	518	19
	8	4	279	518	19
	9	4	279	518	19
	10	4	279	518	19
	11	4	279	518	19
	12	4	279	518	19

* Material Codes: 0 = Ceramics, 1 = Ground Stone, 2 = Flaked Stone, 4 = Shell, 6 = Animal Bone

Figure Number	Object	Material Code	Structure	PD	FS
10.6, *cont'd*	13	4	279	518	19
	14	4	279	518	19
	15	4	279	518	19
	16	4	279	518	19
	17	4	279	518	19
	18	4	288	562	14
	19	4	288	562	19
	20	4	279	518	19
	21	4	279	518	19
	22	4	279	518	19
	23	4	279	518	19
	24	4	279	518	19
	25	4	279	518	19
10.7	1	4	286	237	21
	2	4	222	193	12

* Material Codes: 0 = Ceramics, 1 = Ground Stone, 2 = Flaked Stone, 4 = Shell, 6 = Animal Bone